REVISION CHECKLIST—*Considering Your Whole Essay—Chap*

Using the <u>FACT</u> acronym, ask yourself these questions:

- ✓ Does my essay <u>F</u>IT together, presenting a central point for a specific audience? Does my thesis statement accurately reflect the content of my essay, or have I included material that has no bearing on the main point?
- ✓ Have I included all the material my reader will need to grasp my meaning, or do I need to <u>A</u>DD information or examples?
- ✓ Have I included material that fits the thesis but needs to be <u>C</u>UT because it is uninteresting, uninformative, or repetitious?
- ✓ Does a <u>T</u>EST of my organization show that the writing flows smoothly, with clear transitions between the various ideas?

Responding to Your Peers' Drafts—Chapter 3

If you'll be evaluating your peers' drafts, ask yourself these questions:

- ✓ What is the main point of this essay?
- ✓ What is the biggest problem?
- ✓ What is the greatest strength?
- ✓ What material doesn't seem to fit the main point or the audience?
- ✓ What questions has the author not answered?
- ✓ Where should more details and examples be added? Why?
- ✓ At what point does the paper fail to hold my interest? Why?
- ✓ Where is the organization confusing?
- ✓ Where is the writing unclear or vague?

Strengthening Paragraph Structure and Development—Chapter 14

- ✓ Does each paragraph have only one central idea?
- ✓ Is the idea stated in a topic sentence or clearly implied ?
- ✓ Does the topic sentence help to develop the thesis statement?
- ✓ Do the sentences within each paragraph advance the topic sentence?
- ✓ Does each paragraph contain enough supporting detail?
- ✓ Is each paragraph appropriately organized?
- ✓ Is the relationship between successive sentences clear?
- ✓ Is each paragraph clearly and smoothly related to those that precede and follow it?
- ✓ Does the introduction arouse interest and set the appropriate tone?
- ✓ Does the conclusion reflect the content of the essay and provide a sense of completeness?

Sharpening Sentences and Words—Chapters 15 and 16

- ✓ Are my sentences clearly and effectively constructed?
- ✓ Have I varied the pattern and length of my sentences?
- ✓ Do I know the meanings of the words I use?
- ✓ Do I explain meanings my reader may not know?
- ✓ Have I used the appropriate tone and level of diction?
- ✓ Does/would figurative language enhance my style?
- ✓ Have I avoided wordiness, euphemisms, clichés, mixed metaphors, and sexist language?

Editing the Draft—Handbook

- ✓ Have I inspected my writing for the types of errors listed in the editing symbols on the back endpapers?

Third Edition

STRATEGIES FOR SUCCESSFUL WRITING

A Rhetoric, Reader, and Handbook

James A. Reinking
Andrew W. Hart
Robert von der Osten

All of Ferris State University

Prentice Hall
Englewood Cliffs, New Jersey 07632

Acquisitions Editor: *Phil Miller*
Development Editor: *Joyce Perkins*
Interior design: *Suzanne Behnke*
Editorial/production supervision: *Margaret Antonini*
Cover design: *Tom Nery*
Prepress buyer: *Herb Klein*
Manufacturing buyers: *Patrice Fraccio, Robert Anderson*
Cover photo: *Reginald Wickham*

Printed in the United States of America
10 9 8 7 6 5 4 3 2 1

ISBN 0-13-847674-8

ACKNOWLEDGMENTS

R. T. Allen, "The Porcupine," from *Children, Wives, and Other Wildlife* by Robert Thomas Allen.
  Copyright © 1970 by Robert Thomas Allen (N.Y.: Doubleday, 1970).
Bonnie Angelo, "Those Good Ole Boys," *Time*, Sept. 27, 1976, p. 47.
Maya Angelou, "Momma's Encounter," from *I Know Why the Caged Bird Sings.* Copyright
  © 1969 by Maya Angelou. Reprinted by permission of Random House, Inc.
"Antigen," *Encyclopaedia Britannica*, 1974, I, 417.

(Acknowledgments continue on page 628, which constitutes an extension of the copyright page.)

Prentice-Hall International (UK) Limited, *London*
Prentice-Hall of Australia Pty. Limited, *Sydney*
Prentice-Hall Canada Inc., *Toronto*
Prentice-Hall Hispanoamericana, S.A., *Mexico*
Prentice-Hall of India Private Limited, *New Delhi*
Prentice-Hall of Japan, Inc., *Tokyo*
Simon & Schuster Asia Pte. Ltd., *Singapore*
Editora Prentice-Hall do Brasil, Ltda., *Rio de Janeiro*

In celebration of Diann

Contents

21 *Business Letters and Résumés* 340

READER

RHETORICAL TABLE OF CONTENTS

Narration 361

Description 372

THEMATIC TABLE OF CONTENTS

Our Relationship to Nature

American Crises

Ethnic, Gender, and Cultural Diversity

HANDBOOK

Sentence Elements 499

Editing to Correct Sentence Errors 529

Editing to Correct Faulty Punctuation and Mechanics 556

Preface

The third edition of *Strategies for Successful Writing: A Rhetoric, Reader, and Handbook* is a comprehensive textbook that offers ample material for a full year of freshman composition. Instructors teaching a one-term course can make selections from Chapters 1–16, from whatever types of specialized writing suit the needs of their students, and from appropriate essays in the Reader.

Because we strongly believe that an effective composition textbook should address the student directly, we have aimed for a style that is conversational yet clear and concise. We believe that our style invites students into the book, lessens their apprehensions about writing, and provides a model for their own prose.

*C*HANGES IN THE THIRD EDITION

The enthusiastic response to the two previous editions by both teachers and students has been most gratifying. The third edition retains the many popular features of the previous ones and incorporates a number of improvements, suggested by users and reviewers, that should considerably enhance the utility of the text. Among these changes the following are especially significant.

- A new chapter on interview, questionnaire, and direct observation reports offers detailed planning and writing guidelines on these widely used primary research strategies. Student models, complete with margin notes that highlight key features, illustrate each type.
- The chapter on mixing the writing strategies now includes planning and writing guidelines for problem/solution and evaluation reports, two prevalent types that rely on a combination of strategies. Students can see the practical value of learning how to mix different types of writing.
- The argument chapter, reorganized and strengthened, now unifies the discussion of the rational appeal by positioning argumentative support with induction, deduction, and analogy. We have also added a discussion of the different purposes of argument and how best to achieve them, as well as an introduction to Rogerian argument.

PRINT SUPPLEMENTS FOR INSTRUCTORS

Annotated Instructor's Edition (84767-3)

The *Annotated Instructor's Edition* consists of the entire student edition as well as strong instructional support. The material in the margins of the text consists of background information on particular aspects of writing; key insights into how students view writing projects and why they experience difficulties; assorted ethical issues that should spark lively class discussions; answers to all discussion questions and to appropriate exercises in the text; supplementary exercises; teaching strategies and classroom activities that instructors may want to consider; Reader/theme strategies that show how to use the Reader to build writing assignments based on themes; and lists of readings for instructors. Some of our suggestions begin with "you might"; others, to avoid potentially annoying repetition, do not. All suggestions have worked well for us over the years. Taken together, these resources should simplify the planning and enhance the classroom performance of instructors charting their course or refining their direction. Seasoned instructors may also wish to examine the many suggestions and sample those that seem intriguing.

We cordially invite instructors to participate in the next edition of the *Annotated Instructor's Edition*. Please share your teaching resources or comments with us by sending them to James Reinking, c/o College English Editor, Prentice Hall, Englewood Cliffs, NJ 07632. Items published will be acknowledged.

Teaching Composition with Strategies for Successful Writing, 3/E Supplementary Exercises (84765-7)

This supplement offers various suggestions for teaching freshman composition, sample syllabi for a sequence of three ten-week trimesters and two fifteen-week semesters, numerous guidelines for responding to student writing, and a detailed set of grading standards. In addition, it contains an extra set of twenty-item exercises that parallel those in the Handbook section of *Strategies*. These exercises can be used either in the classroom or as assignments.

PRINT SUPPLEMENTS FOR STUDENTS

The Research Organizer *Revised* (81395-6)

This convenient new tool is designed to help students assemble their research paper notes and drafts in an organized and efficient manner. It offers guidance on the research process and provides space for students to record their search strategy, notes, citations, outlines, and drafts. This newly revised supplement will make preparing for a research paper easier and more efficient by allowing students to categorize the majority of their materials.

Model Research Papers for Writers *Revised* (81398-0)

This newly revised collection of reproducible student research papers, in fields ranging from biology and political science to art history and English literature, provides clear examples of documentation, stylistic conventions, and formal requirements for various disciplines.

- Chapters 4–13 now point out various classroom and on-the-job uses for the writing strategies, validating their practicality.
- The Reader now opens with a unit entitled "Strategies for Successful Reading." We discuss how to read for different purposes—for information/evaluation, to critique—and explain how students can use their reading to improve their writing. Several of our guidelines are applied to a writing sample. Instructors can, of course, assign this unit at any point during the term.
- A new Thematic Table of Contents for the Reader groups essays into five categories: Life's Changes; Who We Are; Our Relationship to Nature; American Crises; and Ethnic, Gender, and Cultural Diversity. Instructors who center their writing courses around themes that serve as a focal point for reading, discussion, and writing should find these groupings useful. Furthermore, Chapters 4–13 in the Instructor's Edition now contain annotations that suggest how to use the Reader essays and writing strategies to build assignments around themes.
- The Reader contains one new essay for each writing strategy. These additions significantly increase the number of selections that deal with minority concerns.
- The individual-sentence exercises in the Handbook are all new. In addition, the section on sentence elements now explains how students can use these elements to improve their writing skills.

*T*HE RHETORIC

In addition to these improvements, the text offers many other noteworthy features. The Rhetoric consists of twenty-one chapters, grouped into four parts. The first part includes three chapters. Chapter 1 introduces students to the purposes of writing, the need for audience awareness, and the qualities of good writing. Chapter 2 looks at the planning and drafting stages of the composing process. Chapter 3 takes students through the various revision stages, starting with a systematic procedure for revising the whole essay and then moving to pointers for revising its component parts. Sets of checklists pose key questions for students to consider. Chapters 2 and 3 are unified by an unfolding case history that includes the first draft of a student paper, the initial revision marked with changes, and the final version. Notes in the margin highlight key features of the finished paper. Students can relate the sequence of events to their own projects as they work through the various stages. Both chapters offer suggestions for using a word processor, and Chapter 3 explains and demonstrates peer evaluation of drafts.

The ten chapters in the second part (Chapters 4–13) feature the various strategies, or modes, used to develop papers. These strategies, which follow a general progression from less to more complex, are presented as natural ways of thinking, as problem-solving strategies, and therefore as effective ways of organizing writing. A separate chapter is devoted to each strategy. This part concludes with a chapter on mixing the writing strategies, which explains and shows that writers frequently use these patterns in assorted combinations for various purposes.

Except for Chapter 13, the discussion in each chapter follows a similar approach, first explaining the key elements of the strategy and then providing detailed planning, drafting, and revising guidelines. Practical heuristic questions are also posed. A complete student essay, accompanied by questions, follows the discussion section. These essays represent realistic, achievable goals and spur student confidence, while the questions reinforce the general principles of good writing and underscore the points we make in our discussions. Each chapter ends with fifteen carefully chosen writing suggestions.

In the third part, we shift from full-length essays to the elements that make them up. Chapter 14 first discusses paragraph unity; it then takes up the topic sentence, adequate development, organization, and coherence, and finally introductory, transitional and concluding paragraphs. Throughout this chapter, as elsewhere, carefully selected examples and exercises form an integral part of the instruction.

Chapter 15 focuses on various strategies for creating effective sentences. Such strategies as coordinating and subordinating ideas and using parallelism help students to increase the versatility of their writing. The concluding section offers practical advice on crafting and arranging sentences so that they work together harmoniously.

Chapter 16, designed to help students improve their writing style, deals with words and their effects. We distinguish between abstract and concrete words as well as between specific and general terms, and we also discuss the dictionary and thesaurus. Levels of diction—formal, informal, and technical—and how to use them are explained, as are tone, various types of figurative language, and irony. The chapter concludes by pointing out how to recognize and avoid wordiness, euphemisms, clichés, mixed metaphors, and sexist language.

The fourth and final part of the Rhetoric concentrates on seven specialized types of college and on-the-job writing. Chapter 17 offers practical advice on studying for exams, assessing test questions, and writing essay answers. To facilitate student comprehension, we analyze both good and poor answers to the same exam question and provide an exercise that requires students to perform similar analyses.

Chapter 18 uses Stephen Crane's "The Bride Comes to Yellow Sky" as a springboard for its discussion. The chapter focuses on plot, point of view, character, setting, symbols, irony, and theme—the elements students will most likely be asked to write about. For each element, we first present basic features and then offer writing guidelines. The chapter ends with a section that details the development of a student paper.

Chapter 19 is a thorough and practical guide to writing library research papers. The chapter covers both the MLA and APA systems of documentation and includes a detailed discussion of plagiarism and how to avoid it. A sample pacing schedule not only encourages students to plan their work and meet their deadlines but also enables them to track their progress. As in Chapters 2 and 3, a progressive case history gradually evolves into an annotated student paper. Reflecting recent technological advances, the expanded discussion of periodical indexes notes the formats—print, microform, computerized—in which each is available. Our detailed treatment should make supplemental handouts or a separate research paper guide unnecessary.

Chapter 20, new to this edition, offers an in-depth discussion of interview, questionnaire, and direct-observation reports. After pointing out the nature, usefulness, and requirements of primary research, we explain how to plan and write each report, concluding with an annotated student model that illustrates the guidelines.

Contemporary View Program

This 32-page collection of articles from *The New York Times* provides students with timely reading selections that serve as both writing models and springboards for discussion.

Supplementary Essays for Writers (70705-9)

This collection of 31 essays by well-known professional writers is available at a nominal price to students using *Strategies for Successful Writing*. Each essay is accompanied by questions for discussion and writing, and each rhetorical section ends with several writing suggestions. Instructors adopting *Strategies* receive a free copy of *Supplementary Essays for Writers* and may reproduce individual essays for their students.

Webster's New World Dictionary, Third College Edition (94978-4)

This authoritative, hardcover dictionary contains more than 6,500 American words and phrases and more than 176,000 entries. Instructors may provide their students with this outstanding resource at a substantially discounted price when it is ordered with *Strategies for Successful Writing*.

SOFTWARE

Blue Pencil *Revised*

This acclaimed interactive editing program allows students to practice their writing skills by making revisions in paragraph-length passages on the computer screen. The program is organized around skills that students use most often in their writing. A counter at the bottom of the screen keeps track of the remaining corrections, and feedback is given for each response that students enter.

If students encounter difficulty with a particular topic or concept, they can receive additional instruction from the program. Blue Pencil includes a final review in which all skill categories are presented together. A site license can be provided for computer labs. Available for both IBM® and Macintosh®.

Blue Pencil Authoring System

This program allows instructors to modify existing Blue Pencil exercises or to create entirely new ones customized for the needs of their students. It includes two Blue Pencil exercise disks totaling 80 passages, 40 on each disk, representing many skill areas. Instructors may customize the existing passages by adding or deleting errors to be corrected and/or modifying the feedback and hints available to students. On-line directions and a helpful manual are included. Available for IBM® as a sale item to instructors only.

Webster's New World Writer

The student edition of this easy-to-learn and easy-to-use commercial word-processing package includes an extensive spelling checker. Ideal for student writers, the program won *PC Magazine's* Literary Choice Award. Students may purchase the documentation book and either 5¼″ or 3½″ disks as a complete package. As a special promotion, adopters of *Strategies for Successful Writing* can obtain a site license free, and students may purchase the documentation booklet at a special low price. Available for IBM®.

Book/disk package 5¼″ disk (94983-4)
Book/disk package 3½″ disk (94727-5)
Book only (94982-6)

Like other parts of the text, Chapter 21 speaks to a practical reality by reminding students that the value of writing extends beyond the English classroom. Example letters address a variety of practical situations—for example, applying for a summer job.

*T*HE READER

The Reader, sequenced to follow the order of the strategies as presented in the Rhetoric, expands the utility of the text by providing a collection of forty-one carefully selected professional models that illustrate the various writing strategies and display a wide variety of styles, tones, and subject matter. These essays, together with the nine student models that accompany the various strategy chapters, should make a separate reader unnecessary.

Each of the essays clearly illustrates the designated pattern, each has been thoroughly class tested for student interest, and each provides a springboard for a stimulating discussion. In making our selections we have aimed for balance and variety:

1. Some are popular classics by acknowledged prose masters; some, anthologized for the first time, are by fresh, new writers.
2. Some are straightforward and simple, some challenging and complex.
3. Some adopt a humorous, lighthearted approach, some a serious, thoughtful one.
4. Some take a liberal stance, some a conservative one, and some address ethnic, gender, and cultural diversity.
5. A few are rather lengthy; most are relatively brief.

In addition, we have aimed for a balance within the group of essays representing each writing strategy. For example, three of the narratives feature an unstated point and one a stated point. One of the cause-and-effect essays highlights causes, two deal with effects, and one explores both. The argument essays display various types of appeals and evidence. This section includes paired essays that propose different solutions to the drug problem, thus demonstrating the controversial nature of argument and allowing students to weigh the evidence and engage in debate.

For each writing strategy, the essays are arranged generally from simple to more complex, with the first one in each section annotated in the margin to show which features of the strategy are included. These annotations not only facilitate student understanding but also help link the Rhetoric and Reader into an organic whole. A brief biographical note about the author precedes each selection, and stimulating questions designed to enhance student understanding of structure and strategy follow it, along with a writing assignment suggested by the essay's topic.

*T*HE HANDBOOK

The comprehensive Handbook, which features tab indexing on each page for easy access to all material, consists of five parts: "Sentence Elements," "Editing to Correct Sentence Errors," "Editing to Correct Faulty Punctuation and Mechanics," "Spelling," and "Glossary of Word Usage." Explanations skirt unneeded grammatical terminology and are reinforced by sets of sentence exercises in the first three sections. We also include connected-discourse exercises—unfolding narratives that engage and retain student interest and therefore facilitate learning—in the "Sentence Errors" and "Punctuation and Mechanics" sections. A separate booklet containing extra sets of 20-item exercises that parallel those in the Handbook is available upon request to instructors who adopt the book. The spelling unit presents four useful spelling rules and an extensive list of commonly misspelled words. The glossary of word usage offers similarly comprehensive coverage of troublesome usages. Instructors can use the Handbook either as a reference guide or as a basis for class discussion.

ACKNOWLEDGMENTS

Like all textbook writers, we are indebted to many people. Our colleagues at Ferris State University and elsewhere, too numerous to mention, have assisted us in several ways: critiquing the manuscript; testing approaches, essays, and exercises in their classrooms; and suggesting writing models for the text. In addition, we would like to thank our reviewers, whose many suggestions have greatly improved our text: Rita Guida, Howard Community College; Daniel M. Huble, DeVry Institute of Technology; Arden Jensen, Gulf Coast Community College; William Lamb, Johnson County Community College; John W. Martin, Moraine Valley Community College; Teddie McFerrin, Collin County Community College; Joyce M. Miller, Collin County Community College; Michael A. Miller, Longview Community College; Kay Mizell, Collin County Community College; Kin Norman, DeVry Institute of Technology; Barbara J. Podkowka, Commonwealth College (Virginia Beach campus); and Keflyn X. Reed, Bishop State Community College.

Many thanks are also due to the outstanding team at Prentice Hall, whose editorial expertise, genial guidance, and promotional efforts have been vital to this project: Phil Miller, Editor-in-Chief for Humanities, who first saw the potential in our approach, proposed the Annotated Instructor's Edition, and suggested and supported many other improvements; Joyce Perkins, Senior Development Editor for English, whose keen judgment and experienced hand are reflected throughout the book; Margaret Antonini, our Production Editor, whose remarkable efficiency and meticulous attention to detail made our job much easier; Jim Tully, who copyedited our manuscript with exceptional precision; and Tracy Augustine and Gina Sluss, whose marketing expertise will help our book find its way. Finally, we'd like to thank Norma Reinking for her conscientious proofreading of the entire text.

J. A. R.
A. W. H.
R. v. d. O.

Write Now™ (97109-3)

The student edition of this full-featured word-processing program includes such features as a 50,000 word dictionary, automatic and immediate repagination, and autonumbering footnotes. *Write Now* is the winner of *MacUser* magazine's Best New Word Processor Award. A book/disk package is available to students at a substantially discounted price with the purchase of *Strategies for Successful Writing*. Available for Macintosh®.

Prentice Hall/Simon & Schuster Transparencies for Writers (70320-7)

This set of 100 two- and four-color transparencies features exercises, examples, and suggestions for student writing that focus on aspects of the writing process—from generating ideas and shaping an outline, to preparing a draft and revising and editing the final paper, to effectively using research sources. These transparencies also cover grammar, punctuation, and mechanics through overlays that show how sentence and paragraph errors can be corrected most effectively.

The Prentice Hall Critical Thinking Audio Study Cassette

This 60 minute cassette helps students develop their critical thinking skills—from asking the right questions to helpful tips on how to become a more effective learner.

THE NEW YORK TIMES and **PRENTICE HALL** are sponsoring **A CONTEMPORARY VIEW**, a program designed to enhance student access to current information of relevance in the classroom.

Through this program, the core subject matter provided in the text is supplemented by a collection of time-sensitive articles from one of the world's most distinguished newspapers, **THE NEW YORK TIMES**. These articles demonstrate the vital, ongoing connection between what is learned in the classroom and what is happening in the world around us.

So that students can enjoy the wealth of information of **THE NEW YORK TIMES** daily, a reduced subscription rate is available. For information, call toll-free: 1-800-631-1222.

PRENTICE HALL and **THE NEW YORK TIMES** are proud to co-sponsor **A CONTEMPORARY VIEW**. We hope that it will make the reading of both textbooks and newspapers a more dynamic, involving process.

RHETORIC

Writing: A First Look

Why write? Hasn't the tempest of technology swept all of us into a brave, new electronic world? Aren't its telephones, portable cassette recorders, and computer networks—all the magical devices of our new electronic estate—fast dooming ordinary writing? Not long ago, some people thought and said so, but events haven't supported those predictions. Although electronic devices have made some writing unnecessary, the written word flourishes both on campus and in the world of work. Furthermore, there's every evidence that writing will become even more important in the future.

Writing offers very real advantages to both writers and readers:

1. It provides a permanent record of thoughts, actions, and decisions.
2. It makes communication more precise and effective.
3. It saves the reader's time; we absorb information more swiftly when we read it than when we hear it.

Many people will expect you to write for them. College instructors ask you to write reports, research papers, and essay exams. Job hunting usually requires you to write application letters. And once you're hired, writing will probably figure in your duties. You might be asked to discuss the capabilities of new computer equipment, report on a conference you attended, or explain the advantages of new safety procedures to supervisors or staff. Perhaps you'll propose that your organization install a new security system, conduct a market survey, or develop an alternate traffic flow pattern. The ability to write will help you earn better grades, land the job you want, and advance afterwards in your career.

Furthermore, writing ability yields personal benefits. You might need to defend a medical reimbursement claim that you filed with your health insurer, request clarification of an inadequate or ambiguous set of directions, or document a demand for replacement of a faulty product. Skill in writing will help you handle these matters.

As you can see, we usually write in response to a situation. This situation often determines the purpose and audience of our paper as well as its content, style, and organization. We don't, then, write in isolation but rather to communicate with

PERSPECTIVE

Students seldom recognize how writing ability will influence their careers. Your course will be more likely to engage student interest if its practical value is readily apparent. To demonstrate this value, you might reproduce the following quotation as a class handout or on the board. We have found that it primes students for the upcoming term. They begin to sense the usefulness of writing in the "real" world and become more receptive to the instruction that will follow.

As soon as you move one step up from the bottom, your effectiveness depends on your ability to reach others through the spoken or written word. And the further away your job is from manual work, the larger the organization of which you are an employee, the more important it will be that you know how to convey your thoughts in writing or speaking. In the very large organizations, whether it is the government, the large business corporation, or the Army, this ability to express oneself is perhaps the most important of all the skills a person can possess.

Peter Drucker, "How to Be an Employee"

TEACHING STRATEGY

Have students interview either working professionals or their advisors on the importance of writing and then share their findings with the class. The interview could double as the first writing assignment.

3

others who have an interest in our message. To do an effective job, you will need to understand the different situations that can prompt a piece of writing and respond accordingly.

THE PURPOSES OF WRITING

Whenever you write, some clear purpose should guide your efforts. If you don't know why you're writing, neither will your reader. Fulfilling an assignment doesn't qualify as a real writing purpose, although it may well be what sends you to your desk. Faced with a close deadline for a research paper or report, you may tell yourself, "I'm doing this because I have to." An authentic purpose, however, requires you to answer this question: What do I want this piece of writing to do for both my reader and me?

Purpose, as you might expect, grows out of the writing situation. You explore the consequences of the greenhouse effect in a report for your science instructor. You write an editorial for the college newspaper to air your frustration over inadequate campus parking. You propose that your organization replace an outdated piece of equipment with a state-of-the-art model. Clearly, your purpose stems from the writing situation.

Here are four common *general writing purposes*, two or more of which often join forces in a single piece:

To Inform.   Presenting information is one of the most common writing purposes. The boating enthusiast who tells landlubber classmates how to handle a skiff plays the role of teacher, as does the researcher who summarizes the results of an investigation for co-workers. Some professional writers carve careers out of writing articles and books that fill gaps in the public's knowledge of timely topics. Instructors often ask you to write exams and papers so that they can gauge how well you have mastered the course material.

To Persuade.   You probably have strong views on many issues, and these feelings may sometimes impel you to try swaying your reader. In a letter to the editor, you might attack a proposal to establish a nearby chemical waste dump. Or, alarmed by a sharp jump in state unemployment, you might write to your state senator and argue for a new job-training program.

To Express Yourself.   Creative writing includes personal essays, fiction, plays, and poetry, as well as journals and diaries. But self-expression has a place in other kinds of writing, too. Almost everything you write offers you a chance to display your mastery of words and to enliven your prose with vivid images and fresh turns of phrase.

To Entertain.   Some writing merely entertains; some writing couples entertainment with a more serious purpose. A light-hearted approach can help your reader absorb dull or difficult material. Satire lets you expose the shortcomings of individuals, ideas, and institutions by poking fun at them. An intention to entertain can add savor to many kinds of writing.

CLASSROOM ACTIVITIES
1. Pair students and have them orally exchange a brief personal history. Next time the class meets, have students write down what they remember of their partner's history. They will quickly see the importance of an accurate, written record.
2. Bring in copies or overheads of a week's worth of interoffice memos to demonstrate the variety of situations that require writing.
3. Have each student identify some personal situations (beyond those listed in the text) that require writing. This type of activity, along with the previous two, helps set the stage for a writing course.

TEACHING STRATEGY
Students often overgeneralize their purpose for writing; they merely state, for instance, that they want to inform the reader. To help students crystallize their thoughts for an essay, require that they precisely state their purpose, the writing occasion, and how these variables influence their plans. You might have them complete a pre-writing sheet, which you either respond to before they write or examine when you read the final copy. Or you could supply the purpose and occasion as part of the assignment and refer to them as you respond to drafts. Either approach reinforces the notion that purpose is *not* merely fulfilling an assignment.

Besides having one or more *general purposes*, each writing project has its own *specific purpose*. Consider the difference in the papers you could write about solar homes. You might explain how readers could build one, argue that readers should buy one, express the advantages of solar homes to urge Congress to enact a tax credit for them, or satirize the solar home craze so that readers might reevaluate their plans to buy one.

Having a specific purpose assists you at every stage of the writing process. It helps you define your audience, select the details, language, and approach that best suit their needs, and avoid going off in directions that won't interest them. The following example from the newspaper *USA Today* has a clear and specific purpose.

We'll Trash *USA Today*, Too

J. Winston Porter

1   What will you do with *USA Today* after you finish reading it? If you're like most of us, you'll put the paper out with the garbage and it'll end up buried in a landfill. Over 80% of all household and commercial garbage ends up this way, and this is a problem.

2   The USA is relentlessly producing more and more trash, and we are rapidly running out of landfill space. At the same time, new landfills and incinerators are encountering local opposition. Before we are truly wallowing in waste, we need to declare a war on garbage.

3   The first battle we need to win is for public acceptance of a strategy that includes reducing the amount of waste generated and increasing the amount recycled. EPA is pushing a national goal of recycling 25% of all garbage within the next four years. But waste reduction and recycling aren't enough to stem the tide of trash that threatens to engulf us. We will continue to need safe landfilling of some garbage and incineration, preferably with energy recovery, as another option. EPA and the states are working to strengthen environmental controls on these facilities. The appropriate mix of waste reduction and recycling, landfilling and incineration should be "custom designed" by states and localities.

4   How can we all do our part? To begin with, we must recognize that we all contribute to the garbage problem. Next, we should cooperate in efforts to reduce the amount of trash requiring disposal. Finally, we must adopt new attitudes about disposal, because there will always be trash to be handled. This means that instead of simply opposing any new disposal facilities, citizens should assist in choosing the best options.

5   Recycling is the cornerstone of a sound waste-management strategy. We all have special responsibilities to make recycling work. Individuals must be willing to participate in local programs. Local governments should plan programs and operate required facilities. States should do statewide planning and enforce their own laws and regulations. Industry should step up its recycling efforts. The federal government should provide national leadership, research and information-sharing as well as develop certain underlying regulations.

6   No one segment of society can, alone, lead us to victory in the war on garbage. Instead, we need a coordinated national effort to confront the solid-waste issue head-on.

From *USA Today*, July 11, 1988, page 8A.

CLASSROOM ACTIVITIES

1. Select any essay from the Reader and have students (possibly in small groups) identify its purpose and the features that signal it.
2. Have students discuss what changes would be required in a sample essay if it had a different purpose (which you could specify).
3. Bring in samples of writing, perhaps student papers with names deleted, that fail to fulfill their purpose. Have students identify how the writing fails and suggest necessary changes.
4. Start with a topic, such as going to college, and have students indicate how they would approach a writing project if its purpose were to (a) tell stories that make friends laugh; (b) explain to high school students how to prepare for college; (c) explain to college professors why students have difficulty adjusting. The class will see that different purposes require different approaches.

SUGGESTED INSTRUCTOR READING

Kinneavy, J. "The Basic Aims of Discourse." College Composition and Communication 20 (1969): 297–304. A briefer version of A Theory of Discourse, this article classifies types of discourse and how they relate to purpose.

Porter hints at his purpose in the first paragraph by noting that the disposal of garbage in landfills poses a problem. The last sentence of paragraph 2 states the purpose clearly. The remaining paragraphs name the strategies that he recommends to wage war on garbage and explain how individuals, government, and industry can all contribute. Everything Porter has written relates to his purpose.

Now examine the next paragraph, which does *not* have a firmly fixed specific purpose.

> Community is a sea in which people swim unconsciously, like fish. We fail
> to recognize our neighbors as fellow humans, and they show the same lack
> of fellow-feelings for us. A complete lack of concern for one another is
> evident in today's complex society. What is community? Is it a plant? A
> building? A place? A state of being? Knowing what it is, we can see if
> such a place exists. To know community, one must realize who he or she
> is. Identity of a person is the first step in establishing a community.

This student writer can't decide what aspect of community to tackle. The opening sentence attempts a definition, but the next two veer onto the shortcomings of the modern community. Notice how aimlessly the thoughts drift. The vague leadoff sentence asserts "Community is a sea . . . ," but the later question "What is community?" contradicts this opening. Also, if community is a plant, a building, or a place, why must we realize who we are in order to know it? This contradictory and illogical paragraph reveals a writer groping for a purpose.

The paragraph, however, isn't a wasted effort. These musings offer several possibilities. By developing the first sentence, the writer might show some interesting similarities between community and a sea so that instead of taking community for granted, readers can see it in a new light. By pursuing the idea in the second and third sentences, the writer might show the callous nature of modern society to encourage readers to act more humanely. The last two sentences might lead to a statement on the relationship between individual and community in order to overcome the common view that the two are in conflict. A specific purpose can sometimes emerge from preliminary jottings.

THE AUDIENCE FOR YOUR WRITING

Everything you write is aimed at some audience—a person or group you want to reach. The ultimate purpose of all writing is to have an effect on a reader (even if that reader is you), and therefore purpose and audience are closely linked. Our discussion on page 4 makes this point clear by noting that your purpose can be to inform *someone* of something, to persuade *someone* to believe or do something, to express feelings or insights to *someone*, or to entertain *someone*. Any of these objectives requires that you *know* that someone, the audience for your writing.

Writing operates on a delayed-action fuse, detonating its ideas in the readers' minds at a later time and place. Sometimes problems follow. In face-to-face conver-

TEACHING STRATEGY

Many students have trouble finding things to say, and as a result they feel they have no purpose for writing except to fulfill the assignment. You could have them list or free-write things they would like to tell people but haven't or can't: personal experiences that others might not initially understand, activities they believe they can do better than others, and the like. Such beginnings can often lead to a specific purpose.

PERSPECTIVE

Audience is a difficult concept for students since they are most familiar with writing that is aimed exclusively at their instructor. The classroom situation often ties them to that assumption. You might attempt therefore to broaden their sense of audience. Students should understand that assorted readers with a variety of characteristics will receive and react to their writing and that reader response must be anticipated.

sations, you can observe your listeners' reactions, and whenever you note signs of hostility, boredom, or puzzlement, you can alter your tone, offer some examples, or ask a question. You can also use gestures and facial expressions to emphasize what you're saying. When you write, however, the words on the page carry your message. Once written work has left your hands, it's on its own. You can't call it back to clear up a misunderstanding or satisfy a disgruntled reader.

Establishing rapport with your audience is easy when you're writing for your friends or someone else you know a great deal about. You can then judge the likely response to what you say. Often, though, you'll be writing for people you know only casually or not at all: employers, customers, fellow townsfolk, and the like. In such situations, you'll need to assess your audience before starting to write and/or later in the writing process.

A good way to size up your readers is to develop an audience profile. This profile will emerge gradually as you answer the following questions:

1. What are the educational level, age, social class, and economic status of the audience I want to reach?
2. Why will this audience read my writing? To gain information? Learn my views on a controversial issue? Enjoy my creative flair? Be entertained?
3. What attitudes, needs, and expectations do they have?
4. How are they likely to respond to what I say? Can I expect them to be neutral? Opposed? Friendly?
5. How much do they know about my topic? (Your answer here will help you gauge whether you're saying too little or too much.)
6. What kind of language will communicate with them most effectively? (See "Level of Diction" section in Chapter 16.)

College writing assignments sometimes ask you to envision a reader who is intelligent but lacking specialized knowledge, receptive but unwilling to put up with boring or trite material. Or perhaps you'll be assigned, or choose, to write for a certain age group or one with particular interests. At other times, you'll be asked to write for a specialized audience—one with some expertise in your topic. This difference will affect what you say to each audience and how you say it.

Let's see how audience can shape a paper. Suppose you are explaining how to take a certain type of X-ray. If your audience is a group of lay readers who have never had an X-ray, you might note at the outset that taking one is much like taking an ordinary photograph. Then you might explain the basic process, including the positioning of the patient and the equipment, comment on the safety and reliability of the procedure, and note how much time it takes. You probably would use few technical terms. If, however, you were writing for radiology students, you might emphasize exposure factors, film size, and required views. This audience would understand technical terms and want a detailed explanation of the procedure. You could speak to these readers as colleagues who appreciate precise information.

Audience shapes all types of writing in similar fashion, even your personal writing. Assume you've recently become engaged, and to share your news you write two letters: one to your clergyman, the other to your best friend back home. You can imagine the differences in details, language, and general tone of each

TEACHING STRATEGIES

1. Have students write to actual readers who might supply a response. They could complain about a defective product, request a free product, or write to a state representative.
2. Have students identify what needs, attitudes, and expectations they have as readers and how these factors influence their response.
3. To show your class that an audience can be other than the instructor, you might specify an assumed audience for a paper and then respond to student efforts as if you belonged to that audience.
4. Have students develop an audience profile for their papers and indicate how it will affect their planning.

CLASSROOM ACTIVITIES

1. Bring in writing samples aimed at a non-student audience. Have students identify how they respond and why.
2. Bring in samples of communication that are clearly inappropriate to their audience. Any faculty member's mailbox is full of examples. Have students identify the problems and suggest changes.
3. Bring in samples of sales literature and have students identify the assumptions being made about audience and how they have influenced the writing.
4. Bring in a writing example that has no clear sense of audience. Have students identify the problems they have with it and suggest needed changes. An excellent example appears in Flowers' article cited below.

SUGGESTED INSTRUCTOR READINGS

Eda, L., and A. Lunsford. "Audience Addressed/ Audience Invoked: The Role of Audience in Composition Theory and Practice." College

8

Composition and Communication 32 (1981): 365–68. Shows how the writer not only addresses the audience but determines the role the audience is to assume.

Flowers, L. "Writer-Based Prose: A Cognitive Basis for Problems in Writing." College English 41 (1979): 19–37. Shows how students can go from writer-oriented prose to reader-oriented prose and supplies excellent examples.

Gibson, W. "Authors, Speakers, Readers, and Mock Readers." College English 11 (1950): 254–69. Distinguishes the different roles an audience can assume in reading a work.

Maimon, E. P. "Talking to Strangers." College Composition and Communication 30 (1979): 364–69. Indicates how important it is for students to recognize that they are addressing strangers who will not necessarily share their experiences or their present context.

EXERCISE ANSWERS

Passage 1 is aimed at a broad, general audience, including young people. To reach this audience, Hamilton has used short sentences and everyday words and, to help his readers understand the term being discussed, has likened antigens to "foes." Passage 2 is aimed at an audience of educated adults. Its sentences are longer and more intricate than those in passage 1, and it uses a number of technical terms— helminths, polysaccharides, lipids—that would puzzle most readers in a general audience. Passage 3 is aimed at students in the field of immunology. Because these readers will become specialists, the authors use more technical

letter. Further, think how inappropriate it would be if you accidentally sent the letter intended for one to the other. Without doubt, different readers call for different approaches.

EXERCISE ■ **The three excerpts below deal with the same subject—antigens—but each explanation is geared to a different audience. Read the passages carefully; then answer the following questions:**

1. What audience does each author address? How do you know?
2. Identify ways in which each author appeals to a specific audience.

1.   The human body is quick to recognize foreign chemicals that enter it. "Foes" must be attacked or otherwise got rid of. The most common of these foes are chemical materials from viruses, bacteria, and other microscopic organisms. Such chemicals, when recognized by the body, are called *antigens*. To combat them, the body produces its own chemicals, protein molecules called *antibodies*. Each kind of antigen causes the production of a specific kind of antibody. Antibodies appear in the body fluids such as blood and lymph and in the body's cells.

L. D. Hamilton, "Antibodies and Antigens,"
The New Book of Knowledge

2.   [An] *Antigen* [is a] foreign substance that, when introduced into the body, is capable of inducing the formation of antibodies and of reacting specifically in a detectable manner with the induced antibodies. For each antigen there is a specific antibody, the physical and chemical structure of which is produced in response to the physical and chemical structure of the antigen. Antigens comprise virtually all proteins that are foreign to the host, including those contained in bacteria, viruses, protozoa, helminths, foods, snake venoms, egg white, serum components, red blood cells, and other cells and tissues of various species, including man. Polysaccharides and lipids may also act as antigens when coupled to proteins.

"Antigen," *Encyclopaedia Britannica*

3.   The substance which stimulates the body to produce antibodies is designated *antigen* (antibody stimulator). . . .

Most complete antigens are protein molecules containing aromatic amino acids, and are large in molecular weight and size. However, it has been demonstrated that other macromolecules, such as pure polysaccharides, polynucleotides, and lipids, may serve as complete antigens.

However, certain other materials, incapable of stimulating antibody formation by themselves can, in association with a protein or other carrier, stimulate antibody formation and are the antigenic determinants. These determinants are referred to as *incomplete antigens* or *haptens* and they are able to react with antibodies which were produced by the determinant-protein complex.

However, before an antigen can stimulate the production of antibodies, it must be soluble in the body fluids, must reach certain tissues in an unaltered form, and must be, in general, foreign to the body tissues. Protein taken by mouth loses its specific foreign-protein characteristics when digested in the alimentary tract. It reaches the tissues of the body as amino acids or other altered digested products of protein. Consequently, it no longer meets the requirements for antigenic behavior.

Orville Wyss and Curtis Eklund,
Microorganisms and Man

Just as you would not dial a telephone number at random and then expect to carry on a meaningful conversation, so you should not expect to communicate effectively without a specific audience in mind.

One other note: as you shape your paper, it is important that the writing please you as well as your audience—that it satisfy your sense of what good writing is and what the writing task requires. You are, after all, your own first reader.

THE QUALITIES OF GOOD WRITING

Three qualities—fresh thinking, a sense of style, and effective organization—help to ensure that a piece of prose will meet your reader's expectations.

Fresh Thinking.   You don't have to astound your readers with something never before discussed in print. Genuinely unique ideas and information are scarce commodities. You can, however, freshen your writing by exploring personal insights and perceptions. Using your own special slant, you might show a connection between seemingly unrelated items, as Kathleen Fury does when she likens office "paper pushers" to different kinds of animals (pages 412–13). Keep the expression of your ideas credible, however; farfetched notions spawn skepticism.

Sense of Style.   Readers don't expect you to display the stylistic flair of Erma Bombeck or Art Buchwald. Indeed, such writing would impair the neutral tone needed in certain kinds of writing, such as technical reports and legal documents. Readers *do*, however, expect you to write in a clear style. And if you strengthen it with vivid, forceful words, readers will absorb your points with even greater interest. The chapters ahead show you how to use language in ways that project your own views and personality. Chapters 15 and 16, in particular, will help you develop a sense of style, as will the many readings throughout the book.

Effective Organization.   A paper should have a beginning, a middle, and an end; that is, an introduction, a body, and a conclusion. The introduction sparks interest and acquaints the reader with what is to come. The body delivers the main message and exhibits a clear connection between ideas so that the reader can easily follow your thoughts. The conclusion ends the discussion so the reader feels satisfied rather than suddenly cut off. Overall, your paper should follow a pattern that is suited to its content. Organizational patterns, or strategies of development, are the subject of Chapters 4–13. Pages 186–92 discuss introductions and conclusions.

terms and provide a more detailed explanation than do the first two writers. Wyss and Eklund assume that the reader understands the basics of antigens and concentrate on presenting specialized information concerning them.

PERSPECTIVE

Good writing, of course, depends on the writer's grasp of purpose and audience. No one would expect a letter to a friend to approximate a magazine article. You can help students understand that good writing is a function of context. Students and instructors often have a different sense of what makes for good writing. What we see as well developed and significant they might see as tedious and pompous. Good writing instruction helps students to understand that our sense of good writing is not arbitrary but stems from how readers receive writing.

CLASSROOM ACTIVITIES

1.   Bring in a newspaper article, magazine article, and professional essay on the same topic. Have students identify textual differences, account for them, and identify what is common to the texts. Suggest that the common qualities are features of good writing; also suggest the qualities that are specific to particular writing situations.
2.   Have students rank three different versions of the same paper or memo. One version might be vague and general, another ineffectively organized, and the third a clear example of good writing. Compare student rankings and discuss the reasons for their decisions.

SUGGESTED INSTRUCTOR READINGS

Booth, W. C. "The Rhetorical Stance." College Composition and Communication 14 (1963): 139–145. Defines the quality of writing as a balance among subject, object, and the writer's persona.

Dillon, G. L. Constructing Texts. Bloomington: Indiana UP, 1981. Insists that good writing reflects social conventions and should be taught accordingly.

Hirsch, E. D. The Philosophy of Composition. Chicago: U of Chicago P, 1977. Attempts to deduce a definition of good writing based on how we supposedly read texts.

Freshness, style, and organization are weighted differently in different kinds of writing. A writer who drafts a proposal to pave a city's streets will probably attach less importance to fresh thinking than to clear writing and careful organization. On the other hand, fresh thinking can be very important in a description of an autumn forest scene. You will learn more about these qualities throughout this book.

Planning and Drafting Your Paper

Many students believe that good essays are dashed off in a burst of inspiration by born writers. Students themselves often boast that they cranked out their topnotch papers in an hour or so of spare time. Perhaps. But for most of us, writing is a process that takes time and work. Better writers are not born with their gift but learn through informed practice how to incorporate their ideas into a paper.

Although successful writers can often describe how they go about their work, writing is a flexible process. No one order guarantees success, and no one approach works for every writer. Some writers establish their purpose and draft a plan for carrying it out at the start of every project. Others begin with a tentative purpose or plan and discover their final direction as they write. As a project proceeds, the writer is likely to leapfrog backward and forward one or more times rather than to proceed in an orderly, straightforward sequence. Part way through a first draft, for instance, a writer may think of a new point to present, then pause and jot down the details needed to develop it. Similarly, part of the conclusion may come to mind as the writer is gathering the details for supporting a key idea.

Regardless of how it unfolds, the writing process consists of the following stages. Advancing through each stage will guide you if you have no plan or if you've run into snags with your approach. Once you're familiar with these stages, you can combine or rearrange them as needed.

Understanding the assignment
Zeroing in on a topic
Gathering information
Organizing the information
Developing a thesis statement
Writing the first draft

UNDERSTANDING THE ASSIGNMENT

Instructors differ in making writing assignments. Some specify the topic, some give you several topics to choose from, and still others offer you a free choice. Likewise, some instructors dictate the length and format of the essay, whereas others don't.

3. Have students, working in small groups, review one another's logs, then formulate and present to the class some general observations about the practice of writing.

PERSPECTIVE

Some assignments can be very detailed and even include the information students are to use in their papers. Others can be very general, allowing students to shape the project to their own ends. General assignments can encourage students to produce vague pieces of writing that reflect ill-defined purposes and audiences. However, if *all* assignments are restrictive, students won't learn to use writing for their own purposes. Perhaps the best compromise is a mixture of general and specific assignments. Good writing assignments should allow students to draw upon their background and interests; have a genuine, clearly evident purpose and be aimed at a real audience; provide a learning experience for students; tailor any research requirements to the ability of students; gradually increase in difficulty as the course progresses; be clear about what students must do to develop the paper; stem from reading and discussions.

TEACHING STRATEGY

It often helps to have students read about and discuss a subject that can serve as a seedbed for a variety of topics. For example, the influence of television on viewers' lives might lead to papers about its influence on our buying habits, dating practices, views of minorities, attitudes toward violence, and health concerns.

Whatever the case, be sure you understand the assignment before you go any further.

Think of it this way: if your boss asked you to report on ways of improving the working conditions in your office and you turned in a report on improving worker benefits, would you expect the boss's approval? Following directions is crucial, so if you have any questions about the assignment, ask your instructor to clear them up right then. Don't be timid; it's much better to ask for directions than to receive a low grade for failing to follow them.

Once you understand the assignment, consider the project *yours.* If you are asked to describe a favorite vacation spot for a local newspaper, here is your chance to inform others about a place special to you. By asking yourself what the assignment allows you to accomplish, you can find your purpose.

ZEROING IN ON A TOPIC

A subject is a broad discussion area: sports, college life, culture, and the like. A topic is one small segment of a subject; for example, testing athletes for drug use, Nirvana College's academic probation policy, the videocassette phenomenon. If you choose your own topic, pick one narrow enough so that you can develop it properly within any length limitation. Avoid sprawling, slippery issues that lead to a string of trite generalities.

In addition, choose a familiar topic or one you can learn enough about in the time available. Avoid overworked topics such as arguments about open visitation in dormitories or the legal drinking age, which generally repeat the same old points. Instead, select a topic that lets you draw upon your unique experiences and insights and offer a fresh perspective to your reader.

Strategies for Finding a Topic

Whenever your instructor assigns a general subject, you'll need to stake out a limited topic suitable for your paper. If you're lucky, the right one will come to mind immediately. More often, though, you'll need to resort to some special strategy. Here are six proven strategies that many writers use. Not all of them will work for everyone, so experiment to find those that produce a topic for you.

Tapping Your Personal Resources.   Personal experience furnishes a rich storehouse of writing material. Over the years, you've packed your mind with memories of family gatherings, school activities, movies, concerts, plays, parties, TV programs, dates, discussions, arguments, and so on. All these experiences can provide suitable topics. Suppose you've been asked to write about some aspect of education. Recalling the difficulties you had last term at registration, you might argue for better registration procedures. Or if you're a hopeless TV addict who must write on some advertising topic, why not analyze video advertising techniques?

Anything you've read in magazines or journals, newspapers, novels, short stories, or textbooks can also trigger a topic. O. Henry's short story "The Last Leaf," in which a character almost dies of pneumonia, might suggest a paper on some miracle drug or a bout of illness you had. An article reviewing the career of a well-known politician might stir thoughts of a friend's experience in running for the student council. Possibilities crowd our lives, waiting for us to recognize and seize them.

EXERCISE ■ **Select five of the subjects listed below. Tapping your personal resources, name one topic suggested by each. For each topic, list three questions that you might answer in a paper.**

Life on a city street	A best-selling book
A particular field of work	Some aspect of nature
Some branch of the federal bureaucracy	Marriage
Concern for some aspect of the environment	Contemporary forms of dancing
Parents	Youth gangs
Saving money	Fashions in clothing
Home ownership	Trendiness
Schools in your town	Human rights
Leisure activities	Public transportation
The two-income family	Childhood fears
	A new scientific discovery
	A religious experience

Keeping a Journal.   Many writers, not comfortable relying on their memories, record their experiences in a journal—a private gathering of entries accumulated over a period of time. Journal keeping provides an abundance of possible writing topics as well as valuable writing practice.

The hallmark of the journal entry is the freedom to explore thoughts, feelings, responses, attitudes, and beliefs. In your own private domain you can express your views without reservation, without concern for "doing it right." *You* control the content and length of the entry without being held to a specified topic or number of words. Furthermore, depending on your instructor's preference, you usually don't have to worry about correct spelling or grammar. Journal writing does not represent a finished product but rather an exploration.

A few simple guidelines ensure effective journal entries:

1. Write in any kind of notebook that appeals to you; the content, not the package, is the important thing.
2. Write on a regular basis—at least five times a week if possible. In any event don't write by fits and starts, cramming two weeks' entries into one sitting.
3. Write for ten to twenty minutes, longer if you have more to say. Don't aim for uniform entry length; for example, three paragraphs or a page and a half. Simply explore your reactions to the happenings in your life or to what you have read, heard in class, or seen on television. The length will take care of itself.

Let's examine a typical journal entry by Sam, a freshman composition student.

PERSPECTIVE

Unless students understand just what their journals are meant to accomplish, they aren't likely to use them properly. Several kinds of journals are possible. *Personal response:* allows students to record stray thoughts and ideas as well as interesting experiences. Beyond having students write a certain amount each day, instructors impose no restrictions. *Focused response:* features a collection of responses to topics set by the instructor and is tailored toward future writing assignments or specific skills being introduced. Thus students who will write comparison and description essays may be asked to write a page or two contrasting two family members or describing a fellow student. *Reading log:* allows students to summarize reading assignments, possibly connect readings to their own experience, compare different readings, or record their thoughts while reading. Such a log helps prepare for a paper based on readings.

TEACHING STRATEGIES

1. Students are likely to confuse journals with diaries and jot down diary-type entries. To counter this tendency, show them examples of what you'll expect and specify the purpose of journal assignments. Focused responses avoid this problem.
2. Many students are likely to write as little as possible and dash off all their entries at the last minute. It is therefore a good idea to review journals frequently.

CLASSROOM ACTIVITIES

1. To use journal entries in class, set up small groups and have students share their focused responses to a reading assignment or a specific question. A discussion aimed at developing a topic for a paper could follow.

Last week went back to my hometown for the first time since my family moved away and while there dropped by the street where I spent my first twelve years. Visit left me feeling very depressed. Family home still there, but its paint peeling and front porch sagging. Sign next to the porch said house now occupied by Acme Realtors. While we lived there, front yard lush green and bordered by beds of irises. Now an oil-spattered parking lot. All the other houses on our side of the street gone, replaced by a row of dumpy buildings housing dry cleaner, bowling alley, hamburger joint, shoe repair shop, laundromat. All of them dingy and rundown looking, even though only a few years old.

Other side of street in no better shape. Directly across from our house a used-car dealership with rows of junky looking cars. No trace left of the Little League park that used to be there. Had lots of fun playing baseball and learned meaning of sportsmanship. To left of the dealership my old grade school, now boarded and abandoned. Wonder about my fifth-grade teacher Mrs. Wyrick. Is she still teaching? Still able to make learning a game, not a chore? Other side of dealership the worst sight of all. Grimy looking plant of some sort pouring foul smelling smoke into the air from a discolored stack. Smoke made me cough.

Don't think I'll revisit my old street again.

This journal entry could spawn several essays. Sam might explore the causes of residential deterioration, define sportsmanship, explain how Mrs. Wyrick made learning a game, or argue for stricter pollution control laws.

EXERCISE ■ Write journal entries over the next week or two for some of the following items that interest you. If you have trouble finding a suitable topic for a paper, review the entries for possibilities.

Pleasant or unpleasant conversations
Developing relationships

Cultural or sporting events
College life: myth vs. reality

Single or married life
Parents
Financial or occupational
considerations
Ideas gained through reading

Public figures—politicians; movie,
rock, or sports stars
World trouble spots
Courses you are taking

Sorting Out a Subject.   All of us sort things. We do it whenever we tackle the laundry, clear away a sinkful of dishes, or tidy up a basement or garage. Let's see how we might handle a cluttered basement. To start off, we'd probably sort the contents according to type: books in one spot, clothing in a second, toys in a third. That done, chances are we'd do still more sorting, separating children's books from adults' and stuffed animals from games. As we looked over and handled the different items, long-buried, bittersweet memories might start flooding from our subconscious. Memories of an uncle, now dead, who sent this old adventure novel . . . of our parents' pride when they saw their child had learned to ride that now battered bicycle . . . of the dance that marked the debut of the evening gown over there.

Sorting out a subject follows a similar scenario. First, we break our broad subject into categories and subcategories, then allow our minds to roam over the different items and see what topics we can turn up. The chart on page 16 shows what one student found when she explored the general topic of public transportation.

As you'll discover for yourself, some subjects yield more topics than others; some, no topics at all.

EXERCISE ■ **Select two of the following subjects; then subdivide those two into five topics.**

Advertising	Movies	The space program
Dwellings	Occupations	Sports
Fashions	Popular music	Television programs
Magazines	Social classes	Vacations

Asking Questions.   Often, working your way through these basic questions will lead you to a manageable topic.

1. Can I define my subject?
2. Does it break into categories?
3. If so, what comparisons can I make among these categories?
4. If my subject is divided into parts, how do they work together?
5. Does my subject have uses? What are they?
6. What are some examples of my subject?
7. What are the causes or origins of my subject?
8. What impact has my subject had?

Results of Sorting out the Subject Public Transportation

Land			Water		Air	
Buses	Taxis	Trains	Sea-going	Lake, River	Airplanes	Helicopters
County bus service for the handicapped	Rights of passengers	The Orient Express, the Twentieth Century Limited	The Titanic		Airline deregulation	Air taxis
Bus tours	Preventing crimes against drivers	Monorails	Luxury liners		Overbooking flights	Cargo
Jitney buses		Preventing subway crimes	Theme cruises		Making air travel safer	
Problem of smoking on buses		Guardian Angels	Modern sea pirates		Coping with hijacking	
Improving bus terminals		Amtrak	Traveling by freighter		Causes and prevention of jet lag	
Designing buses to accommodate the handicapped		Japan's high speed trains	The impact of overseas flights on ship travel		Development of the Stealth bomber	
		Deterioration of railroad trackbeds			Noise pollution around airports	

Let's convert these general questions into specific questions about telescopes, a broad general subject:

1. What is a telescope?
2. What are the different kinds of telescopes?
3. How are they alike? How do they differ?
4. What are the parts of each kind of telescope, and how do they work together?
5. What are telescopes used for?
6. What are some well-known telescopes?
7. Who invented the telescope?
8. What impact have telescopes had on human life and knowledge?

Each of these questions offers a starting point for a suitably focused essay. Question 3 might launch a paper comparing reflecting and refracting telescopes; question 6 might be answered in a paper about the planning and construction of the 200-inch reflecting telescope at California's Mount Palomar observatory.

PERSPECTIVE

Students find it easier to write about questions than topics. Questions require us to generate ideas; topics can be tombstones to thought. It often helps to have students translate topics into questions and then develop a set of related questions.

EXERCISE ■ **Convert the general questions into specific questions about two of the following subjects; then suggest two essay topics for each of your two subjects.**

Astrology	Games	Shopping malls
Books	Microorganisms	Stars
Colleges	Plays	Television
Emotions	Religion	Warships

Freewriting. The freewriting strategy snares thoughts as they race through your mind, yielding a set of sentences that you then look over for writing ideas. To begin, turn your pen loose and write for about five minutes on your general subject. Put down everything that comes into your head, without worrying about grammar, spelling, or punctuation. What you produce is for your eyes alone. If the thought flow becomes blocked, write "I'm stuck, I'm stuck . . ." until you break the mental logjam. When your writing time is up, go through your sentences one by one and extract potential topic material. If you draw a blank, write for another five minutes and look again.

The following example shows the product of one freewriting session. Jim's instructor had assigned a two- or three-page paper on some sports-related topic, and since Jim had been a member of his high school tennis team, his thoughts naturally turned toward this sport.

> Sports. If that's my subject, I'd better do something on tennis. I've played
>
> enough of it. But what can I say that would be interesting? It's very
>
> popular, lots of people watch it on TV. Maybe I could write about the
>
> major tennis tournaments. I'm stuck. I'm stuck. Maybe court surfaces.
>
> That sounds dull. I'm stuck. Well, what about tennis equipment, clothing,
>
> scoring? Maybe my reader is thinking about taking up the game. What do

PERSPECTIVE

Freewriting was heralded by Peter Elbow, who initially used it as a strategy to help MIT engineers whose writing anxiety blocked their writing. A useful way to unlock the mind and bring up interesting and new associations, it can be used at any point in the writing process to help students develop new approaches to papers in progress. Don't expect splendid results every time: students who think trite thoughts produce trite freewriting. And like any activity, freewriting becomes more effective with repeated use. It can be unfocused, with students writing whatever comes into their heads, or focused on some subject or topic.

TEACHING STRATEGIES

1. Have students freewrite on anything, circle sentences that interest them, and then freewrite on those sentences. Ask them to repeat the process until a potential topic emerges.
2. To ingrain the habit of freewriting, ask students to freewrite for five minutes at the beginning of the class, perhaps during the first couple of weeks of the term.

You might also have students freewrite before class discussions in order to develop things to say.

3. Some students can't believe that the instructor doesn't want perfect writing; others view the activity as a waste of time since it doesn't immediately result in a finished paper. Explain the rationale for freewriting and distribute far-from-perfect samples. You could freewrite with the class and share your results.

4. Other students might see freewriting as a green light to produce essays that are merely tidied up freewriting. Maintain a clear distinction between freewriting designed to uncover topics, the drafts that are increasingly audience oriented, and the final draft—developed, organized, and polished.

SUGGESTED INSTRUCTOR READING

Elbow, P. Write Without Teachers. New York: Oxford UP, 1973. The classic account of the rationale for freewriting and how to use it effectively to develop a draft.

PERSPECTIVE

Students are surprised to learn that brainstorming, both by individuals and groups, is widely used in corporations to generate ideas, especially for advertisements.

TEACHING STRATEGIES

1. Brainstorming and freewriting can be combined. A student can brainstorm, select an item from the resulting list, freewrite about it, and then brainstorm an item from the freewriting list.

I like about tennis? The strategy, playing the net, when to use a topspin or a backspin stroke, different serves. I'm stuck. I'm stuck. Maybe I could suggest how to play a better game of singles. I used to be number one. I can still remember Coach harping on those three Cs, conditioning, concentration, consistency. I'm stuck. I'm stuck. Then there's the matter of special shots like lobs, volleys, and overheads. But that stuff is for the pros.

This example suggests at least three papers. For the beginning player, Jim could focus on equipment and scoring. For the intermediate player, he might write on conditioning, concentration, and consistency; for the advanced player, on special shots.

Brainstorming.   Brainstorming, a close cousin of freewriting, captures fleeting ideas in words, fragments, and sometimes sentences, rather than in a series of sentences. Brainstorming garners ideas faster than the other strategies do. But unless you move immediately to the next stage of writing, you may lose track of what some of your fragmentary jottings mean.

To compare the results of freewriting and brainstorming a topic, we've converted our freewriting example into this list, which typifies the results of brainstorming.

Popularity of tennis	Equipment
Major tournaments	Clothing
Court surfaces	Scoring
Doubles strategy	Conditioning
Singles strategy	Concentration
Playing the net	Consistency
Topspin	Special shots—lobs, drop volleys,
Backspin	overheads
Different serves	

EXERCISE ■ **Return to the five subjects you selected for the exercise on page 13. Freewrite or brainstorm for five minutes on each one; then choose a topic suitable for a two- or three-page essay. State your topic, intended audience, and purpose.**

Narrowing a familiar subject may yield not only a topic but also the main divisions for a paper on it. Jim's freewriting session uncovered several possible tennis topics as well as a way of approaching each: by focusing on lobs, drop volleys, and overheads when writing about special shots, for example. Ordinarily, though, the main divisions will emerge only after you have gathered material to develop your topic.

Identifying Your Audience and Purpose

You can identify your purpose and audience at several different stages in the writing process. Sometimes both are set by the assignment and guide your selection of a topic. For example, you might be asked to write the college president to recommend improvements in the school's registration system. At other times, you may have to write a draft before you can determine either. Usually, though, the selection of audience and purpose goes hand in hand with determining a topic. Think of the different types of information Jim would gather if he wrote for (1) beginning players to offer advice on improving their game, (2) tennis buffs to point out refinements of the game, (3) a physics professor to show the physical forces controlling the behavior of tennis balls in flight.

2. Following the practice of business, have the class brainstorm a subject as a group, write their responses on the board, weed out ideas inappropriate for papers, then brainstorm some more.
3. Some students claim to be stuck after listing just two or three ideas. Nudge them into jotting down *any* ideas, no matter how absurd they seem. They can always be deleted later.

CASE HISTORY

Now that you're familiar with some narrowing strategies, let's examine the first segment of a case history that shows how one student handles a writing assignment. This segment illustrates the use of a narrowing strategy to find a topic. Later segments focus on the remaining stages of the writing process.

George's writing class has been talking and reading about the importance people attach to their recreation and the many forms it can take. His instructor asks the class to write a three- or four-page paper on some aspect of recreation. To begin, George uses the sorting strategy and comes up with two major categories of topics: those based primarily on reading and those based on personal experience. Under the first category, he includes legalized casino gambling, vacationing in national parks, and collecting baseball cards; under the second he lists his hobby of coin collecting, his interest in playing bridge, and the recreational possibilities of his hometown, Mt. Pleasant. Because he has only marginal interest in the topics in the first category, he rules all of them out. After weighing the possibilities of the items in the second category, he concludes that Mt. Pleasant offers the most potential and elects to pursue that topic for a high school audience.

This case history continues on page 22.

*G*ATHERING INFORMATION

Once you have a topic, you'll need things to say about it. This supporting material can include facts, ideas, examples, observations, sensory impressions, memories, and the like. Without the proper backup, papers lack force, vividness, and interest and may confuse or mislead readers.

PERSPECTIVE

Lack of supporting material is one of the most evident weaknesses in student writing. Even when you point out that they must support their ideas, many students don't know how, particularly when they dash off a paper the night before it is due. Some think that support consists

Strategies for Gathering Information

If you are writing on a familiar topic, much of your supporting material may come from your own head. Brainstorming is the best way to retrieve it. With unfamiliar topics, brainstorming won't work. Instead, you'll have to do some background reading. Whatever the topic, familiar or unfamiliar, talking with friends, parents, neighbors, or people knowledgeable about the topic can also produce useful ideas.

Brainstorming.   Brainstorming a topic, like brainstorming a subject, yields a set of words, fragments, and occasionally sentences that will furnish ideas for the paper. Assume that Jim, the student who explored the subject of tennis, wants to show how conditioning, concentration, and consistent play can improve one's game. His brainstorming list might look like this:

keeping ball in play	temper distractions
don't try foolish shots	don't continually drive ball with
placing ball so opponent runs	power
staying in good condition yourself	two-on-one drill
running	lobbing ball over opponent's head
jogging	returning a down-the-line passing
skipping rope	shot
keeps you on your toes	don't try spectacular overheads
keeping your mind only on the	chance for opponent to make
game	mistake
personal distractions	game of percentages
courtside distractions	games are lost, not won

You can see how some thoughts have led to others. For example, the first jotting, "keeping ball in play," leads naturally to the next one, "don't try foolish shots." "Placing ball so opponent runs" leads to "staying in good condition yourself," which in turn leads to ways of staying in condition and so forth.

Branching is a helpful and convenient extension of brainstorming that allows you to add details to any item in your list. Here's how you might use this technique to approach "courtside distractions."

only of library research. Students should understand that a four-page paper can be the crystallization of eight pages of notes. The problem for them is to get those eight pages. You might allot time in your syllabus and also classroom time for gathering support. Students need to know not only the expectation of support but also the process of gathering it.

TEACHING STRATEGY

After initial brainstorming or freewriting, ask students to develop a list of questions they want their paper to answer, then propose how they will address these questions—perhaps by further brainstorming, talking, observing, or reading. You might ask them to propose a timetable for gathering this information.

CLASSROOM ACTIVITIES

1. Introduce a possible topic for a paper, perhaps student attitudes toward writing, and have students, working in small groups, suggest various ways to obtain information for a paper. A classroom discussion could then ensue.
2. You might allow students to talk in small groups about their developing papers. Peer questions and opinions help them formulate their own ideas and discover where they need more information.

Don't worry if your brainstorming notes look chaotic and if some seem irrelevant. Sometimes the most unlikely material turns out to be the freshest and most interesting. As you organize and write your paper, you'll probably combine, modify, and omit some of the notes, as well as add others.

EXERCISE ■ **Prepare a brainstorming sheet of supporting details for one of the topics you developed for the exercise on page 18.**

Reading. When you have to grapple with an unfamiliar topic, look in the library for material to develop it. Before going there, however, turn to Chapter 19, The Library Research Paper, and read what we say under the headings "The Card Catalog," "Computerized Card Catalogs," and "Periodical Indexes." These sections tell you how to unearth promising references to investigate. Once you have a list of references, start searching for the books or articles. Look through each one you find and jot down any information that looks useful, either as direct quotations or in your own words.

Whenever you use a direct quotation or rephrased material in your paper, you must give proper credit to the source. If you don't, you are guilty of plagiarism, a serious offense that can result in a failing grade for the course or even expulsion from college. Unless you're doing a library research paper, your instructor will probably require only that you name the speaker or writer and the publication in which the material appeared. (See "Handling Quotations" and "Avoiding Plagiarism," Chapter 19.)

Talking with Others. You can expand the pool of ideas gained through brainstorming or reading by talking with some of the people around you. Imagine you're writing a paper about a taxpayers' revolt in your state. After checking the leading state newspapers at the library, you find that most of the discontent centers on property taxes. You then decide to supplement what you've read by asking questions about the tax situation in your town.

Your parents and neighbors tell you that property taxes have jumped 50 percent in the last two years. The local tax assessor tells you that assessed valuations have risen sharply and that state law requires property taxes to keep pace. She also notes that this situation is causing some people on fixed incomes to lose their homes. A city council member explains that part of the added revenue is being used to repair city streets, build a new library wing, and buy more fire-fighting equipment. The rest is going to the schools. School officials tell you they're using their extra funds to offer more vocational courses and to expand the program for learning-disabled students. As you can see, asking questions can broaden your perspective and provide information that will help you to write a more worthwhile paper.

SUGGESTED INSTRUCTOR READING

Reither, J.A. "Writing and Knowing: Toward Redefining the Writing Process." College English 47 (1985): 620–28. Argues that we err in expecting students to create papers entirely by techniques such as brainstorming and that we should have them write as a result of primary or library research.

READER/THEME STRATEGIES

Students should understand that they can also glean ideas from their reading. If you are building your course around one theme, you might assign a Reader essay, such as "The Boy and the Bank Officer," and have students jot down any ideas or personal experiences that the essay triggers. If students draw a blank, first discuss the essay's theme; then ask the class to freewrite how it relates to their experience. This exercise can also help students become more interactive readers.

CASE HISTORY *(Continued from page 19)*

After choosing to write about the recreational possibilities of his hometown, George brainstorms to gather appropriate material. The result is a twenty-item list. After checking it over, George decides that three items—the local chamber-music orchestra, little theater, and barbershop quartet—would hold little interest for his teenage audience, and he drops them. The remaining items are as follows:

End-of-World parties	crazy activities of party-goers
crowded streets	Mt. Pleasant Mall
Cold Water Lake	Embers Restaurant
Lake Isabella Dam	Holiday Inn
Island Park activities	Nelson Park Zoo
live bands	Mt. Pleasant Speedway
baseball games	mall parking
small gatherings	Boomer's Nightclub
Mt. Pleasant Meadows	

This case history continues on pages 24–25.

ORGANIZING THE INFORMATION

If you have ever listened to a rambling speaker spill out ideas in no particular order, you probably found it hard to pay attention to the speech, let alone make sense of it. So, too, with disorganized writing. A garbled listing of ideas serves no one; an orderly presentation highlights your ideas and helps communication succeed.

Your topic determines the approach you take. In narrating a personal experience, such as a mishap-riddled vacation, you'd probably trace the events in the order they occurred. In describing a process, say caulking a bathtub, you'd take the reader step by step through the procedure. To describe a hillside view near your home, you might work from left to right. Or you could first paint a word picture of some striking central feature and then fan out in either direction. Other topics dictate other patterns, such as comparison and contrast, cause and effect, and illustration. Chapters 4–12 describe the basic patterns in detail.

You can best organize long pieces of writing, such as library research papers, by following a formal outline. (See Chapter 19, "Organizing and Outlining.") For shorter papers, however, a simple, informal system of *flexible notes* will do nicely.

The Flexible Notes System

To create a set of flexible notes, write each of your key points at the top of a separate sheet of paper. If you have a thesis statement, refer to it for your key points. Next, list under each heading the supporting details that go with that heading. Drop any details that don't fit and expand any points that need more support. When your sheets are finished, arrange them in the order you expect to follow in your essay. The notes for the tennis paper might look like this:

1. Ask students to break a sample essay, perhaps from the Reader, into a set of flexible notes or an outline. This exercise helps students see that even professional writers develop their work from basic, ordered information.
2. Have students, working in small groups, develop two alternate organization plans for the tennis essay and then explain their rationale.
3. Discuss with the class when to follow and when to revise a plan. Give students a premature plan and have them determine whether the writer should follow it or bypass it and start drafting to discover new ideas and possible structures. What are the consequences in each case? While plans can be useful, students need to understand that they aren't engraved on marble.

<u>Conditioning</u>

staying in good condition yourself	two-on-one drill
running	lobbing ball over opponent's head
jogging	returning a down-the-line passing
skipping rope	shot
keeps you on your toes	

<u>Concentration</u>

keeping your mind only on the game
overcome distractions: personal, courtside, temper

<u>Consistency</u>

keeping ball in play
don't try foolish shots
placing ball so opponent runs
don't continually drive ball with power
don't try spectacular overheads
chance for opponent to make mistake
game of percentages
games are lost, not won

Since conditioning, concentration, and consistency are simultaneous concerns, this listing arranges them according to their probable importance—starting with the least important.

Now you're ready to draft a plan showing how many paragraphs you'll have in each part of the essay and what each paragraph will cover. Sometimes the number of details will suggest one paragraph; other times you'll need a paragraph block—two or more paragraphs. Here's a plan for the tennis essay.

SUGGESTED INSTRUCTOR READINGS

Kinneavy, J. "Tagmemic Rhetoric: A Reconsideration." <u>College Composition and Communication</u> 29 (1978): 141–45. Critiques the Young, Becker and Pike approach (below) to heuristics.
Young, R. E., A. L. Becker, K. L. Pike. <u>Rhetoric: Discovery and Change.</u> New York: Harcourt, 1970. Suggests that patterns become heuristic ways of solving the problems posed by the subject.

<u>Conditioning</u>

staying in good condition yourself
running
jogging   } Off-the-court
skipping rope   conditioning
keeps you on your toes
two-on-one drill
lobbing ball over opponent's head
returning a down-the-line passing } On-the-court
  shot   conditioning

<u>Concentration</u>

keeping your mind only on the game
overcome distractions: personal, courtside, temper

Consistency

keeping ball in play
don't try foolish shots
placing ball so opponent runs   } Placing shots
don't continually drive ball with power
don't try spectacular overheads
chance for opponent to make mistake   } Playing
game of percentages   percentages
games are lost, not won

These groupings suggest two paragraphs about conditioning, one about concentration, and two about consistency.

EXERCISE ■ **Organize into flexible notes the supporting details that you prepared for the exercise on page 21. Arrange your note pages in a logical sequence and draft a plan showing the number and content of the paragraphs in each section.**

CASE HISTORY   *(Continued from page 22)*

A careful look at his brainstorming list shows George that its items fall into six categories: parties, swimming, parks, shopping, racing, and dining. After sorting the items into these categories, he draws up the following paragraph-by-paragraph plan:

Parties

End-of-World parties   One
crowded streets   paragraph
crazy antics of party-goers   on partying

Swimming

Cold Water Lake   One paragraph
Lake Isabella Dam   on each
                              swimming spot

Parks

Island Park activities   One paragraph
   live bands   on each park
   baseball games
   small gatherings
Nelson Park Zoo

Shopping

Mt. Pleasant Mall   One paragraph
plenty of parking   on shopping

Racing

Mt. Pleasant Meadows   One paragraph on
Mt. Pleasant Speedway   each racing spot

Dining

Embers Restaurant   One paragraph
Holiday Inn   on each dining
Boomer's Nightclub   spot

This case history continues on page 27.

DEVELOPING A THESIS STATEMENT

A thesis statement presents the main idea of a piece of writing, usually in one sentence. The thesis statement points you in a specific direction, helping you to stay on track and out of tempting byways. In addition, it tells your reader what to expect.

Thesis statements can emerge at several points in the writing process. If an instructor assigns a controversial topic on which you hold strong views, the statement may pop into your head right away. At other times it may develop as you narrow a subject to a topic. Occasionally, you even have to write a preliminary draft to determine your main idea. Usually, though, the thesis statement emerges after you've gathered and examined your supporting information.

As you examine your information, search for the central point and the key points that back it up; then use these to develop your thesis statement. Converting the topic to a question may help you to uncover backup ideas and write a thesis statement. For example:

Topic:	The uncertain future of robots in American industry.
Question:	What are some of the drawbacks of using robots in American industry?
Thesis statement:	The expense of producing robots, the lack of qualified personnel to service them, and the moral problems of replacing workers with them—all cloud the future of robots in American industry.

The thesis statement stems from the specifics the student unearthed while answering the question.

TEACHING STRATEGIES

1. Students often have trouble focusing on and then narrowing a thesis statement. You might have them freewrite what they want to say in the paper, boil that writing down to one or two sentences, check to see whether those sentences say what's wanted, and then make necessary modifications in the thesis statement. Further, have them question each term of the thesis to see if it is clear and conveys the right message. Have them check off in their planning notes what does and does not fit under the thesis.

2. If some students develop their thesis statements before gathering support, have them write down what information they will need in the papers. This exercise helps launch the drafting stage.

3. Some students can become fixated on the thesis statement, constantly reworking it as though it were a replacement for the draft. Others will never get beyond the most general restatement of a topic. In both cases, encourage students to write a preliminary draft before formulating a thesis statement.

4. Other students resist modifications in their thesis because changes require additional effort. You might show them how one of your thesis statements evolved as new information surfaced or ideas developed.

5. A thesis statement, of course, does not have to be a simple sentence but could actually encompass two or more sentences. Give students writing samples that contain such thesis statements and have them discuss why more than one sentence is needed and how effective the choice is.

CLASSROOM ACTIVITIES

1. Have the class brainstorm a topic, formulate several possible thesis statements, evaluate them against the requirements of a good thesis statement, and select the best one.

2. Have students review one another's thesis statements, write down any questions about their scope and adequacy, then return the responses to their authors. This exercise can help students redefine and redirect their efforts.

Requirements of a Good Thesis Statement

Unless intended for a lengthy paper, a thesis statement *focuses on just one central point or issue.* Suppose you prepare the following thesis statement for a two- or three-page paper:

> Centerville College should reexamine its policies on open admissions,
>
> vocational programs, and aid to students.

This sprawling statement would commit you to grapple with three separate issues. At best, you could make only a few general remarks about each one.

To correct matters, consider each issue carefully in light of how much it interests you and how much you know about it. Then make your choice and draft a narrower statement. The following thesis statement would do nicely for a brief paper. It shows clearly that the writer will focus on *just one issue.*

> Because of the rising demand among high school graduates for job-related
>
> training, Centerville College should expand its vocational offerings.

A good thesis statement also *tailors the scope of the issue to the length of the paper.* No writer could deal adequately with "Many incoming college freshmen face crucial adjustment problems" in two or three pages. The idea is too broad to yield more than a smattering of poorly supported general statements. Paring it down to "Free time is a responsibility that challenges many college freshmen," however, results in an idea that could probably be developed adequately.

A good thesis statement further provides *an accurate forecast of what's to come.* If you plan to discuss the effects of overeating, don't say that "Overeating stems from deep-seated psychological factors and the easy availability of convenience foods." Such a statement, incorrectly suggesting that the paper will focus on causes, would only mislead and confuse your reader. On the other hand, "Overeating leads to obesity, which can cause or complicate several serious health problems" accurately represents what's to follow.

Finally, a good thesis statement is *precise, often previewing the organization of the paper.* Assertions built on fuzzy, catchall words like *fascinating, bad, meaningful,* or *interesting,* or statements like "My paper is about . . ." tell neither writer nor reader what's going on. To illustrate:

- New York is a fascinating city.
- My paper is about no-fault divorce.

These examples raise a host of questions. Why does the writer find New York fascinating? Because of its skyscrapers? Its night life? Its theaters? Its restaurants? Its museums? Its shops? Its inhabitants? And what about no-fault divorce? Will the writer attack it, defend it, trace its history, suggest ways of improving it? To find out, we must journey through the paper, hoping to find our way without a road-map sentence.

Now look at the rewritten versions of those faulty thesis statements:

■ I love New York because of its many theaters and museums.

■ Compared to traditional divorce, no-fault divorce is less expensive, promotes fairer settlements, and reflects a more realistic view of the causes of marital breakdown.

These statements tell the reader not only what points the writer will make but also the order they will follow.

Omission of Thesis Statement

Not all papers have explicit thesis statements. Narratives and descriptions, for example, often merely support some point that is unstated but nevertheless clear, and professional writers sometimes imply their thesis rather than state it openly. Nonetheless, a core idea underlies and controls all effective writing.

Changing Your Thesis Statement

Unlike diamonds, thesis statements aren't necessarily forever. Before your paper is in final form, you may need to change your thesis statement several times. If you draft the thesis statement during the narrowing stage, you might change it to reflect what you uncovered while gathering information. Or you might amend it after writing the first draft so that it reflects your additions and deletions.

Tentative or final, formulated early or late, the thesis statement serves as a beacon that spotlights your purpose.

CASE HISTORY *(Continued from page 25)*

His paragraph-by-paragraph plan completed, George now drafts a thesis statement that names all categories.

> Mt. Pleasant offers parties, great swimming spots, pleasant parks, race tracks, fine dining, and excellent shopping.

After carefully examining this initial effort, he realizes that three of the categories could be lumped together under the umbrella category "recreation spots." He alters the statement to read as follows.

> Mt. Pleasant offers parties, great recreation spots, fine dining, and excellent shopping.

This case history continues on pages 29–31.

EXERCISE ANSWERS (p. 28)

1. This statement is not precise. It could mean that the writer will discuss (a) the causes of absenteeism; (b) the effects of absenteeism; (c) the efforts industry is making to reduce absenteeism. Any attempt to discuss these aspects adequately would require far more than two or three pages.

2. This thesis statement is satisfactory. Its topic is narrow enough to be covered adequately in two or three pages, and it signals the organization of the paper.

3. This thesis statement offers no clue to why Acme College is not well run. Does the writer mean that (a) The administrators are doing a poor job? (b) The faculty is underpaid and poorly motivated? (c) The course offerings are inadequate? (d) The school doesn't provide adequate recreational facilities? Furthermore, by saying "Although I don't know much about running a college," the student undermines his or her credibility.

4. This thesis statement fails on two counts. First, it makes two separate assertions—about war and taxes. Second, each assertion is too complex to be discussed adequately in a short paper.

5. This is a good thesis statement. It could be explained in two or three pages, and the phrase "motivated by the desire to begin a new and more virtuous life" signals the approach that the writer will take.

6. This thesis statement, like 3, is far too imprecise. Vacationing in Britain might be nice for several reasons, including the opportunity to (a) meet and mingle with the British people; (b) enjoy London's theaters and nightlife; (c) tour the nation's historic cities and shrines; (d) enroll for a summer program at Oxford or Cambridge. A better thesis statement might be, "Vacationing in Britain offers the traveler a chance to visit the birthplaces of some of the world's foremost literary figures."

7. This thesis statement commits the writer to deal with three separate issues, any one of which would require two or three pages. The discussion needs narrowing to just one issue.

8. Another good thesis statement, this one restricts the writer to a topic that suits the length limitations. The paper might include paragraphs about channels devoted to sports, religion, movies, and children's programs.

EXERCISE

A. Write a thesis statement for the flexible notes that you developed for the exercise on page 24.

B. Reread "Requirements of a Good Thesis Statement"; then explain why each of the following does or does not qualify as an effective thesis statement for a two- or three-page essay.

1. My paper discusses the problem of employee absenteeism in American industry.
2. Living on a small island offers three advantages: isolation from city problems, the opportunity to know your neighbors, and the chance to go fishing whenever you want.
3. Although I don't know much about running a college, I know that Acme College is not run well.
4. Expanding our nation's armaments increases the chance of nuclear war and imposes an unneeded tax burden on the American taxpayer.
5. Many people, motivated by the desire to begin a new and more virtuous life, have abandoned the established modes of life and set up communities based on utopian ideals.
6. Vacationing in Britain is a nice way to spend a summer.
7. Extending Middletown's intracity transit system will save consumers money, reduce pollution, and increase city revenues.
8. Most cable TV companies provide subscribers with several specialized-program channels.

WRITING THE FIRST DRAFT

Now on to the first draft of your essay. The writing should go rather quickly. After all, you have a topic you're qualified to write about, a thesis statement that indicates your purpose, enough information to develop it, and a written plan to follow.

But sometimes when you sit down to write, the words won't come, and all you can do is doodle or stare at the blank page. Perhaps the introduction is the problem. Many writers are terrified by the thought of the opening paragraph. They want to get off to a good start but can't figure out how to begin. If this happens to you, additional brainstorming or freewriting can make you more comfortable and may suggest an opening. Keep in mind that any lead-in you write now can be changed later. If these suggestions don't solve your problem, skip the introduction for the time being. Once you have drafted the body of the paper, an effective opening should come more easily.

Here are some general suggestions for writing a first draft.

1. Stack your thesis statement, flexible notes, and written plan in front of you. They will start you thinking.
2. Skip every other line (double-space) and leave wide margins. Then you'll have room to revise later.

3. Write quickly; capture the drift of your thoughts. Concentrate on content and organization. Get your main points and supporting details on paper in the right sequence. *Don't* spend time correcting grammatical or punctuation errors, improving your language, or making the writing flow smoothly. You might lose your train of thought and end up doodling or staring again.

4. Take breaks at logical dividing points, for example, when you finish discussing a key point. Before you start to write again, scan what you've written.

Now for some specific suggestions that will help you with the actual writing:

1. Rewrite your thesis statement at the top of your first page to break the ice and build momentum.

2. Write your first paragraph, introducing your essay and stating your thesis. If you get stuck here, move on to the rest of the paper.

3. Follow your plan as you write. Begin with your first main point and work on each section in turn.

4. Look over the supporting details listed under the first heading in your flexible notes. Write a topic sentence stating the central idea of the paragraph.

5. Turn the details into sentences; use one or more sentences to explain each one. Add other related details, facts, or examples if they occur to you.

6. When you move from one paragraph to the next, try to provide a transitional word or sentence that connects the two.

7. Write your last paragraph, ending your essay in an appropriate fashion. If you get stuck, set your conclusion aside and return to it later.

EXERCISE ■ **Using the plan you prepared for the exercise on page 24, write the first draft of an essay.**

CASE HISTORY   (Continued from page 27)

George now uses his thesis statement and paragraph-by-paragraph plan to write the following draft. Notice the slight changes in the thesis statement wording and in paragraphing, a common occurrence at this writing stage. Without question this draft needs extensive revision. We'll return to it early in the next chapter to discuss the necessary changes.

Mt. Pleasant

Welcome to Mt. Pleasant, the home of Central Michigan University and the oil capital of this state. You have chosen the right town to visit because there are so many things for a high school student here. There are parties, great recreation spots, fine places to dine, and even excellent shopping.

I am sure you have all heard of Mt. Pleasant's famous "End-of-the-World Parties," which have been featured in nationwide news

PERSPECTIVE

Reiterate that a first draft is not a final draft, might not be anything like a final draft, can be subject to massive change, might be thrown out entirely, is an experiment. Despite these caveats, many students will attempt to get it right on the first try in order to save time. You might jokingly label this version the zero draft, fertilizer draft, or overhaul draft. Students approach drafting differently. Some use notes and plans to build a more organized draft; others merely refer to notes and then experiment with getting ideas on paper, well aware that the draft will probably need reorganization and more information.

TEACHING STRATEGIES

1. If you have basic students, you might show them how *you* write a draft, perhaps using an overhead. Students are amazed to discover that even teachers write in a series of fits and starts and change direction.

2. Have basic writers prepare a draft in class. If you see them repeatedly making corrections at the sentence and word level, encourage them to move on with their ideas and reassure them that they can work on mechanics later.

3. If students get stuck, have them write about what they want to say in the paper, then use the results along with their written plan to develop a draft. Many who are stuck need to consider whether they have enough information.

SUGGESTED INSTRUCTOR READINGS

Perl, S. "The Composing Processes of Unskilled College Writers." Research in the Teaching of English 13 (1978): 317–36. A good case study of why and how students have trouble developing drafts.

Pianko, S. "Reflection: A Critical Component of the Composing Process." College Composition and Communication 30 (1979): 275–78. Discusses how students need to reflect when writing and how instructors can encourage such reflection.

PERSPECTIVE

Several kinds of computer programs—including those that focus on interactive planning, outlining, and mechanics—are available to help students. The word-processing program, however, is the most useful because it makes planning, drafting, and revising so much easier. Various programs that differ in power and complexity are available. If your class is scheduled for a word-processing lab, review the literature and available programs with the lab director and select the one that best suits the needs of your class.

TEACHING STRATEGIES

1. Rather than relying only on the manual to teach students how to use the word processor, develop simple handouts that build computer skills step by step. It helps if you are in the lab while students learn the program and draft a brief practice paper. Students need to become familiar with the functions of the computer before being assigned a longer paper.

stories. These parties are a riot, both literally and figuratively. At the end of the school year, all the CMU students gather on fraternity row to celebrate the start of summer. For blocks and blocks, the streets are filled to overflowing with people pushing their way along with drinks in their hands to yet another bash. It is probably one of the rowdiest parties you could attend. People do all kinds of crazy things including climbing on rooftops and burning couches in the street. There was even one party-goer who stripped naked. That's what I call rowdy.

If you are not into partying, maybe a mellow day on the beach would do you some good. There is a beautiful lake called Cold Water Lake that has crystal clear water and a scenic beach. This beach is the "hit spot" on a sunny day, so you will want to be there.

If you're out for some wet-n-wild swimming fun, then Lake Isabella Dam is the place for you. It is a huge slippery slide about a hundred yards long pitched at a 160-degree angle. One could spend all day there and not get bored of sliding away.

After swimming, you could go to Island Park in the center of town. This park is unique because it is surrounded by a river that flows around it; it is Mt. Pleasant's own Island of Paradise. There are many activities at the park including live bands, small gatherings, and baseball games. This park is the main hangout for teens in Mt. Pleasant. For the children, there is also Nelson Park which has a small zoo with bear, deer, badger, and many other kinds of North American wildlife.

If you are a person who likes to shop, then you will want to visit the Mt. Pleasant Mall at the edge of town. It has all the convenience stores necessary for a fulfilling day of shopping. There is always plenty of parking.

Mt. Pleasant also has places for those of you who like to gamble. Mt. Pleasant Meadows has fun-filled, action-packed horse races all weekend long. There is also a concession stand and a bar. The Meadows is just waiting for you to bet and win big.

If you like horse racing, then you might also enjoy the car racing at Mt. Pleasant Speedway. On Fridays there is a high-speed stock car race all night long. So come see the fast cars, bright lights, and the excitement of racing waiting for you.

Let's not forget about the fine dining Mt. Pleasant has to offer. There is an elegant restaurant called The Embers that matches all the fine cuisine in the world. There is also a Holiday Inn which hosts a class A restaurant and nightclub. The club is called Boomers and presents well-known comedians to entertain you throughout the night.

Mt. Pleasant has much to offer you: fine dining, excitement, and relaxation. Why not come and see for yourself.

This essay will be revised in the next chapter.

PLANNING AND DRAFTING WITH A WORD PROCESSOR

Using a computer and word-processing software allows you to compose, save what you write, insert new material, delete unwanted material, move sections around, and when you are ready, print out copies. If you can use your college's equipment and software, read the manual for your unit to discover its capabilities before you attempt to compose with it. Trying to write a paper while simultaneously learning about a word-processing program is a fast route to frustration.

Many word-processing programs can help you plan and draft an essay as well as revise and edit it. You can brainstorm or freewrite, entering words, phrases, and ideas as they come to mind. Do this for about ten minutes and then print out a copy to comb for promising bits and pieces.

If you approach a topic through the set of questions on page 15, convert them into specific questions related to the broad subject area, and then enter them and your answers to them into your document. If you don't find a topic in the answers, brainstorm or freewrite further.

When you draft, experiment with your ideas by trying out new arrangements of material. If your writing stalls, note the spot with an asterisk or other marker so that you can easily find it later with a "Search" command; then continue to write. Always save each draft in a file, if not in hard copy. You may want to use parts of an early draft in a later version.

2. If students plan and draft using their own word processor, ask them to print out the different stages of their work so that you can review them and offer pointers. Often students view a computer as an electronic hot rod and speed prematurely into a draft.

TEACHING STRATEGIES

1. Because changes can be made so easily, some students become compulsive about reworking words and sentences and therefore lose any sense of the overall paper. Encourage them to push forward.
2. Other students, seeing their ideas first on screen and then in print, prematurely conclude that their work is finished. Remind them that typed doesn't necessarily mean finished.
3. Still other students find that words and ideas flow so readily that they forget to edit or limit their work. Remind these students to make choices.
4. Dogs may not have eaten student homework, but far too often computers do. Students need frequent reminders to save. It's helpful if they keep a print copy, the saved original, and a backup of major work.

SUGGESTED INSTRUCTOR READINGS

Daiute, C. Writing and Computers. Reading, MA: Addison-Wesley, 1985. Includes a section on using computers in the composition classroom.
Schwartz, H. J., and L. S. Bridwell-Bowles. "A Selected Bibliography on Computers in Composition: An Update." College Composition and Communication 38 (1987): 453–57. A helpful annotated bibliography of computer programs for the composition classroom.

Revising and Editing Your Paper

3

PERSPECTIVE

Students often view themselves as poor writers if they can't complete a quality draft in one attempt. They are skeptical about revision because they don't know how to identify necessary changes, gear changes to their goals for the work, and implement the necessary modifications. Students need to learn how to revise as much as they need to learn any other aspect of writing.

TEACHING STRATEGIES

1. Because students often blur the distinction between revision and proofreading/editing, try to maintain a clear difference between the two in your syllabus, class discussions, and responses to their drafts.

2. Students benefit greatly when you *show* them how to revise. You might use an overhead to make and explain revision decisions or to present several drafts of a paper, identifying the changes that were made. The best drafts are those closest to the types of writing students will actually do.

CLASSROOM ACTIVITY

You might give students useful metaphors for the writing process. Writing could be described as working with clay, where one shapes and reshapes a figure; as gardening, where constant weeding, watering, and waiting are required; as a relationship, where people meet, slowly get to know each other, and kiss only after they are comfortable. The more plastic the metaphor, the better. Ask students to jot down their metaphors for writing (often very punitive) and discuss their features, making it clear that writing is not a straight line from first idea to final draft.

All of us at one time or another have said something careless to a friend or date and then spent the rest of the night regretting our words. In contrast, when we write we can make sure we say exactly what we mean. Good writers don't express themselves perfectly on the first try, but they do work hard at revising their initial efforts.

Just what is revision? Don't confuse it with proofreading or editing, the final stage of the writing process, where you carefully inspect your word choice, spelling, grammar, and punctuation. Revision is much more drastic, often involving an upheaval of your draft as you change its content and organization in order to communicate more effectively.

Most of what you read, including this book, has been considerably altered and improved as the writers progressed through early drafts. This fact shouldn't surprise you. After all, a rough copy is merely a first attempt to jot down some ideas in essay form. No matter how well you gather and organize your material, you can't predict the outcome until you've prepared a draft. Sometimes only touch-up changes are required. More often though, despite your efforts, this version will be incomplete, unclear in places, possibly disorganized. You might even discover an entirely different idea, focus, or approach buried within it. During revision you keep changing things—your focus, approach to the topic, supporting material, and thesis statement—until the results satisfy you.

Inexperienced writers often mistakenly view initial drafts as nearly finished products rather than as experiments to alter, or even scrap, if need be. As a result, they often approach revision with the wrong attitude. To revise successfully, you need to control your ego and your fear and become your own first critical reader. Set aside natural feelings of accomplishment ("After all, I've put a great deal of thought into this") and dread ("Actually, I'm afraid of what I'll find if I look too closely"). Instead, recognize that revision offers an opportunity to upgrade your strong features and strengthen your weak ones.

PREPARING TO REVISE

To distance yourself from your writing and sharpen your critical eye, set your first draft aside for at least a half day, longer if time permits. When you return to it, gear up for revision by jotting down your intended purpose and audience before you read your paper. These notations will help keep your changes on track. In addition, note any further ideas that have occurred to you.

The right attitude is vital to effective revision. Far too many students hastily skim their essays to reassure themselves that "Everything sounds O.K." Avoid such a quick-fix approach. If your draft appears fine on first reading, probe it again with a more critical eye. Try putting yourself in your reader's place. Will your description of a favorite getaway spot be clear to someone who has never seen it? Will your letter home asking for money really convince parents who might think they've already given you too much? Remember: If you aren't critical now, anticipating confusion and objections, your reader certainly will be later.

Read your essay at least three times, once for each of these reasons:

To improve the development of the essay as a whole
To strengthen paragraph structure and development
To sharpen sentences and words

When you finish reading your paper for content, make a final, meticulous sweep to search for errors and problems that mar your writing. Use the Personal Revision Checklist on the inside back cover of this book to note your own special weaknesses, perhaps some problem with punctuation or a failure to provide specific support. Later chapters discuss paragraphs, sentences, and words in detail. Check these chapters for more information about the points introduced here.

CONSIDERING THE WHOLE ESSAY

If you only inspect your draft sentence by sentence, you can easily overlook how its parts work together. A better approach is to step back and view the overall essay rather than its separate parts, asking questions such as "Does the beginning mesh with the end?" "Does the essay wander?" "Has anything been left out?" In this way you can gauge how part relates to part and to the whole. Use the acronym *FACT* to guide this stage of your revision.

F. Ask yourself first whether the whole essay *FITS* together, presenting a central point for a specific audience. Have you delivered what the thesis statement promises? First drafts often include paragraphs, or even large sections, that have little bearing on the main point. Some drafts contain the kernels of several different essays. Furthermore, one section of a draft might be geared to one audience (parents, for example) and another section to an entirely different audience (students, perhaps). As you read each part, verify its connection to your purpose and students to suggest, and then carry out, a plan for making changes in their drafts.

3. Students find it easy to learn from acronyms. The editors of *Fortune,* noted for quality reporting and superb prose, encourage their writers to think about DARK (Don't Assume the Reader Knows) and AGO (Acute Grasp of the Obvious) when preparing an article. These acronyms can also alert students to the common problems of inadequate support and trite information.

4. Generally it is best to strike a balance between supplying the responses students need in order to develop, on the one hand, and increasing their responsibility over their own work, on the other. To achieve this goal, you could have students revise a draft before they receive any feedback.

CLASSROOM ACTIVITIES

1. You might take the lead and show students how to mark up a draft while revising.

2. Before students revise their own drafts, have the class apply revision guidelines to sample drafts similar to the ones students will write.

CLASSROOM ACTIVITIES

1. Before students begin to read the FACT analysis of this essay, you might have them complete their own FACT sheet. Then have the class (perhaps in small groups) compare their analyses to the text analysis.

2. Have students candidly state their feelings about all the changes this draft is undergoing. Many will be discouraged by all the work, but they should recognize that if this draft can be salvaged, almost anyone's writing can be improved (one of the reasons we use this realistic example).

audience. Don't hesitate to chop out sections that don't fit, redo stray parts so they accord with your central idea, or alter your thesis statement to reflect better your supporting material. Occasionally, you might even expand one small, fertile section of your draft into an entirely new essay.

A. Whenever we write first drafts, we unwittingly leave out essential material. As we revise, we need to identify and fill these gaps. Ask yourself: "Where will the reader need more information or examples to understand my message?" Then *ADD* the appropriate sentences, paragraphs, or even pages.

C. First drafts often contain material that fits the thesis but doesn't contribute to the essay. Writing quickly, we tend to repeat ourselves, include uninteresting or uninformative examples, and crank out whole paragraphs when one clear sentence would suffice. As you revise, *CUT* away this clutter with a free hand. Such paring can be painful, especially if you're left with a skimpy text, but your message will emerge with much greater clarity. As you've probably guessed, revising a draft often requires both adding and cutting.

T. Carefully *TEST* the organization of your essay. The text should flow smoothly from point to point with clear transitions between the various ideas. Test the organization by outlining your major and minor points, then checking the results for logic and completeness. Alternatively, read the draft and note its progression. Look for spots where you can clarify connections between words and thus help your readers.

Chapters 4–12 explain nine different writing strategies, each concluding with revision questions geared specifically to that strategy. Use these questions, together with the *FACT* of revision, to help you revise more effectively.

CASE HISTORY (Continued from page 31)

Now let's apply the *FACT* approach to the first draft of George's Mt. Pleasant essay, which you read on pages 29–31. As we indicated there, the draft needs extensive work.

FIT. Much of George's draft doesn't fit his high school audience. Most of these students won't care about Mt. Pleasant being the oil capital of Michigan, won't be able to attend "End-of-the-World Parties" (which some will find distasteful), and won't have money for fine dining or nightclubs, even assuming they would be admitted. How then to proceed? George has two choices: target his intended audience more accurately or change it entirely. Either decision requires drastic revisions.

ADD. Assuming George keeps his high school audience, he needs to expand the essay at several points. As things stand, he offers only skimpy details about the water activities and never indicates where the different attractions are located or why the mall is appealing. These shortcomings must be corrected and other attractions introduced and discussed—for example, affordable places for teens to eat. Another audience would of course require different additions.

CUT. With cutting as with adding, audience determines what parts of the essay go and what parts stay. For high schoolers, George should drop any mention of Mt. Pleasant's oil status, "End-of-the-World Parties," and night-clubs. Similarly, fine dining has no place in the essay except perhaps as something reserved for special occasions. For a different audience, some of the sections mentioned under ADD might be deleted.

TEST. The introduction suggests that the essay will first discuss parties, then recreation spots and places to dine, and finally places to shop. However, the body reverses the order of the last two, and the conclusion summarizes these features in a different order. Such false signals only confuse a reader. George also errs in opening with "End-of-the-World Parties," which could cause some readers to react negatively. The essay does flow well from point to point although too many paragraphs begin with "If you."

Without question, George's essay requires considerable work, whatever audience he chooses. After weighing his choices, he elects to stay with teen-agers and zero in on Mt. Pleasant as a summer fun spot.

TEACHING STRATEGY
You may encounter a few students who become so involved in revising that they fail to complete a final draft. Probably they are confused about the nature of revision or subconsciously fear having their draft evaluated. Show them this gravestone and caption, which we saw many years ago and never forgot.

As you read your own essay, note on a separate sheet of paper problems to solve, ideas to add, and changes to try. When you mark the actual essay, make your job easier by using these simple techniques.

1. To delete something, cross it out lightly; you may decide to resurrect it later.
2. To add a section of text, place a letter (A, B, C, D) at the appropriate spot and write the new material on a separate sheet, keyed to the letter. Make changes within sections by crossing out what you don't want and writing the replacement above it or nearby.
3. To rearrange the organization, draw arrows showing where you want things to go, or cut up your draft and rearrange the sections by taping them on new sheets of paper. Use whatever method works best for you.

When you finish revising your draft, you might want to team up with one or more classmates and read one another's work critically. The fresh eye you bring to the task can uncover shortcomings that would otherwise go unnoticed. Pages 49–56 discuss peer editing in detail.

CASE HISTORY *(Continued from above)*

After setting his draft aside for a couple of days, George revises it carefully. The original draft, showing deleted material, some added information, and a series of letters that mark where other new material should go, appears on pages 36 and 38. The other new material, keyed to the letters on the draft, appears on facing pages.

Mt. Pleasant

Welcome to Mt. Pleasant, the home of ~~Central~~ Michigan University and the ~~oil capital of this~~ state. You have chosen the right town to visit ~~because there~~ are so many things for a high school student here. There are parties, ~~great~~ recreation spots, fine places to dine, and even excellent shopping. (A)

I am sure you have all heard of Mt. Pleasant's famous "End-of-the-World Parties," which have been featured in nationwide news stories. These parties are a riot, both literally and figuratively. At the end of the school year, all the CMU students gather on fraternity row to celebrate the start of summer. For blocks and blocks, the streets are filled to overflowing with people pushing their way along with drinks in their hands to yet another bash. It is probably one of the rowdiest parties you could attend. People do all kinds of crazy things including climbing on rooftops and burning couches in the street. There was even one party-goer who stripped naked. That's what I call rowdy.

If you ~~are not into partying, maybe a mellow day on~~ like to swim or just lie on the beach, just a few miles west of Mt. Pleasant off Beal City Road ~~the beach would do you some good. There~~ is ~~a~~ beautiful ~~lake~~ with its ~~called~~ Cold Water Lake ~~that has~~ crystal clear water and a surrounded by hills and woods. scenic beach. This beach is the "hit spot" on a sunny day. You can always find a volleyball game to join; or you can simply throw around a frisbee, do ~~so.~~ You will want to be there. some boy or girl watching, or just bask in the sun. The swimming, of course, is

If you're out for some wet-n-wild swimming fun, then great. , just down the road from Cold Water Lake, The dam forms Lake Isabella Dam is the place for you. ~~It is~~ a huge slippery slide about a hundred yards long pitched at a 160-degree angle. ~~One could~~ You can spend ~~all~~ a whole day there and not get bored of sliding away. (B)

If you want to stay closer to town, can ~~After swimming,~~ you ~~could~~ go to Island Park in the off Main Street. center of town. This park is unique because it is surrounded by a river that flows around it; it is Mt. Pleasant's

A.   If you get tired of driving out to the same old Lake Michigan beach this summer, you might think about giving Mt. Pleasant a try for something different. The Mt. Pleasant area offers swimming, canoeing, and hiking; a chance to get together with other teens; horse and auto racing; a college campus to wander around; movies, museums, video games, and shopping for rainy days; and lots of places to eat. What more can you ask for?

B.   Canoeing can be great fun. Near the Mt. Pleasant area there are a number of scenic rivers that are a delight to canoe. There is the Chippewa River, the Cold Water River, the north and south branches of the Salt River, and further to the west the exciting white-water Pine River. Near or on each river are places that rent canoes at a reasonable rate and even provide you with transportation from your destination back to your cars.

      For those of you who like to hike, Deerfield Park, a few miles west of town on M-20, provides 25 miles of nature trails. These secluded trails that meander through a natural forest and gentle, rolling hills can be a great place to take someone special for a quiet stroll. You will be sure to spot a variety of birds as well as squirrels, raccoons, and chipmunks. If you are really lucky, you might even spot a deer or two. Closer to town, on Harris Street, Mission Creek Woodland Park offers 60 acres of forest trails, a creek, and picnicking area.

C.   For those of you who will be going to college in a few years, you might want to take the time to wander around the Central Michigan University campus and try college on for own Island of Paradise. There are many activities at the park

including live bands, small gatherings, and baseball games.

This park is the main hangout for teens in Mt. Pleasant. ~~For~~ ,so you will

~~always find something to do. If you want a break, nearby~~ *always find something to do. If you want a break, nearby*

~~the children, there~~ is also Nelson Park which has a small zoo

with bear, deer, badger, and many other kinds of North

American wildlife.

If you are ~~a~~ person who likes to ~~shop~~, then you will want

to visit the Mt. Pleasant ~~Mall at~~ the edge of town. It has all

the convenience stores ~~necessary~~ for a fulfilling day of

shoping. There ~~is~~ always plenty of parking.   Ⓒ

If you are looking for something different, on Mission Road north of M-20

~~Mt. Pleasant also has places for those of you who like to~~

~~gamble.~~ Mt. Pleasant Meadows has fun-filled, action-packed

for only $2.00, you can enjoy the suspense of cheering your favorite to victory.

horse races all weekend long. ^There is also a concession stand.

~~and a bar. The Meadows is just waiting for you to bet and win~~

~~big.~~

~~If you like horse racing, then~~ you might also enjoy the

car racing at Mt. Pleasant Speedway. On Fridays there ~~is a~~ *are*

high-speed stock car race*s* all night long. So come see the fast

cars, bright lights, and the excitement of racing waiting for

you.   Ⓓ

Let's not forget about the fine dining Mt. Pleasant has to

offer. There is an elegant restaurant called The Embers that

matches all the fine cuisine in the world. There is also a

Holiday Inn which hosts a class A restaurant and nightclub. Ⓔ

The club is called Boomers and presents well-known comedians

to entertain you throughout the night.

swimming, hiking, parks,

Mt. Pleasant has much to offer you: ~~fine dining,~~

racing. It is a fun alternative to whatever you are doing this summer.

~~excitement, and relaxation~~. Why not come and see for

yourself.

size. Its ivy-covered brick buildings and tree-lined walkways give you the feel of real college life. When summer semester is in session, you might also want to stroll through a few buildings, look around the library, and visit the bookstore. If you stop to watch students bustle to class, you could be watching your own future.

D.   On rainy days, there is still a lot to do in Mt. Pleasant. There are several multi-screened movie theaters that give you a choice of the most recent releases. You can also engage in a little time travel at the Center for Cultural and Natural History in Rowe Hall on the CMU campus. This museum includes lumbering tools, Civil War artifacts, a variety of household items from different historical periods, and an exhibit of wildlife, including the remains of a mastodon. You can play video games at the Royal Oasis Family Amusement Center in the campus mall on Mission Street. Or you can spend some time shopping.

E.   Because Mt. Pleasant is a college town, there are a number of great cheap places to eat. The McDonald's on Mission Street is the wildest place to get a Big Mac you will ever see. With fancy chrome palm trees and glossy plastic cutouts of people having a great time, it is like an Art Deco scene. You have to see it to believe it. There are, of course, all the great fast-food places and pizza shops. If you are interested in taking a date to some place special and don't mind spending a little money in the process, you might try The Embers, a restaurant rated as "one of Michigan's finest." When you are looking for a place to eat in Mt. Pleasant, you have many great choices.

Case history continues on page 45–47.

Although this draft is not perfect, George's revisions have considerably improved the paper. He does, however, have more to do. (The final, polished version of the essay appears on pages 45–47.) Never stop revising your work until you are completely satisfied with the results.

"NOW THAT WE'VE BOILED YOUR PAPER DOWN TO THE RELEVANT MATERIAL, I THINK YOU'RE READY TO RE-WRITE."

Reprinted by permission of Richard N. Bibler.

EXERCISE ■ **List George's other options for revising this draft; then indicate the necessary changes if he had decided to write for readers between the ages of thirty-five and forty-five.**

EXERCISE ■ **Use the FACT acronym to revise the draft you prepared for the exercise on page 29.**

STRENGTHENING PARAGRAPH STRUCTURE AND DEVELOPMENT

Once you finish considering the essay as a whole, examine your paragraphs one by one, applying the *FACT* approach that you used for the whole paper. Make sure each paragraph *FITS* the paper's major focus and develops a single central idea. If a paragraph needs more support or examples, *ADD* whatever is necessary. If a paragraph contains ineffective or unhelpful material, *CUT* it. *TEST* the flow of ideas from paragraph to paragraph and clarify connections, both between and within paragraphs, as necessary. Ask the basic questions in the checklist that follows about each paragraph, and make any needed revisions.

REVISION CHECKLIST FOR PARAGRAPHS

- Does the paragraph have one, and only one, central idea?
- Does the central idea help to develop the thesis statement?
- Does each statement within the paragraph help to develop the central idea?
- Does the paragraph need additional explanations, examples, or supporting details?
- Would cutting some material make the paragraph stronger?
- Would reorganization make the ideas easier to follow?
- Can the connections between successive sentences be improved?
- Is each paragraph clearly and smoothly related to those that precede and follow it?

Don't expect to escape making any changes; some readjustments will undoubtedly be needed. Certain paragraphs may be stripped down or deleted, others beefed up, still others reorganized or repositioned. Chapter 14 contains more information on writing effective paragraphs.

EXERCISE ■ Here are three sample student paragraphs. Evaluate each according to the Revision Checklist for Paragraphs and suggest any necessary changes.

1.   I can remember so many times when my father had said that he was coming to pick me up for a day or two. I was excited as a young boy could be at the thought of seeing my father. With all the excitement and anticipation raging inside of me, I would wait on the front porch. Minutes would seem like hours as I would wait impatiently.

2.   Going to high school for the first time, I couldn't decide if I should try out for the cheerleading team or wait a year. Since I had time and had been on other squads, I decided "why not?" I had nothing to lose but a lot to gain. Tryouts were not as hard as I thought, but I just knew I had to be

2. This paragraph, touching briefly on several different ideas, is in reality the skeleton of a short paper that needs fleshing out with more details. The writer should explain the reasons for her indecision, tell what she had to gain by joining the team, add a more descriptive account of the tryouts and selection process, and redo the conclusion. What did she do when her name was finally read? What did she feel? "More than happy" doesn't say much. What would being selected have meant to her?

3. This paragraph seems to have one basic idea (the hikers making a dash for "it"), but the sentences are not clearly connected. For example, "Earlier in the day it had been a perfectly clear day" is out of logical order. Furthermore, additional information about the rainstorm, which is implied but never discussed, is obviously needed.

Possible Revision

For hours we had been waiting under the overhang of an abandoned hut while the rain poured down. Earlier in the day it had been perfectly clear, so none of us had brought ponchos on our short hike through the woods. The downpour had caught us unprepared. We had thought it would let up as sudden storms usually do, but no relief was in sight. Worse, it would soon be dark. None of us wanted to stand there all night, so we didn't have much choice. Even if we were going to get thoroughly soaked, we had to make a dash for the car.

PERSPECTIVE

Many students think sentences and words are revised only to correct errors. They should understand that their sentence

on the squad. The tryout consisted of learning the routine they made up, making up your own routine, doing splits, and making a chant. Yet although these things were not that hard, I still was not sure whether I would make the team or not. The time came for the judges to make their decisions on who made the squad. Totaling the votes, they handed the results to the coach. She gave her speech that all coaches give. We were all good, but only a few could be picked for the team. As she started to read the names, I got hot. When she called my name, I was more than happy.

3.   For hours we had been waiting under the overhang of an abandoned hut. None of us had thought to bring ponchos on our short hike through the woods. Soon it would be dark. Earlier in the day it had been a perfectly clear day. We all agreed that we didn't want to stand here all night in the dark, so we decided to make a dash for it.

SHARPENING SENTENCES AND WORDS

Next, turn your attention to sentences and words. You can improve your writing considerably by finding and correcting sentences that convey the wrong meaning or are stylistically deficient in some way. Consider, for example, the following sentences.

Just Mary was picked to write the report.
Mary was just picked to write the report.
Mary was picked to write just the report.

The first sentence says that no one except Mary will write the report, the second says that she was recently picked for the job, and the third says that she will write nothing else. Clearly, each of these sentences expresses a different meaning.

Now let's look at a second set of sentences.

Personally, I am of the opinion that the results of our membership drive will prove to be pleasing to all of us.
I believe the results of our membership drive will please all of us.

The wordiness of the first sentence slows the reader's pace and makes it harder to grasp the writer's meaning. The second sentence, by contrast, is much easier to grasp.

Like your sentences, your words should also convey your thoughts precisely and clearly. Words are, after all, your chief means of communicating with your reader. Examine the first draft and revised version of the following paragraph, which describe the early morning actions of the writer's roommate. The underlined words identify points of revision.

■ First Draft

Coffee cup in hand, she <u>moves</u> toward the bathroom. The coffee spills <u>noisily</u> on the tile floor as she <u>reaches</u> for the light switch and <u>turns</u> it on. After <u>looking</u> briefly at the face in the mirror, she <u>walks</u> toward the bathtub.

■ Revised Version

Coffee cup in hand, she <u>stumbles</u> toward the bathroom. The coffee she spills on the tile floor makes <u>a slapping sound</u> as she <u>gropes</u> for the light switch and <u>flips</u> it on. After <u>squinting</u> briefly at the face in the mirror, she <u>shuffles</u> toward the bathtub.

Note that the words in the first draft are general and imprecise. Exactly how does she move? With a limp? With a strut? With a spring in her step? And what does "noisily" mean? A thud? A roar? A sharp crack? The reader has no way of knowing. Recognizing this fact, the student revised her paragraph, substituting vivid, specific words. As a result, the reader can visualize the actions more sharply.

Don't confuse vivid, specific words with "jawbreaker words"—those that are complex and pretentious. (Most likely all of the words in the revised version are in your vocabulary.) Words should promote communication, not block it.

Reading your draft aloud will force you to slow down, and you will often hear yourself stumble over problem sections. You'll be more likely to uncover errors such as missing words, excessive repetition, clumsy sentences, and sentence fragments. Be honest in your evaluation; don't read in virtues that aren't there or that exaggerate the writing quality.

REVISION CHECKLIST FOR SENTENCES

- ■ What sentences are not clearly expressed or logically constructed?
- ■ What sentences seem awkward, excessively convoluted, or lacking in punch?
- ■ What words require explanation or substitution because the reader may not know them?
- ■ Where does my writing become wordy or use vague terms?
- ■ Where have I carelessly omitted words or mistakenly used the wrong word?

Chapters 15 and 16 discuss sentences and words in detail.

structure and word choice can usually be improved so as to have greater impact on readers. On the other hand, students must keep this level of revision in its place—as a type of polish applied after the body work of major revision has been completed.

TEACHING STRATEGIES

1. If you take up the different sentence strategies discussed in Chapter 15, you might have students select several sentences from their text and rewrite them using the different strategies.
2. Because students have different abilities, some teachers prefer to identify each one's problems on his or her draft rather than addressing such matters in the classroom.

CLASSROOM ACTIVITIES

1. Have students exchange papers and circle sentences that seem ineffective. The writer could then prepare several improved versions of each.
2. Have students circle vague or ineffective words in their own drafts or those of others and then develop a list of possible substitutes.
3. Use examples from your own writing to demonstrate how you might revise a sentence. Put the changes on the board and explain why each was made.
4. Provide students with several versions of the same sentence. Have them rank the sentences according to effectiveness and explain their decisions.

EXERCISE ANSWER

See the suggested rewrite, answer 1, page 41.

SUGGESTED INSTRUCTOR READING

Christensen, F., ed. The Sentence and the Paragraph. Urbana, IL: NCTE, 1963. Includes not only an account of the generative sentence and paragraph but provides excellent examples of revised paragraphs and sentences.

TEACHING STRATEGIES

1. It usually pays dividends if you allow five to ten minutes of class time for one final proofreading, perhaps to look for sentence errors. Make it clear that you expect the other proofreading to be done outside class.
2. Make sure students know that errors will be penalized and just how severe the penalty will be.
3. Encourage students to use the Personal Revision Checklist on the inside back cover of the text to record any errors they discover.

EXERCISE ■ **Reread exercise paragraph 1 on page 41 and revise the sentence structure and word choice to create a more effective paragraph.**

Proofreading your draft

After revising your draft, proofread or edit it to correct errors in grammar, punctuation, and spelling. Since we often overlook our own errors simply because we know what we meant, proofreading can be difficult. Inch through your draft deliberately, moving your finger along slowly under every word. Repeat this procedure several times, looking first for errors in grammar, then for sentence errors and problems in punctuation and mechanics, and finally for mistakes in spelling. Be especially alert for problems that have plagued your writing in the past.

Effective proofreading calls for you to assume a detective role and probe for errors that weaken your writing. If you accept the challenge, you will certainly improve the quality of your finished work.

Writing the introduction and conclusion

If you've put off writing your introduction, do it now. Generally, short papers begin with a single paragraph that includes the previously drafted thesis statement, which sometimes needs to be rephrased so that it meshes smoothly with the rest of the paragraph. The introduction acquaints the reader with your topic; it should clearly signal your intention as well as spark the reader's interest. Pages 186–88 discuss and illustrate effective introductions.

The conclusion wraps up your discussion. Generally a single paragraph in short papers, a good ending summarizes or supports the paper's main idea. Pages 189–92 discuss and illustrate effective conclusions.

Selecting a title

PERSPECTIVE

Because they are used in different publications that serve different purposes for different readers, titles obviously differ in character.

CLASSROOM ACTIVITY

Have students bring in titles from a variety of publications. Either in small groups or as a

All essays require titles. Unless a good title unexpectedly surfaces while you are writing, wait until you finish the paper before choosing one. Since the reader must see the connection between what the title promises and what the essay delivers, a good title must be both accurate and specific.

Titling the Mt. Pleasant essay "Shopping in Mt. Pleasant" would mislead the reader, as shopping is mentioned only briefly. A specific title suggests the essay's focus rather than just its topic. For example, "Teenage Fun in Mt. Pleasant" is clearer and more precise than simply "Mt. Pleasant." The essay is geared to teenage activities, not a description of the city as a whole.

To engage your reader's interest, you might try your hand at a clever or catchy title, but don't get so carried away with creativity that you forget to relate the title to the paper's content. Here are some examples of common and clever titles:

Common   "Handling a Hangover"

  Clever   "The Mourning After"

Common   "Buying Your Home with Other People's Money"

  Clever   "Home Free"

Use a clever title only if its wit or humor doesn't clash with the overall purpose and tone of the paper.

class they could sort the titles to establish their distinctive characteristics for varying contexts. You might also have students assess the effectiveness of different kinds of titles.

CASE HISTORY   *(Concluded)*

After carefully proofreading and fine-tuning the second draft of his Mt. Pleasant essay, George prepares the final version, which follows. Margin notes highlight key changes. Compare the revised and final versions to see how these changes have improved the essay.

Teenage Fun in Mt. Pleasant

If you get tired of driving out to the same old Lake Michigan beach this summer, you might think about trying Mt. Pleasant for something different. The Mt. Pleasant area offers swimming, canoeing, and hiking; a city park where you can socialize with other teens; a college campus to wander around; horse and auto racing; movies, a museum, video games, and shopping for a rainy day; and many places to eat. What more can you ask?

For swimming or merely lying on the beach, you can't beat Cold Water Lake, just a few miles west of Mt. Pleasant off Beal City Road. This lake boasts crystal clear water and a scenic beach surrounded by hills and woods. Here you can always find a volleyball game to join, throw a frisbee around, do some boy or girl watching, or bask in the sun. The swimming, of course, is great.

If you prefer some wet-and-wild swimming fun, then Lake Isabella Dam, a short drive down the road from Cold Water Lake, is

General title made specific

Slightly rearranged listing reflects organization of essay

First sentence rephrased and divided into two to avoid repeated "if you" paragraph openings and lessen awkwardness the place for you. The dam forms a slippery slide about 100 yards long which is pitched at a 160-degree angle. You can spend a whole day there and not get bored with sliding.

Canoeing can be wonderful fun, and the Mt. Pleasant area offers a number of rivers that will delight anyone who likes this activity. If you prefer calm-water canoeing, you can try the Chippewa River, the Cold Water River, or the north or south branches of the Salt River. If your taste runs to the exciting white-water variety, you will find the Pine River made to order. Near or on each river are places that rent canoes at reasonable rates and even provide you with transportation from your destination back to your car.

For anyone who likes to hike, Deerfield Park, a few miles west of town on M-20, provides 25 miles of nature trails. These secluded trails that meander through a natural forest and gentle, rolling hills can be a fine place to take someone special for a quiet stroll. You will no doubt see a variety of birds as well as squirrels, raccoons, and chipmunks. If you're really lucky, you might spot a deer or two. Closer to town, on Harris Street, Mission Creek Woodland Park offers 60 acres of forest trails, a creek, and a picnicking area.

Island Park, located in the Pine River just off Main Street, offers you a chance to meet other teenagers without going out of town. Here you can listen to live bands, play or watch baseball games, have picnics, or just get together and talk. This park is the main hangout for Mt. Pleasant teens, so you should have no trouble making new friends. Nearby is Nelson Park, which has a small zoo where you can see deer, bear, badger, and many other kinds of local wildlife.

Planning to attend college? If you are, then you might want to spend some time wandering around the Central Michigan University campus and giving it a close look. Strolling past ivy-covered buildings and along tree-lined walkways will give you the feel of real college life. When summer semester is in session, you might also want to walk through a few buildings, look around the library, and visit the

---

Last sentence reworded to lessen awkwardness

Paragraph rewritten to liven and add variety to phrasing

"fine place" substituted because "great" overused in essay. "see" substituted to avoid using "spot" twice

Paragraph rewritten to avoid "if you" opening, liven and tighten phrasing. Opportunity to make friends added.

Opening reworded to eliminate cliché and liven phrasing

bookstore. If you stop to watch students bustle to class, you could be watching your own future.

To sample something different, pay a visit to Mt. Pleasant Meadows on Mission Road north of M-20 some weekend and enjoy the fun-filled, action-packed horse races you'll find there. For just two dollars, you can enjoy the thrill of cheering your favorite to victory. The Mt. Pleasant Speedway offers you the chance to sample a second kind of racing. Each Friday the speedway puts on a night-long program of high-speed stock car races. Fast horses or fast cars—either ensures you an evening of high excitement.

On rainy days, you can still find much to do in Mt. Pleasant. Several multi-screen movie theaters give you a choice of the most recent releases. You can also do a little time traveling at the Center for Cultural and Natural History in Rowe Hall on the college campus. This museum includes lumbering tools, Civil War artifacts, a variety of household items from different historical periods, and an exhibit of wildlife, including the remains of a mastodon. You can play video games at the Royal Oasis Family Amusement Center in the campus mall on Mission Street. Or you can spend some time shopping for clothing, books, records, or gifts in the many mall stores.

Mt. Pleasant has a wide range of great eating places. The McDonald's on Mission Street is the most striking place that you will probably ever see to get a Big Mac. With fancy chrome palm trees and glossy plastic cutouts of people having a good time, it resembles an Art Deco movie set. There are, of course, many other fast-food places such as Arby's, Burger King, Taco Bell, Kentucky Fried Chicken, and Little Caesar's. If you are interested in taking a date to some place special and don't mind spending the money to do it, you might try The Embers, a restaurant rated as "one of Michigan's finest." There you'll find cloth napkins and tablecloths, soft lights, and a menu offering an outstanding selection of meat and seafood. Your date will be sure to like it.

Mt. Pleasant offers enough diversions to satisfy any teenager. Why not come and investigate for yourself?

First two sentences reworded and combined to avoid "if you" opening and tighten phrasing

Third sentence made smoother

Final sentence replaced to strengthen ending

First two sentences rewritten to liven phrasing

Final sentence: types of shopping added

Word "cheap" omitted; Embers restaurant expensive. "wildest" replaced with "most striking" for more accuracy

Other fast-food restaurants named

Details about Embers added

Weak ending sentence replaced with stronger one

Conclusion changed to reiterate audience

It is crucial that you view revision not as a hasty "touch up" job or as a quick sweep through your draft just prior to handing it in. Instead, revision should be an ongoing process that often involves an upheaval of major sections as you see your draft through your reader's eyes and strive to write as well as you can. Only when you reach that summit have you finished revising.

REVISING WITH A WORD PROCESSOR

Many writers prefer the advantages of revising on a word processor. All word-processing programs allow you to write over unwanted sections of your draft, add new information, delete useless material, and move parts of the text around. Learn all the commands of your particular program and experiment to see exactly what your options are. The following practical tips will improve your efficiency.

1. Always keep a backup copy of everything. Accidentally erasing a file or losing your work to an electrical power surge is not uncommon. In addition, save copies of your earlier drafts, either as printouts or on disk; selected parts may prove useful later, and new papers sometimes sprout from old drafts. You can either save each draft under variations of your file name—"COPY A, COPY B, COPY C"—or keep deleted sections in specially labeled files.

2. Jot down helpful ideas or comments in your text as you revise. Enclose them with a special symbol, such as < >, and either save them in a separate file or delete them later if they serve no purpose.

3. If you struggle with a section of the text, write two or three versions and then pick your favorite. You might even open a new file, experiment freely, and then use the best version in your draft.

4. Don't allow the program to control how you revise. The easy-to-use, gentle-touch keyboards can lull you into a lapse of judgment and cause you to forget whether your words are worth writing. Pages of worthless material could pile up. Furthermore, don't be tempted to do what the commands make easiest: fiddle endlessly with sentences and words, never develop the essay as a whole, and move blocks of writing around indiscriminately. Avoid being electronically bewitched and make only those additions and changes that improve your writing.

5. Always revise using a printout. If you use just the computer, you are limited to only one screen at a time. A printed page has a different look. In addition, a printout allows you to compare several pages at once: you can see, for example, how the second paragraph might be more effective if repositioned on page 4.

6. When you finish revising, check the coherence of your draft. The writing must flow smoothly at the points where you have added, deleted, or moved sections of text. In addition, altered sentences must be clearly written and logically constructed. You can best check the essay's flow with a printout.

7. Proofreading with a word processor poses certain dangers. For example, a spelling check function can't judge whether you used the wrong word (*form* instead of *from*) or confused identical sounding but differently spelled words (their, there, they're). Furthermore, the unit will sometimes flag words that are not misspelled but are simply not in the computer's list. In addition, there are few good programs to check grammar or punctuation. *You* are still the ultimate proofreader.

PEER EVALUATION OF DRAFTS

At various points in the writing process, your instructor may ask you and your classmates to read and respond to one another's papers. Peer response often proves useful because even the best writers cannot always predict how their readers will react to their writing. For example, magazine articles designed to reduce the fear of AIDS have, in some cases, increased anxiety about the disease. Furthermore, we often have difficulty seeing the problems with our own drafts because so much hard work has gone into them. What seems clear and effective to us can be confusing or boring to our readers. Comments from our peers can frequently launch a more effective essay.

Just as the responses of others help you, so will your responses help them. You don't have the close, involved relationship with your peers' writing that you do with your own. Therefore, you can gauge their drafts objectively. This type of critical evaluation will eventually heighten your awareness of your own writing strengths and weaknesses. And knowing how to read your own work critically is one of the most important writing skills you can develop.

Responding to Your Peer's Drafts

Responding to someone else's writing is easier than you might imagine. It's not your job to spell out ways to make the draft more effective, how to organize it, what to include, and the type of language to use. The writer must make these decisions. Your job is to *identify* problems, *not solve* them. You can do that best by responding honestly to the draft.

Some responses are more helpful than others. You don't help the writer by casually observing that the draft "looks O.K." Such a response doesn't point to problem areas; rather it suggests that you didn't read the paper carefully and critically. Wouldn't you inform a friend who was wearing clothes that looked terrible *why* they looked terrible? The same attitude should prevail about the writing of others, something that makes a statement just as clothes do. Nor is a vague comment such as "the introduction is uninteresting" helpful. Point out *why* it is uninteresting. For instance, you might note that "The introduction doesn't interest me in the paper because it is very technical, and I get lost. I ask myself why I should read on." Below are two more examples of ineffective responses and their more effective counterparts.

Ineffective

The paper was confusing.

2. You can set up peer groups in different ways. If students form their own groups, those of like ability might join together, as might friends, who could be reluctant to respond critically to each other's papers. Alternatively, you could organize the groups so that different levels of ability are represented, making sure that every strong writer is matched with another strong writer who can provide effective responses. Groups of three to five participants are best.

3. You can direct groups to respond in different ways. Some instructors prefer to have the writer read the paper aloud and "readers" respond orally. Oral responses, however, often cause student minds to wander, and most writers forget the comments. Another alternative is to have students exchange papers and respond in writing. This procedure reinforces the importance of written communication, allows students more time to reflect on their response, provides more responses, and establishes a written record of the responses.

4. Just as you can guide students to respond generally to a draft, you can also guide peer responses by posing a set of specific questions, similar to the revision questions in each chapter, which are keyed to particular features of the assignment.

5. To prevent students from ignoring peer responses, have all writers review the comments they receive, prepare a written plan that incorporates them, and turn in peer responses along with their revised draft.

6. You may have to speak to students who are not making an effort to provide quality peer responses.

Effective

Paragraphs 2, 3, and 4 confused me. You jumped around too much. First you wrote about your experience on the first day of college, then you went on to how much you enjoyed junior high school, and finally you wrote about what you want to do for a career. I don't see how these ideas relate or why they are in the order that they are.

Ineffective

More examples would help.

Effective

When you indicate that college can be a scary place, I get no real idea of why or how. What are the things that you think make college scary? I would like some examples.

Here are some steps to follow when responding to someone else's draft. First, read the essay from beginning to end without interruption. On a separate sheet of paper, indicate what you consider the main idea. The writer can then see whether the intended message has come through. Next, identify the biggest problem and the biggest strength. Writers need both negative and positive comments. Finally, reread the paper and write either specific responses to each paragraph or your responses to general questions such as the ones that follow. In either case, don't comment on spelling or grammar unless it really inhibits your reading.

PEER RESPONSE CHECKLIST

- What is the main point of this essay?
- What is the biggest problem?
- What is the biggest strength?
- What material doesn't seem to fit the main point or the audience?
- What questions has the author not answered?
- Where should more details or examples be added? Why?

■ At what point does the paper fail to hold my interest? Why?
■ Where is the organization confusing?
■ Where is the writing unclear or vague?

SUGGESTED INSTRUCTOR READINGS

Bruffee, K. "Peer Tutoring and the 'Conversation of Mankind.'" Writing Center. Ed. Gary Olsen. Urbana, IL: NCTE, 1984. 3–15. Argues that peer tutors can, in some cases, be more effective than the instructor.

Using Student Writing Response Groups in the Classroom. Curriculum Publication no. 12. Berkeley: Bay Area Writing Project, U of California P, 1980.

As you learn the various strategies for successful writing, new concerns will arise. Questions geared to these concerns appear in the revision section that concludes the discussion of each strategy.

An Example of Peer Response

The following is the first draft of a student essay and a partial peer response to it. The response features three of the nine general questions and also comments on one paragraph. Before you read the response, try evaluating this essay yourself and then compare your reactions to those of the other student.

Captive Breeding in Zoos

This paper is about captive breeding. Today, humans hinder nature's species right to survive. Man is making it hard for over one hundred species of animals to continue to exist. But captive breeding in the worlds zoos may be just what the doctor ordered. This rescue attempt is a complex and difficult undertaking. Captive breeding of endangered species is complicated by the special social and physical requirements of individual species.

There are many social problems that have to be solved for the successful reproduction of endangered species in zoos. Mating is one of the most important of these problems. One propagation "must" for many felines, pandas, and pygmy hippopotami is the complete separation of sexes until they're "ready." Leland Stowe says that cheetahs almost never get together unless they can't see or smell each other ahead of time. When females exhibit a certain behavior, they bring on the male.

Male-female compatibility is a social problem. Great apes seem to be as particular as people in choosing mates. Stowe tells about an orangutan that turned a cold shoulder on the females in the National Zoo located in Washington, D.C. Then they shipped him to a zoo in Colorado. There, he took up with one of the females. The curator of the zoo, William Zanten, says he's "been siring offspring ever since."

Social factors hurt care of infant primates. Sheldon Campbell   4
talks about this in <u>Smithsonian</u> magazine. He writes about the
problems of breeding golden marmosets. These are monkeys that live
in Brazil. The scientists found that captive-born parents neglected
their young. Sometimes they even killed them. The problem was due
to the fact that the marmosets had no experience living in a family
situation. They didn't know what to do. Emily Hahn writes about
gorillas in <u>The New Yorker</u>. She says that those raised by humans
make poor mothers. Those raised by dutiful mothers make good
parents.

The second important stumbling block to successful captive   5
breeding is physical problems. Ignorance of dietary needs can be bad.
Stowe talks about the captive breeding of gorillas and says that when
this breeding was first getting started, infants exhibited a very high
mortality rate. Then the babies were given iron and meat protein,
the latter rich in Vitamin B-12. They were sprinkled on bananas,
and the bananas were fed to the babies. The survival rate markedly
improved.

Animals can be bred more easily if they are in an   6
environment that duplicates that animal's natural habitat. Hooved
and horned animals are an easy job because of the similarity in
terrain and climate of their natural habitats to zoo habitats. Polar
bears are a lot tougher. Mothers want to be let alone until their cubs
are up and about. Because of this fact, the bears often kill their
babies. Stowe says they solved this problem by building replicas of
arctic ice caves. The mothers and cubs are left alone until they
emerge from the cave. John Perry, Director of the National Zoo, said
this:

The world is our zoo—a zoo that must be well-managed, its
resources carefully husbanded, for these are the only resources it
can ever have. We have appointed ourselves the keepers of this
zoo, but we cannot live outside its gates. We are of it. Our lives
are inextricably intertwined with the lives of all that live within.
Their fate will be ours.

Our endangered species can survive only by nature's implacable test—sustained births by second and third generations. It will take decades to reach such a verdict of success. Thus we can see that captive breeding is beset by many problems.

What is the main point of this essay?

I think this paper is saying that the only chance for endangered species is that they reproduce in zoos but that it is hard to get them to breed in captivity.

What is the biggest problem?

I can't see how each paragraph connects to the main point of the paper or to each other. They seem disconnected. What does "Male-Female compatibility is a social problem" have to do with the problem of reproduction or with the previous paragraph on mating? Also, there are a number of very unclear statements that leave me with many questions. How is man making it hard for over a hundred species to exist? What do you mean when you say "almost never get together," "bring on the male," "took up with," and "an easy job?"

What is the biggest strength?

I hadn't thought much about this question, so it was something new for me. I liked the examples about specific animals and the problems that they have in captivity. I especially liked the fact that the writer gave me several problems that occur when animals are bred in captivity. The writer didn't oversimplify.

Response to paragraph 4

Do social factors always hurt the care of infant primates? Your statement seems too general. Shouldn't you combine some of your sentences? The first six sentences seem to abruptly jump from one point to the next; the writing is not smooth. How did you get from marmosets to gorillas? The jump confuses me. Also, were the "dutiful mothers" humans or gorillas?

Acting upon Your Peer's Response

Sometimes you need strong nerves to act upon a peer response. You can easily become defensive or discount your reader's comments as foolish. Remember, however, that as a writer you are trying to communicate with your readers, and that means taking seriously the problems they identify. Of course, you decide which responses are appropriate, but even an inappropriate criticism sometimes sets off a train of thought that leads to good ideas for revision.

Examine the revised version of the captive breeding essay which follows and note how some of the peer responses have been taken into account. Clear transition sentences link paragraphs to the thesis statement and to each other. Vague statements identified in the earlier draft have been clarified. In the fourth paragraph the writer connects the discussion of the marmosets to that of the gorillas by changing the order of the two sentences that precede the final one and combining them, thereby identifying poor parenting as the key problem with both kinds of primates. Finally, she indicates what she means by "dutiful mother."

As you read this version, carefully examine the margin notes, which highlight key features of the revision.

Title: specific and accurate

Introduction: arresting statement

Captive Breeding: Difficult But Necessary

Today, as in the past, humans encroach upon the basic right   1
of nature's species to survive. Through ignorance, oversight, and
technological developments, we are threatening the survival of over
one hundred animal species. Until their environments can be
safeguarded against harmful human intrusion, the last chance for
the threatened species may be captive breeding in zoos. But this
rescue attempt is a complex and difficult undertaking. In particular,

each species presents social and physical problems that must be
solved if breeding is to succeed.

> Thesis statement and statement of organization

    Among the social problems that complicate successful
reproduction, mating problems loom especially large. For instance,
the male and female of many feline species must be kept completely
separated until both animals are ready to mate. Leland Stowe,
writing in National Wildlife magazine, notes that cheetahs almost
never mate unless kept where the one cannot see or smell the other.
Once the female shows signs of receptivity, a male is placed in her
cage, and mating then occurs. Pandas and pygmy hippopotami show
the same behavior.

2

> Topic sentence with link to thesis statement

> Specific details: problems with cheetahs

> Mention of other species with mating problems

    A related social problem with certain species is male-female
compatibility. Great apes, for instance, seem to be as particular as
human beings in choosing mates. Stowe relates an amusing case of a
male orangutan that totally spurned the females in the Washington,
D.C. National Zoo. Shipped to a zoo in Colorado, he succumbed to the
charms of a new face and has, according to curator William Zanten,
''been siring offspring ever since.''

3

> Topic sentence, with link to preceding paragraph. Linking device

> Specific example: problem with particular orangutan

    Social factors can also imperil proper care of infant primates.
In a Smithsonian magazine article, Sheldon Campbell talks about the
problems scientists encountered in trying to breed golden marmosets,
a species of Brazilian monkey. Early attempts failed because the
captive-born parents neglected and sometimes accidentally killed
their babies. Observation showed that the problem occurred because
the marmosets had no experience living in a family situation—they
simply didn't know how to handle their offspring. Gorillas reared by
humans may also make poor mothers, reports Emily Hahn in The
New Yorker. On the other hand, those reared by dutiful mothers,
whether human or gorilla, are usually good parents themselves.

4

> Topic sentence, with link to preceding paragraph

> Specific details: problems with marmosets

> Mention of other species with rearing problems

> Linking device

    Physical problems rival social problems as stumbling blocks to
successful captive breeding. Ignorance of a species' dietary needs, for
instance, can have disastrous consequences. Early in the captive
breeding of gorillas, infants exhibited a very high mortality rate,

5

> Transition sentence: signals switch to discussing physical problems

> Topic sentence, with link to transition sentence

Specific details: problems with gorillas

Linking device

Topic sentence

Linking device

Conclusion: quotation plus statement reinforcing idea that captive breeding presents difficulties

Stowe notes. Then meat protein and iron, the former rich in Vitamin B-12, were sprinkled on bananas and fed to the babies. <u>As a result,</u> the survival rate markedly improved.

<u>An environment that duplicates a species' natural habitat favors easy propagation.</u> Hooved and horned animals present few breeding problems because the zoo habitats are similar in terrain and climate to their natural habitats. Polar bears, <u>on the other hand,</u> present difficult problems. Unless the mothers have complete privacy until the cubs can get around, they often kill the babies. To prevent this from happening, Stowe says, zoos now construct replicas of arctic ice caves and leave mothers and cubs completely alone until the new family emerges from the cave.

6

In his book <u>The World's a Zoo</u> John Perry, director of the National Zoo, has spoken of the need to save our endangered species.

7

The world is our zoo—a zoo that must be well-managed, its resources carefully husbanded, for these are the only resources it can ever have. We have appointed ourselves the keepers of this zoo, but we cannot live outside its gates. We are of it. Our lives are inextricably intertwined with the lives of all that live within. Their fate will be ours.

The difficulty, unfortunately, is as great as the urgency of this problem. Only sustained births by second- and third-generation captive animals can ensure the survival of our endangered species. And it will take decades to achieve the necessary success.

CHAPTER 4

Narration: Relating Events

PERSPECTIVE

Narratives provide a convenient launch point for many writing courses since most students find it relatively easy to tell stories about their lives. The confidence they gain can help lessen apprehension about later assignments.

TEACHING STRATEGIES

1. Have each student bring to class an example of a narrative.

2. You might generate a class discussion that attempts to answer exactly what we gain when we exchange stories about ourselves with others. Some possible answers: (a) the story helps us pull our life into a pattern; (b) hearing about someone else's life gives us perspective on our own; (c) narratives help us understand how other people live; (d) swapping narratives binds us together as a community.

3. To prepare students for writing a narrative, ask them to freewrite in their journals about memorable events in their lives. Emphasize that they include as much detail as possible. These journal entries can become background material for the narrative assignment.

4. You could progress from narratives to types of expository writing. For example, students could write a narrative about what it means to grow up. Then they might write a process essay on the stages of adolescence or a cause-and-effect essay on the problems of growing up.

5. Some students have trouble writing personal narratives because they feel uncomfortable writing about themselves. A number of alternative narrative assignments can work well for such students. They can interview and report on the life of someone else, investigate and trace the development of some professional's career, or narrate a campus or community event.

Clicking off the evening news and padding toward bed, Heloise suddenly glimpsed, out of the corner of her eye, a shadow stretching across the living room floor from under the drawn curtains.

"Wh—who's there?"

No response.

Edging backward toward the phone, her eyes riveted on the shadow, she stammered, "I—I don't have any money."

Still no answer.

Reaching the phone, she gripped the receiver and started to lift it from its cradle. Just then. . . .

Just now you've glimpsed the start of a *narrative*. A narrative relates a series of events. The events may be real—as in histories, biographies, or news stories—or imaginary, as in short stories and novels. The narrative urge stirs in all of us, and like everyone else, you have responded almost from the time you began to talk. As a child, you probably swapped many stories with your friends, recounting an exciting visit to a circus or amusement park or an unusually funny experience with your pet. Today you may tell a friend about the odd happening in your biology laboratory or on the job.

Many classroom and on-the-job writing occasions call for narratives. Your English instructor might want you to trace the development of some literary character. Your history instructor might have you recap the events leading to a major war, your sociology instructor have you relate your unfolding relations with a stepparent or someone else, your psychology instructor ask you to report on society's changing attitudes toward the treatment of insanity. At work, a police officer may record the events leading to an arrest, a scientist recount the development of a research project, a nurse report on a patient's changing attitudes toward surgery, and a department manager prepare a brief history of an employee's work problems.

PURPOSE

A narrative, like any other kind of writing, makes a point or has a purpose. The point can either be stated or left unstated, but it always shapes the writing.

Some narratives simply tell what happened or establish an interesting or useful fact. The reporter who writes about a heated city council meeting or a lively congressional committee hearing usually wants only to set facts before the public.

Most narratives, however, go beyond merely reciting events. Writers of history and biography delve into the motives underlying the events and lives they portray, while narratives of personal experience offer lessons and insights. In the following conclusion to a narrative about an encounter with a would-be mugger, the writer offers an observation on self-respect.

> I kept my self-respect, even at the cost of dirtying my fists with violence, and I feel that I understand the Irish and the Cypriots, the Israelis and the Palestinians, all those who seem to us to fight senseless wars for senseless reasons, better than before. For what respect does one keep for oneself if one isn't in the last resort ready to fight and say, "You punk!"?

Harry Fairlie, "A Victim Fights Back"

ACTION

Action plays a central role in any narrative. Other writing often only suggests action, leaving readers to imagine it for themselves:

> A hundred thousand people were killed by the atomic bomb, and these six were among the survivors. They still wonder why they lived when so many others died. Each of them counts many small items of chance or volition—a step taken in time, a decision to go indoors, catching one streetcar instead of the next—that spared him. And now each knows that in the act of survival he lived a dozen lives and saw more death than he ever thought he would see. At the time, none of them knew anything.

John Hersey, *Hiroshima*

This passage suggests a great deal of action—the flash of an exploding bomb, the collapse of buildings, screaming people fleeing the scorching devastation—but *it does not present the action.* Narration, however, re-creates action:

> When I pulled the trigger I did not hear the bang or feel the kick—one never does when a shot goes home—but I heard the devilish roar of glee that went up from the crowd. In that instant, in too short a time, one would have thought, even for the bullet to get there, a mysterious, terrible change had come over the elephant. He neither stirred nor fell, but every line of his body had altered. He looked suddenly stricken, shrunken, immensely old, as though the frightful impact of the bullet had paralyzed him without knocking him down. At

last, after what seemed a long time—it might have been five seconds, I dare say—he sagged flabbily to his knees. His mouth slobbered. An enormous senility seemed to have settled upon him. One could have imagined him thousands of years old. I fired again into the same spot. At the second shot he did not collapse but climbed with desperate slowness to his feet and stood weakly upright, with legs sagging and head drooping. I fired a third time. That was the shot that did for him. You could see the agony of it jolt his whole body and knock the last remnant of strength from his legs. But in falling he seemed for a moment to rise, for as his hind legs collapsed beneath him he seemed to tower upward like a huge rock toppling, his trunk reaching skywards like a tree. He trumpeted, for the first and only time. And then down he came, his belly towards me, with a crash that seemed to shake the ground even where I lay.

George Orwell, "Shooting an Elephant"

Orwell's account offers a stark, vivid replay of the slaying, leaving nothing significant for the reader to infer.

A few words of caution are in order here. Action entails not only exotic events such as the theft of mass-destruction weapons, then the ransom demand, then the recovery of the weapons and the pursuit of the villains. A wide variety of more normal events also qualify as action: a long, patient wait that comes to nothing, an unexpected kiss after some friendly assistance, a disappointing gift that signals a failed relationship. Furthermore, the narrative action must all relate to the main point—not merely chronicle a series of events.

CONFLICT

The events in our lives and our world are often shaped by conflicts that need to be overcome. It should not be surprising then that conflict and its resolution, if any, is crucial to a narrative since it motivates and often structures the action. Some conflicts pit one individual against another or against a group, such as a union, company, or religious body. In others, the conflict may involve either an individual and nature or two clashing impulses in one person's head. Read the following student paragraph and note how common sense and fear struggle within the writer, who has experienced a sharp, stabbing pain in his side.

> Common sense and fear waged war in my mind. The first argued that a pain so intense was nothing to fool with, that it might indicate a serious or even life-threatening condition. Dr. Montz would be able to identify the problem and deal with it before it worsened. But what if it was already serious? What if I needed emergency surgery? I didn't want anyone cutting into me. "Now wait a minute," I said. "It's probably nothing serious. Most aches and pains aren't. I'll see the doctor, maybe get some pills, and the problem will clear up overnight. But what if he finds

CLASSROOM ACTIVITY

Students often have an exaggerated sense of what conflict entails. Introduce a simple conflict, such as confronting an unruly computer, and show how it can lead to a narrative. Have students then list, in small groups or as an entire class, the kinds of conflicts people encounter.

something major, and I have to spend the night in the hospital getting ready for surgery or recovering from it? I think I'll just ignore the pain."

Luis Rodriguez

POINT OF VIEW

PERSPECTIVE

Point of view can be a complex matter to discuss. The first-person narrator, of course, need not be the author, or even the main character, of a narrative. Third-person narrators can possess various degrees of omniscience. With a capable class you might examine different points of view and their effects on a narrative.

Narrative writers may adopt either a first-person or third-person point of view. In first-person narratives, one of the participants tells what happened, whereas with third-person narration the storyteller stays completely out of the tale. Narratives you write about yourself use the first person, as do autobiographies. Biographies and histories use the third person, and fiction embraces both points of view.

In first-person narration, pronouns such as *I, me, mine, we,* and *ours* identify the storyteller. With the third person, the narrator remains unmentioned, and the characters are identified by nouns and such pronouns as *he, she, him,* and *her.* These two paragraphs illustrate the difference.

First-Person Narration

We would go to the well and wash in the ice-cold, clear water, grease our legs with equally cold stiff Vaseline, then tiptoe into the house. We wiped the dust from our toes and settled down for schoolwork, cornbread, clabbered milk, prayers and bed, always in that order. Momma was famous for pulling the quilts off after we had fallen asleep to examine our feet. If they weren't clean enough for her, she took the switch . . . and woke up the offender with a few aptly placed burning reminders.

Maya Angelou, "Momma's Encounter"

As this example shows, first-person narrators may refer to other characters in the narrative by using nouns and third-person pronouns.

Third-Person Narration

In the depths of the city walk the assorted human creatures who do not suspect the fate that hangs over them. A young woman sweeps happily from store to store, pushing a baby carriage along. Businessmen stride purposefully into their office buildings. A young black sulks down the sidewalks of his tenement, and an old woman tugs her shopping basket across a busy thoroughfare. The old woman is not happy; she has seen better days. Days of parks and fountains, of roses and grass, still stir in her memory. Reaching the other side, she stops and strains her neck upward, past the doorways, past the rows and rows of mirror glass, until her eyes rest on the brilliant blue sky so far away. She looks intently at the sky for a few minutes, noting every cloud that rolls past. And the jet plane. She follows the plane with her deep-socketed eyes and for some unexplainable reason suspects danger. She brings her gaze back to earth and walks away as the jet releases a large cloud of brownish-yellow gas. The gas hangs ominously in the air for a while, as if wanting to give humankind just a few more seconds. Then the cloud slowly descends to the surface, dissipating as it goes. By the time it reaches the glittering megalopolis, it is a colorless, odorless blanket of death.

Richard Latta

EXERCISE ■ **Identify the point of view in each of the following excerpts.**

1.   The bus screeched to a stop, and Pat stepped out of it and onto the sidewalk. Night enveloped the city, and a slight drizzle fell around her as she made her way to Al's office. Turning the corner, she stepped into the dark entryway. The receptionist had gone home, so she proceeded directly to the office. She knocked on the door and entered. Al, standing behind his desk and looking out the window, turned toward her with a startled look on his face.

Jennifer Webber

2.   It had really begun back in the Charlestown Prison, when Bimbi first made me feel envy of his store of knowledge. Bimbi had always taken charge of any conversation he was in, and I had tried to emulate him. But every book I picked up had few sentences which didn't contain anywhere from one to nearly all of the words that might as well have been in Chinese. When I just skipped those words, of course, I really ended up with little idea of what the book said. So I had come to the Norfolk Prison Colony still going through only book-reading motions. Pretty soon, I would have quit even these motions, unless I had received the motivation that I did.

Malcolm X, *The Autobiography of Malcolm X*

*K*EY EVENTS

Any narrative includes many separate events, enough to swamp your narrative boat if you try to pack them all in. Suppose you wish to write about your recent attack of where to begin and end. You might suggest that they identify the narrative's major conflict or focal point, then select the events relevant to it.

2. Other students have trouble because they aren't skilled in using transitions. They might recognize that the appendicitis narrative doesn't need to include opening the garage, but they simply don't know how to move the narrative from home to office. Introduce transition devices that will allow them to skip extraneous material. They could say, "After that brief attack, everything seemed fine. I even made it to work a little early that morning, as if nothing had happened."

3. Have students identify the key events in some of the essays in the Reader and discuss why they were used. Discuss how the writers handled transitions to avoid unwanted details.

4. Ask students to identify a central event in their lives that might be the basis for a narrative, list all the events related to it, and then select the key events.

TEACHING STRATEGY

Students often have trouble going from events to ideas. After they outline an important event, have them freewrite or brainstorm their reasons for the action and any thoughts they have about what happened.

appendicitis in order to make a point about heeding early warnings of an oncoming illness. Your list of events might look like this:

Awakened	Greeted fellow	Returned to work
Showered	employees	Began afternoon's
Experienced acute but	Began morning's	work
passing pain in	work	Collapsed at work
abdomen	Felt nauseated	station
Dressed	Met with boss	Was rushed to
Ate breakfast	Took coffee break	hospital
Opened garage door	Visited bathroom	Underwent diagnostic
Started car	Experienced more	tests
Drove to work	prolonged pain in	Had emergency
Parked in employee	abdomen	operation
lot	Walked to cafeteria	
Entered building	Ate lunch	

A narrative that included all, or even most, of these events would be bloated and ineffective. To avoid this outcome, identify and build your narrative around its key events—those that bear directly on your purpose. Include just enough secondary events to keep the narrative flowing smoothly, but treat them in sketchy fashion. The pain and nausea certainly qualify as key events. Here's how you might present the first attack of pain.

> My first sign of trouble came shortly after I stepped out of the shower. I had just finished toweling when a sharp pain in my lower right side sent me staggering into the bedroom, where I collapsed onto an easy chair in the corner. Biting my lip to hide my groans, I sat twisting in agony as the pain gradually ebbed, leaving me gray faced, sweat drenched, and shaken. What, I asked myself, had been the trouble? Was it ulcers? Was it a gallbladder attack? Did I have stomach cancer?

This passage *convinces*, not just tells, the reader that an attack has occurred. Its details vividly convey the nature of the attack as well as the reactions of the victim. As in any good narrative, the reader shares the experience of the writer, and the two communicate.

TEACHING STRATEGIES

1. To introduce students to effective dialogue techniques, you might have them review the narrative essays in the Reader in light of directed questions such as "How do

DIALOGUE

Dialogue, or conversation, animates many narratives, livening the action and helping draw the reader into the story. Written conversation, however, doesn't duplicate real talk. In speaking with friends, we repeat ourselves, throw in irrelevant comments, use slang, lose our train of thought, and overuse expressions like "you know," "uh," and "well." Dialogue that reproduced real talk would weaken any narrative.

Good dialogue resembles real conversation without copying it. It features simple words and short sentences while avoiding the over-repetition of phrases like "he said" and "she replied." If the conversation unfolds smoothly, the speaker's identity will be clear. To heighten the sense of reality, the writer may use an occasional sentence fragment, slang expression, pause, and the like, as in this passage.

> Mom was waiting for me when I entered the house.
>
> "Your friends. They've been talking to you again. Trying to persuade you to change your mind about going into baseball. Honey, I wish you'd listen to them. You're a terrific ballplayer. Just look at all the trophies and awards you've. . . ." She paused. "Joe's mother called me this morning and asked if you were playing in the game on Saturday. Davey, I wish you would. You haven't played for two weeks. Please. I want you to. For me. It would be so good for you to go and--and do what you've always. . . ."
>
> "O.K., Mom, I'll play. But remember, just for you."
>
> Diane Pickett

Note the mother's use of the slang expression "terrific" and of sentence fragments like "your friends" and "for me" as well as the shift in her train of thought and the repetition of "and." These strategies lend an air of realism to the mother's words.

*W*RITING A NARRATIVE

Planning and Drafting the Narrative

Most of the narratives you write for your composition class will relate a personal experience and therefore use the first person. On occasion, though, you may write about someone else and therefore use the third person. In either case make sure the experience you pick illustrates some point. A paper that indicates only how you violated a friend's confidence may meander along to little purpose. But if that paper is shaped by some point you wish to make—for instance, that you gained insight into the obligations of friendship—the topic can be worthwhile. To get started, do some guided brainstorming, asking yourself these questions.

What experience in my life or that of someone I know would be worth narrating?

various authors indicate who is speaking?" See the Teaching Strategies accompanying "The Boy and the Bank Officer," page 363.
2. Have students record an interesting conversation as best they can remember and then transform it into effective dialogue. Ask them to observe the changes they needed to make.

PERSPECTIVE

While writing a narrative seems like a straightforward activity, the process can be difficult for some students. They don't feel that there is anything in their lives worth writing about, and they find it hard to link their events to a purpose.

TEACHING STRATEGY

To prepare students for writing a narrative, you might focus class discussion, and even journal writing, around a common theme such as "What does it really take to be a friend?" Such preparation often convinces students that they have something to say and provides a purpose for their papers.

ETHICAL ISSUES

How responsible is a writer for the content of a narrative? Is it acceptable to extol the virtues of, for instance, a destructive rampage, racist activities, or the joys of substance abuse? To explore this matter, have students role play, some representing the writer, some potential readers, some actual readers whose lives were influenced by the narrative. On the other hand, is it deceptive to present a fictional narrative as though it were factual? Take, for instance, the fictional biographies and endorsements common in advertising. What responsibility does the company have to indicate the basis of the ad accurately? Again, have students role play and represent the various positions.

READER/THEME STRATEGIES

Many essays in the Reader can lead to interesting narrative topics. Selections such as "The Boy and the Bank Officer," "Momma's Encounter," "Can People Be Judged by Their Appearance?" or "Black Men and Public Space" could prompt students to discuss occasions when they judged others or were judged and the ensuing results. Students could then develop narratives based on their experiences.

What point does this experience illustrate? (Try to state the point in one or two sentences.)

What people were involved and what parts did they play?

When you have pinpointed a topic, use further brainstorming to garner supporting material. Here are some helpful questions:

What background information is necessary to understand the events?

What action should I include?

What is the nature of the conflict? Was it resolved? If so, how?

Which events play key roles, which are secondary, and which should go unmentioned?

Is any dialogue necessary?

Before you start to write, develop a plot outline showing the significant events in your narrative. For each one, jot down what you saw, heard, or did, and what you thought or felt.

Use the opening of your paper to set the stage for what follows. You might tell when and where the action occurred, provide helpful background information, note the incident that activated the chain of events, or identify the problem from which the action grew. If you state your main point directly, do it here or in the conclusion.

The body of the narrative should move the action forward until a turning point is about to be reached. Build the body around your key events. To avoid stranding your reader, use time signals whenever the development of the action might be unclear. Words, phrases, and clauses like *now, next, finally, after an hour,* and *when I returned* help the reader understand the sequence of events. Don't get carried away, though; a paper loaded with time signals makes the sequence seem more important than the events themselves. Finally, think about how you can best use conflict and dialogue to heighten narrative interest.

The conclusion should tie up any loose ends, settle any unresolved conflicts, and lend an air of completion to the narrative. Effective strategies to think about include introducing a surprise twist, offering a reflective summary of the events, noting your reaction to them, or discussing the aftermath of the affair.

Revising the Narrative

As you revise, follow the guidelines in Chapter 3, and in addition ask yourself these questions:

Have I made the point, stated or unstated, that I intended?

Does all of the action relate to the main point?

Is the conflict handled appropriately?

Have I included all of the key events that relate to my purpose? Given each the right emphasis? Used time indicators where needed?

Is my point of view appropriate?

Does my dialogue ring true?

EXAMPLE STUDENT ESSAY OF NARRATION

The Beach Bum

Gail Bartlett

Pete Miller was his name. I met him that summer on the   1
beach of Sanford Lake. I was lying on my extra-large towel, letting
the hot sun soak the water droplets off my body, when some clumsy
fool flopped by and flipped sand all over me. Jerking up, an angry
glare on my face, I was ready to scream at the clod when my mouth
opened wide in surprise. This fox was tall with jet-black hair and
sky-blue eyes. The summer sun had tanned his body to a golden
brown which made me envious as I compared it to my own vague
coloring. It was clearly evident that he had spent most of his
summer on this beach. Immediately my anger evaporated, and a
smile came to my face. In a flirting tone I joked, "Hey, Bud, watch
where you're kicking that sand."

He grinned back and said, "Come on out in the water, and I'll   2
help you wash it off, unless, of course, you want it left on. I can see
you've already discovered it helps for a deep tan. Ha!"

I decided I had nothing to lose and hopped off my towel. As   3
we raced to the water, I could sense him glancing at me, and I knew
at once that he had intentionally tripped in the sand only to get my
attention. This pleased me but made me even more self-conscious
than usual. Not many guys noticed me, and I never was quite sure
how to act.

For the rest of the afternoon, we swam in the warm water.   4
Never before would I have wasted a good tanning sun like that day's
to play in the water, but for some reason I felt this day was
different. He must have been all alone, for I didn't meet any of his
friends. It was only the two of us, and I was very grateful, for I
knew I would not be so much at ease if there were others around. To
my amazement, he asked me out for the next night to go to a
bonfire he and his buddies were having farther down the beach. I
accepted hesitantly, as I had dated only a few times before.

With great pains I tried to decide what I should wear. Wanting   5 to impress him, I didn't wear my usual jeans and grubby sweatshirt. Instead I chose my new plaid slacks and halter top, which were not at all comfortable. While nervously waiting for him, I dabbed on a little extra perfume and a few extra swishes of blusher. The doorbell rang, and instantaneously I was on my feet and at the door. The introduction to my parents wasn't exactly what I would describe as smooth, and I certainly was not at ease.

We arrived at the fire about 9:00 P.M., and already twenty of   6
his friends had gathered. They were just beginning to pass the beer, and when he handed me one I accepted for fear of disappointing him if I said no. It was not normal for me to drink, and I didn't feel myself at all. I became afraid of what his friends would think of me. They were laughing and telling jokes, but, not wanting to say something that would embarrass him, I sat silent. When asked a question by his closest friend, I could only shake my head in answer. The first hour went by quickly, for my date stayed by my side and tried in vain to include me in the conversation. I could not force myself to act normally. It was as though I were being rated, and I wanted a high score so badly I would not allow my true personality to show through for fear of not fitting in and being rejected. I felt as if I were going to suffocate. It was hard for me to hold back my laughter as the jokes grew increasingly funny. Only a timid giggle would I let escape my lips. My date became discouraged—I now can see why—but at that time the reason puzzled me. He left me to talk to a girl on the other side of the fire who was casually telling a joke. She spoke freely and with the confidence I wished I had. He enjoyed her easy manner, and so did many of the others. I could tell this by the way they were attracted to her side of the fire. Everyone was having a jolly time, and there I sat, suppressing myself in fear. Finally the guy I had wanted so much to impress returned and asked in a cold tone, "Are you about ready to go?"

I answered with disappointment, "I am, if you are."   7

We slowly trudged to the car, making trite comments along the   8
way. On the way home I wanted so badly to tell him that I was not usually so quiet and shy. I wanted to tell him how much fun I really

could be and that I had acted as I had only because I was afraid he or his friends would think me odd or different in some way. But instead of saying all this, I only sat in a quiet closet, drawing myself farther into the corner with every mile.

As I climbed into bed, I was angry with myself and vowed that I would never be that way again. I would force myself to be natural, no matter what anyone thought. It seemed certain that I would never be given another chance with this fox. Two weeks passed without my seeing or hearing a word from him. Every day I sat and daydreamed of what could have happened that night had I been myself and a little more at ease. Things could have worked out so nicely for me.

Two weeks later, after I had given up all hope, I answered the ringing phone one night with a bored hello. Lo and behold, it was the beach bum! My nerves shook and my eyes watered as I told him I would be happy to go to a skating party with him that weekend. Hanging up the phone, I released an exultant scream and ran to my room to think in quiet. This time I was not going to wear anything but my usual jeans, and I would act the way I felt.

Through my upstairs bedroom window, I watched him slowly advance to the door, and I could feel that this was going to be the night I wanted so badly. We left the house, and I glanced quickly over at him with a confident smile as we strolled down the sidewalk. The skating rink was crowded, and I recognized most of the people there as his friends whom I had met before. I was surprised at how much friendlier they were to me than at our previous meeting. It was all because I wore a smile and not only listened to them talk but also offered a few quips of my own. When one of the guys skated up beside me and put his arm around me, I didn't look at the floor and shy away as I had done before but returned his warmness by putting my arm around him. My date seemed to enjoy my company and stayed near me the whole evening, glancing at me every now and then in disbelief that I could be the girl he had taken out two weeks before. We laughed and joked the night away, and things went much more smoothly than the last time.

9

10

11

DISCUSSION QUESTIONS (p. 68)
1. The writer adopts the first-person point of view, as shown by her use of "I," "me," and "my." At times she makes judgments concerning her date's attitude and feelings, but these are always based on his actions, tone of voice, or the like. At no time does she adopt an omniscient stance and enter her date's mind.
2. The writer uses time indicators frequently—for example, in the fourth and next-to-the-last sentences of paragraph 1, the second sentence of paragraph 3, the first sentence of paragraph 4, the fourth sentence of paragraph 5, the first sentences of paragraphs 6, 9, and 10, as well as in a number of other places. These indicators tell the reader precisely when each event occurs.
3. The writer says nothing about the events that occurred between the time she accepted the first date and the time she selected the clothing to wear on it. Similarly, she says nothing about the automobile ride to the bonfire, what she did between the time her date left her and she climbed into bed, or the two weeks between her first and second

dates. These events were omitted because they would do nothing to move the narrative forward.

4. The next-to-the-last sentence states the point of the narrative. As positioned, it is effective because it draws a lesson from the events that have occurred, providing a climax to the narrative.

SUGGESTED INSTRUCTOR READINGS

Beach, R. "Differences in Autobiographical Narratives of English Teachers, College Freshmen, and Seventh Graders." College Composition and Communication 38 (1987): 56–69. Discusses the differences in the three groups' self-concepts and knowledge of literary conventions.

Bret, C. "Remedial Writers and Fictive Techniques." College Composition and Communication 39 (1988): 27–30. Shows less experienced writers how to use such techniques as plot, characterization, and dialogue to develop a personal narrative.

Campbell, J. "Stepping Through a Mirror: The Historical Narrative Assignment." College Composition and Communication 38 (1987): 95–97. Historical narratives in which students present the events through the persona of historical figures can provide a research-oriented alternative to the personal narrative.

Crew, L. "Rhetorical Beginnings: Professional and Amateur," College Composition and Communication 38 (1987): 346–49. Reviews the opening paragraphs of a number of essays and concludes that professional writers often begin their essays with narrative while students frequently begin with rhetorical questions.

While returning to my home he said, "I had a wonderful time tonight and would like to see you again sometime. You're really a lot more fun than I thought you were. Why were you so quiet at the bonfire?"   12

Slyly I answered, "Oh, was I quiet that night?" With a grin and a look from the corner of his eye, he squeezed my hand. To myself I said, "How much better it is to be yourself and act the way you feel rather than to try to please others." It had seemed such a hard ordeal to get the others to like and accept me in the beginning, but now I realized that it hadn't been their fault at all—only mine.   13

DISCUSSION QUESTIONS

1. Identify the point of view of the narrative.
2. List the words, phrases, and clauses that serve as time signals. What has the writer accomplished by using them?
3. This narrative spans about two weeks. At what points has the writer omitted events? Why?
4. What sentence states the point of the narrative? Why is it positioned where it is?

SUGGESTIONS FOR WRITING

1. Write a personal narrative about an experience that

   a. altered either your opinion of a friend or acquaintance or your views about some important matter
   b. taught you a lesson or something about human nature
   c. caused you great sorrow or joy
   d. exposed you to the danger of serious injury or death
   e. acquainted you with some previously unrecognized facet of your character or personality
   f. brought about a significant change in your way of life

Keep in mind all the key narrative elements: purpose, action, conflict, point of view, key events, and dialogue.

2. A maxim is a concise statement of a generally recognized truth. Noting the key elements above, write a personal narrative that illustrates one of the following maxims or another that your instructor approves.

   a. A little learning is a dangerous thing.
   b. The more things change, the more they stay the same.
   c. It's an ill wind that blows no good.
   d. Don't judge a book by its cover.
   e. The road to hell is paved with good intentions.
   f. Pride goeth before a fall.

CHAPTER 5

Description: Presenting Impressions

TEACHING STRATEGY

To show students how the writer's perspective affects observation and description, you might have several students, or the entire class, describe one campus feature. Then have students read the descriptions out loud and discuss why the descriptions varied.

SUGGESTED INSTRUCTOR READING

Berthoff, A. Forming, Thinking, Writing: The Composing Imagination. Rochelle Park, NJ: Hayden, 1978. Explores relationships among observing, thinking and writing and provides several interesting activities to help students become self-conscious observers and thinkers.

PERSPECTIVE

Students should recognize that purpose dictates how we observe and describe. While an advertising copywriter might search for dramatic embellishments, a scientist writing a lab report will try to remain objective. Students often have difficulty with description because they lose sight of their purpose.

TEACHING STRATEGIES

1. Ask students to review their reading material for a week, note where description is used, why, and how that purpose shaped the description.

2. Ask students to select an advertising description and rewrite it as if they were objective observers, or do the reverse. Then discuss the changes they made and why.

The sound of sizzling hot dogs, cooking on a grease-spattered grill, gave way to the whirling buzz of a cotton-candy machine. Fascinated, we watched as the white cardboard cone was slowly transformed into a pink, fluffy cloud. Despite their Fiberglas appearance, the sticky puffs melted on my tongue into sweet sugar. Soon our faces and hands were gummed with goo.

You are there. Seeing, hearing, touching, tasting. This is one student writer's *description* of a small segment of a county fair. Effective description creates sharply etched word pictures of objects, persons, scenes, events, or situations. Sensory impressions—reflecting sight, sound, taste, smell, and touch—form the backbone of descriptive writing. Often, they build toward one dominant impression that the writer wants to evoke.

The human mind is not merely a logical thinking machine. Because of our emotional makeup, we react with shock to a photo of a battered victim of child abuse. We feel stirrings of nostalgia upon hearing a song from our past. We smile with satisfaction when quenching our summer thirst with tart sips from a tall, frosted drink. Responses like these, as much as the ability to think rationally, help define the human makeup.

Many occasions call for description. Your chemistry instructor might ask you to characterize the appearance and odor of a series of substances prepared in the laboratory; your art instructor might want you to describe a painting; your hospitality management instructor might have you portray an appealing banquet room. On the job, a realtor might write a glowing advertisement to sell a house, a nurse describe the postoperative status of a surgical incision, and a journalist describe the eruption of a volcano. All are attempts to capture the world through description.

PURPOSE

Sometimes description stands alone; sometimes it enriches other writing. It appears in histories and biographies, fiction and poetry, journalism and advertising, and occasionally even in technical writing. Some descriptions merely create images and mood, as when a writer paints a word picture of a boggy, fog-shrouded moor. But description can also stimulate understanding or lead to action. A historian may juxtapose the splendor of French court life with the wretchedness of a Paris slum to help explain the French Revolution. And everyone knows the persuasive power of advertising's descriptive enticements.

Description will provide effective backup for the writing you do in your composition classes, helping you to drive home your points with force and vividness.

SENSORY IMPRESSIONS

Precise sensory impressions begin with close physical or mental observation. If you can reexamine your subject, do it. If not, recall it to mind; then capture its features with appropriate words. When you can't find the right words, try a comparison. Ask yourself what your subject (or part of it) might be likened to. Does it smell like a rotten egg? A ripe cantaloupe? Burning rubber? Does it sound like a high sigh? A soft rustle? To come across, the comparison must be accurate and familiar. If the reader has never smelled a rotten egg, the point is lost.

Here is a passage marked by particularly vivid sight impressions.

> After our meal we went for a stroll across the plateau. The day was already drawing to a close as we sat down upon a ledge of rock near the lip of the western precipice. From where we sat, as though perched high upon a cloud, we looked out into a gigantic void. Far below, the stream we had crossed that afternoon was a pencil-thin trickle of silver barely visible in the gloaming. Across it, on the other side, the red hills rose one upon another in gentle folds, fading into the distance where the purple thumblike mountains of Adua and Yeha stretched against the sky like a twisting serpent. As we sat, the sun sank fast, and the heavens in the western sky began to glow. It was a coppery fire at first, the orange streaked with aquamarine; but rapidly the firmament expanded into an explosion of red and orange that burst across the sky sending tongues of flame through the feathery clouds to the very limits of the heavens. When the flames had reached their zenith, a great quantity of storks came flying from the south. They circled above us once, their slender bodies sleek and black against the orange sky. Then, gathering together, they flew off into the setting sun, leaving us alone in peace to contemplate. One of the monks who sat with us, hushed by the intensity of the moment, muttered a prayer. The sun died beyond the hills; and the fire withdrew.

> Robert Dick-Read, *Sanamu: Adventures in Search of African Art*

At first, the western sky glows with a "coppery fire," which then expands into "an explosion of red and orange" that sends "tongues of flame" heavenward and then withdraws as the sun disappears. Comparisons strengthen the visual impression: the "pencil-thin" stream, the "thumblike" mountains stretching across the sky "like a twisting serpent." The familiar pencil, thumb, and serpent help us to visualize the unfamiliar landscape.

Most descriptions blend several sense impressions rather than focusing on just one. In the following excerpt, Mark Twain, reminiscing about his uncle's farm, includes all five. As you read it, note which impressions are most effective.

> As I have said, I spent some part of every year at the farm until I was twelve or thirteen years old. The life which I led there with my cousins was full of charm, and so is the memory of it yet. I can call back the solemn twilight and mystery of the deep woods, the earthy smells, the faint odors of the wild flowers, the sheen of rain-washed foliage, the rattling clatter of drops when the wind shook the trees, the far-off hammering of woodpeckers and the muffled drumming of wood pheasants in the remoteness of the forest, the snapshot glimpses of disturbed wild creatures scurrying through the grass—I can call it all back and make it as real as it ever was, and as blessed. I can call back the prairie, and its loneliness and peace, and a vast hawk hanging motionless in the sky, with his wings spread wide and the blue of the vault showing through the fringe of their end feathers. I can see the woods in their autumn dress, the oaks purple, the hickories washed with gold, the maples and the sumachs luminous with crimson fires, and I can hear the rustle made by the fallen leaves as we plowed through them. I can see the blue clusters of wild grapes hanging among the foliage of the saplings, and I remember the taste of them and the smell. I know how the wild blackberries looked, and how they tasted, and the same with the pawpaws, the hazelnuts, and the persimmons; and I can feel the thumping rain, upon my head, of hickory nuts and walnuts when we were out in the frosty dawn to scramble for them with the pigs, and the gusts of wind loosed them and sent them down. I know the stain of blackberries, and how pretty it is, and I know the stain of walnut hulls, and how little it minds soap and water, also what grudged experience it had of either of them. I know the taste of maple sap, and when to gather it, and how to arrange the troughs and the delivery tubes, and how to boil down the juice, and how to hook the sugar after it is made, also how much better hooked sugar tastes than any that is honestly come by, let bigots say what they will.

> Mark Twain, *Autobiography*

2. Have students, working in small groups, list the distinctive features of the day. Encourage them to look closely at the kinds of light, types of clouds, atmospheric conditions, and the like.
3. Have students jot down their precise impressions of the classroom using one sense at a time; then have them compare results.
4. Senses other than sight can, of course, be difficult to convey because our vocabulary is more limited. Have the class bring in devices such as bells or whistles that create distinctive sounds; then work with students on how to describe the sounds they make, paying close attention to how we formulate useful comparisons.

EXERCISE ■ Spend some time in an environment such as one of the following. Concentrate on one sense at a time. Begin by observing what you see; then jot down the precise impressions you receive. Now do the same for impressions of touch, taste, smell, and sound.

1. The woods in the early morning
2. A city intersection
3. A restaurant or cafeteria
4. A scenic spot under a full moon
5. A storm

EXERCISE ANSWER

Explain to students that the rationale for this exercise is to sharpen perception and word choice. Point out that some of their observations might be useful in a paper, depending on the purpose.

ALTERNATE EXERCISE

Provide students with pictures of scientific objects—a chemical solution, the back of the eye, a particular rock, a galaxy formation—and have them describe as objectively as possible what they observe. To make the exercise more challenging, bring in paired pictures of very similar objects, such as two types of viruses, and have students describe them accurately enough so the reader can match the description with the appropriate object.

6. A pool or other recreation area
7. A crowded classroom or hallway
8. A grocery store
9. A park or playground
10. A holiday gathering

DOMINANT IMPRESSION

Skillful writers select and express sensory perceptions in order to create a *dominant impression*—an overall mood or feeling such as joy, anger, terror, or distaste. This impression may be identified or left unnamed for the reader to deduce. Whatever the choice, a verbal picture of a storm about to strike, for example, might be crafted to evoke feelings of fear by describing sinister masses of slaty clouds, cannon salvos of thunder, blinding lightning flashes, and viciously swirling wind-caught dust.

The following paragraph establishes a sense of security as the dominant impression:

> A marvellous stillness pervaded the world, and the stars together with the serenity of their rays seemed to shed upon the earth the assurance of everlasting security. The young moon recurved, and shining low in the west, was like a slender shaving thrown up from a bar of gold, and the Arabian Sea, smooth and cool to the eye like a sheet of ice, extended its perfect level to the perfect circle of a dark horizon. The propeller turned without a check, as though its beat had been part of the scheme of a safe universe; and on each side of the *Patna* two folds of water, permanent and sombre on the unwrinkled shimmer, enclosed within their straight and diverging ridges a few white swirls of foam bursting in a low hiss, a few wavelets, a few ripples, a few undulations that, left behind, agitated the surface of the sea for an instant after the passage of the ship, subsided splashing gently, calmed down at last into the circular stillness of water and sky with the black speck of the moving hull remaining everlastingly in its centre.
>
> Joseph Conrad, *Lord Jim*

The first sentence directly identifies the impression, "security," to which the "stillness" and the "serenity" contribute. Other details also do their part: the "smooth" sea, the "perfect circle" of the horizon, the "safe universe," the quick calming of the water, and the moving hull "everlastingly" in the center of water and sky.

To help students complete the exercise in this section, encourage them to list all their observations, then select the relevant details, and finally write the paragraph. Stu-

EXERCISE ■ **Select one of the following topics and write a paragraph that evokes a particular dominant impression. Omit any details that run counter to your aim.**

1. A multi-alarm fire
2. A repair facility (automobile, appliance, and so on)

3. A laboratory
4. Some aspect of summer in a particular place
5. A religious service
6. A doctor's or dentist's office
7. A dark street
8. A parade or other celebration
9. Some landmark on your college campus
10. A municipal night court or small-claims court

dents could draw on the material from the previous exercise for this assignment.

VANTAGE POINT

You may write a description from either a fixed or a moving vantage point. A fixed observer remains in one place and reports only what can be perceived from there. Here is how Marilyn Kluger describes the Thanksgiving morning sounds she remembers hearing from her bed as a child.

> On the last Thursday in November, I could stay in bed only until the night chill left the house, hearing first the clash of the heavy grates in the huge black iron range, with its flowery scrolls and nickled decorations, as Mother shook down the ashes. Then, in their proper sequence, came the sounds of the fire being made—the rustle of newspaper, the snap of kindling, the rush of smoke up the chimney when Mother opened the damper, slid the regulator wide open, and struck a match to the kerosene-soaked corncobs that started a quick hot fire. I listened for the bang of the cast-iron lid dropping back into place and for the tick of the stovepipes as fierce flames sent up their heat, then the sound of the lid being lifted again as Mother fed more dry wood and lumps of coal to the greedy new fire. The duties of the kitchen on Thanksgiving were a thousandfold, and I could tell that Mother was bustling about with a quicker step than usual.
>
> Marilyn Kluger, "A Time of Plenty"

A moving observer views things from a number of positions, signaling changes in location with phrases such as "moving through the turnstile" and "as I walked around the corner." Below, H. L. Mencken takes us with him as he observes from a moving express train.

> On a Winter day some years ago, coming out of Pittsburgh on one of the expresses of the Pennsylvania Railroad, I rolled eastward for an hour through the coal and steel towns of Westmoreland county. It was familiar ground; boy and man, I had been through it often before. But somehow I had never quite sensed its appalling desolation. Here was the very heart of industrial America, the center of its most lucrative and characteristic activity, the boast and pride of the richest and grandest nation ever seen on earth—and here was a scene so dreadfully hideous, so intolerably bleak and forlorn that it reduced the whole aspiration of man to a macabre and depressing joke. Here was wealth beyond computation, almost beyond imagination—and here were human habitations so abominable that they would have disgraced a race of alley cats.

TEACHING STRATEGY

Using the essays in the Reader, have students identify the vantage points assumed by different writers, how they signal these vantage points, and how they indicate changes in location.

I am not speaking of mere filth. One expects steel towns to be dirty. What I allude to is the unbroken and agonizing ugliness, the sheer revolting monstrousness, of every house in sight. From East Liberty to Greensburg, a distance of twenty-five miles, there was not one in sight from the train that did not insult and lacerate the eye. Some were so bad, and they were among the most pretentious— churches, stores, warehouses, and the like—that they were downright startling; one blinked before them as one blinks before a man with his face shot away. A few linger in memory, horrible even there: a crazy little church just west of Jeannette, set like a dormer-window on the side of a bare, leprous hill; the headquarters of the Veterans of Foreign Wars at another forlorn town, a steel stadium like a huge rat-trap somewhere further down the line. But most of all I recall the general effect—of hideousness without a break. There was not a single decent house within eyerange from the Pittsburgh suburbs to the Greensburg yards. There was not one that was not misshapen, and there was not one that was not shabby.

H. L. Mencken, "The Libido for the Ugly"

The phrase "on one of the expresses of the Pennsylvania Railroad" signals that Mencken will be a moving observer, and "From East Liberty to Greensburg" pinpoints the extent of his journey. "West of Jeannette," "another forlorn town," and "somewhere further down the line" specify the positions from which he views the church, the headquarters of the veterans' organization, and the stadium.

Whatever your vantage point, fixed or moving, report only what would be apparent to someone on the scene. If you describe how a distant mountain looks from a balcony, don't suddenly leap to a description of a mountain flower: you couldn't see it from your vantage point.

EXERCISE

1. **Writing as a fixed observer, describe in a paragraph your impressions of one of the following. Be sure to indicate your vantage point.**

   a. A post office lobby two weeks before Christmas
   b. The scene following a traffic accident
   c. A classroom when the bell rings
   d. A campus lounge
   e. An office
   f. The entrance to some building

ALTERNATE EXERCISE

Have students describe the same object or scene from several different vantage points and then write a brief account of the differences and the impact on the description.

2. **Writing as a moving observer, describe in a paragraph or two your impressions as you do one of the following things. Clearly signal your movements to the reader.**

   a. Walk from one class to another
   b. Shop in a grocery store
   c. Walk from your home to the corner
   d. Cross a long bridge
   e. Water-ski
   f. Go through a ticket line and enter a theater, auditorium, or sports arena

SELECTION OF DETAILS

Effective description depends as much on exclusion as on inclusion. Don't try to pack every possible detail into your paper by providing an inventory of, for example, a room's contents or a natural setting's elements. Such an approach shows only that you can see, not write. Instead, select details that deliberately point toward the mood or feeling you intend to create. Read the following student description of nighttime skiing.

> The glowing orb of the moon, shedding its pale, silvery radiance on the ski slope, seemed to cast a spell. Crystal iridescence of powdered snow twinkled in the night. Shadows cast by the skiers appeared as mysterious silhouettes darting in and out among snow-covered trees. The gentle breeze combing through the branches created a lulling musical chant which drifted into my head, taking control. Delicate snowflakes danced by, kissed me on the face, and seemed to beckon me up the hill.
>
> Sue Mutch

This writer evokes a sense of enchantment by noting the "pale, silvery radiance" of the moon, the "crystal iridescence" of the snow, the "mysterious silhouettes" of the skiers, and the "lulling musical chant" of the wind. She ignores such details as the boisterous snatches of conversation among the skiers, the crunch of ski poles digging into the snow, and the creaking towline moving to the top of the slope. Mentioning these things would detract from the desired mood.

ARRANGEMENT OF DETAILS

Description, like any other writing, must have a clear pattern of organization to guide the reader and help you fulfill your purpose. Often some spatial arrangement works nicely. You might, for example, move systematically from top to bottom, left to right, front to back, nearby to far away, or the reverse of these patterns. To describe Saturday afternoon at the football game, you might start with the crowded parking lot, move into the bustling stadium, and finally zoom in on the sights, sounds, and smells of the playing field. Or if you wanted to highlight the surroundings rather than the central event, the order could be reversed. Going another route, you might start with some striking central feature and then branch out to the things around it. To capture the center of a mall, you might first describe its ornate fountain illuminated with flashing, multicolored lights, shift to the reflection of the lights on the skylight above, and end by portraying the surrounding store fronts.

Sometimes a description follows a time sequence. A writer might, for example, portray the changes in a woodland setting as winter gives way to spring and spring, in turn, yields to summer.

TEACHING STRATEGIES

1. You might provide both a purpose and an audience in your assignment. You could ask students to describe their favorite vacation spot for the Sunday supplement of a local newspaper in order to help readers decide whether they'd like to visit it. The class can then observe and discuss how other writers have solved a similar writing problem. Or you might give a more technically oriented assignment: for example, to describe a dangerous intersection as part of a report to the local road commission.

2. Encourage students to develop extensive lists of sensory details. Such lists provide excellent raw materials for essays.

CLASSROOM ACTIVITY

To prepare for this assignment, choose a site that every student knows and have the class brainstorm and plan. Then show students how they can progress from notes to draft.

READER/THEME STRATEGIES

A descriptive essay could emerge from the exploration of a theme. For the theme "Life's Changes," students might read such essays as "Once More to the Lake," "Momma's Encounter," and "Grant and Lee: A Study in Contrasts" and discuss how the places where people reside help shape their identity. The class could then write essays describing places important to their development. If you'd like to investigate "American Crises," you could have students read "What to Do About Drugs," "Facing up to Drugs . . . ," "The Company Man," and "Why We Have Failed," discuss influences shaping the quality of American life, and then describe areas where they see harm or health.

*W*RITING A DESCRIPTION

Planning and Drafting the Description

If you're choosing your own topic, always select one that is familiar. Don't describe the inside of a restaurant kitchen or Old Faithful geyser in Yellowstone National Park if you've never seen either one. Instead, opt for some place where you've actually worked or a locale you've recently visited. If you keep a journal, thumb through it for possible leads.

For each potential topic that surfaces, ask yourself the following questions. They will direct your attention to matters you'll need to address.

What do I want to accomplish by writing this description? Create one or more impressions? Help the reader understand something? Persuade the reader to act?
Who is my audience and why would this topic interest them?
What dominant impression will I develop?

To help gather and organize support for your topic, pose these additional questions.

What details should I include?
What sensory impressions are associated with each detail? (Jot down any words that you feel will best convey the impressions.)
How does each detail contribute to the dominant impression?
What sequence should I follow in presenting my impressions? (Map out the sequence, setting up a 1-2-3 listing or possibly a paragraph-by-paragraph plan.)

After brainstorming a list of potential details, you might use branching (see page 20) to start accumulating sensory impressions. Here's how Kim Swiger, who wrote the passage on page 77, used this technique.

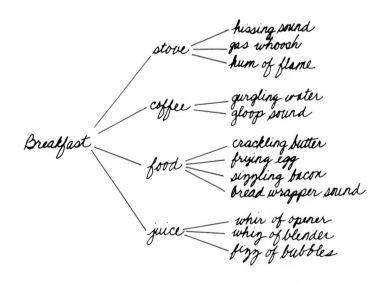

Begin your paper with an introduction that eases the reader into your topic. You might, for example, provide a historical overview, ask a provocative question, or snare the reader's attention with an arresting statement.

Develop each major feature in one or more paragraphs. Present each feature in the order you've mapped out. To ensure that the reader follows your thoughts, clearly signal any shifts in vantage point or time. As you write, aim for vivid, original language. We've all encountered writers who tell us that raindrops "pitter-patter," clouds are "fleecy white," and the sun is "a ball of fire." Such stale, worn out language does nothing to sharpen our vision of the rain, the clouds, or the sun. In contrast, read how one student describes the sounds in her kitchen at breakfast time:

> Sure signs of a new day are the sounds in the kitchen as breakfast is prepared. The high sigh of the gas just before it whooshes into flame and settles into a whispering hum blends with the gurgling of the water for the morning coffee. Soon the gloop, gloop, gloop of the coffee sets up a perky beat. Then in mingles the crackle of creamy butter on a hot skillet and the shush of an egg as it meets this fiery foe. Ribbons of bacon start to sizzle in the spitting grease. The soft rustle of plastic as bread is removed from its wrapper floats on the air and seems to form part of the atmosphere. The can opener whirs, and the orange juice concentrate drops with a splat into the blender, which whizzes together the orange cylinder and splashed-in water. For minutes after the blender stops, tiny effervescing bubbles fizz.
>
> Kim Burson Swiger

You are there in the kitchen, hearing the carefully selected and freshly described sounds.

A word of caution about making your writing vivid. Some students are tempted to enhance their descriptions by stringing together a chain of adjectives without considering the effect on a reader. Think how you'd react if told that

> "A dented, cylindrical, silver-gray, foul-smelling, overloaded trash can sat in the alley."

As you can see, more than the garbage can is overloaded here. Resist the temptation to inject similar sentences into your description. Carefully examine your adjectives and eliminate those that don't advance your purpose.

End your paper by pulling your material together in some way. If you've created an impression or mood, you might offer your reaction to it. If you want your reader to understand something, you might spell your message out. If you wish to persuade, you might urge some action.

TEACHING STRATEGIES

1. Since students usually under-write descriptions, you might have them freewrite additional sensory details for key parts of their papers and then incorporate the best material into their draft.
2. Peer responses can reveal under-written or misplaced description, especially if peers are asked to write down their questions and identify vague passages.
3. Have students circle their key descriptive terms and brainstorm possible substitutes.

ETHICAL ISSUES

How responsible is a writer for accurate, nondistorted description? Is it acceptable to exaggerate the merits of a place in order to encourage tourism or sell real estate? How much can the writer omit and still be fair to the reader? Have students role-play a situation where some represent the tourist bureau, others the ad writer, and still others the disappointed tourists who spent money only to discover a place that fails to match the description.

DISCUSSION QUESTIONS (p. 80)

1. The writer's movements are indicated in paragraph 2 (". . . I found myself in the familiar grass lot bordering the fairground."), paragraph 3

Revising the Description

As you revise, apply the guidelines in Chapter 3 and ask the following questions.

Have I written with a clear sense of purpose and audience in mind?

Have I conveyed how my topic looks, sounds, feels, tastes, or smells? Would comparisons or more precise descriptive terms help convey my perceptions?

Have I evoked one dominant impression? Can I strengthen this impression by adding certain selected details? By eliminating details that detract from the impression?

Have I used an appropriate vantage point? If the observer is moving, have I signaled changes in location? Have I included only details that would be visible to the observer?

Have I arranged my details in an order appropriate to the topic?

EXAMPLE STUDENT ESSAY OF DESCRIPTION

The Big One

Rebecca Mutch

With a final crack of a bat and a lofting fly ball, baseball 　1
ended for the year. The last swirl of water gurgling down the drain
of the community pool marked the end of its season. These closings
marked the beginning of another event, the county fair. This season
I was elected to take my little brother on a ride—"the big one," in
his words.

Once again I found myself in the familiar grass lot bordering 　2
the fairground. The fair itself was completely surrounded by a fence.
No one could see what was inside. The only clues were carried in the
wind. Muffled echoes of carnies hawking their games, excited squeals
of children, and blaring carnival tunes, frequently punctuated by
sharp, crackling static, blended with the tantalizing fragrance of
popcorn, the spicy aroma of pizza, and the sweet molasses smell of
caramel corn.

As we entered the main gate and handed our tickets to the 　3
men whose baskets already overflowed with torn stubs, my eyes
immediately confirmed what my ears and nose had already reported.
In one step we had gone from a semiquiet and relaxed world into an
ever-revolving one. Dazzling lights, blinking out of control, seemed to
flirt with anyone and everyone. Children, their white T-shirts

covered with splotches of chocolate and mustard, dashed ahead of their parents and returned shortly, screaming about the giant bear that waited ahead. The distant, shuffling crowds appeared as moving shadows, their features blurred.

The little tug on my sleeve reminded me of that big ride that waited ahead. The path up the midway, packed with a cushion of sawdust, was strewn with empty popcorn boxes, scraps of papers, and crumpled cigarette packages.

Game booths and food huts, their pennants whipping and snapping in the wind, dotted the path on both sides and formed two long serpent-like strings of pleasure. BB's clinked against tin objects in the shooting gallery. Hawkers with greased hands and pudgy fingers tried to lure suckers toward their gaudy booths. A backboard thudded and a hoop clanked as still another young man tried to win the enormous purple teddy bear which smiled down mockingly from its perch above. The sound of sizzling hot dogs, cooking on a grease-spattered grill, gave way to the whirling buzz of a cotton-candy machine. Fascinated, we watched as the white cardboard cone was slowly transformed into a pink, fluffy cloud. Despite their Fiberglas appearance, the sticky puffs melted on my tongue into sweet sugar. Soon our faces and hands were gummed with goo.

We scuffled along with the rhythm of the crowd and before long arrived at those metallic contraptions of nuts and bolts—the rides. The sounds of metal clanging and banging filled the air. Sparks shot out from where the metal pieces slapped together. Swirling and whirling, these pieces caught the reflection of the neon lights and, together with the sparks, produced a world of spectrum colors.

This was it. The Ferris wheel stood towering before us. As the seat gently swayed, we waited for the ride to begin. The motor belched and then slowly started to turn; goose bumps formed on my brother's bare arms, and his eyes grew larger as the ride picked up speed. The fairground was soon a kaleidoscope of fantastic images and colors. The wind whipped through my hair and snapped it back, stinging my face at times. Both of us were screaming uncontrollably.

("As we entered the main gate . . ."), paragraph 4 ("The path up the midway. . ."), paragraph 5 ("The sound of sizzling hot dogs . . . gave way to the whirling buzz . . ."), paragraph 6 ("We scuffled along with the rhythm of the crowd and before long arrived at . . . the rides."), paragraph 7 (". . . we made our way dizzily to the car.").

2. Like most descriptions, this one relies primarily on impressions of sight. Particularly vivid sight details occur in paragraph 3 ("Dazzling lights, blinking out of control . . ." and ". . . white T-shirts covered with splotches of chocolate and mustard . . ."), paragraph 4 ("The path . . . was strewn with empty popcorn boxes . . ."), paragraph 5 ("The enormous purple teddy bear which smiled down mockingly . . ." and ". . . the white cardboard cone was slowly transformed into a pink fluffy cloud."), paragraph 6 ("Sparks shot out" and "Swirling and whirling, these pieces caught the reflection of the neon lights, and . . . produced a world of spectrum colors."), and paragraph 7 ("The fairground was soon a kaleidoscope of fantastic images and colors.").

Vivid sound impressions occur in paragraph 1 (". . . a final crack of a bat" and "The last swirl of water gurgling down the drain"), paragraph 2 ("Muffled echoes of carnies," "excited squeals of children," "blaring carnival tunes," and "sharp, crackling static"), paragraph 3 ("children . . . screaming about the giant bear . . ." and "shuffling crowds"), paragraph 5 ("pennants whipping and snapping," "BBs clinked," "A backboard thudded and a hoop clanked," "The sound of sizzling hot dogs," and "the whirling buzz of a cotton-candy machine"), paragraph 6 ("The sounds of metal clanging and banging" and "the metal pieces slapped together"), and paragraph 7 ("The motor belched.").

Vivid impressions of smell and taste occur in paragraph 2 ("the tantalizing fragrance of popcorn, the spicy aroma of pizza, and the sweet molasses smell of caramel corn.") and paragraph 5 ("the sticky puffs melted on my tongue into sweet sugar.").

Finally, impressions of touch appear in paragraph 4 ("The little tug on my sleeve . . ."), paragraph 5 ("Soon our faces and hands were gummed with goo."), paragraph 7 ("As the seat gently swayed," "goose bumps formed on my brother's bare arms," and "The wind whipped through my hair . . . stinging my face at times.").

3. Perceptive observations in paragraph 7 include the bulk of the towering Ferris wheel, the swaying of its seat, the belching of the motor as the huge contraption slowly starts to turn, the kaleidoscopic view from its top, and the whipping of the wind through the writer's hair. The observations help re-create, in the reader's mind, the experience of riding on a Ferris wheel.

4. The organization takes the reader inside the fairgrounds, down the midway and finally to the rides—an appropriate pattern since the climactic event of the essay is the ride on the Ferris wheel.

SUGGESTED INSTRUCTOR READINGS

Brand J. "Descriptive Experiment," School Arts 12 (1979): 44–45. Provides a provocative and imaginative assignment that uses description.

Taylor, M. "Draw: A Heuristic for Expressive Writing." Journal of Teaching Writing 4 (1985): 210–14. Demonstrates how a form of creative description can help students to develop ideas for expressive writing.

Suddenly, with no apparent slowdown, the ride was over, and we made our way dizzily to the car.

My brother talked about the big one for weeks. For me it brought back many fond memories and let me, just for an evening, be a child again.   8

DISCUSSION QUESTIONS

1. This description features a moving observer. Where are the writer's movements indicated?
2. Point out details that appeal to each of the five senses.
3. Reread paragraph 7. Identify perceptive observations used to describe the Ferris wheel ride.
4. How is the essay organized? For its purpose, is this pattern appropriate?

SUGGESTIONS FOR WRITING ■ Choose one of the following topics or another that your instructor approves for an essay of description. Create a dominant impression by using carefully chosen, well-organized details observed from an appropriate vantage point. Try to write so that the reader actually experiences your description.

1. Holiday shopping
2. A rock concert
3. An exercise class
4. A graduation audience
5. A shopping center
6. A pet store or zoo
7. A busy city intersection
8. The view from your bedroom window
9. Getting caught in a storm
10. A fast-food restaurant
11. Your house after a party
12. An outdoor place of special importance to you
13. A run-down part of town
14. An automobile
15. An arcade

CHAPTER 6

Process Analysis: Explaining How

PERSPECTIVE

Explaining a process helps students develop some of the key qualities of good writing. They learn to be complete in their information, precise in their statements, and careful about their organization as well as to consider the background knowledge of their intended audience, especially when preparing instructions. Finally, in writing about a process students assume the role of an authority, a role essential to better writing.

"Hey Bill, I'd like you to take a look at Mr. Gorgerise's car. He's really fuming. Says the engine's burning too much oil, running rough, and getting poor mileage. Check it out and see what you can find."

Bill begins by removing the spark plugs, hooking a remote-control starter to the starter in the car, and grounding the ignition to prevent the car's starting accidentally. Next, he fits a compression pressure gauge into the sparkplug hole by cylinder number one, starts the engine, and reads and records the pressure; then he does the same for each of the other cylinders. Finally, he compares the readings with one another and the auto maker's engine specs. The verdict? An excessively worn engine that needs rebuilding. Bill has carried out a *process*, just one among many that fill his workdays.

As we pursue our affairs, we perform processes almost constantly, ranging from such daily rituals as brewing a pot of coffee and flossing our teeth to taking a picture, taping a compact disc, preparing for a date, or replacing a light switch. Often we share our special technique for doing something—for example, making chicken cacciatore—by passing it on to a friend.

Many popular publications feature process analyses which help readers to sew zippers in garments, build catamarans, live within their means, and improve their wok technique. Process analysis also frequently helps you meet the writing demands of your courses. A political science instructor may ask you to explain how your state's governor won nomination, or a biology instructor may want an explanation of how bees find their way back to the hive. Another instructor may call for directions relating to some process in your field—for example, analyzing a chemical compound, taking fingerprints, or obtaining a blood sample.

On the job, a greenhouse crew leader may provide summer employees with directions for planting various kinds of shrubs and flowers. A technical writer may prepare a list of steps for workers to follow when unloading a particular solvent from a tank car. A Sanitation Department technician may write a brochure telling city residents how to get paper, glass, and metal trash ready for recycling.

As these examples show, a process can be nontechnical, historical, scientific, natural, or technical.

TEACHING STRATEGIES

1. You might have students review their assignments, exams, or lecture notes from other classes to see where process analysis would be useful.
2. To prepare students for the research demands of later courses, assign each to research the use of a different library reference tool and write a paper incorporating the explanation. These papers could then be bound together and distributed as a resource.
3. Because so many "how to" articles appear in the popular press, students find it tempting to plagiarize. How, after all, is the teacher to know that the explanation of how to change oil came from an obscure car magazine? To counter this problem, you might have students write about some unique procedure at your school or on topics that are less likely to be readily available in print, such as how to break a date or patch up a quarrel with a friend.

KINDS OF PROCESS ANALYSIS PAPERS

Some process analysis papers offer directions for readers who will carry out the procedure. These readers may be technical or professional personnel who need the information to perform a work-related task. Other papers detail procedures for audiences that won't perform them.

A how-to-do-it paper must include everything the reader needs to know in order to ensure a successful outcome. Its directions take the form of polite commands, often addressing readers directly as "you." This approach helps involve readers in the explanation and emphasizes that the directions must, not merely should, be followed. Here is an illustration.

> To prepare a bacterial smear for staining, first use an inoculating loop to place a drop of distilled water on a clean glass microscope slide. Next, pass the loop and the opening of the tube containing the bacterial culture to be examined through a Bunsen burner flame to sterilize them. From the tube, remove a small bit of culture with the loop, and rub the loop in the drop of water on the slide until the water covers an area one and one-half inches long and approximately the width of the slide. Next, reflame the opening of the culture tube to prevent contamination of the culture, and then plug it shut. Allow the smear to air dry, and then pass the slide, smear side up, through the flame of the burner until it is warm to the touch. The dried smear should have a cloudy, milky-white appearance.
>
> Darryl Williams

A process analysis paper directed at nondoers tells how a process is or was performed or took place. These papers can serve a wide range of purposes—for example, to satisfy popular curiosity; to point up the importance, difficulty, or danger of a process; or to cast a process in a favorable or unfavorable light. Such papers, though often quite detailed, do not provide enough information for the reader to perform the task successfully.

Papers of this sort do not issue polite commands or address the reader as "you." Instead, the writer uses the first person (*I, we*), the third person (*he, she, it,* or some noun), or the passive voice, in which the subject of the sentence receives, rather than performs, the action, and the doer is unnamed ("Two samples were used for testing"). Three examples follow.

TEACHING STRATEGIES

1. Ask students to evaluate the two kinds of process writing in the Reader. "How to Adopt a Stray" and "How to Give a Speech" offer directions; "The Knife" and "The Spider and the Wasp" tell how processes are carried out. Have students identify the different purposes of these essays and how they influence the form of address, material included, and organization.

2. Students might consider the changes needed if "How to Give a Speech" explained how a process was performed.

3. In some high school English classes, students have been warned endlessly not to use "you" in their writing. You might reassure them that "you" can be appropriate, identify works that follow the "you approach," but also establish where "you" is not appropriate.

First Person, Active Voice

Thus, when I now approach a stack of three two-inch cinder blocks to attempt a breaking feat, I do not set myself to "try hard," or to summon up all my strength. Instead I relax, sinking my awareness into my belly and legs, feeling my connection with the ground. I breathe deeply, mentally directing the breath through my torso, legs, and arms. I imagine a line of force coming up from the ground through my legs, down one arm, and out through the stone slabs, and down again into the ground, penetrating to the center of the earth. I do not focus any attention on the objects to be broken. Although when I am lifting or holding them in a normal state of consciousness the blocks seem tremendously dense, heavy, and hard, in the course of my one- or two-minute preparation their reality seems to change, as indeed the reality of the whole situation changes. . . . When I make my final approach to the bricks, if I regard them at all they seem light, airy, and friendly; they do not have the insistent inner drive in them that I do.

Don Ethan Miller, "A State of Grace:
Understanding the Martial Arts"

Third Person, Active Voice

To define a word . . . the dictionary editor places before him the stack of cards illustrating that word; each of the cards represents the use of the word by a writer of some literary or historical importance. He reads the cards carefully, discards some, re-reads the rest, and divides up the stack according to what he thinks are the several senses of the word. Finally, he writes his definition, following the hard-and-fast rule that each definition must be based on what the quotations in front of him reveal about the meaning of the word.

S. I. Hayakawa, *Language in Thought and Action*

Third Person, Passive Voice

The analyzer was adjusted so the scale read zero and was connected to the short sampling tube which had previously been inserted into the smoke stack. The sample was taken by depressing the bulb the requisite number of times, and the results were then read and recorded. The procedure was repeated, this time using the long sampling tube and sampling through the fire door.

Charles Finnie

EXERCISE ■ **Examine your favorite newspaper or magazine for examples of process analysis. Bring them to class for group discussion of which kind each represents and the writer's purpose.**

PERSPECTIVE
When writing process papers, students often assume the reader is somewhat familiar with the process. When explaining how to prepare for skin diving, they might take for granted that the reader has had diving instruction. Thus they are tempted to omit information that "the reader will already know." Tell students that most process papers are written for novices who will need all the help they can get.

TEACHING STRATEGIES

1. Ask students to examine some of the essays in the Reader and list their apparent assumptions about an audience. Or bring to class some instructions that don't assume the reader's limited background knowledge, perhaps instructions for installing or operating electronic equipment or computers.

2. To help students see how a process is developed, break down a finished essay, such as "How to Give a Speech," into a chart similar to the one on this page.

3. To help students understand process writing, you could have them break down a complex process from one of their textbooks into its component parts. Alternatively, ask them to become knowledgeable about some procedure, such as how to use a library tool, change majors, or gain certification in some occupation. They might conduct interviews (see pages 323–27) as part of the assignment.

4. To demonstrate the consequences of imprecise instructions, point out that the official review of the Three Mile Island incident cited ambiguity in the operating manual as one of the causes of the disaster.

*W*RITING A PROCESS ANALYSIS

Planning and Drafting the Process Analysis

As always, when the choice is yours, select a familiar topic. If you're not the outdoor type and prefer a Holiday Inn to the north woods, don't try to explain how to plan a campout. Muddled, inaccurate, and inadequate information will result. On the other hand, if you've pitched many a tent, you might want to share your technique with your readers.

Finding a suitable topic should be easy. But if you do hit a snag, turn to the strategies on pages 12–18. In any event, answer the following questions for each potential choice:

Will the reader find this process useful or interesting?
Should I provide directions for the reader to follow or simply explain how others perform the process?
Can I explain the process adequately within any assigned length?

To help accumulate the necessary details for the body of your paper, ponder this second set of questions.

What separate actions make up the process? (Be especially careful not to omit any action that is obvious to you but wouldn't be to your reader. Such an oversight can ruin your reader's chances of success.)
What is the reason for each action?
If I'm providing directions, what warnings will the reader need in order to perform the process properly and safely?

When you have your answers, record them in a chart similar to this one.

Action	*Reason for Action*	*Warning*
First action	First reason	First warning
Second action	Second reason	Second warning

Sometimes a reason will be so obvious no mention is necessary, and many actions won't require warnings. When you've completed the chart, review it carefully and supply any missing information. If necessary, make a revised chart.

EXERCISE

1. Develop a complete list of the actions involved in one of the following processes; then arrange them in an appropriate order.

   a. Baking bread
   b. Assembling or repairing some common household device

c. Carrying out a process related to sports
d. Breaking a bad habit
e. Building a fire in a fireplace

2. Examine your favorite newspaper or magazine for examples of process analysis. Bring them to class for group discussion of how they illustrate step-by-step directions.

Start your paper by identifying the process and arousing your reader's interest. You might, for instance, note the usefulness of the process or the ease of carrying it out. If the reader will perform the process, list any items needed to do the work and note any special conditions required for a successful outcome. A paper explaining how to grill hamburgers might begin as follows.

> Grilling hamburgers on an outdoor charcoal grill is a simple process that almost anyone can master. Before starting, you will need a clean grill, charcoal briquets, charcoal lighter fluid and matches, hamburger meat, a plate, a spatula, and some water to put out any flames caused by fat drippings. The sizzling, tasty patties you will have when you finish are a treat that almost everyone will enjoy.

DISCUSSION QUESTION ■ How does the writer try to induce the reader to perform the process?

Use the body of the paper to discuss the procedure in detail. Before starting to write, however, scrutinize your list of actions and group related ones together to form steps, the major subdivisions of the procedure. The following actions constitute the first step—getting the fire going—of the hamburger-grilling paper.

remove grill rack	light briquets
stack charcoal briquets	spread out briquets

Present each step in one or more paragraphs so each is distinct and easily grasped.

Develop each step in appropriate detail. For information-only papers, merely provide a good general idea of what the process entails and, where it would be helpful, the reason for an action. Papers providing directions to follow are another matter. If you've ever muttered under your breath as you struggled to assemble something that came with fuzzy or inadequate directions, you know the importance of presenting steps clearly, accurately, and fully. Therefore, think hard about what the reader needs to know. Note the reason for any action unless the reason is obvious. Flag each difficult or dangerous step with a cautionary warning. If two steps must be performed simultaneously, tell the reader at the start of the first one. In some places you may want to tell readers what to expect if they have completed

CLASSROOM ACTIVITIES

1. Have students brainstorm (in small groups or as the entire class) instructions for an activity that they all know. List the results on the board and check them as a group for completeness, accuracy, and organization.
2. To demonstrate the importance of writing exact instructions, hand out a simple diagram to the class. Have students write instructions for drawing it, exchange just the instructions, and then follow them *exactly* as they attempt to reproduce the diagram. If the instructions don't call for pen or pencil and paper, for example, the reader would not proceed. Once students finish drawing their shapes, have them compare their results with the original to determine the differences.
3. No law decrees that process must be serious. Perhaps have students try brainstorming humorous instructions for avoiding muggers, staying up late, cramming for an exam, or the like.

ETHICAL ISSUE

Who is responsible if a writer produces unclear or inaccurate instructions for a company's product and a reader, following those instructions, is injured? Have students role play this scenario, with some representing the writer, others the company, and still others the injured party. Have the class establish criteria for when a writer is, and is not, responsible.

DISCUSSION QUESTION

The writer notes that grilling hamburgers is "a simple process that almost anyone can master" and that the grilled patties are "a treat that almost everyone will enjoy."

A process paper could follow the discussion of a theme. To explore "Who We Are," for example, the class might read "Courtship Through the Ages" and discuss the strange (or typical) steps involved in courting rituals. In addition, students might read "How to Give a Speech" and then talk over the ways in which people interact. Finally, students could be asked to write about the steps that occur when people meet each other, the stages involved in a date or in the collapse of a relationship, or the like. If you choose to examine the theme "Our Relationship to Nature," students could read "A Total Eclipse" or "Dawn Watch" and then observe and explain such changes in nature as the development of cloud patterns or the progression of erosion. You could explain that such observations require the use of effective description.

DISCUSSION QUESTIONS

1. The writer has provided reasons for stacking the briquets, waiting to light the briquets, allowing them to sit for fifteen minutes, and spreading them.
2. He warns against squirting more lighter fluid on the briquets after burning has started.

the instructions properly. Feedback lets readers know they are on track or that they need to redo something.

Let's see how the first step of the hamburger-grilling paper might unfold.

> The first step is to get the fire going. Remove the grill rack and stack about twenty charcoal briquets in a pyramid shape in the center of the grill. Stacking allows the briquets to burn off one another and thus produces a hotter fire. Next, squirt charcoal lighter fluid over the briquets. Wait about five minutes so that the fluid has time to soak into the charcoal. Then toss in a lighted match. The flame will burn for a few minutes before it goes out. When this happens, allow the briquets to sit for another fifteen minutes so that the charcoal can start to burn. Once the burning starts, do not squirt on any more lighter fluid. A flame could quickly follow the stream back into the can, causing it to explode. As the briquets begin to turn from pitch black to ash white, spread them out with a stick so that they barely touch one another. Air can then circulate and produce a hot, even fire, the type that makes grilling a success.

DISCUSSION QUESTIONS

1. At what points has the writer provided reasons for doing things?
2. Where has he included a warning?

Some processes can unfold in *only one order*. When you shoot a free throw in basketball, for example, you step up to the line and receive the ball before lining up the shot, and you line up the shot before releasing the ball. Other processes can be carried out in an *order of choice*. When you grill hamburgers, you can make the patties either before or after you light the charcoal. If you have an option, use the order that has worked best for you.

End your paper with a few brief remarks that provide some perspective on the process. A summary of the steps often works best for longer, multi-step processes. Other popular choices include evaluating the results of the process or discussing its importance. The paper on hamburger grilling ends the latter way.

> Once the patties are cooked the way you like them, remove them from the grill and place them on buns. Now you are ready to enjoy a mouthwatering treat that you will long remember.

E. M. Pryzblyo

Revising the Process Analysis

To revise, follow the guidelines in Chapter 3 and pose these questions.

Have I written consistently for someone who will perform the process or someone who will merely follow it?

Have I included every necessary action? Explained any purpose that is unclear?

Have I warned about any steps that are dangerous or might be performed improperly?

Are my steps presented in an appropriate order? Developed in sufficient detail?

EXAMPLE STUDENT ESSAY OF PROCESS ANALYSIS

The ABC's of CPR

Kathy Petroski

A heart attack, drowning, choking, or an electric shock—any of these can stop a person's breathing. The victim, however, need not always die. Many lives that would otherwise be lost can be saved simply by applying the ABC's of CPR—cardiopulmonary resuscitation. CPR requires no special equipment. However, no one should attempt it without first receiving qualified instruction on a mannequin. Here's how it is performed. When you are certain that the victim's breathing and pulse have stopped, start CPR immediately. If breathing and circulation aren't restored within five minutes, irreversible brain damage occurs.

A stands for opening the airway. Lay the victim in a supine (face up) position on a firm surface. Then tilt the head as far back as possible by gently lifting the chin with one hand. In an unconscious person, the tongue falls to the back of the throat and blocks the air passages. Hyperextending the head in this fashion pulls the tongue from that position, thus allowing air to pass. At the same time tilt the forehead back with the other hand until the chin points straight upward. The relaxed jaw muscles will then tighten, opening the air passage to the lungs. Remove your hand from the forehead and, using your first two fingers, check the mouth for food,

TEACHING STRATEGIES

1. Students should know that they can revise their process papers effectively by following the instructions and seeing if everything works.
2. If the assignment allows it, have students exchange essays and then attempt to follow each other's instructions, reporting on any failures. If this exchange isn't possible, peer response works especially well with process papers since the peer is more likely than the writer to identify omissions and point out other problems.

TEACHING STRATEGY

You might have students identify the warnings and feedback that accompany the actual steps. Suggest that they reread the directions, omit these elements, and note the effectiveness of the essay with and without the omissions.

dentures, vomitus, or a foreign object. Remove any obstruction with a sweeping motion. These measures may cause the patient to start breathing spontaneously. If they do not, mouth-to-mouth resuscitation must be started.

<u>B</u> stands for breathing. Position one hand on the forehead and pinch the victim's nostrils shut with the index finger and thumb of your other hand. Open your mouth, and place it over the victim's mouth so that a tight seal is formed. Such contact allows air to reach and expand the lungs. If the seal is incomplete, you will hear your own breath escaping. Deliver two quick, full breaths without allowing the victim's lungs to deflate completely between breaths; then remove your mouth and allow him to exhale passively. At this point, check the carotid pulse to determine whether the heart is beating. To do so, place the tips of your index and middle fingers laterally into the groove between the trachea (windpipe) and the muscles at the side of the neck. If no pulse is evident, artificial circulation must be started.

3

<u>C</u> means circulation. Locate the lower end of the sternum (breastbone), and move upward approximately the width of two fingers. At this point, firmly apply the heel of one hand, positioning the fingers at right angles to the length of the body and keeping them slanted upward. If the hand is positioned any higher or lower on the sternum, serious internal injuries in the abdomen or chest are possible. Now place the heel of your second hand on top of your first. The fingers may be interlaced or interlocked, but they must not touch the chest, or the force of your compressions may fracture ribs.

4

Keeping your elbows straight and pushing down from the shoulders, apply firm, heavy pressure until the sternum is depressed approximately one and one-half to two inches. Rock forward and backward in a rhythmic fashion, exerting pressure with the weight of your body. This action squeezes the heart against the immobile spine with enough pressure to pump blood from the left ventricle of the heart into general circulation. Compress the chest, and then immediately release the pressure, fifteen times. Do not, at any point

5

in the cycle, remove your hands from the chest wall. Counting the compressions aloud will help develop a systematic cycle, which is essential for success. When the fifteen have been completed, pinch the nose as described above, seal the victim's mouth with your own, and deliver two quick breaths of air. Then compress the chest an additional fifteen times. Alternate respiration and compression steps, timing yourself so as to deliver approximately eighty compressions per minute.

At various intervals, quickly check the effectiveness of your   6
CPR technique. Lift the eyelids and notice if the pupils are constricted—a key sign that the brain is receiving enough oxygen. In addition, if the bluish color of the victim is decreasing and spontaneous breathing and movement are increasing, the victim has responded favorably.

To maximize the chances for survival, do not interrupt this   7
technique for more than five or ten seconds. Continue the ABC's of CPR until competent medical help or life-support equipment arrives.

DISCUSSION QUESTIONS

1. How does the writer use the letters *A*, *B*, and *C* from the CPR technique in this paper?
2. How does the opening paragraph prepare the reader for what follows?
3. Where does the essay indicate the purposes of actions?
4. What order has the writer used? Explain why this order is a good choice.
5. Is the writer merely explaining how the process is carried out, or does she intend for the reader to follow the directions? Defend your answer.

SUGGESTIONS FOR WRITING ■ Write a process analysis on one of the topics below or one approved by your instructor. The paper may provide instructions for the reader to follow or tell how a process is performed. Prepare a complete list of steps, arrange them in an appropriate order, and follow them as you write the body of your essay.

1. Succeeding at pinball or your favorite video game
2. Programming a computer
3. Making a good impression on a first date
4. Breaking a bad habit
5. Dealing with a bite of a poisonous snake

DISCUSSION QUESTIONS

1. The letters *A, B,* and *C* in the title suggest the step-by-step procedure that the paper develops. Furthermore, *A, B,* and *C* are linked to "airway," "breathing," and "circulation."
2. The introduction points out that the process requires no special equipment but that one should receive instruction before performing it. In addition, the opening paragraph clarifies why the process is useful—a life could be saved—and why action must occur within a five-minute span: to prevent brain damage.
3. The essay indicates the purposes of actions in sentences five and seven of paragraph 2, sentence four of paragraph 3, sentences four and six of paragraph 4, sentences three and six of paragraph 5, and sentence two of paragraph 6.
4. The writer used fixed order because the process must follow one particular sequence.
5. This essay explains a procedure for the reader to follow. It addresses the reader as "you" and presents directions in the form of polite commands.

SUGGESTED INSTRUCTOR READINGS

Berman, N. "Language, Process, and Tinkertoys." College Composition and Communication 26 (1975): 390–92. To help students develop language skills, Berman suggests that they construct something with tinkertoys and then write instructions so others can duplicate their product.

Kroll, B. "Explaining How to Play a Game: The Development of Informative Writing Skills." Written Communication 3 (1986): 195–218. To show how students develop as writers, Kroll uses an assignment in which they are taught to play a game and then asked to write instructions for it.

6. Training a dog or another pet
7. Preparing for a two-week vacation
8. Growing a particular type of fruit or vegetable in a home garden
9. Carrying out a process related to your hobby
10. Preparing your favorite meal
11. Studying for an examination
12. Performing a process required by your job
13. Achieving some important goal
14. Building the body beautiful
15. Being the life of a party

CHAPTER 7

Illustration: Making Yourself Clear

PERSPECTIVE

Illustration isn't merely a writing strategy. Often we understand a general assertion only when we connect it to one or more specific examples. Illustration is therefore the cornerstone of all writing that deals with ideas and of all the writing strategies discussed in this book. Students should understand the importance of connecting general ideas to specific examples and the pivotal role that illustration will play in much of their college and on-the-job writing.

TEACHING STRATEGIES

1. Have students review their textbooks and lecture notes to determine where illustration is used effectively to clarify and where it is either missing or badly used. Ask students to evaluate communication effectiveness with and without illustration.
2. To strengthen their illustrations, writers often use narration or description as support. If you've already covered these strategies, you might ask students to examine the illustration essays in the Reader, point out any instances where narration and description are used, and explain why.
3. Have students list communication situations in their lives, other classes, or careers where illustration would be either helpful or essential.

"It doesn't pay to fight City Hall. For example, my friend Josie. . . ."

"Many intelligent people lack common sense. Take Dr. Brandon. . . ."

"Topnotch women tennis players are among the biggest moneymakers in sports. Last year, for instance, Steffi Graff. . . ."

"Predicting the weather is far from an exact science. Two winters ago, a surprise snowstorm. . . ."

Have you ever noticed how often people use *illustrations* (examples) to clarify general statements?

Ordinary conversations teem with "for example . . ." and "for instance . . . ," often in response to a furrowed brow or puzzled look. Hank Cassidy serves as the perfect example of a good ole boy, or Chicago's Watertower Plaza illustrates a vertical shopping mall. But illustration is not limited to concrete items. Teachers, researchers, and writers often present an abstract principle or natural law, then supply concrete examples that bring it down to earth. An economics instructor might illustrate compound interest by an example showing how much $100 earning 5 percent interest would appreciate in ten years. Examples can also persuade, as when advertisers trot out typical satisfied users of their products to induce us to buy.

Many classroom writing assignments can benefit from the use of illustration. A business student writing a paper on effective management can provide a better grasp of the topic by including examples of successful managers and how they operate. A paper defining democracy for a political science course will be more effective if it offers examples of several democratic governments. An explanation of irony for a literature course will gain force and clarity through examples taken from stories and poems. Illustration plays a similarly important role in work-related writing. A teacher wanting a bigger student-counseling staff might cite students who need help but can't get it. An advertising copywriter urging that new copiers be bought might mention different instances of copier breakdown and the resulting delays in customer service. A union steward wanting a better company safety program might call attention to several recent accidents.

The old saw that a picture is worth a thousand words best explains the popularity of illustration. The concrete is always easier to grasp than the abstract, and examples add savor to what might otherwise be flat and vague.

SELECTING APPROPRIATE EXAMPLES

CLASSROOM ACTIVITY

Ask students to bring in different examples of illustration and then either in small or large groups compare them to determine the different types, their purposes, their relative effectiveness, and any problems.

TEACHING STRATEGIES

1. You might have students examine the essays in the Reader and then evaluate the appropriateness, number, and organization of the examples.
2. Examples can, of course, be selected to make specific points. Discuss what examples might be used to create a positive impression of hackers or how the description of Bob Shaw could be rewritten to make a positive point.
3. Discuss the different possible effects on a specific essay if it was developed with different numbers and lengths of examples.

Make sure that your examples stay on target, that is, actually support your general statement and do not veer off into an intriguing side issue. For instance, if you're making the point that the lyrics in a rock group's latest album are not in good taste, don't inject comments on the fast life-style of one of its members. Instead, provide examples of lyrics that support your claim, chosen from different songs in the album to head off objections that your examples aren't representative.

Furthermore, see that your examples display all the chief features of whatever you're illustrating. Don't offer Hank Cassidy as an example of a typical good ole boy unless he fits the general mold by being a fun-loving, easy-going beer guzzler who likes to hang out with other men. Alternatively, consider this example of a hacker, a compulsive computer programmer.

> Bob Shaw, a 15-year-old high-school student, is a case in point. Bob was temporarily pulled off the computers at school when he began failing his other courses. But instead of hitting the books, he continues to sulk outside the computer center, peering longingly through the glass door at the consoles within.
>
> Pale and drawn, his brown hair unkempt, Bob speaks only in monosyllables, avoiding eye contact. In answer to questions about friends, hobbies, school, he merely shrugs or mumbles a few words aimed at his sneakered feet. But when the conversation turns to the subject of computers, he brightens—and blurts out a few full sentences about the computer he's building and the projects he plans.
>
> Dina Ingber, "Computer Addicts"

Clearly, Shaw fits the general description of hackers, programmers who have "a drive so consuming it overshadows nearly every other part of their lives and forms the focal point of their existence."

NUMBER OF EXAMPLES

How many examples will you need? One long one, several fairly brief ones, or a large number of very short ones? Look to your topic for the answer. To illustrate the point that a good nurse must be compassionate, conscientious, and competent, your best bet would probably be one example, since one person must possess all these traits.

When dealing with trends, however, you'll need several examples. To show that parents have been rearing children more and more permissively over the last half century, at least three examples are called for: one family from around 1940, a second from about 1965, and a third from the present time. Sometimes topics that do not involve trends require more than one example, as when you demonstrate the sharp differences between Japanese and American attitudes toward work.

Finally, some topics require a whole series of examples. If you're contending that many everyday expressions have their origins in the world of gambling, you'd need many examples to demonstrate your point.

EXERCISE

1. **Choose one of the following topic sentences. Select an appropriate example and write the rest of the paragraph.**

   a. Sometimes a minor incident drastically changes a person's life.
   b. _____'s name exactly suits (her/his) personality.
   c. I still get embarrassed when I remember _____ .
   d. Not all education goes on in the classroom.
   e. I learned the value of _____ the hard way.

2. **Explain why you would use one extended illustration, several shorter ones, or a whole series of examples to develop each of the following statements. Suggest appropriate illustrations.**

   a. Many parents I know think for their children.
   b. The hamburger isn't what it used to be.
   c. The ideal pet is small, quiet, and affectionate.
   d. Different college students view their responsibilities differently.
   e. The hotels in Gotham City run the gamut from sumptuous to seedy.
   f. Modern English includes any number of words taken directly from foreign languages.

ORGANIZING THE EXAMPLES

A single extended example often assumes the narrative form, presenting a series of events in time sequence. One person's unfolding experience might show that "doing your thing" doesn't always work out for the best. Sets of examples that trace trends also rely on time sequence, moving either forward or backward. This arrangement would work well for the paper on the growing permissiveness in child rearing.

On the other hand, a paper showing that different individuals exhibit some characteristic to different extents would logically be organized by order of climax (from the least to the greatest extent) or perhaps the reverse order. To demonstrate how salesclerks differ in their attitudes toward customers, you might first describe a hostile clerk, then a pleasant one, and finally an outstandingly courteous and helpful one.

Sometimes any arrangement will work equally well. Suppose you're showing that Americans are taking various precautions to ward off heart attacks. Although

EXERCISE ANSWERS

2. **a.** One illustration would work if the parent tried to run every important aspect of the child's life: dating, diet, recreation, friends, and the like. This paper could also present several examples of parents, all of whom tried to control one aspect of their children's lives.
   b. At least two examples would be needed. The first might describe hamburgers the writer could buy ten years ago at a since-vanished neighborhood hamburger shop; the second might describe a typical hamburger from Burger King or McDonald's.
   c. One example is needed here: that of a small animal, probably a cat or dog, that has the characteristics mentioned in the statement.
   d. At least two examples would be required. The writer could provide one illustration of an irresponsible student and another of a responsible student. A third example could be added—of a student who is responsible part of the time (or about some things) and irresponsible part of the time (or about other things).
   e. "Run the gamut" suggests perhaps a paper with three illustrations: one of a luxury hotel, another of a hotel serving a middle-class clientele, and the third of a rundown hotel.
   f. This statement would require a whole series of examples—for instance, kimono, bungalow, perestroika, and kindergarten.

you might move from a person who exercises to one who diets and finally to one who practices relaxation techniques, no special order is preferable.

Large numbers of examples might first be grouped into categories and the categories then arranged in a suitable order. For example, the expressions from the world of gambling could be grouped according to types of gambling: cards, dice, horse racing, and the like. Depending upon the specific categories, one arrangement may or may not be preferable to another.

*W*RITING AN ILLUSTRATION

Planning and Drafting the Illustration

Assertions, unfamiliar topics, abstract principles, natural laws—as we've seen, all of these can form the foundation for your paper. If you have a choice, you should experience little difficulty finding something suitable. After all, you've observed and experienced many things—for example, how people can be TV junkies and the ways students manage the stresses of college life. As always, the strategies on pages 12–18 can help generate some possibilities, which you can then evaluate by asking these questions.

Exactly what point am I trying to make? (Write it down in precise terms.)
Why do I want to make this point? To show how bad something is? To encourage something? To scare people into or away from something?
Who is my prospective audience?
Should I use one extended example, or will I need more? Why?

Once you've picked your topic, ask yourself, "What example(s) will work best with my audience?" Then brainstorm each one for supporting details. Use a chart patterned after the one below to help you.

Example 1	*Example 2*	*Example 3*
First supporting detail	First supporting detail	First supporting detail
Second supporting detail	Second supporting detail	Second supporting detail

Review your details carefully and add any new ones you think of; then make a new chart and re-enter the details into it, arranged in the order you intend to present them.

Your introduction should identify your topic and draw your reader into the paper. If you're illustrating a personal belief, you might indicate how you developed it. If you're trying to scare the reader into or away from something, you might open with an arresting statement.

Present your examples in the body of your paper, keeping your purpose firmly in mind as you plan your organization. If you have many brief examples, perhaps group them into related categories for discussion. The paper on expres-

TEACHING STRATEGY

Students often believe that simply stating an example is sufficient; they are not likely to provide adequate supporting details. Even though the brainstorming chart will help, you might caution them about the problems caused by vague writing.

ETHICAL ISSUES

Is it acceptable to fabricate an example in order to illustrate a point? If so, when? Some politicians and many advertisers contrive examples to support their views. The class might discuss situations where fictional examples created problems, then develop criteria for the appropriate use of fictional examples. Similarly, is it appropriate to use as an example of a distasteful person someone the readers might know? A class discussion could ensue.

sions from gambling, for instance, might devote one paragraph each to terms from the worlds of cards, dice, and horse racing. If you're dealing with a few relatively brief examples—say to show a trend—put each in its own paragraph. For a single extended example, use the entire body of the paper, suitably paragraphed. Thus, an extended example of someone with an eccentric life-style might include paragraphs on his mode of dress, living accommodations, and public behavior.

Conclude in whatever way seems most appropriate. You might express a hope or recommendation that the reader implement or avoid something, or you might issue a personal challenge that grows out of the point you've illustrated.

Revising the Illustration

Think about the following questions and the general guidelines in Chapter 3 as you revise your paper.

Exactly what idea am I trying to put across? Have I used the examples that best typify it?
Do my examples illuminate my idea without introducing irrelevant material?
Are my examples interesting?
Have I used an appropriate number of examples?
Have I organized my paper effectively?

EXAMPLE STUDENT ESSAY OF ILLUSTRATION

A Lesson from Nature

Mike Braendle

As I was growing up, my parents often passed along little 1
maximlike sayings to me. Most of these have since slipped my mind, but I still remember the exact words of my father's favorite: "The door to success is labeled Push." Although for a while these were just words to me, I came to understand their true meaning as I observed the struggles of a crayfish while I was fishing one day.

There it lay, trapped in the small plastic compartment of my 2
steel tackle box, which was sitting on the bank of the river. The sun had been shining for some time, and the plastic of the compartment surrounding the crayfish intensified the heat. In fact, the heat had become so great that the skin covering the small hard-shelled body was beginning to wrinkle. Nevertheless, the pinching claws continually groped about, trying to find something to grasp, some

READER/THEME STRATEGIES

Because almost all writing relies on examples, an illustration paper might follow your discussion of a theme. If you're dealing with the theme "Life's Changes," you might assign "The Boy and the Bank Officer," "The Company Man," and "Private Language, Public Language." Drawing upon their observations of themselves and others, students might then write papers that explain and illustrate how we respond to the different stages of life. If you explore the theme "American Crises," students could read "Why Women Managers Are Bailing Out," discuss various college problems they've encountered, and then explain and illustrate the problems, perhaps in articles directed toward the college newspaper.

means of escape. The hard and heavy shell, acting like an anchor, burdened the crayfish greatly. The two small eyes, always moving, searched wildly for some way out, but found none. The segmented tail, as large as the rest of the body, was constantly pushing, trying to hoist the heavy body over the edge of the compartment.

The eyes at last fell upon a possibility for escape: the back wall of the compartment was slightly lower than the other three walls. Sensing an advantage, the crayfish seemed to labor more deliberately. The tail, pushing vigorously, tried to lift the heavy shell out of the plastic compartment. As the tail struggled, the claws slashed savagely back and forth, searching for something to grab.   3

Finally, after some time and struggle, the crayfish grasped the back wall. As it pulled, with every muscle straining, the hard shell edged up and over the wall of the compartment. Stopping abruptly and gazing at its surroundings, the crayfish tried to orient itself. Off to one side in another compartment lay a strange-looking creature, unmoving. The crayfish did not recognize this odd-shaped thing as a fishing lure, but it did sense that the creature, with its bright metallic tint and protruding hooks, was not alive.   4

It took only a moment for the determined crustacean to figure out which way to go. It moved, as if driven by instinct, across this compartment and then others, occasionally getting caught on a protruding hook. These hooks slowed its progress, scratching grooves and gouges in the hard shell.   5

As the crayfish moved steadily toward the edge of the box, the thought of cold water seemed to excite it. It moved faster, more deliberately now. When reaching the edge of the box, it stopped for a moment, as if pondering what to do next. Then, defiantly, it flopped over the edge, landing on its hard shell. It stayed on its back for some time but then turned over and dragged itself to the water.   6

The crayfish lay there for a long time, soaking in the cool and refreshing river. Then with a powerful flap of its tail, it disappeared into the depths. Here, where there was no threat of drying out, it could and probably would recuperate from this tiring experience.   7

DISCUSSION QUESTIONS

1. What general statement does this essay illustrate?
2. Why is one extended illustration effective here?
3. Explain the organization of the essay and why it is appropriate.
4. In paragraph 2, the writer says the crayfish "continually groped" and "searched wildly" with its tail "constantly pushing." How do these descriptions relate to the writer's purpose?
5. Point out specific sentences in paragraphs 3 and 4 that seem particularly effective in engaging the reader's interest.
6. Would a concluding paragraph which restated the main idea make this essay more effective? Why or why not?

SUGGESTIONS FOR WRITING ■ Use one of the ideas below or another that your instructor approves for your illustration essay. Select appropriate examples, determine how many you will use, and decide how you will organize them.

1. Americans are a wasteful people.
2. If you want something done, ask the busiest person around.
3. People often choose strange places to vacation.
4. Women are becoming increasingly prominent (in politics, business, sports, or some other field).
5. Dedication is the secret of success for many athletes (or use any other field or occupation).
6. People have many strange remedies for hangovers.
7. An adult never stands so tall as when stooping to help a child.
8. A good nurse must be compassionate, conscientious, and competent (or use another occupation with appropriate characteristics).
9. _____ is a demanding profession.
10. Many intelligent people lack common sense.
11. It does not (or does) pay to fight City Hall.
12. Successful people are often self-made.
13. "Doing your thing" does not always work out for the best.
14. _____ is the most (or least) effective teacher I have ever had.
15. Not to decide is to decide.

DISCUSSION QUESTIONS

1. The essay illustrates the idea that "Dedicated effort is the key to accomplishing your goals." This can, of course, be phrased in various ways. In the essay we are told that "The door to success is labeled Push."

2. This single illustration is sufficient because the crayfish's struggle and eventual escape from the tackle box completely exemplify the writer's point. Additional examples would have been redundant.

3. Chronological organization is the only feasible way to present the series of events that make up the struggle.

4. Struggle, or "push," is the key to success. These phrases show the crayfish struggling for its objective: freedom.

5. The third and fourth sentences of paragraph 3 and the second sentence of paragraph 4 engage the reader's interest. These sentences offer vivid sight impressions that depict the struggle of the crayfish.

6. The illustration exemplifies the point effectively; a restatement of the idea would be superfluous.

Classification: Grouping into Categories

PERSPECTIVE

While we all classify our world into functional categories, students often find working with classification to be an abstract task. You can help them approach this strategy by reinforcing what the text points out: since they classify on a regular basis, they already have considerable experience with the method. Furthermore, some students find it difficult to think hierarchically in terms of categories divided into subcategories. By using drawings and charts, you can demonstrate the relationship among categories and prepare your students for writing.

TEACHING STRATEGIES

1. Over a week's time have students record where they rely on classification, whether it is selecting a type of doctor, determining what store would have a coat, or finding a radio station that plays their kind of music.
2. Have students go to a local grocery store and see whether they can determine how the merchandise is classified. For example, some stores group health and beauty products together; some group them separately. Students could develop a list of the different categories, noting examples of the items in each one.
3. Have students examine popular writing and note any classifications that the writers use. Possibilities include types of parents, stereo systems, or food groups.
4. Classification can be a useful learning tool. Have students identify where direct or implied classification is used in their other courses. You might help them chart the classification system.

Help Wanted, Situations Wanted, Real Estate, Personal. Do these terms look familiar? They do if you've ever scanned the classified ads of the newspaper. Ads are grouped into categories, and each category is then subdivided. The people who assemble this layout are *classifying*. Figure 8.1 shows the main divisions of a typical classified ad section and a further breakdown of one of them.

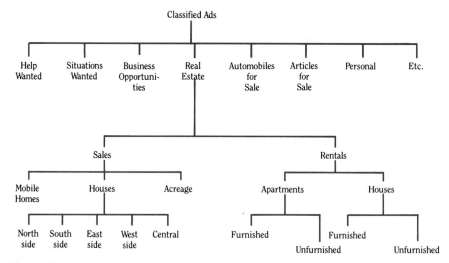

Figure 8.1

As this figure indicates, grouping allows the people who handle ads to divide entries according to a logical scheme and helps readers find what they are looking for. Imagine the difficulty of checking the real estate ads if all the entries were run in the order the ads were placed.

Our minds naturally sort information into categories. Within a few weeks after their birth, infants can tell the faces of family members from those of outsiders. Toddlers learn to distinguish between cats, dogs, and rabbits. In both cases the classification rests solely on physical differences. As we mature we start classifying in more abstract ways, and by adulthood we are constantly sorting things into categories: dates or mates, eating places, oddballs, friends, investments, jobs, political views.

Classification also helps writers and readers come to grips with large or complex topics. It breaks a broad topic into categories according to some specific principle, presents the distinctive features of each category, and shows how the features vary among categories. Segmenting the topic simplifies the discussion by presenting the information in small, neatly sorted piles rather than in one jumbled and confusing heap.

Furthermore, classification helps people make choices. Identifying which groups of consumers—students, accountants, small business owners—are most likely to buy some new product allows the manufacturer to advertise in appropriate media. Knowing the engine size, maneuverability, seating capacity, and gas mileage of typical subcompact, compact, and intermediate-size cars helps customers decide which one to buy. Examining the features of term, whole-life, and endowment insurance enables prospective buyers to select the policy that best suits their needs.

Because classification plays such an important part in our lives, it is a useful writing tool in many situations. Your accounting instructor may ask you to categorize accounting procedures for retail businesses. In a computer class, you may classify computer languages and then specify appropriate applications for each grouping. For an industrial hygiene class, you might categorize different types of respiratory protective equipment and indicate when each type is used. On the job, a state health department employee may prepare a brochure grouping illegal drugs into categories based on their effects. The communications director of an investment firm might write a customer letter categorizing investments according to their degree of risk. An employee of a textbook publisher might prepare a catalog grouping new books by field of study.

SELECTING CATEGORIES

People classify in different ways for different purposes, which generally reflect their interests. A clothing designer might classify people according to their fashion sense, a representative of the National Organization for Women according to their views on women's rights, and the Secretary of Labor according to their occupations. A college's director of housing might classify students according to their type of residence, the dean of students according to their behavior problems, and the financial aid officer according to their sources of income.

When you write a classification paper, choose a principle of classification that's suited to your audience. To illustrate, if you are writing for students, don't classify instructors according to their religion, dietary choices, or investment habits. These breakdowns probably wouldn't interest most students and certainly wouldn't serve their needs. Instead, develop a more useful principle of classification—perhaps by teaching styles, concern for students, or grading policies.

Sometimes it's helpful or necessary to divide one or more categories into subcategories. If you do, use just one principle of classification for each level. Both levels in Figure 8.2 meet this test because each reflects a single principle: place of origin for the first, number of cylinders for the second.

PERSPECTIVE

Students tend to see classification systems as immutable and without alternatives. They should understand that these systems are human creations designed to serve particular purposes but are sometimes modified or even rejected when they are not appropriate.

TEACHING STRATEGIES

1. Charting a classification system helps students organize and test it. Such a chart helps ensure that everything is connected, stresses the hierarchical nature of classification, and allows students to determine whether all relevant items have an appropriate place. Encourage students to verify their classification systems.

2. A helpful way to think of categories is as mail slots grouped according to Zip Code; each and every item would have one, and only one, place.

3. Although students often confuse classification with comparison, it is probably better not to introduce the distinction. If the question does come up, however, you might point out that classification always shows the relationships among categories of things, while comparison shows how specific things are similar and/or different. To illustrate, comparison would be used to evaluate the performance of two instructors, classification to present the characteristics of good and bad instructors. If a good instructor is fired and a bad one becomes a dean, the two classification categories remain intact.

CLASSROOM ACTIVITIES

1. Ask students to list how they (as students) might be classified by (a) the administration, (b) financial aid, (c) housing, (d) the instructor in

a particular class, (e) fraternities or sororities. Have them
point out how the different
purposes for classification
yield different categories.
2. Have students, working in
groups, establish what classification systems would be
helpful for marketing several
new products or services to
the student population. Possible services or products include a new tutoring
service, pizza or newspaper
delivery, research assistance,
perfume, mini-refrigerators,
stereo equipment.

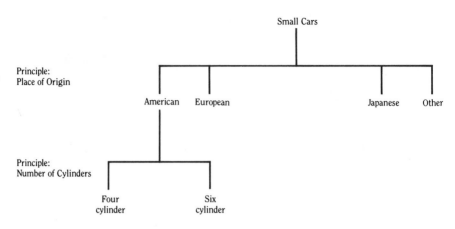

Figure 8.2 Proper Classification of Small Cars

EXERCISE ANSWERS

1. Classifying the families in
Anytown, USA:
a. The Roman Catholic bishop would probably classi-
fy the families by
religious preference: Catholic, Protestant, Jewish,
Moslem, no religion.
b. The state senator would
probably categorize the
families by political preference: Democratic, Re-
publican, Libertarian,
independent.
c. The NAACP representative would probably cate-
gorize them by race:
Caucasian, Black, Orien-
tal.
d. The director of the local
credit bureau would
probably categorize them
by their credit ratings:
good credit risks, ques-
tionable credit risks, poor
credit risks.
You might remind students
that in all cases the same
group of people is being cat-
egorized. An individual might
be a Catholic, a Republican, a
black, and a good credit risk.
In addition, these groupings
might be expanded. The population of Anytown might include Buddhists, socialists,
American Indians, and people
who have no credit rating of
any sort.

Now examine Figure 8.3. This classification is *improper* because it groups cars in two ways—by place of origin and by kind—making it possible for one car to end up in two different categories. For example, the German Porsche is both a Euro-pean car and a sports car. When categories overlap in this way, confusion reigns and nothing is clarified.

Figure 8.3 Improper Classification of Small Cars

EXERCISE

1. How would each of the following people be most likely to classify the families in Anytown, USA?

a. The bishop of the Roman Catholic diocese in which the city is located
b. The state senator who represents the city
c. A field worker for the NAACP
d. The director of the local credit bureau

2. The following lists contain overlapping categories. Identify the incon-sistent item in each list and explain why it is faulty.

Nurses	*Pictures*	*Electorate in Midville*
Surgical nurses	Oil paintings	Republicans
Psychiatric nurses	Magazine illustrations	Democrats
Emergency room nurses	Lithographs	Nonvoters
Terminal care nurses	Watercolors	Independents
Night nurses	Etchings	

"SEE ME TOMORROW—I'M BUSY GRADING FINALS NOW."

Reprinted by permission of Richard N. Bibler.

2. Identifying the overlapping category:

Nurses: The overlapping category is "night nurses"; these might work as surgical nurses, emergency room nurses, etc.

Pictures: The overlapping category is "Magazine Illustrations"; the illustration may be an oil painting, a lithograph, etc.

Electorate in Midville: The overlapping category is "non-voters"; these people may favor Republicans, Democrats, or they may take a neutral position.

NUMBER OF CATEGORIES

Some classification papers discuss every category included within the topic. Others discuss only selected categories. Circumstances and purpose dictate the scope of the discussion. Suppose you work for the commerce department of your state and are asked to write a report that classifies the major nonservice industries in a certain city and assesses their strengths and weaknesses. Your investigation shows that food processing, furniture making, and the production of auto parts account for over 95 percent of all nonservice jobs. Two minor industries, printing and toy making, provide the rest of the jobs. Given these circumstances, you'd probably focus on the first three industries, mentioning the others only in passing. But if printing and toy making were significant industries, they too would require detailed discussion.

TEACHING STRATEGIES

1. You might point out that specific details help writers avoid stereotyping, particularly when the essay features types of people.
2. Have students visit a bookstore and note what classification schemes were used to organize the books. Then have them examine some of the titles in each section and use their findings as the basis of a writing assignment.

DEVELOPING CATEGORIES

Develop every category you include with specific, informative details that provide a clear picture of each one and help the reader grasp the distinctions and relationships among them. The following excerpt from a student paper classifying public restrooms for women discusses two of the writer's three categories.

Luxurious restrooms are found in top-drawer business establishments such as fancy department stores, chic boutiques, and the better restaurants. This aristocrat of public facilities usually disdains the term "restroom," masquerading instead under the alias of "lounge" or "powder room." Upon entering its plush environs, the user is captivated by its elegance. Thick carpet reaches up to cushion tired feet, wood paneled or brocade velvet walls beckon invitingly, and dimly twinkling chandeliers or wall sconces soothe the eyes. Narrow little divans and gold-and-velvet tables add to the restful, welcoming atmosphere, and the latest issues of upscale magazines like Vogue, The New Yorker, and Vanity Fair entice resters into their pages. Mirrors in carved frames, designer lavatories with richly ornamented faucets, and creamy scented soap go hand in hand with the attendant who quietly dispenses thick, white towels as soft as suede. Her detached air deserts her only when she sneaks a furtive glance toward the silver tip dish as the patron passes it on the way out.

The adequate restroom offers utility without the swankiness of its lavish cousin. Typically located in a large shopping mall or mass-market department store, it is a stark world of hard, unadorned surfaces—tile floors, tile walls, and harshly glaring fluorescent lights recessed in the ceiling. For those who wish to rest, there is a garishly colored Naugahyde couch and next to it a battered metal or wood table holding a few tattered copies of Family Circle, People, Reader's Digest, and similar publications. The mirrors have steel frames, the lavatories, set in a formica counter, have plain chrome faucets, and the soap dispenser emits a thin stream of unscented liquid. Paper toweling pulled from a wall-mounted metal holder replaces the cloth article, and no maid stands by to offer her help or to exact tips from departing visitors.

Student Unknown

The concrete details in these paragraphs effectively characterize each category and clearly distinguish between them. Imagine how vague and indistinct the categories would be without these details.

WRITING A CLASSIFICATION

Planning and Drafting the Classification

Many topics that interest you are potential candidates for classification. If you're selecting your own topic, you might explain the different kinds of rock music to novices, take a humorous look at different types of teachers, or, in a more serious vein, identify different types of discrimination. As always, use one or more of the narrowing strategies on pages 12–18 to help stimulate your thinking. As possibilities come to mind, examine each one in light of these questions.

What purpose will this classification serve?
Who is my audience and what will interest them?
What are the categories of this topic?
What features distinguish my categories from one another?

Next, determine whether you'll discuss every category or only selected ones, and then set up a classification chart similar to the one following.

Category 1	*Category 2*	*Category 3*
First distinguishing feature	First distinguishing feature	First distinguishing feature
Second distinguishing feature	Second distinguishing feature	Second distinguishing feature

Such a chart helps you see the relationships among categories and provides a starting point for developing your specific details. Proceed by jotting down the details that come to mind for each distinguishing feature of every category. Then prepare a second chart with the distinguishing features and details arranged in the order you want to present them.

Begin your paper by identifying your topic and capturing your reader's attention in some way. A paper classifying hair dyes might point out their growing popularity among both men and women. One classifying snobs might offer an anecdote showing how far snobbery can go. Or you could cite a personal experience that relates to your topic. As always, circumstances dictate your choice.

TEACHING STRATEGY

Students often view writing a classification as a formal activity without a real purpose or audience. To correct this mistaken belief, you might specify both or guide students to do so. For example, students could classify the different types of sororities or fraternities for those thinking of pledging. A more challenging assignment is to have them research the different categories of jobs in their chosen fields (what are the different kinds of medical technicians or accountants?) in order to help others in the field select a specialty.

READER/THEME STRATEGIES

The discussion of a theme could lead to a classification. If you'd like to explore the theme "Who We Are," students might read such essays as "The Company Man," "The Bureaucrat," and "The Handicap of Definition" and then follow these up with "Can People Be Judged by Their Appearance?" These readings could launch a discussion that attempts to equate individuals in various occupations with particular body types and lead to papers that present the class's conclusions. If you prefer to explore the theme "Our Relationship to Nature," the class could read essays like "Innocence and Experience . . . ," "When the Full Moon . . . ," and "Why We Have Failed," and then, after a discussion, write papers classifying the stances that humans take toward nature.

In the body discuss your categories in whatever order best suits your purpose. Order of climax—least important, more important, most important—often works well. Or perhaps your topic will suggest arranging the categories by behavior, income, education, or physical characteristics. Whatever your arrangement, signal it clearly to your reader. Don't merely start the discussions of your categories by saying first . . . , second . . . , another . . . , next . . . , and the like. These words offer no hint of the rationale behind your order.

In addition, make sure the arrangement of material within the categories follows a consistent pattern. Recall the two categories of restrooms discussed on pages 102–3. In each case, after noting where the restroom can be found, the writer discusses its floor, walls, and lighting, moves to the furniture, and ends by discussing the lavatories, soap, and toweling.

The strategies for ending a classification paper are as varied as those for starting it. A paper on hair dyes might conclude by predicting their continued popularity. One on snobs might end with your recommendations for dealing with them. In other cases, you might express a hope of some kind or advise your reader to do something.

Revising the Classification

Revise your paper by following the guidelines in Chapter 3 as well as by pondering these questions.

Does my classification have a clear sense of purpose and audience?
Does my principle of classification accord with my purpose?
Do any of my categories overlap?
Have I chosen an appropriate number of categories?
Are these categories developed with sufficient details?
Are the categories and details arranged in an effective order?

EXAMPLE STUDENT ESSAY OF CLASSIFICATION

Undesirable Produce Market Customers

Clarence DeLong

You will find almost as large a variety of customers at a   1
produce market as you will find fruits and vegetables. Undesirable
produce market customers fall into three main categories—those who
squeeze the fruit, those who complain constantly, and those who try
to cheat the market—and when you meet them all in one day, you
have one big headache. Perhaps you will recognize these people as I
describe them.

"Sammy Squeezer" is the least annoying of these   2
undesirables. He wants to make sure that everything he buys is

"just right." He pokes his thumbs into the top of a cantaloupe. If they penetrate very deeply, he won't buy this particular specimen, considering it to be overripe. He squeezes the peaches, plums, nectarines, and any other fruit he can get his hands on. After ten of these people squeeze one piece of fruit, it will surely be soft, even if it wasn't originally. Moving on to the corn, Sammy carefully peels back the husk to examine the kernels inside. If they don't suit him, he doesn't bother to fold the husk back to protect the kernels; he simply tosses the ear back into the basket. The problems he creates for the employees are primarily physical—removing the damaged items after he leaves.

A more annoying customer is "Betty Bitcher." She is never satisfied with the quality of the produce: the bananas are too green, the lettuce has brown spots, the berries are too ripe, and the potatoes have green spots. Sometimes you wonder if Betty would have been satisfied with the fruit grown in the Garden of Eden.

3

The produce has no monopoly on her complaints, however. Betty also finds fault with the service she receives from the employees. Talking to other customers or directly to the clerks, she can be heard saying such things as "Why is this the only place I ever have to wait in line? They must have trouble getting good help here." Even as she leaves the market, which is none too soon, she must make one last complaint: "You mean I have to carry my own potatoes to the car?" The problems she creates for the employees are primarily mental--she can make your nerves quite active.

4

Perhaps the most annoying customer of all is "Charlie Cheater." You have to keep your eye on him constantly because he knows all the tricks of cheating. He will add berries to an already full basket. He will take 6/79¢ oranges and tell you they're the 6/59¢ ones. He will put expensive grapes in the bottom of a sack and add cheaper ones on top. Then he'll tell you that they are all the cheaper variety. Likewise, he will put expensive nectarines in a sack, place a few cheaper peaches on top, and try to pass them all off as peaches. If he is caught, he usually says, "I don't know how that happened. My little girl (or boy) must have put them in there."

5

The child usually looks dumbfounded.

The problem Charlie creates for the market is twofold: 6
financial and legal. If you don't catch him, your profits suffer. If you
do catch him, you almost have to prosecute, usually for amounts of
only a dollar or two, or you'll have every Charlie in town at your
door.

Did you recognize any of these customers? If you didn't and 7
would like to see some of them in action, stop in at Steve's Produce
Market. That's where I work, and that's where I meet them.

DISCUSSION QUESTIONS

1. What is the writer's purpose in developing this classification? Where does he state it?

2. In what order has he arranged his categories? Refer to the essay when answering.

3. Demonstrate that the writer has avoided overlapping categories.

4. How do you know he hasn't discussed every category of undesirable customers?

SUGGESTIONS FOR WRITING ■ Write a classification paper on one of the topics below or one approved by your instructor. Determine your purpose and audience, select appropriate categories, decide how many you'll discuss, develop them with specific details, and arrange them in an effective order.

1. College teachers
2. Pet owners
3. House designs
4. Drivers
5. Churchgoers
6. Pocket calculators
7. Patrons of singles bars
8. Eating places
9. Parents
10. Sports announcers (or fans)
11. Television comedies
12. Attitudes toward death
13. Salesclerks
14. People waiting in line
15. Bores

Comparison: Showing Relationships

Which candidate for senator should get my vote, Ken Conwell or Jerry Mander?

Let me know whether this new shipment of nylon thread meets specs.

Doesn't this tune remind you of a Kenny Rogers song?

How does high school in Australia stack up against high school in this country?

Everyone makes *comparisons*, not just once in a while but day after day. When we compare, we examine two or more items for likenesses, differences, or both.

Comparison often helps us choose between alternatives. Some issues are trivial: whether to plunk the first quarter into Star Wars or Space Ace, whether to order pizza or a sub sandwich. But comparison also influences our more important decisions. We weigh majoring in chemistry against majoring in physics, buying against renting, working for Apple Computer against working for IBM. An instructor may ask us to write a paper comparing the features of two word-processing systems. An employer may have us weigh two proposals for decreasing employee absenteeism and write a report recommending one of them.

Comparison also acquaints us with unfamiliar things. To help American readers understand the English sport of rugby, a sportswriter might compare its field, team, rules, and scoring system with those for football. To teach students about France's government, a political science textbook might discuss the makeup and election of its parliament and the method of picking its president and premier, using our own government as a backdrop.

Both your classes and your job will call for comparison writing. Your humanities instructor may ask you to compare baroque and classical music and their contributions to later musical developments. Your psychology instructor may want you to compare two different types of psychosis and assess the legal and medical ramifications of each. Your biology instructor may have you consider how the features of two different kinds of body cells enable them to perform their functions. Comparisons in the workplace are common because they help people make decisions. An office manager may compare several phone systems to determine which

"WE'D LIKE TO TAKE YOU UPSTAIRS AND SHOW YOU THE REAL GRACIOUSNESS OF FRATERNITY LIFE, BUT IT'S SORT OF A RULE AROUND HERE TO WAIT UNTIL THE RUSHEE IS PLEDGED."

Reprinted by permission of Richard N. Bibler.

PERSPECTIVE

Purpose dictates the items selected for a comparison and also how they are developed. It is therefore crucial that students start and proceed with a clear purpose in mind.

TEACHING STRATEGIES

1. Without guidance, students often lean toward superficial or self-evident comparisons—winter and summer, day and night—that produce inane generalities. Since such pointless papers serve neither students' interests nor yours, caution against them.
2. Using the subject matter in their other courses or the significant activities or events in their own lives as a basis, students could develop lists of possible purposes for writing comparisons and perhaps lists of points to include. This activity might be the starting point for actual papers.

one the company should install, a nurse assess the condition of a patient before and after a new medicine is given, an insurance agent point out the features of two insurance policies to highlight the advantages of one.

SELECTING ITEMS FOR COMPARISON

Any items you compare must share some common ground. For example, you could compare two golfers on driving ability, putting ability, and sand play, or two cars on appearance, gas mileage, and warranty; but you can't meaningfully compare a golfer with a car, any more than you could compare guacamole with Guadalajara or chicken with charcoal. There's simply no basis for comparison.

Any valid comparison, on the other hand, presents many possibilities. Suppose you head the record and tape department of a large store and have two excellent salespeople working for you. The manager of the store asks you to prepare a one- or two-page report that compares their qualifications for managing the record department in a new branch store. Assessing their abilities becomes the guiding purpose that motivates and controls the writing. On the spot you can rule out points such as eye color, hair style, and religion, which have no bearing on job performance. Instead, you must decide what managerial traits the job will require and the extent to which each candidate possesses them. Your thinking might result in a list like this.

Points of Similarity or Difference	*Pat*	*Mike*
1. Ability to deal with customers, sales skills	Excellent	Excellent
2. Effort: regular attendance, hard work on the job	Excellent	Excellent
3. Leadership qualities	Excellent	Good
4. Knowledge of ordering and accounting procedures	Good	Fair
5. Musical knowledge	Excellent	Good

This list tells you which points to emphasize and suggests Pat as the candidate to recommend. You might briefly mention similarities (points 1 and 2) in an introductory paragraph, but the report would focus on differences (points 3, 4, and 5), since you're distinguishing between two employees.

EXERCISE ■ **Say you want to compare two good restaurants in order to recommend one of them. List the points of similarity and difference that you might discuss. Differences should predominate because you will base your decision on them.**

DEVELOPING A COMPARISON

Successful comparisons rest upon ample, well-chosen details that show just how the items under consideration are alike and differ. Such support helps the reader grasp your meaning. Read the following two student paragraphs and note how the concrete details convey the striking differences between south and north 14th Street.

On 14th Street running south from P Street are opulent department stores, such as Woodward and Lothrop and Julius Garfinkle, and small but expensive clothing stores with richly dressed mannequins in the windows. Modern skyscraping office buildings harbor banks and travel bureaus on the ground floors and insurance companies and corporation headquarters in the upper stories. Dotting the concretescape are high-priced movie theaters, gourmet restaurants, multilevel parking garages, bookstores, and candy-novelty-gift shops, all catering to the prosperous population of the city. This section of 14th Street is relatively clean: the city maintenance crews must clean up after only a nine-to-five populace and the Saturday crowds of shoppers. The pervading mood of the area is one of bustling wealth during the day and, in the night, calm.

Crossing P Street toward the north, one notes a gradual but disturbing change in the scenery of 14th Street. Two architectural features assault the eyes and automatically register as tokens of trouble: the floodlights that leave no alley or doorway in shadows and the riot screens that cage in the store windows. The buildings are old, condemned, decaying monoliths, each occupying an entire city block. Liquor stores, drugstores, dusty television repair shops, seedy pornographic bookstores that display photographs of naked bodies with the genital areas blacked out by strips of tape, discount stores smelling perpetually of stale chocolate and cold popcorn, and cluttered pawnshops—businesses such as these occupy the street level. Each is separated from the adjoining stores by a littered entranceway that leads up a decaying wooden stairway to the next two floors. All the buildings are three stories tall, all have most of their windows broken and blocked with boards or newspapers, and all reek of liquor, urine, and unidentifiable rot. And so the general atmosphere of this end of 14th Street is one of poverty and decay.

Student Unknown

Vivid details depict with stark clarity the economic differences between the two cultures.

ORGANIZING A COMPARISON

You can use either of two basic patterns to organize a comparison paper: block or alternating. The paper may deal with similarities, differences, or some combination of them.

The Block Pattern. The block pattern first presents all of the points of comparison for one item and then all of the points of comparison for the other.

Here is the comparison of the two salespeople, Pat and Mike, outlined according to the block pattern.

I.   Introduction: mentions similarities in sales skills and effort but recommends Pat for promotion.
II. Specific points about Mike
     A. Leadership qualities
     B. Knowledge of ordering and accounting procedures
     C. Musical knowledge
III. Specific points about Pat
     A. Leadership qualities
     B. Knowledge of ordering and accounting procedures
     C. Musical knowledge
IV. Conclusion: reasserts that Pat should be promoted.

The block pattern works best with short papers or ones that include only a few points of comparison. The reader can easily remember all the points in the first block while reading the second.

The Alternating Pattern.   The alternating pattern presents a point about one item, then follows immediately with a corresponding point about the other. Organized in this way, the Pat-and-Mike paper would look like this:

I.   Introduction: mentions similarities in sales skills and effort but recommends Pat for promotion.
II. Leadership qualities
     A. Mike's qualities
     B. Pat's qualities
III. Knowledge of ordering and accounting procedures
     A. Mike's knowledge
     B. Pat's knowledge
IV. Musical knowledge
     A. Mike's knowledge
     B. Pat's knowledge
V.   Conclusion: reasserts that Pat should be promoted.

For longer papers that include many points of comparison, use the alternating method. Discussing each point in one place highlights similarities and differences; your reader doesn't have to pause and reread in order to grasp them. The alternating plan also works well for short papers.

Once you select your pattern, arrange your points of comparison in an appropriate order. Take up closely related points one after the other. Depending on your purpose, you might work from similarities to differences or the reverse. Often, a good writing strategy is to move from the least significant to the most significant point so that you conclude with punch.

EXERCISE ■ **Using the points of comparison you selected for the exercise on page 109, prepare outlines for a paper organized according to the block and then the alternating pattern.**

TEACHING STRATEGY

Transitions are important in comparisons. Therefore, you might have students outline the comparison essays in the Reader, identify the key transition devices, and determine their contribution to the organization.

CLASSROOM ACTIVITY

In small groups students might brainstorm a comparison and then work out an effective outline, perhaps one that incorporates several similarities and differences. This activity could be the starting point for a paper.

EXERCISE ANSWERS
Block Method

I.   Introduction
II. Restaurant A
     A. Location
     B. Type and quality of food
     C. Decor
     D. Service
     E. Prices
III. Restaurant B
     A. Location
     B. Type and quality of food
     C. Decor
     D. Service
     E. Prices
IV. Conclusion: recommends one of the restaurants

PERSPECTIVE

Analogy can be seen as a key to creativity and effective problem solving. Insights often come from seeing the connections between two seemingly different things. And because an analogy shows a relationship between the familiar and unfamiliar, it is a powerful tool for explaining things.

TEACHING STRATEGIES

1. Have students jot down over a week's time the analogies they observe in writing or speech and determine whether they were or were not effective, and why.
2. Have students identify difficult concepts from another class and attempt to work out an analogy that might facilitate understanding.

CLASSROOM ACTIVITY

Have students complete, with something concrete and physical, sentences such as "Writing is like _____" or "Education is like _____ ." Then the class can discuss and modify the analogies. This activity shows students that an analogy requires careful thinking and that there are many ways of viewing writing and education.

USING ANALOGY

An *analogy*, a special type of comparison, calls attention to one or more similarities underlying two different kinds of items that seem to have nothing in common. While some analogies stand alone, most clarify concepts in other kinds of writing. Whatever their role, they follow the same organizational pattern as ordinary comparisons.

An analogy often explains something unfamiliar by likening it to something familiar. Here is an example.

> The atmosphere of Earth acts like any window in serving two very important functions. It lets light in, and it permits us to look out. It also serves as a shield to keep out dangerous or uncomfortable things. A normal glazed window lets us keep our houses warm by keeping out cold air, and it prevents rain, dirt, and unwelcome insects and animals from coming in. . . . Earth's atmospheric window also helps to keep our planet at a comfortable temperature by holding back radiated heat and protecting us from dangerous levels of ultraviolet light.
>
> Lester del Ray, *The Mysterious Sky*

Conversely, an analogy sometimes highlights the unfamiliar in order to help illuminate the familiar. The following paragraph discusses the qualities and obligations of an unfamiliar person, the mountain guide, to shed light on a familiar practice—teaching:

> The mountain guide, like the true teacher, has a quiet authority. He or she engenders trust and confidence so that one is willing to join the endeavor. The guide accepts his leadership role, yet recognizes that success (measured by the heights that are scaled) depends upon the close cooperation and active participation of each member of the group. He has crossed the terrain before and is familiar with the landmarks, but each trip is new and generates its own anxiety and excitement. Essential skills must be mastered; if they are lacking, disaster looms. The situation demands keen focus and rapt attention: slackness, misjudgment, or laziness can abort the venture.
>
> Nancy K. Hill, "Scaling the Heights: The Teacher as Mountaineer"

When you develop an analogy, keep these points in mind.

1. Your readers must be well acquainted with the familiar item. If they aren't, the point is lost.
2. The items must indeed have significant similarities. You could develop a meaningful analogy between a kidney and a filter or between cancer and anarchy but not between a flicker and a flapjack or a laser and limburger cheese.
3. The analogy must truly illuminate. Overly obvious analogies, such as one comparing a battle to an argument, offer few or no revealing insights.
4. Over-extended analogies can tax the reader's endurance. A multi-page analogy between a heart and a pump would likely overwhelm the reader with all its talk of valves, hoses, pressures, and pumping.

Writing a Comparison

Planning and Drafting the Comparison

Don't write merely to fulfill an assignment; if you do, your paper will likely ramble aimlessly and fail to deliver a specific message. Instead, build your paper around a clear sense of purpose. Do you want to show the superiority of one product or method over another? Do you want to show how sitcoms today differ from those twenty years ago? Purpose governs the details you choose and the organization you follow.

Whether you select your own topic or write on an assigned one, answer these questions.

What purpose will my comparison serve?
Who will be my audience and why will they want to read the essay?
What points of similarity or difference will I discuss?

To develop the comparison, draw up a chart similar to this one.

Item A	Item B
First point of comparison	First point of comparison
Second point of comparison	Second point of comparison

Next, brainstorm each point in turn, recording appropriate supporting details. When you finish, stand back and ask these questions.

Do all the details relate to my purpose?
Do any new details come to mind?
In what order should I organize the details?

When you decide upon an order, copy the points of comparison and the details, arranged in the order you will follow, into a chart like the one below.

Item A	Item B
First point of comparison	First point of comparison
First detail	First detail
Second detail	Second detail
Second point of comparison	Second point of comparison

Use the introduction to identify your topic and arouse the reader's interest. If you intend to establish the superiority of one item over the other, you might call attention to your position. If you're comparing something unfamiliar with something familiar, you might explain the importance of understanding the unfamiliar item.

differences in the treatment accorded male and female workers. If you prefer the theme "Our Relationship to Nature," the essay "Innocence and Experience: Two Views of the River" could lead to a discussion, and then to papers, about how technology has altered our rapport with nature.

Depending on your class, you might help students learn to write from sources by having them compare essays in various ways. For instance, the class might discuss the ways people can relate to places and then, using examples from "Once More to the Lake" and "When the Full Moon . . . ," compare how E. B. White and John V. Young do so. As another option, students might read "The Company Man" and "The Sweet Smell of Success" and then compare the authors' views of our success-driven society. Assignments like these will require that you help students identify, use, and document key ideas in a source. Such assignments, while admittedly difficult, will make the writing of longer research papers less intimidating and help students handle future comparisons.

Organize the body of your paper according to whichever pattern—block or alternating—suits its length and the number of points you're planning to take up. If you explain something familiar by comparing it with something unfamiliar, start with the familiar item. If you try to show the superiority of one item over another, proceed from the less to the more desirable one. Note that both of the Pat-and-Mike outlines (page 111) put Mike ahead of Pat, the superior candidate.

Write whatever kind of conclusion will round off your discussion effectively. Many comparison papers end with a recommendation or a prediction. A paper comparing two brands of stereo receivers might recommend purchasing one of them. A paper comparing a familiar sport, such as football, with an unfamiliar one, such as rugby, might predict the future popularity of the latter. Unless you've written a lengthy paper, don't summarize the likenesses and differences you've presented. If you've done a proper writing job, your reader already has them clearly in mind.

Revising the Comparison

Revise your paper in light of the general guidelines in Chapter 3 and the questions that follow.

Have I accomplished my purpose, whether to choose between alternatives or acquaint the reader with something unfamiliar?
For something unfamiliar, have I shown clearly just how it is like and unlike the familiar item?
Have I consistently written with my audience in mind?
Have I considered all points of similarity and difference that relate to my purpose?
Have I included appropriate supporting details?
Are my comparisons arranged effectively?

EXAMPLE STUDENT ESSAY OF COMPARISON

Different Shifts, Different Actions

Claire Mutter

The nursing team in a small hospital meets the routine and special daily needs of patients. A registered professional nurse usually leads the team, and members often include registered and practical nurses, nurse's aides, and attendants. Although all nurses care for patients, the duties and working conditions of team members on the first and second shifts differ considerably.

The first shift begins at 7:00 A.M., when nurses awaken patients and prepare them for laboratory tests, X-rays, or medications. Additional nursing duties include taking temperatures, pulses, and respirations and giving enemas or preoperative injections. Team members also serve breakfast and then administer medications such as pain pills.

By this time doctors have arrived to visit their patients. The   3
nursing station swirls with activity. Doctors write new orders at desks cluttered with their patients' charts. Laboratory and X-ray technicians explain test results. The pharmacist brings medications and inquires about any new orders for drugs. Inhalation and physical therapists check charts for their new orders. The dietitian asks why Mr. Bowers is not eating his prescribed foods. Telephones ring and patients' signal lights flash continually. The members of the nursing team, all with their own duties, try desperately to keep up with these frenzied activities, which leaves little time to spend with their patients. This pace continues through most of the first shift.

Second shift team members, starting work at 3:00 P.M.,   4
usually can devote more attention to their patients' personal needs. To prepare for supper, nurses clear flowers and cards from tables, wash faces and hands where necessary, and position patients for eating comfort. After supper, when visitors have departed, team members inform patients about their conditions and teach them how to care for themselves after discharge. For example, they show diabetic patients how to administer insulin injections and to care for their skin, and tell them what foods to eat.

To prepare patients for the night, nurses straighten and   5
change beds and give back rubs and last medications. By 10:00 most patients are asleep. Calmness and quiet prevail at the nursing station, with only two or three nurses doing their charting— recording how patients have tolerated treatment and medication. Except for an occasional signal light from a patient, activities cease for the night.

Although both shifts have the same responsibilities, the care   6
and welfare of the patient, the second shift usually works in a much more relaxed atmosphere. Fewer staff people and a slower pace result in more personalized treatment.

DISCUSSION QUESTIONS

1. This phrase signals both the focus and the organization of the essay. The writer compares the first and second shifts on these two points of difference and in the indicated order.

2. Paragraphs 2–5 all contain effective supporting details. These details graphically show the differences between the two shifts.

3. This essay uses the block pattern. Paragraphs 2 and 3 discuss the first shift, paragraphs 4 and 5 the second shift.

4. The writer ends her third sentence by explaining a specialized term. Students should learn that when they introduce a term or concept the reader may not know, they should clarify its meaning in order to ensure communication.

DISCUSSION QUESTIONS

1. Comment on the significance of the phrase "the duties and working conditions" in paragraph 1.
2. Point out effective supporting details in the essay. What do they accomplish?
3. What pattern of organization does the writer use?
4. Explain why the writer ends the third sentence of paragraph 5 as follows: "recording how patients have tolerated treatment and medication." What can you learn from this explanation?

SUGGESTIONS FOR WRITING

1. **Write a comparison essay on one of the topics below or another that your instructor approves. Determine the points you will discuss and how you will develop and arrange them. Emphasize similarities, differences, or both.**

   a. A liberal arts versus a technical education
   b. The physical or mental demands of two jobs
   c. Two advertisements
   d. Parents versus teachers as educators
   e. Something natural and something artificial
   f. A novel and a movie that tell the same story
   g. Two instructors
   h. Two sportscasters or news commentators
   i. A television family and your family
   j. The business, residential, or slum districts of two cities or a wealthy and a working-class residential district in the same city
   k. A favorite social spot during the day and during the evening
   l. Suburban home life versus apartment life
   m. The effectiveness of two pieces of writing
   n. The working conditions on two jobs
   o. Two techniques for doing something in your field

2. **Develop an analogy based on one of the following sets of items or another set that your instructor approves. Proceed as you would for any other comparison.**

   a. The offerings in a college catalog and a restaurant
   b. A conquering army and a swarm of locusts
   c. An electric current and water flowing through a pipe
   d. A heart and a pump
   e. The structure of an atom and that of the solar system
   f. A teacher and a merchant
   g. Cancer and anarchy
   h. A parent and a farmer
   i. A brain and a telephone switchboard
   j. Earth and a spaceship

k. A camera and the human eye
  l. A workaholic and an alcoholic
m. A mob and a storm
  n. A kidney and a filter
  o. A cluttered attic and a disorderly mind

Cause and Effect: Explaining Why

Cause and effect, like the two sides of a coin, are inseparably linked and together make up *causation*. Cause probes the reasons why actions, events, attitudes, and conditions exist. Effect examines their consequences. Causation is important to us because it can explain historical events, natural happenings, and the actions and attitudes of individuals and groups. It can help us anticipate the consequences of personal actions, natural phenomena, or governmental policies.

Everyone asks and answers questions of causation. Scott wonders why Sue *really* broke off their relationship, and Jennifer speculates on the consequences of changing her major. People wonder why freeway shootings and homelessness are on the rise, and millions worry about the effects of escalating health care costs and budget deficits.

Inevitably, therefore, you will need to write papers and reports that employ causation. Your instructors might ask you to write on topics such as the causes of the American Revolution, the consequences of the federal budget deficit, the reasons why so many couples are divorcing, or the effects of different fertilizers on plant growth. An employer may want a report on why a certain product malfunctions, what might happen if a community redesigns its traffic pattern, or how a school closing might affect business.

PATTERNS IN CAUSAL ANALYSIS

Several organizational patterns are possible for a causal analysis. Sometimes, a single cause produces several effects. For instance, poor language skills prevent college students from keeping up with required reading, taking adequate notes, and writing competent papers and essay exams. To explore such a single cause–multiple effect relationship, construct an outline similar to the one following.

I. Introduction: identifies cause
II. Body
    A. Effect number 1
    B. Effect number 2
    C. Effect number 3
III. Conclusion

118

Alternatively, you might discuss the cause after the effects are presented.

On the other hand, several causes may join forces to produce one effect. Zinc production in the United States, for example, has decreased over the last few years because it can be produced more cheaply abroad than it can here, it is being replaced on cars by plastics and lighter metals, and it cannot be recycled. Here's how you might organize a typical multiple cause–single effect paper.

I.   Introduction: identifies effect
II. Body
    A. Cause number 1
    B. Cause number 2
    C. Cause number 3
III. Conclusion

Sometimes discussion of the effect follows the presentation of causes.

At times a set of events forms a causal chain, with each event the effect of the preceding one and the cause of the following one. For example, a student sleeps late and so misses breakfast and ends up hungry and distracted, which in turn results in a poor performance on an exam. Interrupting the chain at any point halts the sequence. Such chains can be likened to a row of upright dominoes that fall one after the other when the first one is pushed. Belief in a domino theory, which held that if one nation in Southeast Asia fell to the communists all would, one after the other, helped bring about U.S. entry into the Vietnam War. Causal chains can also help explain how devices function and some social changes proceed. The following outline typifies the arrangement of a paper explaining a causal chain.

I.   Introduction
II. Body
    A. Cause
    B. Effect
    C. Cause
    D. Effect
III. Conclusion

Papers of this kind resemble process analyses, but process is concerned with *how* the events occur, cause and effect with *why*.

In many situations the sequence of causes and effects is too complex to fit the image of a chain. Suppose you are driving to a movie on a rainy night. You approach an intersection screened by bushes and, because you have the right-of-way, start across. Suddenly a car with unlit headlights looms directly in your path. You hit the brakes but skid on the slippery pavement and crash into the other car, crumpling its left fender and damaging your own bumper. Later, as you think about the episode, you begin to sense its complexities.

Obviously, the *immediate cause* of the accident was the other driver's failure to heed the stop sign. But other causes also played roles: the bushes and unlit headlights that kept you from seeing the other car sooner; the starts and stops, speedups and slowdowns that brought the two cars to the intersection at the same time; the wet pavement you skidded on; and the movie that brought you out in the first place.

CLASSROOM ACTIVITIES

1. As with comparison, have students approach writing problems through a class discussion (possibly starting with small group projects) that helps establish the causes of a well-known problem—bad study habits, environmental pollution, or high absenteeism. Once these causes, and possibly the associated effects, are placed on the board, students can begin to determine the most coherent pattern to use. Similarly, such an activity could concentrate on the effects of an action or trend—raising the entrance requirements at a college, establishing or eliminating a class attendance policy, marrying later in life.

2. For an especially good class, you might note that causes fall into three categories: necessary causes, which must be present for an event to occur but may not be solely responsible for it; contributory causes, which help bring about, but cannot by themselves produce, an effect, which may also occur independently; sufficient causes, which can bring about effects all by themselves. To illustrate the first type, you might point out that watering a houseplant is necessary because it would otherwise die. For survival, though, the plant also needs proper sunlight, drainage, nutrients, and temperature. To illustrate a contributory cause, you could note that high winds may intensify but can't start a brush fire and also that the fire might occur without any wind. To illustrate a sufficient cause, you could point out that a dose of potassium cyanide by itself will kill a person. Indicate that the great majority of causes are either necessary or contributory.

You also realize that the effects of the accident go beyond the fender and bumper damage. After the accident, a police officer ticketed the other driver. As a result of the delay, you missed the movie. Further, the accident unnerved you so badly that you couldn't attend classes the next day and therefore missed an important writing assignment. Because of a bad driving record, the other driver lost his license for sixty days. Clearly, the effects of this accident rival the causes in complexity.

Here's how you might organize a multiple cause–multiple effect essay.

I.   Introduction
II. Body
   A. Cause number 1
   B. Cause number 2
   C. Cause number 3
   D. Effect number 1
   E. Effect number 2
   F. Effect number 3
III. Conclusion

In some situations, however, you might first present the effects, then turn to the causes.

EXERCISE

1. Read the following selection and then arrange the events in a causal chain.

> Although some folk societies still exist today, similar human groups began the slow process of evolving into more complex societies many millennia ago, through settlement in villages and through advances in technology and organizational structure. This gave rise to the second level of organization: civilized preindustrial, or "feudal," society. Here there is a surplus of food because of the selective cultivation of grains—and also because of the practice of animal husbandry. The food surplus permits both the specialization of labor and the kind of class structure that can, for instance, provide the leadership and command the manpower to develop and maintain extensive irrigation systems (which in turn makes possible further increases in the food supply). . . .

> Gideon Sjöberg, "The Origin and Development of Cities"

2. Trace the possible effects of the following occurrences:

a. You pick out a salad at the cafeteria and sit down to eat. Suddenly you notice a large green worm on one of the lettuce leaves.
b. As you leave your composition classroom, you trip and break your arm.
c. Your boss has warned you not to be late to work again. You are driving to work with ten minutes to spare when you get a flat tire.

EXERCISE ANSWERS

1.

Folk → societies	Settlement in villages, technological and organizational advances (effect)
Technological and organizational advances (cause)	Surplus of food (effect)
Feudal society, surplus of food (cause)	Specialization of labor, improved class structure (effect)
Specialization of labor, improved class structure (cause)	Irrigation systems, greater surplus of food (effect)

2. **a.** You might complain to the manager, become ill and have to cancel a shopping trip, scream and leave the restaurant, or remove the worm from the leaf and eat the salad.

REASONING ERRORS IN CAUSAL ANALYSIS

Ignoring Multiple Causes

An effect rarely stems from a single cause. The person who believes that permissive parents have caused the present upsurge of venereal disease or the one who blames television violence for the climbing numbers of emotionally disturbed children oversimplifies the situation. Permissiveness and violence perhaps did contribute to these conditions. Without much doubt, however, numerous other factors also played important parts.

Mistaking Chronology for Causation

Don't assume that just because one event followed another the first necessarily caused the second. This kind of faulty thinking feeds many popular superstitions. Horace walks under a ladder, later stubs his toe, and thinks that his path caused his pain. Sue breaks a mirror just before Al breaks their engagement; then she blames the cracked mirror. Many people once believed that the election of Herbert Hoover as President in 1928 brought on the Great Depression in 1929. Today some people believe that the testing of atomic weapons has altered our weather patterns. Don't misunderstand: one event *may* cause the next; but before you go on record with your conclusion, make sure that you're not dealing with mere chronology.

Confusing Causes with Effects

Young children sometimes declare that the moving trees make the wind blow. Similarly, some adults may think that Pam and Paul married because they fell in love, when in reality economic necessity mandated the vows, and love came later. Scan your evidence carefully in order to avoid such faulty assertions.

EXERCISE

1. **Which of the following statements point toward papers that will focus on causes? Which point toward papers focusing on effects? Explain your answers.**

   a. Most of the problems that plague newly married couples are the direct outgrowth of timidity and pride.

   b. The Marshall Plan was designed to aid the economic recovery of Europe after World War II.

   c. The smoke from burning poison ivy can bring on a skin rash and lung irritation.

   d. Popularity in high school stems largely from good looks, a pleasing personality, participation in school activities, the right friends, and frequent dates.

b. You might have to leave school for the remainder of the term, drop out of some kind of athletic competition, suffer complications that cause you to lose use of the arm, or, if the break is a simple one, merely miss a day's classes.
c. You might lose your job, fail to find another one that pays as well, and have to settle for a less comfortable and desirable lifestyle; your boss might impose a two-week layoff without pay, forcing you to postpone or cancel the purchase of some household item; or you might convince your boss that the tardiness was unavoidable.

PERSPECTIVE

A vast amount of faulty thinking stems from inept causal analysis. It's rather alarming to hear students reason that since they did better on a test when they didn't study, why bother in the future? As part of our responsibility to teach students how to think about causes, we should help them identify such errors.

TEACHING STRATEGY

Ask students to record examples of faulty causal analysis that they find in their academic and personal lives. Have them write a short paper identifying such errors, explaining why they are errors and examining the consequences.

EXERCISE ANSWERS
1. **a.** The phrasing "are the direct outgrowth of" identifies timidity and pride as *causes* of marital discord.
   b. The phrasing "was designed to aid" denotes a paper that will deal with *effects*, concentrating

on the ways in which the Marshall Plan aided European recovery.

c. The phrasing "can bring on" denotes that a skin rash and lung irritation are the *effects* of exposure to burning poison ivy.

d. This paper would explain the *causes* of high school popularity.

2. a. This paragraph deals with effects. These effects include making a color lighter by using a filter of the same color; making a color darker by using a filter of a complementary color; reducing or increasing atmospheric haze by the appropriate filter.

b. This paragraph deals with causes. The causes include the overfeeding of children by their parents; the availability of fast foods; the advertising of snack foods on TV; psychological factors such as nervousness, boredom, loneliness, insecurity, discontent with life, and indolence.

2. Identify which of the following paragraphs deals with causes, which with effects. List the causes and effects.

a.   Color filters offer three advantages in black-and-white photography. First, a particular color will be lightened by a filter of the same color. For example, in a photograph of a red rose in a dark blue vase, both will appear almost the same shade of gray if no filter is used. However, when photographed through a red filter, the rose will appear much lighter than the vase; and through a blue filter the vase will appear much lighter than the rose. This effect can be useful in emphasizing or muting certain objects in a photograph. Second, a particular color filter will darken its complementary color in the scene. Consequently, any orange object will appear darker than normal if a blue filter is used. Finally, color filters can reduce or increase atmospheric haze. For example, in a distant aerial shot there will often be so much haze that distant detail is obscured. To eliminate haze almost entirely, the photographer can use a deep red filter. On the other hand, if more haze is desired in order to achieve an artistic effect, varying shades of blue filters can be used.

Timothy Kelly

b.   Overeating, which has become a national pastime for millions of Americans, has several roots. For example, parents who are concerned that their children get enough to eat during the growing years overfeed them and thereby establish a lifetime overeating habit. The child who is constantly praised for cleaning up his plate experiences a sort of gratification later on as he cleans up all too many plates. The easy availability of so much food is a constant temptation for many people, especially the types of food served at fast food restaurants and merchandised in the frozen food departments of supermarkets. Equally tempting are all the snack foods constantly advertised on TV. But many people don't need temptation from the outside; their overeating arises from such psychological factors as nervousness, boredom, loneliness, insecurity, an overall discontent with life, or an aversion to exercise. Thus, overeating can actually be a symptom of psychological surrender to, or withdrawal from, the complexities and competition of modern life.

Kenneth Reichow

Writing a Causal Analysis

Planning and Drafting the Causal Analysis

Because you have probably speculated about the causes and effects of several campus, local, state, or national problems, writing this type of paper should pose no great difficulty. If you choose your own topic, perhaps your personal experience will suggest something promising. Topics such as "Why I Dislike (or Like) Foreign Cars" and "How My Father's (or Someone Else's) Death Has Changed My Life" might work well. Nonpersonal topics also offer writing possibilities. For instance, "What's Behind Teenage Suicides?" and "The Impact of Trade Tariffs on American Corporations" would allow you to draw on library resources.

The strategies on pages 12–18 can also help you find several topics. Answer these questions about each potential candidate.

What purpose will guide this writing?
Who is my audience? Will the topic interest them? Why or why not?
Shall I focus on causes, effects, or both?

Brainstorming your topic for supporting details should be easy. If you're dealing with causes, pose these questions about each one.

How significant is this cause?
Could it have brought about the effect by itself?
Does it form part of a chain?
Precisely how does it contribute to the effect?

For papers dealing with effects, substitute the following questions for the ones above.

How important is this effect?
What evidence will establish its importance?

Charting your results can help you prepare for writing the paper. To tabulate causes, use an arrangement like this one.

Cause	*Contribution to Effect*
First cause	Specific contribution
Second cause	Specific contribution

For effects, use this chart.

Effect	*Importance*
First effect	Why important
Second effect	Why important

TEACHING STRATEGIES

1. Spending class time on interesting issues can help students find a topic. You might assign the cause-and-effect essays in the Reader and then have the class discuss the ways people are affected by what they own or how they perceive others, the causes of the current fitness fad, or the problems women experience in business or school. Most students can relate to and write about these topics. Such discussions can also be personalized. For example, students might list, and then determine the underlying causes of, their goals or financial requirements.

2. Reinforce the notion of the writing purpose. It's one thing to write the Board of Control showing the negative effects of a certain school policy; it's quite another to objectively review the effects for an impartial judge.

3. Encourage students to write a short paragraph explaining why their target audience would be interested and what it would want to know.

4. Even after students analyze causes and effects, they often under-write their papers. Show students how to describe cause and effect and how to establish that one resulted from the other. It isn't enough to state that bad study habits affect grades. The writer must describe what these habits are and then show how they result in poor grasp of the material, poor test answers, and ultimately poor test scores.

ETHICAL ISSUES

Sometimes groups with vested interests issue reports that deliberately emphasize effects that support their position. Those opposed to a policy, for example, highlight its potentially negative effects, no matter how slim, and overlook the positive ones. Is this ethical? Does it make a difference if the report falsely pretends to be objective? What if the bias were overt? Is it ethical for a writer to oversimplify causes in order to lay blame on a particular individual or organization? Is it ethical for a gubernatorial candidate to attribute an increase in state crime to his/her opponent's policies, when in fact the nationwide crime rate rose by the same amount?

READER/THEME STRATEGIES

If you'd like to take up the themes "Who We Are" and "Life's Changes," you could explore the factors that contribute to a person's identity. Students could, after reading and discussing "My Wood" and "She's Your Basic L.O.L. in N.A.D.," write essays that deal with how their environments have shaped them. As another possibility, students could read and talk about "The Sweet Smell of Success Isn't All That Sweet," then do papers that tell why they picked their majors. If you prefer the theme "American Crises," essays such as "Why Women Managers Are Bailing Out" and "Why We Have Failed" can provide backdrops for a detailed discussion of an important problem facing the country and to papers about its causes and effects. Depending on your class, you might even have students do short research papers that build on one of the essays. They might explore the racial attitudes that underlie the conflict in "Momma's

Once your items are tabulated, examine them carefully for completeness. Perhaps you've overlooked a cause or effect or have slighted the significance of one you've already mentioned. Think about the order in which you'd like to discuss your items and prepare a revised chart that reflects your decision.

Use the opening of your paper to identify your topic and indicate whether you plan to discuss causes, effects, or both. You can signal your intention in a number of ways. To prepare for a focus on causes, you might use the words *cause, reason,* or *stem from,* or you might ask why something has occurred. To signal a paper on effects, you might use *effect, fallout,* or *impact,* or you might ask what has happened since something took place. Read these examples:

> ***Signals*** Midville's recent increase in street crime stems primarily from
> ***causes*** its curtailed educational program, lack of job opportunities for
> young people, and high rate of drug addiction.
>
> ***Signals effects*** Since my marriage to Rita, how has my social life changed?

At times you may choose some dramatic attention-getter. For a paper on the effects of radon, a toxic radioactive gas present in many homes, you might note that "Although almost everyone now knows about the hazards associated with smoking, eating high-cholesterol foods, and drinking excessively, few people are aware that just going home could be hazardous to one's health." If you use an arresting statement, be sure the content of your paper warrants it.

How you organize the body of the paper depends on your topic. Close scrutiny may reveal that one cause was indispensable; the rest merely played supporting roles. If so, discuss the main cause first. In analyzing your automobile mishap, which fits this situation, start with the failure of the other driver to yield the right-of-way; then fan out to any other causes that merit mentioning. Sometimes you'll find that no single cause was essential but that all of them helped matters along. Combinations of this kind lie at the heart of many social and economic concerns: inflation, depression, and urban crime rates, to name just a few. Weigh each cause carefully and rank them in importance. If your topic and purpose will profit from building suspense, work from the least important cause to the most important. Otherwise, reverse the order. For analyzing causal chains, chronological order works effectively.

If space won't permit you to deal adequately with every cause, pick out the two or three you consider most important and limit your discussion to them. To avoid giving your reader an oversimplified impression, note that other causes exist. Even if length poses no problem, don't attempt to trace every cause to some more remote cause and then to a still more remote one. Instead, determine some sensible cutoff point that accords with your purpose, and don't go beyond it.

Treat effects as carefully as you do causes. Keep in mind that effects often travel in packs, and try to arrange them in some logical order. If they occur together, consider order of climax. If one follows the other in a chainlike sequence, present them in that fashion. If space considerations dictate, limit your discussion to the most interesting or significant effects. Whatever order you choose for your paper, don't jump helter-skelter from cause to effect to cause in a way that leaves your reader bewildered.

As you write, don't restrict yourself to a bare-bones discussion of causes and effects. If, for instance, you're exploring the student parking problem on your campus, you might describe the jammed lots or point out that students often miss class by having to drive around and look for spots. Similarly, don't simply assert that the administration's insensitivity contributes to the problem. Instead, cite examples of the college's refusal to answer letters about the situation or to discuss it. To provide statistical evidence of the problem's seriousness, you might note the small number of lots, the limited spaces in each, and the approximate number of student cars on campus.

Causal analyses can end in several ways. A paper discussing the effects of acid rain on America's lakes and streams might specify the grave consequences of failing to deal with the problem or express the hope that something will be done. Frequently, writers use their conclusions to evaluate the relative importance of their causes or effects.

Revising the Causal Analysis

Follow the guidelines in Chapter 3 and answer these questions as you revise your causal analysis.

Have I made the right decision in electing to focus on causes, effects, or both?

Have I ferreted out all important causes and effects? Mistakenly labeled something as an effect merely because it follows something else? Confused causes with effects?

Am I dealing with a causal chain? An immediate cause and several supporting causes? Multiple causes and effects?

Have I presented my causes and effects in an appropriate order?

Have I supported my discussion with sufficient details?

EXAMPLE STUDENT ESSAY OF CAUSE AND EFFECT

Why Students Drop Out of College

Diann Fisher

Each fall a new crop of first-year college students, wavering   1
between high hopes for the future and intense anxiety about their
new status, scan college maps searching for their classrooms. They
have been told repeatedly that college is the key to a well-paying job,
and they certainly don't want to support themselves by flipping
hamburgers or working at some other dead-end job. So, notebooks at
the ready, they await what college has in store. Unfortunately many
of them—indeed over thirty percent—will not return after the first
year. Why do so many students leave? There are several reasons.

Encounter" or examine, after reading "The Company Man," the social and financial costs of workaholism. Finally, they might read "Momma's Encounter," "For My Indian Daughter," and "The Boy and the Bank Officer" and then look into the effects of various kinds of stereotyping.

Some find the academic program too hard, some lack the proper study habits or motivation, others fall victim to the temptations of the college environment, and a large group leave for personal reasons.

Not surprisingly, the academic shortcomings of college students have strong links to high school. In the past, a high-school student who lacked the ability or desire to take a college-preparatory course could settle for a diploma in general studies and afterward find a job with decent pay. Now that possibility scarcely exists, so many poorly prepared students feel compelled to try college. Getting accepted by some schools isn't difficult. Once in, though, the student who has taken nothing beyond general mathematics, English, and science faces serious trouble when confronted with college algebra, freshman composition, and biological or physical science. Most colleges do offer remedial courses and other assistance that may help some weaker students to survive. In spite of everything, however, many others find themselves facing ever-worsening grade-point averages and either fail or just give up.

Like academic shortcomings, poor study habits have their roots in high school, where even average students can often breeze through with a minimum of effort. In many schools, outside assignments are rare and so easy that they require little time or thought to complete. To accommodate slower students, teachers frequently repeat material so many times that slightly better students can grasp it without opening their books. And when papers are late, teachers often don't mark them down. This laxity produces students who can't or don't want to study, students totally unprepared for the rigorous demands of college. There, courses may require several hours of study each week in order to be passed with even a "C." In many programs, outside assignments are commonplace and demanding. Instructors expect students to grasp material after one explanation, and many won't accept late papers at all. Students who don't quickly develop disciplined study habits face a flood of low grades and failure.

Poor student motivation aggravates faulty study habits.

Students who thought high school was boring find even less allure in the more challenging college offerings. Lacking any commitment to do well, they shrug off assigned papers, skip classes, and avoid doing required reading. Over time, classes gradually shrink as more and more students stay away. With final exams upon them, some return in a last-ditch effort to salvage a passing grade, but by then it is too late. Eventually, repetition of this scenario forces the students out.

The wide range of freedoms offered by the college   5
environment can overwhelm even well-prepared newcomers. While students are in high school, parents are on hand to make them study, push them off to class, and send them to bed at a reasonable hour. Once away from home and parents, however, far too many students become caught up in a constant round of parties, dates, bull sessions, and other distractions that seem more fascinating than school work. Again, if such behavior persists poor grades and failure result.

Personal reasons also take a heavy toll of students who might   6
otherwise complete their programs successfully. Often, money problems are at fault. For example, a student may lose a scholarship or grant, fail to obtain needed work, or find that the family can no longer afford to help out. Some students succumb to homesickness; some are forced out an by illness, injury, or death in the family; and yet others become ill or injure themselves and leave to recuperate. Finally, a considerable number become disillusioned with their programs or the size, location, or atmosphere of their schools and decide not to return.

What happens to the students who drop out? Some re-enroll in   7
college later, often in less demanding two- and four-year schools that offer a better chance of academic success. Of the remainder, the great bulk find civilian jobs or enlist in the armed forces. Most, whatever their choice, go on to lead productive, useful lives. In the meantime, campus newcomers need to know about the dangers that tripped up so many of their predecessors and make every effort to avoid them.

DISCUSSION QUESTIONS

1. The thesis statement is the final two sentences of paragraph 1. Your better students may recognize that thesis statements sometimes consist of more than one sentence. You might point out that the second of these sentences forecasts the reasons for dropping out that the essay will discuss.
2. The causal chain is as follows: Failure of college-bound high-school students to take appropriate preparatory courses → difficulties of these students when faced with college courses → worsening grade-point average → final failure or decision to leave college.
3. This sentence, the topic sentence of the paragraph, links both the first and second reasons for students dropping out to high school.
4. Paragraphs 2–6 discuss causes, and paragraph 7 discusses effects.

**SUGGESTED
INSTRUCTOR READING**

Buchan, U. "Why and Because Method Really Works." Improving College and University Teaching 21 (1973): 273–74. Explains how a basic why–and–because question–answer strategy can be an effective teaching tool.

DISCUSSION QUESTIONS

1. Identify the thesis statement in this essay.
2. Trace the causal chain that makes up paragraph 2.
3. What is the function of the first sentence in paragraph 3?
4. In which paragraphs does the writer discuss causes? Effects?

SUGGESTIONS FOR WRITING ■ Use one of the topics below, or another that your instructor approves, to develop a causal analysis. Determine which causes and/or effects to consider. Scrutinize your analysis for errors in reasoning, settle on an organization, and write the essay.

1. Reasons why students fail college
2. The effect of some friend, acquaintance, or public figure on your life
3. Causes behind some disciplinary action
4. Effects of some choice you made
5. Why you are a _____ major
6. Effects of living in a dormitory, in your own apartment, or at home
7. Reasons why you are a Democrat, a Republican, or an Independent
8. Effects of pollution in your hometown or some other familiar place
9. Effects of your choice of college or of your decision to go to college
10. Reasons why you have a particular habit or participate in a particular sport
11. Effects on your life of winning the grand prize in a state lottery
12. Reasons why _____ is a popular public figure
13. Effects of some family crisis on your life
14. Causes or effects or both of some disease
15. Causes or consequences or both of some decision made by you or your family

CHAPTER 11

Definition: Establishing Boundaries

PERSPECTIVE

It's no accident that definition precedes argument since no rational argument, scientific theory, or philosophical position is possible without a precise definition of the terms involved. For Plato, knowledge is attained only when humans recognize the true nature of virtue or the good; his pursuit of wisdom was a search for definition. On the other hand, where there is confusion about the meaning of key terms, such as the often-disputed idea of "free elections," then communication, and even international negotiations, can break down. Many students, however, regard definitions as merely the subject matter of dictionaries, to be utilized only in moments of complete bewilderment. Besides knowing how to write definitions, students need to understand their relevance to thought and communication.

That movie was egregious.

Once the bandage is off the wound, swab the proud flesh with the disinfectant.

Speaking on statewide television, Governor Blaine called his opponent a left-winger.

Do you have questions? You're not alone. Many people would question the sentences above: "What does *egregious* mean?" "How can flesh be *proud?*" "What does the governor mean by *left-winger?* What specific policies does the opponent support that warrant this label?" To avoid puzzling and provoking your own readers, you'll often need to explain the meaning of some term. The term may be unfamiliar (egregious), used in an unfamiliar sense (proud flesh), or mean different things to different people (left-winger). Whenever you clarify the meaning of some term, you are *defining*.

Humans are instinctively curious. We start asking about meanings as soon as we can talk, and we continue to seek, as well as supply, definitions all through life. In school, instructors expect us to explain all sorts of literary, historical, scientific, technical, and social terms. On the job, a member of a company's Human Resources Department might prepare a brochure that explains the meaning of such terms as *corporate responsibility* and *product stewardship* for new employees. An accountant might define *statistical sampling inventory* in a report calling for a change in the inventory system. A special education teacher might write a memo explaining *learning disabled* to the rest of the staff.

When you define, you identify the features that distinguish a term, thereby putting a fence around it, establishing its boundaries, and separating it from all others. Knowing these features enables both you and your reader to use the term appropriately.

Sometimes a word, phrase, or sentence will settle a definition question. To clear up the mystery of "proud flesh," all you'd need to do is insert the parenthetical phrase (excessively swollen and grainy) after the word *proud*. But when you're dealing with new terms—*leveraged buyout, gene splicing,* and *computer virus* are

TEACHING STRATEGIES

1. Ask students where they have observed confusion or conflicts triggered by differing perceptions of what a term means. For a short assignment, they could write a report that names the term involved, identifies the different definitions, and describes the resulting difficulties.

2. Have students identify several key terms in their major field and report on their meaning and significance. This exercise demonstrates the practical importance of precise definitions in every occupation.

3. To demonstrate that words change meaning and can have several meanings, have students use the *Oxford English Dictionary* and report on the evolution of a particular word.

examples—brief definitions won't provide the reader with enough information for proper understanding.

Abstract terms—those standing for things we can't see, touch, or otherwise detect with our five senses—often require extended definitions, too. It's impossible to capture the essence of *democracy* or *hatred* or *bravery* in a single sentence: the terms are too complex, and people have too many differing ideas about what they mean. The same holds true for some concrete terms—those standing for actions and things we can perceive with our five senses. Some people, for instance, limit the term *drug pusher* to full-time sellers of hard drugs like cocaine and heroin. Others, at the opposite extreme, extend the term to full- and part-time sellers of any illegal drug. Writing an argument recommending life sentences for convicted drug pushers would require you to tell just what you mean by the term so that the reader would have solid grounds for judging your position.

TYPES OF DEFINITIONS

Three types of definitions—synonyms, essential definitions, and extended definitions—serve writers' needs. Although the first two seldom require more than a word or a sentence, an extended definition can run to several pages. The three types, however, are related. Synonyms and essential definitions share quarters between the covers of dictionaries, and both furnish starting points for extended definitions.

Synonyms

Synonyms are words with very nearly the same meanings. *Lissome* is synonymous with *lithe* or *nimble*, and *condign* is a synonym of *worthy* and *suitable*. Synonyms let writers clarify meanings of unfamiliar words without using cumbersome explanations. To clarify the term *expostulation* in a quoted passage, all you'd have to do is add the word *objection*, in brackets, after it. Because synonyms are not identical twins, using them puts a slightly different shade of meaning on a message. For example, to "protest" and to "object" are certainly similar in many ways. Yet the claim that we "object" to the establishment of a nuclear power plant in our area fails to capture the active and sustained commitment implied in our willingness to "protest" against the same plant. Still, synonyms provide an easy, convenient means of breaking communications logjams.

Essential Definitions

An essential definition does three things: (1) names the item being defined, (2) places it in a broad category, and (3) distinguishes it from other items in that category. Here are three examples.

Item Being Defined	Broad Category	Distinguishing Features
A howdah	is a covered seat	for riding on the back of an elephant or camel.
A voiceprint	is a graphical record	of a person's voice characteristics.
To parboil	is to boil meat, vegetables, or fruits	until they are partially cooked.

Writing a good essential definition requires careful thought. Suppose your instructor has asked you to write an essential definition of one of the terms listed in an exercise, and you choose "vacuum cleaner." Coming up with a broad category presents no problem: a vacuum cleaner is a household appliance. The hard part is pinpointing the distinguishing features. The purpose of a vacuum cleaner is to clean floors, carpets, and upholstery. You soon realize, however, that these features alone do not separate vacuum cleaners from other appliances. After all, carpet sweepers also clean floors, and whisk brooms clean upholstery. What then does distinguish vacuum cleaners? After a little thought, you realize that, unlike the other items, a vacuum cleaner works by suction. You then write the following definition.

A vacuum cleaner is a household appliance that uses suction to clean floors, carpets, and upholstery.

The same careful attention is necessary to establish the distinguishing features of any essential definition.

Limitations of Essential Definitions.
Essential definitions have certain built-in limitations. Because of their brevity, they often can't do full justice to abstract terms such as *cowardice, love, jealousy, power*. Problems also arise with terms that have several settled meanings. To explain *jam* adequately, you'd need at least three essential definitions: (1) a closely packed crowd, (2) preserves, and (3) a difficult situation. But despite these limitations, an essential definition can be useful by itself or as part of a longer definition. Writers often build an extended definition around an essential definition.

Pitfalls in Preparing Essential Definitions.
When you prepare an essential definition, guard against these flaws:

Circular definition. Don't define a term by repeating it or changing its form slightly. Saying that a psychiatrist is "a physician who practices psychiatry" will only frustrate someone who's never heard of psychiatry. Repress circularity and provide the proper insight by choosing terms the reader can relate to, for example, "A psychiatrist is a physician who diagnoses and treats mental disorders."

Overly broad definition. Shy away from definitions that embrace too much territory. If you define a skunk as "an animal that has a bushy tail and black fur with white markings," your definition is not precise. Many cats and dogs also fit this description. But if you add "and that ejects a foul-smelling secretion when threatened," you will clear the air, of any misconceptions at least.

fundamental to Western analytic thought. Although most obvious in the sciences, this approach is crucial in every other field. Thus filmmakers use it to distinguish camera shots and bankers to categorize mortgages. Because nearly every idea they encounter will involve one or more essential definitions, students should appreciate the power of these definitions to organize the conceptual world.

TEACHING STRATEGIES

1. You might point out that this chapter functions as an extended definition by providing several distinguishing features of the strategy it discusses.
2. Students often believe that dictionary definitions are completely objective and unchanging. You might point out that dictionaries are compiled on the basis of common usage. It is interesting to compare the definitions of controversial words—"rebel" for instance—in dictionaries from several different historical periods. Students might also examine several definitions to determine any latent, and possibly questionable, assumptions. Those, for example, who have faith in astrology would dispute a definition calling it "a pseudoscience claiming that the relative positions of the stars, planets, sun, and moon can be used to foretell the future."

EXERCISE ANSWERS (p. 132)

1. Key: broad category// distinguishing traits
a. Gangue is useless rock// accompanying valuable minerals in a deposit.
b. A catbird is a small American songbird//with a slate-colored body, a black cap, and a catlike cry.

c. A soldier is a man or woman//serving in an army.
d. Myelin is a white, fatty substance//that forms a sheath around some nerve fibers.
e. A gargoyle is a waterspout//carved in the likeness of a grotesque animal or imaginary creature and projecting from the gutter of a building.
f. A magnum is a wine bottle//that holds about two-fifths of a gallon.
2. Identifying good and bad essential definitions and correcting the bad ones.
a. This definition is good.
b. This is a circular definition. A person who didn't know the meaning of "puritan" would not know the meaning of "puritanical." Change to "A puritan is a person with strict moral and religious views."
c. This definition does not name a broad category. Change to "A kraal is a fenced enclosure where South African tribes keep large domestic animals."
d. This definition is too narrow; rifles are used for other purposes besides hunting. Change to "A rifle is a firearm that has a grooved barrel and is used primarily for hunting large game and as a military weapon."
e. This definition is too broad; bicycles also fit the definition. Change to "A motorcycle is a two-wheeled vehicle powered by a gasoline engine and used mainly for human transportation."
f. This definition does not name a broad category. Change to "Fainting is a condition in which a person loses consciousness due to an inadequate flow of blood to the brain."

Overly narrow definition. Don't hem in your definition too closely, either. "A kitchen blender is a bladed electrical appliance used to chop foods" illustrates this error. Blenders perform other operations, too. To correct the error, add the missing information. "A kitchen blender is a bladed electrical appliance used to chop, mix, whip, liquefy, or otherwise process foods."

Omission of main category. Avoid using "is where" or "is when" instead of naming the main category. Here are examples of this error. "A bistro is where food and wine are served" and "An ordination is when a person is formally recognized as a minister, priest, or rabbi." The reader will not know exactly what sort of thing (a bar? a party?) a *bistro* is and may think that *ordination* means a time. Note the improvement when the broad categories are named: "A bistro is a small restaurant where both food and wine are served" and "An ordination is a ceremony at which a person is formally recognized as a minister, priest, or rabbi."

EXERCISE

1. Identify the broad category and the distinguishing traits in each of these essential definitions.

   a. Gangue is useless rock accompanying valuable minerals in a deposit.
   b. A catbird is a small American songbird with a slate-colored body, a black cap, and a catlike cry.
   c. A soldier is a man or woman serving in an army.
   d. Myelin is a white, fatty substance that forms a sheath around some nerve fibers.
   e. A gargoyle is a waterspout carved in the likeness of a grotesque animal or imaginary creature and projecting from the gutter of a building.
   f. A magnum is a wine bottle that holds about two-fifths of a gallon.

2. Indicate which of the following statements are acceptable essential definitions. Explain what is wrong with those that are not. Correct them.

   a. A scalpel is a small knife that has a sharp blade used for surgery and anatomical dissections.
   b. A puritan is a person with puritanical beliefs.
   c. A kraal is where South African tribespeople keep large domestic animals.
   d. A rifle is a firearm that has a grooved barrel and is used for hunting large game.
   e. A motorcycle is a two-wheeled vehicle used mainly for human transportation.
   f. Fainting is when a person loses consciousness owing to inadequate flow of blood to the brain.

3. Write an essential definition for each of the following terms.

   a. groupie   c. hit man   e. pushover
   b. happy hour d. jock   f. hard grader

Extended Definitions

Sometimes it's necessary to go beyond an essential definition and write a paragraph or whole paper explaining a term. New technical, social, and economic terms often require extended definitions. To illustrate, a computer scientist might need to define *data integrity* so that computer operators understand the importance of maintaining it. Terms with differing meanings also frequently require extended definitions. To let voters know just what he means by *left-winger*, Governor Blaine might detail the kinds of legislation his opponent favors and opposes. Furthermore, extended definition is crucial to interpretation of the law, as we see when courts clarify the meaning of concepts such as obscenity.

Extended definitions are not merely academic exercises; they are fundamental to your career and your life. A police officer needs to have a clear understanding of what counts as *reasonable grounds for search and seizure*; an engineer must comprehend the meaning of *stress*; a nuclear medical technologist had better have a solid grasp of *radiation.* And all of us are concerned with the definition of our basic rights as citizens.

Extended definitions are montages of other methods of development—narration, description, process analysis, illustration, classification, comparison, and cause and effect. Often, they also define by negation: explaining what a term *does not* mean. The following paragraphs show how one writer handled an extended definition of "sudden infant death syndrome." The student began by presenting a case history (illustration), which also incorporated an essential definition and two synonyms.

> Jane and Dick Smith were proud, new parents of an eight-pound, ten-ounce baby girl named Jenny. One summer night, Jane put Jenny to bed at 8:00. When she went to check on her at 3:00 A.M., Jane found Jenny dead. The baby had given no cry of pain, shown no sign of trouble. Even the doctor did not know why she had died, for she was healthy and strong. The autopsy report confirmed the doctor's suspicion—the infant was a victim of the "sudden infant death syndrome," also known as SIDS or crib death. SIDS is the sudden and unexplainable death of an apparently healthy, sleeping infant. It is the number-one cause of death in infants after the first week of life and as a result has been the subject of numerous research studies.

DISCUSSION QUESTIONS

1. What synonyms does the writer use?
2. Which sentence presents an essential definition?

In the next paragraph, the writer turned to negation, pointing out some of the things that researchers have ruled out about SIDS.

> Although researchers do not know what SIDS is, they do know what it is <u>not</u>. They know it cannot be predicted; it strikes like a thief in the night. Crib deaths occur in seconds, with no sound of pain, and they always happen when the child is sleeping. Suffocation is <u>not</u> the cause, nor

3. Writing essential definitions
a. A groupie is a girl who follows after rock bands or celebrities in the hope of forming a close attachment.
b. A happy hour is a period of time, usually from late afternoon to early evening, when a bar or restaurant sells alcoholic drinks at reduced prices.
c. A hit man is a criminal who specializes in assassinations.
d. A jock is a man or woman who is dedicated to athletic participation.
e. A pushover is a person who is easily swindled, defeated, or persuaded *OR* a pushover is anything that can be accomplished without significant effort.
f. A hard grader is an instructor who sets especially high standards for his or her students.

TEACHING STRATEGY

A common problem in student and professional writing is purposeful or accidental equivocation, that is, subtly changing the meaning of a term. In opposing the legalization of drugs, a writer might start by using "drugs" to refer to heroin, cocaine, and the like, but later, after establishing the danger of these drugs, shift the term so that it also covers marijuana. The arguments against legalizing marijuana then become the same as those directed against the harder drugs, despite the real differences between marijuana and the others. You could ask students to look for instances of equivocation in their own, and even professional, writing, or bring in illustrative examples yourself.

DISCUSSION QUESTIONS
1. The writer uses the synonym "crib death" for "sudden infant death syndrome."
2. The next-to-the-last one.

is aspiration or regurgitation. Researchers have found no correlation between the incidence of SIDS and the mother's use of birth control pills or tobacco or the presence of fluoride in water. Since it is not hereditary or contagious, only a slim chance exists that SIDS will strike twice in the same family.

Finally, the student explored several proposed causes of SIDS as well as how parents may react to the loss of their child.

As might be expected, researchers have offered many theories concerning the cause of crib death. Dr. R. C. Reisinger, a National Cancer Institute scientist, has linked crib deaths to the growth of a common bacterium, E. coli, in the intestines of newborn babies. The organisms multiply in the intestines, manufacturing a toxin that is absorbed by the intestinal wall and passes into the bloodstream. Breast milk stops the growth of the organism, whereas cow's milk permits it. Therefore, Dr. Reisinger believes, bottle-fed babies run a higher risk of crib death than other babies. . . .

The loss of a child through crib death is an especially traumatic experience. Parents often develop feelings of guilt and depression, thinking they somehow caused the child's death. To alleviate such feelings, organizations have been established to help parents accept the fact that they did not cause the death.

Trudy Stelter

*W*RITING AN EXTENDED DEFINITION

Planning and Drafting the Extended Definition

If you choose your own topic, pick an abstract term or one that is concrete but unfamiliar to your reader. Why, for instance, define *table* when the discussion would likely ease the reader into the Land of Nod? On the other hand, a paper explaining *computer virus* might well prove interesting and informative. Use one of the strategies on pages 12–18 to unearth promising topics. Then answer these questions about them.

Which topic holds the most promise? Why?
What purpose will guide my writing? To clarify a technical or specialized concept? To show what the term means to me? To persuade the reader to adopt my attitude toward it? To discuss some neglected facet of it?
For what audience should I write?

PERSPECTIVE
As with all writing, having a clear purpose and a definite audience helps ensure the success of student definition papers. In addition, students need to spend considerable time evaluating their particular concepts or terms—reading what others have written, discussing aspects with peers, and doing ample brainstorming. Students often assume that because of their general familiarity with terms such as "friendship," "stubbornness," "greed," or "stress," they can crank out papers defining them off the tops of their heads. Not so.

Here's a helpful process to follow as you think your definition through. First, select a clear example that illustrates what you wish to define: the United States could exemplify *democracy*. Then brainstorm to uncover major identifying characteristics. For democracy your list might include majority rule, free elections, a separately elected chief executive, and basic human rights. Next, test these characteristics against other legitimate examples and retain only the characteristics that apply. Britain is clearly a democracy but doesn't have a separately elected chief executive. Finally, test the unfolding definition against a clear counter example, perhaps the People's Republic of China. If the definition fits the example, something is wrong.

Now evaluate what methods you might use to develop your definition. Each method has its own set of special strengths, as the following list shows.

Narration. Tracing the history of a new development or the changing meaning of a term

Description. Pointing out interesting or important features of a device, an event, or an individual

Process. Explaining what a device does or how it is used, how a procedure is carried out, or how a natural event takes place

Illustration. Tracing changes in meaning and defining abstract terms

Classification. Pointing out the different categories into which an item or an event can be grouped

Comparison. Distinguishing between an unfamiliar and a familiar item

Cause and effect. Explaining the origins and consequences of events, conditions, problems, and attitudes

Negation. Placing limitations on conditions and events and correcting popular misconceptions

Examine your topic in light of this listing and select the methods of development that seem most promising. Don't hesitate to use a method for some purpose not mentioned here. If you think that a comparison will help your reader understand some abstract term, use it.

Chart the methods of development you'll use, and then brainstorm each method in turn to gather the details that will inform the reader. When you've finished, look everything over, rearrange the details as necessary, add any new ones you think of, and prepare a revised chart. The example below is for a paper utilizing four methods of development.

Narration	*Classification*	*Process*	*Negation*
First supporting detail	First supporting detail	First supporting detail	First supporting detail
Second supporting detail	Second supporting detail	Second supporting detail	Second supporting detail

Definition papers can begin in various ways. If you're defining a term with no agreed-upon meaning (for example, *conservatism*), you might note some differing views of it and then state your own. If the term reflects some new social, political, a politician might exaggerate a definition of "liberal" or "conservative" and then apply it to an opponent who only marginally fits the embellished definition but who would, under more traditional uses of the term, be considered liberal or conservative. Are such equivocations ethical?

READER/THEME STRATEGIES

If you elect to deal with the theme "Who We Are," many reading selections could lead to a definition paper. Students might read and discuss such essays as "The Bureaucrat," "The Company Man," and "The Sweet Smell of Success Isn't All That Sweet" and then write their definitions of such personal characteristics as charisma, cuteness, aggressiveness, or assertiveness or of such personal accomplishments as success and happiness. If you prefer the theme "Our Relationship to Nature," students might read essays like "Innocence and Experience," "Once More to the Lake," and "Why We Have Failed," discuss them, and then define waterway, wilderness area, or environmentalism.

Depending on your class, you could develop an assignment that calls for writing from sources. Students could compare implicit and explicit definitions of success in "The Company Man" and "The Sweet Smell of Success" and even "How to Give a Speech," which has to do with achieving success at the podium. Here too is an opportunity for students to discuss and define successful writing.

economic, or technological development (such as *macroengineering*), you might mention the events that brought it into being. A colloquial or slang term often lends itself nicely to an attention-getting opener. A paper defining *chutzpah* might begin by illustrating the brash behavior of someone with this trait. Often an introduction includes a short definition, perhaps taken from a dictionary. If you do include a dictionary definition, use the dictionary's full name (*Webster's New World Dictionary* says . . .). Several dictionary titles include the word *Webster*, and unless you use the full name your reader won't know which one you mean. Draw on a dictionary definition, however, only as a last resort.

In writing the body of the paper, present the methods of development in whatever order seems most appropriate. A paper defining *drag racing* might first describe the hectic scene as the cars line up for a race, then classify the different categories of vehicles, and finally explain the steps in a race. One defining *intellectual* might start by showing the differences between intellectuals and scholars, then name several prominent intellectuals and note how their insights have altered our thinking, and conclude by trying to explain why many Americans hold intellectuals in low regard.

Definition papers can end, as well as begin, in a number of ways. If you're defining some undesirable condition or event (such as the "sudden infant death syndrome"), you might express hope for a speedy solution. If you're reporting on some new development (like macroengineering), you might predict its economic or social impact. Often, a summary of your main points is effective. Choose whichever type of ending best supports your main idea.

Revising the Extended Definition

Use the general guidelines in Chapter 3 and these specific questions as you revise your extended definition.

Are my purpose and audience clear and appropriate?
If I've used an essential definition, does it do what it should and avoid the common pitfalls?
Are the methods of development suitable for the topic?
Is the paper organized effectively?
Are there other factors or examples I need to consider?

EXAMPLE STUDENT ESSAY OF DEFINITION

The Food Chain

Michael Galayda

It is a truism that we must eat to stay alive and that all the   1

plants and animals we dine on must do the same. How many of us,

though, ever stop to consider whether or not any pattern underlies

all the cross-dining that goes on? There is a pattern, and to understand it we must first familiarize ourselves with the concept of a food chain. Such a chain can be defined as a hierarchy of organisms in a biological community, or ecosystem, with each member of the chain feeding on the one below it and in turn being fed upon by the one above it. To put the matter more simply, a food chain starts with a great quantity of plant stuffs which are eaten by a large number of very hungry diners. These diners are then eaten by a lesser number of other animals, which in turn fall prey to an even smaller number of creatures. With the passage of time, the uneaten organisms die and become part of the soil for the plant to grow in.

To illustrate, let's look for a moment at one particular biological community, a marshy ecosystem, and a few events that might take place there. First, there are the marsh grasses, with millions of grasshoppers busily feeding upon them. When one grasshopper isn't looking, a shrew sneaks up and eats it. This process is repeated many times as the day wears on. Later, toward sunset, as the stuffed and inattentive shrew is crossing an open stretch of ground, a hawk swoops out of the sky and eats the rodent. The food chain is completed when the marsh hawk dies and its corpse fertilizes the marsh grasses.

This illustration is not meant to suggest that hawks eat only shrews or shrews eat only grasshoppers; the cycle is much more complicated than that, involving what biologists call trophic levels— the different feeding groups in an ecosystem. For example, some creatures eat green plants and some eat meat. There are five major trophic levels. The beginning point for any food chain is green plants, known as producers, which absorb sunlight and through the process of photosynthesis turn carbon dioxide, water, and soil nutrients into food, especially carbohydrates, that animals can assimilate.

All of the other life forms subsist either directly or indirectly on the producers. Animals that feed directly on green plants are the herbivores, called primary consumers. This group includes, among other creatures, most insects, most rodents, and hooved animals. The

2

3

4

TEACHING STRATEGY
Given the difficult and often slippery nature of extended definitions, caution students to revise not only the form but also the substance of their drafts with great care. They could write out a revision plan that details appropriate questions they've asked and answered.

secondary consumers are the carnivores and omnivores. The term "carnivore," meaning an animal that eats only flesh, is more familiar than the term "omnivore," which designates an animal that eats both green plants and flesh. Carnivores include such animals as lions, leopards, eagles, and hawks; whereas omnivores are represented by foxes, bears, humans, and so on.

The last feeding group in the food chain consists of the decomposers: bacteria and fungi. These microorganisms recycle the waste products of living animals and the remains of all dead things—plants, herbivores, omnivores, and carnivores alike—into fertilizers that plants, the producers, can use. 5

Obviously each trophic level must produce more energy than it transfers to the next higher level. With animals, a considerable part of this energy is lost through body heat. The muscles that pump the lungs, continually pushing air out of the body and sucking it back in, consume energy. The muscles in the arms and legs sweat out energy. All of the life-supporting systems of the organism use energy to keep it going. Everything from worms to people lives in accordance with this law of energy loss. As long as life's fires burn, energy is lost, never to be regained. 6

Throughout history we humans have tried to manipulate the food chain so as to provide ever-greater outputs of energy. On the one hand, we have tried, by whatever means we could employ, to rid our fields of harmful birds, insects, and rodents, and our animals of diseases and parasites. On the other, we have constantly striven to produce healthier and more productive strains of plants and animals. Often these attempts have been spectacularly successful. Sometimes, though, the results have proved disastrous, as with the insecticide DDT. 7

Farmers first began using DDT on a large scale in 1946, right after it had proved its effectiveness in tropical military operations in World War II. As expected, the product proved equally effective as an agricultural pesticide, but there were some unexpected and disastrous side effects. The difficulties were caused by excessive DDT washing off crops, entering irrigation canals, and from there flowing 8 to streams, rivers, and lakes. All living creatures in the path of the chemical were contaminated—worms, fish, ducks, indeed all forms of aquatic life. Contaminated worms poisoned songbirds, causing massive dieoffs of birds, and many humans developed serious health problems from eating contaminated aquatic animals. Although Congress has severely restricted the use of DDT in this country, the whole episode stands as a warning of what can happen when humans manipulate the food chain.

As time continues and the population grows, efforts will be made to further increase the food supply. Let us hope that in doing so we won't act in haste and create catastrophes of even greater magnitude.

9

DISCUSSION QUESTIONS

1. Identify the essay's essential definition and explain how it functions.
2. What is accomplished by the last three sentences in paragraph 1?
3. What method of development does the writer use in paragraph 2?
4. What methods of development are combined in paragraphs 3–5?
5. Cite three places in the essay where the writer uses brief definitions.

SUGGESTIONS FOR WRITING ■ Write an extended definition using one of the following suggestions or one approved by your instructor. The term you define may be new, misused, misunderstood, or may have a disputed meaning. Develop the essay by any combination of writing strategies.

1. Liberal arts (or vocational) education
2. 50s and 60s nostalgia
3. Routine
4. Culture
5. Stress
6. Charisma
7. Marriage
8. Boss
9. Greed in America
10. Computer virus
11. Macho man
12. Feminist
13. Angst
14. Fax communication
15. Some term from your field

DISCUSSION QUESTIONS

1. The essential definition occurs in paragraph 1: "Such a chain can be defined. . . ." The definition is proper because it names the chain, places it in a broad category ("a hierarchy of organisms"), and distinguishes it from other items (each member "feeding on the one below it and in turn being fed upon by the one above it.").

2. The writer shows the operation of the food chain in general terms. The chain assumes more concrete form later in the essay.

3. The writer uses the illustrations of the marsh grass, grasshopper, shrew, and marsh hawk to define the operation of the food chain. "To illustrate" at the start of the paragraph signals this method.

4. Paragraphs 3–5 rely primarily on process analysis. The food chain is traced from "The beginning point" (paragraph 3) to "The last feeding group" (paragraph 5), which starts the whole cycle over again. Illustrations and specific examples are also used to clarify the process. Students should note that two methods of development are often interwoven in an extended definition.

5. Brief definitions include "trophic levels" in paragraph 3 and "herbivore," "carnivore," and "omnivore" in paragraph 4.

Argument: Convincing Others

The idea of argument poses a dilemma for some students. Used to being tested on factual matters, they often view an argumentative position as either completely justified or completely unjustified. Students need to understand that such is rarely the case, that justification is a matter of degree, with some positions more justified than others. This knowledge can in turn create further confusion, for if there is some justification for both of two opposing positions, isn't any final judgment of their merits arbitrary? At times such confusion can become emotionally distressing to students. Who are they, after all, to reach a conclusion, and won't someone attack their position? For these students, argument is a problem because it presents an unfamiliar situation which forces them to deal with matters that are not cut and dried.

TEACHING STRATEGIES

1. Have students list the issues they have debated or read about. They might point out the different positions and assess their relative strengths.
2. Bring in the "Debate" page of *USA Today.* Each day this paper publishes an editorial on some current, controversial issue as well as one or more differing viewpoints. By reading this page, students will see the essence of argument.
3. Have students write summaries of arguments they read. When they identify the various claims and evidence, students begin to appreciate the nature and structure of argument and can start thinking about possible topics for their own papers.

"What did you think of that movie?"

"Great!"

"What do you mean, *great*? I thought the acting was wooden and the story completely unbelievable."

"That's about what I'd expect from you. You wouldn't know a good movie if it walked up and bit you."

"Oh yeah? What makes you think you're such a great . . . ?"

Argument or quarrel? Many people would ask, "What's the difference?" To them, the two terms convey the same meaning, both calling to mind two angry, red-faced people, shouting, trading insults, and sometimes slugging it out. In writing, however, *argument* stands for something quite different: a paper, grounded on logical, structured evidence, that attempts to convince the reader to accept an opinion, take some action, or do both.

A knowledge of argument will help you succeed both in class and on the job. A business instructor may ask students to defend a particular management style. A political science instructor may want you to support or oppose limiting the number of terms that members of Congress can serve. A special education instructor may have students make a written case for increased funding for exceptional students. In the workplace, a computer programmer may argue that the company should change its account-keeping program, an automotive service manager call for new diagnostic equipment, and a union president make a case that a company's employees merit raises.

Arguments don't always involve conflicts. Some simply support a previously established decision or course of action, as when a department manager sends her boss a memo justifying some new procedure that she implemented. Others try to establish some common ground, just as you might do when you and your date weigh the pros and cons of two films and pick one to see.

When preparing to write an argument, you need to be aware that certain kinds of topics just aren't arguable. There's no point, for instance, in trying to tackle questions of personal preference or taste (is red prettier than blue?) Such contests quickly turn into "it is," "it isn't" exchanges that establish nothing except the silliness of the contenders. Questions of simple fact (Was Eisenhower first elected

President in 1952?) don't qualify either; one side has all the ammunition. Bickering will never settle these issues; reference books quickly will. We turn to argument when there is room for disagreement.

When you write an argument, you don't simply sit down and dash off your views as though they came prefabricated. Instead, argument represents an opportunity to think things through, to gradually, and often tentatively, come to some conclusions, and then, in stages, begin to draft your position with the support you have discovered. You should try to keep an open mind as you formulate and then express your views.

The most successful arguments rest on a firm foundation of solid, logical support. In addition, many arguments include emotion because it can play an important part in swaying reader opinion. Furthermore, writers often make ethical appeals by projecting favorable images of themselves since readers form conclusions based on their judgments of the writer.

THE RATIONAL APPEAL

In society, and certainly in professional circles, you are usually expected to reach your conclusions on the basis of good reasons and appropriate evidence. Reasons are the key points you'll use to defend your conclusions. If, for instance, you oppose the Strategic Defense Initiative anti-missile system, one reason may be its staggering cost. If you favor SDI, one reason may be the need to defend our country as well as its bases and fighting forces stationed around the globe, perhaps against a Third World missile attack.

To convince readers, your reasons must be substantiated by evidence. If you're against SDI, you could cite figures that project the large cost; if you're for the system, you might quote a respected authority on the Third World threat.

When you appeal to reason in an argument, then, you present your reasons and evidence in such a way that if your readers are also reasonable they will agree with you. That assumes, of course, that you and your readers start with some common ground about the principles you share and what you count as evidence. Evidence falls into several categories: established truths, opinions of authorities, statistical findings, and personal experience. The strongest arguments usually combine several types of evidence.

Established Truths

These are facts that no one can seriously dispute. Here are some examples.

Historical fact   The First Amendment to the United States Constitution prohibits Congress from abridging freedom of the press.

Scientific fact   The layer of ozone in the earth's upper atmosphere protects us from the sun's harmful ultraviolet radiation.

jection seems reasonable, the student might reconsider the "truth." Or students might develop their own lists of established truths on a given topic and verify them.

CLASSROOM ACTIVITY

You could list so-called established truths on the board and have students discuss which ones qualify. Or students might develop their own list on a given topic, which could be discussed in class.

Geographical fact   The western part of the United States has tremendous reserves of coal.

Established truths aren't arguable themselves but do provide strong backup for argumentative propositions. For example, citing the abundant coal supply in the western regions could support an argument that the United States should return to coal to supply its energy needs.

Some established truths, the result of careful observations and thinking over many years, basically amount to enlightened common sense. The notion that everyone possesses a unique combination of interests, abilities, and personality characteristics illustrates this kind of truth. Few people would seriously question it.

Opinions of Authorities

An authority is a recognized expert in some field. Authoritative opinions—the only kind to use—play a powerful role in winning readers over to your side. The views of metropolitan police chiefs and criminologists could support your position on ways to control urban crime. Researchers who have investigated the effects of air pollution could help you argue for stricter smog-control laws. Whatever your argument, don't settle for less than heavyweight authorities, and indicate their credentials to your reader.

The following paragraph, from an article arguing that extra-high-voltage electric transmission lines pose a health hazard, illustrates the use of authority.

CLASSROOM ACTIVITY

You might present students with the names, and brief biographies, of authorities who might address a specific topic. In small groups students could assess the knowledge and possible biases of each authority and then do a ranking. Groups could then compare their conclusions in a class discussion.

Robert Becker, a physician and director of the Orthopedic–Biophysics Laboratory at the Syracuse, New York, Veterans Administration Hospital—Upstate Medical Center, has been researching the effects of low-frequency electric fields (60 Hz) for fifteen years. Testifying at health and safety hearings for proposed lines in New York, he said that exposure to the fields can produce physiological and functional changes in humans—anything from increased irritability and fatigue to raised cholesterol levels, hypertension and ulcers. Studies of rats exposed to low-level electric fields showed tumor growths and abnormalities in development. Dr. Becker believes we are performing unauthorized medical experiments by exposing people to the electromagnetic fields surrounding the transmission lines.

Kelly Davis, "Health and High Voltage: 765 KV Lines"

Beware of biased opinions. The agribusiness executive who favors farm price supports or the labor leader who opposes any restrictions on picketing may be writing merely to guard old privileges or garner new ones. Unless the opinion can stand especially close scrutiny, don't put it in your paper; it will just weaken your case with perceptive readers.

Because authorities don't always see eye to eye, their views lack the finality of established truths. Furthermore, their opinions will convince only if the audience accepts the authority *as* authoritative. Although advertisers successfully present football stars as authorities on shaving cream and credit cards, most people would not accept their views on the safety of nuclear energy.

Statistical Findings

Statistics—data showing how much, how many, or how often—can also buttress your argument. Most statistics come from books, magazines, newspapers, handbooks, encyclopedias, and reports, but you can use data from your own investigations as well.

Because statistics are often misused, many people distrust them, so any you offer must be reliable. First, make sure your sample isn't too small. Don't use a one-day traffic count to argue for a traffic light at a certain intersection. City Hall might counter by contending that the results are atypical. To make your case, you'd need to count traffic for perhaps two or three weeks. Take care not to push statistical claims too far. You may know that two-thirds of Tarrytown's factories pollute the air excessively, but don't argue that the same figures probably apply to your town. There's simply no carryover. Keep alert for biased statistics; they can cause as serious a credibility gap as biased opinions. Generally, recent data are better than old data, but either must come from a reliable source. Older information from the *New York Times* would probably be more accurate than current data from some publication that trades on sensationalism. Here's how one writer used statistics:

> The United States is losing its war against cocaine. Since this war is fought in the marketplace, percentages and statistics are needed to describe the dimensions of the defeat. The federal anti-drug budget grew by more than 300 percent from 1980 to 1988, but the cocaine supply multiplied tenfold in the same period. As a result, cocaine prices have plunged to barely 20 percent of what they were in 1980. In that year there were about 220,000 acres under coca cultivation in Peru, Bolivia, and Colombia; by 1984 the number had increased to 380,000, and by 1988, according to very conservative estimates, to at least 520,000. The supply of cocaine to the United States grew correspondingly: about 40 to 48 metric tons of cocaine entered the U.S. market in 1980, anywhere from 70 to 120 tons in 1984, and possibly as much as 350 to 400 tons in 1988. Plummeting prices reflected the supply glut: in 1980 the wholesale price at the port of entry was $50,000 to $55,000 a kilogram, by 1984 it had dropped to about $35,000, and in 1988 wholesale prices in Florida hit an all-time low of $10,000 to $12,000. . . .

Gustavo A. Garroti, "How to Fight the Drug War"

Personal Experience

Sometimes personal experience can deliver an argumentative message more forcefully than any other kind of evidence. Suppose that two years ago a speeder ran into your car and almost killed you. Today you're arguing for stiffer laws against speeding. Chances are you'll rely mainly on expert opinions and on statistics showing the number of people killed and injured each year in speeding accidents. However, describing the crash, the slow, pain-filled weeks in the hospital, and the months spent hobbling around on crutches may well provide the persuasive nudge that wins your reader over.

Often the experiences and observations of others, gathered from books, magazines, or interviews, can support your position. If you argue against chemical waste dumps, the personal stories of people who lived near them and suffered the consequences—black ooze in the basement, children with birth defects, family members who developed a rare form of cancer—can help sway your reader.

Despite its usefulness, personal experience generally reinforces but does not replace other kinds of evidence. Unless it has other support, readers may reject it as atypical or trivial.

An argument, then, consists of a conclusion you want to support, your reasons for that conclusion, and the evidence that supports your reasons. But how are reasons and evidence fitted together? Rational appeals include three reasoning strategies: induction, deduction, and analogy.

Induction

Induction moves from separate bits of evidence to a general observation. Suppose that on a hot, humid summer day you go to the kitchen to eat some potato chips from a bag opened the day before. As you start to munch, you make these observations:

Chip #1: limp and stale
Chip #2: limp and stale
Chip #3: limp and stale
Chip #4: limp and stale
Chip #5: limp and stale

At this point, you decide that the rest of the chips are probably stale too, and you stop eating. Inductive reasoning has led you, stale chip by stale chip, to a conclusion about the whole bag.

But probability is not proof. To prove something by induction, we must check every bit of evidence, and often that's just not practical or possible. Nonetheless, induction has great value for the conduct of human affairs. Say a food company has test marketed a new spaghetti sauce and now wants to decide whether it should start selling the product nationwide. A poll of 1,200 users, representing a cross section of the market, indicates that 78 percent rate the sauce "excellent." As a result, the company decides to go ahead. Induction has led them to conclude that future customers will favor the sauce as much as past customers did. Polls that sample political preferences and other public attitudes also operate inductively.

You have several options for organizing an inductive argument. You might begin by posing some direct or indirect question in order to snare your reader's interest, or you might simply state the position you will argue. The body of the paper provides the supporting evidence. In the conclusion you could reaffirm your position or suggest the consequences of that position. The following short example illustrates inductive argument.

Bologna is perhaps the most popular of all luncheon meats. Each day, thousands of individuals consume bologna sandwiches at noontime without ever considering the health consequences. Perhaps they should.

The sodium content of bologna is excessively high. On the average, three ounces contain over 850 milligrams, three times as much as a person needs in a single day. In addition, bologna's characteristic flavor and reddish color are caused by sodium nitrite, which is used to prevent the growth of botulism-causing organisms. Unfortunately, sodium nitrite combines with amines, natural compounds already in most foods, to form nitrosamines, which have been proven to cause cancer in laboratory animals. Finally, from a nutrition standpoint, bologna is terrible. The fat content is around 28 percent, the water content ranges upward from 50 percent, and the meat includes very little protein.

Health conscious people, then, will choose better fare for lunch.

Alison Russell

Deduction

Deduction is the reverse of induction. Instead of formulating a conclusion after considering pieces of evidence, you start with an observation that most people accept as true and then show how certain conclusions follow from that observation. For example, to convince a friend to study harder, you begin with the assumption that a profitable career requires a good education; proceed to argue that for a good education students must study diligently; and conclude that, as a result, your friend should spend more time with the books. Politicians who assert that we all want to act in ways beneficial to future generations, then point out how the policies they favor will ensure that outcome, argue deductively.

As with induction, you have several options when organizing a deductive argument. You might begin with the position you intend to prove, with a question that will be answered by the argument, or with a synopsis of the argument. The body of the paper works out the implications of your assumption. In the conclusion you could directly state (or restate, in different words) your position, suggest the consequences of adopting or not adopting that position, or pose a question that is easily answered after reading the argument. Here is a short example of deductive argument.

The recent spot-checks of our rooms by the dorm's head advisor are an unacceptable invasion of privacy. This practice should stop immediately.

The United States Constitution prohibits searches by police officers unless these officers have adequate evidence. That is why the police need a search warrant before they can search our home. If they fail to obtain one, a case that ends up in court will likely be thrown out. Our right to privacy, then, is guaranteed unless adequate evidence suggests otherwise.

lift-off that ended in an explosion. Management apparently favored the launch, arguing inductively that the O-rings had functioned without difficulty in several lift-offs under similar circumstances. Some engineers opposed the launch, arguing deductively about how the O-ring materials should behave in cold weather. Unfortunately, the engineers were correct.

TEACHING STRATEGIES

1. Some students tend to use shaky assumptions in their major premises and then move rather haphazardly to a conclusion. Caution against these flaws.
2. You could discuss the extent to which syllogisms are used in arguments, and why. Bring in and discuss syllogisms with a missing premise, a very common occurrence.
3. Have students record where they or others have argued deductively. Students could write down the major and minor premises, the conclusions, and the connections between them. Have them test the truth and validity of the syllogism.

CLASSROOM ACTIVITY

You might present the class with views that some students hold ("Since I'm paying for this class, I'm entitled to determine when I'll attend.") and then discuss what absurd consequences could follow.

CLASSROOM ACTIVITIES

1. Starting from some agreed-upon premise, such as "Grading should be based only on the objective quality of course work," ask students to reach and justify reasonable conclusions. The validity of the conclusions could then be discussed in class.
2. Provide the class with copies of the Bill of Rights. In small groups have students

> If the police can't search our homes without good reason, why should our head advisor spot-check our rooms for signs of wrongdoing?
>
> Sammy Borchardt

A common and powerful form of deduction called *reductio ad absurdum* (to reduce to absurdity) is used to attack an opponent's position by showing that its consequences are absurd if carried to their possible conclusion. To counter the position that the government should impose no restrictions on the public's right to bear arms, you might point out that, carried to its logical extreme, such a policy would allow individuals to own bazookas, cannons, and nuclear bombs. This absurd result makes it clear that certain restrictions should apply to our right to bear arms. The question then becomes where we should draw the ownership line.

Often, a deductive argument is built around a categorical syllogism, a set of three statements that follow a fixed pattern to ensure sound reasoning. The first statement, called the *major premise*, names a category of things and says that all or none of them shares a certain characteristic. The *minor premise* notes that a thing or group of things belongs to that category. The *conclusion* states that the thing or group shares the characteristics of the category. Here are two examples.

Major premise	All persons are mortal.
Minor premise	Sue Davis is a person.
Conclusion	Therefore, Sue Davis is mortal.
Major premise	No dogs have feathers.
Minor premise	Spot is a dog.
Conclusion	Therefore, Spot does not have feathers.

Note that in each case both major and minor premise are true and the conclusion follows logically.

Syllogisms frequently appear in stripped-down form, with one of the premises or the conclusion omitted. The following example omits the major premise: "Because Wilma is a civil engineer, she has a strong background in mathematics." Obviously the missing major premise is as follows: "All civil engineers have strong backgrounds in mathematics."

Syllogistic Argument at Work. A syllogism can occur anywhere in an essay: in the introduction to set the stage for the evidence, at various places in the body, even in the conclusion in order to pull the argument together. Here is an example that uses a syllogism in the introduction.

> In 1966, when the Astrodome was completed in Houston, Texas, the managers concluded that it would be impossible to grow grass indoors. To solve their problem, they decided to install a ruglike synthetic playing surface that was fittingly called Astroturf. In the ensuing years, many

other sports facilities have installed synthetic turf. Unfortunately, this development has been accompanied by a sharp rise in the number and severity of injuries suffered by athletes—a rise clearly linked to the surface they play upon. <u>Obviously, anything that poses a threat to player safety is undesirable. Because synthetic turf does this, it is undesirable and should be replaced by grass.</u>

Denny Witham

To support his position, the writer then notes that turf, unlike grass, often becomes excessively hot, tiring players and increasing their chances of injury; that seams can open up between sections of turf and lead to tripping and falling; that players can run faster on artificial turf and thus collide more violently; and that the extreme hardness of the turf leads to torn ligaments and tissues when players slam their toes into it.

Avoiding Misuse of Syllogisms.   Two cautions are in order. *First*, make sure any syllogism you use follows the proper order. The writer of the following passage has ignored this caution.

> And that's not all. Newton has stated openly that he favors federally funded abortions for the poor. Just the other day, the American Socialist party took this same stand. In my book, Newton's position puts him squarely in the Socialist camp. I strongly urge anyone supporting this man's candidacy to reconsider. . . .

Restated in syllogistic form, the writer's argument goes like this:

Socialists favor federally funded abortions for the poor.

Newton favors federally funded abortions for the poor.

Therefore, Newton is a Socialist.

The last two statements reverse the proper order, and as a result the syllogism proves nothing about Newton's politics: he may or may not be "in the Socialist camp."

Second, make sure the major premise of your syllogism is in fact true. Note this example.

All conservatives are opposed to environmental protection.

Mary is a conservative.

Therefore, Mary is opposed to environmental protection.

But is every conservative an environmental Jack the Ripper? In some communities, political conservatives have led fights against air and water pollution, and most conservatives agree that at least some controls are worthwhile. Mary's sympathies, then, may well lie with those who want to heal, rather than hack, the environment.

determine what the principles mean and what follows from them. Students might be asked to apply these principles to specific issues.

TEACHING STRATEGY

Have students watch for the misuse of syllogisms in their reading and then bring any examples they find into class for discussion. Alternatively, you might bring in such examples, perhaps ones that you draft yourself.

EXERCISE ANSWERS

1. Syllogism is faulty because its initial statement is untrue: Singers are not necessarily happy.
2. Syllogism is satisfactory.
3. Syllogism is faulty because the final two statements reverse the proper order.
4. Syllogism is faulty because its initial statement is untrue: Salespeople sometimes misrepresent the products they sell.

EXERCISE ■ **Which of these syllogisms is satisfactory, which have false major premises, and which is faulty because the last two statements reverse the proper order?**

1. All singers are happy people.
Mary Harper is a singer.
Therefore, Mary Harper is a happy person.
2. All cowards fear danger.
"Chicken" Cacciatore is a coward.
Therefore, "Chicken" Cacciatore fears danger.
3. All cats like meat.
Towser likes meat.
Therefore, Towser is a cat.
4. No salesperson would ever misrepresent a product to a customer.
Sabrina is a salesperson.
Therefore, Sabrina would never misrepresent a product to a customer.

Analogy in Argument

PERSPECTIVE

While an argument from analogy is never totally conclusive, it is extraordinarily common and, in some ways, unavoidable. We can't always do medical research on humans, and even when we do, it is often in controlled situations dissimilar to daily life. If we learn lessons from history, it can only be on the basis of analogy since historical situations are rarely identical. Economists, political scientists, and sociologists all regularly attempt to reach conclusions and make predictions on the basis of analogy. Indeed, any attempt to work from a scientific model implicitly relies on an analogy since few scientists confuse the model with the real world. More practically, when business executives review the potential for a marketing strategy based on the previous performance of other plans, they are probably drawing on an implicit analogy. For these reasons, students should understand, work with, and evaluate arguments from analogy.

An analogy compares two unlike situations or things. Arguers often use analogies to contend that because two items share one or more likenesses, they are also alike in other ways. Familiar analogies assume that humans respond to chemicals as rats do and that success in school predicts success on the job. You have used analogy if you ever pressed your parents for more adult privileges, such as a later curfew, by arguing that you were like an adult in many ways.

Because its conclusions about one thing rest upon observations about some different thing, analogy is the weakest form of rational appeal. Analogies never prove anything. But they often help explain and show probability and therefore are quite persuasive.

For an analogy to be useful, it must feature significant similarities that bear directly on the issue. In addition, it must account for any significant differences between the two items. It is often helpful to test an analogy by listing the similarities and differences. Here's an effective analogy, used to back an argument that a liberal education is the best kind to help us cope successfully with life.

> Suppose it were perfectly certain that the life and fortune of every one of us would, one day or other, depend upon his winning or losing a game of chess. Don't you think that we should all consider it to be a primary duty to learn at least the names and the moves of the pieces; to have a notion of a gambit, and a keen eye for all the means of giving and getting out of check? Do you not think that we should look with a disapprobation amounting to scorn, upon the father who allowed his son, or the state which allowed its members, to grow up without knowing a pawn from a knight?
>
> Yet it is a very plain and elementary truth, that the life, the fortune, and the happiness of every one of us, and, more or less, of those who are connected with us, do depend upon our knowing something of the rules of a game infinitely more difficult and complicated than chess. It is a game which has been played for

untold ages, every man and woman of us being one of the two players in a game of his or her own. The chessboard is the world, the pieces are the phenomena of the universe, the rules of the game are what we call the laws of Nature. The player on the other side is hidden from us. We know that his play is always fair, just, and patient. But also we know, to our cost, that he never overlooks a mistake, or makes the smallest allowance for ignorance. To the man who plays well, the highest stakes are paid, with that sort of overflowing generosity with which the strong shows delight in strength. And one who plays ill is checkmated—without haste, but without remorse. . . .

Well, what I mean by Education is learning the rules of this mighty game. In other words, education is the instruction of the intellect in the law of Nature, under which name I include not merely things and their forces, but men and their ways; and the fashioning of the affections and of the will into an earnest and loving desire to move in harmony with those laws. For me, education means neither more nor less than this. Anything which professes to call itself education must be tried by this standard, and if it fails to stand the test, I will not call it education, whatever may be the force of authority, or of numbers, upon the other side.

Thomas Henry Huxley, "A Liberal Education and Where to Find It"

THE EMOTIONAL APPEAL

Although effective argument relies mainly on reason, an emotional appeal can lend powerful reinforcement. Indeed, emotion can win the hearts and the help of people who would otherwise passively accept a logical argument but take no action. Each Christmas, newspapers raise money for local charities by running stark case histories of destitute families. Organizations raise funds to fight famine by displaying brochures that feature skeletal, swollen-bellied children. Still other groups use emotion-charged stories and pictures to solicit support for environmental protection, to combat various diseases, and so on. Less benignly, advertisers use emotion to play upon our hopes, fears, and vanities in order to sell mouthwash, cars, clothes, and other products. Politicians paint themselves as God-fearing, honest toilers for the public good while lambasting their opponents as the uncaring tools of special interests. In evaluating or writing an argument, ask yourself whether the facts warrant the emotion. Is the condition of the destitute family truly cause for pity? Is any politician unwaveringly good, any other irredeemably bad?

The following paragraph from "Letter from Birmingham Jail" illustrates an appropriate use of emotion:

We have waited for more than 340 years for our constitutional and God-given rights. The nations of Asia and Africa are moving with jetlike speed toward gaining political independence, but we still creep at horse-and-buggy pace toward gaining a cup of coffee at a lunch counter. Perhaps it is easy for those who have never felt the stinging darts of segregation to say, "Wait." But when you have

TEACHING STRATEGIES

1. Both Reader essays on the legalization of drugs include analogies to prohibition. You might have students read the essays and evaluate the analogies.
2. Ask students to review their textbooks and several newspaper editorials to observe where and how appropriately arguments from analogy were used.

CLASSROOM ACTIVITY

Choose a current controversy—for example, the legalization of drugs, the death penalty, surrogate mothers—and have the class determine what analogies, if any, would be helpful in thinking through the issue. Are the current laws against marijuana similar to prohibition? Is the electrocution of criminals murder? Is receiving money to have a baby for others the same as prostitution? Have students carefully test the analogies by listing the points of similarity and dissimilarity.

PERSPECTIVE

Some have argued that emotion has no place in any rational exchange. But we might take into account that many issues involve values that lie close to our hearts, and thus trigger emotional responses. A writer planning an argument that favors aid for the homeless may intend to rely only on facts about their difficult circumstances. These circumstances, however, can stir deep feelings regarding the value of human life and cause the writer to include emotion in the argument. Indeed, such feelings may have sparked the decision to write in the first place. Emotional appeals can, however, backfire. The movie *Reefer Madness*, designed to discourage marijuana use, became an underground cult film because its portrayal of the drug as stimulating an uncontrollable, often sexual, frenzy was overdone and did not match the experience of those who had tried marijuana.

TEACHING STRATEGIES

1. Ask students to record examples of emotional appeal they observe and comment on their effectiveness, paying particular attention to appeals that have backfired.
2. Have students identify what kinds of appeals might move them or their parents to a specific action, perhaps an act of charity.

ETHICAL ISSUES

Is it acceptable to deliberately manipulate someone's emotional response in order to encourage a specific action? What if the manipulation is for the person's own good, as in ads stressing the risks of AIDS? What about cases where subliminal appeals are used?

TEACHING STRATEGIES

1. Have students examine their own responses to arguments included in the Reader and in the news media. How do they evaluate the character of the author? How do those judgments influence their responses to the argument?
2. Many students are not sure of their ethical credibility; thus, they feel uncomfortable trying to demonstrate it. In discussing potential topics, have students write down the ethical appeals they would like to project and then suggest ways they might do so.
3. Some students have a tendency to come across as extremely judgmental, excessively rigid, and uncomfortably self-righteous, often because they have not explored their topic. Help them recognize this tendency by pointing out examples in their writing.

seen vicious mobs lynch your mothers and fathers at will and drown your sisters and brothers at whim; when you have seen hate-filled policemen curse, kick, and even kill your black brothers and sisters; when you see the vast majority of your twenty million Negro brothers smothering in an airtight cage of poverty in the midst of an affluent society; when you suddenly find your tongue twisted and your speech stammering as you seek to explain to your six-year-old daughter why she can't go to the public amusement park that has just been advertised on television, and see tears welling up in her eyes when she is told that Funtown is closed to colored children, and see ominous clouds of inferiority beginning to form in her little mental sky, and see her beginning to distort her personality by developing an unconscious bitterness toward white people; when you have to concoct an answer for a five-year-old son who is asking, "Daddy, why do white people treat colored people so mean?"; when you take a cross-country drive and find it necessary to sleep night after night in the uncomfortable corners of your automobile because no motel will accept you; when you are humiliated day in and day out by nagging signs reading "white" and "colored"; when your first name becomes "nigger," your middle name becomes "boy" (however old you are) and your last name becomes "John," and your wife and mother are never given the respected title "Mrs."; when you are harried by day and haunted by night by the fact that you are a Negro, living constantly at tiptoe stance, never quite knowing what to expect next, and are plagued with inner fears and outer resentments, when you are forever fighting a degenerating sense of "nobodiness"—then you will understand why we find it difficult to wait. There comes a time when the cup of endurance runs over, and men are no longer willing to be plunged into the abyss of despair. I hope, sirs, you can understand our legitimate and unavoidable impatience.

Martin Luther King, Jr., "Letter from Birmingham Jail"

*T*HE ETHICAL APPEAL

Before logic can do its work, the audience must be willing to consider the argument. If a writer's tone offends the audience, perhaps by being arrogant or mean-spirited, the reasoning will fail to penetrate. But if the writer comes across as pleasant, fair-minded, and decent, gaining reader support is much easier. The image that the writer projects is called the *ethical appeal.*

If you write with a genuine concern for your topic, a commitment to the truth, and a sincere respect for others, you will probably come across reasonably well. When you finish writing, check to see that an occasional snide comment or bitter remark didn't slip unnoticed onto the page. In the following introductory paragraph, from an essay arguing that many universities violate the Constitution by imposing campus rules that restrict freedom of speech, the student establishes an appealing ethical image.

Most of us would agree that educated people should not indulge in

name-calling and stereotyping in their speaking and writing. To do so is an

essential mark of irrational prejudice. Nevertheless, such speaking and writing are protected by the United States Constitution, which prohibits anyone from abridging freedom of expression. Today, many colleges and universities, in a well-meaning attempt to shield particular groups from unwelcome or insensitive words, are subverting this prohibition. Supreme Court Justice William Brennan, noted for his liberal views, recently said, "If there is a bedrock principle underlying the First Amendment, it is that the government may not prohibit the expression of an idea simply because society finds the idea offensive or disagreeable."

Linda Kimrey

The writer opposes on constitutional grounds any attempts to ban the expression of two forms of "irrational prejudice." Nevertheless, she characterizes these attempts as "well-meaning" and acknowledges that they are prompted by worthy motives. As a result, she emerges as fair-minded, decent, sensitive, and concerned, an image she maintains throughout the essay.

ETHICAL ISSUES

Is it ethical to fabricate a character or ethical credentials that are not yours? What if such fabrication is for the public good?

FERRETING OUT FALLACIES

Fallacies are lapses in logic that reflect upon your ability to think clearly, and therefore they weaken your argument. The fallacies described below are among the most common. Correct any you find in your own arguments, and call attention to those used by the opposition.

CLASSROOM ACTIVITY

Bring in advertisements or political speeches and have students identify the fallacies and their intended effect on the reader. This exercise makes an excellent short writing assignment.

Hasty Generalization

Hasty generalization results when someone bases a conclusion on too little evidence. The student who tries to see an instructor during one of her office hours, finds her out, and goes away muttering, "She's never there when she should be" is guilty of hasty generalization. Perhaps the instructor was delayed by another student, attended a special department meeting, or went home ill. Even if she merely went shopping, that's not a good reason for saying she always shirks her responsibility. Several more unsuccessful office visits would be needed to make such a charge stick.

Non Sequitur

From the Latin "It does not follow," this fallacy draws unwarranted conclusions from seemingly ample evidence. Consider this example: "Bill's been out almost every night for the last two weeks. Who is she?" These evening excursions, however numerous, point to no particular conclusion. Bill may be studying in the library, participating in campus organizations, taking night classes, or walking. Of course, he *could* be charmed by a new date, but that conclusion requires other evidence.

Stereotyping

A person who commits this fallacy attaches one or more supposed characteristics to a group or one of its members. Typical stereotypes include "Latins make better lovers," "blondes have more fun," and "women are lousy drivers." Stereotyping racial, religious, ethnic, or nationality groups can destroy an argument. The images are often malicious and always offensive to fair-minded readers.

Either/Or Fallacy

The either/or fallacy asserts that only two choices exist when, in fact, several options are possible. A salesperson who wants you to buy snow tires may claim, "Either buy these tires or plan on getting stuck a lot this winter." But are you really that boxed in? You might drive only on main roads that are plowed immediately after every snowstorm. You could use public transportation when it snows. You could buy radial tires for year-round use. If very little snow falls, you might not need special tires at all.

Not all either/or statements are fallacies. The instructor who checks a student's record and then issues a warning, "Make at least a *C* on your final or you'll fail the course," is not guilty of a reasoning error. No other alternatives exist. Most situations, however, offer more than two choices.

Begging the Question

A person who begs the question asserts the truth of some unproven statement. Here is an example: "Vitamin A is harmful to your health, and all bottles should carry a warning label. If enough of us write the Food and Drug Administration, we can get the labeling we need." But how do we know Vitamin A does harm users? No evidence is offered. People lacking principles often use this fallacy to hit opponents below the belt: "We shouldn't allow a right-wing sympathizer like Mary Dailey to represent us in Congress." Despite a lack of suitable evidence, voters often accept such faulty logic and vote for the other candidate.

Circular Argument

Circular argument, a first cousin to begging the question, supports a position merely by restating it. "Pauline is a good manager because she runs the company effectively" says, in effect, that "something is because something is." Repetition replaces evidence.

Arguing off the Point

The writer who commits this fallacy, which is sometimes called "ignoring the question" or "a red herring," sidetracks an issue by introducing irrelevant information. To illustrate: "The Ford Thunderbolt is a much better value than the Honda Harmony. Anyway, the Japanese are becoming too prominent in our country. They're buying up businesses and real estate on both the East and West Coasts.

Many Americans don't want to work for a Japanese boss." The writer sets out to convince that the American car is superior in value but then abruptly shifts to Japanese ownership in America—a trend which has no bearing on the argument.

The Argument *Ad Hominem*

The Latin term "to the man" designates an argument that attacks an individual rather than that individual's opinions or qualifications. Note this example: "Sam Bernhart doesn't deserve promotion to Personnel Manager. His divorce was a disgrace, and he's always writing letters to the editor. The company should find someone more suitable." This attack completely skirts the real issue—whether Sam's job performance entitles him to the promotion. Unless his personal conduct has caused his work to suffer, it should not enter into the decision.

Appeal to the Crowd

An appeal of this sort arouses an emotional response by playing on the irrational fears and prejudices of the audience. Terms like *communists, fascists, bleeding hearts, right-winger, welfare chiselers*, and *law and order* are tossed about freely to sway the audience for or against something. Consider:

> The streets of our country are in turmoil. The universities are filled with students rebelling and rioting. Communists are seeking to destroy our country. Russia is threatening us with her might, and the public is in danger. Yes, danger from within and without. We need law and order. Yes, without law and order our nation cannot survive. Elect us, and we shall by law and order be respected among the nations of the world. Without law and order our republic shall fall.

Tapping the emotions of the crowd can sway large groups and win acceptance for positions that rational thinking would reject. Think what Adolf Hitler, the author of the foregoing excerpt, brought about in Germany.

Guilt by Association

This fallacy points out some similarity or connection between one person or group and another. It tags the first with the sins, real or imagined, of the second. The following excerpt from a letter protesting a speaker at a lecture series illustrates this technique:

> The next slated speaker, Dr. Sylvester Crampton, was for years a member of the Economic Information Committee. This foundation has very strong ties with other ultraright-wing groups, some of which have been labeled fascistic. When he speaks next Thursday, whose brand of Americanism will he be selling?

Post Hoc, ergo Propter Hoc

The Latin meaning, "after this, therefore because of this," refers to the fallacy of assuming that because one event follows another, the first caused the second. Such shoddy thinking underlies many popular superstitions ("If a black cat crosses your path, you'll have bad luck") and many connections that cannot be substantiated ("I always catch cold on Easter"). Sometimes one event does cause another: a sudden thunderclap might startle a person into dropping a dish. At other times, coincidence is the only connection. Careful thinking will usually lay farfetched causal notions to rest.

Faulty Analogy

This is the error of assuming that two circumstances or things are similar in all important respects, when in fact they are not. Here's an example. Harvey Thompson, high school football coach, tells his players, "Vince Lombardi won two Super Bowls by insisting on perfect execution of plays and enforcing strict disciplinary measures. We're going to win the conference championship by following the same methods." Thompson assumes that because he and Lombardi are coaches, he can duplicate Lombardi's achievements by using Lombardi's methods. Several important differences, however, mark the two situations:

1. Lombardi had very talented players, obtained through the player draft or trades; Thompson can choose only from the students in his high school.
2. Lombardi's players were paid professionals who very likely were motivated, at least in part, by the financial rewards that came from winning the Super Bowl; Thompson's players are amateurs.
3. "Perfect execution of plays" is probably easier to attain on the professional level than in high school because of the players' experience.
4. Despite Lombardi's rigid disciplinary measures, very few of his players quit, perhaps because they were under contract. Could Thompson expect his players, essentially volunteers, to accept the kind of verbal and physical rigors Lombardi was famous for?

EXERCISE ■ **Identify and explain the fallacies in the following examples. Remember that understanding the faulty reasoning is more important than merely naming the fallacy.**

1. While eating a Golden Glow orange, Nancy discovers that it is rotten. "I'll never buy another Golden Glow product," she declares emphatically.
2. A campaigning politician states that unless the federal government appropriates funds to help people living in poverty, they will all starve.
3. A husband and wife see an X-rated movie called *Swinging Wives*. A week later the husband discovers that his wife, while supposedly attending an evening class, has been unfaithful to him. He blames the movie for her infidelity.
4. "Look at those two motorcycle riders trying to pick a fight. All those cycle bums are troublemakers."
5. "Bill really loves to eat. Some day he'll have a serious weight problem."
6. "Because no-fault divorce is responsible for today's skyrocketing divorce rate, it should be abolished."
7. "This is the best-looking picture in the exhibit; it's so much more attractive than the others."

EXERCISE ANSWERS

1. A hasty generalization. Nancy has reached her conclusion after eating just one orange. Such a conclusion would be justified only after she had tried a number of oranges and found all of them rotten.
2. The either–or fallacy. Failure of the federal government to help poverty-stricken people would not necessarily cause starvation for all of them. Some might receive help from relatives or private charities, or state and local governments might provide financial assistance.
3. The *post hoc, ergo propter hoc* fallacy. The wife might have been unfaithful not because she had attended the X-rated movie but because she was angry with her husband or infatuated with the person with whom she was unfaithful.
4. Stereotyping and hasty generalization. The speaker has condemned all motorcycle riders because of the behavior of just two of them.
5. A *non sequitur*. Bill may love to eat, but we can't conclude that he will have a serious weight problem someday. He may be a person who never puts on weight regardless of his food intake, or he may alter his eating habits.
6. Begging the question. The statement assumes, without any supporting evidence, that no-fault divorce has caused the divorce rate to jump sharply.
7. A circular argument. The statement that the picture

8. "I do not support this school millage proposal. It's sponsored by James McAndrews, who's about the most ill-tempered, quarrelsome person I've ever met. I'd never favor anything he supports."

9. "My position on social and economic issues is easy to state. I am against wooly-brained do-gooders and big-spending, pie-in-the-sky welfare programs that have brought us to the brink of social disaster. I stand foursquare behind our free enterprise system, which has given us a standard of living the whole world envies, and if elected, I will defend it with everything at my command."

10. "I am against the proposed ban on smoking in public places. As long as I don't inhale and I limit my habit to 8–10 cigarettes a day, my health won't suffer."

*W*RITING AN ARGUMENT

Planning and Drafting the Argument

Some instructors assign argumentative topics, and some leave the choice of topic to you. If you will be choosing, many options are available. Interesting issues—some local, some of broader importance—crowd our newspapers, magazines, and TV airways, vying for attention. Because several of them have probably piqued your interest, there's a good chance you won't have to rely on the strategies on pages 12–18 for help.

Some students approach an argument with such strong attitudes that they ignore evidence that contradicts their thinking. Don't make this mistake. Instead, maintain an open mind as you research your issue, and then, after careful thought, choose the position you'll take. Often, several possible positions exist. On the question of whether handguns should be banned, the positions might include (1) banning the possession of handguns by anyone except law officers and military personnel, (2) eliminating all restrictions on handgun possession, (3) banning handguns for persons with criminal records or a history of mental problems, and (4) banning certain types of handguns, such as "Saturday night specials" and all-plastic handguns. Even if you don't shift your position, knowing the opposition's strengths allows you to counter or neutralize them, and thus enhance your argument. Suppose you favor the first position. You need to know that half of our state constitutions grant citizens the right to own guns. Unless you acknowledge and somehow counter this fact, your case will suffer and perhaps even founder.

As you investigate the various positions, ask and answer the following questions about each:

What kinds of evidence support it?
How substantial is the evidence?
If the evidence includes statistics and authoritative opinions, are they reliable? Flawed for some reason?
What are the objections to each position, and how can they be countered?
If the issue involves taking some action, what might be its consequences?

is "much more attractive than the others" essentially repeats the statement "This is the best-looking picture in the exhibit."

8. Argument *ad hominem.* Instead of attacking McAndrews' position on the bill, this critic attacks McAndrews' personality, which would seem irrelevant. Unless the critic can show that McAndrews' personality has led him to sponsor a faulty proposal (a task that would appear impossible), personality should not be mentioned.

9. Appeal to the crowd. This statement attempts to sway its readers by playing upon their dislike of "wooly-brained, do-gooders" and "big spending pie-in-the-sky welfare programs," as well as upon their favorable attitudes toward our free-enterprise system.

10. Arguing off the point and also begging the question. The writer sets out to argue against the ban on public smoking and then abruptly shifts to his own health—an entirely different matter. Furthermore, he asserts that his health won't suffer but cites no evidence.

PERSPECTIVE

Some students, confused by the controversy surrounding an issue, are eager to reach a conclusion even when they don't have much support. Encourage students to collect and evaluate evidence for the different positions and consider potential objections to each. A few might need special attention as they confront a particularly difficult issue.

To help with this stage of the process, prepare a chart that summarizes your findings for each position; then examine it carefully to pick the position you'll argue for. The example below illustrates a three-position issue.

Position 1	Position 2	Position 3
Evidence and evaluation	Evidence and evaluation	Evidence and evaluation
Objections and how countered	Objections and how countered	Objections and how countered
Consequences	Consequences	Consequences

TEACHING STRATEGY

Ask students to identify and bring to class the different types of arguments they discover in their reading. Have them point out the purpose of each argument and how it dictated the organization and techniques that the writer used. Writing assignments emphasizing the various argument purposes could follow.

As you contemplate your position and evidence, consider the purpose of your argument and how that might affect the strategies you choose to employ. Arguments are written for several purposes, each requiring a different approach. Some arguments try to establish that something is a fact—nursing is hard work, dormitories are poor study places, bologna is an unhealthy food. This type of paper usually relies on assorted evidence, perhaps some combination of statistics, authoritative opinion, and personal experience. To prove that nursing is quite demanding, you might narrate and describe some of the strenuous activities in a typical nursing day, cite hospital nursing supervisors who verify the rigors of the job, and perhaps give statistics on nurses who quit the profession because of stress.

Other arguments defend or oppose some policy—for example, whether freshmen should be allowed cars on campus or a company should begin drug-testing its employees—or support or oppose some action or project, such as the construction of a study lounge for students or the purchase of more microfiche readers for the library. In this type of paper, you usually discuss the need for the policy or action, how it can best be met, the cost or feasibility of your recommendation, and the benefits that will result. For instance, if you believe the library needs more microfiche readers, you might explain the problems that students currently experience (perhaps long lines, papers turned in late), cite the number of new microfiche readers you think necessary, indicate the cost of purchasing them, and then detail the improvements that will follow (perhaps shorter waiting time, fewer late papers).

Still other arguments assert the greater value of someone or something, as when a supervisor ranks one candidate for promotion ahead of another. To write this type of paper, generally you would indicate what you're trying to prove, identify the points on which the items will be evaluated, and then, using reasons along with details, examples, or statistics, demonstrate that one of the items has greater worth than the other. Often such an argument will be deductive as you show how your conclusions follow from agreed-upon values.

With an argument, as with any essay, purpose and audience are closely linked. For example, imagine that your audience is a group of readers who are neutral or opposed to your position; there's no point in preaching to the converted.

Take a little time to analyze these readers so that you can tailor your arguments appropriately. Pose these questions as you proceed.

> What are the readers' interests, expectations, and needs concerning this issue?
> What evidence is most likely to convince them?
> What objections and consequences would probably weigh most heavily with them?
> How can I answer the objections?

To convince an audience of farmers that the federal school lunch program needs expanding, you might stress the added income they would gain. For nutritionists, you might note the health benefits that would result, and for school officials, the improved class performance of the students. Even though you are unlikely to convince everyone, it is best to adopt the attitude that most readers are willing to be convinced if your approach is appealing and your evidence is sound.

If you're arguing an emotionally charged issue such as gun control or federally funded abortions for the poor, you may want to use *Rogerian argument*. Named for psychologist Carl Rogers, this type of argument attempts to reduce the antagonism that people with opposing views might feel toward your position. To succeed, you must show that you understand and respect the opposing position as well as acknowledge its good points. You try to establish some common point of agreement, then present a position that addresses opposing concerns without compromising your views. For example, if you want stricter gun-control laws, you might begin by acknowledging that the Constitution grants citizens the right to bear arms and that you believe anyone with legitimate uses for guns—hunters, target shooters, and the like—should have access to them. Moving on, you might point to the serious crime problem that the spread of handgun ownership has helped create. Finally, you might propose outlawing the sale of "Saturday night specials," enacting more severe penalties for possessing unlicensed handguns, and establishing a central computer facility to run a criminal record check on individuals wanting handgun permits.

When you have a good grasp on your position, reasons, evidence, and the approach you want to take, you're ready to draft your paper. A typical introduction arouses the reader's interest and may also present the proposition—a special thesis statement that names the issue and indicates which position the writer will take. It can declare that something is a fact, support a policy, call for a certain action, or assert that something has greater value than something else. Here are examples.

1. Carron College does not provide adequate recreational facilities for its students. (*declares something is fact*)
2. Our company's policy of randomly testing employees for drug use has proved effective and should be continued. (*supports policy*)
3. Because the present building is overcrowded and unsafe, the people of Midville should vote funds for a new junior high school. (*calls for action*)
4. The new Ford Fire-Eater is superior to the Honda Harmony in performance, appearance, and economy. (*asserts value*)

Any of the techniques on pages 186–88 can launch your paper. For example,

TEACHING STRATEGY

Many students will benefit if they are guided through the stages of writing an argument. You might want to schedule conferences to help students deal with the challenge of this assignment.

in arguing for stepped-up AIDS education, you might jolt your reader by describing a dying victim. If your issue involves unfamiliar terms, you might define them up front, and if the essay will be long, you could preview its main points.

After the introduction comes the evidence, arranged in whatever order you think will work best. If one of your points is likely to arouse resistance, hold it back and begin by making points your reader can more easily accept. Argument always goes more smoothly if you first establish some common ground of agreement that recognizes the values of your reader. Where strong resistance is not a factor, you could begin or end with your most compelling piece of evidence.

The strategies discussed in earlier chapters can help you develop an argument. Some papers incorporate one strategy, while others rely on several. Let's see how you might combine several in an argument against legalized casino gambling. You might open with a brief *description* of the frantic way an all-too-typical gambling addict keeps pulling the lever of a slot machine, his eyes riveted on the spinning dials, his palms sweating, as flashing lights and wailing sirens announce winners at other machines. Next, you could offer a brief *definition* of gambling fever so that the writer and reader are on common ground, and, to show the dimensions of the problem, *classify* the groups of people who are especially addicted. Then, after detailing the negative *effects* of the addiction, you might end by *comparing* gambling addiction with drug addiction, noting that both provide a "high" and both kinds of addicts know their habits hurt them.

Whatever strategies you use, make sure that substantiating evidence is embedded within them. Strategies by themselves won't convince. To illustrate, in discussing the negative effects of gambling, you might cite statistics that show the extent and nature of the problem. An expert opinion might validate your classification of addicts. Or you might use personal experience to verify gambling's addictive effects.

Besides presenting evidence, use this part of your paper to refute; that is, to point out weaknesses or errors in the opposing position. Typical examples include evidence that undermines that position, faulty assumptions, and flaws in the logic. You can sprinkle refutations throughout the body of the paper or group them together just ahead of the conclusion. Whatever you decide, don't adopt a gloating or sarcastic tone that will alienate a fair-minded reader. Resist the urge to engage in *straw man* tactics—calling attention to imaginary or trivial weaknesses of the opposing side so that you can demolish them. Shrewd readers easily spot such ploys. Finally, don't be afraid to concede secondary or insignificant points to the opposition. Arguments have two or more sides; you can't have all the ammunition on your side. (If you discover you must concede major points, however, consider switching sides.) Here is a sample refutation from a student paper.

> Not everyone agrees with workplace drug testing for employees in
> public transportation companies, electric utilities, nuclear power plants,
> and other industries involving public safety. Critics assert that such tests
> invade privacy and therefore violate one of our cherished freedoms. While
> the examination of one's urine does entail inspection of something private,
> I believe such a test is a reasonable compromise because it helps ensure

public safety and calm public fears. The individual's privacy should be tempered by concern for the community—a concern that benefits all of us.

Annie Louise Griffith

Conclude in a manner that will sway the reader to your side. Depending on the argument, you might restate your position, summarize your main points, predict the consequences if your position does or doesn't prevail, or make an emotional appeal for support or action.

Revising the Argument

Review the guidelines in Chapter 3 and ponder these questions as you revise your argument paper.

- Is my topic controversial? Have I examined all of the main positions? Assessed the evidence supporting each one? Considered the objections to each position and how they can be countered? Weighed the consequences if a position involves taking some action?
- Is the paper aimed at the audience I want to reach? Have I tailored my argument to appeal to that audience?
- Is my evidence sound, adequate, and appropriate to the argument? Are my authorities qualified? Have I established their expertise? Are they biased? Will my audience accept them as authorities? Do my statistics adequately support my position? Have I pushed my statistical claims too far?
- If I've used analogy, are my points of comparison pertinent to the issue? Have I noted any significant differences between the items being compared?
- If I've included an emotional appeal, does it center on those emotions most likely to sway the reader?
- Have I made a conscious effort to present myself in a favorable light?
- Is my proposition clearly evident and of the appropriate type; that is, one of fact, policy, action, or value? If the proposition takes the form of a syllogism, is it sound? If faulty, have I started with a faulty premise? Reversed the last two statements of the syllogism?
- Is my evidence effectively structured? Have I adequately refuted opposing arguments? Developed my position with one or more writing strategies?
- Is my argument free of fallacies?

EXAMPLE STUDENT ESSAY OF ARGUMENT

The Right to Bear Arms

Brenda Buehrle

The right of citizens to bear arms is often discussed in heated 1
tones and emotional language. Political assassinations, for example, inevitably spark an outcry for control of firearms, as do soaring

TEACHING STRATEGY

If you teach this essay, you might generate a class discussion by asking whether the right to bear arms includes the right to purchase assault rifles and armor-piercing bullets.

ETHICAL ISSUES

Are there circumstances when it is ethical to deliberately (1) engage in card stacking, i.e., emphasize all the positive evidence and completely ignore any other? (2) exaggerate or fabricate evidence to support a position? (3) use a fallacy to trick unwary readers? (4) misrepresent an opponent's position in order to more easily refute it?

crime statistics. These appeals are frequently countered by jingles such as "When guns are outlawed, only outlaws will have guns." If we bypass such purely emotional pleas and examine the issue objectively, we find that there is ample legal justification for the right to bear arms.

The first thing we should consider is the original intent of the Second Amendment to the United States Constitution, which states: "A well-regulated militia being necessary to the security of a free State, the right of the people to keep and bear arms shall not be infringed." When the purpose of any constitutional provision or law is in question, a good procedure is to return to the thoughts and words of those who originally framed it. For the Second Amendment, it is necessary to examine the ideas of George Mason, the Virginia constitutionalist. Mason wrote several specific safeguards of individual rights into the Virginia constitution of 1776. The Bill of Rights—that is, the first ten amendments added to the United States Constitution in 1791—incorporates many of Mason's safeguards. R.A. Rutland's edition of Mason's papers reveals clearly that his conception of the militia—that group empowered by law to bear arms—went far beyond an organized group of men in uniform. During a debate in Richmond on June 16, 1788, Mason rhetorically said: "I ask who are the militia?" and then answered his own question with these words: "They consist now of the whole people, except a few public officials." There can be little doubt that George Mason, "Father of the Bill of Rights," never intended to restrict the right to bear arms to a relatively few men in uniform. Therefore, the original concept of the Second Amendment was that the militia consisted of all people; and to ensure security of a free country, the people had the right to keep and bear arms.

Early in this century Congress interpreted the militia more narrowly than Mason did. On January 23, 1903, Congress defined the militia as all able-bodied male citizens more than eighteen and less than forty-five years of age. These men were divided into two classes: the organized militia, to be known as the National Guard of the State, Territory, or District of Columbia, and the remainder, to

2

3

be known as the Reserve Militia. Thus, the Congress classified all males within certain age limits, and not in the National Guard, as members of the militia. These men would now seem to be the "people to keep and bear arms" whose right to firearms "shall not be infringed" under the Second Amendment. Furthermore, under the broad doctrine of equal rights, it would appear that women should also be included, if they fall into the proper age groups eligible for military service.

Since no definite laws in the United States Constitution define   4
the rights of gun owners throughout the fifty states, the state constitutions certainly would seem to be the highest law in such cases, as provided in the Ninth and Tenth Amendments. These reserve to the states and the people all rights and powers not spelled out in the United States Constitution. Because the Second Amendment does not definitely state the rights of gun owners, the federal government cannot alter the rights that are defined in individual state constitutions. At least half of these state constitutions go beyond the Second Amendment by spelling out that the right to bear arms is an individual right for personal protection or defense of home and property and has nothing to do with a "well-regulated militia." Among these states are Arizona, Michigan, and Pennsylvania. For example, Arizona's constitution states, "The right of the individual citizen to bear arms in defense of himself or the State shall not be impaired. . . ." Michigan's says, "Every person has a right to keep and bear arms for the defense of himself and the State." Pennsylvania's constitution is emphatic: "The right of the citizens to bear arms in defense of themselves and the State shall not be questioned." Given such declarations, the states with these and similar provisions could not possibly prohibit ownership of handguns or any other arms.

It should be clear that the Second Amendment was not   5
originally intended to apply only to militia but to the "whole people." In addition, Congress has indicated that the militia consists of all able-bodied young and middle-aged males (and now perhaps females also). Furthermore, 50 percent of the state constitutions define and

protect the rights of individual gun owners. Is it not evident that the right to bear arms is rooted in solid legal precedent?

DISCUSSION QUESTIONS

1. Identify the writer's proposition. Is it one of fact, policy, action, or value?
2. In paragraph 1, the writer cites two approaches to the issue. What are they? Could they have been presented in reverse order? Why or why not?
3. What type of evidence does the writer use in her argument?
4. Reread the last two sentences in paragraph 3. Indicate why the phrasing "would now seem" and "it would appear" is appropriate here.
5. What type of conclusion does the writer use? Why is the question that ends it effective?

SUGGESTIONS FOR WRITING ■ Write an argument on some topic you feel strongly about. Study all sides of the issue so you can argue effectively and appeal to a particular audience. Support your proposition with logical evidence. Here are some possibilities to consider if your instructor gives you a free choice.

1. Compulsory composition courses in college
2. Unmarried couples living together
3. Banning whale hunting
4. Requiring students to pass a general competency test in order to graduate from high school
5. Some aspect of native American affairs
6. Capital punishment
7. Government funding of noncommercial television
8. Gay rights
9. Legislation banning throwaway bottles
10. Bilingual instruction in schools
11. Legalizing prostitution (or gambling)
12. Mandatory airbags in cars
13. Guardian Angels patrolling city streets
14. Sobriety checklanes for nabbing drunk drivers
15. A local or campus issue

DISCUSSION QUESTIONS

1. The proposition, one of fact, is the final sentence in paragraph 1.

2. The writer cites emotional and objective approaches. They could not have been reversed. She introduces, and then bypasses, the emotional approaches in favor of her objective approach, which ends the first paragraph and sets up her arguments to follow.

3. She uses established truths and authoritative opinions.

4. The writer suggests her position rather than insisting upon it. You might point out that a writer who tries to force something on the reader will probably generate backlash. Note the difference if she had said "Only a fool couldn't see. . . ."

5. This conclusion summarizes the main points. The concluding question is effective because, in view of the evidence, the answer will probably be "yes," prompting the reader to acknowledge the strength of the argument.

Mixing the Writing Strategies

PERSPECTIVE

One of our goals is to offer students a variety of conceptual and writing tools that they can use to handle more complex writing projects. Students should understand that using the proper combination of strategies offers a way of approaching many writing situations, including the research paper assignment. When students discover that they have already blended various strategies in earlier papers and that complex writing tasks can be broken down into segments, any apprehension they may have about mixing the strategies should be lessened considerably.

TEACHING STRATEGIES

1. Have students go over their previous essays to determine and annotate where they used more than one strategy. They might find that in an earlier narrative, for example, they implicitly referred to a cause and explicitly used description.

2. Ask students to review a number of professional pieces of writing (perhaps even a proposal or a business report), establish the writer's purpose, and then determine what strategies were used and why. This could also be a classroom activity with the material presented on an overhead.

WHY AND HOW TO MIX STRATEGIES

Writing strategies seldom occur in pure form. Writers nearly always mix them in assorted combinations for various purposes, not just in papers of definition and argument, as we've noted in Chapters 11 and 12, but also in papers of narration, description, process analysis, illustration, classification, comparison, and cause and effect. An essay that is primarily narration might contain descriptive passages or note an effect. A comparison might include illustrations or carry an implied argument. The purpose, audience, and occasion of the individual essay dictate the mixture, which can't be predetermined. Your best bet is to familiarize yourself with the individual strategies and use them as needed.

Let's see how you'd go about combining the various strategies in an actual writing situation. Suppose you've been assigned a description paper and you decide to write about the place your family vacationed last year. You might start your essay by noting what *caused* you to pick that locale and offering a brief *comparison* between it and previous vacation spots. You could then *narrate* your activities on a typical day and conclude by indicating the *effects* the whole experience had on you. Note that not all the strategies are used—only the ones that suit your purpose.

Assignments in other classes and on the job will also require you to mix the writing strategies. Your political science professor might ask for a paper that evaluates the advantages of a democratic state over a totalitarian one. You could open with contrasting *definitions* of the two forms of government and then, to make them more concrete, offer XYZ as an *illustration* of a typical democracy, ABC as a typical totalitarian state. After *describing* the key characteristics of each type, you might *compare* their social, economic, and religious effects on their citizens.

At work, a sales manager might have to write a year-end analysis that *compares* sales trends in the first and second quarters of the year, suggests the *causes* of any areas of weakness, and *classifies* the regions with superior potential in the upcoming year. And almost any employee could be asked to compose a report that

163

PERSPECTIVE

Problem/solution and evaluation reports can introduce students to more complex
writing tasks that, because of
their highly organized nature,
students are capable of doing.
These reports also allow students to adopt the voice of
an authority, a stance crucial
to their growth as writers.
Furthermore, such assign-
ments provide an opportunity
to write for actual readers,
not "just for my composition
teacher." Still, given the complexity of these reports, students will often have to be
guided through their various
stages.

TEACHING STRATEGIES

1. Assignments that draw on
the actual experience of students work best. You could
ask students to identify a
problem at their college or in
their community and then
write to those in authority to
explain the problem and suggest a specific course of action.
2. Have students work on
their problem/solution project
in stages. First they might describe the problem and explain why it is a problem.
Make sure they define all key
terms or concepts. Then have
them determine the causes.
Finally they could consider
several possible solutions, explain them in detail to show
how they work, suggest the
process by which each might
be implemented, and then
consider the consequences.
Only when students have
done the necessary investigative work are they ready to
write a draft.

CLASSROOM ACTIVITY

As a class, investigate a common problem. Students can
then share ideas in group
brainstorming and see the effort involved in working on
this type of paper.

defines and *illustrates* a problem, examines its *causes*, and *argues* for a particular solution.

When tackling a multi-strategy writing assignment, break the project into separate stages. Determine first what you need to accomplish, then which strategies will serve your purpose, and finally how best to implement and organize them. It also helps to list all the strategies before you start reflecting on which ones to use. Let's apply these guidelines to the writing of a problem/solution report and then to an evaluation report, two common projects that rely on a mix of writing strategies.

PROBLEM/SOLUTION REPORT

Suppose many students have experienced serious delays in getting to use the microfiche readers in your college library and you want to report the situation to the administration. Your goal is to eliminate the problem. After a little thought, you realize that you must first demonstrate that a problem exists and that it warrants action.

Before you can write such a report, you need to investigate the extent of the problem (does it really need solving?), look for its causes (possibly hidden causes), and determine the possible effects. Almost always these are your first steps before you decide on any solutions. Often you can find effective solutions by addressing the causes of the problem, but you might also explore new ways of improving the situation. You'll want to consider carefully whether your solution will work. After you review your options, you decide to use illustration and description to demonstrate the problem, and then to examine the effects and their causes.

Here's how you might proceed as you write the report. Your introduction states the problem. Then you portray a typical evening with long lines of students waiting to use the microfiche readers, while others mill around, grumble, and sometimes leave in disgust. Next, you take up effects, noting a number of occasions when both you and your friends have turned in late papers due to unavailable readers and received low grades. Turning to causes, you report your findings. Perhaps the library lacks funds to buy more microfiche readers. Perhaps it needs to expand its hours, or instructors need to schedule research projects at differing times.

The solution you recommend will, of course, depend on the cause(s). If extending the library hours would solve the problem, then purchasing more readers would just waste funds. The best solution may consist of several actions: buying a few readers, extending the library hours, and persuading instructors to stagger their research assignments. In some cases, you may have to explain the process of implementing your solution and/or defend (argue) its feasibility by showing that it will not have unacceptable consequences. For instance, in our microfiche example, you would need to consider the costs of keeping the library open and staffed for longer hours.

EVALUATION REPORT

Imagine that your school has been experimenting with metal whiteboards that use markers instead of chalk. The administration has asked you to assess how effectively these boards serve student and instructor needs and to present your findings in an evaluation report.

As you think the project through, you realize that you first need to determine the key criteria for evaluation, which you decide are glare, the quality of the writing left by the markers, and the effectiveness of erasing. Because these boards compete with conventional blackboards, you decide that you need a comparison of the two that includes a description of the whiteboards and illustrations supporting your observations. You also decide that a discussion of the effects the boards have on students would be in order.

After drawing your conclusions, you begin your report by indicating why it's being written, providing a definition and description of the whiteboards, and noting the criteria you will use. Following this introduction, you discuss each criterion in turn, describing with illustrative examples how well the whiteboard measures up in comparison to conventional blackboards. You also note the effects of any shortcomings on students. In your conclusion, you argue that the irregular performance of the markers, the glare of the whiteboard surfaces, and the difficulty of erasing the marking frustrate students and make classes more difficult for instructors to conduct. You recommend that the college discontinue using whiteboards except in computer classrooms where chalk dust damages the units.

EXERCISE ■ Suggest what combination of writing strategies you might use in each of the situations below.

1. The company you work for, school you attend, or club you belong to has a serious morale problem. You have been asked to evaluate its various dimensions, propose feasible solutions, and then make a recommendation to the appropriate person.
2. Your company, school, or club is about to purchase some specific type of new equipment. You have been asked to write a report examining the available brands and recommending one.
3. Your local newspaper has asked you to write about your college major or occupation and how you regard it. The article will help high school students decide whether this major or occupation would be appropriate for them.
4. Your general science instructor has asked you to study and report on some industrial chemical. The report must answer typical questions a layperson would likely ask about the chemical.

The margin notes on the following essay show the interplay of several writing strategies.

TEACHING STRATEGIES

1. There are many excellent opportunities for evaluation assignments. Students could be asked to review movies, television shows, textbooks, classes, restaurants, products, or to evaluate the different options for providing incoming freshmen with a guide to college life.
2. Students often experience considerable difficulty identifying evaluation criteria. You might want to spend class time explaining these criteria and helping students distinguish between criteria and subjective responses.
3. Evaluations serve different purposes and come in different forms. Have students compare movie reviews from <u>Consumer Reports</u> to determine the different purposes, styles, and organization.

CLASSROOM ACTIVITY

Have students work in small groups to prepare an evaluation of a common object, perhaps this textbook. They should develop, define, and apply the criteria and then support their conclusions with specific examples.

EXERCISE ANSWERS

Here are *possible* approaches to the writing situations.

1. You'd probably begin by *defining* the problem and offering a few *illustrations* of it. Then you might suggest its *causes* and *effects, compare* the alternative solutions, and *argue* for (recommend) implementing one of them.
2. You might begin by examining the reasons why (*causes*) the old equipment is obsolete and projecting the beneficial *effects* if new equipment is purchased. After *comparing* the features of several competing brands, you could review the *process* of operation for one of them and then *argue* for (recommend) its purchase.

3. For starters, you might mention the reasons (*causes*) that led to your choice. Next, you could *classify* your duties, *narrate* a typical work day,' and finally move to *effects* by noting how your occupation benefits the public. You might enhance your account with plenty of enticing *descriptive* details.

4. A layperson would most probably want to know the following: What does the chemical look like? How is it made? What is it used for? Is it harmful in any way? The paper should therefore include a brief physical *description* of the compound, analyze the *process* by which it's made, *classify* its uses, and note any *effects* it can have on the environment or those working with it.

Illustration in narrative form

Definition

Description

Effect

EXAMPLE ESSAY USING SEVERAL WRITING STRATEGIES

Bruce Jay Friedman

EATING ALONE IN RESTAURANTS

Bruce Jay Friedman (born 1930) is a native of New York City and a 1951 graduate of the University of Missouri, where he majored in journalism. Between 1951 and 1953, he served in the U.S. Air Force and for the next decade was editorial director of a magazine management company. He now freelances. A versatile writer, Friedman has produced novels, plays, short stories, and nonfiction, earning critical acclaim as a humorist. In our selection, taken from The Lonely Guy's Book of Life *(1979), he offers the urban male who must dine out alone witty advice on coping with the situation.*

1   Hunched over, trying to be as inconspicuous as possible, a solitary diner slips into a midtown Manhattan steakhouse. No sooner does he check his coat than the voice of the headwaiter comes booming across the restaurant.

2   "Alone again, eh?"

3   As all eyes are raised, the bartender, with enormous good cheer, chimes in: "That's because they all left him high and dry."

4   And then, just in case there is a customer in the restaurant who isn't yet aware of the situation, a waiter shouts out from the buffet table: "Well, we'll take care of him anyway, won't we fellas!"

5   *Haw, haw, haw,* and a lot of sly winks and pokes in the ribs.

6   Eating alone in a restaurant is one of the most terrifying experiences in America.

7   Sniffed at by headwaiters, an object of scorn and amusement to couples, the solitary diner is the unwanted and unloved child of Restaurant Row. No sooner does he make his appearance than he is whisked out of sight and seated at a thin sliver of a table with barely enough room on it for an hors d'oeuvre. Wedged between busboy stations, a hair's breadth from the men's room, there he sits, feet lodged in a railing as if he were in Pilgrim stocks, wondering where he went wrong in life.

8   Rather than face this grim scenario, most Lonely Guys would prefer to nibble away at a tuna fish sandwich in the relative safety of their high-rise apartments.

9   What can be done to ease the pain of this not only starving but silent minority—to make dining alone in restaurants a rewarding experience? Absolutely nothing. But some small strategies *do* exist for making the experience bearable.

■ Before You Get There

10   Once the Lonely Guy has decided to dine alone at a restaurant, a sense of terror and foreboding will begin to build throughout the day. All the more reason for him to get there as quickly as possible so that the experience can soon be forgotten and he can resume his normal life. Clothing should be light and loose-fitting, especially around the neck—on the off chance of a fainting attack during the appetizer. It is best to dress modestly, avoiding both the funeral-director-style suit as well as the bold, eye-arresting costume of the gaucho. A single cocktail should suffice; little sympathy will be given to the Lonely Guy who tumbles in, stewed to the gills. (The fellow who stoops to putting morphine in his toes for courage does not belong in this discussion.) En route to the restaurant, it is best to play down dramatics, such as swinging the arms pluckily and humming the theme from *The Bridge on the River Kwai.*

■ Once You Arrive

11   The way your entrance comes off is of critical importance. Do not skulk in, slipping along the walls as if you are carrying some dirty little secret. There is no need, on the other hand, to fling your coat arrogantly at the hatcheck girl, slap the headwaiter across the cheeks with your gloves and demand to be seated immediately. Simply walk in with a brisk rubbing of the hands and approach the headwaiter. When asked how many are in your party, avoid cute responses such as "Jes lil ol' me." Tell him you are a party of one; the Lonely Guy who does not trust his voice can simply lift a finger. Do not launch into a story about how tired you are of taking out fashion models, night after night, and what a pleasure it is going to be to dine alone.

12   It is best to arrive with no reservation. Asked to set aside a table for one, the restaurant owner will suspect either a prank on the part of an ex-waiter, or a terrorist plot, in which case windows will be boarded up and the kitchen bomb-swept. An advantage of the "no reservation" approach is that you will appear to have just stepped off the plane from Des Moines, your first night in years away from Marge and the kids.

13   All eyes will be upon you when you make the promenade to your table. Stay as close as possible to the headwaiter, trying to match him step for step. This will reduce your visibility and fool some diners into thinking you are a member of the staff. If you hear a generalized snickering throughout the restaurant, do not assume automatically that you are being laughed at. The other diners may all have just recalled an amusing moment in a Feydeau farce.

14   If your table is unsatisfactory, do not demand imperiously that one for eight people be cleared immediately so that you can dine in solitary grandeur. Glance around discreetly and see if there are other possibilities. The ideal table will allow you to keep your back to the wall so that you can see if anyone is laughing at you. Try to get one close to another couple so that if you lean over at a 45-degree angle it will appear that you are a swinging member of their group. Sitting opposite a mirror can be useful; after a drink or two, you will begin to feel that there are a few of you.

15   Once you have been seated, and it becomes clear to the staff that you are alone, there will follow The Single Most Heartbreaking Moment in Dining Out Alone—when the second setting is whisked away and yours is spread out a bit to

Step in process

Description

Step in process

Comparison

Effect

Definition

make the table look busier. This will be done with great ceremony by the waiter—angered in advance at being tipped for only one dinner. At this point, you may be tempted to smack your forehead against the table and curse the fates that brought you to this desolate position in life. A wiser course is to grit your teeth, order a drink and use this opportunity to make contact with other Lonely Guys sprinkled around the room. A menu or a leafy stalk of celery can be used as a shield for peering out at them. Do not expect a hearty greeting or a cry of "huzzah" from these frightened and browbeaten people. Too much excitement may cause them to slump over, curtains. Smile gently and be content if you receive a pale wave of the hand in return. It is unfair to imply that you have come to help them throw off their chains.

Effect

16   When the headwaiter arrives to take your order, do not be bullied into ordering the last of the gazelle haunches unless you really want them. Thrilled to be offered anything at all, many Lonely Guys will say "Get them right out here" and wolf them down. Restaurants take unfair advantage of Lonely Guys, using them to get rid of anything from withered liver to old heels of roast beef. Order anything you like, although it is good to keep to the light and simple in case of a sudden attack of violent stomach cramps.

Step in process

■ Some Proven Strategies

17   Once the meal is under way, a certain pressure will begin to build as couples snuggle together, the women clucking sympathetically in your direction. Warmth and conviviality will pervade the room, none of it encompassing you. At this point, many Lonely Guys will keep their eyes riveted to the restaurant paintings of early Milan or bury themselves in a paperback anthology they have no wish to read.

Effect

18   Here are some ploys designed to confuse other diners and make them feel less sorry for you.

Classification

19   ■ After each bite of food, lift your head, smack your lips thoughtfully, swallow and make a notation in a pad. Diners will assume you are a restaurant critic.

20   ■ Between courses, pull out a walkie-talkie and whisper a message into it. This will lead everyone to believe you are part of a police stake-out team, about to bust the salad man as an international dope dealer.

21   ■ Pretend you are a foreigner. This is done by pointing to items on the menu with an alert smile and saying to the headwaiter: "Is good, no?"

22   ■ When the main course arrives, brush the restaurant silverware off the table and pull some of your own out of a breastpocket. People will think you are a wealthy eccentric.

23   ■ Keep glancing at the door, and make occasional trips to look out at the street, as if you are waiting for a beautiful woman. Half-way through the meal, shrug in a world-weary manner and begin to eat with gusto. The world is full of women! Why tolerate bad manners! Life is too short.

Step in process

■ The Right Way

24   One other course is open to the Lonely Guy, an audacious one, full of perils, but all the more satisfying if you can bring it off. That is to take off your dark glasses, sit erectly, smile broadly at anyone who looks in your direction,

wave off inferior wines, and begin to eat with heartiness and enormous confidence. As outrageous as the thought may be—enjoy your own company. Suddenly, titters and sly winks will tail off, the headwaiter's disdain will fade, and friction will build among couples who will turn out to be not as tightly cemented as they appear. The heads of other Lonely Guys will lift with hope as you become the attractive center of the room.

25   If that doesn't work, you still have your fainting option.

Implied argument

READER/THEME STRATEGIES

Any of the themes explored in the Reader could lead to a mixed-strategy paper. Because of student apprehension about such a complex assignment, it might help to provide specific guidance. Students could, for example, consider the cause of some American crisis and recommend a solution. The pattern we suggest for the microfiche paper—illustration, description, effects, causes, and then a recommendation—might provide a model. If you prefer the theme "Who We Are," the class could discuss and write on the different behaviors displayed by restaurant employees toward different types of customers. These essays could classify the customers, describe and compare the treatment received by each group, speculate on the causes of the difference, and consider the effects on the customers.

After finishing this part of the book, you might wish to have students discuss and establish anew the criteria for good writing. They could then examine two Reader essays on the same general topic or two samples of their own writing and judge which meets the criteria better.

Paragraphs

Imagine the difficulty of reading a magazine article or book if you were faced with one solid block of text. How could you sort its ideas or know the best places to pause for thought? Paragraphs help guide readers through longer pieces of writing. Some break lengthy discussions of one idea into segments of different emphasis, thus providing rest stops for readers. Others consolidate several briefly developed ideas. Yet others begin or end pieces of writing or link major segments together. Most paragraphs, though, include a number of sentences that develop and clarify one idea. Throughout a piece of writing, paragraphs relate to one another and reflect a controlling purpose. To make paragraphs fit together smoothly, you can't just sit down and dash them off. Instead, you first need to think in terms of the entire essay, then channel your thoughts toward its different segments. Often you'll have to revise your paragraphs after you've written a draft.

CHARACTERISTICS OF EFFECTIVE PARAGRAPHS

Unity

A paragraph with unity develops one, and only one, key controlling idea. To ensure unity, edit out any stray ideas that don't belong and fight the urge to take interesting but irrelevant side trips; they only create confusion about your destination.

The following paragraph *lacks unity:*

> The psychiatric nurse deals with dangerous mental patients, pathological personalities who may explode into violence at any moment. Sigmund Freud was one of the first doctors to study mental disorders. Today psychotherapy is a well established medical discipline.

What exactly is this writer trying to say? We can't tell. Each sentence expresses a different, undeveloped idea:

1. Job of the psychiatric nurse
2. Freud's pioneering work in studying mental disorders
3. Present status of psychotherapy

In contrast, the following paragraph develops and clarifies only one central idea: the professional responsibilities of a psychiatric nurse.

> The psychiatric nurse deals with dangerous mental patients, pathological personalities who may explode into violence at any moment. For this reason, the nurse must remain on guard at all times. When a patient displays anger or violence, she cannot respond in kind but must instead show tolerance and understanding. Furthermore, she must be able to recognize attempts at deception. Sometimes a mentally ill person, just prior to launching an attack, will act in a completely normal way in order to deceive the intended victim. The nurse must recognize this behavior and be alert for any possible assault.
>
> Peggy Feltman

Because no unrelated ideas sidetrack the discussion of responsibilities, the paragraph has unity. To check your paragraphs for unity, ask yourself what each one aims to do and whether each sentence helps that aim.

EXERCISE ■ **After reading the next two paragraphs, answer the questions that follow.**

1.   The legend--in Africa--that all elephants over a large geographical area go to a common "graveyard" when they sense death is approaching led many hunters to treat them with special cruelty. Ivory hunters, believing the myth and trying to locate such graveyards, often intentionally wounded an elephant in the hopes of following the suffering beast as it made its way to the place where it wanted to die. The idea was to wound the elephant seriously enough so that it thought it was going to die but not so seriously that it died in a very short time. All too often, the process resulted in a single elephant being shot or speared many times and relentlessly pursued until it either fell dead or was killed when it finally turned and charged its attackers. In any case, no wounded elephant ever led its pursuers to the mythical graveyard with its hoped-for booty of ivory tusks.

Kris Hurrell

EXERCISE ANSWERS (p. 172)
1. This paragraph is unified. The first sentence is the topic sentence, and the rest develop the point that many hunters treated elephants cruelly in hopes of locating the elephants' "graveyard."
2. This paragraph lacks unity. The topic sentence, stated at the outset, indicates that the paragraph will focus on jungle games in the woodlot. The next three sentences do this, but the paragraph then veers off course and discusses the woodlot as a source of fuel, a hunting ground, and a place to keep cool. The final sentence returns to jungle games. The paragraph could be improved by dropping the material that has nothing to do with the woodlot as a playground.

2.   When I was growing up, I spent many happy hours with my brothers and sisters playing jungle games in the woodlot behind our farm home. This lot, ten acres of dense-set poplars and birches standing amidst the blackened stumps of an old pine forest, provided a perfect setting for our jungle adventures. At times we acted out African versions of cowboys and Indians; at others we sought the long-lost treasurers of fabled diamond mines. Often our adventures pitted Tarzan against tomb robbers and poachers. Besides serving as a playground, our woodlot furnished most of the fuel for the iron stoves in our kitchen and living room. I can still remember the back-breaking work of chopping up stumps and fallen trees and hauling them to the house. In the winter, the woodlot offered fine small-game hunting. In the summer, it provided a cool refuge from the heat that blistered the fields and farmhouse. Today, farm and woodlot are gone, swallowed up by a sprawling suburb. I wonder whether the children who live there ever want to play jungle games or regret that there's no place for them.

Student Unknown

1. Which of these paragraphs lacks unity? Refer to the paragraphs when answering.
2. How would you improve the paragraph that lacks unity?

PERSPECTIVE

Alexander Bain (English Composition and Rhetoric , 1866) was the first person to offer a systematic theory of the paragraph. Among other things, he stressed the essential role of the topic sentence. More recently, some researchers have questioned whether topic sentences are as crucial or prevalent as traditional paragraph theory suggests. While it is true that in some writing topic sentences are noticeably absent, it's probably best if students guide their paragraphs with clearly stated topic sentences, at least initially. Later they can advance to implied topic sentences. Writing topic sentences isn't always a conscious act. During the drafting stage, students may automatically create them for

The Topic Sentence

The topic sentence states the main idea of the paragraph. Think of the topic sentence as a rallying point, with all supporting sentences developing the idea it expresses. A good topic sentence helps you gauge what information belongs in a paragraph, thus ensuring unity. At the same time, it informs your reader about the point you're making.

Placement of the topic sentence varies from paragraph to paragraph, as the following examples show. As you read each, note how supporting information develops the topic sentence, which is italicized.

Topic Sentence Stated First.   Many paragraphs open with the topic sentence. The writer reveals the central idea immediately and then builds from a solid base.

Starting about one million years ago, the fossil record shows an accelerating growth of the human brain. It expanded at first at the rate of one cubic inch of additional gray matter every hundred thousand years; then the growth rate doubled; it doubled again; and finally it doubled once more. Five hundred thousand years ago the rate of growth hit its peak. At that time, the brain was expanding at the phenomenal rate of ten cubic inches every hundred thousand years. No other organ in the history of life is known to have grown as fast as this.

Robert Jastrow, *Until the Sun Dies*

Topic Sentence Stated Last.

In order to emphasize the support and build gradually to a conclusion, a topic sentence can end the paragraph. This position creates suspense as the reader anticipates the summarizing remark.

> An experience of my own comes handily to mind. Some years ago, when the Restaurant de la Pyramide in Vienne was without question one of the best half-dozen restaurants in the world, I visited it for the first time. After I had ordered my meal, the sommelier [wine steward] appeared to set before me a wine list of surpassing amplitude and excellence. But as I cast my eyes down this unbelievable offering of the world's most tantalizing wines, the sommelier bent over me and pointed out a wine of which I had never heard, ticketed at a price one-fifth that of its illustrious neighbors. "Monsieur," said the sommelier, "I would suggest this one. It is a local wine, a very good wine. It is not a great wine, but after all, monsieur, you are likely to pass this way only once. The great wines you will find everywhere; this wine you will find only in Vienne. I would like you to try it, while you have the opportunity." *This, to my mind, was true sophistication—on the part of M. Point for having the wine and on the part of the waiter for offering it.*

Stephen White, "The New Sophistication: Defining the Terms"

Topic Sentence Stated First and Last.

Some paragraphs lead with the main idea and then restate it, usually in different words, at the end. This technique allows the writer to repeat an especially important idea.

> *Everything is changing.* . . . This is a prediction I can make with absolute certainty. As human beings, we are constantly in a state of change. Our bodies change every day. Our attitudes are constantly evolving. Something that we swore by five years ago is now almost impossible for us to imagine ourselves believing. The clothes we wore a few years ago now look strange to us in old photographs. The things we take for granted as absolutes, impervious to change, are, in fact, constantly doing just that. Granite boulders become sand in time. Beaches erode and shape new shorelines. Our buildings become outdated and are replaced with modern structures that also will be torn down. Even those things which last thousands of years, such as the Pyramids and the Acropolis, also are changing. This simple insight is very important to grasp if you want to be a no-limit person, and are desirous of raising no-limit children. *Everything you feel, think, see, and touch is constantly changing.*

Wayne Dyer, *What Do You Really Want for Your Children?*

Topic Sentence Stated in the Middle.

On occasion, the topic sentence falls between one set of sentences that provides background information and a follow-up set that develops the central idea. This arrangement allows the writer to shift the emphasis and at the same time preserve close ties between the two sets.

many paragraphs as they try to achieve unity. The remaining topic sentences are then deliberately added during revision as students check for paragraphs that lack them.

TEACHING STRATEGIES

1. Ask students to review several different kinds of writing, including essays in the Reader, business essays, magazine articles, and textbooks to determine where topic sentences tend to be located. Some paragraphs, of course, will contain no topic sentence.

2. Students could follow the same procedure as they review their own writing.

CLASSROOM ACTIVITIES

1. You might rewrite a short essay so that the topic sentences are removed or reworded so as not to function as topic sentences. Have students identify where they have trouble reading the essay and why, develop topic sentences for the paragraphs, and then compare these sentences with those in the original essay.

2. Have students revise several of the sample paragraphs, reposition the topic sentence, and then evaluate the results. This activity shows that placement of the topic sentence can influence the effect, and even the meaning, of the paragraph.

SUGGESTED INSTRUCTOR READINGS

Braddock, R. "The Frequency and Placement of Topic Sentences in Expository Prose." Research in the Teaching of English (Winter 1974): 287–302. Braddock reports that in the professional writing he examined, topic sentences were used less than 15% of the time but that "percentages vary greatly among individual writers."

174

PARAGRAPHS

D'Angelo, F. "The Topic Sentence Revisited." College English 37 (1986): 431–41. Answering critics, D'Angelo argues that we should teach topic sentences since they enhance readability.

Over the centuries, China has often been the subject of Western fantasy. In their own way, a number of scholars, journalists, and other travelers have perpetuated this tradition in recent years, rushing to rediscover the country after its long period of isolation. Some of these visitors, justifiably impressed by the Communists' achievements in eliminating the exploitative aspects of pre-1949 mandarin society, propagated the view that the revolution, after its initial successes, had continued to "serve the people," and that China was "the wave of the future"—a compelling alternative to the disorder and materialism of contemporary Western society. Human rights were not at issue, they argued, because such Western concepts were inapplicable to China. *In the past year, however, the Chinese have begun to speak for themselves, and they are conveying quite a different picture.* In the view of many of its own people, China is a backward and repressive nation. "China is Asia's Gulag Archipelago," an elderly Chinese scholar said to me shortly after I had arrived in China last spring. "I was in Germany right after the Second World War, and I saw the horrors of Buchenwald and other concentration camps. In a way—in its destruction of the human spirit these past two decades—China has been even worse."

David Finkelstein, "When the Snow Thaws"

Topic Sentence Implied.
Some paragraphs, particularly in narrative and descriptive writing, have no topic sentence. Rather, all sentences point toward a main idea that readers must grasp for themselves.

[Captain Robert Barclay] once went out at 5 in the morning to do a little grouse shooting. He walked at least 30 miles while he potted away, and then after dinner set out on a walk of 60 miles that he accomplished in 11 hours without a halt. Barclay did not sleep after this but went through the following day as if nothing had happened until the afternoon, when he walked 16 miles to a ball. He danced all night, and then in early morning walked home and spent a day partridge shooting. Finally he did get to bed—but only after a period of two nights and nearly three days had elapsed and he had walked 130 miles.

John Lovesey, "A Myth Is as Good as a Mile"

The details in this paragraph collectively suggest a clear central idea: that Barclay had incredible physical endurance. But writing effective paragraphs without topic sentences challenges even the best writers. Therefore, control most of your paragraphs with clearly expressed topic sentences.

EXERCISE ANSWERS

1. The topic sentence is the third sentence of the paragraph. The first two sentences explain why the writer started to grow sunflowers. The four sentences following the topic sentence develop the idea that the plot is magnificent. The last two sentences talk about the writer's plans for next season.

EXERCISE ■ **Identify the topic sentences in each of the following paragraphs and explain how you arrived at your decisions. If the topic sentence is implied, state the central idea in your own words.**

1.   Last winter, while leafing through the Guinness Book of World Records, I came across an item stating that the tallest sunflower ever had been grown by G. E. Hocking, an Englishman. Fired by a competitive urge, I planted a half acre of sunflower seeds. That half acre is now a magnificent 22,000 square feet of green and gold flowers. From the

elevated rear deck of my apartment, I can look out over the swaying mass of thick, hairy green stalks and see each stalk thrusting up through the darker heart-shaped leaves below and supporting an ever-bobbing imitation of the sun. In this dwarf forest, some of the flower heads measure almost a foot in diameter. Though almost all my plants are now blooming, none will top the sixteen feet, two inches reached by Hocking's plant. My tallest is just thirteen feet even, but I don't think that's too bad for the first attempt. Next year, however, will be another matter. I plan to have an automatic watering system to feed my babies.

Joseph Wheeler

2.　　What my mother never told me was how fast time passes in adult life. I remember, when I was little, thinking I would live to be at least as old as my grandmother, who was dynamic even at ninety-two, the age at which she died. Now I see those ninety-two years hurtling by me. And my mother never told me how much fun sex could be, or what a discovery it is. Of course, I'm of an age when mothers really didn't tell you much about anything. My mother never told me the facts of life.

Joyce Susskind, "Surprises in a Woman's Life"

3.　　In fact, the separation between the scientists and non-scientists is much less bridgeable among the young than it was even thirty years ago. Thirty years ago the cultures had long ceased to speak to each other: but at least they managed a kind of frozen smile across the gulf. Now the politeness has gone, and they just make faces. It is not only that the young scientists now feel that they are part of a culture on the rise while the other is in retreat. It is also, to be brutal, that the young scientists know that with an indifferent degree they'll get a comfortable job, while their contemporaries and counterparts in English or History will be lucky to earn 60 percent as much. No young scientist of any talent would feel that he isn't wanted or that his work is ridiculous, as did the hero of *Lucky Jim;* and in fact, some of the disgruntlement of Amis and his associates is the disgruntlement of the underemployed arts graduate [Kingsley Amis is the author of the novel *Lucky Jim*].

C. P. Snow, *The Two Cultures: A Second Look*

4.　　The first hostage to be brought off the plane was a dark little man with a bald head and a moustache so thick and black that it obliterated his mouth. Four of the masked terrorists were guarding him closely, each with a heavy rifle held ready for fire. When the group was about fifty feet from the plane, a second hostage, a young woman in flowered slacks and a red blouse, was brought out in clear view by a single terrorist, who held a pistol against the side of her head. Then the first four pushed the dark little man from them and instructed him to kneel on the pavement. They

2. The topic sentence is the last sentence in the paragraph. The preceding sentences deal with two things Susskind's mother never told her: that time flies and sex can be fun. These sentences provide specific examples that support the general point made in the final sentence.

3. The first sentence is the topic sentence. The remaining sentences point out reasons for the widening gap.

4. This paragraph has an implied topic sentence. A suitable topic sentence might be "The terrorists, ignoring all efforts to negotiate the release of the passengers, began carrying out their threat to execute hostages."

looked at him as they might an insect. But he sat there on his knees, seemingly as indifferent as if he had already taken leave of his body. The shots from the four rifles sounded faintly at the far end of the field where a group of horrified spectators watched the grisly proceedings.

Bradley Willis

EXERCISE ■ **Develop one of the ideas below into a topic sentence. Then write a unified paragraph that is built around it.**

1. The career (or job or profession) I want is _____ .
2. The one quality most necessary in my chosen field is _____ .
3. The most difficult aspect of my chosen field is _____ .
4. One good example of the American tendency to waste is _____ .
5. The best (or worst) thing about fast-food restaurants is _____ .
6. The college course I find most useful (or interesting) is _____ .
7. Concentration (or substitute your own term here) is an important part of a successful golf game (or substitute your own sport).
8. The one place where I feel most at home is _____ .
9. More than anything else, owning a pet (or growing a garden) involves _____ .

Write a topic sentence that would control a paragraph on each of the following:

1. Preparations for traveling away from home
2. Advantages of having your own room
3. Some landmark of the community in which you live
4. The price of long-distance telephone calls
5. Registering for college courses
6. A cherished memento or souvenir
7. High school graduation
8. New Year's resolutions

PERSPECTIVE

The amount of development needed varies according to the situation. Students, for various reasons, consistently underdevelop their paragraphs. Students simply may not take the time to gather the necessary information. Or they may be afraid of going into too much detail "for fear of boring the reader." (The short, pithy paragraphs of the

Adequate Development

Students often ask for guidelines on paragraph length: "Should I aim for fifty to sixty words? Seven to ten sentences? About one-fourth of a page?" The questions are natural, but the approach is wrong. Instead of targeting a particular length, ask yourself what the reader needs to know. Then supply enough information to make your point clearly. Developing a paragraph inadequately is like inviting guests to a party but failing to tell them when and where it will be held. Skimpy paragraphs force readers to fill in the gaps for themselves, a task that can both irritate and stump them. On the other hand, a paragraph stuffed with useless padding dilutes the main idea. In all cases, the reader, the information being presented, and the publication medium determine the proper amount of detail. A newspaper might feature short paragraphs including only key facts, whereas a scientific journal might have lengthy paragraphs that offer detailed development of facts.

The details you supply can include facts, figures, thoughts, observations, steps, lists, examples, and personal experiences. Individually, these bits of information may mean little, but added together they clearly illustrate your point. Keep in mind, however, that development isn't an end in itself but instead advances the purpose of the entire essay.

Here are two versions of a paragraph, the first inadequately developed.

Underdeveloped Paragraph

Most of the delegates to the Constitutional Convention of 1787 feared too much democracy. As a result, they drafted the Constitution as a document outlining a limited democracy. Indeed, some of the provisions were simply undemocratic. But despite reflecting the delegates' distrust of popular rule, the Constitution did provide a framework in which democracy could evolve.

Adequately Developed Paragraph

Most of the delegates to the Constitutional Convention of 1787 feared too much democracy. As a result, they drafted the Constitution as a document outlining a limited democracy. Indeed, some of the provisions were simply undemocratic: *universal suffrage was denied; voting qualifications were left to the states; and women, blacks, and persons without property were denied the federal franchise. Until the passage of the Seventeenth Amendment in 1913, senators were not popularly elected but were chosen by state legislators.* But despite reflecting the delegates' distrust of popular rule, the Constitution did provide a framework in which democracy could evolve.

The first paragraph lacks examples of undemocratic provisions, whereas the second one provides the needed information.

Readability also helps set paragraph length. Within a paper, paragraphs signal natural dividing places, allowing the reader to pause and absorb the material presented up to that point. Too little paragraphing overwhelms the reader with long blocks of material. Too much creates a choppy Dick-and-Jane effect that may seem simplistic, even irritating. To counter these problems, writers sometimes use several paragraphs for an idea that needs extended development, or they combine several short paragraphs into one.

EXERCISE

1. Indicate where the ideas in this long block of material divide logically; explain your choices.

During the summer following graduation from high school, I could hardly wait to get to college and "be on my own." In the first weeks of my freshman year at State University, however, I found that independence occupation. . . ." The remaining material constitutes the final paragraph and deals with the writer's sense of being alone.

2. Possible details to use in expanding inadequately developed paragraphs. Paragraph 1: Strangers smile, say "hello"; Neighbors are friendly, visit back and forth, have block parties, baby-sit one another's children, borrow household items; Doors are seldom locked; Salesclerks and waiters are cheerful and helpful, as are public servants such as police officers and trash collectors. Paragraph 2: Strangers never smile or speak; Neighbors keep to themselves, almost never talk; Often neighbors' names are not known; Neighbors keep doors locked and bolted; Salesclerks and waiters are impersonal, often discourteous; Public servants also impersonal or discourteous.

can be tough and painful. I had expected raucous good times and a carefree collegiate life, the sort depicted in old beach movies and suggested by the selective memories of sentimental alumni. Instead, all I felt at first was the burden of increasing responsibilities and the loneliness of "a man without a country." I discovered that being independent of parents who kept at me to do my homework and expected me to accomplish certain household chores did not mean I was free to do as I pleased. On the contrary, living on my own meant that I had to perform for myself all the tasks that the family used to share. Studying became a full-time occupation rather than a nightly duty to be accomplished in an hour or two, and my college instructors made it clear that they would have little sympathy for negligence or even for my inability to do an assignment. But what was more troubling about my early college life than having to do laundry, prepare meals, and complete stacks of homework was the terrifying sense of being entirely alone. I was independent, no longer a part of the world that had seemed to confine me, but I soon realized that confinement had also meant security. I never liked the feeling that people were watching over me, but I knew that my family and friends were also watching out for me—and that's a good feeling to have. At the university no one seemed particularly to be watching, though professors constantly evaluated the quality of my work. I felt estranged from people in those first weeks of college life, desperately needing a confidant but fearful that the new and tenuous friendships I had made would be damaged if I were to confess my fears and problems. It was simply too early for me to feel a part of the university. So there I was, independent in the fullest sense, and thus "a man without a country."

2. The following short, choppy units are inadequately developed. List some details you could use to expand one of them into a good paragraph.

> I like living in a small town because the people are so friendly. I can always get the latest gossip from the local busybody. In addition, there's always the telephone party line.
>
> In a big city, people are afraid to get too friendly. Everything is very private, and nobody knows anything about anybody else.

3. Scan the compositions you have written in other classes for paragraphs that are over- or underdeveloped. Revise any you find.

Organization

An effective paragraph unfolds in a clear pattern of organization so that the reader can easily follow the flow of ideas. Here are some options:

1. The strategies discussed in Chapters 4–12
2. Order of climax

The choice you make depends upon your material and purpose in writing.

Writing Strategies. These include all of the following patterns:

Time sequence (narration)
Space sequence (description)
Process analysis
Illustration
Classification
Comparison
Cause and effect
Definition
Argument

Four example paragraphs follow. The first, organized by *time sequence,* traces the final years of the Model T Ford, concluding with a topic sentence that sums up its impact.

> In 1917 the Model T lost much of its attraction when its exterior appearance was drastically altered. The famous flat-sided brass radiator disappeared and the new style featured (in the words of the catalogue) "The stream-line hood, large radiator and enclosed fan, crown fenders, black finish and nickel trimmings" ("crown fenders" would be described in England as domed mudguards). Electric lighting and starting followed in 1919, and the model then continued with little alteration until 1927, when it was finally withdrawn. After a considerable pause it was replaced by the Model A, a very conventional machine with wire wheels, three-speed gearbox and four-wheel brakes (the "T" had never made this concession to progress and continued to the last with two minute brake drums on the back wheels only). While it was in preparation, others had taken the lead and the "A" never replaced the immortal "T" in the public fancy. Indeed, the "Tin Lizzy" or "Flivver" had become almost a national characteristic, and at the end of its eighteen years in production the total number sold was fifteen million.
>
> Cecil Clutton and John Stanford,
> *The Vintage Motor-Car*

The next paragraph, organized by *space sequence,* describes a ceramic elf, starting from the bottom and working up to the top. Other common spatial arrangements include top to bottom, left to right, right to left, nearby to far away, far away to nearby, clockwise, and counterclockwise.

> The ceramic elf in our family room is quite a character. His reddish-brown slippers, which hang over the mantel shelf, taper to a slender point.

which reaches a peak whenever the home team makes a basket.

2. Every now and then a shrill referee whistle silences the crowd, or a stabbing buzzer signals a timeout.

2. At every major turn in the game, the pep band strikes up the school fight song, and the fans join in.

Point out that each supporting sentence refers to the topic sentence, carries the same weight, and describes a different noise.

To explain subordination, you might use the following sentence from Lewis Thomas's Lives of a Cell: Notes of a Biology-Watcher as an example.

1. The microorganisms that seem to have it in for us in the worst way . . . turn out on close examination to be rather more like bystanders, strays, strangers in from the cold.

2. They will invade and replicate if given the choice . . . but it is our response to their presence that makes the disease.

3. Our arsenals for fighting off bacteria are so powerful, and involve so many different defense mechanisms, that we are in more danger from them than from the invaders.

4. We live in the midst of explosive devices; we are mined.

Point out that each supporting sentence refers to and throws light on the preceding sentence. Thus, *they* and *their* in the second sentence refer to *microorganisms* in the first sentence, *arsenals for fighting off bacteria* and *defense*

Pudgy, yellow-stockinged legs disappear into a wrinkled tunic-style, olive-green jacket, gathered at the waist with a thick, brown belt that fits snugly around his roly-poly belly. His short, meaty arms hang comfortably, one hand resting on the knapsack at his side and the other clutching the bowl of an old black pipe. An unkempt, snow-white beard, dotted by occasional snarls, trails patriarch-fashion from his lower lip to his belt line. A button nose capped with a smudge of gold dust, mischievous black eyes, and an unruly snatch of hair peeking out from under his burnt-orange stocking cap complete Bartholomew's appearance.

Maria Sanchez

Although descriptive paragraphs, like those developed by narration, often lack topic sentences, our example leads off with the central idea.

Here is a paragraph showing *process* development.

Making beer nuts is a quick, simple procedure that provides a delicious evening snack. You'll need six cups of raw peanuts, three cups of sugar, and one-and-one-half cups of water. To begin, combine the sugar and water in a two-quart saucepan and stir to dissolve the sugar. Next, add the peanuts and stir again until all of the peanuts are covered by the sugar-water solution. Leave the pan, uncovered, on a burner set at medium-high heat for ten to twelve minutes, until the sugar crystallizes and coats the peanuts thoroughly. Stay at the stove during the heating process and stir the mixture every two or three minutes to ensure even coating of the nuts. When the peanuts are thoroughly coated, pour them onto an ungreased cookie sheet and bake at 350 degrees for about thirty minutes, stirring and lightly salting at ten-minute intervals. Serve your beer nuts fresh out of the oven or eat them at room temperature.

Kimberlee Walters

Again, the topic sentence comes first.

The final example illustrates development by *comparison* and also proceeds from an opening topic sentence.

There is an essential difference between a news story, as understood by a newspaperman or a wire-service writer, and the newsmagazine story. The chief purpose of the conventional news story is to tell what happened. It starts with the most important information and continues into increasingly inconsequential details, not only because the reader may not read beyond the first paragraph but because an editor working on galley proofs a few minutes before press time likes to be able to cut freely from the end of the story. A newsmagazine is very different. It is written to be read consecutively from beginning to end, and each of its stories is designed, following the critical theories of Edgar Allan Poe, to create one emotional effect. The news, what happened that week, may be told in the beginning, the middle, or the end; for the purpose is not to throw information at the reader but to seduce him into reading the whole story, and into accepting the dramatic (and often political) point being made.

Otto Friedrich, "There Are 00 Trees in Russia"

Order of Climax. Climactic order creates a crescendo pattern, starting with the least emphatic detail and progressing to the most emphatic. The topic sentence can begin or end the paragraph, or it can remain implied. This pattern holds the reader's interest by building suspense. On occasion, writers reverse the order, landing the heaviest punch first; but such paragraphs can trail off, leaving the reader dissatisfied.

Here is a paragraph illustrating climactic order:

The speaking errors I hear affect me to different degrees. I'm so conditioned to hearing "It don't make any difference" and "There's three ways to solve the problem" that I've almost accepted such usage. However, errors such as "Just between you and I, Arnold loves Edna" and "I'm going back to my room to lay down" still offend my sensibility. When hearing them, I usually just chuckle to myself and walk away. The "Twin I's"--irrevelant and irregardless--are another matter. More than any other errors, they really grate on my ear. Whenever I hear "that may be true, but it's irrevelant" or "Irregardless of how much I study, I still get C's," I have the urge to correct the speaker. It's really surprising that more people don't clean up their language act.

Valerie Sonntag

EXERCISE ■ **From a magazine or newspaper article, select four paragraphs that illustrate different patterns of organization. Identify the topic sentence in each case; or if it is implied, state it in your own words. Point out the organization of each paragraph.**

Coherence

Coherent writing flows smoothly and easily from one sentence and paragraph to another, clarifying the relationships among ideas and thus allowing the reader to grasp connections. Because incoherent writing fails to do this, it confuses, and sometimes even irritates, the reader.

Here is a paragraph that lacks coherence:

I woke up late. I had been so tired the night before that I had forgotten to set the alarm. All I could think of was the report I had stayed up until 3 A.M.

PERSPECTIVE

mechanisms in the third sentence are linked to *response to their presence* in the second, and *explosive devices* and *mined* in the final sentence tie in with *danger* in the third.

Incoherence assumes several forms. Individual sentences might not make sense; they might not be linked by a common idea; some might shift the point too radically; essential information may be missing; or there might be an organization problem. It's easy to see how such prob-

182

lems arise. Sometimes students don't really understand their topic, or they haven't adequately thought it through. Often, they omit material they take for granted, assuming that because they can fill in the gaps, readers can too. On the other hand, some students expect too much from transitions. To demonstrate that connectors will not change complete nonsense into coherent writing, you might reproduce the following passage.

> It is always important for us to consider the will of the populace. Certainly, we can find that the populace is by nature popular. But is the popular willful? This is an issue we need to carefully consider since the will of the populace is often a diet soft drink. The populace, after all, is comprised of lost cows in a meadow. Further, the populace is comprised of wolves baying at the moon. With these definitions of the populace, we have to doubt their will and go off willynilly to our own picnic.

TEACHING STRATEGIES

1. As they study coherence in individual paragraphs, you might remind students that body paragraphs are interconnected units developed in relation to some overall essay purpose, not a string of discrete units that exist in a vacuum.
2. Many students probably use most of these transitions in their paragraphs. You can help them diversify by having them review their writing, identify these techniques, and circle those they repeat excessively.
3. Advise students to deal with coherence problems primarily during the revision stage. They should read their

typing, and how I could possibly get twenty copies ready for next morning's 9 o'clock sales meeting. I panicked and ran out the door. My bus was so crowded I had to stand. Jumping off the bus, I raced back up the street. The meeting was already underway. Mr. Jackson gestured for me to come into the conference room. Inserting the first page of the report into the copier, I set the dial for twenty copies and pressed the print button. The sign started flashing CALL KEY OPERATOR. The machine was out of order. Mr. Jackson asked whether the report was ready. I pointed to the flashing red words. Mr. Jackson nodded grimly without saying anything. He left me alone with the broken machine.

This paragraph has some degree of unity: most of its sentences relate to the writer's disastrous experience with the sales report. Unfortunately, though, its many gaps in logic create rather than answer questions, and in very bumpy prose, at that. Note the gap between the third and fourth sentences. Did the writer jump out of bed and rush right out the door? Of course not, but the reader has no real clue to the actual sequence of events. Another gap occurs between the next two sentences, leaving the reader to wonder why the writer had to race up the street upon leaving the bus. And who is Mr. Jackson? The paragraph never tells, but the reader will want to know.

Now read this rewritten version, additions italicized:

> I woke up late *because* I had been so tired the night before that I had forgotten to set the alarm. All I could think of was the report I had stayed up until 3 A.M. typing, and how I could possibly get twenty copies ready for next morning's 9 o'clock sales meeting. *When I realized it was 8:30,* I panicked. *Jumping out of bed, I threw on some clothes, grabbed the report,* and ran out the door. My bus was so crowded I had to stand *and could not see out the window. Two blocks beyond my stop, I realized I should have gotten off. "Stop!" I cried and,* jumping off the bus, raced back up the street. *When I reached the office, it was 9:15, and* the meeting was already underway. Mr. Jackson, *the sales manager, saw me and* gestured for me to come into the conference room. *"One moment," I said as calmly as I could and hurried to the copier.* Inserting the first page of the report into it, I set the dial for twenty copies and pressed the print button. *Immediately,* the sign started flashing CALL KEY OPERATOR. The machine was out of order. *The next thing I knew,* Mr. Jackson *was at my side* asking whether the report was ready. I pointed to the flashing red words*, and* Mr. Jackson nodded grimly without saying anything. *Turning on his heel,* he *walked away and* left me alone with the broken machine.

As this example shows, correcting an incoherent paragraph may call for anything from a single word to a whole sentence or more.

Coherence derives from a sufficient supply of supporting details and your firm sense of the way your ideas go together. If you brainstorm your topic thoroughly and think carefully about the relationships between sentences, incoherence isn't likely to haunt your paragraphs.

As you write, and especially when you revise, signal connections to the reader by using *transitions*—devices that link sentences to one another. These are the most common transitional devices:

1. Connecting words and phrases
2. Repeated key words
3. Pronouns and demonstrative adjectives
4. Parallelism

You can use them to furnish links both within and between paragraphs.

Connecting Words and Phrases. These connectors clarify relationships between sentences. The following list groups them according to function:

Showing similarity: in like manner, likewise, moreover, similarly
Showing contrast: at the same time, but, even so, however, in contrast, instead, nevertheless, still, on the contrary, on the other hand, otherwise, yet
Showing results or effects: accordingly, as a result, because, consequently, hence, since, therefore, thus
Adding ideas together: also, besides, first (second, third . . .), furthermore, in addition, in the first place, likewise, moreover, similarly, too
Drawing conclusions: as a result, finally, in brief, in conclusion, in short, to summarize
Pointing out examples: for example, for instance, to illustrate
Showing emphasis and clarity: above all, after all, again, as a matter of fact, besides, in fact, in other words, indeed, nonetheless, that is
Indicating time: at times, after, afterward, from then on, immediately, later, meanwhile, next, now, once, previously, subsequently, then, until, while
Conceding a point: granted that, of course, to be sure, admittedly

Don't overload your paper with connectors. In well-planned prose, your message flows clearly with only an occasional assist from them.

In the following excerpt, which clarifies the difference between workers and workaholics, the connectors are italicized.

> My efforts to define workaholism and to distinguish workaholics from other hard workers proved difficult. *While* workaholics do work hard, not all hard workers are workaholics. Moonlighters, *for example,* may work 16 hours a day to make ends meet, but most of them will stop working when their financial circumstances permit. Accountants, *too,* seem to work non-stop, but many slow down after the April 15 tax deadline. Workaholics, *on the other hand,* always devote more time and thought to their work than their situation demands. Even in the absence of deadlines to meet, mortgages to pay, promotions to earn, or bosses to please, workaholics still work hard. What sets them apart is their attitude toward work, not the number of hours they work.
>
> Marilyn Machlowitz, "Workaholism: What's Wrong with Being Married to Your Work?"

DISCUSSION QUESTIONS

1. What ideas do each of the italicized words and phrases connect?
2. What relationship does each show?

drafts as a stranger would, particularly noting places where someone might be confused.

4. All of us have encountered students who have problems with coherence. In some cases, the material in each paragraph seems linked by free association rather than logic. Problems can occur because students are anxious or depressed about the thought of writing or because they simply lack experience with any logical discipline. Such problems need to be addressed in an individual conference. In some cases, students may need to change topics. In others, they may need practice with exercises that require them to arrange pre-selected sentences under appropriate topic headings and discard those that don't fit.

CLASSROOM ACTIVITY

Bring in several paragraphs that lack coherence. Have students identify the reasons for the incoherence and suggest ways to correct the problem.

SUGGESTED INSTRUCTOR READINGS

Bamberg, B. "What Makes a Text Coherent?" College English 34 (1983): 417–30. Elaborates on the role meaning plays in determining coherence.

Markels, R. B. A New Perspective on Cohesion in Expository Paragraphs

Carbondale, IL: Southern Illinois UP, 1984. Details both the semantic and syntactic considerations that produce cohesion.

DISCUSSION QUESTIONS

In this paragraph, *while* picks up the contrast suggested in the first sentence and provides a link to the specific contrast in the sentence in which it appears. *For example* links the illustration presented in its sentence with the general idea stated in the second. *Too* in the fourth sentence indicates that the writer is adding another example to illustrate her point. *On the other hand* in the fifth sentence sets up the contrast between hard workers and workaholics that is at the heart of the paragraph.

Repeated Key Words.　　Repeating key words, especially those that help convey a paragraph's central idea, can smooth the reader's path. The words may appear in different forms, but their presence keeps the main issues before the reader. In the following paragraph, the repetition of *majority, minority,* and *will* aids coherence, as does the more limited repetition of *government* and *interests.*

> Whatever fine-spun theories we may devise to resolve or obscure the difficulty, there is no use blinking the fact that the *will* of the *majority* is not the same thing as the *will* of all. *Majority* rule works well only so long as the *minority* is *willing* to accept the *will* of the *majority* as the *will* of the *nation* and let it go at that. Generally speaking, the *minority* will be *willing* to let it go at that so long as it feels that its essential *interests* and rights are not fundamentally different from those of the current *majority,* and so long as it can, in any case, look forward with confidence to mustering enough votes within four or six years to become itself the *majority* and so redress the balance. But if it comes to pass that a large *minority* feels that it has no such chance, that it is a fixed and permanent *minority* and that another group or class with rights and *interests* fundamentally hostile to its own is in permanent control, then *government* by *majority* vote ceases in any sense to be *government* by the *will* of the people for the good of all, and becomes *government* by the *will* of some of the people for their own *interests* at the expense of the others.
>
> Carl Becker, *Freedom and Responsibility in the American Way of Life*

EXERCISE ■ **Write a paragraph using one of the following sentences as your topic sentence. Insert the missing key word and then repeat it in your paragraph to help link your sentences together.**

1. _____ is my favorite relative.
2. I wish I had (a, an, some, more) _____ .
3. _____ changed my life.
4. _____ is more trouble that it's worth.
5. A visit to _____ always depresses me.
6. Eating _____ is a challenge.
7. I admire _____ .

Pronouns and Demonstrative Adjectives.　　Pronouns stand in for nouns that appear earlier in the sentence or in previous sentences. Mixing pronouns and their nouns throughout the paragraph prevents monotony and promotes clarity. We have italicized the pronouns in the following excerpt from an article about Dolores Huerta and Cesar Chavez, two leaders of The United Farm Workers union.

> A book could be written on *their* [Huerta's and Chavez's] complex relationship. *Both* are stubborn and opinionated. *She* is notorious in the union for combativeness. (Stories are told of growers begging to face anyone at the negotiating table except Huerta.) Chavez jokes of "unleashing Dolores"; but *he* respects *her* opinions and *they* generally agree on larger issues. Dolores says *they* fight a lot because "*he* knows *I*'ll never quit, so *he* uses *me* to let off steam; *he* knows *I*'ll

fight back anyway." Chavez, a traditionalist in *his* own home life, is said to privately disapprove of Dolores's divorces, *her* living now with *his* brother Richard, and *her* chaotic way of raising *her* kids. But *he* knows that the union is the center of *her* life, just as *it* is with *his.* "Dolores is absolutely fearless, physically and emotionally," *he* says.

> Judith Coburn, "Dolores Huerta: La Pasionaria of the Farm Workers"

Except for *it* in the second sentence from the end, all the pronouns refer to Huerta, Chavez, or both.

Four demonstrative adjectives—*this, that, these,* and *those*—also help hook ideas together. Demonstratives are special adjectives that identify or point out nouns rather than describe them. Here is an example from the Declaration of Independence:

> We hold *these* truths to be self-evident, that all men are created equal, that they are endowed by their Creator with certain unalienable Rights, that among *these* are Life, Liberty, and the pursuit of Happiness. That to secure *these* rights, Governments are instituted among Men, deriving their just powers from the consent of the governed. That whenever any Form of Government becomes destructive of *these* ends, it is the Right of the People to alter or to abolish it, and to institute new Government, laying its foundation on such principles and organizing its power in such form, as to them shall seem most likely to effect their Safety and Happiness.

EXERCISE ■ **In a magazine, newspaper, textbook, or some other written source, find two paragraphs that use pronouns and demonstrative adjectives to increase coherence. Copy the paragraphs, underline the pronouns and demonstrative adjectives, and explain what each refers to.**

Parallelism. Parallelism uses repetition of grammatical form to express a series of equivalent ideas. Besides giving continuity, the repetition adds rhythm and balance to the writing. Note how the following italicized constructions tie together the unfolding definition of poverty.

> *Poverty is staying* up all night on cold nights to watch the fire, knowing one spark on the newspaper covering the walls means your sleeping children die in flames. In summer *poverty is watching* gnats and flies devour your baby's tears when he cries. The screens are torn and you pay so little rent you know they will never be fixed. *Poverty means* insects in your food, in your nose, in your eyes, and crawling over you when you sleep. *Poverty is hoping* it never rains because diapers won't dry when it rains and soon you are using newspapers. *Poverty is seeing* your children forever with runny noses. Paper handkerchiefs cost money and all your rags you need for other things. Even more costly are antihistamines. *Poverty is cooking* without food and cleaning without soap.

> Jo Goodwin Parker, "What Is Poverty?"

PARAGRAPHS WITH SPECIAL FUNCTIONS

Special-function paragraphs include introductions, transitional paragraphs, and conclusions. One-paragraph introductions and conclusions appear in short, multi-paragraph essays. Transitional paragraphs occur primarily in long compositions.

Introductions

A good introduction acquaints and coaxes. It announces the essay's topic and may directly state the thesis. In addition, it sets the tone—somber, lighthearted, angry—of what will follow. An amusing anecdote would not be an appropriate opening for a paper about political torture.

With essays, as with people, first impressions are important. If your opening rouses interest, it will draw the reader into the essay and pave the way for your ideas. If, instead, you'd like to try your hand at turning the reader away, search for a beginning that is mechanical, plodding, and dull. Your success will astonish you. Here are some bad openings.

In this paper I intend to . . .

Wars have always afflicted mankind.

As you may know, inflation is a problem for many of us.

In the modern world of today . . .

How would you respond to these openings? Ask yourself that same question about every opening you write.

Gear the length of the introduction to that of the essay. Although longer papers sometimes begin with two or more introductory paragraphs, generally the lead-in for a short essay is a single paragraph. Here are some possibilities for starting an essay. The type you select depends on your purpose, subject, audience, and personality.

A Directly Stated Thesis. This is a common type of opening, orienting the reader to what will follow. After providing some general background, the writer of our example narrows her scope to a thesis that previews the upcoming sections of her essay.

An increasing number of mid-life women are reentering the
workforce, pursuing college degrees, and getting more involved in the
public arena. Several labels besides ''mid-life'' have been attached to this
type of person: the mature woman, the older woman, and, more recently,
the reentry woman. By definition, she is between thirty-five and fifty-five
years old and has been away from the business or academic scene
anywhere from fifteen to thirty years. The academic community, the

media, marketing people, and employers are giving her close scrutiny, and it is apparent that she is having a greater impact on our society than she realizes.

Jo Ann Harris

A Definition. This kind of introduction works particularly well in a paper that acquaints the reader with an unfamiliar topic.

> You are completely alone in a large open space and are struck by a terrifying, unreasoning fear. You sweat, your heart beats, you cannot breathe. You fear you may die of a heart attack, although you do not have heart disease. Suppose you decide you will never get yourself in this helpless situation again. You go home and refuse to leave its secure confines. Your family has to support you. You have agoraphobia—a disabling terror of open spaces.
>
> "Controlling Phobias Through Behavior Modification"

A Quotation. A beginning quotation, particularly from an authority in the field, can be an effective springboard for the ideas that follow. Make sure any quote you use relates clearly to your topic.

> The director of the census made a dramatic announcement in 1890. The Nation's unsettled area, he revealed, "has been so broken into by isolated bodies of settlement that there can hardly be said to be a frontier line." These words sounded the close of one period of America's history. For three centuries before, men had marched westward, seeking in the forests and plains that lay beyond the settled areas a chance to begin anew. For three centuries they had driven back the wilderness as their conquest of the continent went on. Now, in 1890, they were told that a frontier line separating the settled and unsettled portions of the United States no longer existed. The west was won, and the expansion that had been the most distinctive feature of the country's past was at an end.
>
> Ray Allen Billington, "The Frontier Disappears"

An Anecdote or Personal Experience. A well-told personal anecdote or experience can lure readers into the rest of the paper. Like other introductions, this kind should bear on what comes afterward. Engle's anecdote, like the stories she reviews, demonstrates that "women also have dark hearts."

> My mother used to have a little china cream and sugar set that was given to her by a woman who later killed her children with an axe. It sat cheerfully in the china cabinet, as inadequate a symbol as I have ever seen of the dark mysteries within us. Yet at least it was there to remind us that no matter how much Jesus wanted us for a sunbeam, we would still have some day to cope with a deeper reality than common sense could explain. It stood for strange cars not to get into, running shoes to wear when you were out alone at night and the backs of Chinese restaurants you were not supposed to go into.
>
> Marian Engle, review of *The Goddess and Other Women* by Joyce Carol Oates

An Arresting Statement.   Sometimes you can jolt the reader into attention, using content, language, or both, particularly if your essay develops an unusual or extreme position.

> It's like Pearl Harbor. The Japanese have invaded, and the U.S. has been caught short. Not on guns and tanks and battleships—those are yesterday's weapons—but on mental might. In a high-tech age where nations increasingly compete on brainpower, American schools are producing an army of illiterates. Companies that cannot hire enough skilled workers now realize they must do something to save the public schools. Not to be charitable, not to promote good public relations, but to survive.
>
> Nancy Perry, "Saving the Schools: How Business Can Help"

Interesting Details.   These details pique curiosity and draw the reader into the paper.

> It is Friday night at any of the ten thousand watering holes of the small towns and crossroads hamlets of the South. The room is a cacophony of the ping-pong-ding-dingding of the pinball machine, the pop-fizz of another round of Pabst, the refrain of "Red Necks, White Socks and Blue Ribbon Beer" on the juke box, the insolent roar of a souped-up engine outside and, above it all, the sound of easy laughter. The good ole boys have gathered for their fraternal ritual—the aimless diversion that they have elevated into a life-style.
>
> Bonnie Angelo, "Those Good Ole Boys"

A Question.   A provocative question can entice the reader into the essay to find the answer.

> When you leave your apartment or house, do you begin to feel better? If you leave for a week-long trip, do you find your head clears, your migraine disappears, dizziness stops, your aches and pains subside, depression fades away, and your entire attitude is better? If so, chemical pollution of the atmosphere in your home may be making you ill.
>
> Marshall Mandell, "Are You Allergic to Your House?"

EXERCISE

1. **Explain why each of the preceding introductions interests or does not interest you. Does your response stem from the topic or the way the author introduces it?**

2. **Find magazine articles with effective introductory paragraphs illustrating at least three different techniques. Write a paragraph explaining why each impresses you.**

Transitional Paragraphs

In the midst of a lengthy essay, you may need a short paragraph that announces a shift from one group of ideas to another. Transitional paragraphs summarize previously explained ideas, repeat the thesis, or point to ideas that follow. In our example, Bruno Bettelheim has been discussing a young boy named Joey who has turned into a kind of human machine. After describing Joey's assorted delusions, Bettelheim signals his switch from the delusions to the fears that caused them.

> What deep-seated fears and needs underlay Joey's delusional system? We were long in finding out, for Joey's preventions effectively concealed the secret of his autistic behavior. In the meantime we dealt with his peripheral problems one by one.
>
> Bruno Bettelheim, "Joey: 'A Mechanical Boy' "

The following transitional paragraph looks back as well as ahead.

> Certainly these three factors—exercise, economy, convenience of short-cuts—help explain the popularity of bicycling today. But a fourth attraction sometimes overrides the others: the lure of the open road.
>
> Mike Bernstein

Conclusions

A conclusion rounds out a paper and signals that the discussion has been completed. Not all papers require a separate conclusion; narratives and descriptions, for example, generally end when the writer finishes the story or concludes the impression. But many essays benefit from a conclusion that drives the point home a final time. To be effective, a conclusion must mesh logically and stylistically with what comes earlier. A long, complex paper often ends with a summary of the main points, but any of several other options may be used for shorter papers with easy-to-grasp ideas. Most short essays have single-paragraph conclusions; longer papers may require two or three paragraphs.

Here are some cautions about writing your conclusion:

1. Don't introduce new material. Draw together, round out, but don't take off in a new direction.
2. Don't tack on an ending in desperation when the hour is late and the paper is due tomorrow—the so-called midnight special. Your reader deserves better than "All in all, skiing is a great sport" or "Thus we can see that motorcycle racing isn't for everyone."
3. Don't apologize. Saying that you could have done a better job makes a reader wonder why you didn't.
4. Don't moralize. A preachy conclusion can undermine the position you have established in the rest of your composition.

The following examples illustrate several common types of conclusions.

TEACHING STRATEGIES

1. Students experience difficulty writing conclusions. Part of the reason is that they believe they have nothing more to say. You might reassure them that it is acceptable, even useful, to repeat their main point in new language.
2. When students are working on a paper, have them freewrite on the kind of final impression they want to leave with the reader. Then they could try writing several conclusions until one meets their objectives.
3. You might have students try to write different conclusions to some of the essays in the Reader to note the effect that the new endings have on the impact of the work. Encourage students to stick as closely as possible to the style of the author.

Restatement of the Thesis. The following conclusion reasserts Jordan's thesis that "a mood of antisocial negativism is creeping through the structure of American life, corroding our ideals, and suffocating the hopes of poor people and minorities."

> There is room for honest differences about each of these key issues, but the new negativism's overt greed and the implicit racism of its loud "No" to minority aspirations indicate that this is a poisonous movement that denies the moral ideals and humane values that characterize the best in America's heritage.
>
> Vernon E. Jordan, Jr., "The New Negativism"

A Summary. A summary draws together and reinforces the main points of a paper.

> There are, of course, many other arguments against capital punishment, including its high cost and its failure to deter crime. But I believe the most important points against the death penalty are the possibility of executing an innocent man, the discriminatory manner in which it is applied, and the barbaric methods of carrying it out. In my opinion, capital punishment is, in effect, premeditated murder by society as a whole. As the old saying goes, two wrongs don't make a right.
>
> Diane Trathen

A Question. The paragraph below concludes an argument that running should not be elevated to a religion, that its other benefits are sufficient. A final question often prompts the reader to think further on the topic. If your essay is meant to be persuasive, be sure to phrase a concluding question so that the way a reasonable person would answer emphasizes your point of view.

> Aren't those gifts enough? Why ask running for benefits that are plainly beyond its capacity to bestow?
>
> James Fixx, "What Running Can't Do for You"

A Quotation. A quotation can capture the essence of your thought and end the essay with authority.

> "We had no idea of the emotional involvement and the commitment of these women," Richard says. "Suddenly a constituency arose. Suddenly there are thousands and thousands of women who don't care about your moral position or mine—they want a baby."
>
> David Zimmerman, "Are Test-Tube Babies the Answer for the Childless?"

Ironic Twist or Surprising Observation. These approaches prompt the reader to think further about a paper's topic. The following paragraph points out the ironic refusal of the government to confront poverty that exists a mere ten blocks away from its offices.

Thus, a stark contrast exists between the two cultures of 14th Street, which appears to be like an earthworm with half of its body crushed by poverty but the other half still alive, wriggling in wealth. The two are alike only in that each communicates little with the other because of the wide disparity between the lives of the people and the conditions of the environments. The devastating irony of the situation on 14th Street lies in the fact that only ten blocks away sit the very governmental institutions that could alleviate the poverty—the Senate, the House of Representatives, and the White House.

Student Unknown

Clever or Lighthearted Ending. In our example, the writer, capitalizing on the essay's topic, ends by exaggerating the fault being criticized.

Because using clichés is as easy as falling off a log, it goes without saying that it would be duck soup to continue in this vein till hell freezes over. However, since that would be carrying coals to Newcastle, let's ring down the curtain and bid adieu to the fair topic of the cliché. (No use beating a dead horse.)

Student Unknown

Personal Challenge. A challenge often prompts the reader to take some action.

And therein lies the challenge. You can't merely puff hard for a few days and then revert to the La-Z-Boy recliner, smugly thinking that you're "in shape." You must sweat and strain and puff regularly, week in and week out. They're your muscles, your lungs, your heart. The only caretaker they have is you.

Monica Duvall

Hope or Recommendation. Both a hope and a recommendation may restate points already made in the essay or suggest actions to take in order to arrive at a solution.

Periodically my pilot and I climb into our aircraft and head out over the Minnesota wilderness, following a succession of electronic beeps that lead to some of the last remaining wolves in the lower 48 states. We hope that the data we collect will provide a better understanding of the wolf. We especially hope that our work will help guide authorities into a management program that will insure the perpetuation of the species in the last vestiges of its former range.

L. David Mech, "Where Can the Wolves Survive?"

I who am blind can give one hint to those who can see—one admonition to those who would make full use of the gift of sight: Use your eyes as if tomorrow you would be stricken blind. And the same method can be applied to the other senses. Hear the music of voices, the song of the bird, the mighty strains of an orchestra, as if you would be stricken deaf tomorrow. Touch each object you want to touch as if tomorrow your tactile sense would fail. Smell the perfume of flowers, taste with relish each morsel, as if tomorrow you could never smell and taste again. Make the most of every sense; glory in all the facets of pleasure and beauty which the world reveals to you through the several means of contact which Nature provides. But of all the senses, I am sure that sight must be the most delightful.

Helen Keller, "Three Days to See"

EXERCISE

1. **Explain why each of the foregoing conclusions does or does not interest you. Does your response stem from the topic or from the author's handling of it?**

2. **Copy effective concluding paragraphs, illustrating at least three different techniques, from magazine articles. Then write a paragraph explaining why each impresses you.**

Effective Sentences

A sentence is a group of words that begins with a capital letter, ends with a period, question mark, or exclamation point, and makes sense by itself. The elements that comprise sentences include subjects, predicates, direct objects, indirect objects, subject complements, object complements, phrases, and clauses.

Sentences take many forms, some straightforward and unadorned, others intricate and ornate, each with its own stylistic strengths. Becoming familiar with these forms and their uses gives you the option to

- emphasize or de-emphasize an idea
- combine ideas into one sentence or keep them separate in more than one sentence
- make sentences sound formal or informal
- emphasize the actor or the action
- achieve rhythm, variety, and contrast.

Effective sentences bring both exactness and flair to your writing.

SENTENCE STRATEGIES

Effective sentences stem, at least in part, from selecting the right word order for independent clauses, coordinating and subordinating effectively, correctly positioning movable modifiers, using parallel structures, choosing the right verb voice, and avoiding fragments except for particular effects. Usually it's best to work on these different strategies as you revise rather than pausing to refine each sentence after you write it.

Word Order in Independent Clauses

Most independent clauses follow a similar arrangement. First comes the subject, then the verb, and finally any other element needed to convey the main message.

Barney blushed. *(subject, verb)*

They built the dog a kennel. *(subject, verb, indirect object, direct object)*

Samantha is an architect. *(subject, verb, subject complement)*

This arrangement puts the emphasis on the subject, right where it's usually wanted.

But the pattern doesn't work in every situation. Occasionally, a writer wants to emphasize some element that follows the verb, create an artistic effect, or give the subject unusual emphasis. Enter inverted order and the expletive construction.

Inverted Order. To invert a sentence, move to the front the element you want to emphasize. Sometimes the rest of the sentence follows in regular subject-then-verb order; sometimes the verb precedes the subject.

Lovable he isn't. *(subject complement, subject, verb)*

This I just don't understand. *(direct object, subject, verb)*

Tall grow the pines in the mountains. *(subject complement, verb, subject)*

Sentences that ask questions typically follow an inverted pattern.

Is this your coat? *(verb, subject, subject complement)*

Will you let the cat out? *(verb, subject, verb, direct object)*

Most of your sentences should follow normal order: readers expect it and read most easily through it. Furthermore, don't invert a sentence if the result would sound strained and unnatural. A sentence like "Fools were Brett and Amanda for quitting college" will only hinder communication.

Expletives. An expletive fills a vacancy in a sentence without contributing to the meaning. English has two common expletives, *there* and *it.* Ordinarily, *there* functions as an adverb, *it* as a pronoun, and either can appear anywhere in a sentence. As expletives, however, they alter normal sentence order by beginning sentences and anticipating the real subjects or objects.

Expletives are often used unnecessarily, as in the following example:

There were twenty persons attending the sales meeting.

This sentence errs on two counts: its subject needs no extra emphasis, and it is very clumsy. Notice the improvement without the expletive and the unneeded words:

Twenty persons attended the sales meeting.

When the subject or object needs highlighting, leading off with an expletive will, by altering normal order, call it more forcefully to the reader's attention.

| *Normal order* | A fly is in my soup. |
| | He seeks her happiness. |

| *Expletive construction* | There is a fly in my soup. *(expletive anticipating subject)* |
| | It is her happiness he seeks. *(expletive anticipating object)* |

Once in a while you'll find that something just can't be said unless you use an expletive.

There is no reason for such foolishness.

No other construction can express exactly the same thought.

EXERCISE ■ **Indicate which of these sentences follow normal order, which are inverted, and which have expletive constructions. Rewrite so that all will be in normal order.**

1. Dick Lewis is a true friend.
2. It was her car in the ditch.
3. An intelligent person is she.
4. May I go to the movie with you?
5. A sadder but wiser man he became.
6. There are many dead fish on the beach.
7. The instructor gave the class a long reading assignment.
8. The Willetts have bought a new house.
9. It is Marianne's aim to become a lawyer.
10. Harry works at a supermarket.

Coordination and Subordination

Coordination and subordination are ways to rank ideas in sentences. Coordination makes ideas equal; subordination makes them unequal. To understand coordination and subordination, you need to know about four kinds of sentences: simple, compound, complex, and compound–complex.

Simple Sentences. A simple sentence has one subject and one predicate. Some simple sentences consist merely of a single noun and a single verb.

Millicent shouted.

Others can include elements such as compound subjects, compound verbs, direct objects, indirect objects, and subject complements.

Jim and Sue have bought a car. (*compound subject, direct object*)

Lucretia Borgia smiled and mixed her guests a cocktail. (*compound verb, indirect object, direct object*)

Autumn is a sad season. (*subject complement*)

Most simple sentences are rather short and easy to understand. This trimness can add punch to your writing, but it can also make your writing sound childish and may waste words.

The audience was young and friendly. It was responsive. It cheered for each speaker.

Combined into a single simple sentence, the information is easier to follow and more interesting to read:

The young, friendly, responsive audience cheered for each speaker.

ple sentences that have a relationship which can be demonstrated through
coordination and subordination. Ask the class to determine ways of establishing the
relationship, and then introduce the structure you wish
to teach. For example, "The
ball was over. Arthur collapsed on the sofa." might
become "After the ball was
over, Arthur collapsed on the
sofa." Have students try to
explain what is gained con-
ceptually and stylistically by
the new sentence.

**SUGGESTED INSTRUCTOR
READING**

O'Hare, F. Sentence-
  Combining: Improving
  Student Writing Without
  Formal Grammar
  Instruction. Urbana, IL:
  NCTE, 1973. Perhaps the
  most effective introduction
  to the sentence-combining
  technique.

**ADDITIONAL SENTENCE-
COMBINING EXERCISES**

1. It had rained for four
days.
All the snow had melted.
The dog sled race had to be
cancelled.
Because it had rained for four
days, all the snow had melted
and the dog sled race had to
be cancelled.
2. Mr. James is the accountant for our company.
He vanished mysteriously.
The auditors discovered an
accounting fraud.
The fraud was in excess of a
million dollars.
Mr. James, the accountant for
our company, vanished mysteriously before the auditors
discovered an accounting
fraud that was in excess of a
million dollars.
3. Jason said he didn't believe in ghosts.
He refused to walk past the
Karnes mansion.
Many people believe the
mansion is haunted.

Compound Sentences.   A compound sentence contains two or more independent clauses, each holding the same (coordinate) rank. As a result, the idea in the first clause receives the same emphasis as the idea in the second.

In some cases, a comma and a coordinating conjunction *(and, but, or, nor, for, yet, so)* link successive clauses.

Name the baby Huey, *or* I'll cut you out of my will.

The audience was young, friendly, and responsive, *so* it cheered for each speaker.

In others, a semicolon and a conjunctive adverb *(for example, however, in fact, likewise, meanwhile, instead,* and the like) furnish the connection.

Tod wants to see the play; *in fact,* he's talked about it for weeks.

Today, many young women do not rush into marriage and motherhood; *instead,* they spend several years establishing careers.

Finally, a writer may omit any connecting word and separate the clauses with a semicolon.

The sky grew pitch black; the wind died; an ominous quiet hung over the whole city.

Be sure to read this Hemingway novel; it suggests how to cope gracefully with pressure.

As the preceding sentences show, compound sentences allow writers to express simple relationships among simple ideas. However, such sentences have one important limitation: it is impossible to highlight one particular idea. To do this, we need to use complex sentences.

Complex Sentences.   A complex sentence has one independent clause and one or more dependent clauses. Relegating an idea to a dependent clause shows that the writer wishes it to receive less emphasis than the idea in the main clause.

Because the young, friendly audience was responsive, it cheered for each speaker.

After the ball was over, Arthur collapsed on the sofa.

Once they had reached the lakeshore, the campers found a level spot *where they could pitch their tent.*

Unlike compound sentences, complex ones allow writers to vary the emphasis of ideas.

While I watered the grass, I discussed stock options with Liz.

I watered the grass while I discussed stock options with Liz.

The first sentence emphasizes the talk with Liz, the second watering the lawn.

Often, shifting sights allows a writer to make changes in meaning as well as in emphasis.

While his bicycle was damaged, Pat walked to work.

While Pat walked to work, his bicycle was damaged.

Furthermore, complex sentences signal *how* ideas relate. Note the various relationships in the following sentences:

Because she was swimming well, Millicent did 200 laps today. *(reason)*

The Sears Tower is taller *than the Empire State Building. (extent)*

Ms. Yoshira is the executive *for whom I am working. (relationship between persons)*

Compound–Complex Sentences.

This type of sentence features two or more independent clauses and one or more dependent clauses. Here are two examples with the dependent clauses italicized.

Ms. Harris works as an investment manager, and Mr. Williams, *who lives next door to her,* owns a jewelry store.

If you are to communicate properly, your thoughts must be clear and correct; thoughts are wasted *when language is muddled.*

Compound–complex sentences allow writers to present more intricate relationships than do other kinds of sentences. In the following example, three sentences—one compound and two simple—have been rewritten as a compound–complex sentence. Notice how subordination improves the compactness and smoothness of the final version.

Mary hated to be seen in ugly clothing, but she wore an ugly dress with red polka dots. She had received the dress as a Christmas present. Her Aunt Ida had given it to her.

Mary hated to be seen in ugly clothing; nevertheless, she wore an ugly red-polka-dot dress that her Aunt Ida had given her for Christmas.

The second version condenses thirty-five words to twenty-six.

EXERCISE

A. Label the independent and dependent clauses in the sentences below. Then identify each sentence as simple, compound, complex, or compound–complex.

1. A career in broadcasting requires good verbal skills, an extensive wardrobe, and a pleasant smile.
2. Because its bag was too full, the vacuum cleaner backfired, leaving the room dirtier than it had been before.
3. Leave your boots in the back hall, please.
4. When Tom arrived home, his roommate asked him where he had really gone; six hours seemed too long a time to spend in the library.
5. My orange tree blossomed last week; however, the grapefruit trees have withered, probably because of the freeze last month.

Though Jason said he didn't believe in ghosts, he refused to walk past the Karnes mansion which many people believe is haunted.

4. Amy looks forward to her third class in economics. Economics is her best subject. Other students say the class is extremely difficult.

Amy looks forward to her third class in economics, which is her best subject, even though other students say the class is extremely difficult.

5. Travis had worked as a police officer for many years. He was used to investigating murder scenes. This scene was particularly hard to take. The murdered man was his best friend.

Travis, who had worked as a police officer for many years, was used to investigating murder scenes; but this one was particularly hard to take since the murdered man was his best friend.

EXERCISE ANSWERS

A. 1. This is a simple sentence and so has one independent clause.
   2. This is a complex sentence with two dependent clauses: "Because its bag was too full" and "than it had been before."
   3. This is a simple sentence and so has one independent clause.
   4. This is a compound–complex sentence with one dependent clause, "When Tom arrived home," and two independent clauses, "his roommate . . . gone" and "six hours . . . library."
   5. This is a compound sentence with two independent clauses: "my orange trees blossomed last week" and "the grapefruit trees have withered." The word group following "withered" is a phrase.

6. This is a compound–complex sentence. The independent clauses are "kites make good gifts for children" and "a second will come in handy." The two dependent clauses are "even if a child already has a kite" and "if the first one becomes tangled in a tree."

7. This is a complex sentence. The independent clause is "It's risky to confide in a co-worker." The rest of the sentence consists of two dependent clauses: "because one can never be sure" and "that the confidence will be kept."

8. This is a compound–complex sentence. The first independent clause is "I know," and the second consists of everything following the colon. The dependent clause is "why he moved here." (Note: some instructors would classify this sentence as compound because the dependent clause serves as a direct object of "I know.")

9. This is a simple sentence and so has one independent clause.

10. This is a compound sentence. The first independent clause precedes the semicolon; the second one follows it.

B. **1.** He played the piano, organ, and French horn but not the viola.

2. Although the weather was icy cold and windy, Lee was wearing only a T-shirt and athletic shorts.

3. Life on Venus and Mars may be possible, but it will not be the kind of life we know on Earth.

4. Feeling that his classmates were laughing at his error, he ran out of the room, vowing never to return to that class.

5. Albert lay in bed, staring at the ceiling and

6. Kites make good gifts for children; even if a child already has a kite, a second one will come in handy if the first one becomes tangled in a tree.

7. It's risky to confide in a co-worker because one can never be sure that the confidence will be kept.

8. I know why he moved here: he likes having the only dental practice in this part of the state.

9. The pencil and the stapler are on the table next to the window in Mr. Brigg's office.

10. Don't add bleach to your load of colored shirts; the colors will fade and the fibers weaken.

B. Using coordination and subordination, rewrite the following passages to reduce words and/or improve smoothness.

1. He played the piano. He played the organ. He played the French horn. He did not play the viola.

2. The weather was icy cold and windy. Lee was wearing only a T-shirt and athletic shorts.

3. Life on Venus may be possible. It will not be the kind of life we know on Earth. Life on Mars may be possible. It will not be the kind of life we know on Earth.

4. He felt his classmates were laughing at his error. He ran out of the room. He vowed never to return to that class.

5. Albert lay in bed. He stared at the ceiling. Albert thought about the previous afternoon. He had asked Kathy to go to dinner with him. She is a pretty, blonde-haired woman. She sits at the desk next to his. They work at Hemphill's. She had refused.

6. I went to the store to buy a box of detergent. I saw Bill there, and we talked about last night's game.

7. Tim went to the newsstand. He bought a magazine there. While he was on the way home, he lost it. He had nothing to read.

Positioning of Movable Modifiers

Movable modifiers can appear on either side of the main statement or within it.

Modifiers After Main Statement. Sentences that follow this arrangement, frequently called *loose sentences,* occur more commonly than either of the others. They mirror conversation, in which a speaker first makes a statement and then adds on further thoughts. Often, the main statement has just one modifier.

Our company will have to file for bankruptcy *because of this year's huge losses. (phrase as modifier)*

Or it can head up a whole train of modifiers.

He burst suddenly into the party, *loud, angry, obscene. (words as modifiers)*

The family used to gather around the hearth, *doing such chores as polishing shoes, mending ripped clothing, reading, chatting, always warmed by one another's presence as much as by the flames. (words and phrases as modifiers)*

Sally stared in disbelief, and then she smiled, *slowly, tremulously, as if she couldn't believe her good fortune. (words and clause as modifiers)*

There are three essential qualities for buzzard country: *a rich supply of unburied corpses, high mountains, a strong sun. (noun-base groups as modifiers)*

John D. Stewart, "Vulture Country"

A sentence may contain several layers of modifiers. In the following example, we've indented and numbered to show the different layers.

1. The men struggled to the top of the hill,
    2. thirsty,
    2. drenched in sweat,
    2. and cursing in pain
        3. as their knapsack straps cut into their raw, chafed shoulders
            4. with every step.

In this sentence, the terms numbered 2 refer back to *men* in the item numbered 1. Item 3 is linked to *cursing* in the preceding item 2, and item 4 is linked to *cut* in item 3.

The modifiers-last arrangement works well for injecting descriptive details into narratives and also for qualifying, explaining, and presenting lists in other kinds of writing.

Modifiers Before Main Statement.

Sentences that delay the main point until the end are called *periodic*. In contrast to loose sentences, they lend a formal note to what is said, slowing its pace, adding cadence, and making it more serious.

> *If you can keep your head when everyone around you is panicking,* you probably don't understand the situation. *(clauses as modifiers)*

> *From the onset of his journey to the heart of darkness,* Marlow witnesses many incidents that reveal the human capacity for evil. *(phrases as modifiers)*

> *The danger of sideswiping another vehicle, the knowledge that a hidden bump or hole could throw me from the dune buggy,* both of these things added to the thrill of the race. *(noun plus phrase and noun plus clause as modifiers)*

> *When so large a percentage of our college students admits to cheating, when so many professors practice grade inflation, when administrators fail to face up to these problems,* our colleges are in serious trouble. *(clauses as modifiers)*

1. *When the public protests,*
    2. *confronted with some obvious evidence of the damaging results of pesticide applications,* it is fed little tranquilizing pills of half truth. *(clause and phrase as modifiers)*

Rachel Carson, *Silent Spring*

As shown in the Carson example, periodic sentences can also have layers of modifiers.

Positioning the modifiers before the main point throws the emphasis upon the end of the sentence, adding force to the main point. The delay also lets the

thinking about the previous afternoon when he had asked Kathy, the pretty blonde who sits at the desk next to him at Hemphill's, to go to dinner with him. She had refused.

6. While buying a box of detergent at the store, I saw Bill, and we talked about last night's game.

7. Tim bought a magazine at the newsstand, but on the way home he lost it, so he had nothing to read. *Or:* On the way home from the newsstand, Tim lost the magazine he had bought there, so he had nothing to read.

TEACHING STRATEGIES

1. You might review different kinds of writing with students, first observing what modifier structures are employed and then discussing the results of each approach. Have students review their own writing to determine how and where they place modifiers and whether they might vary their word order.

2. Francis Christensen argues that having students add modifiers to simple sentences is an effective way of getting them to generate richer sentences of their own. This is an easy approach to teach. Give students fill-in-the-blank sentences and ask them to provide effective modifiers. For example: We have had to postpone our trip to London _____ . _____ , Marvin and Mary have become committed environmentalists. Harry Travis, _____ , signed a three-year contract with the Boston Celtics.

SUGGESTED INSTRUCTOR READING

Christensen, F. "A Generative Rhetoric of the Sentence." College Composition and Communication 14 (1963): 155–61.

EXERCISE ANSWERS

1. Interrupted order. Rewritten as a periodic sentence: Cast out by family and friends, without the strength to make a new life in a new place, Victoria calmly and carefully injected the lethal drug into her thigh.

2. Periodic. Rewritten as a loose sentence: The woman gasped when told she had to have her spleen removed.

3. Loose. Rewritten as a periodic sentence: Because his wife had forgotten to set the alarm after she got up and he had cut himself several times shaving, Tom missed the bus.

4. Periodic. Rewritten in interrupted order: The best things—good health, warm friends, a beautiful summer evening—cannot be purchased.

5. Interrupted. Rewritten as a periodic sentence: Redfaced and perspiring, a customer stormed up to the claims desk.

6. Periodic. Rewritten in interrupted order: The freight train, stopping just short of the tunnel entrance, avoided a collision with the crowded commuter train stalled inside.

7. Loose. Rewritten as a periodic sentence: Determination in his eyes and glory in his fists, the new kid hammered away at the fading champ.

8. Loose. Rewritten as a periodic sentence: Pink and trim, its lawn immaculate, its two bushes and newly planted crab apple tree making by their very tininess the yard look vaster than its actual size, the new tract house sparkled in the sunlight.

9. Periodic. Rewritten in interrupted order: Steve, bright red and skin stinging after a day at the beach, will remember the tanning oil next time.

10. Interrupted. Rewritten as a periodic sentence: Gaudily painted and beckoning with

writer create sentences that, like the first example, carry stings, ironic or humorous, in their tails.

Modifiers Within Main Statement.   Inserting one or more modifiers into a main statement creates a sentence with *interrupted order*. The material may come between the subject and the verb or between the verb and the rest of the predicate.

> The young girl, *wearing a tattered dress and looking anything but well-off herself,* gave the beggar a ten-dollar bill. *(phrases between subject and verb)*

> Dewey declared, *in a loud, happy voice,* that the concert was the best he'd ever heard. *(phrase between verb and rest of predicate)*

> The bedsprings, *bent and rusted, festooned with spider webs,* lay on top of the heap. *(words and phrase between subject and verb)*

> The evolutionists, *piercing beneath the show of momentary stability,* discovered, *hidden in rudimentary organs,* the discarded rubbish of the past. *(one phrase between subject and verb, another between verb and rest of predicate)*

By stretching out the main idea, inserted modifiers slow the forward pace of the sentence, giving it some of the formality and force of a periodic sentence.

EXERCISE ■ **Identify each sentence as loose, periodic, or interrupted. Rewrite each as one of the other kinds.**

1. Victoria, cast out by family and friends, without the strength to make a new life in a new place, calmly and carefully injected the lethal drug into her thigh.

2. When told that she had to have her spleen removed, the woman gasped.

3. Tom missed the bus because his wife had forgotten to reset the alarm after she got up and he had cut himself several times while shaving.

4. Good health, warm friends, a beautiful summer evening—the best things cannot be purchased.

5. A customer, red-faced and perspiring, stormed up to the claims desk.

6. Stopping just short of the tunnel entrance, the freight train avoided a collision with the crowded commuter train stalled inside.

7. The new kid hammered away at the fading champ, determination in his eyes and glory in his fists.

8. The new tract house sparkled in the sunlight, pink and trim, its lawn immaculate, its two bushes and newly planted crab apple tree, by their very tininess, making the yard look vaster than its actual size.

9. Bright red and skin stinging after a day at the beach, Steve will remember the tanning oil next time.

10. Saloons, gaudily painted and beckoning with promises of extraordinary pleasures, lined the town's main street.

11. In being whisked from Lyons, France, to Tel Aviv to Sri Lanka for location shots, the Hollywood star gave new force to the phrase "international celebrity."

12. The first graders stood in line, talking and giggling, pushing at one another's caps and pencil boxes and kicking one another's shins, unmindful of the drudgery that awaited them within the old schoolhouse.

Using Parallelism

Parallelism presents equivalent ideas in grammatically equivalent form. Dressing them in the same grammatical garb calls attention to their kinship and adds smoothness and polish. The following sentence pairs demonstrate the improvement that parallelism brings:

Nonparallel   James's outfit was *wrinkled, mismatched,* and *he needed to wash it. (words and independent clause)*

Parallel   James's outfit was *wrinkled, mismatched,* and *dirty. (words)*

Nonparallel   Oscar likes *reading books, attending plays,* and *to search for antiques. (different kinds of phrases)*

Parallel   Oscar likes *reading books, attending plays,* and *searching for antiques. (same kind of phrases)*

Nonparallel   Beth performs her tasks *quickly, willingly,* and *with accuracy. (words and phrase)*

Parallel   Beth performs her tasks *quickly, willingly,* and *accurately. (words)*

Nonparallel   The instructor complimented me *for taking part in class discussions and because I had written a superb theme. (phrase and clause)*

Parallel   The instructor complimented me *for taking part in class discussions and for writing a superb theme. (phrases)*

As the examples show, revising nonparallel sentences smooths out bumpiness while binding the ideas together more closely and lending them a more finished look.

Parallelism doesn't always stop with a single sentence. Writers sometimes use it in a series of sentences:

> He had never lost his childlike innocence. He had never lost his sense of wonder. He had never lost his sense of joy in nature's simplest gifts.

For an example of parallelism that extends over much of a paragraph, see page 185.

Repeating a structure through several sentences of a paragraph beats a tattoo that drums the points home more forcefully and adds rhythm to the prose. But don't overuse the technique, or it will lose its impact and seem irritating and artificial.

Balance, a special form of parallelism, positions two grammatically equivalent ideas on opposite sides of some pivot point, such as a word or punctuation mark.

Hope for the best, and prepare for the worst.

Many are called, but few are chosen.

When I'm right, nobody ever notices; when I'm wrong, nobody ever forgets.

The sheep are in the meadow, and the cows are in the corn.

promises of extraordinary pleasures, saloons lined the town's main street.

11. Periodic. Rewritten as a loose sentence: The Hollywood star gave new force to the phrase "international celebrity" in being whisked from Lyons, France, to Tel Aviv to Sri Lanka for location shots.

12. Loose. Rewritten as a periodic sentence: Talking and giggling, pushing at one another's caps and pencil boxes, kicking one another's shins, unmindful of the drudgery that awaited them within the old schoolhouse, the first graders stood in line.

PERSPECTIVE

The attempt to produce parallel structures can prompt students to ask a rhetorical "What else?" and expand one modifier into a parallel series. As a result, "He cleared the table" can become "He cleared the table, washed the dishes, then put his daughter to bed." In attempting to achieve parallelism, however, students can strain syntax and verb forms. Encourage them to check parallel structures for other faults.

TEACHING STRATEGY

You can encourage students to generate parallel sentences by providing them with fill-in-the-blank exercises like the following: ___ and ___ are essential to every college student. To gain victory our team will ___ , ___ , and even ___ . Today we celebrate our victories, but tomorrow ___ .

Like regular parallel sentences, balanced sentences sometimes come in series:

> The tension in this city is not between white people and Negro people. The tension is, at bottom, between justice and injustice, between the forces of light and the forces of darkness. And if there is a victory, it will be a victory not merely for fifty thousand Negroes, but a victory for justice and the forces of light.

> Martin Luther King, Jr., "Pilgrimage to Nonviolence"

Balance works especially well for pitting contrasting or clashing ideas against each other. It sharpens the difference between them while achieving compactness and lending an air of insight to what is said.

EXERCISE ■ **Identify each sentence as nonparallel, parallel, or balanced; then rewrite each nonparallel sentence to make it parallel.**

1. Professor Bartlett enjoys helping students, counseling advisees, and participation in faculty meetings.
2. I can still see Aunt Alva striding into the corral, cornering a cow against a fencepost, try to balance herself on a one-legged milking stool, and butt her head into the cow's belly.
3. The city plans on building a new fishing pier and on dredging the channel of the river.
4. Elton plans on vacationing in New York, but Noreen wants to raft down the Colorado River.
5. Being half drunk and because he was already late for work, Tom called his boss and said he was too ill to come in that day.
6. The novel's chief character peers through a tangle of long hair, slouches along in a shambling gait, and gets into trouble constantly.
7. You can take the boy out of the country, but you can't take the country out of the boy.
8. Joe's problem is not that he earns too little money but spending it foolishly.
9. The room was dark, gloomy, and everything was dusty.
10. The apparition glided through the wall, across the room, and up the fireplace chimney.

Choosing the Right Verb Voice

A sentence's verb voice derives from the relationship between the subject and the action. A sentence in the *active voice* has a subject that does something plus a verb that shows action.

The boy hit the target.

The girl painted the garage.

This pattern keeps the key information in the key part of the sentence, making it strong and vigorous and giving the reader a close-up look at the action.

The *passive voice* reverses the subject–action relationship by having the subject receive, rather than perform, the action. It is built around a form of the verb *to* be; for example, *is, are, was, were*. Some sentences identify the actor by using a prepositional phrase; others don't mention the actor at all.

The target was hit by the boy. *(actor identified)*

The federal debt limit is to be increased. *(actor unidentified)*

Demoting or banishing the actor dilutes the force of the sentence, puts greater distance between the action and the reader, and almost always adds extra words to the message.

Most writers who overuse the passive voice simply don't realize its effects on their writing. Read the following paragraph, written mainly in the passive voice.

> Graft becomes possible when gifts are given to police officers or favors are done for them by persons who expect preferential treatment in return. Gifts of many kinds may be received by officers. Often free meals are given to them by the owners of restaurants on their beats. During the Christmas season, they may be given liquor, food, or theater tickets by merchants. If favored treatment is not received by the donors, no great harm is done. But if traffic offenses, safety code violations, and other infractions are overlooked by the officers, corruption results. When such corruption is exposed by the newspapers, faith is lost in law enforcement agencies.

This impersonal, wordy passage plods across the page and therefore lacks any real, persuasive impact. Now note the livelier, more forceful tone of this rewritten version.

> Graft becomes possible when police officers accept gifts or favors from persons who expect preferential treatment in return. Officers may receive gifts of many kinds. Restaurant owners often provide free meals for officers on the beat. During the Christmas season, merchants may give them liquor, food, or theater tickets. If donors do not receive favored treatment, no great harm is done. But if officers overlook traffic offenses, safety code violations, and other infractions, corruption results. When the newspapers expose such corruption, citizens lose faith in law enforcement agencies.

Don't misunderstand: the passive voice does have its uses. It can mask identities—or at least try to. A child may try to dodge responsibility by saying, "Mother, while you were out, the living room lamp got broken." Less manipulatively, reporters may use it to conceal the identity of a source.

Technical and scientific writing customarily uses the passive voice to explain processes.

> In the production of steel, iron ore is first converted into pig iron by combining it with limestone and coke and then heating the mixture in a blast furnace. Pig iron, however, contains too many impurities to be useful to industry, and as a result must be refined and converted to steel. In the refining process, manganese, silicon, and aluminum are heated with the pig iron in order to degas it, that is, to remove excess oxygen and impurities from it. The manganese, silicon, and aluminum are vaporized

sively in scientific, legal, and administrative writing where the doer is often irrelevant or difficult to identify. Because much of what college students read makes extensive use of the passive voice, it seems to them the mark of more advanced writers. No wonder they become confused when we encourage them to write more effective prose but at the same time chide them about using the passive voice.

TEACHING STRATEGY

To end confusion over the use of the passive voice, have students review several kinds of writing and determine which voice predominates. Then ask them to explain whether that voice helps or hinders communication and why.

while the iron remains in the liquid state and the impurities are carried away by the vapors. Once this step has been completed, the molten steel is poured into ingots and allowed to cool. The steel is now ready for further processing.

Greg Langford

Putting such writing in the passive voice provides a desirable objective tone and puts the emphasis where it's most important: on the action, not the actor.

On occasion, everyday writing also uses the passive voice.

The garbage is collected once a week, on Monday.

These caves were formed about 10 million years ago.

In the first case, there's no need to tell who collects the garbage; obviously, garbage collectors do. In the second, the writer may not know what caused the formation, and saying "Something formed these caves about 10 million years ago" would sound ridiculous. In both situations, the action, not the actor, is paramount.

Unless special circumstances call for the passive voice, however, use the active voice.

EXERCISE ■ **After determining whether each sentence below is in active or passive voice, rewrite the passive sentences as active ones.**

1. Mary's parents gave her a sports car for her sixteenth birthday.
2. Fires were left burning by negligent campers.
3. The new ice arena will be opened by the city in about two weeks.
4. Harry left the open toolbox out in the rain.
5. Corn was introduced to the Pilgrims by friendly American Indians.
6. Maude took a trip to Sante Fe, New Mexico.
7. We have just installed a new computer in our main office.
8. The club president awarded Tompkins the Order of the Golden Mace.
9. The sound of war drums was heard by the missionaries as they floated down the river.
10. Objections were raised by some members of the legislature to the ratification of the proposed amendment.

Using Fragments

A fragment is a part of a sentence that is capitalized and punctuated as if it were a complete sentence.

Although fragments are seldom used in formal prose, they form the backbone of most conversations. Here's how a typical bit of dialogue might go:

"Where are you going tonight?" *(sentence)*
"To Woodland Mall." *(fragment)*

"What for?" *(fragment)*
"To buy some shoes." *(fragment)*
"Alone?" *(fragment)*
"No, with Maisie Perkins." *(fragment)*
"Can I come too?" *(sentence)*
"Sure." *(fragment)*

As with most conversations, the sprinkling of complete sentences makes the fragments clear.

Writers of nonfiction use fragments to create special effects. In the following passage, the fragment emphasizes the importance of the question it asks and varies the pace of the writing:

> Before kidney transplants, people had an ethical unease about renal dialysis—the artificial kidney machine. Unquestionably it was a great technical advance making it possible to treat kidney dysfunctions from which thousands die. But the machine was, and is, expensive and involves intensive care of the patient by doctors and nurses. For whom the machine? In the United States the dilemma was evaded but not solved by having lay panels, like juries, making life-or-death choices. In Britain, where the National Health Service entitles everyone, rich or poor, to have access to any necessary treatment, the responsibility rests on the medical staff. It was (and still is) a difficult decision.
>
> Lord Ritchie-Calder, "The Doctor's Dilemma"

Once in a while, as in the following examples, a writer will use a whole series of fragments. In the Ciardi selection, the fragments heighten the ironic effect. In the other one, they create a kaleidoscopic effect that mirrors the kaleidoscopic impressions offered by the Jazz Age itself.

> Or look at any of the women's magazines. There, as Bernard DeVoto once pointed out, advertising begins as poetry in the front pages and ends as pharmacopoeia and therapy in the back pages. The poetry of the front matter is the dream of perfect beauty that must be hers. These, the flawless teeth. This, the baby skin that must be hers. This, the perfumed breath she must exhale. This, the sixteen-year-old figure she must display at forty, at fifty, at sixty, and forever.
>
> John Ciardi, "What Is Happiness?"

> The Jazz Age offers a kaleidoscope of shifting impressions. Of novelties quickly embraced and quickly discarded. Of flappers flaunting bobbed hair and short skirts. Of hip flasks and bootleg whisky, fast cars and coonskin coats, jazz and dancing till dawn. And overall a sense of futility, an uneasy conviction that all the gods were dead.
>
> Elliott L. Smith and Andrew W. Hart, *The Short Story: A Contemporary Looking Glass*

Before using any fragment in your own writing, think carefully about your intended effect and explore other ways of achieving it. Unless only a fragment will serve your needs, don't use one; fragments are likely to be viewed as unintentional—and thus errors—in the work of inexperienced writers.

fragments. Generally, fragments are more acceptable in informal writing but even then only if they are extremely clear. Whether to allow "intentional" fragments in student writing depends, of course, on your attitude and your class. Overall, it may be best to acknowledge the use of fragments but caution against them until students first master complete sentences.

TEACHING STRATEGIES

1. You could open the discussion of fragments with a statement such as, "If you want to get a good grade on the final exam" and then stop. Puzzled looks will, of course, abound. When someone asks for the missing information, acknowledge the fragment and tell the class that written fragments often create the same confusion as your oral one just did.

2. Have students check textbooks, newspaper and magazine articles, and advertisements for fragments. Where do they occur most frequently? Why are they used? Are they effective?

3. Break a formal text, such as a piece of business correspondence, into fragments and have students read the result and assess the competence of the author. Then provide them with the original and ask for a reassessment.

EXERCISE ANSWERS

1. The fragment "To the library?" ends the paragraph and heightens the irony of the wry observation that anthropologists were a worse enemy of the American Indian than the cavalry. To demonstrate the impact of the fragment, ask students to read the passage with this ending: "Would he go to the library?"
2. The fragments are "Not for criticism. For applause." These fragments give added emphasis to why Wagner summoned his friends and highlight his egotism.

SUGGESTED INSTRUCTOR READING

Kline, C. R., Jr., and W. D. Memering. "Formal Fragments: The English Minor Sentence." Research in the Teaching of English 11 (1977): 97–110. Provides a useful catalog of the conditions under which fragments are effectively used.

EXERCISE ■ **Each of the following passages includes one or more fragments. Identify each and explain its function.**

1.   Anthropologists came to Indian country only after the tribes had agreed to live on reservations and had given up their warlike ways. Had the tribes been given a choice of fighting the cavalry or the anthropologists, there is little doubt as to whom they would have chosen. In a crisis situation, men always attack the biggest threat to their existence. A warrior killed in battle could always go to the happy hunting grounds. But where does an Indian laid low by an anthro go? To the library?

Vine Deloria, Jr., "Custer Died for Your Sins"

2.   He [Richard Wagner] wrote operas; and no sooner did he have the synopsis of a story, but he would invite—or rather summon—a crowd of his friends to his house and read it aloud to them. Not for criticism. For applause. When the complete poem was written, the friends had to come again, and hear *that* read aloud. Then he would publish the poem, sometimes years before the music that went with it was written. He played the piano like a composer, in the worst sense of what that implies, and he would sit down at the piano before parties that included some of the finest pianists of his time, and play for them, by the hour, his own music, needless to say. He had a composer's voice. And he would invite eminent vocalists to his house, and sing them his operas, taking all the parts.

Deems Taylor, "The Monster"

*B*EYOND THE SINGLE SENTENCE

What makes a team successful? Skilled players, to be sure, but teamwork as well. Most sentences are part of a team; and unless they work in harmony, the composition will suffer, however good each of them may be.

Harmony—the rhythmic interplay of sentences—demands, first of all, sentences of different lengths. If all your sentences drag on and on, your reader may bog down and lose the train of thought. If all are clipped, the ideas may seem simplistic, and the sentences will jerk along like a car with a misfiring engine. And if all of them are middling long, their plodding, monotonous pace may bring boredom and inattention.

Content sets the pattern of sentence lengths, and often your ideas will lead naturally to the proper mix of long and short sentences. But don't count on it. Chances are you will need to make adjustments. Once you have finished a draft of your paper, read it over, see how its rhythms strike your inner ear, and put check marks by stretches that "sound" wrong. For instance, you might need to condense a set of jolting primer-book sentences into one or two sentences that present their ideas in a series:

Original Version

Members of the Unification Church actively recruit converts. They do it in shopping malls. College campuses are also recruiting sites. They talk about the benefits of world unity and sell books as well as records. Donations are also solicited. Listeners receive invitations to a dinner. There the guests learn more about the sect.

Revised Version

Members of the Unification Church recruit converts in such places as shopping malls and college campuses. They talk about the benefits of world unity, sell books and records, ask for donations, and invite listeners to a dinner to learn more about the sect.

If a key point is submerged in a long sentence, highlight it as a separate thought, thereby giving it the recognition it deserves. Here is an example:

Original Version

Employers find mature women to be valuable members of their organizations. They are conscientious, have excellent attendance records, and stay calm when things go awry, *but unfortunately many employers exploit them.* Despite their desirable qualities, most remain mired in clerical, sales, and elementary teaching positions. On the average they earn two-thirds as much as men.

Revised Version

Employers find mature women to be valuable members of their organizations. They are conscientious, have excellent attendance records, and stay calm when things go awry. *Unfortunately, though, many employers exploit them.* Despite their desirable qualities, most remain mired in clerical, sales, and elementary teaching positions. On the average they earn two-thirds as much as men.

In the following paragraph, the sentences differ considerably in length.

To protest that some fairly improbable people, some people who could not possibly respect themselves, seem to sleep easily enough is to miss the point entirely, as surely as those people miss it who think that self-respect has necessarily to do with not having safety pins in one's underwear. There is a common superstition that "self-respect" is a kind of charm against snakes, something that keeps those who have it locked in some unblighted Eden, out of strange beds, ambivalent conversations, and trouble in general. It does not at all. It has nothing to do with the face of things, but concerns instead a separate peace, a private reconciliation.

Joan Didion, "On Self-Respect"

Much of the appealing rhythm of this passage stems from varied sentence length. The first two rather long sentences (49 and 36 words) are followed by the very brief "It does not at all," which gains emphasis by its position. The last sentence adds variety by means of its moderate length (19 words), quite apart from its interesting observation on the real nature of self-respect.

Look to the structures of your sentences as well as their length. Do they resemble a streetful of row houses built from the same blueprint? If they are all simple, with few modifiers, your readers may underrate the importance of your message. To correct row-house sentences, draw upon the patterns you learned about earlier in this chapter. Try inverting sentence order or positioning modifiers at different points. Combine sentences. Turn a statement into a question. Build from several blueprints. Try anything as long as the structures go together and you don't warp meanings.

The following example illustrates how sentence combining adds smoothness and interest to a piece of writing.

Original Version

Before deaf children can speak, they must learn the speech sounds of the English language. This is a process that requires them to practice breath control, to mouth vowels, and to study the speech positions of the mouth and tongue for many hours. A speech specialist helped my brother do these things. The specialist started with him before he was two years old. She built up his vocabulary by teaching him a series of related words. Each of these words identified something in his environment. My brother proved to be an apt student. He soon learned to talk.

Revised Version

Before deaf children can speak, they must learn the speech sounds of the English language, a process that requires them to practice breath control, mouth vowels, and study the speech positions of the mouth and tongue for many hours. A speech specialist helped my brother do these things. Starting before he was two years old, she built up his vocabulary by teaching him a series of related words, each identified with something in his environment. My brother proved to be an apt student and soon learned to talk.

EXERCISE ■ Revise the following passages to improve their style.

1. Andrew Carnegie came to America from Scotland. He worked as a factory hand, a telegrapher, and a railway clerk to support himself. His savings from these jobs were invested in oil and later in the largest steel works in the country. Historians do not agree in their assessments of Carnegie. Some have considered him as a cruel taskmaster and others as a benevolent benefactor. His contributions to American society, however, cannot be denied. He established public libraries all across the country and spent much time in promoting peace. Good or bad, he ranks as one of our most noteworthy nineteenth-century immigrants.

2. She went to the seashore. She found some seashells. She picked up the seashells. She put the seashells into a basket. She had a whole basketful of seashells. She went home with the basket. She took the shells out of the basket. She put the shells on a dinette table. She brought jeweler's tools to the table. She pierced holes in the shells. She strung the shells on small chains. The chains were gold and silver. She made twenty necklaces. The selling price of the necklaces was $10 apiece. She earned $175 profit. She used her profits to go to the shore again. She could afford to stay for a week this time.

CHAPTER 16

Diction, Tone, Style

Your decisions about words and sentences set the tone and style of your writing. Not only do you choose sentence strategies for correctness and effectiveness, but you also choose words for accuracy and effect. Sentences must be clear and effective; so must words. Diction deals broadly with words, not in isolation but as parts of sentences, paragraphs, and essays. Every time you write and revise, diction comes into play.

TOWARD CLEAR DICTION

Clear diction stems from choosing words with the right meanings, using abstract and concrete words appropriately, and picking terms that are neither too specific nor too general. Dictionaries and thesauruses can help guide your choices.

Word Meanings

Make sure the words you use mean what you think they do, so that inaccurate words will not distort your message. Sound-alike word pairs often trip up unwary writers. Take "accept" and "except" for example. "Accept" means "to approve." "Except," when used as a verb, means "to exclude or omit." If you want to indicate approval but you say "The following new courses were *excepted* by the committee," think of the obvious consequences. Likewise, consider the distinction between "continual" (frequently or regularly repeated) and "continuous" (uninterrupted). If you illustrate your popularity by saying "My phone rings *continuously*," your reader will wonder why you never answer it and how you ever sleep.

Concrete and Abstract Words

A concrete word names or describes something that we can perceive with one or more of our five senses. A thing is concrete if we can weigh it, measure it, hold it in our hands, photograph it, taste it, sniff it, add salt to it, drop it, smash into it, or borrow it from a neighbor. If it's abstract, we can't do any of these things. *Bob*

PERSPECTIVE

While helping students improve their writing style, we should be wary of laying down excessively absolute rules such as "Never start a sentence with 'and,' 'but,' or 'because' " and "Always keep sentences short." Such rules must often be violated if writing is to be effective. Instead, we might well guide students to more effective choices in diction, tone, and style while helping them understand how to adapt their style to specific writing situations.

PERSPECTIVE

Student vocabularies include words they can (1) understand only in context, (2) understand out of context but not explain, (3) understand and explain, (4) use productively. We should encourage students to learn new words and help them understand the nuances and appropriate contexts of those they already know.

TEACHING STRATEGIES

1. Have students review their essays, circle any words that are improperly used, and then make appropriate substitutions.
2. Ask students to record in their journals new words they encounter, along with their contexts and definitions.
3. Pages 590–613 list and explain commonly confused words. If your students are using the version of this book that includes a Handbook, suggest that they refer to this list as they revise and use a dictionary if they have any doubt about meaning.

SUGGESTED INSTRUCTOR READINGS

Halliday, M. A. K. Learning How to Mean: Explorations in the Development of Language. London: Arnold, 1975. A seminal account of how we acquire mastery over language.
Smith, F. Writing and the Writer. New York: Holt,

1982. Provides a good psycholinguistic account of the writing process. Chapters 4 and 5 concentrate on the nature of language and language learning.

PERSPECTIVE

In our efforts to encourage students to use more concrete words, we shouldn't overlook the role of abstract words, which allow us to clarify general relationships and capture ideas that cannot be expressed concretely.

TEACHING STRATEGIES

1. Have students review a variety of writing—perhaps newspaper stories, science and business articles, and textbooks—to determine where and to what extent abstract and concrete words predominate. Students should recognize that concrete words are important not only in personal and in-class writing but also in scientific and business writing.

2. Have students underline abstract words and circle concrete words in their own writing. When they have finished, ask them to look for places where concrete examples would clarify abstractions and abstract expressions would clarify relationships among concrete items.

CLASSROOM ACTIVITIES

1. Write a number of abstract words on the board and have students, working separately or in small groups, generate as many different concrete manifestations as they can. Point out the implications of having different concrete images for the same abstract term as well as what is uniquely captured by the abstract term and the concrete word.

2. Have students attempt to define an abstract term like self-respect, perhaps by determining its relation to other

Seger is a concrete term, as are *Swiss cheese, petroleum, maple syrup,* and *Dallas.* On the other hand, *jealousy, power, conservatism, size,* and *sadness* are abstract terms.

Concrete words evoke precise, vivid mental images and thus help convey a message. The images that abstract terms create differ from person to person. Try this test: ask several of your friends to describe what comes to mind when they think of *joy, hatred, fear,* or some other abstract term. To illustrate, the word *hatred* might call up images of a person with cold, slitted eyes, a grimly set jaw, and tightly clenched fists. As you can see, concrete terms help us specify what we mean and thus enhance communication.

In the following passage, the concrete diction is italicized:

> To do without self-respect . . . is to be an unwilling *audience of one* to an interminable *documentary* that details one's failings, both real and imagined, with *fresh footage spliced* in for every *screening.* There's *the glass you broke* in anger, there's *the hurt on X's face; watch now, this next scene, the night Y came back from Houston,* see how you muff this one. To live without self-respect is to *lie awake some night,* beyond the reach of *warm milk, phenobarbital,* and *the sleeping hand on the coverlet,* counting up the sins of commission and omission, the trusts betrayed, the promises subtly broken, the gifts irrevocably wasted through sloth or cowardice or carelessness. However long we postpone it, we eventually lie down alone in that notoriously *uncomfortable bed,* the one we make ourselves. Whether or not we sleep in it depends, of course, on whether or not we respect ourselves.
>
> Joan Didion, "On Self-Respect"

Now note how vague and colorless the passage becomes without the concrete diction.

> To do without self-respect is to be continuously aware of your failings, both real and imagined. Incidents stay in your mind long after they are over. To live without self-respect means being bothered by intentional or unintentional failings, trusts betrayed, promises subtly broken, and gifts irrevocably wasted through sloth or cowardice or carelessness. However long we postpone it, we eventually must come to terms with who we are. How we respond to this situation depends, of course, on whether or not we respect ourselves.

EXERCISE ■ **Underline the concrete terms in the following passage.**

The fog which rises from the river has no color, no texture, no taste, smell, or sound. It is sheer vision, a vision of purity, a slow, mesmeric, inexorable erasure of the slate. You see fog mushrooming along the river's course. Gently, it obliterates the alders tangled on the banks, wipes out the road. Buildings without foundations, trees without trunks, hang in the air like mirages. Sun may be shining brightly on them, or rain drenching them, or stars twinkling above or among them. Slowly the fog reaches higher and spreads. Ridgepoles, small topmost branches, and your own dooryard vanish. There is nothing left now but shining mist. It is all, and you float on it, utterly alone, as one imagines he might in empty space if flung off by earth; as the mind does, drifting into sleep; as the spirit does, having escaped its mortal frame.

Gladys Hasty Carroll, *Sing Out the Glory*

Specific and General Terms

One concrete term can be more specific or more general than another. As we move from *Lassie* to *collie* to *dog* to *mammal* and finally to *animal*, we become less and less specific, ending with a term that encompasses every animal on earth. With each step we retain only those features that fit the more general term. Thus, when we move from *collie* to *dog,* we leave out everything that makes collies different from terriers, greyhounds, and other breeds.

The more specific the term, the less difference among the images it calls to mind. If you say *animal* to a group of friends, one may think of a dog, another of a horse, and a third of a gorilla. *Collie,* on the other hand, triggers images of a large, long-haired, brown and white dog with a pointed muzzle.

Ask yourself how specific you need to be and then act accordingly. Often, the more specific term will be the better choice. If, for instance, you're describing a wealthy jet-setter, noting that he drives a Ferrari, not just a car, helps establish his character. But if you're writing a narrative about your flight to New Orleans and your experience at Mardi Gras, nothing is gained by naming the make of car you rented and used uneventfully during your stay.

EXERCISE

1. Arrange each set of words from less specific to more specific.

    a. man, ex-President, human being, Ronald Reagan, American
    b. Forest Hills Apartments, building, structure, condominium, dwelling

2. Expand each of the following words into a series of four or more that become progressively more specific. Use 1a or 1b as a pattern.

a. activity	c. political party	e. device
b. event	d. institution	f. reading matter

Dictionaries and Thesauruses

Get the dictionary habit and learn to use a thesaurus. They'll increase your vocabulary as well as your skill at using words you already know.

Dictionaries. Dictionaries are storehouses of word meanings. In general, dictionary makers do not try to dictate how words should be used. Instead, they note current and past meanings. When a word gains or loses a meaning or a newly minted word enjoys wide circulation, dictionary makers observe and record. Most users, however, regard dictionaries as authorities on correctness.

abstract terms or providing a list of abstract characteristics associated with it. They might, for example, consider the relation of self-respect to self-love and self-awareness.

EXERCISE ANSWERS (p. 210)

The *fog* which rises from the *river* has no color, no texture, no taste, smell, or sound. It is sheer vision, a vision of purity, a slow mesmeric, inexorable erasure of the *slate.* You see fog mushrooming along the *river's course.* Gently, it obliterates the *alders* tangled on the *banks,* wipes out the *road. Buildings* without *foundations, trees* without *trunks,* hang in the *air* like *mirages. Sun* may be shining brightly on them, or *rain* drenching them, or *stars* twinkling above or among them. Slowly the *fog* reaches higher and spreads. *Ridgepoles,* small topmost *branches,* and your own *dooryard* varnish. There is nothing left now but shining *mist.* It is all, and you float on it, utterly alone, as one imagines he might in empty space if flung off by *earth;* as the mind does, drifting into sleep; as the spirit does, having escaped its mortal *frame.*

EXERCISE ANSWERS

1. **a.** Human being, man, American, ex-president, Ronald Reagan
    b. Structure, building, dwelling, condominium, Forest Hills Apartments

2. **a.** activity, sport, skiing, water skiing
    b. event, meeting, stockholders' meeting, GM stockholders' meeting
    c. organization, political party, British political party, Labour Party
    d. institution, school, college, Kendall College
    e. thing, device, typewriter, Olivetti typewriter
    f. reading matter, book, novel, *From Here to Eternity*

PERSPECTIVE

We give students the right message if we require them to purchase and use a dictionary. When they misuse a word in their writing, refer them to the dictionary rather than supply the appropriate definition.

TEACHING STRATEGIES

1. Have students create dictionary entries for modern slang expressions not yet included in most dictionaries (retro, grody). Students will have to familiarize themselves with actual dictionary entries before they compile their own.
2. Few students know the versatility of dictionaries. Have them examine the origins of words in order to gain new insights into their meaning. Or have students use the *OED* to trace the changes in the usage of words like "husband." Then ask them to suggest possible reasons for the changes.
3. Many students regard dictionary entries as unchanging and absolute. To dispel this notion, have students compare how different dictionaries define the same word, especially one likely to generate controversy, such as "communist" or "feminist." Similarly, students could trace the changes in the definition of such a word through successive editions of the same dictionary. They will come to appreciate the role of history and individual perceptions in shaping word definitions.

EXERCISE ANSWERS
(pp. 213–14)

1. Variant spellings: aeroplane, colour, esthete, gayly, grey, theatre, tornados, useable
2. Syllabication and the syllable that receives the main stress: an-a-*cru*-sis, bac-ca-*lau*-re-ate, ca-*den*-za, ex-cla-*ma*-tion, *har*-bin-ger, *i*-on-ize, *mis*-an-thrope, se-*ques*-ter

Dictionaries supply much more than word meanings. Figure 16.1, an annotated entry from a college-level dictionary, shows what they can provide. Some dictionary entries include other information as well.

Idioms. Idioms express meanings that differ from those of the words that make them up. Here are two examples.

I won't *put up with* any foolishness.

The dowager *gave me the cold shoulder.*

Put up with means "tolerate"; *gave me the cold shoulder* means "snubbed me." Looking up the most prominent word of an unfamiliar idiom may lead you to a listing and a definition.

Irregular forms. Any irregular forms are indicated. In *Webster's New World Dictionary,* the entry for the verb *spring* notes that the other forms are *sprang, sprung,* and *springing.* This information helps you use correct forms in your writing.

Usage labels. Usage labels help you determine whether a word suits the circumstances of your writing. Here are the most common labels:

Label	Meaning
Colloquial	Characteristic of informal writing and speaking; should not be considered nonstandard.
Slang	Informal, newly coined words and expressions or old expressions with new meanings.
Obsolete	No longer in use but found in past writing.
Archaic	Still finds restricted use; for example, in legal documents; otherwise not appropriate.
Poetic	Used only in poetry and in prose with a poetic tone.
Dialect	Used regularly only in a particular geographical location such as the southeastern United States or the Scottish Lowlands.

Supplementary information. While focusing primarily on individual words, college-level dictionaries often provide several other kinds of information. These may include a history of the language, lists of standard abbreviations and of colleges and universities, biographical notes on distinguished individuals, and geographical notes on important locations.

While any dictionary is better than none, some clearly outrank others in usefulness. A pocket dictionary is handy but not as comprehensive as a desk dictionary. Excellent desk-sized dictionaries include the following:

The American Heritage Dictionary
Funk and Wagnall's Standard College Dictionary
The Random House Dictionary of the English Language
Webster's Ninth New Collegiate Dictionary
Webster's New World Dictionary of the American Language

Unabridged (complete) dictionaries such as *Webster's Third New International Dictionary* and the *Oxford English Dictionary* can be found in college and public libraries. There you'll also find a variety of specialized dictionaries. Your librarian can direct you to dictionaries that list terms in particular fields.

Spelling, Syllabication. When a word has variant spellings, some dictionaries indicate a preferred version. Alphabetically close variants appear in the same entry. Dots or hyphens separate syllables and tell where to divide a word written on two lines.

Parts of Speech. Each word is classified by grammatical function. Usually, abbreviations such as *n* (noun), *adj.* (adjective), and *vt.* (transitive verb) identify the part of speech.

Pronunciation. Dictionaries indicate preferred as well as secondary pronunciations. Accent marks (') show which syllable gets the primary stress and which the secondary stress, if any. To determine the pronunciation, follow the key at the bottom of the page.

Etymology. This term means the origin and development of words. Most college dictionaries limit the entry to the root (original) word and an abbreviation for the original language. The abbreviation key near the front of the dictionary identifies the language.

man·i·fold (man′ə fōld′) *adj.* [ME. < OE. *manigfeald:* see MANY & -FOLD] 1. having many and various forms, features, parts, etc. *[manifold wisdom]* 2. of many sorts; many and varied; multifarious: used with a plural noun *[manifold duties.]* 3. being such in many and various ways or for many reasons *[a manifold villain]* 4. comprising, consisting of, or operating several units or parts of one kind: said of certain devices —*n.* 1. something that is manifold 2. a pipe with one inlet and several outlets or with one outlet and several inlets, for connecting with other pipes, as, in an automobile, for conducting exhausts from each cylinder into a single exhaust pipe —*vt.* 1. to make manifold; multiply 2. to make more than one copy of *[to manifold* a letter with carbon paper] —*SYN.* see MANY — **man′i·fold′er** *n.* —**man′i·fold′ly** *adv.* —**man′i·fold′ness** *n.*

MANIFOLD
(A. manifold; B. cylinders)

Additional Word Formations. These are words derived from the one being defined. Their parts of speech are also indicated. Because they have the same basic meaning as the parent word, definitions are omitted.

Meanings. Meanings are grouped by parts of speech. Sometimes usage is briefly illustrated (*manifold* duties). Some dictionaries list meanings in historical order, others according to frequency of use. The front part of the dictionary specifies the arrangement.

Synonyms. These are words close in meaning to the one being defined. Although no synonym carries exactly the same meaning as the original, the two may be interchangeable in some situations.

Figure 16.1 From *Webster's New World Dictionary of the American Language,* Third College Edition.

3. Parts of speech:
   before (adverb, preposition, conjunction)
   deep (adjective, noun, adverb)
   fair (adjective, adverb, noun)
   here (adverb, interjection, noun)
   separate (verb, adjective, noun)
   then (adverb, adjective, noun)
   to (preposition, adverb); also serves as sign of infinitive (*to* run)
   where (adverb, conjunction, pronoun)

4. Etymology:
   carnival—based on the French *carnaval* or Italian *carnevale,* which in turn are derived from the Middle Latin *carnelevarium,* meaning "to remove meat."
   fiduciary—based on the Latin *fiducarius,* which is derived from the Latin *fiducia,* meaning "trust" and "thing held in trust." *Fiducia* in turn derives from the Latin *fidere,* meaning "to trust."
   Icarian—based on the Latin *Icarus,* which is derived from the Greek *Ikaros.*
   lethargy—based on the Middle English *litarge,* which is derived from the late Latin *lethargia.* This term in turn derives from the Greek *lethargos,* meaning "forgetful."
   phenomenon—based on the late Latin *phaenomenon,* which is derived from the Greek *phainesthai,* meaning "to appear." The latter word is related to the Greek *phainein,* meaning "fantasy."
   sabotage—based on the French word *sabot,* which designates a kind of wooden shoe. In the past, workers used sabots to damage machines during times of labor strife, hence the present meaning of *sabotage.*

EXERCISE ■ **Use a good desk dictionary to look up the specified information for each of the following lists of words.**

1. Variant spellings:

airplane	aesthete	gray	tornadoes
color	gaily	theater	usable

supercilious—based on the Latin *supercilium*, meaning "eyebrow." The term refers to the raised eyebrows of someone who is prideful or contemptuous of others.

tawdry—based on the name St. Audrey, with special reference to the cheap laces sold at St. Audrey's fair in Norwich, England.

5. Idiomatic phrases:

beat: beat (about, back, down, it, off, out, up [on], the band, on the beat)

ear: be all ears, bend an ear, fall on deaf ears, lend an ear, keep an ear to the ground, have someone's ear, in one ear and out the other, play (it) by ear, set on its ear, turn a deaf ear

get: get (about, across, after, along, around, around to, at, to, away, away with, back at, behind, by, down [to, from], in, together, it, nowhere, off, on with, out of, over, through, up)

high: high and dry, high and low, high and mighty, high on, high, wide, and handsome, on high

jump: jump (a claim, at, bail, in with both feet, off, on [all over], the track, get the jump on)

make: make (a fool of, a meal on, as if, away with, believe, do, it, like, off [with], or break, out, over, up, up to, with, on the make)

put: put (about, across, ahead, aside, away, back, down, forth, forward, in [for], in on, over [on], it there, off, on [to], out, through, up, upon, up with)

set: set (about, against, apart, aside, back, down, forth, in, off, out, straight, to, up, upon, all set)

2. Syllabication and the syllable that receives the main stress:

anacrusis	cadenza	harbinger	misanthrope
baccalaureate	exclamation	ionize	sequester

3. Parts of speech:

before	fair	separate	to
deep	here	then	where

4. Etymology:

carnival	Icarian	phenomenon	supercilious
fiduciary	lethargy	sabotage	tawdry

5. Idiomatic phrases:

beat	get	jump	put
ear	high	make	set

6. Synonyms:

attack	ghastly	mercy	plot
distress	keep	object	range

Thesauruses. Thesauruses list synonyms for words but omit the other elements in dictionary entries. Figure 16.2 shows a typical entry. Note that the items are grouped according to parts of speech, and some are cross-indexed.

247. FORMLESSNESS

.1 NOUNS **formlessness, shapelessness;** amorphousness, amorphism, amorphia; **chaos,** confusion, messiness, orderlessness; disorder 62; entropy; anarchy 740.2; **indeterminateness, indefiniteness,** indecisiveness, vagueness, mistiness, haziness, fuzziness, blurriness, unclearness, obscurity.

.2 unlicked cub, diamond in the rough.

.3 VERBS **deform, distort** 249.5; unform, unshape; disorder, jumble, mess up, muddle, confuse; obfuscate, obscure, fog up, blur.

.4 ADJS **formless, shapeless,** featureless, characterless, nondescript, inchoate, lumpen, blobby *or* baggy [both informal], inform: amorphous, amorphic, amorph(o)-: **chaotic, orderless,** disorderly 62.13, unordered, unorganized, confused, anarchic 740.6; kaleidoscopic; **indeterminate, indefinite,** undefined, indecisive, vague, misty, hazy, fuzzy, blurred *or* blurry, unclear, obscure.

.5 **unformed, unshaped,** unshapen, unfashioned, unlicked; uncut, unhewn.

Figure 16.2 From *Roget's International Thesaurus,* 4th edition, Robert L. Chapman. Copyright © 1977 by Harper & Row, Publishers, Inc. Reprinted by permission of the Publishers.

A thesaurus will help you find a word with just the right shade of meaning or a synonym when you want to avoid repetition. But synonyms are never exactly equal, nor are they always interchangeable. To illustrate, *old* means "in existence or use for a long time"; *antiquated* conveys the notion that something is old-fashioned or outdated. Therefore, use the thesaurus along with the dictionary. Only then can you tell which synonym fits a specific sentence.

Excellent guides to synonyms include the following:

Roget's Thesaurus
Webster's New Dictionary of Synonyms
Modern Guide to Synonyms and Related Words,

TOWARD RHETORICAL EFFECT

Rhetorical effect refers to the response that the manner of writing, not the message, generates in the reader. Successful writers create a desired response through the level of their diction and the tone of their writing.

Level of Diction

What level of diction is best? The answer depends upon the writer's audience and purpose. Think about a safety engineer who investigates a serious industrial accident on which she must write two reports, one for the safety director of the company, who represents a technical audience, and another for the local newspaper, read by a general audience. Although the two accounts would deal with the same matter, clearly they would use very different language: specialized and formal in the first case, everyday and more relaxed in the second. In each case, the language would reflect the background of the audience. As you write, always choose language suited to your audience and purpose.

Edited American English follows the familiar grammatical rules maintained in most formal and academic writing. Generally, everything you write for college courses or on the job should be in edited American English. *Nonstandard English* refers to any version of the language that deviates from these rules. Here is an example from Mark Twain's famous novel *The Adventures of Huckleberry Finn.*

> You don't know about me without you have read a book by the name of *The Adventures of Tom Sawyer*, but that ain't no matter. That book was made by Mr. Mark Twain, and he told the truth, mainly. There was things which he stretched, but mainly he told the truth. That is nothing. I never seen anybody but lied one time or another, without it was Aunt Polly, or the widow, or maybe Mary. Aunt Polly—Tom's Aunt Polly, she is—and Mary, and the Widow Douglas is all told about in that book, which is mostly a true book, with some stretchers, as I said before.

Nonstandard English does have a place in writing. Fiction writers use it to narrate the talk of characters who, if real, would speak that way. Journalists use it to standard English to ease their introduction to writing. It's frequently counterproductive to treat a dialect as wrong, as this often results in a back-lash that hinders learning. Explain that because edited American English is the dialect used in school and business, students must master it to compete effectively. Sometimes it's helpful to have students mimic the speech of an instructor. Another good approach is to compare the rules that govern edited American English and non-standard English. In especially difficult cases, students can benefit from reading a passage in edited American English and deliberately stressing the constructions that differ from those in their dialect.

TEACHING STRATEGY

Have students write different versions of one short assignment, directing them at different audiences and using different levels of diction. If they write about some college problem, one version (informal and colloquial) might be directed to friends at home, a second (informal) to their parents, and a third (formal) to the college president.

SUGGESTED INSTRUCTOR READINGS

Davis, A. L., ed. Culture, Class, and Language Variety. Urbana, IL: NCTE, 1972. This collection of essays on a variety of dialects also classifies key problem areas.

Labov, W. The Study of Nonstandard English. Urbana, IL: NCTE, 1970. Documents the rule-governed nature of nonstandard English, argues for allowing some work in student dialects to help them gain fluency, and provides mechanisms for helping students learn edited American English (referred to as standard English).

report eyewitness reactions to accidents and crimes, and people who compile oral histories use it to record the recollections of people they interview.

Edited American English includes three levels of usage: formal, informal, and technical.

Formal Level.   The formal level, dignified and serious, is suitable for important political, business, and academic occasions. Its vocabulary is marked by many abstract and multisyllabic words but no slang or contractions. Long sentences and deliberately varied sentence patterns help give it a strong, rhythmic flow. Sentences are often periodic, and many have parallel or balanced structures. (See pages 201–2.) Overall, formal prose impresses the reader as authoritative, stately, and graceful.

The following excerpts from John F. Kennedy's inaugural address illustrate the formal level.

> Now the trumpet summons us again—not as a call to bear arms, though arms we need; not as a call to battle, though embattled we are; but a call to bear the burden of a long twilight struggle, year in and year out, "rejoicing in hope, patient in tribulation," a struggle against the common enemies of man: tyranny, poverty, disease, and war itself. . . .
>
> In the long history of the world, only a few generations have been granted the role of defending freedom in its hour of maximum danger. I do not shrink from this responsibility; I welcome it. I do not believe that any of us would exchange places with any other people or any other generation. The energy, the faith, the devotion which we bring to this endeavor will light our country and all who serve it, and the glow from that fire can truly light the world.
>
> And so, my fellow Americans, ask not what your country can do for you; ask what you can do for your country.
>
> John F. Kennedy, "Inaugural Address"

The first sentence opens with parallelism to show contrast: "not as a call to bear arms, though arms we need" and "not as a call to battle, though embattled we are." In the second paragraph, parallelism in the second sentence shows contrast; in the last sentence it does not. Except for the second sentence in paragraph 2, all of the sentences are periodic rather than loose. Thus, not until the end of the opening sentence do we learn the nature of the "long twilight struggle" to which the "trumpet summons us." Time and again Kennedy uses elevated diction—polysyllabic words like *embattled, rejoicing, tribulation, tyranny, poverty, generations, devotion,* and *endeavor,* along with shorter abstract words like *hope, freedom,* and *faith.* These carefully controlled sentence patterns, along with this wording, lend rhythmical dignity to the whole passage.

Informal Level.   Informal writing resembles orderly, intelligent conversation. Earmarked by relatively ordinary words, loose sentences, and numerous shorter, less varied sentence structures than formal prose, informal writing may include contractions or even slang, and it is more likely than formal writing to use the pronouns *I, me, my, you,* and *yours.* Casual and familiar rather than dignified and rhythmic, informal writing does not usually call attention to itself. Nevertheless, the language is precise and effective. Here is an example:

There was a distressing story in the paper a few months ago. I wish I'd clipped it out and saved it. As it is, I can only hope I remember it fairly accurately. There was a group of people who wanted a particular dictionary removed from the shelves of the local library because it contained a lot of obscenity. I think they said there were sixty-five or so dirty words in it. Some poor woman who was acting as a spokesman for the group had a list of offending words, which she started to read aloud at a hearing. She managed to read about twenty of them before she started sobbing uncontrollably and couldn't continue.

> Thomas H. Middleton, "The Magic Power of Words"

Unlike the Kennedy excerpt, this one has relatively uncomplicated sentences. Three of them—the fourth, sixth, and seventh—are loose rather than periodic. The passage includes two contractions, *I'd* and *couldn't,* one casual expression, *a lot of,* and the pronoun *I.* Most of the words are very short, and none would be out of place in an ordinary conversation.

Formal–Informal Level. As life has become less formal, informal diction has become increasingly widespread. Today many articles and books, even ones on relatively serious topics, mix informal and formal elements. Here is an example:

> . . . faith in sports has been vigorously promoted by industry, the military, government, the media. The value of the arena and the locker room has been imposed on our national life. Coaches and sportswriters are speaking for generals and businessmen, too, when they tell us that a man must be physically and psychologically "tough" to succeed, that he must be clean and punctual and honest, that he must bear pain, bad luck, and defeat without whimpering or making excuses. A man must prove his faith in sports and the American Way by whipping himself into shape, playing by the rules, being part of the team, and putting out all the way. If his faith is strong, he will triumph. It's his own fault if he loses, fails, remains poor.
>
> Robert Lipsyte, *Sports World*

All these sentences except the next to last are loose. Two are quite long, four quite short, and only two have parallel phrases or clauses. Although a few expressions—"bear," "the American Way," "triumph"—echo formal diction, most of the words have an informal ring, and two expressions, "whipping himself into shape" and "putting out all the way," skirt the edges of slang.

Technical Level. A specialist writing for others in the same field or for sophisticated nonspecialists writes on the technical level, a cousin to the formal level. Technical language uses specialized words that may be unfamiliar to a general audience. Its sentences tend to be long and complex, but unlike formal diction it doesn't lean toward periodic sentences, parallelism, and balance. Read this example from the field of entomology, the study of insects:

> The light organs of fireflies are complex structures, and recent studies using the electron microscope show them to be even more complex than once supposed. Each is composed of three layers: an outer "window," simply a transparent portion of the body wall; the light organ proper; and an inner layer of opaque,

whitish cells filled with granules of uric acid, the so-called "reflector." The light organ proper contains large, slablike light cells, each of them filled with large granules and much smaller, dark granules, the latter tending to be concentrated around the numerous air tubes and nerves penetrating the light organ. These smaller granules were once assumed by some persons to be luminous bacteria, but we now know that they are mitochondria, the source of ATP [adenosine triphosphate] and therefore of the energy of light production. The much larger granules that fill most of the light cells are still of unknown function; perhaps they serve as the source of luciferin.

Howard Ensign Evans, *Life on a Little-Known Planet*

Note the specialized vocabulary—*granules, uric acid, mitochondria,* and *luciferin*—as well as the length and complexity of the sentences. Five sentences make up the passage, the shortest having twenty-four words. None is periodic, and none has a parallel or balanced structure.

Every field has *jargon,* specialized terms or inside talk that provides a convenient shorthand for communication among its members. For an audience of biologists, you may write that two organisms have a *symbiotic relationship,* meaning "mutually beneficial"; for psychology majors, you might use *catalepsy* instead of "a temporary loss of consciousness and feeling, often accompanied by muscular rigidity." As a general rule, use technical terms only if your audience will know their meanings. If you must use unfamiliar words when writing for a general audience, define them the first time they appear.

Colloquial Language and Slang.

Colloquial originally meant "the language of ordinary conversation between people of a particular region." *Slang,* according to *Webster's Ninth New Collegiate Dictionary,* is "an informal nonstandard vocabulary composed typically of coinages, changed words, and extravagant, forced, or facetious figures of speech." These two categories shade into each other, and even authorities sometimes disagree on whether to label a term *colloquial* or *slang.* The word *bender,* meaning "a drinking spree," seems firmly in the colloquial camp, and *bummer,* a term recently used by young people to mean "a bad time," is just as clearly slang. *Break a leg* is theater slang used to wish a performer success. But what about *guy* and *kid?* Once they were slang, but so many people have used them for so long that they have now become colloquial.

Regardless of their labels, colloquial and slang terms are almost never appropriate in formal writing. They sometimes serve a useful purpose in informal writing by creating a special effect or increasing audience appeal. Even so, careful writers use them sparingly. Some readers may not understand some colloquial language, and slang usually becomes dated quickly. The following paragraph uses colloquial and slang expressions successfully:

. . . When I was just a kid on Eighth Avenue in knee pants . . . [Big Bill] was trying to get himself killed. He was always in some fight with a knife. He was always cutting or trying to cut somebody's throat. He was always getting cut or getting shot. Every Saturday night that he was out there, something happened. If you heard on Sunday morning that somebody had gotten shot or stabbed, you didn't usually ask who did it. You'd ask if Big Bill did it. If he did it, no one paid much attention to it, because he was always doing something like that. They'd say, "Yeah, man. That cat is crazy."

Claude Brown, Manchild in the Promised Land

Kid, yeah, and *cat* reflect the speech of Brown's characters and thus add authenticity to his account. Despite the informal diction, Brown uses parallelism in the second, third, and fourth sentences; repetition of "he was always" emphasizes the single-minded self-destructiveness of Big Bill's behavior.

EXERCISE ■ **Identify the level of diction in each of the following passages. Support your answers with examples from the passages. Point out slang or colloquial expressions.**

1.   We may now recapitulate the reasons which have made it necessary to substitute "space-time" for space and time. The old separation of space and time rested upon the belief that there was no ambiguity in saying that two events in distant places happened at the same time; consequently it was thought that we could describe the topography of the universe at a given instant in purely spatial terms. But now that simultaneity has become relative to a particular observer, this is no longer possible. What is, for one observer, a description of the state of the world at a given instant, is, for another observer, a series of events at various different times, whose relations are not merely spatial but also temporal.

Bertrand Russell, The ABC of Relativity

2.   In some ways I am an exceptionally privileged woman of thirty-seven. I am in the room of a private, legal abortion hospital, where a surgeon, a friend of many years, is waiting for me in the operating room. I am only five weeks pregnant. Last week I walked out of another hospital, unaborted, because I had suddenly changed my mind. I have a husband who cares for me. He yells because my indecisiveness makes him anxious, but basically he has permitted the final choice to rest in my hands: "It would be very tough, especially for you, and it is absolutely insane, but yes, we could have another baby." I have a mother who cares. I have two young sons, whose small faces are the most moving arguments I have against going through with this abortion. I have a doctorate in psychology, which among other advantages, assures me of the professional courtesy of special passes in hospitals, passes that at this moment enable my husband and my mother to stand in my room at a nonvisiting hour and yell at each other over my head while I sob.

Magda Denes, In Necessity and Sorrow: Life and Death in an Abortion Hospital

3.   I have just spent two days with Edward T. Hall, an anthropologist, watching thousands of my fellow New Yorkers short-circuiting themselves into hot little twitching death balls with jolts of their own adrenalin. Dr. Hall says it is overcrowding that does it. Overcrowding gets the adrenalin going, and the adrenalin gets them queer, autistic, sadistic, barren, batty, sloppy, hot-in-the-pants, charred-in-the-flankers, leering, puling, numb—the usual in New York, in other words, and God knows where else. Dr. Hall has the theory that overcrowding has already

EXERCISE ANSWERS
1. This is technical diction. The writing is directed at sophisticated nonspecialists rather than physicists specializing in the matter of relativity. The passage uses words that a general audience would probably have difficulty understanding: *recapitulate, topography, simultaneity,* and *temporal.* For the most part, the expressions are abstract, and there are no contractions or slang. The sentences are long and their patterns varied, but only one of them, the next-to-last sentence, is periodic, and only the last one uses parallelism: "for one observer"—"for another observer."
2. This is formal–informal diction. Informal elements include loose sentences that, except for sentences 6 and 9, are relatively short; the use of the pronouns *I, me,* and *my;* and the colloquial expressions *yells* and *tough.* Formal elements include parallelism ("I am" in sentences 1–3, and "I have" in sentences 5 and 7–9) and the absence of contractions.
3. This is informal diction. The language is casual, familiar, and frantic rather than stately and serious. The passage includes two original and highly figurative examples of slang—"short-circuiting themselves into hot little twitching death balls" and "charred in-the-flankers"—as well as such less flamboyant slang and colloquial expressions as "gets

them queer," "hot-in-the-pants," "God knows where else," and "winds up." The first and third sentences are long, but the remaining five are relatively short. All are loose rather than periodic, and none of them shows parallelism or balanced construction. Although Wolfe uses one term, "ethology," which even a sophisticated audience might not know, he defines it for his readers.

PERSPECTIVE

Students often have trouble mastering tone. Sensitivity to tone requires social awareness, an extensive vocabulary, and a flexible syntax. Students struggling to develop their ideas, express them in appropriate language, and present them in some coherent order often find tone one burden too many. Nevertheless, students should be encouraged to use a tone appropriate to their writing topics, the image they wish to project, and to their audience.

TEACHING STRATEGY

Have students change the wording of several neutral sentences so that their denotations are preserved but their connotations altered. **Samples:** The police officer arrested the suspected felon. The gentleman embraced his young lady friend. Our two nations are engaged in armed conflict.

TEACHING STRATEGIES

1. Bring in several samples of writing—letters to the editor or junk mail sales pitches—in which the tone is inappropriate; then have the class discuss their tonal shortcomings.
2. Assign short pieces of writing that call for different tones. Students might write a brief argument in an objective tone and then recast it as a strongly emotional plea.

thrown New York into a state of behavioral sink. Behavioral sink is a term from ethology, which is the study of how animals relate to their environment. Among animals, the sink winds up with a "population collapse" or "massive die-off." O rotten Gotham.

Tom Wolfe, *The Pump House Gang*

Tone

Tone reveals the author's attitude toward the topic and the reader. Every piece of writing has a tone, intended or otherwise, which stems from the meanings and connotations of words, the sentence patterns, and the rhythm of the prose.

Denotation and Connotation. The denotation of a word is its direct, essential meaning: what the word always stands for. The word *book,* for example, denotes "a set of printed or blank sheets bound together along one edge to form a volume." This definition is objective and neutral: it does not assign any special value or convey any particular attitude toward the word or what the word stands for. Connotations are the values and emotional associations that accompany a word. When the self-made man snorts "book learnin' " at his better-educated junior partner, he assigns a value and an attitude—that he ranks experience higher than the knowledge gained from books.

Some words—*death,* for instance—almost always carry strong connotations or emotional associations. *Webster's Ninth New Collegiate Dictionary* defines it as "a permanent cessation of all vital functions" or "the end of life," but it means much more. All of us have hopes, fears, and memories about death, feelings that color our responses whenever we hear or read the word. Likewise, we have personal responses to words like *sexy, cheap, radical, politician,* and *mother.* Experience, to a considerable extent, conditions how we think and feel about a word. To an Olympic swimmer who has won a gold medal, *swimming* may stir pleasant memories of the victory and the plaudits that went with it. The victim of a near-drowning, however, might react to the same word with something approaching horror.

Nonetheless, cultural connotations are more important than personal ones. Cultural connotations develop the way individual ones do, but on a much larger scale, growing out of the common experiences of many speakers and writers and changing with usage and circumstances.

Context, the parts of a passage that precede and follow a word, also affects connotation. Note, for instance, the different associations of *dog* in these sentences.

That movie is a real dog.

I sure am putting on the dog!

It's a dog-eat-dog world.

Your dog-in-the-manger attitude makes you very unpopular.

Denotation is sometimes called the language of science and technology; connotation, the language of art. But we need both to communicate effectively. Denotation allows us to convey precise, essential meanings. Connotation adds richness, warmth, and bite. Without these qualities our language would be bland and sterile, our lives bleak and mechanical.

Objective Tone.
An objective tone keeps the writer's personality and opinions out of the message. Here is an example.

> Myopia is a condition of the eye which makes distant vision blurry. In brief, the myopic individual is nearsighted. When the eye is normal, rays of light pass through it and come to focus on the retina, located at the back of the eye. With the myopic eye, however, the rays of light come together a little in front of the retina. As a result, the distant image is not seen clearly. Myopia may result from the eye itself being too long or the lens of the eye being too flat. In either case, the rays converge in front of the retina, and the nearsighted individual is likely to have difficulty making out distant objects.
>
> Janine Neumann

This tone suits a popular explanation of a medical condition. The prose is businesslike and authoritative, the sentence patterns uncomplicated, and nothing reveals the person behind the words.

Other Attitudes.
Sometimes you write merely to inform, sometimes to persuade. In persuasive writing, let your attitude toward your topic set the tone. Decide how subtle, flamboyant, or formal your writing should be and what special tone—satiric, cynical, serious, mock pompous, bawdy, playful—will win your reader over.

Every essay has combined characteristics that give it a special tone. The following excerpts illustrate some of tone's many dimensions.

> Unless you have led an abnormally isolated adulthood, the chances are excellent that you know many people who have at one time or another committed an act, or consorted with someone who was committing an act, for which they might have been sent to prison. We do not consider most of these people, or ourselves, criminals; the act is one thing, the criminality of it quite something else. Homicide, for example, is in our law not a crime; murder only is proscribed. The difference between the two is the intention, or to be more accurate, society's decision about the nature of that intention.
>
> Bruce Jackson, "Who Goes to Prison: Caste and Careerism in Crime"

Here we have a sophisticated and rather formal tone. Terms like *consorted* and *proscribed,* while exactly suited to Jackson's meaning, do not form part of most people's word kits. The complexity of the first sentence and the varied patterns of the others add to the air of sophistication. The emphatic *quite,* meaning "entirely," is cultivated usage; and along with *society's decision,* it lends the tone a wry touch.

Cans. Beer cans. Glinting on the verges of a million miles of roadways, lying in scrub, grass, dirt, leaves, sand, mud, but never hidden. Piels, Rheingold, Ballantine, Schaeffer, Schlitz, shining in the sun or picked by moon or the beams of headlights at night; washed by rain or flattened by wheels, but never dulled, never buried, never destroyed. Here is the mark of savages, the testament of wasters, the stain of prosperity.

Who are these men who defile the grassy borders of our roads and lanes, who pollute our ponds, who spoil the purity of our ocean beaches with the empty vessels of their thirst? Who are the men who make these vessels in millions and then say, "Drink and discard"? What society is this that can afford to cast away a million tons of metal and to make a wild and fruitful land a garbage heap?

Marya Mannes, "Wasteland"

Rhythm and word choice contribute equally to the tone of this passage. The excerpt opens with imagistic sentence fragments that create a panoramic word picture of our littered roadways. Then complete sentences and somber commentary follow. Words and patterns are repeated, mixing the dignified language of epic and religion with common derogatory terms—*testament, purity, vessels,* and *fruitful* set against *savages, wasters, defile,* and *garbage heap*—to convey the contradictions Mannes deplores. The rhetorical questions, used instead of accusations, add a sense of loftiness to her outrage, helping create a tone both majestic and disdainful.

Erethizon dorsatus, an antisocial character of the Northern U.S. and Canadian forest, commonly called a porcupine, looks like an uncombed head, has a grumpy personality, fights with his tail, hides his head when he's in trouble, attacks backing up, retreats going ahead, and eats toilet seats as if they were Post Toasties. It's a sad commentary on his personality that people are always trying to do him in.

R. T. Allen, "The Porcupine"

The tone of this passage is affectionately humorous. Allen sets this tone by noting the porcupine's tousled appearance, testy personality, and peculiar habits, such as eating outdoor toilet seats (for their salt content, as Allen later explains). The net effect is to personify porcupines, making them seem like the eccentric reprobate human that others regard with amused toleration.

The final passage begins by referring to a "promissory note": the Constitution and the promise of life, liberty, and the pursuit of happiness spelled out in the Declaration of Independence:

It is obvious today that America has defaulted on this promissory note insofar as her citizens of color are concerned. Instead of honoring this sacred obligation, America has given the Negro people a bad check; a check which has come back marked "insufficient funds." But we refuse to believe that the bank of justice is bankrupt. We refuse to believe that there are insufficient funds in the great vaults of opportunity in this nation. So we have come to cash this check—a check that will give us upon demand the riches of freedom and the security of justice. We have also come to this hallowed spot to remind America of the fierce urgency of *now.* This is no time to engage in the luxury of cooling off or to take the tranquilizing drug of gradualism. *Now* is the time to make real the promises of Democracy. *Now* is the time to rise from the dark and desolate valley of segregation to the sunlit path of racial justice. *Now* is the time to open the doors of opportunity to all of God's children. *Now* is the time to lift our nation from the quicksands of racial injustice to the solid rock of brotherhood.

Martin Luther King, Jr., "I Have a Dream"

This writing speaks passionately for freedom and justice. Its most obvious rhetorical strategy is metaphor, first the extended one of the promissory note, then brief separate metaphors that make the same point. The repetition of *now* sharpens the insistent tone. Eloquence comes through parallelism, repetition, and words like *sacred* and *hallowed*, vividness through figures of speech like "vaults of opportunity" and "sunlit path of racial justice." Like George Orwell, Mark Twain, Joseph Conrad, and other masters of tonal effects whose work appears in this book, King uses both rhythm and diction to create a tone that infuses and invigorates his message.

EXERCISE ■ **Characterize the tone of each of the following paragraphs. Point out how word choice, sentence structure, rhythm, and other elements contribute to it.**

1.   When I awoke, dimly aware of some commotion and outcry in the clearing, the light was slanting down through the pines in such a way that the glade was lit like some vast cathedral. I could see the dust motes of wood pollen in the long shaft of light, and there on the extended branch sat an enormous raven with a red and squirming nestling in its beak.

   The sound that awoke me was the outraged cries of the nestling's parents, who flew helplessly in circles around the clearing. . . . And he, the murderer, the black bird at the heart of life, sat there, glistening in the common light, formidable, unperturbed, untouchable. The sighing died. It was then I saw the judgment. It was the judgment of life against death. I will never see it again so forcefully presented. I will never hear it again in notes so tragically prolonged. For in the midst of protest, they forgot the violence. There, in that clearing, the crystal note of a song sparrow lifted hesitantly in the hush. And, finally, after painful fluttering, another took the song, and then another, the song passing from one bird to another, doubtfully at first, as though some evil thing was being slowly forgotten. Till suddenly they took heart and sang from many throats joyously together as birds are known to sing. They sang under the brooding shadow of the raven. In simple truth they had forgotten the raven, for they were the singers of life, and not of death.

Loren Eiseley, "The Judgment of the Birds"

2.   America, which leads the world in almost every economic category, leads it above all in the production of schlock. Christmas toys broken before New Year's, wash-n-wear suits that neither wash well nor wear well, appliances that expire a month after the guarantee, Barbie dolls, frozen pizza—these are but a few of the shoddy goods whose main contribution to our civilization, apart from a momentary satisfaction to the purchaser, is to swell the sanitary-fill schlock heaps that are the feces of our Gross (and how!) National Product.

Robert Claiborne, "Future Schlock"

EXERCISE ANSWERS

1. This passage is elegiac but undespairing. Eiseley establishes his elegiac tone by first likening the glade in which the drama is played out to a cathedral and by calling the raven "the black bird at the heart of life." This tone is sustained by the strongly rhythmic and repetitious pattern of the sentences ("It was then I saw the judgment. It was the judgment of life against death. I will never see it again so forcefully presented. I will never hear it again in notes so tragically prolonged."). Much of the impact of the passage stems from its allegorical character: like Eiseley's sparrows, all of us exist "under the brooding shadow of the raven" and, again like them, have no choice except to sing in the shadow of death.

2. The tone here is one of deeply felt anger at people who produce the shoddy goods. The anger comes through strongly in the expressions "schlock," "shoddy goods," and, most notable of all, "the sanitary-fill schlock heaps that are the feces of our Gross (and how!) National Product."

3. This passage conveys a strong sense of excitement and adulation, aroused in the opening short, pithy sentences with their stars, capitalized words, and exclamation points. Durocher then sustains this tone by invoking the carnival atmosphere of the games in which Ruth played and by his behavior when he got a hit. The language is highly informal—short sentences, slang and colloquialisms, and contractions—and adds to the excitement of the passage.

PERSPECTIVE

While stylistic techniques create more memorable prose, they also convey meaning that cannot be captured in a more literal fashion. Metaphors help us draw connections between apparently dissimilar ideas and establish a link between abstract ideas and our physical contact with the world. Modern physicists who talk of light as a wave or space as curved speak metaphorically. Overstatement and understatement are bound to our fundamental notion of character; the British traditional understatement and emphasis on a "stiff upper lip" are examples. Irony establishes an outlook that distrusts appearances and envisions a world fraught with contradictions.

TEACHING STRATEGIES

1. Have students record the metaphors and similes they use daily. They should discover that, like most of us, they often think in terms of metaphors and similes without deliberately trying to create them.
2. Students sometimes mistakenly believe that metaphors and similes belong exclusively to more literary writing. To correct this impression, have students review scientific and technical writing for examples of metaphors and then determine

3.   Babe Ruth was *** The Sultan of Swat ***
    Babe Ruth was *** THE BAMBINO ***
    Babe Ruth was what you came to see!!!!
    It was like going to a carnival, with Babe as both the star performer and the side-show attraction. Hell, that's what we called him: "You big ape." He was what a home-run hitter was supposed to look like. Wide, flat nose. Big feet. Little ankles. Belly hanging over his belt. All he had to do was walk on to the field and everybody would applaud. The air became charged with electricity. You just felt that something great was going to happen.
    He'd twirl that big 48-ounce bat around in little circles up at the plate as if he were cranking it up for the Biggest Home Run Ever Hit—*you felt that*—and when he'd hit one he would hit it like nobody has hit it before or since. A mile high and a mile out. I can see him now, as I did so many times, just look up, drop the bat and start to trot, the little pitter-patter pigeon-toed, high-bellied trot that seemed to say, I've done it before and I'll do it again, but this one was for you.

Leo Durocher, *Nice Guys Finish Last*

SPECIAL STYLISTIC TECHNIQUES

The style of a piece of writing is its character or personality. Like people, writing can be many things: dull, stuffy, discordant, sedate, lively, flamboyant, eccentric, and so on. Figurative language and irony can contribute to your own distinctive writing style.

Figurative Language

Figurative language uses concrete words in a nonliteral way to create sharply etched sensory images that catch and hold the reader's attention. Besides energizing the writing, figurative language helps to strengthen the reader's grip on its ideas. Five figurative devices are especially important: simile, metaphor, personification, overstatement, and understatement.

Simile and Metaphor.   A *simile* directly compares two unlike things by the use of *like* or *as*. "Todd is as restless as an aspen leaf in a breeze" and "Her smile flicked on and off like a sunbeam flashing momentarily through a cloudbank" are similes. A *metaphor* also compares unlike things, but without using *like* or *as*. Some metaphors include a linking verb (*is, are, were,* and so on); others do not. "The moon was a wind-tossed bark" and "The curtain of darkness fell over the land" are both metaphors. Here is an excerpt that contains similes and metaphors.

    The field is a sea of deep, dark green, a sea made up of millions of small blades of grass blended together as one. Each blade is a dark green spear, broad at the bottom and narrowing to a needle point at the tip. Its full length is arched so that, viewed from one end, it looks like a shallow trough with paper-thin sides. On the inner side of this trough, small ridges and shallow valleys run from base to tip. To a finger rubbed across them, they feel like short, bristly hairs.

Daniel Kinney

DISCUSSION QUESTIONS

1. Locate the similes in this passage and explain how they help the reader.
2. Locate the metaphors and point out how each heightens the sensory impact of the writing.

Writers too often snatch hastily at the first similes and metaphors that come to mind and end up strewing their pages with overused and enfeebled specimens. Johnny is "as blind as a bat," Mary runs around "like a chicken with its head cut off"—and the writing slips into trite gear. Other comparisons link items that are too dissimilar. For example, "The wind whistled through the trees like a herd of galloping horses" would only puzzle a reader.

Personification.   This is a special sort of metaphor that assigns human qualities or traits to something nonhuman: a plant, an abstraction, a nonliving thing. Here are some examples.

The vine clung stubbornly to the trunk of the tree.

May fortune smile upon you.

The waves lapped sullenly against the base of the cliff.

Each of these sentences assigns its subject a different emotional quality—stubbornness, friendliness, gloom—each figurative rather than literal: vines aren't stubborn, fortune doesn't smile, and waves aren't sullen.

Personification sometimes extends beyond a single sentence. To illustrate, the following passage carries a single image through two paragraphs:

"I figured when my legislative program passed the Congress," [Lyndon] Johnson said in 1971, "that the Great Society had a real chance to grow into a beautiful woman. And I figured her growth and development would be as natural and inevitable as any small child's. In the first year, as we got the laws on the books, she'd begin to crawl. Then in the second year, as we got more laws on the books, she'd begin to walk, and the year after that, she'd be off and running, all the time growing bigger and healthier and fatter. And when she grew up, I figured she'd be so big and beautiful that the American people couldn't help but fall in love with her, and once they did, they'd want to keep her around forever, making her a permanent part of American life, more permanent than the New Deal.

"But now Nixon has come along and everything I've worked for is ruined. There's a story in the paper every day about him slashing another one of my Great Society programs. I can just see him waking up in the morning, making that victory sign of his and deciding which program to kill. It's a terrible thing for me to sit by and watch someone else starve my Great Society to death. She's getting thinner and thinner and uglier and uglier all the time; now her bones are beginning to stick out and her wrinkles are beginning to show. Soon she'll be so ugly

whether they were employed for stylistic effect or to help present an idea.

3.   Students can be spurred to write effective metaphors and similes by completing unfinished statements, then evaluating the results in terms of stylistic effectiveness and the insights provided. For example: Education today is _____ . My life _____ (concrete verb) like _____ (concrete but correlated object). Time _____ our days. Love _____ like a _____ in us. His voice _____ .

DISCUSSION QUESTIONS

1.   The passage has two similes: "like a shallow trough with paper-thin sides" and "like short bristly hairs." They help the reader to visualize unfamiliar things, the curvature of the grass blade and its ridges and valleys, by comparing them to familiar things, a shallow trough and hairs.

2.   There are also two metaphors. The first, "a sea of deep, dark green," points out the vast expanse of the field by likening it to a huge body of water. The second, "a dark green spear. . . ." adds vividness to the overall image of the blade.

PERSPECTIVE

Personification comes naturally to us; we all tend to project human qualities onto other objects. Far from a rhetorical flourish, personification is often our first response to an obstinate motor that refuses to turn over or a computer that is too smart for its own good. The trick is for students to master their impulse to personify instead of wildly exaggerating.

TEACHING STRATEGIES

1.   Have students keep track of when and why they personify and determine whether or not the personifications are appropriate and helpful.

2. Have students examine the Johnson passage to determine why the personification is effective. The key lies in the way the passage plays on our sympathies by drawing a parallel between human life and the life of Johnson's Great Society program, based upon their shared traits of growth and decay.
3. To help students learn to create effective personifications, have them list a number of traits that people might share with education, the night, winter, or a stream, and then construct several personifications, each based upon one of the traits.

SUGGESTED INSTRUCTOR READINGS

Lakoff, G. and M. Johnson. Metaphors We Live By. Chicago: U of Chicago P, 1980. Demonstrates how and why metaphors underlie most of our everyday language.
Ortony, A. ed. Metaphor and Thought. Cambridge, England: Cambridge UP, 1979. Includes some interesting theoretical accounts of the ways we think metaphorically.

TEACHING STRATEGIES

1. Fed a steady diet of media hype which discovers a crisis in even modest events, many students overstate, not for any particular effect but because they don't realize how shrill they sound. Have them read newspapers for examples of overstatements and then discuss the effects on readers.
2. Have students review their own writing for instances of overstatement and tone down any inappropriate examples they find.
3. Have students attempt to turn the following statements into effective overstatements: Students have some mechanical errors in their papers; It can be difficult to register for

that the American people will refuse to look at her; they'll stick her in a closet to hide her away and there she'll die. And when she dies, I too will die."

Doris Kearns, "Who *Was* Lyndon Baines Johnson?"

Through personification, Johnson expresses affection for his social program, disapproval of Nixon's policies, and sorrow over the coming demise of the "child" he has so carefully nurtured.

Personification works best when it is used in moderation and doesn't make outrageous comparisons. Dishes don't run away with spoons except in nursery rhymes.

Overstatement. Overstatement, sometimes called hyperbole, deliberately and drastically exaggerates in order to make a point. An example is "Wilfred is the world's biggest fool."

One of the best examples of sustained overstatement is Mark Twain's essay "Fenimore Cooper's Literary Offences." In it, Twain claims, "In one place in *Deerslayer,* and in the restricted space of two-thirds of a page, Cooper has scored 114 offences against literary art out of a possible 115." Twain also asserts, "There have been daring people in the world who claimed that Cooper could write English, but they are all dead now. . . . " Through such exaggerations, Twain mocks the shortcomings of Cooper's novels.

Used sparingly, overstatement is emphatic, adding real force to an event or situation. Writers who consistently exaggerate, however, risk losing their credibility.

Understatement. Understatement makes an assertion in a humble manner without giving something its due, as when a sportscaster calls a team's 23–2 record "pretty fair." By drawing attention to the thing it appears to slight, this soft-spoken approach offers writers an effective strategy. Here is an example:

To assume that Heidi Mansfield lacks the qualifications for this position is not unwarranted.

Without ever actually calling Mansfield unqualified, the statement suggests that she is. Similarly, when a meat company executive says, "It is not unlikely that beef prices will jump ten cents a pound in the next two months," we might as well count on spending another dime. As these statements show, understatement not infrequently has an ulterior motive.

EXERCISE ■ **Identify the similes, metaphors, personifications, overstatements, or understatements in these sentences.**

1. The old table greedily sucked up the linseed oil.
2. Russia's social and economic system is a giant staircase that leads nowhere.
3. Stanley has the bile of human meanness by the quart in every vein.
4. Their music sounds like the drumming of an infant's fists against the sides of a crib.
5. The foundations of our divorce are as strong as ever.
6. It is not unlike Muriel to be late.

7. You're the world's biggest liar!
8. "Fashion, though folly's child, and guide of fools, Rules e'en the wisest, and in learning rules."
9. Einstein's theories have had some impact on modern science.
10. I'm as tired as a horse at sunset.

Irony

Irony occurs when a writer intentionally states one thing but actually means something different or even opposite. A certain point is thus highlighted. The sportswriter who refers to the "ideal conditions" for a tennis tournament when rain has drenched the courts and forced cancellation of matches speaks ironically. Here is a longer example of the same sort of irony:

> The baron, though a small man, had a large soul, and it swelled with satisfaction at the consciousness of being the greatest man in the little world about him. He loved to tell long stories about the dark old warriors whose portraits looked grimly down from the walls around, and he found no listeners equal to those that fed at his expense. He was much given to the marvellous, and a firm believer in all those supernatural tales with which every mountain and valley in Germany abounds. The faith of his guests exceeded even his own; they listened to every tale of wonder with open eyes and mouths, and never failed to be astonished, even though repeated for the hundredth time. Thus lived the Baron Von Landshort, the oracle of his table, the absolute monarch of his little territory, and happy, above all things, in the persuasion that he was the wisest man of the age.

> Washington Irving, "The Spectre Bridegroom"

Irving never directly states the baron's shortcomings. Rather, suggestive details such as the swelling of the baron's soul, his belief in the supernatural, and his deception by the sponging guests portray one who, far from being "the wisest man of the age," is pompous, superstitious, and gullible.

*E*LIMINATING FLAWED DICTION

Diction flaws include wordiness, euphemisms, clichés, mixed metaphors, and sexist language. As you revise, stay alert for these culprits and eliminate any that you find.

Wordiness

Wordiness is verbal obesity, and like physical obesity it has more than one cause. Some writers overnourish their prose to make it sound more impressive, some to pad an assignment, and some simply because they don't realize they're doing it. Whatever the reason, the results are the same: ponderous, slow-moving papers that lack punch. To inject vigor, strip your prose down to fighting weight by cutting out every word that doesn't serve a purpose. If five words are doing the work of one, drop four.

the class you want; Dorms may be noisy in the evening; Dorm food can occasionally be unappetizing.

TEACHING STRATEGY

Have students attempt to turn the following statements into effective understatements: College can be extremely expensive; This class will be terribly difficult; A serious illness will result in extensive medical bills.

EXERCISE ANSWERS

1. Personification.
2. Metaphor.
3. Overstatement.
4. Simile.
5. Metaphor.
6. Understatement.
7. Overstatement.
8. Personification.
9. Understatement.
10. Simile.

TEACHING STRATEGIES

1. Because students often fail to recognize that they use irony, you might provide them with relevant examples. "Oh, it was a wonderful date. He fascinated me hour after hour with a detailed account of his high school exploits. He was so interesting I never had to say a thing. And what a big spender; he treated me to a meal at McDonald's." Have students record examples of irony they have heard or inadvertently produced themselves.
2. Have students attempt to respond to the following prompts with effective irony: A teacher who never gives a grade higher than a C; A student who attempts to get better grades by sleeping more and studying less; A summer day that never gets above 50°; A fairly unimportant member of the administration of a small college who sees himself as the key to the future.

PERSPECTIVE

Sometimes only a fine line separates excessive wordiness

and essential elaboration. Although students need to cut excess verbiage, encourage them to supply helpful qualifications and useful technical terms. In some kinds of writing, especially legal documents, writers must follow established precedent. As they look for deadwood to chop, students should also check for places where they need to supply qualifications and modifiers to make their writing clearer.

TEACHING STRATEGIES

1. Have students review magazine articles and their textbooks for examples of seeming verbosity and then determine if cutting is needed.

2. Have students review their own writing for deadwood and gobbledygook that can be cut.

PERSPECTIVE

While encouraging students to avoid euphemisms, we do not want them to adopt an excessively rude bluntness that pays no attention to tact. Explain the differences between an undesirable euphemism, a helpful technical term, and basic tact.

TEACHING STRATEGIES

1. Have students list the euphemisms they know well and then indicate circumstances in which each would be appropriate and inappropriate.

2. Have students review the following paired expressions to determine which would probably be most acceptable and under what circumstances.

You did not do very well on that last test. You bombed that exam.

Your hospital tests do not look promising. I'm afraid you're going to die in the near future.

The two major forms of wordiness, deadwood and gobbledygook, often occur together. *Deadwood,* which does nothing but take up space and clutter the writing, is bracketed in the following sentence:

> Responsible parents [of today] neither allow their children [to have] absolute freedom [to do as they please] nor severely restrict their children's activities.

Now read the sentence without the deadwood.

> Responsible parents neither allow their children absolute freedom nor severely restrict their children's activities.

Careful revision has increased the clarity and reduced the words from twenty-three to fourteen.

Gobbledygook consists of long, abstract, or technical words that help create unnecessarily long and complex sentences. Some people who write it mistakenly believe it "dignifies" their thoughts. Others want to conceal their meanings by clouding their statements. And some naively think that long words are better than short ones. All of these writers use gobbledygook, but none of their readers appreciate it. Here are some samples of gobbledygook followed by revised versions in plain English:

Original Version	*Revised Version*
The fish exhibited a 100 percent mortality response.	All of the fish died.
We have been made cognizant of the fact that the experiment will be terminated in the near future.	We have learned that the experiment will end soon.

Euphemisms

Euphemisms take the sting out of something unpleasant or add stature to something humble. Familiar expressions include *pass away* for *die, preowned* for *used*, and *sanitation engineer* for *garbage collector*.

In most cases, the writer simply intends to cushion reality. But euphemisms also have grisly uses. Mobsters don't *beat up* merchants who refuse *protection* (itself a euphemism); they *lean on* them. Hitler didn't talk about *exterminating the Jews* but about *the final solution to the Jewish problem*. These euphemisms don't just blur reality; they blot out images of horror. Of merchants with broken limbs and bloodied faces. Of cattle cars crammed with men, women, and children enroute to death camps. Of barbed wire and gas ovens and starved corpses in the millions.

Any euphemism, however well-intentioned, probably obscures an issue. On occasion you may need one in order to protect the sensitive reader, but usually you will serve readers best by using direct expressions that present reality, not a tidied-up version.

Clichés and Mixed Metaphors

Clichés. Clichés are expressions that have become flat and stale from overuse. Rather than responding to experience with their own perceptions, writers sometimes resort to oft-repeated words or phrases that stem from patterned thinking. Dullness follows. Daily conversation abounds with stale, trite expressions because talk is unplanned, but writing allows you time to find invigorating and effective language. Your individual response is what draws the reader's interest, and only fresh thinking will produce that response. The following list of clichés barely "scratches the surface."

acid test	burn the midnight oil	green with envy
almighty dollar	chip off the old block	last but not least
beat a hasty retreat	clear as a bell	nipped in the bud
better late than never	cool as a cucumber	rears its ugly head
black sheep	easier said than done	set the world on fire
blind as a bat	goes without saying	sick as a dog

Mixed Metaphors. Clichéd writing often suffers as well from mixed metaphors—inappropriate combinations that startle or amuse the reader. How would you respond if you came across this example?

When he opened that can of worms, he bit off more than he could chew.

Can you visualize someone chewing a mouthful of worms? The point is obvious.

Sexist Language

Sexist language assigns roles to people according to sex. It is offensive because it demeans women or reinforces erroneous beliefs that limit the roles they can play. Deliberate or accidental, sexist language must be eliminated from your writing. These guidelines will help you do just that.

1. Don't unnecessarily mention a woman's appearance, husband, or family.

> *Sexist*   The attractive new loan officer at the Godfather Finance Company is a real hit with customers.

> *Sexist*   Monica Helmond, wife of local restauranteur Samuel Helmond, won election to the Beal City Board of Education.

> *Sexist*   After eight years of attending college part time, Angelica Denham, a three-time grandmother, was awarded a Bachelor of Science degree.

> *Nonsexist*   The efficient new loan officer at the Godfather Finance Company is a real hit with the customers.

> *Nonsexist*   Monica Helmond, president of Oakwood Growth Enterprise, won election to the Beal City Board of Education.

> *Nonsexist*   After eight years of attending college part time, Angelica Denham was awarded a Bachelor of Science degree.

Note how, in each case, the sentence has been rewritten to include only relevant information.

2. Use the pronouns *he, him, his,* and *himself* only when referring to antecedents that are clearly masculine.

EXERCISE ANSWERS

1. Mixed metaphor. The American eagle (or "America") will never back down in the face of foreign threats.
2. Wordiness. Last summer, I repaired automobiles.
3. Cliché. You're looking exceptionally bright (very perky, radiant) this morning.
4. Euphemism. My mother died last winter.
5. Sexist language. Students wishing to attend summer school must pay their tuition one week before registration day.
6. Wordiness. My brother is majoring in industrial chemistry.
7. Mixed metaphor. The ball is in your court (the matter is in your hands), and if you fail to handle things properly don't expect any help from me.
8. Sexist language. The efficient clerk quickly filled the order.
9. Cliché. Winning first prize for her essay was a real accomplishment for Peggy.
10. Wordiness. Our company plans to retire 200 employees by year's end.

Sexist   Each tourist must carry *his* passport with *him* at all times.

Sexist   If anyone doesn't understand the instructions, *he* should see me right away.

Correct this type of error by substituting plural antecedents and pronouns for the singular ones or by rewriting the sentence to eliminate the pronouns.

Nonsexist   Tourists must carry *their* passports with *them* at all times.

Nonsexist   Anyone who doesn't understand the instructions should see me right away.

3. Don't use occupational labels that imply the positions are held only by men.

Sexist	*Nonsexist*
chairman	chair
draftsman	drafter
fireman	fire fighter
policeman	police officer
postman	letter carrier
weatherman	weather reporter

A word of caution here. To avoid sexism, some writers substitute the suffix *-person* for *-man* in many job titles (such as *handyperson* for someone who does odd jobs). Such attempts, however, often create awkward expressions that you should avoid.

EXERCISE ■ **The following sentences are flawed by wordiness, euphemisms, clichés, mixed metaphors, and sexist language. When you have identified the faults, revise the sentences.**

1. The American eagle will never, in the face of foreign threats, pull in its horns or draw back into its shell.
2. Last summer, I was engaged in the repair of automobiles.
3. You're looking as bright as a button this morning.
4. My mother was called to her heavenly reward last winter.
5. Any student wishing to attend summer school must pay his tuition one week before registration day.
6. My brother is in the process of pursuing a curriculum of industrial chemistry.
7. The ball's in your court, and if you strike out, don't expect me to pick up the pieces.
8. The blonde, sultry voiced clerk quickly filled the order.
9. Winning first prize for her essay was a real feather in Peggy's cap.
10. Our company plans to confer retirement on 200 employees by year's end.

CHAPTER 17

The Essay Examination

Instructors use essay examinations to gauge your grasp of ideas, noting how well you apply, analyze, challenge, compare, or otherwise handle them. Facts and figures, on the other hand, are more often tested by objective examinations. Writing essay answers under pressure and with minimal time to rethink and revise differs from writing at home. Instructors expect reasonably complete and coherent answers but not models of style or neatness. They do expect legibility. An effective presentation increases your chances for success; the skills learned in composition class can help you achieve it. A plan, a thesis, specific support, staying on track, and the pointers presented in this chapter—all are grade boosters.

STUDYING FOR THE EXAMINATION

Here are some pointers for studying:

1. Allow adequate preparation time. For a comprehensive test, start reviewing several days in advance. For one that covers a small segment of the course, a day or two should be enough.
2. Reread the key points you've marked in your class notes and textbook. Use them to develop a set of basic concepts.
3. Make up a set of sample questions related to these concepts and do some free-writing to answer them. Even if none of the questions appears on the test, your efforts will ease pretest jitters and supply insights that apply to other questions.
4. Answer your questions by drawing upon your concepts and supplying details from your notes and textbook.

TYPES OF TEST QUESTIONS

Some instructors favor narrow, highly focused test questions with detailed answering instructions. Others like broad items, perhaps with simple directions such as "write for twenty minutes." The sample questions below range from very

TEACHING STRATEGY

You might teach this unit before mid-term exams. Students could then interview instructors briefly about why they give essay exams, what they expect of students, and how they evaluate the results. Findings could be discussed orally or submitted in writing, bound, and distributed to the class as a resource.

TEACHING STRATEGY

To help students develop good study habits, have them maintain a study log in which they record when, where, and how long they study, how they go about doing it, and the problems they have. When reading the logs, you will probably find that many students try to study in their dorms, are regularly distracted, have no more than 15 minutes uninterrupted study time, then end up cramming for tests late at night when they are exhausted. Once you identify the problems, you can then offer suggestions for coping with them.

231

broad to very narrow. Note how when answering them you can often use the writing strategies discussed in Chapters 4–12.

1. Analyze the *influences* of the industrial revolution on European society.
2. Discuss the most important *causes* of the Spanish–American War.
3. *Compare and contrast* the David statues of Michelangelo and Bernini.
4. Select three different camera shots used in the movie *Batman*. Identify at least one scene that *illustrates* each shot; then explain how each shot functions by *describing* the relationship between the shot and the action or dialogue.
5. Discuss the stock market crash of October 1987. Consider the major *factors* involved, such as the collapse of the Japanese bond market, the decline in the value of the dollar, and the wide spread between interest rates and stock yields, and how the different *factors* interacted. Use a thesis statement that signals the points you will discuss.

A highly focused question such as item 5 suggests how to organize and develop the essay. If you know the answer, you can begin writing quickly. In contrast, item 1 forces you to focus and narrow the subject before you respond. Answering this type of item requires careful planning.

PREPARING TO WRITE

You can't get from Pocatello to Poughkeepsie without knowing and following an appropriate route. The same principle applies to exam writing. Often students fail to read general directions or to answer what is asked. Low grades follow. To avoid penalizing yourself, scan the test items, noting how many must be answered and which ones, if any, are optional. When you have a choice, select the questions you can answer most thoroughly. Pay attention to any suggestions or requirements concerning length (one paragraph, two pages) or relative weight (25 points, 30 minutes, 40 percent), and budget your time accordingly.

The first requirement for most essay tests is to read the question for *key words*. Does the instructor want you to analyze, compare, criticize, defend, describe, discuss, evaluate, illustrate, explain, justify, trace, or summarize? If you are asked to explain how Darwin's theory of evolution affected nineteenth-century thinking, do just that; you won't like your grade if, instead, you summarize the theory. Merely putting ideas on paper, even perceptive ideas, does not substitute for addressing the question.

EXERCISE ■ **Indicate what each of the following questions calls for. What is required? By what methods—arguing, describing, or the like—would you develop the answer?**

1. Distinguish between mild depression and severe depression. You might focus on the nature, the symptoms, or the potential treatments of each condition.
2. Support or refute the following statement: Because waste incineration generates stack gases and ash that contain high levels of toxic substances, it is not an acceptable solution to waste-disposal problems.

3. Explain how to clean an automobile carburetor.
4. Briefly relate the events in the Book of Job and then explain the significance of the tale. Could the tale be called symbolic? Why or why not?

3. This question calls for a process explanation.
4. This answer would begin with a narrative ("relate the events"), move to an analysis ("explain the significance"), and end with an argument.

When you have the essay question clearly in mind, don't immediately start writing. A jack-rabbit start spells trouble. Instead, take a few moments to plan your answer. Following these steps will help you do this.

1. Jot down specific supporting information from your reading and lecture notes.
2. Make a rough outline that sketches the main points you'll cover and an effective order for presenting them.
3. Prepare a thesis statement that responds to the question and will control your answer.

Writing an essay exam, like writing an essay, is a front-end-loaded process. Much of the brain work occurs before you put your answer on paper. You won't get to Poughkeepsie just by starting to drive.

WRITING THE EXAMINATION ANSWER

Here are some guidelines that will help you write a successful exam.

1. Position your thesis statement at the beginning of your answer. Make sure each paragraph is controlled by a topic sentence tied to the thesis statement.
2. Don't become excessively concerned about your wording. Focus on content and, if time permits, make stylistic changes later.
3. Fight the impulse to jot down everything you know about the general subject. The grader doesn't want to plow through verbiage to arrive at your answer.

The following essay illustrates these guidelines.

PERSPECTIVE

Some students are victims of test anxiety, a psychological problem few instructors are prepared to treat. They may ask repeatedly and nervously about an upcoming test, expressing fears that they will do poorly. During the actual test they may sweat excessively, look nervously about, even become ill. If you notice these symptoms, ask whether the student has had past problems and if so, suggest a counselor.

Question:	Discuss the various appeals described by classical rhetoric that an orator can use. Give a brief example of each kind of appeal.
Answer: **Thesis statement previews focus and order of answer**	Classical rhetoric defines three major appeals—logical, emotional, and ethical—that orators may use to win support from their audience.
Topic sentence **Example 1** **Example 2**	Most rhetoricians agree that any argument must be based on logic; that is, it must appeal to the intellect of the listeners. Unless it does, the orator will fail to convince them. For example, if a speaker who is urging the election of a candidate presents the candidate's voting record, she is appealing to logic. She asks the audience to understand that the voting record predicts how the candidate will continue to vote if elected. Likewise, a candidate for public office who describes how a tax cut will stimulate the economy and create new jobs is using a logical appeal.

TEACHING STRATEGY

Have students bring in previously written exams and revise them as necessary according to the suggestions in this section. If students have no sample exams, you could follow the same practice with one you hand out.

Topic sentence In addition to logic, emotional appeals are a powerful means of swaying people, especially groups. Though emotional appeals work along with logical appeals, they are quite different because they are directed at the listener's ***Example 1*** hopes, fears, and sympathies. When a presidential candidate indicates that a vote for his opponent is a vote to ***Example 2*** increase government spending and risk a financial crisis, he is making an emotional appeal. So, too, is the candidate who asserts that American industry can be revitalized and that our country can assume its rightful place as economic leader of the world.

Topic sentence The ethical appeal is more subtle than either of the other two but probably just as important. The orator must strike the audience as a sensible, good person if they are to be- ***Example 1*** lieve the message. Sometimes the speaker's logic and also the tone—moderate, sensible, or wise—will convey suffi- ***Example 2*** cient ethical appeal. At other times, a speaker will use statements that are deliberately intended to create ethical appeal. "In developing this program, I will work closely with both houses of the legislature, including the members of both political parties" and "Despite our differences, I believe my opponent to be a decent, honest person" are examples of such statements.

Restatement of In any speech, all these appeals—logical, emotional, and ***thesis*** ethical—work together to convince an audience.

Student Unknown

In contrast, the next two responses to the same question illustrate common faults of examination essays.

Answer A

There are three basic appeals that a speaker can make to captivate 1 his audience. These are the ethical appeal, the logical appeal, and the emotional appeal.

The first of these—the ethical appeal—includes all the speaker's 2 efforts to have his audience regard him as rational, wise, good, and generous. Needless to say, the ethical appeal, is very important. Without it, no one would pay attention to the speaker's argument.

The second appeal—logical—is also extremely important. It carries 3 the burden of the argument from speaker to listener and appeals to the intellect of the audience.

Emotional appeal—the third and final one—is made to the passions 4 and feelings of the listeners. The significance of such an appeal is obvious.

A speaker often uses all three appeals to win an audience over. 5

Answer *A* starts with a thesis statement and includes brief definitions of the three appeals; however, it omits any concrete examples and includes no specific details. As a result, the significance of the emotional appeal is not "obvious," as paragraph 4 claims, nor does the answer offer any hints as to why the other appeals are important. This response resembles an outline more than an answer and suggests the student lacked the knowledge to do a good job.

Answer B

Orators may make three different kinds of appeals to win favor from an audience: emotional appeal, logical appeal, and ethical appeal.   1

Let's start with emotional appeal because this is the one that is not essential to a speech. Logical and ethical appeals are always included; emotional appeal may be used to help sway an audience, but without logical and ethical appeals no argument is accepted. This simply makes sense: if there is no logic, there is no argument; and if the speaker doesn't come across as an ethical person—someone to be relied upon—then no one will accept what he or she says. But emotional appeal is different. Unemotional arguments may be accepted.   2

Nevertheless, emotional appeal is important. It includes whatever a speaker does to move the feelings of the audience. The speaker asks, "Don't you want to protect your families?" In doing so, he or she appeals emotionally. A speaker may appeal to the prejudices or biases of listeners. Someone at a Ku Klux Klan rally does that. So does a minister who exhorts people to be "saved." Both speakers address the emotions of the groups they talk to.   3

There is a very fine use of emotional appeal in the "Letter from Birmingham Jail" by Martin Luther King, Jr. At one point King asks his audience of white clergy how they would feel if, like blacks, they had to deny their children treats such as amusement parks and had to fear for the lives of their families, and so on. He also describes the bombings and burnings that blacks are subjected to. All the details move readers emotionally, so that they come to sympathize with blacks who live in fear.   4

Logical appeal, as noted earlier, is crucial. The speaker must seem to have an intelligent plan. The listeners want the plan to meet their needs.   5

The other appeal is the ethical one. It is made when a speaker makes him- or herself seem generous, good and wise.   6

All three appeals can be used in one speech, although the logical and ethical appeals are essential to it.   7

Although the writer opens with an acceptable thesis statement, this answer shows little evidence of advance planning. Does it make sense to begin in paragraph 2 with an appeal tagged "not essential"? And note how the paragraph drifts from the emotional appeal to the other two types, despite its topic sentence. Paragraphs 3 and 4 do focus on the emotional appeal and ironically, through specific examples, make a good case for its importance. Paragraphs 5 and 6 shortchange logical and ethical appeals by saying next to nothing about them. The essay contradicts itself: if logical and ethical appeals are the essential ones and emotional appeals "not essential," why is more than half of the essay about emotional appeal?

EXERCISE

1. Read the examination questions and answers below. Then respond to the questions that follow the answers.

A. Question

Living organisms are composed of cells. On the basis of structure, biologists categorize cells into two groups: the prokaryotic cells and the eukaryotic cells. What are the major differences between prokaryotic cells and eukaryotic cells, and in which living organisms are these cells found?

Answer

ANSWER TO EXAM QUESTION

The student is asked to (1) distinguish between eukaryotic and prokaryotic cells and (2) tell where each is found. The response notes (1) that the first type has a true nucleus containing its genetic material while the second has no nucleus and dispersed genetic material and (2) that the first type is found in all life forms except bacteria and blue-green algae, which have the second type. Thus the student has addressed both parts of the question.

Eukaryotic cells have a true nucleus and their genetic material, the DNA-containing chromosomes, is located within this nucleus, which is surrounded by a nuclear membrane. Prokaryotic cells lack a true nucleus, and their genetic material lies free in the cytoplasm of the cell.   1

Eukaryotic cells are also much more complex than prokaryotic cells. Eukaryotic cells commonly contain organelles such as mitochondria, a Golgi complex, lysosomes, an endoplasmic reticulum, and in photosynthetic cells, chloroplasts. These organelles are typically lacking in the simpler prokaryotic cells.   2

Prokaryotic cells make up the structure of all bacteria and the blue-green algae. These are the simplest of all known cellular organisms. All other cellular organisms, including humans, are composed of eukaryotic cells.   3

Scott Wybolt

a. Does the response answer the question that was asked? Discuss.

B. Question

Analyze the significant relationships between imagination and reality in Coleridge's "This Lime-Tree Bower My Prison." In your answer, you might consider some of the following questions. What is the importance of setting in the poem? Is the speaker's mind a form of setting? How is reality implicitly defined in the poem? How, and through what agencies, can reality be transmitted? What relationship is finally perceived between the spiritual and the concrete? How does friendship or fellow-feeling trigger the essential insights revealed in the poem?

Answer

ANSWERS TO EXAM QUESTIONS

a. The student uses the importance of setting as a springboard for her discussion. After noting the power of imagination to control one's perception of reality and the form the poem takes, she turns her attention to the setting, the lime tree bower "prison" in which the speaker finds himself. Paragraph 3 discusses his reactions to the bower, which lead to imaginative participation in his friends' walks, while paragraph 4 notes his newfound appreciation of the bower itself. Setting has triggered his imaginative faculties and transformed his perception of the setting itself.
b. Indirectly, the answer suggests that the speaker's mind is a sort of setting in

Coleridge's "This Lime-Tree Bower My Prison" shows imagination to be a powerful force that can control one's perception of reality and that is, in itself, a kind of reality—perhaps the most important reality. Thus, imagination and reality are more intimately linked and more similar in Coleridge's poem than they are ordinarily thought to be.   1

The relationship between imagination and reality is revealed by the speaker of "Lime-Tree Bower," although he doesn't openly state it. The technique for revelation is dramatic monologue, with the speaker seemingly talking spontaneously as his situation gives rise to a series of thoughts.   2

As the poem begins, the speaker finds himself "trapped" at home in his lime-tree bower, while his friends go on a walk he had hoped to take with them. This situation at first bothers the speaker, causing him to feel imprisoned. As the poem progresses, however, the speaker begins to imagine all the places his friends are visiting on their walk. Though he laments not being with them, he shows excitement as he describes the scenes his friends are viewing: the "roaring dell," the sea, and so on. Thus the speaker recognizes that he is able to participate imaginatively in the walk and, in doing so, to escape his "prison" reality and enter the reality of his friends.

The moment of recognition occurs at the beginning of stanza three: "A delight / Comes sudden on my heart, and I am glad / As I myself was there!" Interestingly, however, this point marks a turn in the speaker's thoughts. Once again he realizes where he actually is—the lime-tree bower. But now he appreciates its beauties. The natural beauties he imagined have taught him to appreciate the beauties of nature right before him. He has learned that there is "No plot so narrow, be but Nature there." The lime-tree bower is no longer a prison but a rich and beautiful, if somewhat small, world.

Imagination has again shaped the speaker's perceptions of reality. It controls the perception of circumstances—whether one views a place as a prison or a microcosm of a larger world, with beauties and possibilities in its own right. The use of imagination can teach one about reality, as it has Coleridge's speaker. And, if one surrenders to it completely—as the speaker does when he envisions the world of the walkers—imagination is a delightful reality, as valid as the reality of the place in which one sits.

Imagination and reality are merged in "This Lime-Tree Bower My Prison," and though this identification is apparently temporary, one may learn through imagination how to cope with and enjoy reality. Thus, imagination is intimately involved in shaping the perception of reality.

Lori McCue

a. Which of the possible approaches suggested in the question does the student select?
b. Which of the other questions does she indirectly answer? Which ones are not addressed?
c. Identify the thesis statement and explain how it controls the answer.
d. Show how the answer demonstrates careful planning.
e. Point out some effective supporting details.

3 which he walks imaginatively with his friends. Reality is defined as being not just what we perceive with our eyes but what we imagine and how we regard our circumstances. Although the answer does not explain *how* friendship triggers the insights revealed in the poem, it does suggest that friendship plays a role in stimulating the imagination: it's unlikely that one could as easily participate imaginatively in the activities of strangers or casual acquaintances.

4 c. The thesis statement is the first sentence in the answer. Everything that follows supports its contention that imagination shapes reality and is itself a sort of reality. Paragraph 3 notes that imagination allows the speaker to share his friends' reality. Paragraph 4 points out that imagination transforms the speaker's perceptions of his surroundings, and paragraph 5 shows that the reality of imagination is as valid as the reality of one's actual location.

5 d. The answer begins with a thesis sentence which indicates what the writer will discuss and in what order. Then she explains her first point and her second point, using an inductive organization: first she discusses a specific situation and set of reactions, then draws general conclusions. The conclusion reiterates the two points stated in the thesis.

6 e. Paragraph 3 supports the statement that "the speaker begins to imagine all the places his friends are visiting. . . ." The speaker "shows excitement" in describing the scenery viewed by his friends: a "roaring dell" and "the sea." The two quotations cited in paragraph 4 support the student's comments about the relationship between imagination and reality.

CHAPTER 18

Writing About Literature

PERSPECTIVE

While writing about literature builds on and uses the skills and strategies students already know, it is nevertheless a specialized form of writing that utilizes a specific vocabulary and particular analytic skills. As a result, some students who are proficient in other types of writing may have difficulty with this type. In any event, effective performance usually occurs only after extensive discussion and several writing assignments.

TEACHING STRATEGIES

1. Response journals allow students to gain practice in responding to literature and to accumulate information that might be used in later assignments. In a personal response journal, students informally explore various reactions to a work—their feelings about the plot or understanding of the setting, for example. A directed journal features a more structured response to specific questions such as "In what ways did the main character change and why?"

2. A class discussion can help prepare students for the content of a literary work. To illustrate, before reading "The Bride Comes to Yellow Sky," students might discuss the nature of the wild west, what a sheriff and gunslinger were like, and so on.

Teachers of literature generally expect you to write about what you've read. Typically they might ask you to

- show how an author handled one element of a short story, play, or poem
- compare how two different works treat a particular element
- weigh several elements and then determine the writer's intention
- air your reactions to some work.

Writing about literature offers several benefits. Weighing and recording your thoughts on the different elements sharpen your critical thinking ability. Literary papers also pay artistic dividends, as careful reading and subsequent writing deepen your appreciation of the writer's craft. Furthermore, you'll feel a sense of accomplishment as you coherently express your perceptions. Finally, writing a literature paper offers yet another opportunity to apply the writing guidelines discussed in Chapters 1–3. Focusing, gathering information, organizing, writing, revising, and editing—the old familiar trail leads to success here too.

THE ELEMENTS OF LITERATURE

Most writing assignments on literature will probably feature one or more of the following elements:

Plot	Symbols
Point of view	Irony
Character	Theme
Setting	

Depending on the work, some of these will be more important than others. Read the following story by Stephen Crane, "The Bride Comes to Yellow Sky." The discussions that follow it point out the basic features of each element and offer useful writing suggestions.

The Bride Comes to Yellow Sky

Stephen Crane

I

The great Pullman was whirling onward with such dignity of motion that a glance from the window seemed simply to prove that the plains of Texas were pouring eastward. Vast flats of green grass, dull-hued spaces of mesquit and cactus, little groups of frame houses, woods of light and tender trees, all were sweeping into the east, sweeping over the horizon, a precipice.

· A newly married pair had boarded this coach at San Antonio. The man's face was reddened from many days in the wind and sun, and a direct result of his new black clothes was that his brick-colored hands were constantly performing in a most conscious fashion. From time to time he looked down respectfully at his attire. He sat with a hand on each knee, like a man waiting in a barber's shop. The glances he devoted to other passengers were furtive and shy.

The bride was not pretty, nor was she very young. She wore a dress of blue cashmere, with small reservations of velvet here and there, and with steel buttons abounding. She continually twisted her head to regard her puff sleeves, very stiff, straight, and high. They embarrassed her. It was quite apparent that she had cooked, and that she expected to cook, dutifully. The blushes caused by the careless scrutiny of some passengers as she had entered the car were strange to see upon this plain, under-class countenance, which was drawn in placid, almost emotionless lines.

They were evidently very happy. "Ever been in a parlor-car before?" he asked, smiling with delight.

"No," she answered; "I never was. It's fine, ain't it?"

"Great! And then after a while we'll go forward to the diner, and get a big lay-out. Finest meal in the world. Charge a dollar."

"Oh, do they?" cried the bride. "Charge a dollar? Why, that's too much—for us—ain't it, Jack?"

"Not this trip, anyhow," he answered bravely. "We're going to go the whole thing."

Later he explained to her about the trains. "You see, it's a thousand miles from one end of Texas to the other; and this train runs right across it and never stops but four times." He had the pride of an owner. He pointed out to her the dazzling fittings of the coach; and in truth her eyes opened wider as she contemplated the sea-green figured velvet, the shining brass, silver, and glass, the wood that gleamed as darkly brilliant as the surface of a pool of oil. At one end a bronze figure sturdily held a support for a separated chamber, and at convenient places on the ceiling were frescos in olive and silver.

To the minds of the pair, their surroundings reflected the glory of their marriage that morning in San Antonio; this was the environment of their new estate; and the man's face in particular beamed with an elation that made him appear ridiculous to the negro porter. This individual at times surveyed them from afar with an amused and superior grin. On other occasions he bullied them with skill in ways that did not make it exactly plain to them that they were being bullied. He subtly used all the manners of the most unconquerable kind of snobbery. He oppressed them; but of this oppression they had small knowledge,

3. Perhaps start with a general question which leads to a particular insight into the story: "Why do you think Scratchy Wilson backed down?" Student responses can be followed by questions that ask for more detail: "In what ways does this action seem consistent or inconsistent with his character?" "What clues in the text led to your conclusion?"

4. Ask students to identify or explain specific features. For example: "The drummer is calmed by gazing at 'various zinc and copper fittings that bore a resemblance to armorplate.'" "What do you think these fittings symbolize?"

5. Some instructors prefer to ask imaginative questions that call for speculation about what happens after the ending. You might ask students what they think the future holds for Scratchy Wilson and Potter. After they respond, ask what clues in the story led to their conclusion or how their views fit the themes of the story.

and they speedily forgot that infrequently a number of travelers covered them with stares of derisive enjoyment. Historically there was supposed to be something infinitely humorous in their situation.

"We are due in Yellow Sky at 3:42," he said, looking tenderly into her eyes.

"Oh, are we?" she said, as if she had not been aware of it. To evince surprise at her husband's statement was part of her wifely amiability. She took from a pocket a little silver watch; and as she held it before her, and stared at it with a frown of attention, the new husband's face shone.

"I bought it in San Anton' from a friend of mine," he told her gleefully.

"It's seventeen minutes past twelve," she said, looking up at him with a kind of shy and clumsy coquetry. A passenger, noting this play, grew excessively sardonic, and winked at himself in one of the numerous mirrors.

At last they went to the dining car. Two rows of negro waiters, in glowing white suits, surveyed their entrance with the interest, and also the equanimity, of men who had been forewarned. The pair fell to the lot of a waiter who happened to feel pleasure in steering them through their meal. He viewed them with the manner of a fatherly pilot, his countenance radiant with benevolence. The patronage, entwined with the ordinary deference, was not plain to them. And yet, as they returned to their coach, they showed in their faces a sense of escape.

To the left, miles down a long purple slope, was a little ribbon of mist where moved the keening Rio Grande. The train was approaching it at an angle, and the apex was Yellow Sky. Presently it was apparent that, as the distance from Yellow Sky grew shorter, the husband became commensurately restless. His brick-red hands were more insistent in their prominence. Occasionally he was even rather absent-minded and far-away when the bride leaned forward and addressed him.

As a matter of truth, Jack Potter was beginning to find the shadow of a deed weigh upon him like a leaden slab. He, the town marshal of Yellow Sky, a man known, liked, and feared in his corner, a prominent person, had gone to San Antonio to meet a girl he believed he loved, and there, after the usual prayers, had actually induced her to marry him, without consulting Yellow Sky for any part of the transaction. He was now bringing his bride before an innocent and unsuspecting community.

Of course people in Yellow Sky married as it pleased them, in accordance with a general custom; but such was Potter's thought of his duty to his friends, or of their idea of his duty, or of an unspoken form which does not control men in these matters, that he felt he was heinous. He had committed an extraordinary crime. Face to face with this girl in San Antonio, and spurred by his sharp impulse, he had gone headlong over all the social hedges. At San Antonio he was like a man hidden in the dark. A knife to sever any friendly duty, any form, was easy to his hand in that remote city. But the hour of Yellow Sky—the hour of daylight—was approaching.

He knew full well that his marriage was an important thing to his town. It could only be exceeded by the burning of the new hotel. His friends could not forgive him. Frequently he had reflected on the advisability of telling them by telegraph, but a new cowardice had been upon him. He feared to do it. And now the train was hurrying him toward a scene of amazement, glee, and reproach. He glanced out of the window at the line of haze swinging slowly in toward the train.

Yellow Sky had a kind of brass band, which played painfully, to the delight of the populace. He laughed without heart as he thought of it. If the citizens could dream of his prospective arrival with his bride, they would parade the band at the station and escort them, amid cheers and laughing congratulations, to his adobe home.

He resolved that he would use all the devices of speed and plainscraft in making the journey from the station to his house. Once within that safe citadel, he could issue some sort of vocal bulletin, and then not go among the citizens until they had time to wear off a little of their enthusiasm.

The bride looked anxiously at him. "What's worrying you, Jack?"

He laughed again. "I'm not worrying, girl; I'm only thinking of Yellow Sky."

She flushed in comprehension.

A sense of mutual guilt invaded their minds and developed a finer tenderness. They looked at each other, with eyes softly aglow. But Potter often laughed the same nervous laugh; the flush upon the bride's face seemed quite permanent.

The traitor to the feelings of Yellow Sky narrowly watched the speeding landscape. "We're nearly there," he said.

Presently the porter came and announced the proximity of Potter's home. He held a brush in his hand, and, with all his airy superiority gone, he brushed Potter's new clothes as the latter slowly turned this way and that way. Potter tumbled out a coin and gave it to the porter, as he had seen others do. It was a heavy and muscle-bound business, as that of a man shoeing his first horse.

The porter took their bag, and as the train began to slow they moved forward to the hooded platform of the car. Presently the two engines and their long string of coaches rushed into the station of Yellow Sky.

"They have to take water here," said Potter, from a constricted throat and in mournful cadence, as one announcing death. Before the train stopped his eye had swept the length of the platform, and he was glad and astonished to see there was none upon it but the station-agent, who, with a slightly hurried and anxious air, was walking toward the water-tanks. When the train had halted, the porter alighted first, and placed in position a little temporary step.

"Come on, girl," said Potter, hoarsely. As he helped her down they each laughed on a false note. He took the bag from the negro, and bade his wife cling to his arm. As they slunk rapidly away, his hang-dog glance perceived that they were unloading the two trunks, and also that the station-agent, far ahead near the baggage-car, had turned and was running toward him, making gestures. He laughed, and groaned as he laughed, when he noted the first effect of his marital bliss upon Yellow Sky. He gripped his wife's arm firmly to his side, and they fled. Behind them the porter stood, chuckling fatuously.

II

The California express on the Southern Railway was due at Yellow Sky in twenty-one minutes. There were six men at the bar of the Weary Gentleman saloon. One was a drummer[1] who talked a great deal and rapidly; three were Texans who did not care to talk at that time; and two were Mexican sheepherders, who did not talk as a general practice in the Weary Gentleman saloon. The barkeeper's dog lay on the boardwalk that crossed in front of the door. His head was on his paws, and he glanced drowsily here and there with the constant vigilance of a dog that is kicked on occasion. Across the sandy street were some

[1]Traveling salesman

vivid green grass-plots, so wonderful in appearance, amid the sands that burned near them in a blazing sun, that they caused a doubt in the mind. They exactly resembled the grass mats used to represent lawns on the stage. At the cooler end of the railway station, a man without a coat sat in a tilted chair and smoked his pipe. The fresh-cut bank of the Rio Grande circled near the town, and there could be seen beyond it a great plum-colored plain of mesquit.

Save for the busy drummer and his companions in the saloon, Yellow Sky was dozing. The new-comer leaned gracefully upon the bar, and recited many tales with the confidence of a bard who has come upon a new field.

"—and at the moment that the old man fell downstairs with the bureau in his arms, the old woman was coming up with two scuttles of coal, and of course—"

The drummer's tale was interrupted by a young man who suddenly appeared in the open door. He cried: "Scratchy Wilson's drunk, and has turned loose with both hands." The two Mexicans at once set down their glasses and faded out of the rear entrance of the saloon.

The drummer, innocent and jocular, answered: "All right, old man. S'pose he has? Come in and have a drink, anyhow."

But the information had made such an obvious cleft in every skull in the room that the drummer was obliged to see its importance. All had become instantly solemn. "Say," said he, mystified, "what is this?" His three companions made the introductory gesture of eloquent speech; but the young man at the door forestalled them.

"It means, my friend," he answered, as he came into the saloon, "that for the next two hours this town won't be a health resort."

The barkeeper went to the door, and locked and barred it; reaching out of the window, he pulled in heavy wooden shutters, and barred them. Immediately a solemn, chapel-like gloom was upon the place. The drummer was looking from one to another.

"But say," he cried, "what is this, anyhow? You don't mean there is going to be a gun-fight?"

"Don't know whether there'll be a fight or not," answered one man, grimly; "but there'll be some shootin'—some good shootin'."

The young man who had warned them waved his hand. "Oh, there'll be a fight fast enough, if any one wants it. Anybody can get a fight out there in the street. There's a fight just waiting."

The drummer seemed to be swayed between the interest of a foreigner and a perception of personal danger.

"What did you say his name was?" he asked.

"Scratchy Wilson," they answered in chorus.

"And will he kill anybody? What are you going to do? Does this happen often? Does he rampage around like this once a week or so? Can he break in that door?"

"No; he can't break down that door," replied the barkeeper. "He's tried it three times. But when he comes you'd better lay down on the floor, stranger. He's dead sure to shoot at it, and a bullet may come through."

Thereafter the drummer kept a strict eye upon the door. The time had not yet been called for him to hug the floor, but, as a minor precaution, he sidled near to the wall. "Will he kill anybody?" he said again.

The men laughed low and scornfully at the question.

"He's out to shoot, and he's out for trouble. Don't see any good in experimentin' with him."

"But what do you do in a case like this? What do you do?"

A man responded: "Why, he and Jack Potter—"

"But," in chorus the other men interrupted, "Jack Potter's in San Anton'."

"Well, who is he? What's he got to do with it?"

"Oh, he's the town marshal. He goes out and fights Scratchy when he gets on one of these tears."

"Wow!" said the drummer, mopping his brow. "Nice job he's got."

The voices had toned away to mere whisperings. The drummer wished to ask further questions, which were born of an increasing anxiety and bewilderment; but when he attempted them, the men merely looked at him in irritation and motioned him to remain silent. A tense waiting hush was upon them. In the deep shadows of the room their eyes shone as they listened for sounds from the street. One man made three gestures at the barkeeper; and the latter, moving like a ghost, handed him a glass and a bottle. The man poured a full glass of whisky, and set down the bottle noiselessly. He gulped the whisky in a swallow, and turned again toward the door in immovable silence. The drummer saw that the barkeeper, without a sound, had taken a Winchester from beneath the bar. Later he saw this individual beckoning to him, so he tiptoed across the room.

"You better come with me back of the bar."

"No, thanks," said the drummer, perspiring: "I'd rather be where I can make a break for the back door."

Whereupon the man of bottles made a kindly but peremptory gesture. The drummer obeyed it, and, finding himself seated on a box with his head below the level of the bar, balm was laid upon his soul at sight of various zinc and copper fittings that bore a resemblance to armorplate. The barkeeper took a seat comfortably upon an adjacent box.

"You see," he whispered, "this here Scratchy Wilson is a wonder with a gun—a perfect wonder; and when he goes on the wartrail, we hunt our holes—naturally. He's about the last one of the old gang that used to hang out along the river here. He's a terror when he's drunk. When he's sober he's all right—kind of simple—wouldn't hurt a fly—nicest fellow in town. But when he's drunk—whoo!"

There were periods of stillness. "I wish Jack Potter was back from San Anton'," said the barkeeper. "He shot Wilson up once—in the leg—and he would sail in and pull out the kinks in this thing."

Presently they heard from a distance the sound of a shot, followed by three wild yowls. It instantly removed a bond from the men in the darkened saloon. There was a shuffling of feet. They looked at each other. "Here he comes," they said.

III

A man in a maroon-colored flannel shirt, which had been purchased for purposes of decoration, and made principally by some Jewish women on the East Side of New York, rounded a corner and walked into the middle of the main street of Yellow Sky. In either hand the man held a long, heavy, blue-black revolver. Often he yelled, and these cries rang through a semblance of a deserted village, shrilly flying over the roofs in a volume that seemed to have no relation to the ordinary vocal strength of a man. It was as if the surrounding stillness formed the arch of a tomb over him. These cries of ferocious challenge rang against walls of silence. And his boots had red tops with gilded imprints, of the kind beloved in winter by little sledding boys on the hillsides of New England.

The man's face flamed in a rage begot of whisky. His eyes, rolling, and yet keen for ambush, hunted the still doorways and windows. He walked with the creeping movement of the midnight cat. As it occurred to him, he roared menacing information. The long revolvers in his hands were as easy as straws; they were moved with an electric swiftness. The little fingers of each hand played sometimes in a musician's way. Plain from the low collar of the shirt, the cords of his neck straightened and sank, straightened and sank, as passion moved him. The only sounds were his terrible invitations. The calm adobes preserved their demeanor at the passing of this small thing in the middle of the street.

There was no offer of fight—no offer of fight. The man called to the sky. There were no attractions. He bellowed and fumed and swayed his revolvers here and everywhere.

The dog of the barkeeper of the Weary Gentleman saloon had not appreciated the advance of events. He yet lay dozing in front of his master's door. At sight of the dog, the man paused and raised his revolver humorously. At sight of the man, the dog sprang up and walked diagonally away, with a sullen head, and growling. The man yelled, and the dog broke into a gallop. As it was about to enter an alley, there was a loud noise, a whistling, and something spat the ground directly before it. The dog screamed, and, wheeling in terror, galloped headlong in a new direction. Again there was a noise, a whistling, and sand was kicked viciously before it. Fear-stricken, the dog turned and flurried like an animal in a pen. The man stood laughing, his weapons at his hips.

Ultimately the man was attracted by the closed door of the Weary Gentleman saloon. He went to it and, hammering with a revolver, demanded drink.

The door remaining imperturbable, he picked a bit of paper from the walk, and nailed it to the framework with a knife. He then turned his back contemptuously upon this popular resort and, walking to the opposite side of the street and spinning there on his heel quickly and lithely, fired at the bit of paper. He missed it by a half-inch. He swore at himself, and went away. Later he comfortably fusilladed the windows of his most intimate friend. The man was playing with this town; it was a toy for him.

But still there was no offer of fight. The name of Jack Potter, his ancient antagonist, entered his mind, and he concluded that it would be a glad thing if he should go to Potter's house, and by bombardment induce him to come out and fight. He moved in the direction of his desire, chanting Apache scalp-music.

When he arrived at it, Potter's house presented the same still front as had the other adobes. Taking up a strategic position, the man howled a challenge. But this house regarded him as might a great stone god. It gave no sign. After a decent wait, the man howled further challenges, mingling with them wonderful epithets.

Presently there came the spectacle of a man churning himself into deepest rage over the immobility of a house. He fumed at it as the winter wind attacks a prairie cabin in the North. To the distance there should have gone the sound of a tumult like the fighting of two hundred Mexicans. As necessity bade him, he paused for breath or to reload his revolvers.

IV

Potter and his bride walked sheepishly and with speed. Sometimes they laughed together shamefacedly and low.

"Next corner, dear," he said finally.

They put forth the efforts of a pair walking bowed against a strong wind. Potter was about to raise a finger to point the first appearance of the new home when, as they circled the corner, they came face to face with a man in a maroon-colored shirt, who was feverishly pushing cartridges into a large revolver. Upon the instant the man dropped his revolver to the ground and, like lightning, whipped another from its holster. The second weapon was aimed at the bridegroom's chest.

There was a silence. Potter's mouth seemed to be merely a grave for his tongue. He exhibited an instinct to at once loosen his arm from the woman's grip, and he dropped the bag to the sand. As for the bride, her face had gone as yellow as old cloth. She was a slave to hideous rites, gazing at the apparitional snake.

The two men faced each other at a distance of three paces. He of the revolver smiled with a new and quiet ferocity.

"Tried to sneak up on me," he said. "Tried to sneak up on me!" His eyes grew more baleful. As Potter made a slight movement, the man thrust his revolver venomously forward. "No; don't you do it, Jack Potter. Don't you move a finger toward a gun just yet. Don't you move an eyelash. The time has come for me to settle with you, and I'm goin' to do it my own way, and loaf along with no interferin'. So if you don't want a gun bent on you, just mind what I tell you."

Potter looked at his enemy. "I ain't got a gun on me, Scratchy," he said. "Honest, I ain't." He was stiffening and steadying, but yet somewhere at the back of his mind a vision of the Pullman floated: the seagreen figured velvet, the shining brass, silver, and glass, the wood that gleamed as darkly brilliant as the surface of a pool of oil—all the glory of the marriage, the environment of the new estate. "You know I fight when it comes to fighting, Scratchy Wilson; but I ain't got a gun on me. You'll have to do all the shootin' yourself."

His enemy's face went livid. He stepped forward, and lashed his weapon to and fro before Potter's chest. "Don't tell me you ain't got no gun on you, you whelp. Don't tell me no lie like that. There ain't a man in Texas ever seen you without no gun. Don't take me for no kid." His eyes blazed with light, and his throat worked like a pump.

"I ain't takin' you for no kid," answered Potter. His heels had not moved an inch backward. "I'm takin' you for a damn fool. I tell you I ain't got a gun, and I ain't. If you're goin' to shoot me up, you better begin now; you'll never get a chance like this again."

So much enforced reasoning had told on Wilson's rage; he was calmer. "If you ain't got a gun, why ain't you got a gun?" he sneered. "Been to Sunday-school?"

"I ain't got a gun because I've just come from San Anton' with my wife. I'm married," said Potter. "And if I'd thought there was going to be any galoots like you prowling around when I brought my wife home, I'd had a gun, and don't you forget it."

"Married!" said Scratchy, not at all comprehending.

"Yes, married. I'm married." said Potter, distinctly.

"Married?" said Scratchy. Seemingly for the first time, he saw the drooping, drowning woman at the other man's side. "No!" he said. He was like a creature allowed a glimpse of another world. He moved a pace backward, and his arm, with the revolver, dropped to his side. "Is this the lady?" he asked.

"Yes; this is the lady," answered Potter.

There was another period of silence.

"Well," said Wilson at last, slowly, "I s'pose it's all off now."

"It's all off if you say so, Scratchy. You know I didn't make the trouble." Potter lifted his valise.

"Well, I 'low it's off, Jack," said Wilson. He was looking at the ground. "Married!" He was not a student of chivalry; it was merely that in the presence of this foreign condition he was a simple child of the earlier plains. He picked up his starboard revolver, and, placing both weapons in their holsters, he went away. His feet made funnel-shaped tracks in the heavy sand.

Plot

TEACHING STRATEGIES

1. To help students appreciate the importance of plot, have them discuss how the story would change if key plot elements were altered. What would have happened if Potter had arrived an hour earlier? If the men in the saloon had come to watch the showdown?

2. To help students appreciate the different devices of plot organization, have them discuss the effects if significant changes were made in plot structure. For example, how would the story differ if it were told as a flashback from the time Potter confronts Scratchy Wilson?

Plot Factors.   Plot is the series of events that moves a narrative along. The opening of a story with a conventional plot introduces important characters and sets the stage for what happens. Then one or more conflicts develop, some pitting person against person, others setting characters against society, nature, fate or themselves. Action gradually builds to a climax, where events take a decisive turn. The ending can do a number of things—clear up unanswered questions, hint at the future, state a theme, or reestablish some sort of relationship between two foes. In "The Bride," Potter experiences two conflicts: one with Scratchy Wilson and the other within himself over his marriage. The climax comes when Potter and Scratchy meet face to face, and Scratchy learns about his old adversary's marriage. As Scratchy walks away, we sense that the two old foes have had their last confrontation, that Potter's marriage has altered forever the relationship between them.

To organize plots, writers use a number of techniques. In foreshadowing, for example, the writer hints at later developments, thus creating interest and building suspense. In H. H. Munro's short story "The Open Window," a visitor to a country house observes that "An undefinable something about the room seemed to suggest masculine habitation." Yet he accepts the story of a young girl that her uncle, the man of the house, had lost his life in a bog three years before. Because he ignores his observation and accepts the girl's story at face value, the visitor is terrified by the sudden appearance of the uncle, who seems to be a ghost. The careful reader, however, senses what's coming and enjoys the trick more for having been in on it.

When using a flashback, another organizational technique, the writer interrupts the flow of events to relate one or more happenings that occurred before the point at which the story opened, then resumes the narrative at or near the point of interruption. Ernest Hemingway's short story "The Short Happy Life of Francis Macomber" provides an illustration. As the story opens, we meet characters who hint that Macomber displayed cowardice by running from, rather than shooting, a charging, wounded lion. A bit later the story flashes back to detail the actual incident. Flashbacks supply essential information and either create or resolve suspense.

Not every plot unfolds in clear stages. Many modern stories lack distinct plot divisions and focus on psychological, not physical, conflicts. In extreme cases, writers may abandon the traditional plot structure and present events in a disorganized sequence that helps accomplish some literary purpose, such as reflecting a character's disturbed state of mind. Joyce Carol Oates's short story "How I Contemplated the World from the Detroit House of Correction and Began My Life Over Again" fits this mold. To dramatize her chief character's mental turmoil, Oates presents the story as a series of notes for an English composition. These notes, labeled "Events," "Characters," "Sioux Drive," "Detroit," and "That Night," are internally disorganized and arranged in a jumbled sequence.

A poem sometimes includes a series of actions and events, as Edwin Arlington Robinson's "The Miller's Wife" illustrates.

> The miller's wife had waited long,
>   The tea was cold, the fire was dead;
> And there might yet be nothing wrong
>   In how he went and what he said:
> "There are no millers any more,"
>   Was all that she had heard him say:
> And he had lingered at the door
>   So long that it seemed yesterday.
>
> Sick with a fear that had no form
>   She knew that she was there at last;
> And in the mill there was a warm
>   And mealy fragrance of the past.
> What else there was would only seem
>   To say again what he had meant;
> And what was hanging from a beam
>   Would not have heeded where she went.
>
> And if she thought it followed her,
>   She may have reasoned in the dark
> That one way of the few there were
>   Would hide her and would leave no mark;
> Black water, smooth above the weir
>   Like starry velvet in the night,
> Though ruffled once, would soon appear
>   The same as ever to the sight.

Most poems, however, present a series of images, building statements that make a philosophical point rather than tell a conventionally plotted story.

Writing about Plot. Unless your instructor asks for a plot summary, don't merely repeat what happens in the story. Instead, help your reader understand what's special about the plot and how it functions. Does it build suspense, mirror a character's confusion, shape a conflict, show how different lives can intersect, or help reveal a theme?

Before starting to write, answer the following questions:

TEACHING STRATEGY

You might ask students to answer, perhaps as short journal assignments, some of the plot questions posed in the text. This exercise helps them develop an understanding of plot and ingrains the habit of specific textual support.

What are the key events of the story? Do they unfold in conventional fashion or deviate from it in some way?

Does the writer use foreshadowing or flashback? If so, for what purpose?

Is the plot believable and effective, or does it display weakness of some sort?

Does it include any unique features?

Is it similar to the plot of another story or some type of story?

What plot features could I write about? What examples from the story would support my contentions?

As you prepare your analysis, determine the important events and how they relate to your topic. If the story is disjointed or incoherent, arrange the events so that they make sense and ask yourself why the writer chose that sequence. To mirror the main character's disordered state of mind? To show that life is chaotic and difficult to understand? Similarly, assess the reason for any use of foreshadowing or flashback. Does it build, create, or resolve suspense?

Not all plots are successful. A character's actions may not fit his or her personality or the situation. The plot might be too hard to follow or fail to produce the desired effect, as in a mystery where the clues are too obvious to create suspense. Or a writer might rely on chance or coincidence to resolve a conflict or problem: it's unacceptable to have the cavalry charge in gallantly out of nowhere and rescue the hero.

If there's something unique about the plot—perhaps a surprise event that works well—describe it and tell how it functions in the story, or perhaps you can compare the plot with one in another story in order to show how both develop some key insight.

The organization of a paper on plot is simple: you'll either present a thesis and then support it with examples taken from the text, or you'll write a comparison. Writing about "The Bride Comes to Yellow Sky," you could show how foreshadowing moves the story toward an inevitable showdown. As support, you could cite the deliberate, forward motion of the train, the repeated emphasis on clocks and time, the repeated suggestions of Potter's anxiousness, and Scratchy's ongoing conflict with Potter. As a more ambitious project, you might compare the plot of "The Bride" to that of a conventional western showdown, noting any important differences and what they accomplish. A more critical approach would be to argue that the plot is implausible, citing Potter's unplanned marriage and the coincidence of his return to Yellow Sky precisely when Scratchy Wilson was drunk and shooting up the town.

EXERCISE ■ **In a short story with a strong plot line, identify conflicts and climax and tell what the ending accomplishes. Point out any use of foreshadowing or flashback.**

Point of View

Point-of-View Factors. The point of view is the vantage point from which the writer of a literary work views its events. A writer may adopt either a first-person or a third-person point of view. In *first-person* narration, someone in the work tells what happens and is identified by words like *I, me, mine,* and *my.* A *third-person* narrator stays completely out of the story and is never mentioned in any way. "The Bride Comes to Yellow Sky" illustrates third-person narration.

The most common form of first-person narration features a narrator who takes part in the action. This technique puts the readers directly on the scene and is excellent for tracing the growth or deterioration of a character. Instead of participating in the action, the narrator may view it from the sideline, an approach that preserves on-the-scene directness and allows the narrator to comment on the characters and issues. The narrator, however, cannot enter the mind and reveal the unspoken thoughts of anyone else.

Third-person narrators don't participate in the action but can survey the whole literary landscape and directly report events that first-person narrators would know only by hearsay. Most third-person narrators reveal the thoughts of just one character. Others, with *limited omniscience,* can enter the heads of several characters, while still others display *full omniscience* and know everything in the literary work, including all thoughts and feelings of all characters. Omniscience allows the narrator to contrast two or more sets of thoughts and feelings and draw general conclusions from them. The narrator of Stephen Crane's "The Open Boat" is fully omniscient. The story is about four shipwrecked sailors adrift in a lifeboat, and the narrator, knowing what they all think, traces their developing awareness that nature is completely indifferent to their plight.

Yet another type of third-person narration, *dramatic,* has emerged in contemporary fiction. A dramatic narrator, like a motion-picture camera, moves about recording the characters' actions and words but without revealing anyone's thoughts. Stories with surprise endings often use this technique.

Writing about Point of View.   For a paper about point of view, ask and answer these questions.

What point of view is used? Why is it used?
Is it suitable for the situation? Why or why not?
If the story uses first-person narration, is the narrator reliable? What textual evidence supports my answer?
What focus would produce an effective paper? What textual evidence could support its discussion?

Various reasons might prompt the choice of a particular point of view. For example, an author might use the first person to show a character's mental deterioration. A third-person narrator might enter two minds to contrast opposing attitudes toward some incident or enter no minds at all, in order to heighten the emotional impact of a story's climax.

If a point of view seems unsuitable, say so and suggest why. Suppose a man is planning an elopement that will create a surprise ending. A point of view that revealed the man's thoughts would give away that ending.

First-person narrators are sometimes unreliable; that is, they offer the reader a warped view of things. To gauge reliability, compare the narrator's version of the facts with what the work otherwise reveals. The narrator may come off as stupid, psychologically warped, or too biased to view events fairly. If so, speculate on the reasons. A mentally unreliable narrator may be meant, for example, to heighten the horror of events.

Although organization can vary, papers on point of view basically follow a cause-and-effect format, first identifying the point of view used and then demonstrating, with examples, its effect on the story and reader. In "The Bride," the third-person point of view allows Crane to shift from Potter and his new wife to the men in the saloon to the rampaging Scratchy and then to Potter and Scratchy as they confront each other. Shifting scenes in this way builds a sense of impending conflict, which would be difficult to produce with a first-person narrator, who could not move about in this fashion.

EXERCISE ANSWERS

1. The unnamed narrator conveys the mother's attitude by telling the reader not what she thinks but rather how she reacts. We learn that she shows contempt for her son's war fever, that she tries to talk him out of enlisting, and that her way of expressing herself reflects her deep feelings. As a result, the reader has no doubt about the mother's position.

2. The first-person approach allows the reader to enter the mind of the story's main character, a small boy, and learn firsthand the impact that viewing a mysterious, ghostly train has had upon him. A third-person narrator could have told the reader what the boy thought and how he felt, but presenting these reactions directly strengthens their impact on the reader.

EXERCISE ■ **Read the following two excerpts and answer the questions that follow them.**

He had burned several times to enlist. Tales of great movements shook the land. . . . He had read of marches, sieges, conflicts, and he had longed to see it all. His busy mind had drawn for him large pictures, extravagant with color, lurid with breathless deeds.

But his mother had discouraged him. She had affected to look with some contempt on the quality of his war ardor and patriotism. She would calmly seat herself, and with no apparent difficulty give him many hundreds of reasons why he was of vastly more importance on the farm than he was on the field of battle. She had had certain ways of expression that told him that her statements on the subject came from a deep conviction. Moreover, on her side, was his belief that her ethical motive in the argument was impregnable.

Stephen Crane, *The Red Badge of Courage*

Daddy helped me up onto the line and we hurried home. He said, "That was strange. What train was that, I wonder? And I didn't know the driver either." Then he didn't say any more.

I was shaking all over. That had been for me—for my sake. I guessed what it meant. It was all the fear which would come to me, all the unknowns; all that Daddy didn't know about and couldn't save me from. That was how the world would be for me. . . .

Pär Lagerkvist, "Father and I"

1. In Crane's third-person stance, the narrator enters the son's mind but not the mother's. How does he convey the mother's attitude toward her son's desire to enlist?
2. What does Lagerkvist accomplish by using the first-person point of view?

PERSPECTIVE

Students tend to react more strongly to literary characters than to any other element. For that reason, you might begin your analysis with a discussion of the characters and then have students write about them. Students should understand, however, the distinction between actual persons and literary characters that serve a function.

Character

Character Factors. The characters in a literary work function in various ways. Some are centers of physical and mental action. Others furnish humor, act as narrators, provide needed information, act as *foils* who highlight more important characters by contrast, serve as symbols, or simply populate the landscape. In "The

Bride," the drummer helps funnel information to the reader. He asks questions, the bartender answers them, and the reader learns all about Scratchy.

Writers present character in several ways. Some tell the reader point-blank that a person is brave, stupid, self-serving, or the like. But most authors take an indirect approach by indicating how their characters look and act, what they think and say, how they live, and how other characters regard them.

Beware of uncritically accepting Character X's assessment of Character Y. X may be prejudiced, simple-minded, a deliberate liar, or too emotionally involved or disturbed to be objective. To illustrate, Scratchy Wilson, despite the bartender's fearful comments, proves to be something less than a real terror. He makes no real attempt to break down any doors and toys with, rather than shoots, the dog and Potter.

In picturing Potter, Crane first notes his appearance and self-conscious behavior, then delves into his mind to show the turmoil his marriage has stirred. Somewhat later, the bartender adds his brush strokes to Potter's portrait. At the confrontation, we again observe Potter's thoughts and behavior, as well as what he says to Scratchy. From all this, Potter emerges not as a mere one-dimensional lawman but as someone with a recognizably lifelike personality.

Some characters remain static; others mature, gain insight, or deteriorate in some telling way. Potter changes. As the story unfolds he abandons his doubts about the course he's charted and ends up fully committed to "the environment of the new estate." Scratchy, on the other hand, ends just as he started, "a simple child of the earlier plains."

Writing about Character.   Start the process by asking yourself these questions.

What characters offer the potential for a paper?
What are their most important features, and where in the story are these features revealed?
Do the characters undergo any changes? If so, how and why do the changes occur?
Are the characters believable, true to life? If not, why?
What focus would produce an effective paper?
What textual evidence could support the discussion?

Usually, you'll write about the main character, but at times you might choose the chief adversary or some minor character. For a lesser character, point out how that person interacts with the main one.

Most main characters change; most lesser ones do not. But sometimes a main character remains frozen, allowing the writer to make an important point. To show that a certain social group suffers from paralysis of the will, an author might create a main character who begins and ends weak and ineffectual. Whatever the situation, when you determine what purpose your character serves, tell the reader.

Think hard about your character's credibility. Ask yourself if he or she is true to life. Cruel stepmothers, brilliant but eccentric detectives, mad scientists, masked seekers after justice—these and other stereotyped figures don't square with real-life people, who are complex mixtures of many traits. Inconsistent acts or unexplained and unmotivated personality changes don't ring true: most people behave the same

TEACHING STRATEGIES

1. Have students develop, in stages, a comprehensive analysis of a particular character's role. They might first note all the information they can about the character, next identify elements in the text that suggest these traits, and then detail how other characters perceive that character. Finally, they should consider how the character is important to the story, perhaps linking him or her to the plot or themes.

2. Inexperienced readers of literature tend to overemphasize the importance of verisimilitude. You could discuss where it is and isn't important for characters to be realistic. Students might identify the ways in which a character is unrealistic and then show how that character serves the function of the story.

TEACHING STRATEGIES

1. For inexperienced students it is best to give assignments that require thought yet provide some structure, perhaps a comparison of two characters or a cause-and-effect analysis of character change. As students gain experience, increase the complexity of the assignments to include some evaluation. For example: "Is Scratchy Wilson's retreat believable given the way he is characterized?"

2. To help students see the range of options in writing about character, you might start a class discussion centered on possible approaches and how each would be developed.

in similar situations and change only when properly motivated. Not every character needs to be a full-dress creation, but all require enough development to justify their roles.

Start your paper by identifying your character's role or personality; then back your contention with illustrations that support it, possibly following the sequence in which the writer presents them. If a character changes, say so, tell why, and indicate the results of the change, again using supporting examples. Such a paper is usually a cause-and-effect analysis. Papers that evaluate two characters are essentially comparisons.

For an example of a paper analyzing a character, see pages 261–63.

EXERCISE ■ **Write a paragraph describing the personality of the character in the following passage.**

The thousand injuries of Fortunato I had borne as I best could, but when he ventured upon insult, I vowed revenge. You, who so well know the nature of my soul, will not suppose, however, that I gave utterance to a threat. *At length* I would be avenged; this was a point definitely settled—but the very definiteness with which it was resolved precluded the idea of risk. I must not only punish, but punish with impunity. A wrong is unredressed when retribution overtakes its redresser. It is equally unredressed when the avenger fails to make himself felt as such to the one who has done the wrong.

Edgar Allan Poe, "The Cask of Amontillado"

Setting

Setting Factors.   Setting locates characters in a time, place, and culture so they can think, feel, and act against this background. Writers can generate feelings and moods by describing settings. Sunny spring landscapes signal hope or happiness, dark alleys are foreboding, and thunderstorms suggest violent possibilities. Poetry, especially, uses setting to create mood. In the sonnet "Composed upon Westminster Bridge," William Wordsworth evokes the serenity and grandeur of London as the sun breaks over the sleeping city:

> Earth has not anything to show more fair:
> Dull would he be of soul who could pass by
> A sight so touching in its majesty:
> This city now doth, like a garment, wear
> The beauty of the morning: silent, bare,
> Ships, towers, domes, theaters, and temples lie
> Open unto the fields, and to the sky;
> All bright and glittering in the smokeless air.
> Never did sun more beautifully steep
> In his first splendor, valley, rock, or hill;
> Ne'er saw I, never felt, a calm so deep!
> The river glideth at his own sweet will:
> Dear God! the very houses seem asleep;
> And all that mighty heart is lying still!

Setting can also help reveal character. In this excerpt from Sinclair Lewis's novel *Babbitt,* the contents and atmosphere of the library mirror the stiff, self-satisfied formality of its banker-owner:

> . . . The books were most of them standard sets, with the correct and traditional touch of dim blue, dim gold, and glossy calf-skin. The fire was exactly correct and traditional; a small, quiet, steady fire, reflected by polished fire-irons. The oak desk was dark and altogether perfect; the chairs were gently supercilious.

Settings sometimes function as symbols, reinforcing the workings of the other elements. A broad, slowly flowing river may stand for time or fate, a craggy cliff for strength of character, a blizzard-swept plain for the overwhelming power of nature. The following section, a discussion of symbols, points out some symbolic settings in "The Bride."

At times, setting provides a clue to some observation about life. At one point in Stephen Crane's story "The Open Boat," the men spot a nearby flock of seagulls sitting comfortably on the turbulent waves. Juxtaposing the complacent gulls and the imperiled men suggests the philosophical point of the story: that the universe is indifferent to human aspirations and struggles.

Shifts in setting often trigger shifts in a character's emotional or psychological state. Jack Potter, typically calm and assured in Yellow Sky, displays great awkwardness and embarrassment in the unfamiliar environment of the Pullman car.

Writing about Setting.   Begin your search for a topic by identifying the settings in the story and then asking these questions about each one.

What are its key features?
What does it accomplish? Create a mood? Reveal a character? Serve as a symbol?
   Reinforce the story's point? How does it accomplish these things?
In what ways does it support or interfere with the story?
Does the setting seem realistic? If not, why not?
What focus would produce an effective paper? What textual evidence would
   support it?

Check the impact of setting on mood by seeing how well the two match up for each setting. Sometimes, as in "The Bride," the two bear little or no relationship to each other. In other cases, the two intertwine throughout the work.

Try to establish connections between settings and characters. If an emotionally barren individual always appears against backdrops of gloomy furnished rooms, cheerless restaurants, and decaying slums, you can assume that the writer is using setting to convey character. Look for links between changes in characters and changes in settings. If the setting remains the same, point out any shifts in the way the character views it.

Occasionally, a writer drums home settings so insistently that they overpower the characters and story line. A novel about the super rich may linger so lovingly over their extravagant surroundings that the plot lacks force and the characters seem mere puppets. If the setting hobbles the other elements, identify this flaw in your analysis.

When you write about setting, describe it and discuss its impact on the story's other elements, supporting your claims with specific examples. In writing about

"The Bride," you might argue that Crane used as his chief setting a pulp fiction cliché of a western town in order to heighten the atypical nature of the showdown. As support, you could cite such stock features as the train station, saloon, dog, and dusty streets, all of which point toward an actual shootout rather than Scratchy Wilson's backdown.

EXERCISE ■ **What mood does the following description of a room generate? What does it suggest about the situation of the room's inhabitants, two women in an Old Ladies' Home?**

> Marian stood enclosed by a bed, a washstand, and a chair; the tiny room had altogether too much furniture. Everything smelled wet—even the bare floor. She held onto the back of the chair, which was wicker and felt soft and damp. . . . How dark it was! The window shade was down, and the only door was shut. Marian looked at the ceiling. . . . It was like being caught in a robbers' cave. . . .
>
> Eudora Welty, "A Visit of Charity"

Symbols

Symbol Factors.   To strengthen and deepen their messages, writers use symbols: names, persons, objects, places, colors, or actions that have a significance beyond their surface meaning. A symbol may be very obvious—as a name like Mr. Grimm, suggesting the person's character—or quite subtle, as an object representing a universal human emotion.

Some symbols are private and others conventional. A private symbol has special significance within a literary work but not outside it. Conventional symbols are deeply rooted in our culture, and almost everyone knows what they represent. We associate crosses with Christianity and limousines with wealth and power. In "The Bride," the plains pouring eastward past the Pullman windows, Scratchy's eastern clothing, and the mirage-like grass plots in front of the saloon are all private symbols that stand for the passing of the Old West. Because people of Crane's time associated Pullman cars with an urbane, eastern life-style, the Pullman is a conventional symbol that represents the new order of things. Like the Pullman, a symbol may appear more than once in a literary work.

Whether or not a recurring item is a symbol depends upon its associations. In Ernest Hemingway's novel *A Farewell to Arms,* rain may fairly be said to symbolize doom because it consistently accompanies disasters, and one of the main characters says that she has visions of herself lying dead in the rain. But if rain is randomly associated with a rundown lakeside resort, a spirited business meeting, a cozy weekend, and the twentieth-anniversary celebration of a happy marriage, the writer probably intends no symbolism.

Writing about Symbols.   When you examine the symbols in a literary work, think about these questions.

What symbols are used and where do they appear?
Are they private or conventional?

What do they appear to mean?
Do any of them undergo a change in meaning? If so, how and why?
Which symbol(s) could I discuss effectively?
What textual evidence would support my interpretation?

To locate symbols, read the literary work carefully, looking for items that seem to have an extended meaning. You might, for example, discover that the cracked walls of a crumbling mansion symbolize some character's disordered mental state or that a voyage symbolizes the human journey from birth to death. Several symbols often mean the same thing; writers frequently use them in sets. In "Bartleby the Scrivener," for instance, Herman Melville uses windows that look upon walls, a folding screen, and a prison to symbolize Bartleby's alienated condition, that is, his mental separation from those around him. Determining whether each symbol is private or conventional can provide clues to its meaning.

Sometimes a symbol changes meaning during the course of a work. A woman who regards her lover's large, strong hands as symbols of passion may, following an illness that leaves him a dangerous madman, view them as symbols of danger and brute strength. Note any changes you discover, and suggest what they signify.

A word of caution: don't let symbol hunting become an obsession. Before you assert that something has a different and deeper meaning than its surface application, make sure the evidence in the work backs your claim.

For each symbol you discuss, state what you think it means and then support your position with appropriate textual evidence. You could argue, for example, that the Pullman car in "The Bride" symbolizes the Eastern civilization that is encroaching on the West, offering as evidence the car's "figured velvet . . . shining brass, silver, and glass" and darkly gleaming wood appointments.

TEACHING STRATEGIES

1. Examination of a professional or student paper that successfully discusses the symbols in some literary work can help students understand their function. Have students identify the paper's purpose, the writing strategies used to develop it, and the places where the writer points out connections between the symbols and the story's other elements.
2. Point out that discussions of symbols often support an interpretation of a work's themes rather than function as the central focus of a piece of writing.

EXERCISE ■ **Read the following excerpts from Edward Fitzgerald's** *The Rubáiyát of Omar Khayyám* **and answer the questions that follow.**

> Strange, is it not? that of the myriads who
> Before us passed the door of Darkness through,
> Not one returns to tell us of the Road,
> Which to discover we must travel too.

> The Moving Finger writes; and, having writ,
> Moves on: nor all your Piety nor Wit
> Shall lure it back to cancel half a line,
> Nor all your Tears wash out a Word of it.

1. What does the door of Darkness symbolize? The Road? The Moving Finger?
2. What messages are these symbols meant to convey?

EXERCISE ANSWERS
1. The door symbolizes death, the Road symbolizes the world beyond the grave, and the Moving Finger the events written in the book of a person's life.
2. The symbols in stanza 1 indicate that we must die to learn what lies beyond death. The symbols in stanza 2 make the point that what's done is done and that tears, prayers, and reflections can never undo any deed.

Irony

Irony Factors. Irony features some discrepancy, some difference between appearance and reality, expectation and outcome. Sometimes a character

PERSPECTIVE

Many students are slow to identify and understand literary irony because they fail to see the implied contradictions that lie at its heart. Special care and considerable time are often required to help students grasp this element.

TEACHING STRATEGY

You might provide students with blatant examples of irony close to their experience. How ironic if an instructor who because of nervousness appears cold and distant at the first class meeting actually proves to be warm and deeply concerned about students. You could discuss examples in class, first identifying one or two discrepancies yourself and then gradually having students point out those in the remaining examples.

TEACHING STRATEGY

Like symbols, irony is usually discussed in connection with a character or theme rather than as the primary emphasis in a literary paper.

says one thing but means something else. The critic who, tongue in cheek, says that a clumsy dancer is "poetry in motion" speaks ironically.

Irony also results when the reader or a character recognizes something as important, but another character does not. In "The Bride" this situation occurs when Potter, not knowing that Scratchy is on a rampage, flees the station agent, who tries to let him know. A character's behavior sometimes offers ironic contrasts, too. There's high irony in the contrast between Potter's unflinching face-off with Scratchy and his fear of telling the townsfolk about his marriage.

At times the ending of a work doesn't square with what the reader expects: the confrontation between Potter and Scratchy ends not in a fusillade of bullets but a flurry of words. To add to the irony, Potter wins because he is armed with a new and unfamiliar weapon—his wife. The emotional impact of an ironic ending depends upon the circumstances of plot and character. As Scratchy walks off, we're likely to view matters with amusement. In other cases, we might register joy, horror, gloom, or almost anything else.

Writing about Irony.   Start by answering these questions.

Where does irony occur?
What does it accomplish?
What could my thesis be, and how could I support it?

In probing for irony, check for statements that say one thing and mean something else, situations in which one character knows something that another doesn't, and contrasts between the ways characters should and do behave. Review the plot to see whether the outcome matches the expectations.

To prove that irony is intended, examine the context in which the words are spoken or the events occur. Also, tell the reader what the irony accomplishes. In "The Bride," it is ironic that someone as wild as Scratchy Wilson would be awed by, and retreat from, Potter's wife; yet this irony is central to the idea that the Old West, despite its violence, was no match for the civilizing forces of the East.

EXERCISE ANSWER

The ending of "Richard Cory" contradicts the expectations that precede it. The poem's first three stanzas portray Cory as handsome, well-dressed, polite, wealthy, even kingly—in short, a person with everything to live for. This public facade, however, masks a deep inner despair, unsuspected by the townspeople who observe Cory, that drives him to suicide. In the end, it is the townspeople who survive because, unlike Cory, they retain the capacity to hope (wait for the light).

EXERCISE ■ **Discuss the irony in this poem.**

Richard Cory

Edwin Arlington Robinson

Whenever Richard Cory went down town,
We people on the pavement looked at him:
He was a gentleman from sole to crown,
Clean favored, and imperially slim.

And he was always quietly arrayed,
And he was always human when he talked;
But still he fluttered pulses when he said,
"Good-morning," and he glittered when he walked.

And he was rich—yes, richer than a king—
And admirably schooled in every grace:
In fine, we thought that he was everything
To make us wish that we were in his place.

So on we worked, and waited for the light,
And went without the meat, and cursed the bread;
And Richard Cory, one calm summer night,
Went home and put a bullet through his head.

Theme

Theme Factors. The theme of a literary work is its controlling idea, some observation or insight about life or the conditions and terms of living, such as the prevalence of evil, the foolishness of pride, or the healing power of love. Many literary works suggest several themes: sometimes one primary motif and several related ones, sometimes a number of unrelated motifs. Theme is central to a work of literature; frequently all of the other elements help develop and support it.

On occasion, the writer or a character states the theme directly. Mrs. Alving, the main character in Henrik Ibsen's play *Ghosts*, notes that the dead past plays a powerful and evil role in shaping human lives.

> . . . I am half inclined to think that we are all ghosts, Mr. Manders. It is not only what we have inherited from our fathers and mothers that exists again in us, but all sorts of old dead ideas and all kinds of old dead beliefs and things of that kind. They are not actually alive in us; but there they are dormant, all the same, and we can never be rid of them.

Ordinarily, though, the theme remains unstated and must be deduced by examining the other elements of the literary work.

Writing about Theme. Before you begin writing, ask and answer these questions.

What are the themes of this work? Which of these should I write about? Are they stated or unstated?
If stated, what elements support them?
If unstated, what elements create them?
What, if any, thematic weaknesses are present?

Check the comments of the characters and the narrator to see whether they state the themes directly. If they don't, assess the interaction of characters, events, settings, symbols, and other elements to determine them.

Let's see how the elements of Nathaniel Hawthorne's short story "Young Goodman Brown" work together to yield the primary theme. The story has four characters—Goodman Brown; his wife, Faith; Deacon Gookin; and Goody Cloyse—whose names symbolically suggest that they are completely good. Another symbol, Faith's pink hair ribbon, at first suggests innocence and later its loss. The story relates Brown's nighttime journey into a forest at the edge of a Puritan village and subsequent attendance at a baptismal ceremony for new converts to the Devil. He proceeds into the forest, suggestive of mystery and lawlessness, during a dark night, suggestive of evil, where he meets his guide, the Devil in the guise of his grandfather. As he proceeds, Goodman vacillates between reluctance to join the

PERSPECTIVE

Since we read literature not simply as an art form but also for insights into life, much of the writing about literature is about theme. Students, however, experience problems when approaching this element. First, many of them see works as having only one theme. Instead, of course, it is the endless suggestiveness that allows us to go back to the best works repeatedly. Second, students tend to reduce theme to a simple generalization rather than recognize that it emerges from the actual dynamics of the story and how it is developed.

TEACHING STRATEGIES

1. Have students explain in a journal or as a class how the story either confirmed or changed their view of the world. Then have them articulate how that attitude might be a theme and, in turn, how it is realized in the text.
2. After students have identified a theme, have them list some of the associated themes and identify how these themes are developed in the text. Students tend to suppress the conflicts and contradictions in a theme in order to reduce it to the simplest form. Encourage them to note any conflicts and where they are resolved. For example, in "The Bride," there is a clear conflict between eastern society and the wild west.

Devil's party and fascination with it. Innocent and ignorant, he is horrified when he finds that the deacon and Goody seem to be in league with the Devil. Goodman tries to preserve his pure image of his wife, Faith, but her pink ribbon falls out of a tumultuous sky seemingly filled with demons, and Goodman sees her at the baptismal ceremony. He shrieks out to her to "resist the wicked one" and is suddenly alone in the woods, not knowing whether she obeyed. The end of the story finds Brown back in his village, unable to view his wife and neighbors as anything but totally evil.

In light of these happenings, it's probably safe to say that the primary theme of the story is somewhat as follows:

> Human beings are a mixture of good and evil, but some individuals can't accept this fact. Once they realize that "good" people are susceptible to sin, they decide that everyone is evil, and they become embittered for life.

Point out any thematic weakness that you find. Including a completely innocent major character in a story written to show that people are mixtures of good and evil would contradict the writer's intention.

A paper on theme is basically an argument, first presenting your interpretation and then supporting it with textual evidence. You might argue that the primary theme of "The Bride" is the demise of the Old West under the civilizing influence of the East. You could cite the luxurious Pullman car in contrast to the drab town, Potter's uncomfortable submission to the waiter and porter, and Scratchy Wilson's retreat at the story's end. In addition, you could suggest a related theme: people out of their element often founder—sometimes even appear ridiculous. As support, you might point to Potter's behavior on the train, the drummer's subdued attitude when Scratchy's arrival is imminent, and Scratchy's reaction when told about Potter's wife.

EXERCISE ANSWER

The poem offers the observation that time provides us with the opportunity to engage in meaningful or trivial pursuits. The observation emerges through the imagery of the muffled and dumb daughters of time who bring diadems (symbolizing the opportunity for meaningful pursuits) and fagots (symbolizing the opportunity for trivial pursuits). The final sentence presents the point of the poem: that it is shameful to opt for trivial pursuits. When the narrator hastily takes "a few herbs and apples," he earns the scorn of their bearer.

EXERCISE ■ **Ralph Waldo Emerson's "Days" offers an observation on how people should occupy their time. Read the poem carefully, checking any unfamiliar words in your dictionary. Then state Emerson's observation in your own words.**

> Daughters of Time, the hypocritic Days,
> Muffled and dumb like barefoot dervishes,
> And marching single in an endless file,
> Bring diadems and fagots in their hands.
> To each they offer gifts after his will,
> Bread, kingdom, stars, and sky that holds them all.
>
> I, in my pleachéd garden, watched the pomp,
> Forgot my morning wishes, hastily
> Took a few herbs and apples, and the Day
> Turned and departed silent. I, too late,
> Under her solemn fillet saw the scorn.

*W*RITING A PAPER ON LITERATURE

Focusing, gathering information, organizing, writing, revising and editing—the same procedure leads to success in a literature paper as in any other type.

First, make sure you *understand the assignment*. Let's assume you have been asked to do the following:

> Write a 750-word essay that analyzes one of the elements in Stephen Crane's "The Bride Comes to Yellow Sky." Take into account all the pertinent factors of whatever element(s) you choose.

For this assignment you could focus on plot, point of view, character, setting, symbols, irony, theme, or some meaningful combination of two or more of these elements.

Next, *decide upon a suitable topic*. For papers on literature, your best approach is to reread the work carefully and then reflect on it. As you do this for "The Bride" assignment, you rule out a paper centering on plot, setting, irony, point of view, or theme. Because your class has discussed the first three so thoroughly, you doubt you can offer anything more. The matter of the narrator stumps you; you can understand why Crane uses a third-person narrator who airs Potter's thoughts, but you can't see what's accomplished by the brief looks into other characters' minds. Regarding theme, you doubt you can do justice to the topic in 750 words. As you mentally mine character and symbolism for possible topics, your thoughts turn to the many gunfighters you've watched in the movies and read about in western fiction. Because gunfighters have always fascinated you and Scratchy Wilson seems an intriguing example of the breed, you decide to analyze his character.

To complete the next stage, *gathering information,* reread the story again and as you do, list all pertinent information about Scratchy that might help develop a character analysis. Your efforts might yield these results.

1. Scratchy "a wonder with a gun."
2. "about the last one of the old gang that used to hang out along the river here."
3. "He's a terror when he's drunk," the opposite otherwise.
4. Potter "goes out and fights Scratchy when he gets on one of these tears."
5. Has shot Scratchy once, in the leg.
6. Does nothing to stop "tears" from happening.
7. On street, Scratchy "in a rage begot of whisky." Neck works angrily.
8. Utters "Cries of ferocious challenge."
9. Moves with "the creeping movement of the midnight cat."
10. Guns move "with an electric swiftness."
11. Clothes—maroon shirt, gilded red-topped boots—not adult western garb.
12. Doesn't shoot dog.
13. Doesn't try breaking down doors.
14. Warns Potter not to go for gun rather than shooting him.
15. Says he'll hit Potter with gun, not shoot him, if Potter doesn't "mind what I tell you."

PERSPECTIVE

You can help students write a paper about literature by giving them some sense of purpose and audience. If a class discussion of some work has raised questions of interest to your students, clearly the purpose of their writing should be to share their insights. In general, students will write better if they see themselves helping an actual reader gain a new perspective on a work of literature.

TEACHING STRATEGY

An interesting discussion of the work can establish the context for writing assignments. Furthermore, students benefit if you discuss the range of papers they might possibly write and the ways they could approach them. Finished papers might be copied or exchanged as a way of carrying on the discussion.

16. Only sneers when Potter calls him "damn fool," and when Potter says, "If you're goin' to shoot me up, you better begin now; you'll never get a chance like this again."

17. Backs down and walks away when confronted with Potter's marriage.

List in hand, you are now ready to *organize your information*. As you examine your items and answer the questions about character on page 251, you start to realize that Scratchy is not merely a one-dimensional gunslinging menace. To reflect your discovery, you prepare a formal topic outline.

I. Bartender's assessment
   A. Evidence that Scratchy is a menace
      1. A wonder with a gun
      2. Former outlaw gang member
      3. A terror when drunk
   B. Contradictory evidence
      1. Mild when sober
      2. Only one actual shootout with Potter
II. Scratchy's behavior
   A. Evidence that Scratchy is a menace
      1. Rage
      2. Wary movements
      3. Skillful handling of guns
   B. Contradictory evidence
      1. Mode of dress
      2. Failure to shoot dog
      3. Failure to try breaking down doors
      4. Behavior during confrontation
      5. Final retreat

The next stage, *developing a thesis statement,* presents few difficulties. After examining the outline and thinking about its contents, you draft the following sentence:

> A close look at Scratchy Wilson shows that he has much more depth than
>
> his pulp fiction counterparts.

Drawing on your notes and following your outline, you now *write a first draft* of your essay, and then follow up with the necessary revising and editing. In addition, you review the story and verify your interpretation.

As you *prepare your final draft,* follow these guidelines.

Handling Quotations.   Like aspirin, quotations should be used when necessary, but not to excess. Cite brief, relevant passages to support key ideas, but fight the urge to quote huge blocks of material. Place short quotations, less than five lines long, within quotation marks and run them into the text. For longer quotes, omit the quotation marks and indent the material ten spaces from the left-hand margin. When quoting poetry, use a slash mark (/) to show the shift from one line to the other in the original: "A honey tongue, a heart of gall,/ Is fancy's spring, but sorrow's fall." Pages 304–7 provide added information on handling quotes.

Documentation. Document ideas and quotations from outside sources by following the guidelines on pages 299–304.

If your instructor wants you to document quotations from the work you're writing about, include the information within parentheses following the quotations. For fiction, cite the page number on which the quote appeared: (83). For poetry, cite the word "line" or "lines" and the appropriate numbers: (lines 23–24). For plays, cite act, scene, and line numbers, separated by periods: (1.3.18–19). When discussing a work of fiction not in your textbook, identify the book you used as your source. Your instructor can then easily check your information. With short papers like the one below, internal documentation is often omitted.

Tense. Write your essay in the present rather than the past tense. Say "In *The Sound and the Fury,* William Faulkner uses four narrators, each of whom provides a different perspective on the events that take place," not ". . . William Faulkner used four narrators, each of whom provided a different perspective on the events that took place."

EXAMPLE STUDENT ESSAY ON LITERATURE

Scratchy Wilson: No Cardboard Character

Wendell Stone

Stephen Crane's "The Bride Comes to Yellow Sky" is artful on several counts. For one thing, the story is rich in irony. It makes use of an elaborate set of symbols to get its point across. It is filled with vivid language, and in Jack Potter and Scratchy Wilson it offers its readers two very unusual characters. Potter's actions and thoughts clearly show that he is a complex person. In fact, his complexity is so conspicuous that it becomes easy to regard Scratchy as nothing more than a one-dimensional badman. But this judgment is mistaken. A close look at Scratchy shows that he, like Potter, has much more depth than his pulp fiction counterparts.

Nothing in what the bartender says about Scratchy hints that there is anything unusual about the old outlaw. We learn that Scratchy is "a wonder with a gun," that he is "about the last one of the old gang that used to hang out along the river here," and that "He's a terror when he's drunk" but mild-mannered and pleasant at other times. One thing may strike the careful reader as a little odd, though. Although Potter "goes out and fights Scratchy when he gets on one of these tears," he has wounded Scratchy just once, and then only in the leg. Apparently, Potter has been able to talk the supposed terror out of a shootout each of the other times. Nor has Potter apparently tried doing anything to stop Scratchy's "tears."

As he steps onto the main street of Yellow Sky, Scratchy seems every bit as menacing as the bartender has described him. His face flames "in a rage begot of whisky," the cords in his neck throb and bulge with anger, and he hurls "cries of ferocious challenge" at the barricaded buildings. Scratchy is clearly no stranger to either weapons or shootouts. He walks with "the creeping movement of the midnight cat," moves his revolvers with "an electric swiftness," and keeps constantly on the alert for an ambush.

Nevertheless, Scratchy comes across as less than totally menacing. For one thing, his maroon shirt and gilded, red-topped boots make him look not like a westerner but like some child's notion of one. When he sees the dog, he deliberately shoots to frighten rather than to kill it. And in spite of all his bluster, he makes no real attempt to break down any doors and get at the people hiding behind them. Scratchy's clothing shows that eastern ways have touched even this "child of the earlier plains." But one could easily argue that eastern gentleness has had some slight softening influence on him, too. Be that as it may, it seems evident that Scratchy, perhaps without quite realizing it himself, is mainly play-acting when he goes on his rampages and that Potter knows this.

During the whole final confrontation, Scratchy seems more of an actor than a gunman wanting revenge against his "ancient antagonist." Instead of shooting when Potter makes a slight movement, Scratchy warns him not to go for a gun and says that he intends to take his time settling accounts, to "loaf along with no interferin'." Significantly, he threatens to hit Potter with a gun, not shoot him, if the marshal does not "mind what I tell you." Even when Potter, recovered from his brief fright, calls Scratchy a "damn fool" and says "If you're goin' to shoot me up, you better begin now; you'll never get a chance like this again." Scratchy does nothing except sneer. This confrontation, like all but one of the others, ends with no shots fired. But one thing is different. Potter's marriage has forced

Scratchy to realize that something unstoppable is changing the Old West forever. When he drops his revolver to his side, stands silent for a while, and then says, "I s'pose it's all off now," we sense that he means not just this episode but any future clashes as well.

Scratchy is not a cardboard creation. His behavior is by no means as easily explainable as it at first seems, and he is capable of some degree of insight. Nonetheless, Scratchy remains very much a creature of the past, something that time has passed by. As he leaves, his feet make funnel-shaped tracks, reminiscent of hourglasses, in the sand. Soon these tracks, along with Scratchy and his way of life, will disappear.

EXERCISE ■ **Using the guidelines offered in this chapter, write a short essay comparing and contrasting the two writers' assessments of the women in the poems below. (You might find it helpful to review pages 107–17 on comparison.) Limit your focus and back any general statements you make with appropriate support from the poems.**

There Is a Garden in Her Face
Thomas Campion (1617)

There is a garden in her face,
Where roses and white lilies grow;
A heavenly paradise is that place,
Wherein all pleasant fruits do flow.
There cherries grow which none may buy
Till "Cherry ripe" themselves do cry.

Those cherries fairly do inclose
Of orient pearl a double row,
Which when her lovely laughter shows,
They look like rosebuds filled with snow;
Yet them nor peer nor prince can buy,
Till "Cherry ripe" themselves do cry.

Her eyes like angels watch them still;
Her brows like bended bows do stand,
Threat'ning with piercing frowns to kill
All that attempt with eye or hand
Those sacred cherries to come nigh,
Till "Cherry ripe" themselves do cry.

EXERCISE ANSWER

The student should note that Campion presents a highly idealized image of the woman he writes about. Shakespeare presents a much more realistic assessment of his mistress, yet asserts, in the final two lines of the poem, that his love (mistress) is every bit as precious as any woman (she) lied about (belied) through false comparison.

SUGGESTED INSTRUCTOR READINGS

Biatt, G. T., and L. M. Rosen. "The Writing Response to Literature." The Journal of Reading 28 (1984): 8–12. Reviews how writing can serve as an important vehicle for understanding literature.

Lodge, D., ed. 20th Century Criticism. London: Longman, 1972. Contains many of the key twentieth-century essays on literary criticism. While no substitute for reading Richards, Empson, Brooks, and others, it provides an effective overview of many of the key issues in contemporary criticism.

Moran, C. "Teaching Writing/ Teaching Literature." College Composition and Communication 32 (1981): 21–29. Gives helpful suggestions for effectively combining the teaching of writing and the teaching of literature.

Rosenblatt, L. The Reader, The Text, The Poem: The Transactional Theory of the Literary Work. Carbondale, IL: Southern Illinois UP, 1978. Provides helpful insights into how students read literature and experience the literary work.

Scott, P. G. "Flowers in the Path of Science: Teaching Composition Through Traditional High Literature." College English 42 (1980): 1–9. Reviews the important reasons that literature can sometimes be an important ingredient for a successful composition class.

Sonnet 130

William Shakespeare (1609)

My mistress' eyes are nothing like the sun;
Coral is far more red than her lips red;
If snow be white, why then her breasts are dun;
If hairs be wires, black wires grow on her head.
I have seen roses damask'd, red and white,
But no such roses see I in her cheeks;
And in some perfumes there is more delight
Than in the breath that from my mistress reeks.
I love to hear her speak, yet well I know
That music hath a far more pleasing sound;
I grant I never saw a goddess go;
My mistress, when she walks, treads on the ground.
And yet, by heaven, I think my love as rare
As any she belied with false compare.

CHAPTER 19

The Library Research Paper

PERSPECTIVE

The reports of the research paper's demise have been, of course, greatly exaggerated; the research paper is still the key assignment in many courses. Furthermore, many professionals do on-the-job research-report writing: business people detail new production methods, social workers explore the effects of a new law, and hospital pharmacists relate developments in their field. To advance in many fields, students must be able to research, synthesize, and report on published information affecting their occupation.

TEACHING STRATEGY

Students often believe that research papers are busywork. To counter this notion, have them interview faculty or working professionals in their fields to determine the role of research writing and then report back to the class. If this is too impractical, you could have students review publications in their fields to determine what kinds of reports are written and why.

Scene: A dark, sinister-looking laboratory. In the center of the stage stands a large laboratory bench crowded with an array of mysterious chemistry apparatus. Tall, cadaverous, and foreboding, Dr. Frankenslime leers as he pours the contents of a tube through a funnel and into a bubbling flask. A short, hunchbacked figure looks on with interest. Suddenly the doctor spreads his arms wide and flashes a sardonic smile.

Frankenslime: Igor! At last! At last I've got it! With this fluid, I can control. . . .

Research yes. But not all researchers are mad scientists, or scientists, or even mad. You might not be any of these things, but no doubt you'll be asked to prepare a *library research paper* for your composition class. This assignment calls for you to gather information from a variety of sources and then to focus, organize, and present it in a formal paper that documents your sources. The procedure will familiarize you with the mechanics of documentation, and when you finish you'll have a solid grasp of your topic and pride in your accomplishment. In addition, the experience will help you learn how to meet the research demands of other courses and your job.

These demands are more common than you might think. A history professor might require a long report on the causes of the Korean War. A business instructor might ask you to trace the history of a company, evaluate an advertising campaign, or review the Japanese style of management. A building trades instructor might call for a short report that compares the effectiveness of several new insulating materials. At work, a marketing analyst might report on the development costs, sales potential, and competition for a product the company is considering introducing. An engineer might write a journal article that summarizes recent developments in plastic fabrication. A physical therapist might prepare a seminar paper that evaluates different exercise programs to follow arthroscopic surgery.

Whatever the writing project, let your purpose guide your research and determine the information you elect to use. When you write, the conclusions you have reached from thinking about what you have read and your purpose in communicating, not your notes, should dictate what you say.

LEARNING ABOUT YOUR LIBRARY

Before starting a library research paper, take time to familiarize yourself with your library. Many college libraries offer guided tours, and almost all of them display floor plans that show where and how the books are grouped. If your library doesn't have tours, browse through it on your own and scan its contents. As you do, note the following features:

Stacks: These are the bookshelves that hold books and bound periodicals (magazines and newspapers). Stacks are either open or closed. Open stacks allow you to go directly to the books you want, take them off the shelf, and check them out. Closed stacks do not allow you direct access to shelved material. Instead, some staff person brings you what you want.

Circulation Desk: Here's where you check materials in and out, renew books you want to keep longer, and pay overdue fines. If you can't find something you want, the desk clerk will tell you whether it's missing, on reserve, or checked out. If it's out, fill out a hold card, and the library will notify you when it is available.

Reserve Area: This area contains books that instructors have had removed from general circulation so students can use them for particular courses. Ordinarily, you can keep these books for only a few hours or overnight.

Reference Area: This area houses the library's collection of encyclopedias, periodical indexes, almanacs, handbooks, dictionaries, and other research tools that you'll use as you investigate your topic. You'll also find one or more reference guides—Eugene P. Sheehy's *Guide to Reference Books* (1986) is an example— that direct you to useful reference tools. To ensure that these books are always available, they must be used in the library. Someone is always on duty to answer questions.

Periodical Area: Here you'll find current and recent issues of magazines and newspapers. If your topic calls for articles that have appeared within the last few months, you're likely to find them in this area.

Microfilm and Microfiche Files: Microfilm is a filmstrip bearing a series of photographically reduced printed pages. Microfiche is a small card with a set of photographically reduced pages mounted on it. Often, most of a library's magazine and newspaper collection is on film. Ask a librarian how to work the viewing machines. Once you can run them, you'll have access to many library resources.

Card Catalog: The card catalog, located close to the circulation desk, indexes all the library's books and often most of the other holdings as well. Libraries classify and arrange books by either the Library of Congress system or the Dewey Decimal system. Each labels the cards with call numbers that enable you or a librarian to locate items quickly. The card catalog is discussed in detail on pages 271–74.

Computer Terminals: These may include terminals for computerized card catalogs and databases. Ask the librarian how to use the terminals. There may be a small fee for using them.

CHOOSING A TOPIC

Instructors take different approaches in assigning library research papers. Some want explanatory papers, others want papers that address a two-sided question, and still others allow students a free choice. An explanatory paper takes no position but provides information that gives the reader a better grasp of the topic. For example, it may explain the key advantages of solar heating, thereby clearing up popular misconceptions. An argument paper, on the other hand, attempts to sway the reader toward one point of view—for instance, that solar heat is commercially feasible. Some instructors specify not only the type of paper but also the topic. Others restrict students to a general subject area, ask them to pick topics from lists, or give them free choice. If you have little to say in the selection, take a positive view: at least you won't have to wrestle with finding a topic.

Whatever the circumstances, it's a good idea to follow a pacing schedule that establishes completion dates for the various stages of your paper. Such a timetable encourages you to plan your work, clarifies both your progress and the work remaining, and provides an overview of the entire project. You can use the following sample schedule as a guide, modifying the stages or adding other ones as necessary.

Sample schedule for a library research paper

Activity	*Targeted Completion Date*
Topic Selection	_____
Working Bibliography	_____
Tentative Thesis	_____
Note-Taking	_____
Working Outline	_____
First Draft	_____
Revised Drafts	_____ _____ _____
Date Due:	_____

Topics to Avoid

If you have free rein to pick your topic, how should you proceed? To begin, rule out certain types of topics:

- Those based entirely on personal·experience or opinion such as "The Thrills I Have Enjoyed Waterskiing" or "Colorado Has More [or Less] Scenic Beauty than New Mexico." Such topics can't be supported by library research. Don't hesitate, however, to include personal judgments and conclusions that emerge from your reading.
- Those fully explained in a single source. An explanation of a process, such as cardiopulmonary resuscitation, or the description of a place, such as the Gobi Desert, does not require coordination of materials from various sources. Although

TEACHING STRATEGIES

1. To help students avoid dead-end topics, specify that papers must either recommend a solution to a problem or argue one side of a controversial issue. Significant problems and issues are rarely personal or found in a single source. More importantly, you instill the notion that students should utilize their sources for a purpose rather than merely collecting and displaying them.

2. You might show students how to generalize personal or recent topics and restrict broad ones. While "How last night's riot got started" is obviously too current, it might be acceptable if recast as "What causes student riots at sporting events, and how can these riots be prevented?" While "The home computer revolution" is clearly too broad, it could be narrowed to "How are home computers actually being used?"

EXERCISE ANSWERS

1. Suitable. The topic is narrow enough to be discussed adequately, and material is available in periodicals, newspapers, and possibly books.
2. Unsuitable. The topic is too broad.
3. Suitable. See item 1 for reasons.
4. Unsuitable. The topic is too contemporary for sufficient source material to be available. Also, most riots lack sufficient significance to be suitable topics.
5. Unsuitable. This is a process paper, and any articles that might be found would probably repeat the same information.
6. Suitable. See item 1 for reasons. (If the place has become a hot spot *very recently*, it may not be a suitable topic because of lack of source material.)
7. Suitable. See item 1 for reasons.

you may find several articles on such topics, basically they will repeat the same information.

- Those that are brand new. Often it's impossible to find sufficient source material about such topics.
- Those that are overly broad. Don't try to tackle such elephant-sized topics as "The Causes of World War II" or "Recent Medical Advances." Instead, slim them down to something like "The Advent of Jet Fighters" or "Eye Surgery with Laser Beams." The techniques discussed on pages 12–18 can help you reduce a topic to manageable size.
- Those that have been worked over and over, such as abortion and the legal drinking age. Why bore your reader with information and arguments that are all too familiar already?

EXERCISE ■ **Using the advice on topics to avoid, explain why each of the following would or would not be suitable for a library research topic.**

1. Genetic counseling
2. Neoconservatism
3. The home computer revolution
4. How last night's riot got started
5. Building a rock garden
6. A third world hot spot as described on the evening news
7. Reforming the financing of presidential election campaigns

---

Drawing on Your Interests

Let your interests guide your choice. A long-standing interest in baseball might suggest a paper on the pros and cons of expanding the number of teams in the Major Leagues. An instructor's lecture might spark your interest in a historical event or person, an economic crisis, a scientific development, a sociological trend, a medical milestone, a political scandal, or the influences on an author. An argument with a friend might spur you to investigate latch-key children. A television documentary might arouse your curiosity about a group of primitive people. A recent article or novel might inspire you to explore the occult or some taboo.

Be practical in selecting a topic. Why not get a head start on a particular aspect of your major field by researching it now? Some management, marketing, or advertising strategy; the beginnings of current contract law; medical ethics—all of these topics, and many others, qualify. Think about your audience, the availability of information, and whether you can fit it into the guidelines for your paper.

CASE HISTORY

Christine Harding was a freshman composition student when she wrote the library research paper at the end of this chapter. Christine's instructor had limited the class to writing on some recent technological development. After watching a TV rerun of the movie *Star Wars*, she decided to explore some aspect of robots. Because her focus was fuzzy, she decided to sharpen it by doing some brainstorming and background reading in order to explore the many possibilities. Christine brainstormed by drafting a series of questions suggested by the writing strategies she learned about in Chapters 4–12. Perhaps these questions could lead to a focus for her paper.

```
Could I narrate a brief history of robots?
Could I describe a typical robot?
Could I classify robots into categories?
Could I compare robots to anything?
Could I explain a typical process that a robot performs?
What causes led to the development of robots?
What effects are robots likely to have?
What model or example best illustrates a robot?
Is there a widely accepted definition of "robot"?
Could I argue for or against greater industrial use of robots?
```

These writing strategies can often help you narrow a subject to a manageable topic.

For her background reading, Christine turned to two general encyclopedias: the *Encyclopedia Americana* and the *Encyclopaedia Britannica,* where she skimmed the articles on robots. Next, she decided to search out a couple of other general articles in more specialized publications. Not knowing how to proceed, she consulted a reference room librarian who acquainted her with the *McGraw-Hill Encyclopedia of Science and Technology* and *Van Nostrand's Scientific Encyclopedia.*

This reading suggested several areas of focus: the history of robots, the factors involved in designing them, and their possible impact on industry. After a little thought, she elected the third possibility. Unlike the first one, it interested her greatly, and she felt it would also interest her audience—fellow students at the vocationally oriented school she attended. Unlike the second focus, it would not require highly technical source material, which she might not understand.

Her focus in hand, Christine used the branching technique (see page 20) to explore possible research directions and guide her library search.

PERSPECTIVE

Students often focus on their topic without considering their audience and purpose. Such a misplaced emphasis is one reason why many students write anemic papers: they are not writing to anyone but the teacher nor for any reason except the grade.

TEACHING STRATEGIES

1. To show the range of potential audiences, give students specific topics, such as the effectiveness of different cancer treatments, and have them develop lists of possible audiences, such as physicians and families of cancer victims. Then have students indicate how the audience would influence the kind of research they would do and also the final report. Next, do the same thing with purpose. Will they be helping patients select a treatment? Trying to convince legislators to legalize a certain treatment? How would purpose influence the research and final report?

2. Encourage students to transform their topic ideas into questions. Questions call for responses, especially when related ones are clustered. For example, Christine might draft this series of questions: What are robots? Where are they used? Are they effective? Do they replace workers? Have students turn in sets of research questions for topics they have selected.

3. To keep students on track, you might require them to turn in an early prospectus. In it they should identify their topic, why it interests them, their potential audience and purpose, the initial research questions, what they know about the topic, and their next step in the project.

Possible harmful effects —————— Loss of jobs
High purchase costs

Impact of robots on industry

Possible beneficial effects —————— 24-hour-a-day operation
Greater accuracy
No discipline problems
No vacation or sick leave
Lower operating costs

This case history continues on pages 279–80.

This same general procedure—brainstorming with the writing strategies, skimming encyclopedia articles and other background material, and branching—works well in approaching almost any research topic. Other background material depends on your topic: for a historical figure, there are the *Dictionary of American Biography* (for deceased American figures), the *Dictionary of National Biography* (for deceased British figures), and the *McGraw-Hill Encyclopedia of World Biography.* Librarians can suggest appropriate background books.

Brainstorming frequently leads to a number of questions that require answers. Such questions can help guide your research; after all, the purpose of doing research is to answer questions.

More often than not, things won't fall neatly into place when you probe for a topic. False starts and blind alleys are part of the process. Don't be discouraged when you encounter them.

ASSEMBLING A WORKING BIBLIOGRAPHY

TEACHING STRATEGIES

1. Many students plunge ahead, taking notes on the first article they find without adequately surveying the field. Advise students to start by gauging available information about their topic and only then to begin taking notes from the most useful sources. To encourage this approach, have students turn in an annotated bibliography which also includes evaluations of the sources.

Once you have a topic, you're ready to see whether the library has the resources you'll need to complete the project. This step requires you to check additional reference tools and compile a working bibliography—a set of cards that list promising sources of information. This section discusses these reference tools and how to use them.

Encyclopedias

What They Are. Encyclopedias fall into two categories, general and specialized. General encyclopedias, the *Encyclopedia Americana* and the *Encyclopaedia Britannica,* for instance, offer general articles on a wide range of subjects. Specialized encyclopedias cover one particular field, such as advertising or human behavior. Here's a sampling of specialized encyclopedias:

Encyclopedia of Advertising
Encyclopedia of Education
Encyclopedia of Environmental Science
Encyclopedia of Human Behavior: Psychology, Psychiatry, and Mental Health
Encyclopedia of Social Work
Encyclopedia of World Art
Harper's Encyclopedia of Science
International Encyclopedia of the Social Sciences
McGraw-Hill Encyclopedia of Science and Technology

How to Use Them.   Encyclopedias are a convenient launching pad for your investigation because they provide an overview of the broad field your topic fits into. For a nonspecialized topic, like the impact of commercial television during the 1950s, check the articles on television in one or more general encyclopedias. For a specialized aspect of television, say the development of the picture tube, consult one or more specialized encyclopedias, such as *Harper's Encyclopedia of Science* and the *McGraw-Hill Encyclopedia of Science and Technology*, along with the general encyclopedias. During this search you'll re-encounter material you scanned while trying to focus on a topic.

Some instructors allow you to acknowledge encyclopedias as a source, others prohibit their use, and still others allow material from specialized, but not general, encyclopedias. As always, follow your instructor's wishes.

If you will be using encyclopedia sources, jot down the following information for each note you take:

Title of article
Author(s) of article (Not always available. Sometimes only initials at the end of an
    article identify an author. In that case, check the list of contributors at the front
    of the first volume for the full name.)
Name of encyclopedia
Year of publication

Furthermore, check for bibliographies at the ends of articles and copy down any reference that looks promising.

When you've finished your exploratory reading in encyclopedias, turn to the card catalog and periodical indexes—the prime sources of information for library research papers.

The Card Catalog

What It Is.   The card catalog, a file of 3 × 5-inch cards, indexes all of the books in the library. In some libraries, it also lists magazines, newspapers, government documents, college catalogs, records, and tape recordings. In others, these materials are cataloged separately. Your librarian will help you locate any other listings.

The card catalog contains three kinds of cards—author, title, and subject—for each nonfiction item cataloged. Fiction has author and title cards only. Except for

2. When students can't find any material on their topics, suggest an indirect approach. If there is no material on "Robots and the work force," is there any on automation? On robots in a particular industry, such as the auto industry? Have students list all the salient matters related to their questions. Students investigating soccer riots in England might explore riots in general, mob psychology, and even unemployment in England, all of which might provide insights into the topic.
3. Students often encounter problems as they search for sources. Library holdings may be inadequate; periodical issues may have been stolen or articles torn out of magazines; books may be checked out or misshelved. Students can quickly become frustrated. Confront this problem in class by discussing the difficulties students are having and suggesting potential solutions. Could they check the local public library? Look for a nearby organization that would have the information? Ask a faculty member for help? Visit their own city library or another college library while home for the weekend? Encourage students to assess the strengths of their college library and capitalize on them. If it has an inadequate selection of scholarly periodicals but a large collection of popular magazines, encourage students to consider current topics for their papers.

the top line, which differs for the different types of cards, all cards for the same book are identical. The cards are arranged alphabetically, and the three kinds may be filed together, separately, or in some other manner; for example, title and author cards together, subject cards elsewhere. In alphabetizing the cards, librarians follow certain standard practices.

1. Title and subject cards are filed alphabetically according to the first word that is not an article (*a, an, the*).
2. Cards are filed word by word rather than strictly letter by letter. To illustrate, note the following series:

> Chicken and Turkey Tapeworms
> Chicken Beacon
> Chicken Every Sunday
> Chicken Raising Made Easy
> The Chickenbone Special
> Chickens, Chickens, Chickens
> Chickens Come Home to Roost

3. "Mc" names are filed under "Mac."
4. Numbers and abbreviations are filed alphabetically as if they were spelled out. For example, the title card for the novel *Mr. Bridge* is filed under "Mister."
5. Names of people precede identical names of places and things. Thus, "Snow, C. P., *The Masters*" comes before "*Snow at Evening.*"

Knowing these conventions will lessen tedious thumbing through the cards.

The card catalog allows you to gauge your library's holdings on a subject or by an author. The cards themselves also provide helpful information, as Figure 19.1 illustrates.

How to Use It. Start your search for useful books by looking up any book titles gleaned from encyclopedia bibliographies. Next, draw up a list of subject headings that seem likely to yield useful material; then check the headings in the card catalog. If you're investigating satanic cults, your headings might include *devil worship, satanism, diabolism,* and *cult.*

When a check of your subject headings yields nothing, don't give up. Perhaps your list doesn't include any headings that are actually used. To find the right headings, turn to the publications that your library uses in cataloging books. These publications are the *Library of Congress Subject Heading Guide* and, for libraries that follow the Dewey Decimal system, Sears' *List of Subject Headings.* Say you're researching the impact of America's entry into World War I on citizens with German roots. You've come up with the subject headings "World War I" and "First World War" but have not found catalog entries for either of them. Your library uses Dewey Decimal call numbers. Check "World War I" in Sears' *List of Subject Headings* and you'll discover that the books you want are cataloged under "European War, 1914–1918."

For each promising title you turn up, record the following information on a 3 × 5-inch card:

> Author(s)
> Title
> Editor(s) and translator(s), as well as author(s) of any supplementary material

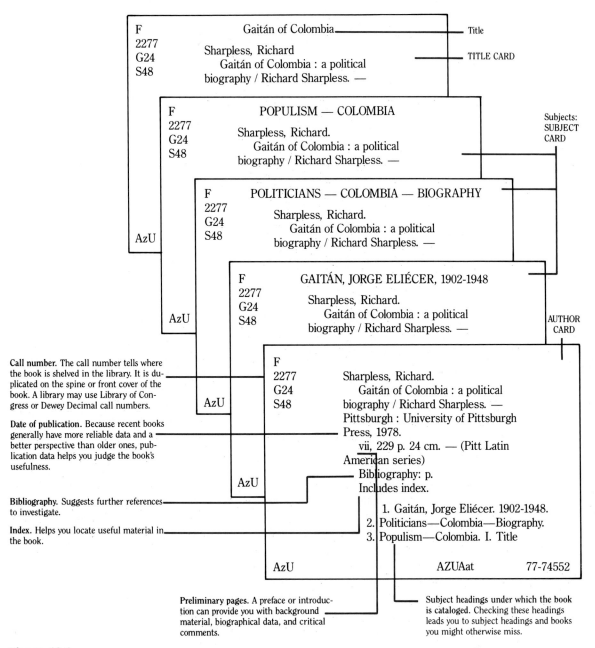

Figure 19.1

Total number of volumes (if more than one) and the number of the specific
    volume that you want to use
City of publication
Name of publisher
Date of publication

Also, copy the book's call number in the upper left-hand corner of the card.

Next, scan the books themselves. If your library stacks are closed, give the librarian a list of your call numbers and ask to see the books. If you can enter the stacks, locate the general areas where your books are shelved. Once you find a number range that includes one of your call numbers, follow the trail of guides on the book spines until you find your book. Spend a few extra minutes browsing in the general area of each book; you may discover useful sources that you over-looked in the card catalog.

Skim each book's table of contents and any introductory material, such as a preface or introduction, to determine scope and approach. Also check the index and note the pages with discussions that relate to your topic. Finally, thumb through any portions that look promising. If the book won't help you, throw away the card.

If you can't find a book you're searching for, don't assume that it's lost or not available. Ask the librarian whether it's been checked out or placed on reserve. If it's on reserve, go to the reserve section and examine it there. If someone has checked it out, find out when it's due back. When that date is some time away, ask the librarian to contact the borrower and try to speed up the return.

Computerized Card Catalogs

More and more colleges now have computerized card catalogs. These units serve the same purposes as conventional catalogs and may provide additional information, such as whether a book has been checked out and, if so, the due date. Some of the catalogs even include the holdings of nearby libraries. Although several systems are available, all have similar terminals that consist essentially of a viewing screen and a keyboard on which the user enters requests for information. To use your library's system properly, read the instructions at the terminal or ask a librarian for help.

Most systems let you conduct searches by author, title, subject, and key terms—those appearing in book titles and descriptions. Typically, you'll begin by typing in a code—say A for "author," T for "title," S for "subject," and KT for "key term"—and then your specific search request. Searching may require you to view a series of screens with increasingly specific information, with the final screen providing the same information as a conventional card catalog.

Because the lists obtained through key-term searches may not include every book on a particular subject, you should also investigate related terms and perhaps also make a subject search. Most systems let you narrow your focus by searching combinations of subject and terms. Thus, for a paper on the role of alcoholism in child abuse, you could enter "child abuse, alcoholism" and avoid calling up unhelpful titles.

Because computerized catalogs use Library of Congress subject headings, you'll need to know the right headings to enter. If you have trouble, the *Library of Congress Subject Heading Guide* (see page 272) or your librarian can help you.

Instead of computerized catalogs, other libraries have their card catalogs on microfiche cards or microfilm, which are read with a special viewing device.

EXERCISE

1. **Select five of the following topics. Go to the card catalog and find one book about each. List each book's call number, author, title, publisher, and date of publication. Because subject headings may vary, investigate related categories, if necessary, to find an entry. To illustrate, if you find nothing under *mountaineering*, check *mountain climbing* or *backpacking*.**

1. Adolescence	11. Pearl Harbor
2. Balkan Peninsula	12. Parapsychological research
3. Child abuse	13. Regional planning
4. Flying saucers	14. Bertrand Russell
5. Mohandas Gandhi	15. Spin fishing
6. Heraldry	16. Taxidermy
7. Doris Lessing	17. Telecommunication
8. Mass transit	18. Underwater exploration
9. Mountaineering	19. Volcanoes
10. Origami	20. Zen Buddhism

2. **Provide your instructor with a list of the books you found that appear useful for developing your paper's topic. For each book, furnish the information specified in Part 1 above, along with a brief note indicating why you think the book will be useful.**

Periodical Indexes

What They Are. Periodical indexes catalog articles in magazines and newspapers. Indexes may be in book form, on microfilm or microfiche, or computerized. Some are offered in two or more forms. Computerized indexes, called *databases*, are available to libraries through subscription. Depending upon the particular database, information may be furnished on compact discs or transmitted via wire from a mainframe computer to the library. The term *online* designates the second kind of system. Databases are accessed through terminals equipped with a keyboard and viewing screen. Some have printers that can supply lists of references or even copies of articles.

In some cases, terminals are intended for student operation; others are operated by library personnel. If you use a database, you may have to pay a service fee, but it's likely to be small.

Updated frequently, sometimes every week, periodical indexes provide access to information that hasn't yet found its way into books and perhaps never will. Their listings allow you to examine new topics, follow developments in older ones, and explore your topic in greater depth than you could by using books alone. In short, indexes help you avoid doing a superficial paper.

The *Readers' Guide to Periodical Literature*, available since 1900 in printed form, is now available online and on compact discs. The *Guide* indexes the material in over 200 widely circulated magazines—*Harper's, Newsweek, Scientific American* and the like—articles by subject and author and other categories by title and author. The *Guide* is especially useful for finding material on historical events (say the Vietnam War or the Iran-Contra hearings) and on social, political, and economic developments (for instance, the assisted-suicide movement and the drive to limit the terms of officeholders). The *Guide* also includes scientific, technical, and even literary articles intended for a general audience rather than specialists, but such articles do not include all the available research.

The first pages in the printed version of the *Guide* identify the abbreviations used for the magazines indexed. Figure 19.2 shows the arrangement of the index and the "see also" cross-references that direct you to related subject headings.

The *Magazine Index*, available on microfilm or online, indexes some 400 popular publications by author, title, and subject. Updated monthly, it covers a five-year period and includes references to articles no more than two weeks old. The viewing machines for units using microfilm resemble small television sets and have motorized controls that allow swift movement through the filmstrip. Accompanying the viewer are coded reels of microfilm containing the indexed articles, together with a reader/printer that allows you to read articles and obtain printed copies. Your librarian will demonstrate how these machines work. The producers of the index also publish a listing of recent articles on twenty to thirty current topics.

Figure 19.2

Subject headings — **PRISONS and Prisoners. Note:** Includes material on juvenile correctional institutions

    See also Political Prisoners. US Armament (for mil prisons). Geog headings (for pol prisoners and mil prisons). Personal names. Types of crimes. War names — Note on scope of coverage

Cross-references

    Alabama
    Selma jailed prisoners are served food from local fast-food restaurants as cost-saving measure (S), Ja 6.11.6:5
    Attys representing Ala prison inmates ask Dist Judge — Summary of article
Robert Varner to hold Gov Fob James in contempt for failure to relieve overcrowding (S), Ag 24.II.5:1
    Draper Correctional Center repts that John Anthony Cruse, 15-yr-old sentenced to life in prison in Feb for murder of his foster mother, is adjusting to incarceration (S), O 10.53:5

Subheading — **Alaska**

Date of publication: the article appeared in the August 24 issue of the paper, Section II, page 5, column 1.

    Alaska is about to settle civil rights suit with agreement that will obligate it to spend millions of dollars to build maximum security prison, including cells for 200 prisoners now housed in Fed prisons outside Alaska; litigation's origins began when territory became state, when law enforcement and penal insts were Fed Govt functions (M), O 11,13:1

Figure 19.3

The *National Newspaper Index* covers five national newspapers: the *Christian Science Monitor*, the *Los Angeles Times*, the *New York Times*, the *Wall Street Journal*, and *The Washington Post*. It is available on microfilm, compact discs, and online. Each monthly issue covers two-and-one-half years of references, and back issues can be obtained on microfiche cards. Microfilm units have the same kind of viewer as the microfilm version of the *Magazine Index*.

The *New York Times Index* comes in printed and online form. It indexes, by subject, all news articles, book reviews, commentaries, and features that have appeared in the paper and briefly summarizes each listing. The index entries refer to the "Late City Edition" of the paper, the one most libraries have on microfilm. If your library subscribes to a regional edition, an article may appear on another page or not at all. Figure 19.3 is a sample entry from this index.

NewsBank may be your best bet for a topic of regional interest. This index covers more than 500 newspapers in all fifty states, indexing articles on politics, economics, business, the environment, and the entertainment world. It is available in loose-leaf notebook form or online. The printed version is accompanied by the articles on microfiche cards.

Info Trac, the most common database, is a compact disc system. It provides access to listings of articles, arranged and subdivided by subject, that have appeared in over 1,100 magazines and newspapers, including the entries in the *Magazine Index*, *National Newspaper Index*, and various other indexes. Because its instructions are so easily followed, *Info Trac* is a good system to use when starting your search for articles.

Specialized indexes are also available. Here is a brief sampling of some of them. They list articles appearing in scholarly journals rather than popular magazines.

Applied Science and Technology Index, 1958–date (indexed by subject)
Education Index, 1929–date (indexed by subject and author)
Humanities Index, 1974–date (indexed by subject and author)

> *International Index to Periodicals*, 1907–1964 (indexed by subject and author; entitled *Social Sciences and Humanities Index*, 1965–1974, and then separated into the *Humanities Index* and the *Social Science Index*)
> *Social Sciences and Humanities Index*, 1965–1974 (indexed by subject and author)
> *Social Sciences Index*, 1975–date (indexed by subject and author)

All come in printed form, and some are also available on compact discs and online.

With periodical indexes, as with the card catalog, don't give up if a subject heading you're exploring yields few or no entries. Instead, explore related headings. For example, if your subject is teenage marriages, look also under "adolescence," "divorce," "teen pregnancies," and the like. Browse through the system and try a variety of options. Use this as an opportunity to gain different perspectives on your research project.

How to Use Them. Start your search for articles by checking general indexes; then move to appropriate specialized indexes. Each time you unearth a promising reference, copy the following information on a 3 × 5-inch note card:

> Author(s), if identified
> Title of article
> Name of periodical
> Volume or issue number (for professional and scholarly journals only)
> Date of periodical
> The page range of the entire article

Obtain printout copies of whatever articles you can and check the topic sentences of paragraphs for essential points. Also, scan any accompanying abstracts or summaries. If an article appears useful, check to see whether it has a bibliography, which might include additional useful sources. Keep the cards for articles that seem promising—and any useful articles—and throw away the others.

Take the remaining cards—and any periodical references that you found in encyclopedia bibliographies—to whatever catalog your library uses for periodicals. There you can determine whether the library subscribes to what you want and, if it does, where the periodicals are shelved. Libraries frequently keep current issues in a periodical room or some other special section. Back issues of magazines are often kept on microfilm or bound into hardcover volumes and shelved. Most newspapers are on microfilm. Check the articles for which you don't have printouts in the same manner that you checked the others.

EXERCISE ■ **Select five of the following topics and find one magazine article about each. Use at least three different periodical indexes to locate the articles. List the author, if given, the title of the article, the name of the magazine, its date, the page range, and the name of the index used.**

1. Acting schools
2. Aeronautical research
3. Black holes
4. Campaign funds
5. Collective bargaining
6. Dow Chemical Company
7. Dwight David Eisenhower
8. Fiber optics
9. Fundamentalism
10. Holography

11. Investment trusts
12. Leveraged buyouts
13. Nuclear fusion
14. Oral history
15. Perestroika

16. Television industry
17. Unemployment
18. Vegetarianism
19. X-ray astronomy
20. Yale University

Adjusting Your Topic

After finishing your search for sources, you may need to adjust the scope and emphasis of your topic. If your start with "America's First Nuclear-Powered Submarine" but fail to turn up enough sources, you might expand your emphasis to "America's First Nuclear-Powered Warships." On the other hand, if you're working with "America's First Nuclear-Powered Warships" and find yourself floundering in an ocean of sources, you might zero in on one type of vessel. Gathering evidence helps to develop your judgment about how many sources you need to do the job.

CASE HISTORY   *(Continued from page 270)*

Once Christine Harding targeted a focus for her paper on robots, she began compiling her working bibliography. First, she reread the encyclopedia articles she had already skimmed but found them uninformative.

Next, Christine turned to the card catalog and checked the listings under the headings "Robots" and "Robots, Industrial." The first heading yielded a cross-reference directing her to the headings "Androids," "Automata," and "Automation"; the second revealed a listing of seven books. A check of all four headings turned up fourteen books, four of which proved upon examination to contain material that looked useful.

Her search for periodical articles took Christine to four indexes: the *Reader's Guide to Periodical Literature*, the *Magazine Index*, the *Applied Science and Technology Index*, and the *National Newspaper Index*. The result: twenty-five articles with promising titles. Of these, sixteen were available in the college library, and eleven appeared useful for her purpose.

Suspecting that the library might have helpful government documents, Christine checked the library's document catalog after having a librarian explain how to use it. Her search led to a single promising publication.

Satisfied that ample information was available, Christine now returned to her sources for a closer look in order to carefully evaluate their content. Her instructor had suggested that one good way to approach a topic is to pose a question about it and then draft a *tentative* answer, if possible. Here's how Christine proceeded.

Q: What impact are robots likely to have on industry?

A: Despite the misgivings of some people, robots will probably have a beneficial effect on industry and its work force.

TEACHING STRATEGIES

1. After students have examined their working bibliographies, ask them if they need to revise their research questions in light of their findings.
2. At this point students might write brief progress reports specifying any problems they are having and outlining their plans for further research. Such reports allow you to provide helpful suggestions.

Her answer provided Christine with a *tentative thesis*, an informed opinion that guided her later note taking, giving her a sense of direction and indicating what information would likely prove useful and what useless. Tentative theses are just that—tentative—and can be altered slightly or changed completely if necessary. If later reading indicated that robots would likely prove a mixed blessing, Christine could alter her tentative thesis accordingly.

This case history continues on pages 286–87.

TAKING NOTES

To take notes, read your references carefully and record significant information. Notes are the raw materials for your finished product, so develop them accurately.

Evaluating Your Sources

Evaluate your sources by considering these factors.

The Expertise of the Author.   Judge an author's expertise by examining his or her professional status. Say you're searching for information on some new cancer-treating drug. An article by the director of a national cancer research center would be a better bet than one by a staff writer for a magazine. Similarly, a historian's account of a national figure will probably have more balance and depth than a novelist's popularized account of that person's life. Gauging a writer's credentials is not difficult. Articles in periodicals often note authors' job titles along with their names. Some even supply thumbnail biographies. For a book, check its title page, preface, or introduction, and—if it's been left on—the dust jacket. Finally, notice whether the writer has other publications on this general subject. If your sources include two or more items by one person or if that person's name keeps cropping up as you take notes, you're probably dealing with an expert.

The Credibility of the Publication.   A book's credibility hinges on its approach and its reception by reviewers. Cast a cautious eye on books that take a popular rather than a scholarly approach. For research papers, scholarly treatments provide more solid fare. Weigh what reviewers said when a book first appeared. Two publications excerpt selected reviews and provide references to others. The *Book Review Digest* (1905–date) deals mainly with nontechnical works, while the *Technical Book Review Index* (1935–date) covers technical and scientific books. Turn first to the volume for the year the book came out. If you don't find any reviews, scan the next year's index. Often books published in the fall are not reviewed until the following year.

Periodical articles can also take a scholarly or popular tack. Editors of specialized journals and of some wide-circulation magazines—for example, *Scientific American* and *The New Yorker*—publish only in-depth, accurate articles. Most newsstand publications, however, popularize to some extent, and some deliberately strive for sensationalism. Popularizing may result in broad, general statements, skimpy details, and a sensational tone.

Don't automatically reject a source because the writer lacks expertise or offers a popularized treatment. Often, especially when writing about a current topic, you'll need to use material that falls short in some way. Remember, though, that you undertake research to become more knowledgeable than general readers are about a topic. When information in popular periodicals provides less than adequate coverage, candidly acknowledge the shortcomings.

Mechanics of Note Taking

Generally your most effective approach to note taking is to use note cards. Copy each note on a 4 × 6-inch card to avoid confusion with the smaller bibliography cards. Record only one note per card, even when you take several notes from a single page: you may use the notes at different points. If you can't fit a note on a single card, continue the note on a second card and paper-clip or staple the two together. Cards allow you to test different arrangements of notes and use the best one.

Before you take a note, indicate its source at the bottom of the card. You will then have all the details necessary for documenting the information if you use it in your paper. Usually, the author's last name and the page number suffice, since the bibliography card contains all other details. To distinguish between two authors with the same last name or between two works by the same author, add initials or partial titles. *Don't forget to include the page number or numbers for each note.* Otherwise, you'll have to waste time looking them up when you cite your sources in the paper.

Summarize briefly the contents of the note at the top of the card. Later, when you construct an outline, these notations will help you sort your cards into categories and subcategories.

Responding to Notes

As you take notes, reflect on your topic and try to come up with new ideas, see connections to other notes, and anticipate future research. Think of yourself as having a conversation with your sources, and jot down your responses on the backs of your note cards. Ask yourself these questions: Does this information agree with what I have learned so far? Does it suggest any new avenues to explore? Does it raise any additional research questions? Does it leave me with questions about what's been said? Although it may take a few minutes to record your responses to a note, this type of analysis will help you write a paper that reflects *your* opinions, decisions, and evaluations, not one that smacks of notes merely patched together from different sources.

Some students prefer to photocopy some or all of their source material and work on it at their leisure while at home. They can then reread as well as underline, highlight, and/or annotate in the margins. While this approach may sound appealing, keep in mind that *you* must still evaluate, select, and organize the material, use it according to your purpose, and draw your conclusions. In addition, excessive duplicating can become expensive.

Types of Notes

A note can be a summary, paraphrase, or quotation. *Whenever you use any kind of note in your paper, give proper credit to your source. Failure to do so results in plagiarism—that is, literary theft—a serious offense even when committed unintentionally.* Pages 307–8 discuss plagiarism, and pages 292–304 explain proper documentation of sources.

TEACHING STRATEGY

As an exercise, you might have students, working in groups, summarize all or part of one of the essays in the Reader. Then have them compare the different versions and prepare a final version.

Summary.   A summary condenses original material, presenting its core ideas *in your own words.* In order to write an effective summary, you must have a good grasp of the information, and this comprehension ensures that you are ready to use the material in your paper. You may include brief quotations if you enclose them in quotation marks. A properly written summary presents the main points in their original order without distorting their emphasis or meaning, and it omits supporting details and repetition. Summaries, then, serve up the heart of the matter.

Begin the summarizing process by asking yourself, "What points does the author make that have an important bearing on my topic and purpose?" To answer, note especially the topic sentences in the original, which often provide essential information. Copy the points in order; then condense and rewrite them in your own words. Figure 19.4 summarizes the Bertrand Russell passage that follows. We have underscored key points in the original.

Under the influence of the romantic movement, a process began about a hundred and fifty years ago, which has continued ever since—a process of revaluing the traditional virtues, placing some higher on the scale than before, and others lower. The tendency has been to exalt impulse at the expense of deliberation. The virtues that spring from the heart have come to be thought superior to those that are based upon reflection: a generous man is preferred to a man who is punctual in paying his debts. *Per contra*, deliberate sins are thought worse than impulsive sins: a hypocrite is more harshly condemned than a murderer. The upshot is that we tend to estimate virtues, not by their capacity for providing human happiness, but by their power of inspiring a personal liking for the possessors, and we are not apt to include among the qualities for which we like people, a habit of reflecting before making an important decision.

The men who started this movement were, in the main, gentle sentimentalists who imagined that, when the fetters of custom and law were removed, the heart would be free to display its natural goodness. Human nature, they thought, is good, but institutions have corrupted it; remove the institutions and we shall all become angels. Unfortunately, the matter is not so simple as they thought. Men who follow their impulses establish governments based on pogroms, clamour for war with foreign countries, and murder pacifists and Negroes. Human nature unrestrained by law is violent and cruel. In the London Zoo, the male baboons fought over the females until all the females were torn to pieces; human beings, left to the ungoverned impulse, would be no better. In ages that have had recent experience of anarchy, this has been obvious. All the great writers of the middle ages were passionate in their admiration of the law; it was the Thirty Years' War that led Grotius to become the first advocate of international law. Law, respected and enforced, is in the long run the only alternative to violent and predatory

> ### Necessity for law
> About a century and a half ago, there began a still-existing preference for impulsive actions over deliberate ones. Those responsible for this development believed that people are naturally good but institutions have perverted them. Actually, unfettered human nature breeds violence and brutality, and law is our only protection against anarchy. The law assumes the responsibility for revenge and settles disputes equitably. It frees people from the fear of being victimized by criminals and provides a means of catching them. Without it, civilization could not endure.
>
> Russell, pp. 63-65

Figure 19.4

anarchy; and it is just as necessary to realize this now as it was in the time of Dante and Grotius.

What is the essence of law? On the one hand, it takes away from private citizens the right of revenge, which it confers upon the government. If a man steals your money, you must not steal it back, or thrash him, or shoot him; you must establish the facts before a neutral tribunal, which inflicts upon him such punishment as has seemed just to the disinterested legislators. On the other hand, when two men have a dispute, the law provides a machinery for settling it, again on principles laid down in advance by neutrals. The advantages of law are many. It diminishes the amount of private violence, and settles disagreements in a manner more nearly just than that which would result if the disputants fought it out by private war. It makes it possible for men to work without being perpetually on the watch against bandits. When a crime has been committed it provides a skilled machine for discovering the criminal.

Without law, the existence of civilized communities is impossible. In international law, there is as yet no effective law, for lack of an international police force capable of overpowering national armies, and it is daily becoming more evident that this defect must be remedied if civilization is to survive. Within single nations there is a dangerous tendency to think that moral indignation excuses the extra-legal punishment of criminals. In Germany an era of private murder (on the loftiest grounds) preceded and followed the victory of the Nazis. In fact, nine-tenths of what appeared as just indignation was sheer lust for cruelty; and this is equally true in other countries where mobs rob the law of its functions. In any civilized community, toleration of mob rule is the first step towards barbarism.

Bertrand Russell, "Respect for Law," *San Francisco Review*, Winter 1958, 63–65.

EXERCISE

A. Select two passages that your instructor approves from any essay in the Reader and prepare summary note cards for them.

B. Submit summaries of three pieces of information that you plan to use in writing your paper; also submit photocopies of the original information.

Paraphrase.   To paraphrase is to restate material *in your own words* without attempting to condense it. Unlike a summary, a paraphrase allows you to present an essentially complete version of the original material. A note of caution, however: Don't copy the original source nearly verbatim, changing only a word here and there. To do so is to plagiarize. To avoid this offense, follow a read, think, and write-without-looking-at-the-original strategy when you take notes so that you concentrate on recording the information in your own words. Then verify the accuracy of your notes by checking them against the original source. Here is a sample passage, and Figure 19.5 is its paraphrase.

> Over time, more and more of life has become subject to the controls of knowledge. However, this is never a one-way process. Scientific investigation is continually increasing our knowledge. But if we are to make good use of this knowledge, we must not only rid our minds of old, superseded beliefs and fragments of magic, but also recognize new superstitions for what they are. Both are generated by our wishes, our fears, and our feelings of helplessness in difficult situations.
>
> Margaret Mead, "New Superstitions for Old," *A Way of Seeing*. New York: McCall, 1970. 266.

EXERCISE ■ **Paraphrase a short passage from one of your textbooks. Make a copy of the passage to hand in with the assignment.**

Quotation.   A quotation is a copy of original material. Since your paper should demonstrate that you've mastered your sources, don't rely extensively on quotations. You need practice in expressing yourself. As a general rule, avoid quotations except when

- the original displays special elegance or force
- you really need support from an authority
- you need to back up your interpretation of a passage from a literary work

Paraphrasing a passage as well-written as the one below would rob it of much of its force.

> Man is himself, like the universe he inhabits, like the demoniacal stirring of the ooze from which he sprang, a tale of desolation. He walks in his mind from birth to death the long resounding shores of endless disillusionment. Finally, the commitment to life departs or turns to bitterness. But out of such desolation

> *Combatting Superstitions*
>
> As time has passed, knowledge has asserted its sway over larger and larger segments of human life. But the process cuts two ways. Science is forever adding to the storehouse of human knowledge. Before we can take proper advantage of its gifts, however, we must purge our minds of old and outmoded convictions, while recognizing the true nature of modern superstitions. Both stem from our desires, our apprehensions, and our sense of impotence under difficult circumstances.
>
> Mead, p. 266

Figure 19.5

emerges the awful freedom to choose beyond the narrowly circumscribed circle that delimits the rational being.

Loren Eiseley, *The Unexpected Universe*

Special rules govern the use of quotations. If, for clarity, you need to add an explanation or substitute a proper name for a personal pronoun, enclose the addition in *brackets*.

> The Declaration of Independence asserts that "the history of the present King of Great Britain [George III] is a history of repeated injuries and usurpations. . . ."

If your typewriter cannot type brackets, insert them neatly with a dark pen.

Reproduce any grammatical or spelling errors in a source exactly as they appear in the original. To let your reader know that the original author, not you, made the mistake, insert the Latin word *sic* (meaning "thus") within brackets immediately after the error.

> As Wabash notes, "The threat to our enviroment [sic] comes from many directions."

If you exclude an unneeded part of a quotation, show the omission with an ellipsis—three spaced periods. Indicate omissions *within sentences* in the following way:

> Writing in *Step by Step, 1936–1939*, Winston Churchill observed, "To France and Belgium the avalanche of fire and steel which fell upon them twenty years ago . . . [was] an overpowering memory and obsession."

When an omission comes *at the end of a sentence* and what is actually quoted can also stand as a complete sentence, use an unspaced period followed by an ellipsis.

> In his second inaugural address, Lincoln voiced his hopes for the nation: "With malice toward none, with charity for all, with firmness in the right as God gives us to see the right, let us strive on to finish the work we are in. . . ."

Do the same when you drop *a whole sentence* within a quoted passage.

> According to newspaper columnist Grace Dunn, "Williamson's campaign will undoubtedly focus primarily on the legalized gambling issue because he hopes to capitalize on the strong opposition to it in his district. . . . Nonetheless, commentators all agree he faces an uphill fight in his attempt to unseat the incumbent."

Don't change or distort when you delete. Tampering like the following violates ethical standards:

Original passage   This film is poorly directed, and the acting uninspired; only the cameo appearance by Laurence Olivier makes it truly worth seeing.

Distorted version   This film is . . . truly worth seeing.

You can summarize or paraphrase original material but retain a few words or phrases to add vividness or keep a precise shade of meaning. Simply use quotation marks but no ellipsis.

> Because of the "passionate advocacy" of its supporters, the push to roll back property taxes has been gaining momentum across the country.

When you copy a quotation onto a note card, put quotation marks at the beginning and the end so you won't mistake it for a paraphrase or a summary when you write the paper. If the quoted material starts on one page and ends on the next, use a slash mark (/) to show exactly where the shift comes. Then if you use only part of the quotation in your paper, you'll know whether to use one page number or two.

Don't expect to find a gold mine of information on every page you read. Sometimes one page will yield several notes, another page nothing. If you can't immediately gauge the value of some material, take it down. Useless information can be discarded later. Place a rubber band around your growing stack of note cards. Store them in a large envelope closed with a snap or string and labeled with your name and address. Submit them with your completed paper if your instructor requests.

TEACHING STRATEGIES

1. After students have done extensive reading but before they make an outline, you might give them a chance to pull their material together.

CASE HISTORY   *(Continued from page 280)*

Working bibliography in hand, Christine Harding began taking notes for her paper. Most were in summary form, but in a few cases she chose quotations because of the importance of the source, the significance of the material, or the force with which it was presented. One quotation offered the Robot Institute of America's definition of the term *robot*. Several spoke optimistically of the impact of robots, while yet another related a landmark agreement between General Motors and the United Auto Workers on the retraining of displaced workers.

As she read, Christine realized that she should focus on (1) the benefits that robots promise and (2) the steps being taken to lessen their harmful effects, while giving passing attention to (3) the history of robots and (4) the fears they have caused. A plan started to emerge: the paper would begin with a historical overview, touch lightly on the fears aroused by robots, and then deal in depth with the other two matters.

This case history continues on pages 288–89.

ORGANIZING AND OUTLINING

Next comes your formal outline, the blueprint that shows the divisions and subdivisions of your paper, the order of your ideas, and the relationships between ideas and supporting details. An outline is a tool that benefits both writer and reader.

A formal outline follows the pattern shown below:

I.
    A.
    B.
        1.
        2.
            a.
            b.
II.

You can see the significance of an item by its numeral, letter, or number designation and by its distance from the left-hand margin; the farther it's indented, the less important it is. All items with the same designation have roughly the same importance.

Developing Your Outline

Developing an outline is no easy job. It involves arranging material from various sources in an appropriate manner. Sorting and re-sorting your note cards is a good way to proceed. First, determine the main divisions of your paper by checking the summarized notations at the tops of your cards, and then make one stack of cards for each division. Next, review each stack carefully to determine further subdivisions and sort it into smaller stacks. Finally, use the stacks to prepare your outline.

There are two types of formal outlines: *topic* and *sentence*. A topic outline presents all entries as words, short phrases, or short clauses. A sentence outline

Have them set aside their notes and write down what they know about their topics; what position, if any, they want to take and why; what questions still need answering; and how they plan to organize their papers. Such an assessment gives students an overview of their projects. It also helps you spot problems, detect potential plagiarists, and place procrastinators on notice. Students could draft this document in class while you review their note cards.
2. Alternatively, have students report on and answer questions about their research, either to the entire class or in small groups. Such a presentation requires them to pull everything together.

TEACHING STRATEGY

Before students construct a formal outline, you might have them draft a more general plan, perhaps just a list of questions to be answered or issues to be addressed. They can then add to or reorganize the plan as they build it into a formal outline.

presents them as complete sentences. To emphasize the relationships among elements, items of equal importance have parallel phrasing. Although neither is *the* preferred form, a sentence outline includes more details and also your attitude toward each idea. The following segments of a topic and a sentence outline for a paper on tranquilizer dependence illustrate the difference between the two.

Topic Outline

II. The tranquilizer abuse problem
    A. Reasons for the problem
        1. Over-promotion
        2. Over-prescription
        3. Patient's misuse
            a. Dosage
            b. Length of usage
    B. Growth of the problem

Sentence Outline

II. Tranquilizers are widely abused.
    A. Several factors account for the abuse of tranquilizers.
        1. Drug companies over-promote their product.
        2. Doctors often unnecessarily prescribe tranquilizers.
        3. Patients often do not follow their doctors' instructions.
            a. Some patients take more than prescribed doses.
            b. Some continue to use tranquilizers beyond the prescribed time.
    B. The problem of tranquilizer abuse appears to be growing.

Note that the items in the sentence outline are followed by periods, but those in the topic outline are not.

Keying Your Note Cards to Your Outline

When your outline is finished, key your note cards to it by writing at the top of each card the letters and numbers—such as IIA or IIIB2—for the appropriate outline category. Now arrange the cards into one stack, following the order shown in the outline. Finally, start with the top card in the stack and number all of them consecutively. If they later fall off the table or slide out of place, you can easily put them in order again. You might have a few stragglers left over when you complete this keying. Some of these may be worked into your paper as you write or revise it.

CASE HISTORY   *(Continued from page 287)*

Sorting and re-sorting was challenging and at times frustrating for Christine. Since some of her material could be arranged in different ways, she found herself experimenting, evaluating, and rearranging as she tested various options. After much thought and some trial and error, the following *initial draft* of her outline evolved.

I. History of robots

    A. Origin of the term "robot"

    B. Who started the robot revolution?

    C. Who were the first purchasers of robots?

    D. Present status of robots and their future prospects

II. Fears about robots

    A. Company managers' fears

    B. Fears of people not working for companies

III. What benefits will robots bring?

    A. Past benefits of automation

    B. Company benefits

    C. What workers can expect

        1. More interesting jobs

        2. Shorter workweek

        3. There will be fewer workers being injured.

IV. The unemployment threat

    A. Reassignment of displaced workers to other jobs

    B. Where displaced workers will be retrained

        1. By industry

        2. By colleges

        3. By others

This version is marked by nonparallelism, poor phrasing, and inadequate attention to some points. Despite these weaknesses, her tentative outline provided an adequate blueprint for the first draft of Christine's paper.

This case history continues on pages 308–18.

WRITING YOUR RESEARCH PAPER

Some students think of a library research paper as a series of quotations, paraphrases, and summaries, one following the other throughout the paper. Not so. Without question, you use the material of others, but *you* select and organize it according to *your purpose. You* develop insights, and *you* draw conclusions about what you've read. You can best express your conclusions by setting your notes aside, stepping back to gain some perspective, and then expressing your sense of what you've learned. Here again you'll make use of the strategies presented earlier in the book.

TEACHING STRATEGY

As students draft their papers, you might set aside class time to discuss problems they are experiencing. Since some students forget their initial audience and purpose, ask the class to redefine both. Sometimes the initial outline won't work, and changes are necessary.

Writing the First Draft

Your final research results will be expressed in a thesis. You've already drafted a tentative thesis (see page 280), and now you'll probably refine or revise it to accommodate any change in perspective. Position the thesis in your introduction unless you're analyzing a problem or recommending a solution; then you might hold the thesis back until the conclusion. If you do hold it back, state the problem clearly at the outset. Because of the paper's length, it's a good idea to reveal your organizational plan in the introduction.

Write the paper section by section, following the divisions of your outline. But keep in mind that you're not locked into its pattern. If you see an opportunity to develop an important idea that you omitted from your outline, try it. If you discover that it might be better to introduce an item earlier than you intended, go ahead. Just be sure to check your organization later. As you write, think of yourself as supporting the conclusions you have reached with the appropriate material on your note cards, not just as stringing note cards together. You will then incorporate the material on your note cards with your own assessments and with transitional elements that clarify your information and orient the reader.

Because of this paper's length, you will probably need to connect its major sections with transitional paragraphs that pull together the material already covered and prepare the reader for what follows. Don't fret if the style bumps along or connections aren't always clear. These problems can be smoothed out when you revise.

You will, of course, need to give proper credit to the sources you use. The section entitled "Acknowledging and Handling your Sources Properly (MLA and APA Formats)" details appropriate guidelines.

On occasion you may want to include supplementary information that would interrupt the flow of thought if you placed it in the paper. When this happens, use an *explanatory note*.[1] A typical explanatory note might clarify or elaborate upon a point, discuss some side issue, or define a term used in a specialized way.

When you finish writing, let this version sit for a day or two. Then revise it, just as you would with a shorter essay. Keep track of all sources so that preparing the bibliography will go smoothly.

TEACHING STRATEGY

You might comment on student drafts in conference sessions. The scope of their projects often makes such sessions particularly helpful to students.

Preparing Your Finished Copy

Follow the revision guidelines in Chapter 3. In addition, verify that you have

- included all key information
- clearly organized your material
- not overloaded your paper with quotations
- worked in your own observations
- put in-text documentation and source information in proper form

---

[1] This is an explanatory note. Position it at the bottom of the page, spaced four lines away from the main text. If more than one note occurs on a page, double-space between them. If the note carries over to the next page, separate it from your text with a solid, full-length line. Put two spaces above the line and two spaces below it.

Prepare your final draft with a typewriter or word-processor printer that produces dark, readable copy. Don't use a dot-matrix printer. Double-space throughout, including indented block quotations and the list of works you used to prepare the paper.

Two systems for formatting and documenting library research papers are in common use: the Modern Language Association (MLA) system, favored by many English and humanities instructors, and the American Psychological Association (APA) system, used by many social science and psychology instructors. For more information, consult the *MLA Handbook for Writers of Research Papers*, 3rd ed., 1988, and *The Publication Manual of the American Psychological Association*, 3rd ed., 1983.

MLA System.　　Number every page in the upper right-hand corner one-half inch from the top, and precede each number with your last name. Beginning one inch from the top of the first page, type your full name, the instructor's name, the course designation, and the date, all flush with the left-hand margin. Two lines below this, center the title; then double-space before starting your first paragraph. Leave one-inch margins on all four sides except at the top of the first page. Indent the first line of each paragraph five spaces.

The MLA system does not require a title page. However, if your instructor wants one, include the title of the paper, centered about two inches below the top of the sheet; your name, centered in the middle of the sheet; and the course designation, instructor's name, and date, centered about two inches from the bottom. Use capital and lowercase letters for everything on the page. Repeat the title, again in capital and lowercase letters, on the first text page, positioning it about two inches from the top.

The bibliography follows the text of the paper. It begins on a new page and has the heading "Works Cited." List each entry alphabetically according to the author's last name or, if no author is given, by the first significant word in the title. For a work with more than one author, alphabetize by the name that comes first. If you include more than one entry for an author, substitute three unspaced hyphens, followed by a period and a double space, for the author's name in the second and subsequent entries. Begin the first line of each entry at the left-hand margin and indent any subsequent lines five spaces.

APA System.　　Under this system, papers require a title page. Center the title about four inches from the top and position your name, similarly centered, two spaces below the title. About three-fourths of the way from the top of the page, provide the course designation, the name of your instructor, and the date, typed flush with the right-hand margin. Two inches from the bottom of the page, type the words "Running Head," without quotation marks, then a colon and a word or phrase that identifies the paper's topic. Center these items. Use capital and lowercase letters for all items on the title page except the identifying word or phrase, which should be typed in capital letters. Number every page of the text in the upper right-hand corner, beginning with the number "2," without quotation marks. Position a shortened form of the title about one and one-half inches from the top of the page and, two spaces below it, the page number. Use one-and-one-half-inch margins at the bottom and at both sides of each page. Indent the first line of each paragraph five spaces.

The APA system uses the heading "References" for the bibliography and follows the same positioning and alphabetizing guidelines as the MLA system. If the listing includes more than one entry for an author, repeat the name. Begin the first line of each entry at the left-hand margin and indent subsequent lines three spaces.

*A*CKNOWLEDGING AND HANDLING *Y*OUR SOURCES PROPERLY (MLA AND APA FORMATS)

PERSPECTIVE
Some instructors prefer to specify the system students are to follow; others leave the choice to students. Whatever the case, the side-by-side presentation of each system allows the class to note the variations between the two.

To give proper credit to your sources, you must know how to (1) prepare source information, (2) document sources within your text, (3) handle quotations, and (4) avoid plagiarism.

Preparing Accurate Source Information

The kind of information included in bibliographical references depends on the type of source and the documentation system. The entries that follow illustrate basic MLA and APA conventions.

Source Information for Books.   The basic bibliographic reference for a book includes the name of the author, the title of the book, the place of publication, the name of the publisher, and the date of publication. Other information is added as necessary. The order of presentation depends upon which system of listing sources, the MLA or APA, is used. Note that the APA system uses initials rather than first and middle names for authors, editors, and translators.

A Book with One Author

MLA   Wilk, Max. <u>Every Day's a Matinee</u>. New York: Norton, 1975.

APA   Wilk, M. (1975). <u>Every day's a matinee</u>. New York: W. W. Norton.

A Book with Two Authors

MLA   Bolt, A. B., and M. E. Wardle. <u>Communicating with a Computer</u>.
Cambridge, Eng.: Cambridge UP, 1970.

APA   Bolt, A. B., & Wardle, M. E. (1970). <u>Communicating with a computer</u>.
Cambridge: Cambridge University Press.

Note that the APA system reverses the name of the second author and uses "&" instead of "and" between the names. In titles and subtitles, only the first word and proper nouns and adjectives are capitalized.

A Book with More Than Three Authors

Alder, Roger William, et al. Mechanisms in Organic Chemistry. New
    York: Wiley, 1971.

> MLA

Alder, R. W., Finn, T., Bradley, M. A., & Li, A. W. (1971). Mechanisms
    in organic chemistry. New York: John Wiley.

> APA

The MLA system uses "et al." for four or more authors or editors; the APA system gives all author or editor names in the reference list. In the body of a paper, APA style gives the first author's surname followed by et al. *only* for a book or an article with six or more authors.

A Book with Corporate Authorship

United Nations, Public Administration Division. Local Government
    Training. New York: UN, 1968.

> MLA

United Nations, Public Administration Division. (1968). Local
    government training. New York: Author.

> APA

When the author of the work is also the publisher, the APA system uses the word "Author" following the place of publication. If the work is published by another organization, its name replaces "Author."

An Edition Other Than the First

Turabian, Kate L. A Manual for Writers of Term Papers, Theses, and
    Dissertations. 4th ed. Chicago: U of Chicago P, 1973.

> MLA

Turabian, K. L. (1973). A manual for writers of term papers, theses,
    and dissertations (4th ed.). Chicago: University of Chicago Press.

> APA

A Book in Two or More Volumes

Bartram, Henry C. The Cavalcade of America. 2 vols. New York: Knopf,
    1959.

> MLA

Bartram, H. C. (1959). The cavalcade of America. (vols. 1–2). New
    York: Alfred Knopf.

> APA

A Reprint of an Older Work

Matthiessen, F.O. American Renaissance: Art and Expression in the Age
    of Emerson and Whitman. 1941. New York: Oxford UP, 1970.

> MLA

Matthiessen, F. O. (1970). American renaissance: Art and expression in

> APA

the age of Emerson and Whitman. New York: Oxford University Press.
(Original work published 1941)

A Book with an Editor Rather Than an Author

MLA

Deetz, James, ed. Man's Imprint from the Past: Readings in the Methods
of Archaeology. Boston: Little, 1971.

APA

Deetz, J. (Ed.). (1971). Man's imprint from the past: Readings in the
methods of archaeology. Boston: Little Brown.

A Book with Both an Author and an Editor

MLA

Melville, Herman. The Confidence Man. Ed. Hershel Parker. New York:
Norton, 1971.

APA

Melville, H. (1971). The confidence man. (H. Parker, Ed.). New York:
W. W. Norton. (Original work published 1857)

A Translation

MLA

Beauvoir, Simone de. All Said and Done. Trans. Patrick O'Brian. New
York: Putnam, 1974.

APA

Beauvoir, S. de. (1974). All said and done. (P. O'Brian, Trans.). New
York: G. P. Putnam. (Original work published 1972)

An Essay or Chapter in a Collection of Works by One Author

MLA

Woolf, Virginia. "The Lives of the Obscure." The Common Reader, First
Series. New York: Harcourt, 1925. 111–18.

APA

Woolf, V. (1925). The lives of the obscure. In V. Woolf, The common
reader, first series (pp. 111–18). New York: Harcourt Brace
Jovanovich.

An Essay or Chapter in a Collection Containing Several Authors' Contributions Compiled by an Editor

MLA

Angell, Roger. "On the Ball." Subject and Strategy. Ed. Paul Eschholz
and Alfred Rosa. New York: St. Martin's, 1981. 34–41.

APA

Angell, R. (1981). On the ball. In P. Eschholz & Rosa, A. (Eds.),
Subject and strategy (pp. 34–41). New York: St. Martin's Press.

Source Information for Periodicals. The basic information for a
periodical article includes the name of the article's author, the name of the periodical, the title of the article, the date of publication, the page range of the entire
article, and, for scholarly journals, the volume number of the periodical. Again, the

order of presentation depends on the documentation system used. Note that the MLA and APA systems capitalize periodical titles identically.

An Article in a Scholarly Journal Consecutively Paged Through the Entire Volume

Alvord, John A. "Literature and Law in Medieval England." PMLA 92   MLA
      (1977): 941-51.

Alvord, J. A. (1977). Literature and law in medieval England. PMLA,   APA
      92, 941-51.

An Article in a Scholarly Journal That Pages Each Issue Separately

Block, Joel W. "Sodom and Gomorrah: A Volcanic Disaster." Journal of   MLA
      Geological Education 23.5 (1976): 74-77.

Block, J. W. (1976). Sodom and Gomorrah: A volcanic disaster. Journal   APA
      of Geological Education, 23(5), 74-77.

An Article in a Magazine

Kraft, Joseph. "Letter from Saudi Arabia." New Yorker 20 Oct. 1975:   MLA
      111-39.

Kraft, J. (1975, October 20). Letter from Saudi Arabia. New Yorker,   APA
      pp. 111-39.

A Signed Article in a Daily Newspaper

Walker-Lynn, Joyce. "The Marine Corps Now Is Building Women, Too."   MLA
      Chicago Tribune 30 Oct. 1977:I5.

Walker-Lynn, J. (1977, October 30). The Marine Corps now is building   APA
      women, too. Chicago Tribune, sec. I, p. 5.

An Unsigned Article in a Daily Newspaper

"Lawmakers Unite on Mileage Rules." Detroit Free Press 21 Oct. 1975: B3.   MLA

Lawmakers unite on mileage rules. (1975, October 21). Detroit Free   APA
      Press, sec. B, p. 3.

Source Information for Encyclopedia Articles.   The basic information includes the name of the article's author, the title of the article, the name of the encyclopedia, and the date of the edition. Here too the order of presentation differs for the MLA and APA systems.

Davis, Harold S. "Team Teaching." The Encyclopedia of Education. 1974   MLA
      ed.

Davis, H. S. (1974 ed.). Team teaching. The encyclopedia of   APA
      education.

For an unsigned article, the reference begins with the title of the article:

MLA

"Hydrography." The American People's Encyclopedia. 1965 ed.

APA

Hydrography. (1965 ed.). The American people's encyclopedia.

Source Information for Other Sources.
The information presented and the order of presentation depend on the type of source and the documentation system.

Book Reviews

MLA

Koenig, Rhoda. "Billy the Kid." Rev. of Billy Bathgate, by E. L. Doctorow. New York 20 Feb. 1989: 20–21.

APA

Koenig, R. (1989, February 20). Billy the Kid. [Review of Billy Bathgate by E. L. Doctorow]. New York, 20–21.

If the review is untitled, follow the above formats but omit the missing element.

Interviews

MLA

Noriega, Manuel. "A Talk with Manuel Noriega." By Felipe Hernandez. News Report 20 March 1987: 28–30.

APA

Hernandez, F. (1987, March 20). A talk with Manuel Noriega. [Interview with Manuel Noriega]. News Report, pp. 28–30.

If the interview in untitled, use the word "Interview," without quotation marks or underlining, for the MLA system. For the APA system, follow the example above, omitting any mention of a title. If you conducted the interview yourself and are using the MLA system, start with the name of the person interviewed and follow it with the kind of interview and the date conducted.

MLA

Newman, Paul. Personal interview. 19 May 1985.

For the APA system, use an in-text parenthetical citation instead of a bibliographical reference. Include the name of the person interviewed, the notation "personal communication," and the date: (P. Newman, personal communication, May 19, 1985).

Films

MLA

Frankenstein. Dir. James Whale. With Boris Karloff, John Boles, Colin Clive, and Mae Clarke. Universal, 1931.

If you are interested in the contribution of a particular person, start with that person's name.

MLA

Whale, James, dir. Frankenstein. With Boris Karloff, John Boles, Colin Clive, and Mae Clarke. Universal, 1931.

In the APA system, the citation begins with an individual's name and his or her contribution to the film.

```
Whale, J.  (Director).  (1931).  Frankenstein [Film].  With Karloff, B.,        APA
     Boles, J., Clive, C., & Clarke, M.  Hollywood: Universal.
```

Television and Radio Programs

```
Murder, She Wrote.  With Angela Lansbury, David McCallum, and Peter             MLA
     Donat.  CBS.  WLNS, Lansing.  26 Feb. 1989.
```

If you are focusing on the work of some individual connected with the program, begin the entry with his or her name.

```
Anderson, Lindsay, dir.  Glory! Glory!  With Richard Thomas, Ellen             MLA
     Greene, and James Whitmore.  HBO, Detroit.  19, 20 Feb. 1989.
```

When citing one episode out of a series, start with its title, in quotation marks.

```
"Forgive Us Our Debts."  Miami Vice.  With Don Johnson, Edward James           MLA
     Olmos, and Olivia Brown.  NBC.  WOTV, Grand Rapids.  20 April 1987.
```

The APA system does not include a documentation format for television and radio programs.

Record Albums and Tapes

```
Smith, Bessie.  The World's Greatest Blues Singer.  Columbia, GP 33,           MLA
     1948.
```

If you mention the name of a particular item on the record or tape, set it off with quotation marks and position it as shown.

```
Smith, Bessie.  "Down Hearted Blues."  The World's Greatest Blues             MLA
     Singer.  Columbia, GP 33, 1948.
```

The APA system calls for these formats.

```
Smith, Bessie.  (Singer).  (1948).  The world's greatest blues singer.        APA
     (Record No. GP 33).  New York: Columbia.
```

```
Smith, B.  (Singer).  (1948).  Down hearted blues.  The world's greatest      APA
     blues singer.  (Record No. GP 33).  New York: Columbia.
```

Computer Software Programs

```
Southwell, Michael G., and John Fox.  GrammarLab.  Computer software.         MLA
     Applied Logic Consultants, 1985.  IBM PC, 48 KB, disk.
```

```
Southwell, M. G., & Fox, J.  (1985).  GrammarLab.  [Computer program].        APA
     New York: Applied Logic Consultants.  IBM PC, 48 KB, Disk.
```

EXERCISE ANSWERS

1. Dow Chemical Company. *Gas Conditioning Fact Book.* Midland, Michigan: Dow, 1962.

2. "Justices Restrict Action by Courts in Nuclear Cases." *The Wall Street Journal* 5 April 1982: 2.

3. Mills, C. Wright. "The Competitive Personality." *Power, Politics, and People.* Ed. Irving Louis Horowitz. New York: Ballantine, 1963. 263–73.

4. "Where Do We Go From Here?" *U.S. News and World Report* 4 Oct. 1982: 30–33.

5. Theroux, Paul. *The Kingdom by the Sea.* Boston: Houghton, 1983.

6. Chopin, Kate. *The Awakening.* Ed. Margaret Culley. New York: Norton, 1976.

7. Schmerdler, Gertrude. "Parapsychology." *International Encyclopedia of the Social Sciences.* 1968 ed.

8. Willcox, Christopher. "Right-to-Die Bill Sparks Hot Debate." *Detroit Free Press* 28 Feb. 1983: B2.

9. Ember, Carol R., and Melvin Ember. *Anthropology.* New York: Appleton, 1973.

10. Descola, Jean. *A History of Spain.* Trans. Elaine P. Halperin. New York: Knopf, 1962.

11. Flanagan, John T., and Raymond L. Grimer. "Mexico in American Fiction to 1850." *Hispania* 23 (1940): 307–18.

EXERCISE

A. Using the MLA system, write a proper reference for each of the following sets of information.

1. A book titled Gas Conditioning Fact Book. The book was published in 1962 by Dow Chemical Company in Midland, Michigan. No author is named.

2. An unsigned article titled Justices Restrict Action by Courts in Nuclear Cases. The article was published in the April 5, 1982, issue of the Wall Street Journal. It appears on page 2.

3. An essay written by C. Wright Mills and titled The Competitive Personality. The essay appeared in a collection of Mills's writings entitled Power, Politics, and People. The collection was published in 1963 by Ballantine Books in New York. The book is edited and introduced by Irving Louis Horowitz. The essay appears on pages 263 through 273.

4. An unsigned article titled Inflation: Where Do We Go from Here? The article was published in the October 4, 1982, issue of U.S. News and World Report. It appears on pages 30 to 33.

5. A book written by Paul Theroux and titled The Kingdom by the Sea. The book was published in 1983 by the Houghton Mifflin Company in Boston.

6. A book written by Kate Chopin and titled The Awakening. The book, edited by Margaret Culley, was published in 1976 by W. W. Norton and Company in New York.

7. An article written by Gertrude R. Schmerdler and titled Parapsychology. The article appears in volume 11 of the International Encyclopedia of the Social Sciences, published in 1968. It appears on pages 386 through 398.

8. An article written by Christopher Willcox and titled Right-to-Die Bill Sparks Hot Debate. The article was published in the February 28, 1983, issue of the Detroit News. It appears on page 2 of Section B.

9. A book written by Carol R. Ember and Melvin Ember and titled Anthropology. The book was published in 1973 by Appleton-Century-Crofts in New York.

10. A book written by Jean Descola and titled A History of Spain. The book, translated by Elaine P. Halperin, was published in 1962 by Alfred A. Knopf in New York.

11. An article written by John T. Flanagan and Raymond L. Grimer and titled Mexico in American Fiction to 1850. The article was published in 1940 in a journal called Hispania. It appears on pages 307 through 318. The volume number is 23.

12. A book written by Babette Deutsch and titled Poetry in Our Time. The second edition of the book was published in 1956 by Columbia University Press in New York.

13. A book written by Joseph Blotner and titled Faulkner: A Biography. The book was published in two volumes in 1974 by Random House in New York.

14. An article written by Jerome L. Singer and titled Fantasy: The Foundation of Serenity. The article was published in the July 1983 issue of Psychology Today. It appears on pages 32 through 37.

15. A book written by Thomas Beer and titled Stephen Crane: A Study in American Letters. The book was published in 1923 and reprinted in 1972 by Octagon Books in New York.

16. A review of a book written by Jacques Barzun and titled The Culture We Deserve. The review, by Beth Winona, appeared in the March 1989 issue of American Issues magazine and was titled Barzun and Culture. It appeared on pages 46 through 50.

17. An interview of play producer Joseph Papp. The interview was titled Joseph Papp on the New York Theater and appeared in the August 21, 1989, issue of the Long Island News, on pages C3-4. The interviewer was Mary Barnes.

18. A Film titled Casablanca. The film was directed by Michael Curtiz and starred Humphrey Bogart, Ingrid Bergman, Claude Rains, and Paul Henreid. It was released in 1942 by Warner Brothers.

19. A television program titled Wolf. It starred Jack Scalia, Joseph Sirola, Mimi Kuzyk, and Nicholas Surovy. It appeared on WNTR, New York, on September 13, 1989. The station is part of the CBS network.

B. Prepare a proper MLA entry for each of the works you plan to use in writing your paper.

12. Deutsch, Babette. *Poetry in Our Time.* 2nd ed. New York: Columbia UP, 1956.

13. Blotner, Joseph. *Faulkner: A Biography.* 2 vols. New York: Random, 1974.

14. Singer, Jerome L. "Fantasy: The Foundation of Serenity." *Psychology Today* July 1983: 32–37.

15. Beer, Thomas. *Stephen Crane: A Study in American Letters.* 1923. New York: Octagon, 1972.

16. Winona, Beth. "Barzun and Culture." Review of *The Culture We Deserve,* by Jacques Barzun, *American Issues* March 1989: 46–50.

17. Papp, Joseph. "Joseph Papp on the New York Theater." By Mary Barnes. *Long Island News* 21 Aug. 1989: C3-4.

18. *Casablanca.* Dir. Michael Curtiz. With Humphrey Bogart, Ingrid Bergman, Claude Rains, and Paul Henreid. Warner Brothers, 1942.

19. *Wolf.* With Jack Scalia, Joseph Sirola, Mimi Kuzyk, and Nicholas Surovy. CBS. WNTR, New York. 13 Sept. 1989.

Handling In-Text Citations

Both the MLA and APA systems use notations that appear within the text and are set off by parentheses. The systems are illustrated by the following examples.

Basic Citation Form.   For the MLA system, the citation consists of the last name of the author and the page numbers of the publication in which the material originally appeared. The APA system adds the year to the citation. At the writer's option, the items may be grouped together or separated, as shown in the following examples. The bibliographic references preceding the passages follow the MLA format.

Bibliographic Reference

Bryan, Christopher. "Big Steel's Winter of Woes." Time 24 Jan. 1983: 58.

Passage and Citation

Steel workers in this country make an average of twenty-four dollars an hour, including benefits, whereas Japanese workers make just over eleven dollars an hour (Bryan 58).

MLA

Bryan notes that steel workers in this country make an average of twenty-four dollars an hour, including benefits, whereas Japanese workers make just over eleven dollars an hour (58).

MLA

. . . make just over eleven dollars an hour (Bryan, 1983, p. 58).

APA

Bryan (1983) notes that . . . Japanese workers make just over eleven dollars an hour (58).

Bibliographic Reference

Weider, Benjamin, and David Hapgood. <u>The Murder of Napoleon</u>. New York: Congdon, 1982.

Passage and Citation

Four different autopsy reports were filed. All the reports agreed that there was a cancerous ulcer in Napoleon's stomach, but none of them declared that the cancer was the cause of death. Nevertheless, cancer has become accepted as the cause (Weider and Hapgood 72).

. . . Nevertheless, cancer has become accepted as the cause (Weider & Hapgood, 1982, p. 72).

If a source has more than three authors (more than six for the APA), use et al., meaning "and others," for all but the first-named one.

Bibliographic Reference

Baugh, Albert C., et al. <u>A Literary History of England</u>. New York: Appleton, 1948.

Passage and Citation

Although no one knows for certain just when Francis Beaumont and John Fletcher started collaborating, by 1610 they were writing plays together (Baugh et al. 573).

. . . writing plays together (Baugh et al., 1948, p. 573).

Authors with the Same Last Name.　If your notes include authors with the same last name, use the initials of their first names to distinguish them.

Bibliographic References

Adler, Jerry. "Search for an Orange Thread." <u>Newsweek</u> 16 June 1980: 32–34.

Adler, William L. "The Agent Orange Controversy." <u>Detroit Free Press</u> 18 Dec. 1979: B2.

Passage and Citation

As early as 1966, government studies showed that dioxin-contaminated 2,4,5-T caused birth defects in laboratory animals.

Later studies also found that this herbicide was to blame for miscarriages, liver abscesses, and nerve damage (J. Adler 32).

. . . miscarriages, liver abscesses, and nerve damage (J. Adler, 1980, p. 32).

> APA

Separate Works by the Same Author.
If your references include two or more works by the same author, add shortened forms of the titles to your in-text citation if you follow the MLA system. Underline shortened book titles and use quotation marks around article and essay titles. For the APA system, use the conventional name-date-page number entry.

Bibliographic References

Mullin, Dennis. "After U.S. Troops Pull Out of Grenada." U.S. News & World Report 14 Nov. 1983: 22-25.

---. "Why the Surprise Move in Grenada--and What Next." U.S. News & World Report 7 Nov. 1983: 31-34.

Passage and Citation

As the rangers evacuated students, the marines launched another offensive at Grand Mal Bay, then moved south to seize the capital and free the governor (Mullin, "Why the Surprise" 33).

> MLA

. . . and free the governor (Mullin, 1983b, p. 33).

> APA

As the APA example illustrates, if the two works appeared in the same year, put an "a" or a "b," without quotes, after the date to identify whether you are referring to the first or second entry for that author in the bibliography.

Two Separate Sources for the Same Citation.
If two sources provide essentially the same information and you wish to mention both in one parenthetical citation, group them together with a semicolon between them and position them as you would any other citation.

Bibliographic References

Bryce, Bonnie. "The Controversy over Funding Community Colleges." Detroit Free Press 13 Nov. 1988: A4.

Warshow, Harry. "Community College Funding Hits a Snag." Grand Rapids Press 15 Nov. 1988: A2.

Passage and Citation

In contending that a 3 percent reduction in state funding for community colleges would not significantly hamper their

> MLA

operations, the governor overlooks the fact that community college
enrollment is expected to jump by 15 percent next year (Bryce A4;
Warshow A2).

In contending that a 3 percent reduction in state funding for
community colleges would not significantly hamper their
operations, the governor overlooks the fact that community college
enrollment is expected to jump by 15 percent next year (Bryce,
1988, p. A4; Warshow, 1988, p. A2).

Unsigned References. When you use a source for which no author is
given, the in-text citation consists of all or part of the title, the appropriate page
numbers, and, for the APA system, the date.

Bibliographic Reference

"Reform in sight for People's Right to Know." American Libraries 4
(1975): 540.

Passage and Citation

In 1974, Congress proposed several amendments to the Freedom of
Information Act, only to have President Ford reject them on the
grounds that they were "unconstitutional and unworkable." But
while Ford was out of the country in early 1975, Congress voted
overwhelmingly to enact them into law ("Reform in Sight" 540).

. . . overwhelmingly to enact them into law (Reform in sight, 1975,
p. 540).

Citing Quotations. When the quotation is run into the text, position the
citation as shown below.

Bibliographic Reference

Verney, Thomas, M.D., and John Kelly. The Secret Life of the Unborn
Child. New York: Simon, 1981.

Passage and Citation

Investigators who have studied mother-child bonding have found
that "women who bond become better mothers, and their babies almost
always are physically healthier, emotionally more stable and
intellectually more acute than infants taken from their mothers
right after birth" (Verney and Kelly 146).

> . . . mothers right after birth" (Verney & Kelly, 1981, p. 146).

APA

With longer, indented quotations, skip two horizontal spaces after the end punctuation and type the reference in parentheses.

Bibliographic Reference

Newhouse, John. "The Diplomatic Round: A Freemasonry of Terrorism."

New Yorker 8 July 1985: 46–63.

Passage and Citation

One commentator offers this assessment of why foreign terrorist

groups don't operate in this country:

MLA

> The reason that America has been spared so far,
> apparently, is that it is less vulnerable than Europe,
> especially to Middle Eastern extremists. Moving in and
> out of most European countries isn't difficult for non-
> Europeans; border controls are negligible. But American
> customs and immigration authorities, being hyper-alert
> to drug traffic, tend to pay attention to even marginally
> doubtful people, and a would-be terrorist . . . could come
> under surveillance for the wrong reason. (Newhouse 63)

> . . . come under surveillance for the wrong reason. (Newhouse,
> 1985, p. 63)

APA

Indirect Citations. If you use a quotation from person A that you obtained from a book or article written by person B, or you paraphrase such a quotation, put "qtd. in" before the name of the publication's author in the parenthetical reference.

Bibliographic Reference

Klein, Joe. "Ready for Rudy." New York 6 Mar. 1989: 30–37.

Passage and Citation

U.S. attorney Rudolph Giuliani favors the death penalty for "the
murder of a law-enforcement officer, mass murder, a particularly
heinous killing" but would impose it only "when there is certainty
of guilt well beyond a reasonable doubt" (qtd. in Klein 37).

MLA

" . . . there is certainty of guilt well beyond a reasonable doubt"
(qtd. in Klein, 1989, p. 37).

APA

Authors Identified in Text. Sometimes you'll want to introduce a paraphrase, summary, or quotation with the name of its author. In this case the page number may be positioned immediately after the name or follow the material cited.

Bibliographic Reference

Jacoby, Susan. "Waiting for the End: On Nursing Homes." New York Times Magazine 31 March 1974: 80.

Passage and Citation

MLA	Susan Jacoby (80) sums up the grim outlook of patients in bad nursing homes by noting that they are merely waiting to die.
MLA	Susan Jacoby sums up the grim outlook of patients in bad nursing homes by noting that they are merely waiting to die (80).
APA	Susan Jacoby (1974, p. 80) sums up . . .
APA	Susan Jacoby (1974) sums up . . . waiting to die (p. 80).

EXERCISE ■ **Using the MLA system, write a proper in-text citation for each of the bibliographic references you prepared for parts A and B on pages 298–99. Assume that you have not used the author's name to introduce the material you cite.**

Handling Quotations

Set off quotations fewer than five lines long (fewer than forty words long for the APA system) with quotation marks and run them into the text of the paper. For longer quotes, omit the quotation marks and indent the material ten spaces from the left-hand margin (four spaces for the APA system). Double-space the typing. If you quote part or all of one paragraph, don't further indent the first line. If you quote two or more consecutive paragraphs, indent each one's first line three additional spaces. Use single quotation marks for a quotation within a shorter quotation and double marks for a quotation within a longer, indented quotation. The following examples illustrate the handling of quotations. The documentation and indentation follow the MLA guidelines.

Short Quotation

Ellen Goodman offers this further observation about writers who peddle formulas for achieving success through selfishness: "They are all Doctor Feelgoods, offering placebo prescriptions instead of strong medicine. They give us a way to live with ourselves, perhaps, but not a way to live with each other" (16).

Quotation Within Short Quotation

The report further stated, "All great writing styles have their wellsprings in the personality of the writer. As Buffon said, 'The style is the man'" (Duncan 49).

Quotation Within Longer, Indented Quotation

Barbara Tuchman's The Proud Tower presents a somewhat different view of the new conservative leaders:

> Besides riches, rank, broad acres, and ancient lineage,
> the new government also possessed, to the regret of the
> liberal opposition, and in the words of one of them, "an
> almost embarrassing wealth of talent and capacity."
> Secure in authority, resting comfortably on their
> electoral majority in the House of Commons and on a
> permanent majority in the House of Lords, of whom four-
> fifths were conservatives, they were in a position,
> admitted the same opponent, "of unassailable strength."
> (4)

Always provide some context for material that you quote. Various options exist. When you quote from a source for the first time, you might provide the author's full name and the source of the quotation, perhaps indicating the author's expertise as well. The passage just above omits the author's expertise; the passage below includes it.

> Writing in Newsweek magazine, Riena Gross, chief psychiatric
> social worker at Illinois Medical Center in Chicago, said, "Kids
> have no real sense that they belong anywhere or to anyone as they
> did ten or fifteen years ago. Parents have loosened the reins, and
> kids are kind of floundering" (74).

Or you might note the event prompting the quotation and then the author's name.

> Addressing a seminar at the University of Toronto, Dr. Joseph
> Pomeranz speculated that "acupuncture may work by activating a
> neural pain suppression mechanism in the brain" (324).

On other occasions you might note only the author's full name and expertise.

> Economist Richard M. Cybert, President of Carnegie-Mellon
> University, offers the following sad prediction about the steel
> industry's future: "It will never be as large an industry as it has

> been. There are a lot of plants that will never come back and many
> laborers that will never be rehired" (43).

When quoting from a source with no author given, introduce the quotation with the name of the source.

> Commenting upon the problems that law enforcement personnel have in
> coping with computer crime, <u>Credit and Financial Management</u>
> magazine pointed out that "A computer crime can be committed in
> three hundredths of a second, and the criminal can be thousands of
> miles from the 'scene,' using a telephone" ("Computer Crime" 43).

After first citing an author's full name, use only the last name for subsequent references.

> In answering the objections of governmental agencies to the Freedom
> of Information Act, Wellford commented, "Increased citizen access
> should help citizens learn of governmental activities that weaken
> our First Amendment freedoms. Some administrative inconvenience
> isn't too large a price to pay for that" (137).

Page numbers are not helpful when you cite passages from plays and poems since these literary forms are available in many editions. When you quote from a play, identify the act, scene, and line numbers. Use Arabic numbers separated by periods. Here's how to cite Act 2, Scene 1, lines 258–63 of Shakespeare's *Othello*:

> That Cassio loves her, I do well believe it;
> That she loves him, 'tis apt, and of great credit:
> The Moor, how be it that I endure him not,
> Is of a constant, loving, noble nature;
> And I dare think he'll prove to Desdemona
> A most dear husband. (<u>Othello</u> 2.1. 258–63)

When quoting from a short poem, use "line" or "lines" and the line number(s):

> In "Dover Beach," Matthew Arnold offers this melancholy assessment
> of the state of religion:
>
>> The Sea of Faith
>> Was once, too, at the full, and round earth's shore
>> Lay like the folds of a bright girdle furl'd.
>> But now I only hear
>> Its melancholy, long, withdrawing roar. (lines 21–26)

In quoting poetry that has been run into the text, use a slash mark (/) to indicate the shift from one line to the next in the original:

In his ode "To Autumn," Keats says that Autumn is the "Season of mists and mellow fruitfulness,/Close bosom-friend of the maturing sun" (lines 1-2).

Avoiding Plagiarism

Plagiarism occurs when a writer uses another person's material without properly acknowledging the debt. Sometimes plagiarism is deliberate, but often it happens because students simply don't understand what must be acknowledged and documented. Deliberate or not, plagiarism is absolutely unacceptable. *Any summary, paraphrase, or quotation you include in your paper must be documented*. The only types of information escaping this requirement are those listed below.

1. Common Knowledge. Common knowledge is information that most educated people would know. For instance, there's no need to document a statement that the Disney theme parks in California and Florida attract thousands of visitors each year. However, if you include precise daily, monthly, or yearly figures, then documentation is necessary.
2. Your own conclusions. As you write your paper, you'll incorporate your own conclusions at various points. (See the margin notes accompanying Christine Harding's library research paper, pages 313, 315, and 316, for example.) Such comments require no documentation. The same holds true for your own research. If you polled students on a campus issue, simply present the findings as your own.
3. Facts found in many sources. Facts such as the year of Shakespeare's death, the size of the 1992 national budget deficit, and the location of the Taj Mahal need not be documented.

Any piece of information not set off with quotation marks must be in your own words. Otherwise, even though you name your source, you plagiarize by stealing the original phrasing.

The following passages illustrate the improper and proper use of source material.

Original Passage

One might contend, of course, that our country's biological diversity is so great and the land is so developed—so criss-crossed with the works of man—that it will soon be hard to build a dam anywhere without endangering some species. But as we develop a national inventory of endangered species, we certainly can plan our *necessary* development so as to exterminate the smallest number possible . . .

James L. Buckley, "Three Cheers for the Snail Darter," *National Review*, September 14, 1979: 1144-45.

Plagiarism

Our country's biological diversity is so great and the land is so developed that it will soon be hard to build a dam anywhere without

PERSPECTIVE

The sad fact of plagiarism, intentional or otherwise, cannot be ignored. Advertisements in many school papers offer to sell term papers, students write them for a fee, and fraternities and sororities often keep "A" models on file. There are, however, several ways of coping with the problem.

TEACHING STRATEGIES
1. Have students bring in the appropriate original sources and proofread in class for instances of unintentional plagiarism in their papers. This activity reinforces the message that plagiarism is unacceptable and also gives students an opportunity to detect and redress problems.
2. Have students turn in the paper in stages—working bibliography, note cards, rough outline, different drafts, and the like. If students are asked to revise according to your responses, they can't simply turn in a pre-written paper. Refuse to accept a finished draft on an entirely new topic "because the old one just wasn't working out."
3. You might add unique requirements that serve as plagiarism fingerprints, such as including faculty interviews (on their topic) in the paper.

SUGGESTED INSTRUCTOR READING

Galles, G. "Psst, Kid! Wanna Buy a Term Paper?" Christian Science Monitor 25 Sept. 1989: 19. Analyzes the operation of term paper mills and the difficulties teachers face in dealing with them. In a separate listing, Galles details some creative "Barriers to Plagiarism" that instructors might like to consider.

```
endangering some species. But as we develop a national inventory of

endangered species, we certainly can plan our necessary

development so as to exterminate the smallest number possible.
```

This writer clearly plagiarizes. The absence of Buckley's name and the failure to enclose his words in quotation marks create the impression that this passage is the student's own work.

Plagiarism

```
Our country's biological diversity is so great and the land so

developed that in the near future we may pose a threat to some

creature whenever we construct a dam. By developing a national

inventory of endangered species, however, we can plan necessary

development so as to preserve as many species as possible (Buckley

1144).
```

This version credits the ideas to Buckley, but the student has plagiarized by failing to put quotation marks around the phrasing (underlined above) that was copied from the original. As a result, readers will think that the passage represents the student's own wording.

Proper Use of Original

```
America has so many kinds of plants and animals, and it is so built

up, that in the near future we may pose a threat to some living

thing whenever we construct a dam. If, however, we knew which of our

nation's plants and animals were threatened, we could use this

information to preserve as many species as possible (Buckley 1144).
```

This student has identified the author and used her own words. As a result, no plagiarism occurs.

Plagiarism is a serious offense because it robs the original writer of recognition. Students caught plagiarizing risk failure in the course or perhaps suspension from school. Whenever you are unsure whether material requires documentation, supply a reference. And always handle direct quotations by following the guidelines beginning on page 304.

EXAMPLE STUDENT RESEARCH PAPER

CASE HISTORY *(Concluded)*

Using her outline and thesis statement as a guide, Christine prepared a first draft of her paper, following the MLA format required by her instructor. After putting it aside for two days, she revised it carefully. She then revised the topic outline she had previously prepared and followed it while drafting the sentence version, which appears on pages 309–10. The final draft of the paper itself is on pages 311–18. Direct your attention to its noteworthy features.

Sentence Outline

Thesis Statement: Despite the misgivings of some people, robots will probably have beneficial effects on industry and its workforce.

I.   Robots have a short but highly successful history.

    A. Karel Capek, a Czech writer, coined the term "robot."

    B. George C. Devol and Joseph F. Engelberger launched the robot revolution.

    C. The first robots were sold to automakers.

    D. Robots are now firmly established in American industry.

    E. Robots will continue to become more sophisticated and important to American industry.

II.   Many people fear the impact that robots will have.

    A. Corporate management often looks with disfavor on robots.

        1. Some managers fear their financial impact.

        2. Some worry about unemployment.

    B. Some people outside of corporations also worry about unemployment.

III.   Robots are another form of mechanization, and mechanization is beneficial, not harmful.

    A. Historical evidence points up the benefits of automation.

        1. The introduction of the assembly line into the auto industry caused manufacturing costs and car prices to plummet and sales and employment to leap.

        2. The invention of the Hargreaves spinning jenny benefited employment in Britain's textile industry.

    B. Robots offer corporate managers a number of advantages.

        1. They are more efficient than human workers.

        2. They are more economical than human workers.

    C. Robots offer advantages to workers as well as managers.

        1. Jobs become more interesting and challenging.

        2. Workers will spend less time on the job.

            3. Workers will face fewer health and safety risks.

IV.   Robots do not pose a serious unemployment threat.

    A. Most displaced workers will move into jobs directly or indirectly associated with robots.

    B. Efforts are now underway to provide the specialized training these workers will need.

        1. Industry is initiating training programs.

        2. Colleges are also rising to the challenge.

           a. Twelve Michigan colleges are offering or considering programs.

           b. Nationwide, over 30 colleges have programs.

        3. Government and private organizations may also play a role in training workers.

Christine Harding
Professor Reinking
English 113
May 7, 1990

Robots in Industry: A Boon for Everyone

Historically, industry has relied on humans to perform its
tasks. In the beginning, productivity depended upon the sheer
muscle power of workers, augmented by a few hand-operated
devices. With the Industrial Revolution, these devices gave way
to ever-larger, ever-more-complicated machines that made modern
factories possible and multiplied enormously the production
capacity of their workers. Now technological advances have
ushered in a new Industrial Revolution, one in which robots will
take over many of the operations now carried out by conventional
machines and their human attendants.

Exactly what is a robot? The Robot Institute of America
defines it as "a reprogrammable multifunctional manipulator
designed to move material, parts, tools, or specialized devices
through variable programmed motions for the performance of a
variety of tasks" (Rosenblatt 349). A robot consists essentially
of a manipulator arm, a pair of grippers, an electrical control
unit, and a power pack to move the mechanical arm (McElroy 43).
Currently, efforts are underway to develop robots that can "see"
and "feel" so that they can respond to changes in the environment
without expensive human assistance (Rosenblatt, 350, 352).
Although the rapid growth in robot technology has aroused some
fears of its consequences, robots will actually benefit
everyone, and efforts are being made to lessen any harmful impact
upon the work force.

As Rosenblatt notes, the term "robot" was coined in 1921 by
Karel Capek, a Czech writer, who used it to designate the
humanoid factory workers in his satirical play R.U.R., or
Rosson's Universal Robots (348). George C. Devol, an engineer,
developed the basic technology that made the robot industry
possible. In 1956, Devol met Joseph F. Engelberger, a physics
student at Columbia University, and shared with him his dream of

Title reflects main thrust
of paper

Context provided for
short, run-in quote within
quotation marks

Thesis statement reflects
content and organization

311

a day when robots would be used for a broad spectrum of industrial tasks. Engelberger, an avid disciple of Devol, went on to become the founder and president of Unimation, Inc., which produced the first robots industry was to buy (Feder F6).

These first robots were sold to auto makers. The pioneer purchaser, General Motors, installed a robot welding line in its Lordstown, Ohio, auto plant, where it was used in respot welding on the 1969 Vega automobile. By 1975, Ford was using robots for a whole range of welding operations, and its Kansas City facility was recognized as the world's most technically advanced auto assembly plant (Weisel 19).

Robots have become firmly established in many industries. By 1982, 29 percent of all automated factories were using robots, 19 percent were planning to install them very soon, and 44 percent were considering them for a later time ("Robot Productivity" 53). Specific functions now performed by robots in automobile plants and elsewhere include die casting, arc and spot welding, machine tool loading and unloading, forging, shot blasting, and spray painting (Weisel 18).

Statistics, forecasts of functions and sales provide interest, depth

As time passes, robots will become more sophisticated, and their industrial role will continue to enlarge. The Robot Institute of America forecasts that by 1990, 25 percent of all robots will have "vision," 20 percent will be able to "feel," and 88 percent will be controlled by computers (McElroy 43). At that time, the Institute says, the nation's robot population will number between 75,000 and 100,000 (Hunt and Hunt 3). Robots will do 15 to 20 percent of all arc welding, 30 to 35 percent of all materials handling, and 35 to 40 percent of all assembly work in our factories (Rosenblatt 360). Annual sales of industrial robots in the United States will be as much as $2.5 billion, as compared to 1984 sales of $190 million (Stepanek 4B). Similarly, annual sales of service robots are expected to top $2 billion by 1995, up from 1987's $120 million (Bylinsky 82).

The swift industrial inroads made by robots have led many people to fear their impact on industry as well as on the overall economy. Corporate management is often reluctant to invest in robots, reasoning that workers are plentiful and that the high initial cost and long payback period could jeopardize the financial position of their companies. Many managers also fear that robots may bring about massive unemployment (Rosenblatt 360). Others outside the corporate fold have criticized the impact of robots upon the employment picture. Thus Harley Shaiken, a labor analyst at the Massachusetts Institute of Technology, wonders, "What of the worker in Flint, Mich.? He's being asked to commit economic suicide so GM can return to profitability" (qtd. in Skrzycki 25). William Wimpisinger, of the International Association of Machinists, goes so far as to declare that "The union worker is the endangered species in the robot revolution" (qtd. in Cromie 16). At first glance, this gloomy assessment of the impact of robotics on the work force seems only too well-founded since, Skrzycki notes, robots may eliminate 1.3 million jobs by the year 2000 (25).

Short quotations put in context, enclosed in quotation marks

These fears would shrink or disappear if the people holding them would only stop to realize that robots are merely another form of automation or mechanization. Historical evidence shows that automation leads to more, not less, employment. Consider, for example, Henry Ford's introduction of the assembly line and mass production into the automobile industry. This innovation proved spectacularly successful, boosting the productivity of the work force by 8.5 percent a year and reducing by 56 percent the number of hours needed to build each vehicle. As a result, the average price of a Ford car dropped by more than 62 percent, sales increased tenfold, and the employment of assembly workers in the Ford factory jumped from 37,000 to 206,000 in just one decade (Vedder 26).

Some 140 years earlier, the invention of the Hargreaves spinning jenny brought about much the same happy outcome in Britain's textile industry. This invention made it possible for one spinner to do as much in a day as 200 could have done previously. But instead of creating mass unemployment, the jenny led to a sharp jump in the work force—from approximately 100,000 in 1770 to 350,000 in 1800 (Deane 90–91). As more and more industries become highly robotized, we can expect this pattern of falling prices and surging sales to repeat itself.

Independent conclusion; no reference necessary

Robots offer corporate managers a number of advantages over human workers. To begin, robots require much less instruction and can outperform even the best humans by working around the clock with precision and at high speed. Furthermore, robots, unlike humans, can be reassigned and reprogrammed for new jobs instantly (Cromie 13). Adopting robots also allows management to avoid production losses that stem from human frailty. A survey cited by Walter Weisel found that 30 percent of the workday is lost because of scheduling problems, misunderstood assignments, improper staffing, and poor discipline (18). Other sources have pointed out the extent to which sickness, vacations, physical disabilities, injuries, carelessness, and boredom cut into productivity. Robots have none of these shortcomings. In fact, they surpass human capabilities by working in hot, dirty, noisy, dangerous, fume-filled areas without any type of safety equipment (Chamberlin 32).

Not surprisingly, robots, despite their high initial cost, are much more economical than human workers. According to the Robot Institute of America, an average human assembly-line worker costs management about $17 per hour in wages, fringe benefits, and the expenses associated with absenteeism, work stoppages, and so on. In contrast, the cost of a robot—including maintenance charges, indirect labor support costs, depreciation, and property tax liabilities—works out to be $5 to $6 per hour (Cromie 13). Often the costs of a robot can be recovered in two years, a small fraction of its working life ("Robots Are Coming" 75).

> Citation for article with no author specified

Robots offer important advantages to workers as well as to corporate management. The introduction of robots into a plant makes it necessary for workers to tend their charges more carefully as well as to show more ability to plan and to exercise good judgment. The result: more interesting and mentally challenging work (Mueller et al. 14-15). Here's what The Economist of London says about this matter:

> Extended quotation, indented ten spaces, without quotation marks, double-spaced

Most of the skilled workers doing 4-7% of American jobs that could be taken over by robots by 1990 should welcome their incursion. Robots will have to be taught to do their jobs and be supervised while they work. American companies are discovering that few people can teach or supervise a robot better than the man who did the job before. Although fewer people are needed in the trade as a whole . . . the skilled people in

> Omission within sentence, ellipsis

factories where robots are welcomed generally get more interesting jobs. . . . Joblessness is created in firms that fail to welcome robots. ("Robots Are Coming" 75)

Omission at end of sentence, period and ellipsis

Besides having more interesting jobs, employees in plants with robots will have to work fewer hours—possibly only a four-day week—and will earn more money (McElroy 43). When this happens, a significant number of workers may well use the extra time in creative and socially useful ways—painting, carpentry, restoring antiques, and becoming involved in public issues such as conservation, for example. If enough of them do so, the result could be a noticeable improvement in the quality of American life.

Independent conclusion; no reference needed

Thanks to robots, workers will face fewer on-the-job health and safety risks. In many factories robots have already taken over welding, spray painting, and other heavy or hazardous work, and efforts are now underway to develop robots that will take over other dangerous tasks. Several robots are on the drawing board for the mining industry, including those that excavate, haul coal, and bolt mine roofs. The nuclear power industry is developing robots that walk up poles and that search out flaws in power plants. For the construction industry, robots that dig around natural gas lines and install tunnel liners are in the offing (Armstrong 6). By 1995, the Society of Manufacturing Engineers says, robots should bring about a 41 percent decrease in factory injuries (McElroy 44).

Despite predictions to the contrary, robots have not created an unemployment problem, nor should they have a significant direct impact on the nation's employment level in the future. Government studies show that by 1990 robots will reduce the overall employment level by less than 1 percent. Many displaced workers will move into jobs building, installing, programming, and serving robots. Still others will become involved in designing and engineering them, while some will provide a backup cadre of clerical workers and managers (Hunt and Hunt 82, 139).

To handle these jobs, workers will have to be more highly trained than in the past. Over one half of the jobs created by robot technology will require two or more years of college, while others will require extensive on-the-job training. Industry has risen to the challenge by initiating training programs to provide the needed technical and scientific know-how. In this connection, General Motors and the United Auto Workers have endorsed a "Statement on Technological Progress," which states that

Context provided for quotation

> In view of the corporation's interest in affording maximum opportunity for employes [sic] to progress with advancing technology, the Corporation shall make available short-range, specialized training programs for those employees who have the qualifications to perform the new or changed work, where such programs are reasonable and practicable. (qtd. in Hunt and Hunt 156-57)

To implement training, GM is providing $80 million annually. This development reflects industry's awareness of the problems workers face from robots and a willingness to help cope with them.

A number of colleges are now instituting programs to train robot technicians. In 1983, Hunt and Hunt report, four Michigan junior colleges were offering such programs, and eight others were considering them. These programs have proved extremely popular; at one school, 600 students enrolled in the semester that the program began, and over 800 enrolled the second semester (159-60). Nationwide, over 30 colleges and universities have robotics programs, including such prestigious institutions as the Massachusetts Institute of Technology and Pittsburgh's Carnegie-Mellon University. Graduates can expect salaries ranging upward from $30,000 (Rosenblatt 360).

Government can also play a role in retraining the victims of robotization for different jobs. Help could, for example, be provided in the form of vouchers to cover the costs of retraining in private or public schools. In addition, government could distribute labor market information and help reshape vocational educational programs to meet the needs of industry (Vedder 20). As time passes, help may come from other sources. Labor unions, for instance, might establish their own retraining programs. Other organizations—churches, service clubs, charitable

groups——might also offer some retraining or help displaced
workers find jobs unconnected with robots.

    Robots are firmly and irreversibly entrenched in industry.
Already they have greatly altered the manufacture of many
products, and in the coming years they could transform the world
of work as greatly as did the first Industrial Revolution in the
18th century. But even greater potential exists. As technology
advances, we can expect robots to move out of the factory and
into the wider world. Someday, household robots may vacuum our
floors, feed our dog, cook our meals, take out our trash, balance
our checkbook, and then, for relaxation, challenge us to
checkers or chess. Out-of-the-home mechanical servants may
include robot security officers, fire fighters, ditch diggers,
trash collectors, and salesclerks, to name just a few
possibilities. Whatever the future of robots, we can be sure of
one thing: the world will never be the same as before they
arrived on the scene.

> Independent conclusion;
> no reference needed

> Stresses future of robots;
> reinforces revolutionary
> aspect

Works Cited

Armstrong, Scott. "Hard-Hat Robots May Take Risk Out of Dangerous
    Jobs." Christian Science Monitor 30 Aug. 1983: 6.

Bylinsky, Gene. "Invasion of the Service Robots." Fortune 14
    Sept. 1987: 81-88.

Chamberlin, Leslie J. "Facing up to Robotation." USA Today Nov.
    1982: 31-33.[1]

Cromie, William J. "Robots: A Growing, Maturing Population."
    Sciquest Mar. 1981: 12-16.

Deane, Phyllis. The First Industrial Revolution. Cambridge, Eng.:
    Cambridge UP, 1979.

Feder, Barnaby J. "He Brought the Robot to Life." New York Times 21
    Mar. 1982: F6.

Hunt, H. Allan, and Timothy L. Hunt. Human Resource Implications
    of Robotics. Kalamazoo, MI: The W.E. Upjohn Institute for
    Employment Research, 1983.

> Entry for newspaper
> article

> Entry for periodical article
> with one author

> Entry for book with one
> author

> Entry for book with two
> authors

[1]This is the magazine USA Today, not the newspaper of that title.

McElroy, John. "Industrial Robot Growth: How Experts See It."
Automotive Industries Sept. 1982: 43–45.

Mueller, Eva, et al. Technological Advance in an Expanding
Economy. Ann Arbor: U of Mich P, 1969.

"Robot Productivity." Production Engineering May 1982: 52–55.

"Robots are Coming to Industry's Service." The Economist 29 Aug.
1981: 71–75.

Rosenblatt, Jean. "The Robot Revolution." Editorial Research
Reports 14 May 1982: 347–62.

Skrzycki, Cindy. "Will Robots Bring More Jobs—Or Less?" U.S. News
& World Report 5 Sept. 1983: 25.

Stepanek, Marcia. "Automotive Leader Directs Invasion of a
Cutthroat Industry." Detroit Free Press 28 May 1984: B1, 4.

Vedder, Richard K. Robotics and the Economy. Subcommittee on
Monetary and Fiscal Policy, Joint Economic Committee, U.S.
97th Cong. 26 Mar. 1982.

Weisel, Walter K. "The Robot's Role in Productivity." Production
Engineering Dec. 1981: 18–19.

Side annotations (left margin):

Entry for book with multiple authors

Entries for periodical journal articles with no author given

Entry for popular magazine article

Entry for government document

USING A WORD PROCESSOR

A word processor can help you with the various stages of library research. Several guidelines will enhance your efficiency as you proceed.

Taking Notes

Students with portable units sometimes take them into the library and enter notes as they read their sources, despite the inconvenience that often results. In most cases, though, it works best to take notes on cards, then afterward enter them and your bibliographical references into your word processor. You can type notes into one central file and distribute them later to separate files by topic or distribute them as you go along. Programs are available that will alphabetize your bibliography after it has been entered.

As you proceed, take great care to distinguish between your notes and your thoughts about them. One good way to do this is to establish some system, such as typing notes in boldface and putting brackets around your thoughts. To avoid inadvertently using the exact words of others without giving proper credit, always put quotation marks around directly quoted material. As an added safeguard you might also use different spacing for quotations. To identify the sources of your notes, you could number them to match the number of the source or end each note with the author's name. For an anonymous source use a shortened title. Finally, don't neglect to keep printout copies of your notes and bibliography to guard against accidental erasure or a power surge.

Outlining

Many word-processing programs provide options that facilitate outlining. With some programs you can compare two arrangements side by side; others enable you to call up your stored and organized notes on one side of the screen and create your outline on the other side.

Don't let any limitations in your program cramp your explorations of possibilities. If your program lets you compare two outlines but you'd like to check more, make a second and if necessary a third printout; then examine them side by side. Similarly, if an outline includes more items than a single screen will accommodate, continue on a second screen and use printouts to check the complete product.

Drafting

Students follow different approaches when drafting on a word processor. Some follow the outline section by section, entering their notes and any thoughts that previously occurred to them, then go through everything again and add more material. Others finish off one section before moving on to the next, some by focusing on their notes and then developing thoughts that elaborate on them, others by developing their thoughts and working in their notes afterward. Follow the procedure that works best for you.

When you write the paper, fight the urge simply to string your notes together. Such an approach results in a draft that lurches from one bit of information to another without any consistent style or proper attention to the underlying thesis. If you find yourself merely typing in notes, stop, open a separate file, read each note carefully, and then enter your thoughts concerning it. When you've examined all the notes, begin the drafting process over again, integrating your notes and your thoughts in the new file.

As you compose, don't overfill any of your files; too many words leave little room for revision. You can avoid this problem by establishing a separate file for each section of your paper.

Revising and Formatting

Students often hesitate to revise research papers because of their length. A word processor gives you an edge. You can isolate different sections and experiment with them; move large sections of the text around; or, if you used separate files for different sections, change transitions to reflect different orders. When you make such changes, check to see that you maintain the flow of the paper. An adjustment in one section must mesh logically and stylistically with what precedes and follows. Reviewing a printout offers the best opportunity to check your paper's continuity. As you revise, always keep copies of earlier versions. Some part that seemed ineffective may fill a gap or take on a new look in view of your changes.

Finally, the formatting capabilities of word processors can be a powerful asset. Most programs will position page numbers, set margins properly, and add your name at the top of each page. Some programs will also indent bibliographic entries properly. Don't, however, neglect your instructor's specifications with regard to spacing, print style, and the like.

Additional Research Strategies: Interviews, Questionnaires, Direct Observations

The library isn't the only source of information for research writing. Investigators also gather information through *primary research*, which includes such activities as consulting public records in local, state, and federal archives, performing experiments, conducting interviews, sending out questionnaires, and making direct observations of various kinds.

This chapter focuses on the latter three types, the most common primary research strategies.

*T*HE VALUE OF PRIMARY RESEARCH

What makes primary research so valuable? First, it allows individuals and organizations to collect recent information, often unavailable elsewhere, that precisely suits their needs. A company that has developed a new product can't turn to published data to estimate its sales prospects; such information simply doesn't exist. But polling test users with a well-crafted questionnaire could suggest some answers and perhaps also some tips for improving the product. Similarly, someone wanting to gauge the success of an ongoing clothing drive by a local charitable organization might interview its director.

Even when published material exists, it may not contain desired information. Although numerous articles discuss student attitudes about required courses, you probably wouldn't find a report that explores student reaction to a new general-education requirement at your school. You could, however, assemble this information by distributing a questionnaire. The findings might even contradict, and therefore cause you to question, the conclusions of others.

Primary research can also yield unexpected and significant material. Suppose you're investigating adult illiteracy, and you interview a professor with a specialty in this area of study. She explains the reasons why people who can't read resist help and supplies several relevant examples. Such information might not appear anywhere in print. Certainly the resulting report would carry more weight and elicit more interest than one without such insights.

requirements they can expect
in their courses and careers.
Students could then share
their findings with the class.
3. As students work on their
library papers, have them determine what types of primary
research form the basis of the
books and articles they read.
Ask students to report their
findings to the class or to
present them in a short
paper.

You can integrate primary research results into a report that consists largely of *secondary research*, the kind that draws on library materials. The student who wrote the research paper on robots (see pages 311–18) might have included information from an interview of a manager at a plant using robot technology, the results of a questionnaire given to factory workers, or even observations of a factory using robots. Often, however, writers detail the methods of their primary research in a separate report. If your employer asked you to interview users of a new computer system to determine their degree of satisfaction, you would present a written summary of your findings.

GENERAL PRINCIPLES FOR PRIMARY RESEARCH

Primary research, like all research, requires well-formulated questions. Such questions must be specifically focused, contain clearly defined terms, and be answerable by the actual research. A vague, general question such as "What attitudes do Americans have about their government?" lacks the necessary precision and therefore can't be resolved. What kind(s) of attitudes? What level or branch of government? Which Americans? How would you gather their opinions? A more realistic question might be "According to the Mason College faculty, how adequate is the new congressional proposal for funding academic research in this country?" You could easily develop and distribute to faculty members a questionnaire addressing the different provisions of the proposal. In addition, you can't resolve ethical or philosophical questions through primary research. While you could use a questionnaire to determine student attitudes about placing cigarette-dispensing machines on campus, such information won't decide the moral and free-choice issue of whether people have the right to smoke in the presence of others.

For valid results, conduct your primary research in an impartial manner. Always aim to determine facts rather than to justify some belief you hold. This means, first of all, that you must develop questions that have no built-in bias. If you poll other students and ask them to tell you "how core-course teachers on this campus marked their papers unreasonably hard," those responding might falsify their answers to give you what you want. Instead, use neutral phrasing such as "Do you believe core-course teachers on this campus marked your paper fairly or unfairly? Explain." Second, don't rely on atypical sources and situations for your data. If you investigate the adequacy of parking space on campus, don't deliberately observe the parking lots on a day when some special event has flooded the campus with visitors. Careful readers will see what you have done and reject your findings.

Just as you avoid bias when gathering information, so also do you report your results fairly. For one thing, don't use inaccurate interpretations of your findings to make them agree with the conclusions you're after. If you believe peer editing produces questionable results, don't claim that the students in a class you observed spent their time sneering at one another's work when in fact they offered constructive criticism. While such criticism can sometimes be straightforward, certainly most people wouldn't consider it sneering. Similarly, don't report conclusions that are unsupported by your actual research. If you observe a large number of violent acts while watching Saturday cartoons, don't leap to the conclusion that the violence in the cartoons causes violent behavior in children. You simply don't have the evidence needed to support that assertion. Finally, don't cover up results that you don't like. If your survey of teachers' marking practices shows that most of your respondents believe core-course instructors mark fairly, don't hide the fact because it doesn't match what you expected to discover. Instead, report your findings accurately and rethink your original position.

*I*NTERVIEWS

During an interview, questions are asked and answered. Some interviews amount to little more than brief, informal chats. Others, like those discussed here, may feature extended conversations, involve a series of questions, and require careful preparation. Interviewing an informed person provides you with firsthand answers to your queries, lets you ask follow-up questions, and gives you access to the most up-to-date thinking.

If you major in a business program, an instructor may require you to question a personnel manager about the company's employee relations program. If your field is social work, you might have to interview a case worker as part of your study of some kind of family problem. On the job, you might have to talk with prospective employees and then assess their suitability for a position in the company. Police officers routinely interview witnesses to accidents and crimes, and journalists do the same in pursuit of stories.

Choosing the Interviewee

Professional and technical personnel are a rich source of interview candidates. The faculty of any university can provide insights into a wide range of subjects. Doctors, pharmacists, and other health professionals can draw upon their expertise to help you, as can lawyers, engineers, researchers, corporation managers, and employees at every level of government—federal, state, and local.

Whom you interview depends, of course, on what you wish to know. For information on the safe disposal of high-level nuclear waste, you might consult a physics professor. If you want an expert view on the causes of homelessness, contact an authority such as a sociologist, who could provide objective information. If, however, you want to gain a sense of what it's like to be homeless, you might interview the manager of a shelter or (in a safe place) one or more homeless people.

Preparing for the Interview

If you don't relish the thought of phoning to request an interview, keep in mind that most interviewees are eager to discuss their areas of expertise and are

PERSPECTIVE

Having students write interview reports yields a number of benefits. Besides acquainting them with a skill that they will use in other classes and on the job, this assignment gives them a glimpse of the process that produces many of the popular articles that they read. Conducting interviews puts them in charge of their research, and turning research notes into an organized report teaches a skill that eliminates the cut-and-paste approach that is all too common when students use secondary sources. More pragmatically, when you require that a research paper include material from an interview, you have a hedge against plagiarism.

TEACHING STRATEGIES

1. Because many students will be apprehensive about conducting interviews, you might set aside class time to talk about their concerns. You could explain that just as they have interests they are willing to discuss with others, so do interviewees.

2. Students often have trouble identifying appropriate interviewees. To help them, select several of the topics students are working on and have the class brainstorm for potential candidates. You could suggest that they examine a campus directory or phone book to pinpoint individuals. Some students may try taking the easy way out by proposing interviews with friends or relatives. Remind them that the candidate must have experience or expertise in the area of interest to the student.

3. Have students evaluate one another's interview questions, or if you prefer, evaluate them yourself. Students often overlook important questions or draft ones that exhibit the shortcomings mentioned in the text.

4. To help students interview properly, you might have select members of the class interview you. You could then follow up by critiquing their performance.

5. Some students will procrastinate on this assignment. To prevent stalling, you could, at intervals of a couple of days, ask which ones haven't scheduled their interviews and the reasons for the delay, and then provide extra assistance for those who need it.

often flattered by the opportunity. The worst that can happen is a turndown, and in that event you can always find someone else in the same field.

Before you phone, review your own upcoming commitments and try to determine which ones you could reschedule if necessary. You may need to make an adjustment to accommodate the schedule of a busy person. When you call, indicate who you are, that you are requesting an interview, the subject of the interview, and how much time you'd like.

If the person agrees to meet with you, then ask when it would be convenient. Carefully record the time, day, and place of the interview, and if for any reason you need to cancel be sure to call well in advance.

Before the interview, do as much background reading as possible. This reading will help you develop a list of key questions and avoid those with obvious and readily available answers. Write out your questions to help ensure that the interview will proceed smoothly.

Good questions permit elaboration and don't call for simple "yes" or "no" answers. To illustrate:

> ***Poor:***   Is it difficult to work with adult illiterates?
> (The obvious answer is "yes.")

> ***Better:***   What have you found most challenging about working with adult illiterates?

On the other hand, don't ask overly broad questions that can't be answered in a relatively brief interview.

> ***Poor:***   What's wrong with primary-school education?

> ***Better:***   Why do you think so many children have trouble learning to read?

Avoid questions that are biased and may insult the interviewee.

> ***Poor:***   Why do you bother to work with adult illiterates?

> ***Better:***   Why did you decide to work with adult illiterates?

Likewise, avoid questions that restrict the interviewee's options for answering.

> ***Poor:***   What do you think accounts for the poor academic performance of so many American secondary-school students—too much TV watching or overly large classes?

> ***Better:***   People often blame the poor academic performance of so many American students on too much TV watching or overly large classes. What importance do you attach to these factors? Do you think other factors contribute to the problem?

The number of questions you prepare depends on the length of the interview. It's a good idea to draft more questions than you think you'll have time to ask, then arrange them from most to least important. If the interviewee keeps to the schedule, you'll obtain your desired information. If the interviewee grants you extra time, your written followup will have even more substance.

Conducting the Interview

Naturally you'll want to arrive on time and to bring a notepad and a pen. Sometimes you can tape-record an interview but only if you ask permission first. Because most people warm up slowly, you might start with one or two brief, general questions that provide you with useful background. Possibilities include "What is the nature of your specialty?" and "How long have you been employed in this field?"

Proceed by asking your most important questions first. If you believe that a question hasn't been answered or that an answer is incomplete, don't hesitate to ask follow-up questions.

As the interview unfolds, take notes but don't attempt to copy everything that's said. Instead, jot down key phrases and ideas that will serve as memory prompts. If you want to capture an essential explanation or some other important material in the interviewee's own words, ask the person to go slowly while you copy them down. When the interview is over, thank the person for talking to you. You may also offer to supply a copy of the finished report. With the answers to your questions fresh in your mind, expand on your notes by filling in details, supplying necessary connections between points that were made, and noting your reactions.

Writing about the Interview

The project you're working on determines how to handle your interview information. If you're preparing a library research paper, include the material, suitably presented, at the appropriate spot and document it according to whatever system, MLA or APA, you're using (see pages 291–307).

Often, however, you'll be asked to prepare a separate report of the interview. Then, as with any other report, you'll need to organize and present the material in an effective order. Your topic, purpose, and audience will determine the arrangement you select. In any event, remember to establish the context for the report, identify the interviewee and his or her position, and present the information accurately.

TEACHING STRATEGY

When writing an interview report, students often will want to report their results by following the pattern of the interview. Point out the differences between speech and writing. If possible, pass out an interview transcript and ask students to identify why they experience difficulty reading it. To make their own reports more effective, have students identify the main points they want to make and the order that will facilitate their presentation.

EXAMPLE STUDENT INTERVIEW REPORT

Budget Cuts Affect State Police: An Interview Report

with Officer Robert Timmons

Holly Swain

Confronted with a billion-dollar budget deficit, Michigan's governor, John Engler, has been forced to make sharp budget cuts. One of these cuts is the allocation to the state police. This decision has threatened the loss of some police jobs and aroused considerable

Paragraph 1: establishes context for interview

controversy. How, many ask, will the police, who were already on a tight budget, be able to provide the public with adequate protection when they have even less money and fewer personnel?

Sentence 1, paragraph 2: identifies interviewee and his position

Remainder of report: presents information provided by interviewee

When Trooper Robert Timmons, a state police officer based in Marywood County, first heard that the governor might call for police cutbacks, he didn't believe they would become a reality. Timmons thought Engler was just making "political noise." Actually, the state police head did at first propose cutting 350 jobs, Timmons' among them, to help meet a $19 million cutback. This proposal was rejected in favor of one that combined demotions, pay cuts, and the elimination of special programs. In addition, the amounts allotted for other purposes were also cut.

All of these actions, Timmons says, have had an unfortunate effect on the operations of the state police. As an example, he mentions a sergeant who was demoted to "Accident Reconstructionist," a job requiring him to review severe accidents and reconstruct what happened for the court. This demotion, Timmons says, has taken an excellent police officer out of the field, where he's most needed, and put him behind a desk.

Timmons notes several bad effects of cuts in the allocation for gasoline. Because of these cuts, troopers are expected to drive just ninety miles a night. Timmons thinks this limitation has a "direct effect on the public." A motorist stranded on a freeway might not be spotted and aided by a trooper who is unable to make another run through his territory. Late-night accidents might go undiscovered, with serious or fatal consequences for those involved. Many more speeders and drunk drivers will escape being caught.

As of now, Timmons says, there are only 3,000 state police, about 400 fewer than needed. Each year, 100 to 200 officers retire. These vacancies need to be filled, but according to Timmons the state academy has been closed for over a year. The personnel shortages that already exist and the cutbacks resulting from the state's budget troubles are making it harder and harder for the state police to do an adequate job of protecting the public.

Officer Timmons understands that the state government needs to control its spending. However, he believes that the present budget cutbacks for a department that is already understaffed are very unwise. "I feel Engler should have given the matter more thought," he says.

*Q*UESTIONNAIRES

A questionnaire consists essentially of a series of statements or questions to which recipients are asked to respond. Questionnaires help individuals and organizations determine what select groups of people think about particular products, services, issues, and personal matters. You yourself have probably completed a variety of questionnaires, including teacher evaluations and market surveys.

Questionnaires are used extensively both on campus and in the workplace. A social science instructor might ask you to prepare a survey that explores community reaction to a recently implemented curfew for teenagers. A business instructor might want you to survey a test-market group to determine its response to some new product. In fact, some marketing classes focus on survey techniques. But even if marketing isn't your specialty, learning how to construct questionnaires can serve you well in your career. If you work in the hotel, restaurant, or health service field, you could use a questionnaire to gauge customer satisfaction. The same holds true if you manage or own a small repair service. As a landscape specialist, you might survey the people in your community to learn what planting and maintenance services they desire.

Developing the Questionnaire

When you develop a questionnaire, you need to target precisely what you want to know and what group you intend to survey. You could survey restaurant customers to determine their attitudes about the service and the quality of the food or to assess the types of food they prefer. Zero in on only one area of interest and then explore it with appropriate questions.

Begin the questionnaire with a clear explanation of what you intend to accomplish, and supply brief but clear instructions on how to respond to each part. Keep the questionnaire as short as possible, preferably no longer than a page or two. The longer the survey, the less likely that people will answer all the questions.

As you draw up your questions, take care to avoid these common errors.

1. Don't ask two questions in the same sentence. Their answers may be different.

> ***Unacceptable:*** Do you find that this year's Ford Taurus has better acceleration and fuel economy than last year's model?

These conclusions might serve as the topic sentences of the paragraphs in the Results section.

5. Depending on your class, you may want to explain how surveys can be slanted, samples skewed, and statistics abused. This understanding is perhaps as important to the development of critical reasoning skills as a sound knowledge of argumentative fallacies.

CLASSROOM ACTIVITIES

1. List several biased and unbiased questions on the board. Have students identify those that are biased and rewrite them in an acceptable fashion. Here are two samples.

Biased: What types of disorderly student behavior occur during a class period in a typical, chaotic high school?

Acceptable: What types of student behavior occur during a class period in randomly selected high schools?

Biased: Given the problems associated with holding student attention during the last month of the school year, do you favor extending the school year from 180 to 220 days?

Acceptable: Do you favor extending the school year from 180 to 220 days?

2. You might suggest several different situations in which someone would gather data and then have students identify the possible bias. Here are some examples. A person in a supermarket hands out food samples and then asks customers if they might buy the product. A professor has students complete a questionnaire on a new course after she enthusiastically supports the course. A principal observes a new teacher's class

To correct this fault, use separate sentences.

> ***Better:*** Do you find that this year's Ford Taurus has better acceleration than last year's model?
>
> ***Better:*** Do you find that this year's Ford Taurus has better fuel economy than last year's model?

2. Don't include vague or ambiguous questions. Since people won't understand your intent, their answers may not reflect their beliefs.

> ***Unacceptable:*** Is assisted suicide a good idea?
>
> ***Better:*** Should assisted suicide be permitted for terminally ill patients?

3. Avoid biased questions. They might antagonize those who don't share your views and cause them not to complete the questionnaire.

> ***Unacceptable:*** Should Century City taxpayers continue to waste money on renovating the North Park Bridge?
>
> ***Better:*** Should Century City taxpayers spend an additional $100,000 to complete the North Park Bridge renovation?

Most questionnaire items fall into the categories that follow. The information you want determines which you choose. Often you'll need to include several or all of the categories in your questionnaire.

Two-Choice Items.   Some items have two possible responses: yes/no, true/false, male/female.

> ***Example:*** Do you plan to repaint your house during the summer months?
> ❏ yes
> ❏ no

Multiple-Choice Items.   Often there are several possible responses to a questionnaire item. When you prepare this type of item, make sure that you include all significant choices and that the choices share some common ground. Don't ask if someone's primary vehicle is a subcompact, compact, full-size, or foreign car as size and place of manufacture are unrelated. To determine whether the vehicle is domestic or foreign, use a separate item.

> ***Example:*** Check the income group that describes your combined family income.
> ❏ less than $10,000 a year
> ❏ $10,000–$20,000 a year
> ❏ $20,000–$30,000 a year
> ❏ $30,000–$40,000 a year
> ❏ $40,000–$50,000 a year
> ❏ over $50,000 a year

Checklists.   Checklists allow respondents to mark more than one option. They can help you determine the range of factors that led to a decision.

Example: Please check any of the following factors that help explain why you decided not to re-enroll your child in Good Growth Private School.
- ❏ can no longer afford tuition
- ❏ moved
- ❏ dissatisfaction with child's progress
- ❏ disagree with school's educational approach
- ❏ conflict with teacher
- ❏ conflict with other staff
- ❏ child unhappy with school
- ❏ child had conflict with other children

Ranking Lists. Sometimes you may need to ask people to rank their preferences. This information will help you select the most suitable option from among several possibilities.

Example: Designating your first choice as "1," please rank your preferences in music from 1 through 5.
- ❏ classical
- ❏ country and western
- ❏ jazz
- ❏ rock and roll
- ❏ new wave

Using the responses to this item, the manager of a local radio station could broadcast the type of music that listeners clearly prefer.

Scale Items. When you are trying to determine the extent to which members of a group support or oppose some issue, using a scale can be helpful. Be sure to have people respond to a statement, *not* a question.

Example: Please circle the response that best reflects your feelings about the statement below. SA = strongly agree, A = agree, N = no opinion, D = disagree, SD = strongly disagree
Women should be allowed to fly combat aircraft in time of war.
SA   A   N   D   SD

Open-Ended Items. When you want to gather ideas from other people, you might turn to open-ended items—those that don't limit the reader's response. If you do, keep such items narrow enough to be manageable. You should know, however, that readers are less likely to complete open-ended items and that they are difficult to sort and tally.

Example: Please list the three improvements that you would most like to see in Lowden's high school curriculum. _____

_____

_____

_____

_____

_____

_____

after giving the teacher two weeks' notice of the pending observation.

3. Students could bring in copies of articles relevant to their research papers. In small groups they might examine the articles for potentially biased reporting. Alternatively, you could bring in an article on a subject known to students, perhaps student behavior, that demonstrates clearcut bias. Students could then evaluate the article and identify the bias.

EXAMPLE STUDENT QUESTIONNAIRE

Survey on Public Smoking

Kelly Reetz

Please take a few minutes to fill out this questionnaire. My purpose is to determine the smoking habits and attitudes toward public smoking of Bartram College male smokers.

| Two-choice item |

1. Do you smoke cigarettes? (check one)

    _____ yes

    _____ no

| Multiple-choice item |

2. If you smoke, indicate how many cigarettes each day. (check one)

    _____ less than half a pack

    _____ between a half and a whole pack

    _____ between one and two packs

    _____ more than two packs

| Multiple-choice item |

3. If you smoke, what are you likely to do upon entering a public place with no posted smoking restrictions? (check one)

    _____ smoke freely

    _____ check to see whether your smoking is bothering others

    _____ ask others whether they would be bothered if you smoke

    _____ not smoke

| Checklist |

4. Check the statements you believe are true.

    _____ My health is at risk only if I am a smoker.

    _____ Secondhand smoke contains the same ingredients as directly inhaled smoke.

    _____ Secondhand smoke poses a health risk to nonsmokers.

    _____ Secondhand smoke poses less of a health risk than directly inhaled smoke.

| Scale items |

5. Please rate each of the statements below, using the following scale: SA = strongly agree, A = agree, N = no opinion, D = disagree, SD = strongly disagree

    _____ There should be no restrictions on public smoking.

    _____ Smoking should be prohibited in stores and banks.

    _____ Smoking and nonsmoking sections in restaurants should be separated by a barrier that smoke cannot penetrate.

_____ Smokers and nonsmokers should have separate workplace lounges.

_____ All public smoking should be prohibited.

6. Please add one or two comments you might have regarding public smoking. _____

_____

_____

Open-ended item

Testing and Administering the Questionnaire

When you have finished making out the questionnaire, ask several people to respond to the items and gauge their effectiveness. Are any items vague, ambiguous, biased, or otherwise faulty? If so, rewrite and retest them.

To ensure that you obtain an accurate assessment, make certain that you select an appropriate cross-section of recipients. To illustrate, assume that you and many of your campus friends dislike early morning classes. You decide to draw up a questionnaire to sample the attitudes of other students. You suspect that many students share your dislike, and you plan to submit your findings to the college president for possible action. To obtain meaningful results, you'll have to sample a sizable group of students. Furthermore, this group will need to include representative numbers of freshmen, sophomores, juniors, and seniors, as these classes may not share a uniform view. Failure to sample properly can call your results into question and cause the administration to disregard them. Proper sampling, on the other hand, pinpoints where dissatisfaction is greatest and suggests a possible response. Thus if freshmen and sophomores register the most objections, the administration might decide to reduce the number of 100- and 200-level classes meeting at 8 A.M.

Totaling the Responses

When the recipients have finished marking the questionnaire, you will need to total the responses. Even without computer scoring, this job is easier than you might think. Simply prepare a table that lists the questionnaire items and the possible responses to each; then go through the questionnaire and add up the number of times each response is marked.

When you finish, turn your numbers into percentages, which provide an easier-to-understand comparison of the responses. Simply divide the number of times each possible response is checked by the total number of questionnaires and then multiply the result by 100.

Writing the Questionnaire Report

When you write your report, don't merely fill it with numbers and responses to the questionnaire items. Instead, look for patterns in the responses and try to draw conclusions from them. Follow the order of the questionnaire items in presenting your findings.

Typically, a report consists of two or three sections. The first, "Purpose and Scope," explains why the survey was performed, how many questionnaires were distributed and returned, and how the recipients were contacted. The second section, "Results," reports the conclusions that were drawn. Finally, if appropriate, a "Recommendations" section offers responses that seem warranted based on the survey findings.

EXAMPLE STUDENT QUESTIONNAIRE REPORT

Findings from Smoking Questionnaire Distributed

to Bartram College Students

Kelly Reetz

Purpose and Scope of Survey

Provides background details on project, profile of respondents

This survey was carried out to determine the smoking habits and attitudes toward public smoking of Bartram College's male students. The assignment was one of my requirements for completing Public Health 201. Each of the 240 male students in Crandall Hall received a copy of the questionnaire in his mailbox, and 72 completed questionnaires were returned. This latter number equals 10 percent of the college's male student population and therefore can be considered a representative sample. Of those responding, 37, or 51 percent, were cigarette smokers. Thirty-five, or 49 percent, were nonsmokers. Of the smokers, all but 11 percent smoked over a pack of cigarettes a day.

Results of Survey

Discusses responses to questionnaire item 3

Smokers seemed fairly considerate of nonsmokers in public places. Only 16 percent said they would smoke freely. In fact, 51 percent said they wouldn't smoke at all. The remaining 33 percent indicated they would either look around to see whether they were bothering others or ask others whether they objected to cigarette smoke.

Discusses responses to questionnaire item 4

In general, respondents seemed aware that secondhand smoke poses a health risk. Seventy-six percent believe that such smoke contains the same ingredients as directly inhaled smoke, and an amazing 96 percent believe that anyone exposed to secondhand smoke may be at risk. Only 3 percent think no health risk is involved.

Opinions were strongly divided on the matter of banning all public smoking, with 79 percent strongly opposed and 21 percent strongly in favor. As might be expected, all of the smokers fell in the first group, but a surprising 51 percent of the nonsmokers did too. A sharp division was equally apparent between supporters and opponents of restaurant barriers, with 81 percent for or strongly for them and 19 percent against or strongly against them. In contrast to the findings on a smoking ban, all of the smokers favored barriers. Respondents overwhelmingly endorsed, 90 percent to 10 percent, prohibiting smoking in stores and banks and providing separate workplace lounges. Nobody registered a "no opinion" vote on any of the statements under item 5.

> Discusses responses to questionnaire item 5

Responses to items 3–5 reveal an awareness among smokers of the dangers posed by secondhand cigarette smoke, a concern for the well-being of nonsmokers, and a willingness to accept restrictions, though not an outright ban, on public smoking. This attitude was consistent for both light and heavy smokers. For their part, about half the nonsmokers showed a tolerant attitude by supporting smoking restrictions but rejecting an outright ban.

> Discusses patterns in responses to items 3–5

No smokers, but 71 percent of the nonsmokers, responded to the request to provide one or two additional comments. All of these comments dealt with how the respondents would act if bothered by someone else's smoke. Two-thirds said they would move to another spot, half of the remainder said they would ask the smoker to stop, and the other half said they would remain silent rather than risk an argument.

> Discusses responses to item 6

Recommendations

As noted previously, this survey included only male students. To determine how its results compare with those for females, the same questionnaire should be administered to a similar group of females.

Direct Observations

Often direct observation is the most effective means of answering research questions. If you want to know the extent and nature of violence in children's TV cartoons, watching a number of shows will tell you. Similarly, a researcher who

PERSPECTIVE

Students often find it easy to make personal observations as part of their library research projects. A student doing a paper on sexism in society could review supermarket magazines to find advertisements showing sexism. Another student, doing a paper on homelessness, might check the newspaper to determine the average rental price of advertised apartments and then compare it with the monthly income of a person making the minimum wage. These activities not only help students better understand how other writers reach their conclusions but also let students know that they too have the ability to answer their own questions.

TEACHING STRATEGIES

1. Using material from the Reader (or secondary sources that students are using in their research), have students identify which claims are based on some form of direct observation. Have them write out the claim, the kinds of observations that were made, and their own evaluations of the observations.
2. Have students identify questions about college life or college students that they could answer by their own observations, then make those observations and report back to the class. This activity could lead to a paper.
3. Have students identify questions that are important to their library research projects, then select which questions can and cannot be answered by direct observation. Students could outline their strategy for gaining the necessary information. If, for instance, a paper is on violence and television, the writer could observe children's programs to determine the extent and nature of any violence.
4. Many students will experience difficulty being objective and specific in reporting their results. You might want to compare more objective and less objective reports on the same data to help students see the difference. You could put a few student reports on the overhead projector and have the class offer suggestions for improvement.

seeks information about living conditions in an inner-city area of some metropolis can obtain it by visiting that locale. Such observations furnish firsthand answers to our questions.

In college and on the job, you may need to report your own observations. If you're majoring in business, an instructor might require a report on the work habits of employees at a small local company. If your field is biology, you might need to assess and report on the environmental health of a marsh, riverbank, or other ecological area. On the job, a factory superintendent might observe and then discuss in writing the particulars of some problem-plagued operation. Police officers routinely investigate and report on accidents, and waste-management specialists inspect and report on potential disposal sites.

The following suggestions will help you make your observations, record them, and then write your report.

Preparing to Make the Observations

First, determine the purpose of your observations and keep the purpose firmly in mind as you proceed. Otherwise, you'll overlook important details and record less-than-helpful information. Obviously, observing a classroom to assess the interaction of students calls for a different set of notes than if you were observing the teacher's instructional style or the student's note-taking habits.

Next, establish the site or sites that will best supply you with the information you need. If you're trying to determine how college students interact in the classroom, then the time of day, kind of class, and types of students will all make a difference. You might have to visit more than one class in order to observe the different types of behavior.

If your observations will take place on private property or will involve an organized group such as a class or a legislative body, you'll need to obtain permission and to make an appointment. Also, you might want to supplement your observations with an interview. Ordinarily, the interview will take place after you make your observations so that you can ask about what you've seen. However, if technical information is needed in advance, the interview should precede the observations.

Because you'll probably be making a great many individual observations, try to develop a chart and a code for recording them. Suppose you're comparing the extent to which students interact with one another and with the instructor in remedial and nonremedial composition courses. After much thought, you might develop a chart like the one following.

Class designation: Composition 100

Minutes into observation when interaction occurred	Classroom location of interacting students	Number and sex of students	Subject of interaction	Length of interaction

With certain kinds of observations, using a chart will not be possible.

In developing your code, you would undoubtedly use M = male and

F = female to distinguish the sexes. To show the location of the interacting students, FC = front of class, MC = middle of class, and BC = back of class would probably work quite well. Coding the kinds of interactions presents a more difficult task. Here, after considering several possibilities, you might decide upon these symbols: CR = class related, SR = school related, SP = sports, D = dating, O = other matters. To save writing time, you'd probably want to use "min." for "minutes" and "sec." for "seconds" when recording the lengths of the interactions.

Making the Observations

If your visit involves a scheduled appointment, be sure to arrive on time and be ready to take notes. Select a location where you can observe without interfering. If you are observing people or animals, remember that they need to adjust to you before they will behave naturally.

Before you begin taking notes, record any pertinent general information. If you're observing a class, you might note the time it is meeting, its size, the name of the instructor, and whether he or she is present when you arrive. If you're observing an apartment, pertinent information would include the location and condition of the building, the time of the visit, and the general nature of the environment. Note also whether the landlord as well as the tenant knew you were coming: it is amazing how much cleanup landlords can carry out when they know an observer will soon arrive.

Don't feel as though you must take extensive notes. Do, however, record enough details to ensure that you won't forget any events, activities, or features that are important. If you have a chart and coding system, rely on it as much as possible when recording information. Here's how the coded notes for part of a classroom visit might look.

Class designation: Composition 100

Minutes into observation when interaction occurred	Classroom location of interacting students	Number and sex of students	Subject of interaction	Length of interaction
O	FC	M-M	SP	1 min., 30 sec.
3 Instructor arrived	MC	F-F	D	
5	FC, MC, BC	M-M-M-F-F	CR	3 min., 45 sec.
20	FC, MC	M-F-M	CR	1 min.

If you haven't developed a chart, take enough notes so that you can produce a thorough report. Try to follow some note-taking pattern. When observing the condition of an apartment, you could proceed from room to room, jotting down observations such as "Front hallway, entranceway: paint peeling in large strips from wall, paint chips on floor. Hallway dark, bulb burned out. Linoleum curling up along sides. Cockroaches running along lower molding." Remain as objective as possible as you take notes. Record what you see, hear, and smell, and avoid loaded language. If you must record a subjective impression, identify it as such.

Ask questions if necessary, but rely primarily on what you observe, not what you're told. If the landlord of a rundown apartment you're visiting tells you that he's repainting the building but you see no signs that this is happening, ignore what he says or report it along with an appropriate cautionary comment. When you finish, thank the person(s) who made your observations possible or helped you in other ways.

When you leave the observation site, expand your notes by adding more details. Supply any needed connections and record your overall impressions. To illustrate, suppose you are expanding your notes on student interactions in a composition class. You might note that the greatest number of interactions occurred before and immediately after the instructor arrived, that all student-student interactions involved individuals seated together, that student-instructor interactions included students in all parts of the room, and that all the latter interactions were about subject-related matters. This information might stimulate interesting speculation concerning the student-student and student-teacher relationships in the class, causing you to conclude that the students were hesitant about having exchanges with the instructor. As you proceed, record only what you actually observed, not what you wanted or expected to observe.

If upon reviewing your notes you find that you require more information, you may need to arrange a second or even a third visit to the observation site.

Writing the Report

Once your notes are in final form, you can start writing your report. On the job your employer may specify a certain form to follow. As a general rule, all such reports reflect their purposes, focus on relevant information, and remain objective.

Usually you begin by explaining the reason for the investigation, noting any preliminary arrangements that were made, and if appropriate, providing an overview of the observation site. Depending upon the nature of the report, the primary means of organization may be as follows.

1. *Narration.* A report on the changing conduct of a child over a three-hour period in a day-care center would probably be organized by narration.
2. *Description.* A report assessing the tornado damage in a large urban area could present its details in spatial order.
3. *Classification.* A visit to a toxic waste dump suspected of violating state regulations might produce a report classifying the types of wastes improperly stored there.
4. *Point-by-point comparison.* If you're comparing two possible sites for a baseball stadium, shopping mall, or other structure, a point-by-point comparison will probably best suit your purpose.
5. *Cause and effect.* This pattern works well for reporting events whose effects are of special concern, such as the testing of a new siren intended to scare birds from an airport runway.

6. *Process.* This arrangement is indicated when readers will want to know step-by-step how some process—for example, a new test for determining the mineral content of water—is carried out.

Conclude the report by discussing the significance of the findings and making any other comments that seem justified.

EXAMPLE STUDENT OBSERVATION REPORT

Observations of an Inner-City Apartment Building

Caleb Thomas

To fulfill part of the requirements for Social Service 321, I observed the housing conditions in an inner-city residential area. The building I selected is located in the city of Grand Mound, at the corner of Division Avenue and Hall Street, an area where most of the residents hold minimum-wage jobs or receive some form of public assistance.

> Gives reason for visit, location of site

I met the building supervisor, who had agreed to this visit, at 9:30 A.M. on Friday, April 19, 1992. The brick sides of the three-story apartment building appeared to be in good repair, but one second-story window was broken out and boarded up. Most windows had standard window shades, but a few were blocked with sheets or black plastic bags. Two had no coverings of any kind. Overall, the building's appearance was similar to that of several nearby apartment buildings.

> Notes preliminary arrangements, provides overview of site location

Heavy traffic clogged Division Avenue at the time of my visit. Next to the apartment building stood three single-story wooden buildings housing an adult video store, a bar, and a novelty shop, all with boarded windows and peeling paint. Across the street, a single-story Goodwill Store occupied the entire block. In front of it, three women in short skirts walked slowly back and forth, eying the cars that passed. Two men sat on crates, their backs to the building, drinking something out of paper bags.

> Continues overview of site location

The supervisor opened the unlocked metal door of the apartment building, and we went in. The hallway was lighted by a single dim bulb located on the wall toward the rear. Other bulbs along the wall and in two light fixtures hanging from the ceiling appeared burned out. Scraps

> Describes building's hallway

of newspaper and chips of paint that had peeled from the ceiling and walls littered the floor. A strong urine-like smell pervaded the air.

| Describes apartment hallway |

Stating that he couldn't show me an occupied apartment because he "respected the privacy of the tenants," the supervisor took me to an unoccupied apartment on the first floor. He had trouble unlocking the wooden door; the key appeared to stick in the lock. The inside of the door had two bolt locks, one a few inches above the door handle and the other one near the floor. The door opened into a short hall with rooms off either side. Here, as in the building entrance, paint chips from the peeling walls and ceiling littered the floor. A battered socket on the wall held a single bulb, but when I flicked its switch, the bulb did not light. On the hall floor, linoleum curled at the edges. When I bent down to examine it more closely, several cockroaches scurried under the curl.

| Describes apartment living room |

The first door on the right-hand side of the hall led into a 10-by-12-foot room that the supervisor identified as the living room. Here the walls had been recently painted—by a former tenant, the supervisor said—and a strong paint smell was still apparent. However, nothing else had been done to the rest of the room. The radiator was unshielded, several nail heads protruded from the stained and uncovered wooden floor, and the sagging ceiling had several long cracks. Plaster chips dotted the floor.

| Describes apartment kitchen |

A small kitchen was situated behind the living room. Again, linoleum floor covering curled from the baseboard, and cockroaches scurried for cover. The kitchen was furnished with a battered-looking gas stove, but there was no refrigerator (the supervisor said one was on order). The surface of the sink was chipped and had many brownish stains. When I turned on the faucet, a rusty brown stream of water spurted out. I asked for a sample to be tested for lead content, but the supervisor refused.

| Describes apartment bathroom |

The bathroom, located at the end of the hall, had no radiator. Its floor tiles, broken in a number of places, exposed a foot-long section of rotted wood. The toilet, with seat missing, would not flush when I tried it but simply made a hissing noise. A brown stain spread over the bottom of the bathtub and a large portion of its sides. The wall tiles around the tub bulged outward and appeared ready to collapse into the tub. The supervisor offered the observation that there had been "some trouble with the plumbing."

Two small bedrooms opened off the left side of the hall. Like the living room both had unprotected radiators, uncovered wooden floors, and cracked ceilings. Walls were papered rather than painted, but long strips of the wallpaper were missing. In one bedroom a piece of plaster board hung on the wall as if covering a hole. The windows in both bedrooms were covered with sheets tacked to the wall.

> Describes apartment bedrooms

When I had finished looking at the bedrooms, the supervisor quickly escorted me from the apartment and the building, declaring that he was too busy to show me any other vacant apartments. He also said he had no time to answer any questions.

Clearly the building I visited fails to meet city housing code: the living conditions are not what most people would consider acceptable. A careful investigation, including a test of the water and of the paint for lead content, seems called for to determine whether this apartment constitutes a health risk.

> Discusses significance of findings

Business Letters and Résumés

Business people aren't the only ones who write business letters. You write quite a few yourself, or soon will, especially to request information, place orders, register complaints, and apply for jobs. There's nothing mysterious or difficult about business correspondence. True, it follows its own special format, but otherwise it breaks no new writing ground. As always, deciding what to say and how to say it is vital to your success.

LETTER LANGUAGE

Effective letter language weaves conciseness, informality, and courtesy into a three-strand finished fabric. Concise writing avoids word clutter and gets directly to the point, saving the reader time and enlivening the message. As you write and revise, guard against two kinds of wordiness: deadwood and gobbledygook. *Deadwood* repeats the same thing or uses excess words to deliver its message. Here are some examples of deadwood and ways of correcting them.

Deadwood	*Correction*
in view of the fact that, due to the fact that	because
had the effect of causing	caused
would you be kind enough to	would you please
I want to take this opportunity to thank you	thank you
in the event that	if
personally, I believe	I believe
I want to make it clear that	[simply state what you want known]

Gobbledygook uses inflated, elaborately polite expressions that make writing stiff, stuffy, and distant. Note how the corrections soften the standoffish tone.

Gobbledygook	Correction
enclosed please find	I am enclosing
pursuant to the purchase of your	after buying your
in accordance with the terms of your warranty	your warranty provides
reference is made herewith	I am referring to
the said lawnmower	this lawnmower

Informal language is everyday language. Friendly and relaxed, it has the air of face-to-face conversation between writer and reader. To achieve it, use simple words and sentence structures; personal pronouns like *I, me, you,* and *your* are appropriate. At the same time, though, don't go overboard and resort to slang or overly casual expressions. Saying "When you guys packed my radio, you must have goofed; when I got it, it was busted" raises questions about your seriousness.

In your business letters, as in direct dealings with others, courtesy plays a key part in helping you gain your ends. Here are some tips to help you avoid antagonizing the reader.

1. Avoid insults and sarcasm.

    Sarcastic   Do you think you could possibly send me the correct size this time?

    Courteous   Would you please replace the dress with one of the correct size?

2. Avoid curt demands.

    Blunt   I want you to send me . . . , I need a copy of . . .

    Courteous   Would you please send me . . .

3. Avoid negative implications. The first example below suggests that the reader will automatically disagree.

    Negative   I take the position that . . .

    Courteous   I think you'll find that . . .

As you prepare your letter, try changing places with your reader. How would you react to the message? If you're pleased with what you see, courtesy should be no problem.

PARTS OF THE BUSINESS LETTER

The letter in Figure 21.1, labeled to show the parts of a business letter, is set up in the modified block format, a very common one for business correspondence.

    Heading.   Spell out every word except for the two-letter state abbreviation used by the postal service. Begin the heading at the center of the sheet.

    Inside Address.   *Ms.* is an acceptable personal title for both married and single women. If you don't know the name of the person you want to reach, begin

If you hadn't been so foolish, you wouldn't have had the problems you describe. The hydrochloric acid you used in the wash had the effect of damaging both your clothes and your washer. In the future, you would be well advised to use only bleach and standard detergents as per instructions. This will protect your machine in the future.

Revised Version

Dear Mr. Maloney:

We are sorry to hear about the damage to your new Maelstrom washing machine and your clothes. Unfortunately, our warranty does not cover the damage, as it was caused by the hydrochloric acid you used in your machine. This strong acid is dangerous and should not be used with any Maelstrom product.

In the future, to protect your washing machine and clothes, please follow the instructions in the owner's manual and use only standard detergents and bleaches.

PERSPECTIVE

The letters in this chapter follow the same format. You might tell students that other formats are used and that they will be expected to use whichever one their company has adopted.

Heading

Inside address

Salutation

Body

Complimentary close

Signature

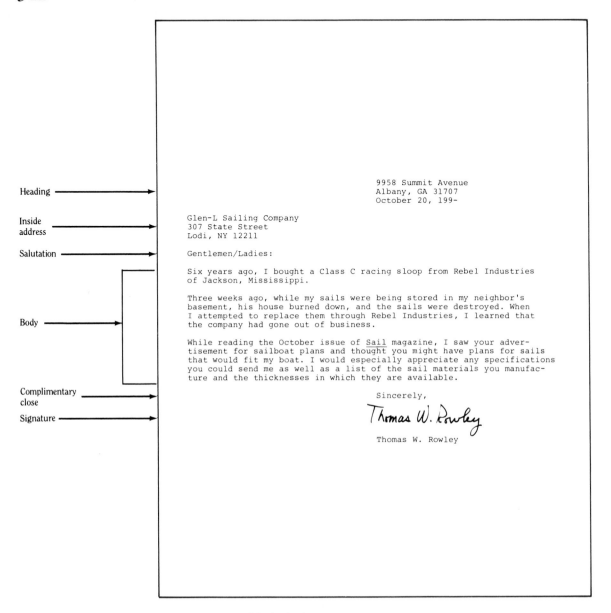

9958 Summit Avenue
Albany, GA 31707
October 20, 199-

Glen-L Sailing Company
307 State Street
Lodi, NY 12211

Gentlemen/Ladies:

Six years ago, I bought a Class C racing sloop from Rebel Industries of Jackson, Mississippi.

Three weeks ago, while my sails were being stored in my neighbor's basement, his house burned down, and the sails were destroyed. When I attempted to replace them through Rebel Industries, I learned that the company had gone out of business.

While reading the October issue of _Sail_ magazine, I saw your advertisement for sailboat plans and thought you might have plans for sails that would fit my boat. I would especially appreciate any specifications you could send me as well as a list of the sail materials you manufacture and the thicknesses in which they are available.

Sincerely,

Thomas W. Rowley

Thomas W. Rowley

Figure 21.1   Modified Block Form

CLASSROOM ACTIVITY

Have students bring in samples of business letters and examine them for differences in style and format. Or use letters you have received.

the inside address with the job title or name of the department, for example, _Vice-president for Research_ or _Sales Department_. If you don't know the job title or department, start with the company name. Use abbreviations only if they are part of the company name. Begin the inside address two spaces below the heading in long letters and three to eight spaces in shorter letters. The shorter the letter, the more space should be left.

Salutation.   Address an individual by title and name. If the inside address begins with a job title or the name of a department, use that title or department name for the salutation, for instance, *Vice-president for Research* or *Sales Department*. If the inside address begins with the name of the company, use the salutation *Gentlemen/Ladies*. The letters on pages 342, 346, and 348 show these kinds of salutations. The salutation comes two spaces below the inside address.

Body.   Most letters are one page or less. Try to keep your paragraphs short—about seven lines at most. Begin the body two spaces below the salutation. If the letter contains only one brief paragraph, double-space the typing. Otherwise use single spacing with double spacing between paragraphs.

Complimentary Close.   Acceptable closings are *Sincerely yours, Sincerely,* and *Yours truly.* Type the complimentary close two spaces below the last line of the body and line it up with the center of the sheet.

Signature.   Both typewritten and handwritten signatures are necessary. Leave four spaces between the complimentary close and the typed signature. Line the typed signature up with the center of the sheet.

Enclosure Notation.   The abbreviation *Enc.,* used in several of our sample letters, indicates that a brochure, drawing, check, money order, or other document accompanies the letter. It starts at the left-hand margin. If more than one item accompanies a letter, the notation should indicate how many there are. Important documents are often named:

Enc. 3
Enc. Money Order

Type business letters on 8½ × 11-inch unlined white paper and center them on the page. For full-page letters, make the side margins one inch wide; for shorter letters, make wider margins. In all cases, establish top and bottom margins of roughly equal width.

```
DJ ASSOCIATES
230 PARK AVE S
NEW YORK NY 10003-1502




                        MS SHARON CUSTOMER
                        806 S ARLINGTON MILL DRIVE APT 1A
                        ARLINGTON VA 22204-2921
```

Figure 21.2

PREPARATION FOR MAILING

To ensure that the Post Office's optical scanners can read your envelope, type the address entirely in capital letters and without punctuation. Position the address between one-half and three inches from the bottom of the envelope and at least one inch from the right-hand edge. Figure 21.2 shows a properly typed address. Use the standard state abbreviations which are readily available.

Proofread your letter carefully, sign it, and then fold it neatly in thirds (Figure 21.3) so that it will fit into a number 10 size business envelope.

TYPES OF LETTERS

Of the many kinds of business letters, the ones you'll most likely write are inquiries, orders, complaints, and job applications. Here are guidelines and models.

Letters of Inquiry

Your letters of inquiry may be written to request information about a vacation spot, a hobby, or a project that you are working on; or you may write for data to be used in a research paper. (See Figure 21.4.) Here's how to proceed:

1. Identify yourself, indicate the kind of information you're after, and explain why you need it.
2. To avoid inconveniencing your reader, keep your questions to a minimum, make them clear, and word them so they can be answered briefly.
3. If you have three or more questions, set them up in a numbered list so the reader is less likely to miss answering one.
4. If you're using the information for a research paper and it's appropriate to do so, offer to supply a copy of your paper. Acknowledge the source of information when you write the paper.
5. Close by expressing appreciation for any help the reader can give.

EXERCISE ■ **Write a letter of inquiry that requests one of the following kinds of information.**

1. More details about a project reported in a magazine or newspaper article
2. Performance data for something you might buy
3. Detailed information about the credit policies of a company
4. Information for a research paper
5. Your congressional representative's, mayor's, or other public official's position on an issue you're concerned about
6. Membership information for a club or professional organization

Figure 21.3

```
                              325 Darrin Hall
                              Prentice College
                              Barstow, ME 04611
                              January 3, 199-

          Mr. John Antwerp
          Antrim Industries, Inc.
          6431 Honeysuckle Avenue
          Modesto, CA 95355

          Dear Mr. Antwerp:

          Your article in the December issue of Modern Health, in which
          you describe the features of your company's new comprehensive
          medical program, greatly interested me.

          I am an environmental health student investigating the benefits
          that small companies have realized by instituting such programs.
          Can you help me by answering the following questions?

               1. To what extent has the number of employees calling in
                  sick increased or decreased since your program began?

               2. To what extent has the program affected worker
                  productivity and efficiency?

               3. How do the costs of the program compare with those of
                  the medical insurance you used to provide through a
                  private insurance company?

          Thank you for any information you can supply. If you wish, I will
          be happy to send you a copy of my finished report.

                              Sincerely,

                              René M. Hewitt

                              René M. Hewitt
```

Figure 21.4 The Pointers Applied: Sample Inquiry Letter

Order Letters

Order letters, used to order sports equipment, hobby supplies, appliances, furniture, clothing, and the like, must be brief and to the point. (See Figure 21.5.) Write the letter as follows:

1. Identify the merchandise by name, model or catalog number, size, weight, color, finish, or whatever else is needed.

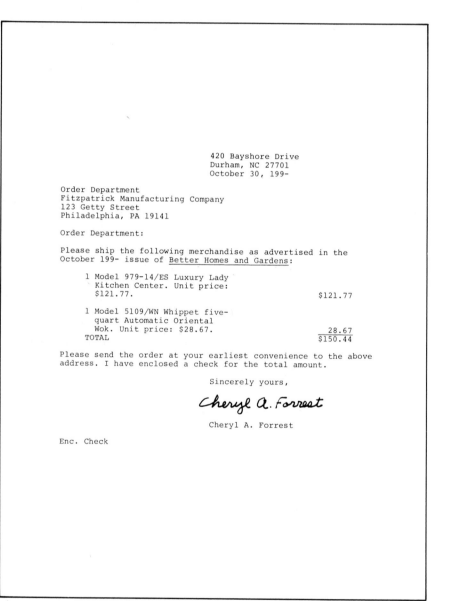

```
                                        420 Bayshore Drive
                                        Durham, NC 27701
                                        October 30, 199-

     Order Department
     Fitzpatrick Manufacturing Company
     123 Getty Street
     Philadelphia, PA 19141

     Order Department:

     Please ship the following merchandise as advertised in the
     October 199- issue of Better Homes and Gardens:

          1 Model 979-14/ES Luxury Lady
            Kitchen Center. Unit price:
            $121.77.                                    $121.77

          1 Model 5109/WN Whippet five-
            quart Automatic Oriental
            Wok. Unit price: $28.67.                      28.67
          TOTAL                                         $150.44

     Please send the order at your earliest convenience to the above
     address. I have enclosed a check for the total amount.

                              Sincerely yours,

                              Cheryl A. Forrest

                              Cheryl A. Forrest

     Enc. Check
```

Figure 21.5   The Pointers Applied: Sample Order Letter

2. To order a single item, write the letter in paragraph form. Otherwise set up a numbered list.

3. Specify how many items of each sort you want, the cost of a single item, and the total cost of the order.

4. Indicate when you wish to pay and how: by check, money order, or credit card. If you are enclosing payment, say so.

5. If you're ordering a gift to be shipped to someone at another address, be sure to include that address in the body of your letter.

EXERCISE ■ Write one of the following letters.

1. Order one or more pieces of furniture, household appliances, garden implements, or automobile accessories.
2. Order a gift to be shipped to a friend or relative.

Claim Letters

Writing a claim (complaint) letter is unpleasant but sometimes necessary. An improperly filled order, damaged or shoddy merchandise, a misunderstanding about prices—these and many other situations can result in claims. The letter points out the problem and asks that it be corrected.

When writing your letter, don't let anger make you discourteous. Remember, you're trying to settle a problem, not antagonize your reader. These guidelines will help you get a quick, favorable response.

1. If you are writing a large company and don't know the name of the department that handles claims, address your letter to "Customer Adjustments Department" or "Claims Department." For small companies, write to the sales department. Your letter should then quickly reach someone who can help you.

2. Begin the body of the letter by identifying the problem precisely. Tell what happened and when, giving size, colors, model numbers, prices—whatever the reader needs to investigate and make an adjustment.

3. If you've suffered serious inconvenience, mentioning it may speed the settlement.

4. Clearly state the adjustment you want.

5. Back your position with supporting evidence or arguments, positioned at whatever point in the letter seems most appropriate.

6. End courteously by expressing hope for a speedy settlement or offering any further information needed to reach that settlement.

Figure 21.6 shows a typical claim letter.

EXERCISE ■ Write a claim letter calling attention to one of the following.

1. An improperly or incompletely filled order
2. An order that was delivered late
3. Merchandise damaged in transit because of improper packing
4. Improper billing by a credit card company or utility

CLASSROOM ACTIVITIES

1. Provide students with information on some individual and then have each one use it to write a cover letter and résumé. Divide the class into groups; then have the groups exchange papers and rank them. The discussion that accompanies the rankings will help illuminate the important features of a good cover letter and résumé.

Sample Biography

John Sims. Age 21. Sims will graduate from Ferris State University this summer with a BA in accounting. He minored in computer science and can program in COBOL, Pascal, and Assembly. His GPA is 2.4. While at Ferris, he has been the treasurer of his fraternity, Sigma Delta Alpha. He worked summers at Friendly Foods in Bangor, Michigan, first as a cashier but for the last two summers as a bookkeeper. He graduated from Bangor High School four years ago but only with a 2.2 GPA.

Job Opening

Accountant wanted for Morton Foods, Inc. Person will need to be responsible for computerized payroll operations. Experience preferred.

2. Have students revise the following cover letter:

Dear Mr. Carter:

I hope you will hire me for a summer position as a sales representative at Beach Paper Products. I know summer is your best sales season since so many people go on picnics. I have also noticed that far too few stores in my neck of the woods sell your paper plates, napkins, and cups. I will do a slam-bang job for you. As you might guess, I am wonderful with people. As president of our college fraternity, I have been responsible for throwing parties,

```
                                       815 Buckaroo Lane
                                       Dallas, TX 75226
                                       July 10, 199-

Customer Relations Department
Carlson Craft
P.O. Box 87
Mankato, MN 56001

Customer Relations Department:

On June 12, I sent a check for $10.19 and an order for 150
imprinted white luncheon napkins, style 7219. These napkins
were intended for my wedding reception.

The napkins came today, but instead of saying "Kathleen and
Ward" they have the wrong imprint--"Kathleen and Lard." I am
enclosing one of them to show you the mistake.

My wedding is less than five weeks off, and I'd like to settle the
details of the reception well before then. Therefore, I'd appreciate
a replacement order as soon as possible.

My fiancé and I both hope you'll take care of this matter promptly.

                        Yours truly,

                        Kathleen M. Van Meer

                        Kathleen M. Van Meer

Enc.
```

Figure 21.6 The Pointers Applied: Sample Claim Letter

Job Application Letters

Once you've finished your academic preparation and started looking for a permanent job, you'll have to write one or more job application letters. In the meantime, you may need to write one to apply for a summer job (see Figures 21.7 and 21.8).

Take great care to do a first-rate job. Companies scan applications carefully and immediately discard those that fail to measure up. Grammatical or punctuation

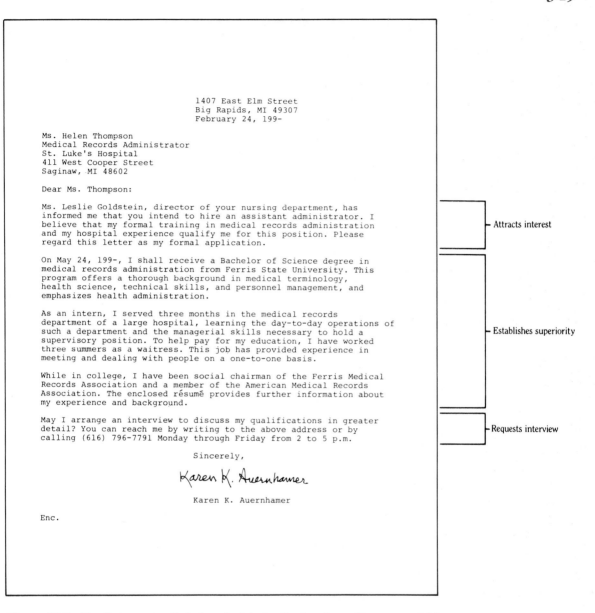

1407 East Elm Street
Big Rapids, MI 49307
February 24, 199-

Ms. Helen Thompson
Medical Records Administrator
St. Luke's Hospital
411 West Cooper Street
Saginaw, MI 48602

Dear Ms. Thompson:

Ms. Leslie Goldstein, director of your nursing department, has informed me that you intend to hire an assistant administrator. I believe that my formal training in medical records administration and my hospital experience qualify me for this position. Please regard this letter as my formal application.

— Attracts interest

On May 24, 199-, I shall receive a Bachelor of Science degree in medical records administration from Ferris State University. This program offers a thorough background in medical terminology, health science, technical skills, and personnel management, and emphasizes health administration.

As an intern, I served three months in the medical records department of a large hospital, learning the day-to-day operations of such a department and the managerial skills necessary to hold a supervisory position. To help pay for my education, I have worked three summers as a waitress. This job has provided experience in meeting and dealing with people on a one-to-one basis.

While in college, I have been social chairman of the Ferris Medical Records Association and a member of the American Medical Records Association. The enclosed résumé provides further information about my experience and background.

— Establishes superiority

May I arrange an interview to discuss my qualifications in greater detail? You can reach me by writing to the above address or by calling (616) 796-7791 Monday through Friday from 2 to 5 p.m.

— Requests interview

Sincerely,

Karen K. Auernhamer

Karen K. Auernhamer

Enc.

Figure 21.7 The Pointers Applied: Sample Job Application Letter [Permanent Job]

errors, misspellings, strikeovers, obvious erasures, smudge marks, beverage stains—all can earn your letter a quick trip to the reject pile. Be sure to include enough information for the employer to evaluate your qualifications. Here are some guidelines.

1. If you know an opening exists, begin by naming the position and how you heard of it—through an advertisement or from an instructor, for example. Using a name implies a recommendation by that person. If you're writing to ask whether an

signing up new members, and making sure everyone gets along well. My college education is appropriate as well since I am getting a degree in marketing. As you probably guessed, I haven't much work experience. I have only had summer jobs as a salesclerk at a local clothing store. But you can give me the break I need. Hire me and you won't regret it. Before long you will want to make me vice-president in charge of sales. I will be happy to hop up and see you at your convenience.

Revised Version

Dear Mr. Carter:

I believe I can help you improve your sales in the Cincinnati area. Your quality line of paper plates, napkins, and cups is not available in most of the area stores, even during the summer months, which are the peak sales period for such products. I would like to help you place your products in these stores by working for you as a sales representative from May to September.

I am experienced in sales, having worked the last four years as a salesclerk for John Atterbury's Clothing Shop. Because of that experience, I not only know sales but am also familiar with many of the area retailers who should be interested in your product. In addition, I will complete my degree in marketing at Forham University next year. While at Forham, I served two years as the president of Sigma Delta Pi fraternity. As president, I was responsible for organizing charity and social functions, managing the affairs of the fraternity, and recruiting new members. These activities have helped prepare me to be an effective sales representative.

May I arrange an interview to discuss how I might use my

2439 South Lake Road
Fenton, MI 48438
March 27, 199-

Mr. Roger Updike
General Manager
Martin Buick-Olds, Inc.
Fenton, MI 48439

Dear Mr. Updike:

According to the weekly bulletin of the Drake College Placement Bureau, you have several summer openings for automotive technicians. I believe my academic training and practical experience have provided me with the qualifications needed to fill one of these positions.

I am a second-year student in the automotive service program at Drake College and expect to receive my Bachelor of Science degree in May 199-. My overall academic average is 3.08 on a 4.0 scale.

I have worked nine months as a co-op auto mechanic, and I owned a lawn-care service for one year. The co-op position has given me hands-on experience working with automobiles, and both positions have taught me the value of teamwork. I am hardworking, responsible, and quick to learn, and I will do an effective job for you.

If you desire further information concerning my background and qualifications, the Drake Placement Bureau can supply you with my college transcripts. Just call (616) 892-2319, extension 2607, and request them.

I will be happy to come in for an interview at some mutually convenient time. My number is (616) 892-9531, or you can reach me at the above address.

Sincerely yours,

Philip Thomas Dieck

Figure 21.8 The Pointers Applied: Sample Job Application Letter [Summer Job]

opening exists, specify exactly what position you're after. In either case, proceed by naming one or two of your qualifications or mentioning some service you can provide.

2. Establish your superiority over other candidates. Elaborate on the qualities mentioned at the start and present others that suit you for the position. If you have earned some or all of your college expenses or had on-the-job supervisory experience, note these facts; employers like candidates who are ambitious and possess leadership potential.

3. Don't take a "hard-sell" approach. Assertions such as "I'm just the person you're looking for" or "You'll be making a mistake if you bypass me" will likely backfire. On the other hand, don't sell yourself short with statements such as "Although I have little on-the-job experience, I think I can probably handle your job." Instead, say something like "I'm confident my academic training has prepared me to handle this job successfully." In short, don't cast yourself in a negative light; accentuate the positive without bragging.

4. Keep your letter short by referring the reader to your résumé for further information. (Summer jobs often don't require résumés.)

5. End by requesting an interview. Provide a phone number so the employer can contact you quickly. If you can be reached only at certain times, specify them.

Résumés

The résumé, sent with the application letter, elaborates on the qualifications mentioned in that letter and presents others that the employer is likely to find useful (see Figure 21.9). Since it, like the letter, helps to sell you as a candidate, spare no effort to ensure that it's attractive, well-organized, and easy to read. Here are some tips.

1. Capitalize the main captions to make them stand out on the page.

2. To condense information, use phrases and clauses rather than complete sentences.

3. List your most recent education and employment experience first and then work backward so the employer can quickly gauge what you've done recently.

4. Don't try to cram too much material onto a page. Ample white space is important.

5. Center the heading at the top of the page.

Typically, information is grouped under the six headings below. If you are a recent graduate with little or no full-time work experience, list education before work experience. If you've worked for a number of years, however, reverse the order.

1. *Heading.* Include your address and phone number. Don't date the résumé; it will then become obsolete more quickly than it otherwise would.

2. *Employment Objective.* State your immediate work goal and the direction you hope your career will take. Avoid any impression that you will soon move on to another organization or try for the boss's job. If you can't specify your objective in a believable manner, leave it out.

3. *Education.* List pertinent facts of your college education. Note any academic honors, such as a good (above 3.0) grade-point average, a scholarship, or a certificate of commendation. If you've taken elective courses in your major or have a minor in a closely related field, so indicate. To demonstrate leadership and a strong commitment to your field of study, name any campus offices you have held and professional organizations to which you belong. Conclude by noting the basic facts of your high school education: date and place of graduation and your program.

4. *Employment Experience.* Highlight your full-time, part-time, volunteer, and summer work experience. If a job was seasonal, note this fact to avoid the impression that you were fired. Mention any promotions or raises you've received and any

sales ability to the benefit of your company? You can reach me by writing to the above address or by calling (616) 796-7791.

TEACHING STRATEGIES

1. Nontraditional students often have difficulty handling gaps in their employment history or education. One solution to employment gaps is to organize the job entries so that they emphasize job titles instead of dates of employment. Here is an example:

Administrative Assistant. John Thorpe and Sons. 1430 West Michigan Drive, Grand Rapids. 1970-1972.

If the gaps can be explained, do this positively in the cover letter, as the following writer does.

After ten years as a housewife, I look forward to putting my interpersonal skills, judgment, and professional training in management at Ferris State University to work for your company.

2. Students applying for technical positions might wish to include in their résumés a special section naming their specific skills as well as the equipment and techniques with which they are familiar. For example, candidates seeking programming jobs might list the computer languages they know. This section, entitled "Special Skills," should follow the "Employment Experience" section.

SUGGESTED INSTRUCTOR READING

Odell, L. and D. Goswami, eds. Writing in Nonacademic Settings. New York: Guilford, 1985. Includes a number of helpful essays on the kinds of nonacademic writing and the concerns and writing processes of nonacademic writers.

Many textbooks on business communication as well as guides for writing résumés and cover letters are available and can provide additional insights and teaching ideas.

```
                    Karen K. Auernhamer
                    1407 East Elm Street
                    Big Rapids, MI 49307
                    Telephone: (616) 796-7791


EMPLOYMENT OBJECTIVE

To work in a technical or an assistant managerial position in a
medical records department, gain experience, and eventually
assume an administrative position.


EDUCATION

May 1991, Bachelor of Science degree, medical records
administration, Ferris State University, Big Rapids, MI 49307


Academic Honors:
    3.85/4.0 G.P.A., medical records courses

Extracurricular Activities:

    Social Chair, Ferris Medical Records Association


June 1987, graduated from Reese High School, Reese, MI 48757,
college preparatory program.


EMPLOYMENT EXPERIENCE

June 1990 to August 1990      Technical trainee (internship
                              program)
                              Saginaw Osteopathic Hospital,
                              Saginaw, MI 48602
                              Assisted with technical duties in
                              the medical records department.


Summers of 1987, 1988, 1989   Waitress, Zehnder's of
                              Frankenmuth,
                              215 South Main Street,
                              Frankenmuth, MI 48734

PERSONAL AND PROFESSIONAL INTERESTS

Member, American Medical Records Association. Enjoy tennis,
reading, biking, skiing, ice skating, and arts and crafts.


REFERENCES

Will be furnished upon request.
```

Figure 21.9 The Pointers Applied: Sample Résumé

supervisory experience you've had. Don't mention any job duties unless they are similar to those of the job you're after.

5. *Personal and Professional Interests.* Cite membership in civic and noncampus professional organizations. In addition, note any special skills like training in life saving or fluency in a foreign language, as well as special interests.

6. *References.* List references only if you are answering an advertisement that asks for them. Otherwise, indicate that they will be furnished on request. Typical references include instructors, supervisors, and prominent community leaders

who know you. Never use names of relatives or name anyone as a reference without first obtaining permission. For each reference, give the person's name, including a personal title, position, business address, and telephone number. An example follows.

Ms. Brenda Pretzer
Director, Medical Records Department
Saginaw Osteopathic Hospital
515 North Michigan Avenue
Saginaw, MI 48602
Telephone: (517) 776-2682

EXERCISE

1. Write a letter applying for an advertised job or one that someone has told you about.
2. Write a letter applying for a position for which there may or may not be a vacancy.
3. Prepare a résumé to accompany your letter.

READER

Strategies for Successful Reading

Effective reading is not the passive process that many people imagine. On the contrary, it requires the ongoing interaction of your mind and the printed page. Bringing your own knowledge and experience to bear on a piece of writing can help you assess its events, ideas, and conclusions. For example, an understanding of marriage, love, and conflict, as well as experience with divorce, can help readers comprehend an essay that explores divorce. As you read, you must also understand each point that's made, consider how the various parts fit together, and try to anticipate the direction the writing will take. Successful reading, then, requires work. Fortunately, you can follow specific strategies to help yourself read better.

*F*OLLOWING AN EFFECTIVE READING STRATEGY

Different purposes require different approaches to reading. When reading for pleasure, you can relax and proceed at your own pace, slowing down to savor a section you especially enjoy, speeding up when you encounter less interesting material, and breaking off when you wish. Even so, you will get more satisfaction out of the material if you can relate it to your own knowledge and experience.

Reading for information/evaluation and to critique the writing call for a more methodical approach. Most of your college reading will require this kind of attention.

Strategies When Reading for Information/ Evaluation

Because of the challenging nature of most college-level reading assignments, you should plan on more than one reading. A good first reading should orient you to the material. Before you begin, scan any accompanying biographical sketch and try to determine the writer's expertise and views on the topic. To illustrate, Eric Berne's background as a psychiatrist and an author of psychoanalytical texts lends authority to his discussion of personality types in the essay "Can People Be Judged by Their Appearance?" (pages 409–11).

Next, see what the title tells you. Most titles identify the topic and often the viewpoint as well. Thus "The Sweet Smell of Success Isn't All That Sweet" (pages 450–52) suggests that the author isn't overly impressed with conventional attitudes toward success. Some titles signal the writer's primary strategy: "Why Women

PERSPECTIVE

Many college students read poorly and need help to overcome this handicap. While writing instructors are limited in what they can do, you can alert students to some common causes of reading problems. Often, noise is the culprit. Successful reading requires careful concentration, impossible against a background of blaring music, loud dorm mates, and other noisy distractions. Similarly, poor eyesight and poor sleep habits can cause difficulties. Not all problems have physical roots, however. Some students lack the knowledge needed to understand an essay's ideas. Others have a limited vocabulary and limited ability to follow complex syntax. Finally, many students don't stop to identify main ideas or to anticipate the direction of the writing, interpret difficult sections in light of what they know, look for connections between ideas, or respond critically to the material. Noting these factors and taking steps to deal with them can improve many students' reading performance.

TEACHING STRATEGIES

1. Have students note the conditions under which they read, how much they read, and their biggest reading problems. Discuss the overall results with the class or address each student's difficulties in individual conferences.
2. Ask students to read an essay in the Reader, answer the discussion questions or others you have given them, and provide their definitions of key words. Check the responses to identify students who missed the main idea or misconstrued the connections between ideas. When students experience considerable difficulty, you may want to refer them to a developmental reading class.

357

3. Have students keep reading journals in which they note the main idea and back-up ideas of each assigned essay, along with their reactions and any questions that come to mind. Spot checks will reveal whether students are doing the reading.

4. Before students read an assigned essay, consider discussing its general topic in class in order to provide needed background information.

CLASSROOM ACTIVITIES

1. Have students read and respond to "Strategies for Successful Reading" by noting its main and secondary ideas in the margins, circling and defining unfamiliar words, marking transitions, and indicating difficult spots. They should then state the unit's key ideas in their own words. Observe students as they write, and offer assistance wherever needed.

2. With authors who develop their own ideas as well as discuss the ideas of others, students often misread the transitions and tangle up the ideas. To remedy this problem, you might first identify and mark the key transitions in a difficult essay like "Why Women Managers Are Bailing Out" and then have students do the same in a second essay, perhaps "Facing Up to Drugs: Is Legalization the Solution?"

3. Small group discussions can help students read more thoughtfully and actively, provided they have specific tasks to perform or questions to answer. If they are reading an argument, for example, you could have them identify the writer's chief claim, supporting claims, and evidence, as well as note any refutations.

CLASSROOM ACTIVITY

Showing students how to identify word meanings by using context can help them

Managers Are Bailing Out" (pages 441–47) indicates development by causation and "How to Adopt a Stray" (pages 385–87) development by process analysis. After evaluating the title, read the introductory paragraph(s) to see if you can determine the writer's main thesis.

Read the body of the essay quickly, noting any likely topic sentences that stand out (often the first or last sentence in a paragraph). Try to gain an idea of the essay's main thrust, the key ideas that support it, and the ways that they are organized. In your first reading, you can skim over the more difficult sections without trying to understand them fully. When you've finished, and before you reread the essay, think about what you've learned and then, either by saying it to yourself or jotting it down, express it *in your own words. For effective reading to take place, this activity is crucial.* You can hardly be said to understand what you've read, and you will be less likely to remember it, until you can state its essence in your own words. Next, go back and underline the thesis statement or, if one is not included, try to formulate one in your own words. Also look for any writing strategies the author has used. Finally, jot down questions that the first reading has raised in your mind.

On the second reading, which will take more time, you carefully absorb the writer's ideas. Read at a pace suitable to the material. Underline significant topic sentences as well as other key sentences but keep in mind that underlining in itself doesn't ensure comprehension. Restating the ideas in your own words is more effective in this regard. As you proceed, carefully examine the supporting sentences to see how well they back up the main ideas. In addition, underline or note in the margin any ideas or facts you feel are important.

Consider reading as a kind of conversation with the text. Develop the habit of asking questions about facts, reasons, ideas—practically anything in the essay. Jot your queries and their answers in the margins. (On the next page you can see how a student interacted with the first page of Amy Gross's essay "The Appeal of the Androgynous Man.") Good writers anticipate your questions and answer them, and because you have posed the questions yourself, you are more likely to see the connections in the text. If the author hasn't answered your questions, there may be problems with the work.

At times, unfamiliar words can hinder your grasp of the material. Whenever you encounter a new word, circle it, use context to help gauge its meaning, check the dictionary for the exact meaning, and then record it in the margin or some other convenient place. If the writing is peppered with words you don't know, you may have to read the whole piece just to figure out its general drift, then look up key words, and finally reread the material.

When the ideas of a single section prove difficult, restate the points of those sections you do understand. Then experiment by stating in your own words different interpretations of the problem section and see which one best fits the writing as a whole. When an entire essay is troublesome, state the ideas that are easier for you to understand and use them as keys to help unlock meanings that are difficult but not unintelligible. Save the most difficult sections until last. You might also want to discuss a difficult essay with others who are reading it.

Whenever you finish a major section of a lengthy essay, express your sense of

AMY GROSS

both male and female in one

■ *The Appeal of the* (Androgynous) *Man*

Amy Gross has been features editor at Vogue *magazine since 1983. A native of Brooklyn, New York, she earned a zoology degree at Connecticut College, then joined Condé Nast Publications where she served on the staffs of* Glamour *and* Mademoiselle. *After a period of freelancing, she became consulting editor for* Mademoiselle, *writing features every month, and then she moved to her present position at* Vogue. *She is currently coauthoring a book on women and surgery. In this selection, which first appeared in* Mademoiselle, *Gross compares androgynous men to "all-men" and finds the former preferable.*

James Dean was my first androgynous man.[1] I figured I could talk to him. He was anguished and I was 12, so we had a lot in common. With only a few exceptions, all the men I have liked or loved have been a certain kind of man: a kind who doesn't play football or watch the games on Sunday, who doesn't tell dirty jokes featuring broads or chicks, who is not contemptuous of conversations that are philosophically speculative, introspective, or otherwise foolish according to the other kind of man. He is more self-amused, less inflated, more quirky, vulnerable and responsive than the other sort (the other sort, I'm visualizing as the guys on TV who advertise deodorant in the locker room). He is more like me than the other sort. He is what social scientists and feminists would call androgynous: having the characteristics of both male and female.

Now the first thing I want you to know about the androgynous man is that he is neither effeminate nor (hermaphroditic.) All his primary and secondary sexual characteristics are in order and I would say he's all-man, but that is just what he is not. He is more than all-man. *both male and female sex organs*

The merely all-man man, for one thing, never walks to the grocery store unless the little woman is away visiting her mother with the kids, or is in the hospital having a kid, or there is no little woman. All-men men don't know how to shop in a grocery store unless it is to buy a 6-pack and some pretzels. Their ideas of nutrition expand beyond a 6-pack and pretzels only to take in steak, potatoes, scotch or rye whiskey, and maybe a wad of cake or apple pie. All-men men have absolutely no taste in food, art, books, movies, theatre, dance, how to live, what are good questions, what is funny, or anything else I care about. It's not exactly that the all-man's man is an uncouth illiterate. He may be educated, well-mannered, and on a first-name basis with fine wines. One all-man man I knew was a handsome individual who gave the impression of being gentle, affectionate, and sensitive. He sat and ate dinner one night while I was doing something endearingly feminine at the sink. At one point, he mutely held up his glass to indicate in a primitive, even ape-like, way his need for a refill. This was in 1967, before Women's Liberation. Even so, I was disturbed. Not enough to break the

1

2

3

[1]James Dean (1931–1955) was a 1950s film star who gained fame for his portrayals of restless, defiant young men.

Handwritten margin notes:

Does she favor androgynous men? What kind of appeal?

She will give a woman's perspective. She writes for and edits women's magazines.

Seems like she is going to talk about the advantages of androgynous men as compared to other men. Sees them as better.

Attempt to counter stereotype> can't androgynous men also be effeminate?

Suggests "all-men" men reject behaviors and interests they consider feminine, but isn't she stereotyping? Are all these men like this? She seems to be exaggerating.

overcome vocabulary problems, as can requiring them to buy a dictionary, showing them how to use it (see pages 211–13), and insisting that they understand the difficult words in writing assignments. Similarly, demonstrating how to parse sentences with complicated structures—for example, compound-complex sentences—can help students determine their meaning. Ultimately, however, only extensive reading experience will help students acclimate to complex sentence structures.

TEACHING STRATEGIES

1. To counter the common but mistaken student belief that professional writing is authoritative and therefore can't be criticized, assign an essay that many students will find objectionable. Provide advance warning of how they are likely to react.

2. Because the argument chapter's discussions of evidence and reasoning provide a foundation for critical reading, you might teach critical reading in connection with argumentation.

CLASSROOM ACTIVITY

Ask students to review a controversial essay in small groups. Have them identify the writer's main claims and their support, note any weakness in either, and list possible objections to the views expressed. The whole class can then discuss whether the writer's position is valid.

TEACHING STRATEGY

When discussing essays developed by a particular strategy, you might ask students guiding questions like "How is the essay organized, and is the organization effective?" and "What other strategies might the writer have used, and what would the effect have been?" Asking such questions helps students learn to read as writers.

what it means. If you have trouble seeing the connections between ideas, try outlining them, using as a starting point the topic sentences you've noted. When you finish an essay, do an overall summary.

To strengthen your grasp of material you'll need to remember for some time, try restating its main points a couple of days after the second reading. If anything has become hazy or slipped your mind, reread the appropriate section(s).

Strategies When Reading to Critique

In college you usually read not only to understand but also to judge. Your instructors will want to know what you think about what you've read.

Much of what written work conveys isn't always immediately apparent. Every writer makes assumptions, implies attitudes and values not directly stated, and has biases. For each major point that you encounter, ask yourself, "Why does the writer think this?" Then examine the supporting material for an answer.

Often, you'll be asked whether you agree or disagree with a piece of writing. Merely because information and ideas are in print does not mean that they are true or acceptable. An essay, for example, might include faulty logic, unreasonable ideas, suspect facts, or unreliable authorities. Don't hesitate to dispute the writer's information. Does it match your experience? Do the pieces of evidence support the claims? Do the ideas appear reasonable? Note any objections that you have. When you agree, try to suggest why, perhaps by citing additional support. A knowledge of the various reasoning fallacies can also help you critique a piece of writing. These fallacies are discussed on pages 151–54.

READING AS A WRITER

All of us who write can use reading as a springboard for improving our writing. You can do several things to make your reading especially useful.

As you read, the views of others, the experiences they relate, and the information they present often deepen your understanding of yourself, your relationships, and your surroundings. In turn, this broadened perspective can supply you with writing ideas. When possibilities surface, be sure to record them. Some writers keep a reading journal in which they summarize what they've read and jot down writing ideas that come to mind. In addition, you can take down specific ideas, facts, and perhaps even a few particularly telling quotations that you discover. You may want to incorporate this material into your own writing at a later time. Carefully record the source so that you can document it properly in order to avoid plagiarism (see pages 307–8). When you read several essays on the same topic, you may notice connections between their ideas. Since these connections can be fertile ground for a later essay, don't neglect to record them.

Because writers solve problems, you'll want to pay attention to the techniques and strategies that other writers use. If you find an introduction, an organizational pattern, a transition, a certain description or comparison unusually engaging, study the writer's technique. Perhaps you can use it yourself. Similarly, observe when a piece of writing fails and try to determine why.

Narration

James Alexander Thom

THE PERFECT PICTURE

James Alexander Thom (born 1933) is a native of Gosport, Indiana, where his parents were physicians, and a graduate of Butler University. Before becoming a freelance writer in 1973, he worked as an editor for the Indianapolis Star *and the* Saturday Evening Post. *In addition, he has been a lecturer at Indiana University. He has authored one volume of essays,* Let the Sun Shine *(1976), and three historical novels,* Long Knife *(1979),* Follow the River *(1981), and* From Sea to Shining Sea *(1984). He is a contributor to many popular magazines and an editor for* Nuggets *magazine. "The Perfect Picture," which first appeared in* Reader's Digest, *depicts an incident and an ethical dilemma that Thom experienced as a cub reporter.*

It was early in the spring about 15 years ago—a day of pale sunlight and trees just beginning to bud. I was a young police reporter, driving to a scene I didn't want to see. A man, the police-dispatcher's broadcast said, had accidentally backed his pickup truck over his baby granddaughter in the driveway of the family home. It was a fatality. [1]

As I parked among police cars and TV-news cruisers, I saw a stocky white-haired man in cotton work clothes standing near a pickup. Cameras were trained on him, and reporters were sticking microphones in his face. Looking totally bewildered, he was trying to answer their questions. Mostly he was only moving his lips, blinking and choking up. [2]

After a while the reporters gave up on him and followed the police into the small white house. I can still see in my mind's eye that devastated old man looking down at the place in the driveway where the child had been. Beside the house was a freshly spaded flower bed, and nearby a pile of dark, rich earth. [3]

"I was just backing up there to spread that good dirt," he said to me, though I had not asked him anything. "I didn't even know she was outdoors." He stretched his hand toward the flower bed, then let it flop to his side. He lapsed back into his thoughts, and I, like a good reporter, went into the house to find someone who could provide a recent photo of the toddler. [4]

A few minutes later, with all the details in my notebook and a three-by-five studio portrait of the cherubic child tucked in my jacket pocket, I went toward the kitchen where the police had said the body was. [5]

1 | Introduction: notes time, locale, and cause of action; first-person point of view

2 | Body: paragraphs 2–12; action begins

3 | Time signal / Key event

4 | Dialogue

5 | Time signal / Secondary event

Key event

Time signal

6   I had brought a camera in with me—the big, bulky Speed Graphic which used to be the newspaper reporter's trademark. Everybody had drifted back out of the house together—family, police, reporters and photographers. Entering the kitchen, I came upon this scene:

7   On a Formica-topped table, backlighted by a frilly curtained window, lay the tiny body, wrapped in a clean white sheet. Somehow the grandfather had managed to stay away from the crowd. He was sitting on a chair beside the table, in profile to me and unaware of my presence, looking uncomprehendingly at the swaddled corpse.

8   The house was very quiet. A clock ticked. As I watched, the grandfather slowly leaned forward, curved his arms like parentheses around the head and feet of the little form, then pressed his face to the shroud and remained motionless.

9   In that hushed moment I recognized the makings of a prize-winning news photograph. I appraised the light, adjusted the lens setting and distance, locked a bulb in the flashgun, raised the camera and composed the scene in the viewfinder.

10   Every element of the picture was perfect: the grandfather in his plain work clothes, his white hair backlighted by sunshine, the child's form wrapped in the sheet, the atmosphere of the simple home suggested by black iron trivets and World's Fair souvenir plates on the walls flanking the window. Outside, the police could be seen inspecting the fatal rear wheel of the pickup while the child's mother and father leaned in each other's arms.

Conflict

11   I don't know how many seconds I stood there, unable to snap that shutter. I was keenly aware of the powerful story-telling value that photo would have, and my professional conscience told me to take it. Yet I couldn't make my hand fire that flashbulb and intrude on the poor man's island of grief.

**Time signal
Action ends**

12   At length I lowered the camera and crept away, shaken with doubt about my suitability for the journalistic profession. Of course I never told the city editor or any fellow reporters about that missed opportunity for a perfect news picture.

Conclusion: paragraphs 13 and 14; indirectly states point; notes writer's reaction

13   Every day on the newscasts and in the papers, we see pictures of people in extreme conditions of grief and despair. Human suffering has become a spectator sport. And sometimes, as I'm watching news film, I remember that day.

14   I still feel right about what I did.

DISCUSSION QUESTIONS

1. Thom's statement shows him to be a sensitive person with empathy for the misfortunes of others. These characteristics lead him to pass up the picture that a more callous photographer would have eagerly snapped.

2. These details, while providing the makings of a perfect picture, also highlight the horror of what has happened and through their impact on his sensitivity help influence his decision.

3. Each person, of course, will have his or her own answer.

DISCUSSION QUESTIONS

1. Thom notes in his opening paragraph that he is "driving to a scene I didn't want to see." How does this statement help explain what happens later?

2. Paragraph 10 contains numerous descriptive details. What bearing do these details have on Thom's decision?

3. Do you think that Thom made the right decision? Why or why not?

SUGGESTION FOR WRITING ■ **Write a personal narrative that features a conflict over a choice between an advantageous and a morally satisfying decision. State your point directly or indirectly and use time signals and dialogue as necessary.**

Philip Ross

THE BOY AND THE BANK OFFICER

Philip Ross (born 1939) has spent his writing career in New York, his birthplace, and in New Jersey. After earning degrees at Princeton (1961) and Columbia (1962), he worked for four years as a newspaper reporter. In 1965, he became a writer for the American Museum of Natural History, and in 1969 he turned to freelance writing, which he has done ever since. His writings include two book-length works: The Bribe *(1976), a nonfiction work about an unsuccessful attempt at municipal bribery, and* The Kreuzeck Coordinates *(1985), a spy thriller. He has contributed articles to* New York, Reader's Digest, New Times, *and the* New York Times. *Our Ross narrative details an episode with an unexpected and highly embarrassing outcome.*

I have a friend who hates banks with a special passion. "A bank is just a store like a candy store or a grocery store," he says, "except that a bank's merchandise happens to be money which is yours in the first place. If banks were required to sell wallets and money belts, they might act less like churches." 1

I began thinking about my friend the other day as I walked into a small, overlighted branch office on the West Side. I had come to open a checking account. 2

It was lunchtime and the only officer on duty was a fortyish black man with short, pressed hair, a pencil mustache, and a neatly pressed brown suit. Everything about him suggested a carefully groomed authority, an eager determination to define himself through his vaulted surroundings. 3

This officer was standing across a small counter from a young white boy who was wearing a crew-neck sweater, khakis, and loafers. He had sandy hair, and I think I was especially aware of him because he looked like he belonged more on the campus of a New England prep school than in a West Side bank. 4

The boy continued to hold my attention because of what happened next. 5

He was clutching an open savings-account book and wearing an expression of open dismay. "But I don't understand," he was saying to the officer. "I opened the account myself, so why can't I withdraw any money?" 6

"I've already explained to you," the officer told him, "that bank regulations prohibit someone who is fourteen years old from withdrawing any funds without a letter from his parents." 7

"But that doesn't seem fair," the boy said, his voice breaking. "It's my money. I put it in. It's my account." 8

"I know it is," the officer said, "but those are the rules. Now if you'll excuse me." 9

He turned to me with a smile. "May I help you, sir?" 10

I didn't think twice. "I was going to open a new account," I said, "but after seeing what's going on here, I think I've changed my mind." 11

"Excuse me?" he said. 12

"Look," I said, "if I understand what's going on here correctly, what you're saying is that this boy is old enough to deposit his money in your bank but he's not old enough to withdraw it. And since there doesn't seem to be any question as 13 to whether it's his money or his account, the bank's so-called policy is patently ridiculous."

14   "It may seem ridiculous to you," he replied in a voice rising slightly in irritation, "but that is the bank's policy and I have no alternative but to abide by the rules."

15   The boy had stood hopefully next to me during this exchange, but now I was reduced to his helplessness. Suddenly I noticed that the open savings book he continued to grasp showed a balance of about $100. It also showed that there had been a series of small deposits and withdrawals.

16   I had my opening.

17   "Have you withdrawn money before by yourself?" I asked the boy.

18   "Yes," he said.

19   I moved in for the kill.

20   "How do you explain that away?" I zeroed in on the officer. "Why did you let him withdraw money before but not now?"

21   He looked exasperated. "Because the tellers were not aware of his age before and now they are. It's really very simple."

22   I turned to the boy with a pained shrug. "You're really getting ripped off," I said. "You ought to get your parents to come in here and protest."

23   The boy looked destroyed. Silently, he put his savings book in a rear-pocket and walked out of the bank.

24   The officer turned to me. "You know," he said, "you really shouldn't have interfered."

25   "Shouldn't have interfered?" I shouted. "Well, it damn well seemed to me that he needed someone to represent his interests."

26   "Someone was representing his interests," he said softly.

27   "And who might that be?"

28   "The bank."

29   I couldn't believe what this idiot was saying. "Look," I concluded, "we're just wasting each other's time. But maybe you'd like to explain exactly how the bank was representing that boy's interests?"

30   "Certainly," he said. "We were informed this morning that some neighborhood punk has been shaking this boy down for more than a month. The other guy was forcing him to take money out every week and hand it over. The poor kid was apparently too scared to tell anyone. That's the real reason he was so upset. He was afraid of what the other guy would do to him. Anyway, the police are on the case and they'll probably make an arrest today."

31   Uh.

32   "You mean there is no rule about being too young to withdraw funds from a savings account?"

33   "Not that I ever heard of. Now, sir, what can we do for you?"

DISCUSSION QUESTIONS

DISCUSSION QUESTIONS

1. The attitude of the friend prejudices Ross against the bank officer and, together with the officer's stuffy appearance, prompts Ross to take the side of the boy. (The developing situation, "bullying" officer and young boy, and the discussion between Ross and the officer also set the reader's mind against banks and add to the surprise of the outcome.)

2. Incomplete sentences occur in paragraph 9 ("Now, if you'll excuse me."), paragraph 21 ("Because the tellers were not aware of his age before and now they are."), paragraph 28 ("The bank."), and the final paragraph ("Not that I ever heard of."). Slang expressions are found in paragraphs 22 ("ripped off") and 30 ("neighborhood punk," "shaking this boy down," "other guy," "poor kid"). Omitting these features, particularly the slang expressions in paragraph 30, would leave the dialogue sounding stilted and artificial.

3. Time signals are unnecessary because the action unfolds in an uninterrupted sequence which the reader can easily follow.

4. Paragraphs 4–9 deal with the first conflict and paragraphs 10–33 with the second. The latter conflict receives more extended treatment because it involves the

1. In his opening paragraph Ross cites a friend's attitude toward banks, and in the third paragraph he describes the bank officer. What does he accomplish by presenting these two aspects of the story?

2. Examine the dialogue in this essay and then point out examples of incomplete sentences and slang. Why are these included?

3. This story has very few time signals. Why are they unnecessary?
4. This narrative features two conflicts: the first between the boy and the bank officer, the second between the officer and the narrator. In which paragraphs does Ross present each conflict? Why does the second conflict receive more extended treatment?
5. Ross provides a good example of a narrative with an unstated point. What is the point? Refer to specific parts of the story when answering.

SUGGESTION FOR WRITING ■ Narrate an experience whose outcome was not at all what you expected. Include material that points toward an ending different from the one that in fact occurred.

Maya Angelou

MOMMA'S ENCOUNTER[1]

Maya Angelou has earned a reputation as one of this country's foremost black writers. Born (1928) Marguerite Johnson in St. Louis, Missouri, she spent much of her childhood in Stamps, Arkansas, the locale of our selection, where her grandmother ran a general store. Angelou has written plays, poems, and a five-part autobiography that includes I Know Why the Caged Bird Sings *(1970),* Gather Together in My Name *(1974),* Singin' and Swingin' and Gettin' Merry Like Christmas *(1976),* The Heart of a Woman *(1981), and* All God's Children Have Traveling Shoes *(1986). She has acted in numerous plays and has served as a television narrator, interviewer, and host. In our selection, taken from her first volume of autobiography, Angelou tells about an encounter in which her grandmother, whom she calls Momma, triumphs over a pack of taunting neighborhood children.*

"Thou shall not be dirty" and "Thou shall not be impudent" were the two commandments of Grandmother Henderson upon which hung our total salvation. 1

Each night in the bitterest winter we were forced to wash faces, arms, necks, legs and feet before going to bed. She used to add, with a smirk that unprofane people can't control when venturing into profanity, "and wash as far as possible, then wash possible." 2

We would go to the well and wash in the ice-cold, clear water, grease our legs with the equally cold stiff Vaseline, then tiptoe into the house. We wiped the dust from our toes and settled down for schoolwork, cornbread, clabbered milk, prayers and bed, always in that order. Momma was famous for pulling the quilts off after we had fallen asleep to examine our feet. If they weren't clean enough for her, she took the switch (she kept one behind the bedroom door for emergencies) and woke up the offender with a few aptly placed burning reminders. 3

[1]Editors' title.

narrator, and the point of the essay hinges on it. You might call attention to an offstage conflict: the one between the boy with the account and the one shaking him down.
5. The unstated point of this narrative is "appearances can be deceiving." Everything preceding paragraph 26 stamps the bank officer as a pompous bureaucrat with no concern for the boy's feelings. Then the writer springs his surprise, and we learn the truth about the teller.

PERSPECTIVE

As the answer to Discussion Question 2 indicates, the disrespectful upbringing of the "powhitetrash" children foreshadows their confrontation with Momma. But race also plays a role in what happens. Because Momma and her family are black, they are regarded as inferior and are thus fair game for humiliation. Momma's reaction in turn is conditioned by the then-prevailing racial climate. Given her firm approach to discipline in her own family, she probably would not have tolerated the taunting words and antics in black children.

TEACHING STRATEGIES

1. Initially you might point out that differences in status influence the ways people behave toward one another. Examples are plentiful: teachers who expect to be addressed as "Ms.," "Doctor," or "Professor" call students by their first names; bosses summon employees to their offices for conferences but not vice versa; people in a courtroom are asked to rise when the judge enters. With this point established, ask the class to read paragraphs 7–13 and discuss their function in the essay.
2. When writing narratives some students become so ab-

sorbed in relating events that they forget about creating and maintaining reader interest. You might discuss how Angelou keeps the reader involved. When students write their own narratives, have them exchange papers within peer groups, get some feedback on the interest level, and then revise accordingly.

4   The area around the well at night was dark and slick, and boys told about how snakes love water, so that anyone who had to draw water at night and then stand there alone and wash knew that moccasins and rattlers, puff adders and boa constrictors were winding their way to the well and would arrive just as the person washing got soap in her eyes. But Momma convinced us that not only was cleanliness next to Godliness, dirtiness was the inventor of misery.

5   The impudent child was detested by God and a shame to its parents and could bring destruction to its house and line. All adults had to be addressed as Mister, Missus, Miss, Auntie, Cousin, Unk, Uncle, Buhbah, Sister, Brother and a thousand other appellations indicating familial relationship and the lowliness of the addressor.

6   Everyone I knew respected these customary laws, except for the powhite-trash children.

7   Some families of powhitetrash lived on Momma's farm land behind the school. Sometimes a gaggle of them came to the Store, filling the whole room, chasing out the air and even changing the well-known scents. The children crawled over the shelves and into the potato and onion bins, twanging all the time in their sharp voices like cigarbox guitars. They took liberties in my Store that I would never dare. Since Momma told us that the less you say to whitefolks (or even powhitetrash) the better, Bailey and I would stand, solemn, quiet, in the displaced air. But if one of the playful apparitions got close to us, I pinched it. Partly out of angry frustration and partly because I didn't believe in its flesh reality.

8   They called my uncle by his first name and ordered him around the Store. He, to my crying shame, obeyed them in his limping dip-straight-dip fashion.

9   My grandmother, too followed their orders, except that she didn't seem to be servile because she anticipated their needs.

10   "Here's sugar, Miz Potter, and here's baking powder. You didn't buy soda last month, you'll probably be needing some."

11   Momma always directed her statements to the adults, but sometimes, Oh painful sometimes, the grimy, snotty-nosed girls would answer her.

12   "Naw, Annie. . ."—to Momma? Who owned the land they lived on? Who forgot more than they would ever learn? If there was any justice in the world, God should strike them dumb at once!—"Just give us some extry sody crackers, and some more mackerel."

13   At least they never looked in her face, or I never caught them doing so. Nobody with a smidgen of training, not even the worst roustabout, would look right in a grown person's face. It meant the person was trying to take the words out before they were formed. The dirty little children didn't do that, but they threw their orders around the Store like lashes from a cat-o'-nine tails.

14   When I was around ten years old, those scruffy children caused me the most painful and confusing experience I had ever had with my grandmother.

15   One summer morning, after I had swept the dirt yard of leaves, spearmint-gum wrappers and Vienna-sausage labels, I raked the yellow-red dirt, and made half-moons carefully, so that the design stood out clearly and mask-like. I put the rake behind the Store and came through the back of the house to find Grandmother on the front porch in her big, wide white apron. The apron was so stiff by virtue of the starch that it could have stood alone. Momma was admiring the yard, so I joined her. It truly looked like a flat redhead that had been raked with a big-toothed comb. Momma didn't say anything but I knew she liked it. She looked over toward the school principal's house and to the right at Mr. McElroy's. She

was hoping one of those community pillars would see the design before the day's business wiped it out. Then she looked upward to the school. My head had swung with hers, so at just about the same time we saw a troop of the po-whitetrash kids marching over the hill and down by the side of the school.

I looked to Momma for direction. She did an excellent job of sagging from her waist down, but from the waist up she seemed to be pulling for the top of the oak tree across the road. Then she began to moan a hymn. Maybe not to moan, but the tune was so slow and the meter so strange that she could have been moaning. She didn't look at me again. When the children reached halfway down the hill, halfway to the Store, she said without turning, "Sister, go on inside." 16

I wanted to beg her, "Momma, don't wait for them. Come on inside with me. If they come in the Store, you go to the bedroom and let me wait on them. They only frighten me if you're around. Alone I know how to handle them." But of course I couldn't say anything, so I went in and stood behind the screen door. 17

Before the girls got to the porch I heard their laughter crackling and popping like pine logs in a cooking stove. I suppose my lifelong paranoia was born in those cold, molasses-slow minutes. They came finally to stand on the ground in front of Momma. At first they pretended seriousness. Then one of them wrapped her right arm in the crook of her left, pushed out her mouth and started to hum. I realized that she was aping my grandmother. Another said, "Naw, Helen, you ain't standing like her. This here's it." Then she lifted her chest, folded her arms and mocked that strange carriage that was Annie Henderson. Another laughed, "Naw, you can't do it. Your mouth ain't pooched out enough. It's like this." 18

I thought about the rifle behind the door, but I knew I'd never be able to hold it straight, and the .410, our sawed-off shotgun, which stayed loaded and was fired every New Year's night, was locked in the trunk and Uncle Willie had the key on his chain. Through the fly-specked screen-door, I could see that the arms of Momma's apron jiggled from the vibrations of her humming. But her knees seemed to have locked as if they would never bend again. 19

She sang on. No louder than before, but no softer either. No slower or faster. 20

The dirt of the girls' cotton dresses continued on their legs, feet, arms and faces to make them all of a piece. Their greasy uncolored hair hung down, uncombed, with a grim finality. I knelt to see them better, to remember them for all time. The tears that had slipped down my dress left unsurprising dark spots, and made the front yard blurry and even more unreal. The world had taken a deep breath and was having doubts about continuing to revolve. 21

The girls had tired of mocking Momma and turned to other means of agitation. One crossed her eyes, stuck her thumbs in both sides of her mouth and said, "Look here, Annie." Grandmother hummed on and the apron strings trembled. I wanted to throw a handful of black pepper in their faces, to throw lye on them, to scream that they were dirty, scummy peckerwoods, but I knew I was as clearly imprisoned behind the scene as the actors outside were confined to their roles. 22

One of the smaller girls did a kind of puppet dance while her fellow clowns laughed at her. But the tall one, who was almost a woman, said something very quietly, which I couldn't hear. They all moved backward from the porch, still watching Momma. For an awful second I thought they were going to throw a rock at Momma, who seemed (except for the apron strings) to have turned into stone herself. But the big girl turned her back, bent down and put her hands flat on the 23

DISCUSSION QUESTIONS (pp. 368–69)

1. This narrative has an unstated main point which might be rendered somewhat as follows: high standards of behavior are an important part of life, and one should not abandon them, even under severe provocation. By maintaining her dignity when confronted with the rudeness of the "powhitetrash" children, Momma triumphs over them. The whole episode has a classic Christian outcome, as Momma's triumph comes through acting humbly and turning the other cheek.

2. Angelou's strict upbringing stresses cleanliness and respect for elders. Each night, even during the winter, she and the other children must wash in the ice-cold water of the well, and all adults have to be addressed by some title. In contrast, the "powhite-trash" children are so dirty that they change "the well-known scents" of the store whenever they enter it. In the store they show disrespect by messing up the merchandise and treating the proprietors disrespectfully, behavior that foreshadows their later abuse of Momma.

3. Angelou is a prisoner of her sociological and familial backgrounds. The first of these dictates deference to whites, and the second prohibits her from responding in kind to the taunts of her grandmother's tormenters. Like Angelou, the "po-whitetrash" children are prisoners of their upbringing. Reared in a society that regards blacks as inferior and lacking any sense of respect for adults, they behave in a manner that fully accords with their upbringing.

4. This dialogue marks the climax of the confrontation between Momma and her tormenters and points up her triumph over them. Having survived their insolent behavior with her dignity intact, she replies courteously to their final taunting "bye's" and in so doing signals their final defeat.

5. The pattern of concentric hearts pierced by an arrow suggests the love that the 10-year-old Angelou bears for her family and perhaps the wish for love to bind everyone together. Momma's "Glory, glory, hallelujah . . ." reflects both her recognition of the difficulty of maintaining her standards of behavior and her determination to do so as long as she lives.

6. At 10, Angelou, as paragraph 35 indicates, realizes

ground—she didn't pick up anything. She simply shifted her weight and did a hand stand.

24   Her dirty bare feet and long legs went straight for the sky. Her dress fell down around her shoulders, and she had on no drawers. The slick pubic hair made a brown triangle where her legs came together. She hung in the vacuum of that lifeless morning for only a few seconds, then wavered and tumbled. The other girls clapped her on the back and slapped their hands.

25   Momma changed her song to "Bread of Heaven, bread of Heaven, feed me till I want no more."

26   I found that I was praying too. How long could Momma hold out? What new indignity would they think of to subject her to? Would I be able to stay out of it? What would Momma really like me to do?

27   Then they were moving out of the yard, on their way to town. They bobbed their heads and shook their slack behinds and turned, one at a time:

28   " 'Bye, Annie."

29   " 'Bye, Annie."

30   " 'Bye, Annie."

31   Momma never turned her head or unfolded her arms, but she stopped singing and said, "'Bye, Miz Helen, 'bye, Miz Ruth, 'bye, Miz Eloise."

32   I burst. A firecracker July-the-Fourth burst. How could Momma call them Miz? The mean nasty things. Why couldn't she have come inside the sweet, cool store when we saw them breasting the hill? What did she prove? And then if they were dirty, mean and impudent, why did Momma have to call them Miz?

33   She stood another whole song through and then opened the screen door to look down on me crying in rage. She looked until I looked up. Her face was a brown moon that shone on me. She was beautiful. Something had happened out there, which I couldn't completely understand, but I could see that she was happy. Then she bent down and touched me as mothers of the church "lay hands on the sick and afflicted" and I quieted.

34   "Go wash your face, Sister." And she went behind the candy counter and hummed, "Glory, glory, hallelujah, when I lay my burden down."

35   I threw the well water on my face and used the weekday handkerchief to blow my nose. Whatever the contest had been out front, I knew Momma had won.

36   I took the rake back to the front yard. The smudged footprints were easy to erase. I worked for a long time on my new design and laid the rake behind the wash pot. When I came back in the Store, I took Momma's hand and we both walked outside to look at the pattern.

37   It was a large heart with lots of hearts growing smaller inside, and piercing from the outside rim to the smallest heart was an arrow. Momma said, "Sister, that's right pretty." Then she turned back to the Store and resumed, "Glory, glory, hallelujah, when I lay my burden down."

DISCUSSION QUESTIONS

1. Does this narrative have a stated or an unstated point? If it is stated, indicate where. If it is unstated, express it in your own words.

2. Point out the contrast between Angelou's upbringing and that of the "powhite-trash" children. How does this contrast prepare the reader for the events that follow?

3. Explain what Angelou means in paragraph 22 when she says ". . . but I knew I was as clearly imprisoned behind the scene as the actors outside were confined to their roles."
4. Discuss the significance of the dialogue in paragraphs 28–31.
5. Suggest the significance of the pattern of hearts that Angelou draws in the front yard. Of Momma singing "Glory, glory, hallelujah, when I lay my burden down."
6. Angelou recalls that she was "around ten years old" when the encounter took place. Explain why her age was significant. How would her perception have differed had she been, say, eighteen?
7. Angelou uses the first-person point of view. Explain why third-person narration would have been inappropriate for this narrative.

SUGGESTION FOR WRITING ■ **Write a narrative that illustrates how a friend, an acquaintance, or a family member achieved a personal triumph through turning the other cheek.**

Lewis Sawaquat

FOR MY INDIAN DAUGHTER

Lewis Sawaquat (born 1935), a Native American who numbers an Indian chief among his ancestors, is an active participant in the affairs of his tribe and in securing scholarships for Native American students. While serving in the United States Army, he completed a program in surveying and then spent the remainder of his enlistment in Korea. Later, he attended the Art Institute of Chicago. He is now a retired United States government surveyor. In "For My Indian Daughter," Sawaquat addresses anti-Indian prejudice and the development of his sense of "what it means to be Indian."

My little girl is singing herself to sleep upstairs, her voice mingling with the sounds of the birds outside in the old maple trees. She is two and I am nearly 50, and I am very taken with her. She came along late in my life, unexpected and unbidden, a startling gift. 1

Today at the beach my chubby-legged, brown-skinned daughter ran laughing into the water as fast as she could. My wife and I laughed watching her, until we heard behind us a low guttural curse and then an unpleasant voice raised in an imitation war whoop. 2

I turned to see a fat man in a bathing suit, white and soft as a grub, as he covered his mouth and prepared to make the Indian war cry again. He was middle-aged, younger than I, and had three little children lined up next to him, grinning foolishly. My wife suggested we leave the beach, and I agreed. 3

I knew the man was not unusual in his feelings against Indians. His beach behavior might have been socially unacceptable to more civilized whites, but his basic view of Indians is expressed daily in our small town, frequently on the editorial pages of the county newspaper, as white people speak out against Indian 4

TEACHING STRATEGY

TEACHING STRATEGY

As a prelude to a writing assignment, ask students to explore the causes of ethnic, racial, religious, and class prejudice and suggest strategies for combatting it.

CLASSROOM ACTIVITIES

1. Divide the class into small groups and have students exchange accounts of unpleasant incidents they have experienced because of race, ethnicity, gender, mode of dress, or lifestyle. When the groups have finished, have them present their incidents to the class. This activity could serve as the springboard for a writing assignment.
2. Ask students to bring in articles that discuss the authors' encounters with prejudice. Divide the class into small groups, distribute the articles, and have students compare the incidents in the articles with those encountered by Sawaquat. This activity will help students gain insight into the basic factors leading to prejudice.

DISCUSSION QUESTIONS

1. The opening section clearly establishes that Sawaquat is writing for his daughter, and the last paragraph of the essay shows why—to arm her against the prejudice she has already unknowingly encountered and will face later. The middle paragraphs support this purpose by explaining why prejudice happens and pointing out that American Indians possess a proud heritage. Sawaquat's title, then, is an obvious choice.
2. Sawaquat offers two reasons: first, hatred is aroused

fishing rights and land rights, saying in essence, "Those Indians are taking our fish, our land." It doesn't matter to them that we were here first, that the U.S. Supreme Court has ruled in our favor. It matters to them that we have something they want, and they hate us for it. Backlash is the common explanation of the attacks on Indians, the bumper stickers that say, "Spear an Indian, Save a Fish," but I know better. The hatred of Indians goes back to the beginning when white people came to this country. For me it goes back to my childhood in Harbor Springs, Mich.

5 　**Theft:** Harbor Springs is now a summer resort for the very affluent, but a hundred years ago it was the Indian village of my Ottawa ancestors. My grandmother, Anna Showanessy, and other Indians like her, had their land there taken by treaty, by fraud, by violence, by theft. They remembered how whites had burned down the village at Burt Lake in 1900 and pushed the Indians out. These were the stories in my family.

6 　When I was a boy my mother told me to walk down the alleys in Harbor Springs and not to wear my orange football sweater out of the house. This way I would not stand out, not be noticed, and not be a target.

7 　I wore my orange sweater anyway and deliberately avoided the alleys. I was the biggest person I knew and wasn't really afraid. But I met my comeuppance when I enlisted in the U.S. Army. One night all the men in my barracks gathered together and, gang-fashion, pulled me into the shower and scrubbed me down with rough brushes used for floors, saying, "We won't have any dirty Indians in our outfit." It is a point of irony that I was cleaner than any of them. Later in Korea I learned how to kill, how to bully, how to hate Koreans. I came out of the war tougher than ever and, strangely, white.

8 　I went to college, got married, lived in La Porte, Ind., worked as a surveyor and raised three boys. I headed Boy Scout groups, never thinking it odd when the Scouts did imitation Indian dances, imitation Indian lore.

9 　One day when I was 35 or thereabouts I heard about an Indian powwow. My father used to attend them and so with great curiosity and a strange joy at discovering a part of my heritage, I decided the thing to do to get ready for this big event was to have my friend make me a spear in his forge. The steel was fine and blue and iridescent. The feathers on the shaft were bright and proud.

10 　In a dusty state fairground in southern Indiana, I found white people dressed as Indians. I learned they were "hobbyists," that is, it was their hobby and leisure pastime to masquerade as Indians on weekends. I felt ridiculous with my spear, and I left.

11 　It was years before I could tell anyone of the embarrassment of this weekend and see any humor in it. But in a way it was that weekend, for all its silliness, that was my awakening. I realized I didn't know who I was. I didn't have an Indian name. I didn't speak the Indian language. I didn't know the Indian customs. Dimly I remembered the Ottawa word for dog, but it was a baby word, *kahgee*, not the full word, *muhkahgee*, which I was later to learn. Even more hazily I remembered a naming ceremony (my own). I remembered legs dancing around me, dust. Where had that been? Who had I been? "Suwaukquat," my mother told me when I asked, "where the tree begins to grow."

12 　That was 1968, and I was not the only Indian in the country who was feeling the need to remember who he or she was. There were others. They had powwows, real ones, and eventually I found them. Together we researched our past, a search that for me culminated in the Longest Walk, a march on Washington

in 1978. Maybe because I now know what it means to be Indian, it surprises me that others don't. Of course there aren't very many of us left. The chances of an average person knowing an average Indian in an average lifetime are pretty slim.

Circle: Still, I was amused one day when my small, four-year-old neighbor 13 looked at me as I was hoeing in my garden and said, "You aren't a real Indian, are you?" Scotty is little, talkative, likable. Finally I said, "I'm a real Indian." He looked at me for a moment and then said, squinting into the sun, "Then where's your horse and feathers?" The child was simply a smaller, whiter version of my own ignorant self years before. We'd both seen too much TV, that's all. He was not to be blamed. And so, in a way, the moronic man on the beach today is blameless. We come full circle to realize other people are like ourselves, as discomfiting as that may be sometimes.

As I sit in my old chair on my porch, in a light that is fading so the leaves are 14 barely distinguishable against the sky, I can picture my girl asleep upstairs. I would like to prepare her for what's to come, take her each step of the way saying, there's a place to avoid, here's what I know about this, but much of what's before her she must go through alone. She must pass through pain and joy and solitude and community to discover her own inner self that is unlike any other and come through that passage to the place where she sees all people are one, and in so seeing may live her life in a brighter future.

DISCUSSION QUESTIONS

1. After reflecting on the entire essay, try to account for Sawaquat's choice of title.
2. Why, according to Sawaquat, are so many whites prejudiced against Indians?
3. The man who ridicules Sawaquat's daughter is described in paragraph 3 as being "white and soft as a grub." What does this description reveal about Sawaquat's attitude toward him?
4. Why was the "powwow" that Sawaquat discusses in paragraphs 9-10 an important event in his life?
5. What is accomplished by the repetition of "I didn't" in four consecutive sentences of paragraph 11?
6. Discuss the significance of the dialogue in paragraph 13.
7. Reflecting on his daughter's future, Sawaquat says in paragraph 14 that "much of what's before her she must go through alone." Explain what he means.

SUGGESTION FOR WRITING ■ Write a narrative that relates an instance when you experienced some form of prejudice and how you coped with it. Your thesis may be stated or unstated.

when Indians have something that whites want (paragraphs 4 and 5); second, bigotry is a product of ignorance (paragraphs 2, 3, and 7).

3. Grubs live underground, and most people consider them ugly. In characterizing the man as he does, Sawaquat points up his ugly behavior and, on a more symbolic level, his lack of enlightenment.

4. This event was important because it made Sawaquat realize that he knew nothing about his Indian heritage and because it led him to begin searching it out.

5. Repetition of "I didn't" lends added force to the point Sawaquat is making: his complete ignorance of his Indian heritage.

6. This dialogue shows that ignorance doesn't necessarily lead to prejudice. The neighbor boy certainly knows nothing about the lifestyle of the Indians who live in his area, but he shows no hostility toward Sawaquat. The boy's question "Then where's your horse and feathers?" suggests that the movies and TV have played a big role in molding mistaken impressions of Indians, not to mention flawed attitudes toward them.

7. Sawaquat means that he can prepare his daughter intellectually but not emotionally for what she will face later. This meaning is made explicit in the sentence following the one from which the quotation comes.

OVERVIEW OF DESCRIPTIVE ESSAYS

Two of the descriptions rely almost entirely on sight impressions, one relies mainly on sight impressions together with a scattering of sound impressions, and one blends all five kinds. Three are written from a fixed vantage point, one from a moving vantage point. Two span intervals of only a few minutes, one covers perhaps a half hour, and one covers about a week. Three culminate in a turning point or climax that brings with it emotional release or some insight. All feature a strong dominant impression.

Title identifies dominant impression: magic

Introduction: paragraphs 1 and 2; identifies when, where, who, why
Touch impression

Sight impression
Comparisons

Body: paragraphs 3–8
Fixed vantage point
Sight impressions

Time signal

Sight impressions

Sound impressions

Time signal
Sight impression
Comparison

John V. Young

WHEN THE FULL MOON SHINES ITS MAGIC OVER MONUMENT VALLEY

John V. Young (born 1909) is a native of Oakland, California. After attending San Jose State Teachers College, he spent twelve years as a reporter and editor for several rural California newspapers, then held a series of personnel and public relations positions. In 1966, he became a full-time freelance writer, specializing in western travel pieces. His books include The Grand Canyon *(1969),* Ghost Towns of the Santa Cruz Mountains *(1979, 1984),* Hot Type and Pony Wire *(1980),* State Parks of New Mexico *(1984), and* State Parks of Arizona *(1986). His articles have appeared in the* New York Times *as well as numerous travel publications. In the article that follows, he focuses on the sensations generated first by his surroundings and then by the moonrise.*

1   We were camped here in early spring, by one of those open-faced shelters that the Navajos have provided for tourists in this part of their vast tribal park on the Arizona–Utah border, 25 miles north of Kayenta. It was cool but pleasant, and we were alone, three men in a truck.

2   We were here for a purpose; to see the full moon rise over this most mysterious and lonely of scenic wonders, where fantastically eroded red and yellow sandstone shapes soar to the sky like a giant's chess pieces and where people—especially white strangers—come quickly to feel like pretty small change indeed.

3   Because all Navajo dwellings face east, our camp faced east—toward the rising sun and the rising moon and across a limitless expanse of tawny desert, that ancient sea, framed by the towering nearby twin pinnacles called The Mittens. We began to feel the magic even before the sun was fully down. It occurred when a diminutive wraith of a Navajo girl wearing a long, dark, velvet dress gleaming with silver ornaments drifted silently by, herding a flock of ghostly sheep to a waterhole somewhere. A bell on one of the rams tinkled faintly, and then its music was lost in the soft rustle of the night wind, leaving us with an impression that perhaps we had really seen nothing at all.

4   Just then, a large woolly dog appeared out of the gloom, seeming to materialize on the spot. It sat quietly on the edge of the glow from our campfire, its eyes shining like mirrors. It made no sound but when we offered food, it accepted the gift gravely and with much dignity. The dog then vanished again, probably to join the girl and her flock. We were not certain it was not part of the illusion.

As the sun disappeared entirely, the evening afterglow brush tipped all the spires and cliffs with magenta, deepening to purple, and the sand ripples stood out like miniature ocean waves in darkening shades of orange. Off to the east on the edge of the desert, a pale saffron glow told us the moon was about to rise behind a thin layer of clouds, slashed by the white contrail of an invisible jet airplane miles away. 5

Time signal
Sight impressions
Comparison
Sight impressions

We had our cameras on tripods and were fussing with light meters, making casual bets as to the exact place where the moon would first appear, when it happened—instant enchantment. Precisely between the twin spires of The Mittens, the enormous globe loomed suddenly, seeming as big as the sun itself, behind a coppery curtain on the rim of creation. 6

Sight impressions
Comparison
Original language

We were as totally unprepared for the great size of the moon as we were for its flaming color, nor could we have prepared ourselves for the improbable setting. We felt like the wizards of Stonehenge, commanding the planets to send their light through the magic orifices in line at the equinox. Had the Navajo medicine men contrived this for our benefit? 7

Sight impressions

Comparison

The massive disk of the moon seemed to rise very fast at first, an optical effect magnified by the crystalline air and the flatness of the landscape between us and the distant, ragged skyline. Then it seemed to pause for a moment, as if it were pinioned on one of the pinnacles or impaled on a sharply upthrusting rocky point. Its blazing light made inky shadows all around us, split by the brilliant wedge of the moon's path between the spires. The wind had stopped. There was not a sound anywhere, nor even a whisper. If a drum had sounded just then, it would not have been out of place, I suppose, but it would have frightened us half to death. 8

Sight impressions

Original language

Absent sound
Impression

Before the moon had cleared the tops of The Mittens, the show was over and the magic was gone. A thin veil of clouds spread over the sky, ending the spell as suddenly as it had come upon us. It was as if the gods had decided that we had seen enough for mere mortals on one spring night, and I must confess it was something of a relief to find ourselves back on mundane earth again, with sand in our shoes and a chill in the air. 9

Conclusion: time signal; renames dominant impression

Notes writer's reaction

Touch impression

DISCUSSION QUESTIONS

1. How does the last sentence in paragraph 7 ("Had the Navajo medicine men contrived this for our benefit?") relate to the purpose of the essay?
2. This description takes the form of a narrative. Where does the climax occur and how does it affect the viewers?

DISCUSSION QUESTIONS

1. This question suggests that the whole episode is a piece of magic deliberately created by the medicine men.
2. The climax occurs in the last sentence of paragraph 6, when the moon suddenly looms between the twin spires of the mountain called "The Mittens." The men are awe-struck, and they liken their reactions to those of the ancient wizards at Stonehenge, in England, "commanding the planets to send their light through the magic orifices in line at the equinox."

SUGGESTION FOR WRITING ■ Select a place you know well and describe it by conveying some dominant impression that emerges during daylight hours. Settle on an appropriate vantage point and either identify the impression or allow readers to determine it for themselves.

Annie Dillard

A TOTAL ECLIPSE[1]

Annie Dillard was born in Pittsburgh (1945) and received her education at Hollins College in Virginia. Between 1965 and 1975, she lived in the Roanoke Valley of Virginia, where she investigated the world of nature and wrote about it. In 1975, she became Distinguished Visiting Professor at Western Washington State University and later became Writer-in-Residence at Wesleyan University. Dillard's first prose book, Pilgrim at Tinker Creek *(1974), was compared favorably with Thoreau's* Walden *and won her the 1974 Pulitzer Prize. Later books include* Teaching a Stone to Talk *(1982), from which "A Total Eclipse" is taken, and* An American Childhood *(1987). She has contributed to a variety of magazines, including* American Scholar, Atlantic Monthly, Chicago Review, Harper's, *and* Poetry. *In "A Total Eclipse" Dillard shares her perceptions about one of nature's most spectacular phenomena.*

1   It began with no ado. It was odd that such a well-advertised public event should have no starting gun, no overture, no introductory speaker. I should have known right then that I was out of my depth. Without pause or preamble, silent as orbits, a piece of the sun went away. We looked at it through welders' goggles. A piece of the sun was missing; in its place we saw empty sky.

2   I had seen a partial eclipse in 1970. A partial eclipse is very interesting. It bears almost no relation to a total eclipse. Seeing a partial eclipse bears the same relation to seeing a total eclipse as kissing a man does to marrying him, or as flying in an airplane does to falling out of an airplane. Although the one experience precedes the other, it in no way prepares you for it. During a partial eclipse the sky does not darken—not even when 94 percent of the sun is hidden. Nor does the sun, seen colorless through protective devices, seem terribly strange. We have all seen a sliver of light in the sky; we have all seen the crescent moon by day. However, during a partial eclipse the air does indeed get cold, precisely as if someone were standing between you and the fire. And blackbirds do fly back to their roosts. I had seen a partial eclipse before, and here was another.

3   What you see in an eclipse is entirely different from what you know. It is especially different for those of us whose grasp of astronomy is so frail that, given a flashlight, a grapefruit, two oranges, and fifteen years, we still could not figure out which way to set the clocks for Daylight Saving Time. Usually it is a bit of a trick to keep your knowledge from blinding you. But during an eclipse it is easy. What you see is much more convincing than any wild-eyed theory you may know.

4   You may read that the moon has something to do with eclipses. I have never seen the moon yet. You do not see the moon. So near the sun, it is as completely invisible as the stars are by day. What you see before your eyes is the sun going through phases. It gets narrower and narrower, as the waning moon

[1]Editors' title.

does, and, like the ordinary moon, it travels alone in the simple sky. The sky is of course background. It does not appear to eat the sun; it is far behind the sun. The sun simply shaves away; gradually, you see less sun and more sky.

The sky's blue was deepening, but there was no darkness. The sun was a wide crescent, like a segment of tangerine. The wind freshened and blew steadily over the hill. The eastern hill across the highway grew dusky and sharp. The towns and orchards in the valley to the south were dissolving into the blue light. Only the thin river held a trickle of sun.   5

Now the sky to the west deepened to indigo, a color never seen. A dark sky usually loses color. This was a saturated, deep indigo, up in the air. Stuck up into that unworldly sky was the cone of Mount Adams, and the alpenglow was upon it. The alpenglow is that red light of sunset which holds out on snowy mountaintops long after the valleys and tablelands are dimmed. "Look at Mount Adams," I said, and that was the last sane moment I remember.   6

I turned back to the sun. It was going. The sun was going, and the world was wrong. The grasses were wrong; they were platinum. Their every detail of stem, head, and blade shone lightless and artificially distinct as an art photographer's platinum print. This color has never been seen on earth. The hues were metallic; their finish was matte. The hillside was a nineteenth-century tinted photograph from which the tints had faded. All the people you see in the photograph, distinct and detailed as their faces look, are now dead. The sky was navy blue. My hands were silver. All the distant hills' grasses were finespun metal which the wind laid down. I was watching a faded color print of a movie filmed in the Middle Ages; I was standing in it, by some mistake. I was standing in a movie of hillside grasses filmed in the Middle Ages. I missed my own century, the people I knew, and the real light of day.   7

I looked at Gary [her husband]. He was in the film. Everything was lost. He was a platinum print, a dead artist's version of life. I saw on his skull the darkness of night mixed with the colors of day. My mind was going out; my eyes were receding the way galaxies recede to the rim of space. Gary was light-years away, gesturing inside a circle of darkness, down the wrong end of a telescope. He smiled as if he saw me; the stringy crinkles around his eyes moved. The sight of him, familiar and wrong, was something I was remembering from centuries hence, from the other side of death: yes, *that* is the way he used to look, when we were living. When it was our generation's turn to be alive. I could not hear him; the wind was too loud. Behind him the sun was going. We had all started down a chute of time. At first it was pleasant; now there was no stopping it. Gary was chuting away across space, moving and talking and catching my eye, chuting down the long corridor of separation. The skin on his face moved like thin bronze plating that would peel.   8

The grass at our feet was wild barley. It was the wild einkorn wheat which grew on the hilly flanks of the Zagros Mountains, above the Euphrates valley, above the valley of the river we called *River*. We harvested the grass with stone sickles, I remember. We found the grasses on the hillsides; we built our shelter beside them and cut them down. That is how he used to look then, that one, moving and living and catching my eye, with the sky so dark behind him, and the wind blowing. God save our life.   9

From all the hills came screams. A piece of sky beside the crescent sun was detaching. It was a loosened circle of evening sky, suddenly lighted from the back. It was an abrupt black body out of nowhere; it was a flat disk; it was almost over the sun. That is when there were screams. At once this disk of sky slid over   10

DISCUSSION QUESTIONS

1. Dillard begins her description with a short arresting statement that captures the reader's attention. The rest of the opening paragraph expands on the discrepancy between the "well-advertised public event" and the lack of fanfare preceding it. Students might note that despite beginning with "no ado" the eclipse turns out to have a profound impact on Dillard. The final sentence of this description echoes the terseness of the first sentence, lending a sense of symmetry to the whole episode.

2. The unfamiliar (the relation of a partial to a full eclipse) is made graphically clear by comparing it with the familiar. In addition, Dillard prepares the reader for the sense of awe she experienced upon viewing this total eclipse.

3. No amount of book learning or "wild-eyed theory" can alter the stark reality of viewing an eclipse.

4. "God save our life" is at the heart of the awe, even terror, that Dillard experiences. Foreshadowed in paragraph 1 ("out of my depth"), the feeling is made explicit in, for example, "that unworldly sky" and "the last sane moment" (paragraph 6), things that were "wrong" and of another time (paragraph 7), viewing her husband from "the other side of death" (paragraph 8), and the observation that "we were the world's dead people. . . ." (paragraph 10).

5. Although each essay creates an other-worldly effect, the effects are very different in kind. Young finds that his experience creates a sense of enchantment. Dillard, far from being enchanted, experiences awe bordering on terror.

the sun like a lid. The sky snapped over the sun like a lens cover. The hatch in the brain slammed. Abruptly it was dark night, on the land and in the sky. In the night sky was a tiny ring of light. The hole where the sun belongs is very small. A thin ring of light marked its place. There was no sound. The eyes dried, the arteries drained, the lungs hushed. There was no world. We were the world's dead people rotating and orbiting around and around, embedded in the planet's crust, while the earth rolled down. Our minds were light-years distant, forgetful of almost everything. Only an extraordinary act of will could recall to us our former, living selves and our contexts in matter and time. We had, it seems, loved the planet and loved our lives, but could no longer remember the way of them. We got the light wrong. In the sky was something that should not be there. In the black sky was a ring of light. It was a thin ring, an old, thin silver wedding band, an old, worn ring. It was an old wedding band in the sky, or a morsel of bone. There were stars. It was all over.

DISCUSSION QUESTIONS

1. Comment on the significance of the opening line: "It began with no ado."

2. In paragraph 2 Dillard observes that "seeing a partial eclipse bears the same relation to seeing a total eclipse as kissing a man does to marrying him, or as flying in an airplane does to falling out of an airplane." Point out why her comparisons are effective.

3. State in your own words what Dillard means when she says in paragraph 3 that "usually it is a bit of a trick to keep your knowledge from blinding you. But during an eclipse it is easy."

4. Explain how the plea "God save our life" at the end of paragraph 9 relates to the dominant impression that emerges from the essay. Cite specific details that help create this impression.

5. The essays of Dillard and John V. Young (pages 372–73) both deal with effects triggered by heavenly bodies. How do the two effects compare?

SUGGESTION FOR WRITING ■ Select some event that had a profound impact on your life—perhaps the launch of a space shuttle or the devastation caused by a storm. Describe the event so that the reader clearly grasps the impression you experienced.

John Ciardi

DAWN WATCH

John Ciardi (1916–1986) was born in Boston and earned degrees from Tufts College (now Tufts University) and the University of Michigan. Following graduation in 1938, he began a college teaching career—broken only by military service during World War II—that lasted until 1961. In that year, he left teaching to pursue a career as a writer and lecturer. Although best known as the author of more than thirty volumes of juvenile and adult poetry, Ciardi also translated the Italian poet Dante, wrote on the American language, and produced many essays. In the following selection, he describes his favorite time of day.

Unless a man is up for the dawn and for the half hour or so of first light, he has missed the best of the day.

The traffic has just started, not yet a roar and a stink. One car at a time goes by, the tires humming almost like the sound of a brook a half mile down in the crease of a mountain I know—a sound that carries not because it is loud but because everything else is still.

It isn't exactly a mist that hangs in the thickets but more nearly the ghost of a mist—a phenomenon like side vision. Look hard and it isn't there, but glance without focusing and something registers, an exhalation that will be gone three minutes after the sun comes over the treetops.

The lawns shine with a dew not exactly dew. There is a rabbit bobbing about on the lawn and then freezing. If it were truly a dew, his tracks would shine black on the grass, and he leaves no visible track. Yet, there is something on the grass that makes it glow a depth of green it will not show again all day. Or is that something in the dawn air?

Our cardinals know what time it is. They drop pure tones from the hemlock tops. The black gang of grackles that makes a slum of the pin oak also knows the time but can only grate at it. They sound like a convention of broken universal joints grating uphill. The grackles creak and speak, and the cardinals form tones that only occasionally sound through the noise. I scatter sunflower seeds by the birdbath for the cardinals and hope the grackles won't find them.

My neighbor's tomcat comes across the lawn, probably on his way home from passion, or only acting as if he had had a big night. I suspect him of being one of those poolroom braggarts who can't get next to a girl but who likes to let on that he is a hot stud. This one is too can-fed and too lazy to hunt for anything. Here he comes now, ignoring the rabbit. And there he goes.

As soon as he has hopped the fence, I let my dog out. The dog charges the rabbit, watches it jump the fence, shakes himself in a self-satisfied way, then trots dutifully into the thicket for his morning service, stopping to sniff everything on the way back.

There is an old mountain laurel on the island of the driveway turnaround. From somewhere on the wind a white morning-glory rooted next to it and has climbed it. Now the laurel is woven full of white bells tinged pink by the first rays through the not quite mist. Only in earliest morning can they be seen. Come out two hours from now and there will be no morning-glories.

Dawn, too, is the hour of a weed I know only as day flower—a bright blue button that closes in full sunlight. I have weeded bales of it out of my flower beds, its one daytime virtue being the shallowness of its root system that allows it to be pulled out effortlessly in great handfuls. Yet, now it shines. Had it a few more hours of such shining in its cycle, I would cultivate it as a ground cover, but dawn is its one hour, and a garden is for whole days.

There is another blue morning weed whose name I do not know. This one grows from a bulb to pulpy stems and a bedraggled daytime sprawl. Only a shovel will dig it out. Try weeding it by hand and the stems will break off to be replaced by new ones and to sprawl over the chosen plants in the flower bed. Yet,

1

2

3

4

5

6

7

8

9

10

PERSPECTIVE

Unlike the other descriptive essays, this one does not culminate in a turning point or an insight. The reason is not hard to understand: repetition lessens the likelihood that happenings will surprise or enlighten, and Ciardi is describing what he has witnessed many times.

TEACHING STRATEGY

To emphasize selection of details, ask students to point out places where Ciardi might have included sight or sound impressions but didn't. Although some students may be from urban environments, none of them should have any particular trouble with this exercise.

now and for another hour it outshines its betters, its flowers about the size of a quarter and paler than those of the day flower but somehow more brilliant, perhaps because of the contrast of its paler foliage.

11   And now the sun is slanting in full. It is bright enough to make the leaves of the Japanese red maple seem a transparent red bronze when the tree is between me and the light. There must be others, but this is the only tree I know whose leaves let the sun through in this way—except, that is, when the fall colors start. Aspen leaves, when they first yellow and before they dry, are transparent in this way. I tell myself it must have something to do with the red-yellow range of the spectrum. Green takes sunlight and holds it, but red and yellow let it through.

12   The damned crabgrass is wrestling with the zinnias, and I stop to weed it out. The stuff weaves too close to the zinnias to make the iron claw usable. And it won't do to pull at the stalks. Crabgrass (at least in a mulched bed) can be weeded only with dirty fingers. Thumb and forefinger have to pincer into the dirt and grab the root-center. Weeding, of course, is an illusion of hope. Pulling out the root only stirs the soil and brings new crabgrass seeds into germinating position. Take a walk around the block and a new clump will have sprouted by the time you get back. But I am not ready to walk around the block. I fill a small basket with the plucked clumps, and for the instant I look at them, the zinnias are weedless.

13   Don't look back. I dump the weeds in the thicket where they will be smothered by the grass clippings I will pile on at the next cutting. On the way back I see the cardinals come down for the sunflower seeds, and the jays join them, and then the grackles start ganging in, gate-crashing the buffet and clattering all over it. The dog stops chewing his rawhide and makes a dash into the puddle of birds, which splashes away from him.

14   I hear a brake-squeak I have been waiting for and know the paper has arrived. As usual, the news turns out to be another disaster count. The function of the wire services is to bring us tragedies faster than we can pity. In the end we shall all be inured, numb, and ready for emotionless programming. I sit on the patio and read until the sun grows too bright on the page. The cardinals have stopped singing, and the grackles have flown off. It's the end of birdsong again.

15   Then suddenly—better than song for its instant—a hummingbird the color of green crushed velvet hovers in the throat of my favorite lily, a lovely high-bloomer I got the bulbs for but not the name. The lily is a crest of white horns with red dots and red velvet tongues along the insides of the petals and with an odor that drowns the patio. The hummingbird darts in and out of each horn in turn, then hovers an instant, and disappears.

16   Even without the sun, I have had enough of the paper. I'll take that hummingbird as my news for this dawn. It is over now. I smoke one more cigarette too many and decide that, if I got to bed now, no one in the family need know I have stayed up for it again. Why do they insist on shaking their heads when they find me still up for breakfast, after having scribbled through the dark hours? They always do. They seem compelled to express pity for an old loony who can't find his own way to bed. Why won't they understand that this is the one hour of any day that must not be missed, as it is the one hour I couldn't imagine getting up for, though I can still get to it by staying up? It makes sense to me. There comes a time when the windows lighten and the twittering starts. I look up and know it's time to leave the papers in their mess. I could slip quietly into bed and avoid the family's headshakes, but this stroll-around first hour is too good to miss. Even my dog, still sniffing and circling, knows what hour this is.

DISCUSSION QUESTIONS

1. This paragraph serves as the thesis statement of the essay and establishes its narrow time frame, the period of sunrise. The remaining paragraphs provide evidence that this interval is indeed "the best of the day" for Ciardi. Paragraphs 8, 9, 10, and 16 further note the time frame.

2. In paragraph 2, Ciardi equates the hum of tires to the sound of a brook; in paragraph 5, he says that a flock of grackles sounds like "a convention of broken universal joints grating uphill"; in paragraph 6, he likens the neighbor's tomcat to a poolroom braggart; in paragraph 10, he notes that a weed has flowers "the size of a quarter"; in paragraph 13, he mentions a "puddle of birds" that "splashes away" from his dog; and in paragraph 15, he calls his favorite lily "a crest of white horns with red dots and red velvet tongues." Except for the conventional fourth example, all of the comparisons are fresh and evoke vivid sight or sound impressions.

3. This question suggests that the dawn air has a mystical, hard-to-pin-down quality, such as he evokes in paragraph 3, where he refers to a "ghost of a mist" that vanishes under a hard look.

4. Except for a fleeting mention of the traffic's "stink" (paragraph 2) and the odor of the lily (paragraph 15), Ciardi relies entirely on impressions of sight and sound. Despite the loud grackles and the boisterous dog, the overall impression is one of serenity.

Come on, boy. It's time to go in. The rabbit won't come back till tomorrow,   17
and the birds have work to do. The dawn's over. It's time to call it a day.

DISCUSSION QUESTIONS

1. What does Ciardi accomplish in his first paragraph?
2. Point out several places where Ciardi uses comparisons and offer reasons for their effectiveness.
3. What function is served by the question that ends paragraph 4?
4. How many kinds of sensory impressions does Ciardi include in his essay?
5. How does Ciardi arrange the details of his description? What kind of vantage point does he use?
6. Cite examples of vivid, original language in paragraph 5.
7. Discuss the significance of the essay's concluding sentence.

SUGGESTION FOR WRITING ■ Carefully observe and then describe a rural or an urban scene at dusk. Try to use vivid, original language to convey your impressions.

E. B. White

ONCE MORE TO THE LAKE

E. B. White (1899–1985) was born in Mount Vernon, New York, and was a graduate of Cornell University. In 1927, he accepted a position with The New Yorker, *which had begun publication about two years before, and in the next several decades he produced a steady flow of short pieces for that magazine. Between 1937 and 1943, he also wrote a column, "One Man's Meat," for* Harper's. *He is the author of three children's books,* Stuart Little *(1945),* Charlotte's Web *(1952), and* The Trumpet of the Swan *(1970), and numerous works for adults, including* The Second Tree from the Corner *(1954),* The Essays of E. B. White *(1977), and* The Poems and Sketches of E. B. White *(1981). In "Once More to the Lake," White creates a vivid and memorable word picture of a summer vacation spot that had great meaning for him and that brought him a sobering insight.*

One summer, along about 1904, my father rented a camp on a lake in   1
Maine and took us all there for the month of August. We all got ringworm from
some kittens and had to rub Pond's Extract on our arms and legs night and
morning, and my father rolled over in a canoe with all his clothes on; but outside

5. Ciardi follows a time sequence, starting with the first traces of dawn and ending after the sun is fully up. Although Ciardi moves about his yard, he never leaves it; therefore, his vantage point is essentially fixed.

6. "Our cardinals . . . drop pure tones," "The black gang of grackles that makes a slum of the pin oak," "They sound like a convention of broken universal joints grating uphill," and "The grackles creak and squeak" are examples of the kind of vivid, original language that makes description memorable. Depending on your class, you may wish to point out the use of alliteration to enhance the rhetorical effect.

7. First, it signals that with dawn's passage, "the best of the day" (paragraph 1) has ended for Ciardi, leaving only unimportant hours to come. Second, it reflects the fact that in writing "through the dark hours" he has in effect done a day's work, which dawn has now ended.

PERSPECTIVE

Narration figures more prominently in this essay than in any of the others in this section. White presents a series of events that cover about a week's time and culminate in a turning point together with its chilling insight. On the other hand, the essay lacks any dialogue or characterization of White's son.

of that the vacation was a success and from then on none of us ever thought there was any place in the world like that lake in Maine. We returned summer after summer—always on August 1st for one month. I have since become a salt-water man, but sometimes in summer there are days when the restlessness of the tides and the fearful cold of the sea water and the incessant wind which blows across the afternoon and into the evening make me wish for the placidity of a lake in the woods. A few weeks ago this feeling got so strong I bought myself a couple of bass hooks and a spinner and returned to the lake where we used to go, for a week's fishing and to revisit old haunts.

2   I took along my son, who had never had any fresh water up his nose and who had seen lily pads only from train windows. On the journey over to the lake I began to wonder what it would be like. I wondered how time would have marred this unique, this holy spot—the coves and streams, the hills that the sun set behind, the camps and the paths behind the camps. I was sure the tarred road would have found it out and I wondered in what other ways it would be deso-lated. It is strange how much you can remember about places like that once you allow your mind to return into the grooves which lead back. You remember one thing, and that suddenly reminds you of another thing. I guess I remembered clearest of all the early mornings, when the lake was cool and motionless, remem-bered how the bedroom smelled of the lumber it was made of and the wet woods whose scent entered through the screen. The partitions in the camp were thin and did not extend clear to the top of the rooms, and as I was always the first up I would dress softly so as not to wake the others, and sneak out into the sweet outdoors and start out in the canoe, keeping close along the shore in the long shadows of the pines. I remembered being very careful never to rub my paddle against the gunwale for fear of disturbing the stillness of the cathedral.

3   The lake had never been what you would call a wild lake. There were cottages sprinkled around the shores, and it was in farming country although the shores of the lake were quite heavily wooded. Some of the cottages were owned by nearby farmers, and you would live at the shore and eat your meals at the farmhouse. That's what our family did. But although it wasn't wild, it was a fairly large and undisturbed lake and there were places in it which, to a child at least, seemed infinitely remote and primeval.

4   I was right about the tar: it led to within half a mile of the shore. But when I got back there, with my boy, and we settled into a camp near a farmhouse and into the kind of summertime I had known, I could tell that it was going to be pretty much the same as it had been before—I knew it, lying in bed the first morning, smelling the bedroom, and hearing the boy sneak quietly out and go off along the shore in a boat. I began to sustain the illusion that he was I, and therefore by simple transposition, that I was my father. This sensation persisted, kept cropping up all the time we were there. It was not an entirely new feeling, but in this setting it grew much stronger. I seemed to be living a dual existence. I would be in the middle of some simple act, I would be picking up a bait box or laying down a table fork, or I would be saying something, and suddenly it would be not I but my father who was saying the words or making the gesture. It gave me a creepy sensation.

5   We went fishing the first morning. I felt the same damp moss covering the worms in the bait can, and saw the dragonfly alight on the tip of my rod as it hovered a few inches from the surface of the water. It was the arrival of this fly that convinced me beyond any doubt that everything was as it always had been, that the years were a mirage and there had been no years. The small waves were

the same, chucking the rowboat under the chin as we fished at anchor, and the boat was the same boat, the same color green and the ribs broken in the same places, and under the floor-boards the same fresh-water leavings and debris—the dead hellgramite,[1] the wisps of moss, the rusty discarded fishhook, the dried blood from yesterday's catch. We stared silently at the tips of our rods, at the dragonflies that came and went. I lowered the tip of mine into the water, tentatively, pensively dislodging the fly, which darted two feet away, poised, darted two feet back, and came to rest again a little farther up the rod. There had been no years between the ducking of this dragonfly and the other one—the one that was part of memory. I looked at the boy, who was silently watching his fly, and it was my hands that held his rod, my eyes watching. I felt dizzy and didn't know which rod I was at the end of.

We caught two bass, hauling them in briskly as though they were mackerel,   6
putting them over the side of the boat in a businesslike manner without any landing net, and stunning them with a blow on the back of the head. When we got back for a swim before lunch, the lake was exactly where we had left it, the same number of inches from the dock, and there was only the merest suggestion of a breeze. This seemed an utterly enchanted sea, this lake you could leave to its own devices for a few hours and come back to, and find that it had not stirred, this constant and trustworthy body of water. In the shallows, the dark, water-soaked sticks and twigs, smooth and old, were undulating in clusters on the bottom against the clean ribbed sand, and the track of the mussel was plain. A school of minnows swam by, each minnow with its small individual shadow, doubling the attendance, so clear and sharp in the sunlight. Some of the other campers were in swimming, along the shore, one of them with a cake of soap, and the water felt thin and clear and unsubstantial. Over the years there had been this person with the cake of soap, this cultist, and here he was. There had been no years.

Up to the farmhouse to dinner through the teeming, dusty field, the road   7
under our sneakers was only a two-track road. The middle track was missing, the one with the marks of the hooves and the splotches of dried, flaky manure. There had always been three tracks to choose from in choosing which track to walk in; now the choice was narrowed down to two. For a moment I missed terribly the middle alternative. But the way led past the tennis court, and something about the way it lay there in the sun reassured me; the tape had loosened along the backline, the alleys were green with plantains and other weeds, and the net (installed in June and removed in September) sagged in the dry noon, and the whole place steamed with midday heat and hunger and emptiness. There was a choice of pie for dessert, and one was blueberry and one was apple, and the waitresses were the same country girls, there having been no passage of time, only the illusion of it as in a dropped curtain—the waitresses were still fifteen; their hair had been washed, that was the only difference—they had been to the movies and seen the pretty girls with the clean hair.

Summertime, oh summertime, pattern of life indelible, the fade-proof lake,   8
the woods unshatterable, the pasture with the sweetfern and the juniper forever and ever, summer without end; this was the background, and the life along the shore was the design, the cottages with their innocent and tranquil design, their tiny docks with the flagpole and the American flag floating against the white clouds in the blue sky, the little paths over the roots of the trees leading from camp to camp and the paths leading back to the outhouses and the can of lime for

[1] Insect used as bait.

sprinkling, and at the souvenir counters at the store the miniature birch-bark canoes and the post cards that showed things looking a little better than they looked. This was the American family at play, escaping the city heat, wondering whether the newcomers in the camp at the head of the cove were "common" or "nice," wondering whether it was true that the people who drove up for Sunday dinner at the farmhouse were turned away because there wasn't enough chicken.

9   It seemed to me, as I kept remembering all this, that those times and those summers had been infinitely precious and worth saving. There had been jollity and peace and goodness. The arriving (at the beginning of August) had been so big a business in itself, at the railway station the farm wagon drawn up, the first smell of the pine-laden air, the first glimpse of the smiling farmer, and the great importance of the trunks and your father's enormous authority in such matters, and the feel of the wagon under you for the long ten-mile haul, and at the top of the last long hill catching the first view of the lake after eleven months of not seeing this cherished body of water. The shouts and cries of the other campers when they saw you, and the trunks to be unpacked, to give up their rich burden. (Arriving was less exciting nowadays, when you sneaked up in your car and parked it under a tree near the camp and took out the bags and in five minutes it was all over, no fuss, no loud wonderful fuss about trunks.)

10   Peace and goodness and jollity. The only thing that was wrong now, really, was the sound of the place, an unfamiliar nervous sound of the outboard motors. This was the note that jarred, the one thing that would sometimes break the illusion and set the years moving. In those other summertimes all motors were inboard; and when they were at a little distance, the noise they made was a sedative, an ingredient of summer sleep. They were one-cylinder and two-cylinder engines, and some were make-and-break and some were jump-spark, but they all made a sleepy sound across the lake. The one-lungers throbbed and fluttered, and the twin-cylinder ones purred and purred, and that was a quiet sound too. But now the campers all had outboards. In the daytime, in the hot mornings, these motors made a petulant, irritable sound; at night, in the still evening when the afterglow lit the water, they whined about one's ears like mosquitoes. My boy loved our rented outboard, and his great desire was to achieve singlehanded mastery over it, and authority, and he soon learned the trick of choking it a little (but not too much), and the adjustment of the needle valve. Watching him I would remember the things you could do with the old one-cylinder engine with the heavy flywheel, how you could have it eating out of your hand if you got really close to it spiritually. Motor boats in those days didn't have clutches, and you would make a landing by shutting off the motor at the proper time and coasting in with a dead rudder. But there was a way of reversing them, if you learned the trick, by cutting the switch and putting it on again exactly on the final dying revolution of the flywheel, so that it would kick back against compression and begin reversing. Approaching a dock in a strong following breeze, it was difficult to slow up sufficiently by the ordinary coasting method, and if a boy felt he had complete mastery over his motor, he was tempted to keep it running beyond its time and then reverse it a few feet from the dock. It took a cool nerve, because if you threw the switch a twentieth of a second too soon you would catch the flywheel when it still had speed enough to go up past center, and the boat would leap ahead, charging bull-fashion at the dock.

11   We had a good week at the camp. The bass were biting well and the sun shone endlessly, day after day. We would be tired at night and lie down in the accumulated heat of the little bedrooms after the long hot day and the breeze

would stir almost imperceptibly outside and the smell of the swamp drift in through the rusty screens. Sleep would come easily and in the morning the red squirrel would be on the roof, tapping out his gay routine. I kept remembering everything, lying in bed in the mornings—the small steamboat that had a long rounded stern like the lip of a Ubangi, and how quietly she ran on the moonlight sails, when the older boys played their mandolins and the girls sang and we ate doughnuts dipped in sugar, and how sweet the music was on the water in the shining night, and what it had felt like to think about girls then. After breakfast we would go up to the store and the things were in the same place—the minnows in a bottle, the plugs and spinners disarranged and pawed over by the youngsters from the boys' camp, the fig newtons and the Beeman's gum. Outside, the road was tarred and cars stood in front of the store. Inside, all was just as it had always been, except there was more Coca-Cola and not so much Moxie and root beer and birch beer and sarsaparilla. We would walk out with a bottle of pop apiece and sometimes the pop would backfire up our noses and hurt. We explored the streams, quietly, where the turtles slid off the sunny logs and dug their way into the soft bottom; and we lay on the town wharf and fed worms to the tame bass. Everywhere we went I had trouble making out which was I, the one walking at my side, the one walking in my pants.

One afternoon while we were there at the lake a thunderstorm came up. It 12
was like the revival of an old melodrama that I had seen long ago with childish awe. The second-act climax of the drama of the electrical disturbance over a lake in America had not changed in any important respect. This was the big scene, still the big scene. The whole thing was so familiar, the first feeling of oppression and heat and a general air around camp of not wanting to go very far away. In mid-afternoon (it was all the same) a curious darkening of the sky, and a lull in everything that had made life tick; and then the way the boats suddenly swung the other way at their moorings with the coming of a breeze out of the new quarter, and the premonitory rumble. Then the kettle drum, then the snare, then the bass drum and cymbals, then crackling light against the dark, and the gods grinning and licking their chops in the hills. Afterward the calm, the rain steadily rustling in the calm lake, the return of light and hope and spirits, and the campers running out in joy and relief to go swimming in the rain, their bright cries perpetuating the deathless joke about how they were getting simply drenched, and the children screaming with delight at the new sensation of bathing in the rain, and the joke about getting drenched linking the generations in a strong indestructible chain. And the comedian who waded in carrying an umbrella.

When the others went swimming my son said he was going in too. He 13
pulled his dripping trunks from the line where they had hung all through the shower, and wrung them out. Languidly, and with no thought of going in, I watched him, his hard little body, skinny and bare, saw him wince slightly as he pulled up around his vitals the small, soggy, icy garment. As he buckled the swollen belt suddenly my groin felt the chill of death.

DISCUSSION QUESTIONS

1. In paragraph 4 White says that while doing or saying things "suddenly it would be not I but my father who was saying the words or making the gesture." Explain what he means.

2. White supplies relatively little information about his son except to mention that his

actions resemble White's own as a child. How do you account for this brief treatment?

3. What is the significance of the missing middle track of the road (paragraph 7) and the "nervous sound of the outboard motors" (paragraph 10)?

4. Throughout the essay White spices his descriptions with precise sensory impressions of sight, hearing, touch, taste, and smell. How do these sensory details enhance his writing?

5. On what audience would this essay likely have the largest impact?

6. White's final sentence provides an indirect statement of his main point. What is the point?

SUGGESTION FOR WRITING ■ **Write an essay describing a place you have revisited after being absent for a number of years. Indicate what was similar and what was different and describe your reactions to the changes. Appeal to at least three of the five senses.**

OVERVIEW OF PROCESS ANALYSIS ESSAYS (pp. 385–96)

Two of the essays use formal-informal language and have a serious tone. One uses informal language laced with colloquialisms and touched with light humor, and one uses formal-informal language that sometimes takes on a formal, poetic cast. Two of the essays offer directions for readers who might carry out the process for themselves. Another tells how a natural process unfolds. The fourth, directed at nondoers, tells how a process is performed, a process that because of circumstances cannot follow a completely predetermined course.

Process Analysis

Kathy Roth

How to Adopt a Stray

Kathy Roth is a cat fancier with special concern for the plight of homeless animals. In this essay, which first appeared in The Cat Catalog *(1976), she tells how to go about turning a stray cat into a healthy, contented house cat.*

Title indicates set of directions

Did you know that for every cat with a home there are twelve strays? We have all seen them—huddled in doorways, foraging through garbage, frightened, sick, unwanted. The average street cat has a limited life expectancy; poorly fed, he risks death from untreated ailments, automobiles, and the cold. It is of no help to think someone else will do something about the stray. In most cases no one does. The A.S.P.C.A. can do no more than pick up some of them. What stray cats need are *homes*.

1

Introduction: paragraphs 1 and 2

Emotional appeal

Adopting a stray can be rewarding and fun for you and the cat, but be aware before you bring the cat home of what the costs will be. Every stray will need at least a check-up, shots and neutering as soon as possible after adoption. Many veterinarians (not all, but many) will reduce fees if you tell them that the animal you have adopted was a stray. If your veterinarian cannot help with costs, find one who can—they do exist. Your local A.S.P.C.A. or humane society can probably make recommendations.

2

Notes rewards, requirements of adoption

The first step in adopting a stray is, of course, getting him home. Approach the cat slowly; talk to him reassuringly. Touch him, pet him. Pick him up by placing your right hand under his rib cage between his two sets of legs, your left hand around his rump supporting his back legs, and lifting gently. If you have a distance to go, wrap him inside your coat or sweater, for a sudden noise on the street might cause him to start and jump from your arms. Hold him close to your body so that he will be comforted by your body heat.

3

Body: paragraphs 3–13; uses polite commands, addressing reader as "you"

First step and its actions

Reasons for actions

The stray in need of help is often the most docile, the most trusting. The seriously injured stray needs help most, yet because people dislike the problems this situation creates, this is the cat most often ignored. Take the injured cat to a veterinarian immediately. Even if it must be euthanized, it is far worse to walk away and leave a cat to suffer.

4

Pregnant cats present other problems, particularly if they are strays. You will not help reduce the stray population by taking in the mother and then plan to abandon the newborn kittens. If you assume responsibility for a cat's welfare, you should be prepared to assume total responsibility. Therefore, if you are unable to deal with the difficulties of finding good homes for kittens (as anyone who has tried knows, it is nearly an impossible job), then it is best to have the kittens aborted.

5

Warning

If you are bringing the stray into a household where there is another cat, totally isolate the stray on arrival and until it has been examined by your vet. The

6

Second step and its actions

385

most frequent health problems one confronts in strays are parasites—ear mites, worms and fleas. Although these can be treated quickly and effectively, they are easily transmitted to other cats. Strays may also suffer from upper respiratory ailments—symptoms are running eyes, sneezing and nasal discharge. Do not think of this as "just a cold." Upper respiratory ailments can kill cats.

Warnings

7   If you already have a cat, you probably know about feline distemper. This is a virus which may be fatal to cats. If your cat has been inoculated, he runs no risk of catching this virus from a stray (nor do you, since it affects only cats). During the past two years, I have rescued fourteen strays. None of these had distemper and only one died from an upper respiratory illness. Do not be overly concerned about the possibilities of the stray being seriously sick. Just follow two simple precautions: keep the stray isolated from other cats for the first few days and have him examined by a doctor as soon as possible.

8   Once treated for ailments and restored to good health, strays require no more special care than any other cat. Some people think that stray cats, like dogs, should be bathed. It is best to let the cat take care of himself unless he has gotten into some terrible mess that only a scrubbing, and not a self-licking, will clean up. Secure in a new home, even the dingiest stray will soon make himself shine again.

9   Stray cats, like all cats, do not need much training to be house-broken. Introduce the stray to the litter pan and he will quickly get the idea. If your stray seems slow catching on, put him in the pan and help him make digging motions in the litter with his front paws, as you would a kitten. One or two lessons should be sufficient.

10   Because of poor diet, strays often suffer from constipation or diarrhea when first picked up. If your cat is suffering from constipation, feed him a half-teaspoon of nonmedicated petroleum jelly. If he is suffering from diarrhea, mix a little cooked white rice with his food. If you notice blood in the cat's stool, it may be the result of the stray's having eaten bones or sharp objects or having gotten worms while living outside on the street. Don't panic; take a stool sample to your veterinarian to be analyzed.

Warning

11   The adoption of a stray should be enjoyable, but it is no fun living with a cat who has not been spayed or neutered. Adult males tend to spray furniture with urine; females cry all night long, particularly when in heat. Do not believe the old stories about how neutering or spaying will change the disposition of a cat. It does not, as your veterinarian will tell you.

Third step and its actions

12   Once you have provided the physical comforts and medical necessities of your new pet, you may begin to worry about his adjustments to his new life. The best advice is not to worry. If this is your first cat, relax and enjoy getting to know him. He will be nervous and shy for a few days, but gradually he will begin to come to you for petting and play sessions. You are providing him with food and shelter, and in a short time he will begin to show his appreciation of your care. If

Warning

you already have a cat, let the new cat adjust gradually. Do not try to force the cats to accept each other—they will want to maintain distance for a time. No matter how much explaining you do, your original cat will feel threatened and jealous. Reassure him by giving him extra attention. There will be growling and hissing, but ignore everything for at least three days. In most cases, by the end of this period the original cat usually tires of hostilities and begins to establish a negotiated peace.

13   As soon as your new cat begins to feel at home, he will sleep a lot. A little food, a little quiet, and you may not see much of your new pet for a few days. I

have known strays to sleep almost uninterruptedly for a week after being rescued from the rigors of street life. If the vet found the cat healthy, do not worry. Let him rest and, in a few days, he will feel more sociable.

People often mistakenly think that cats who have lived on the streets must be permitted to go outside. A former street cat will quickly adjust to life in the home and come to depend on the food and comforts he has been deprived of for so long. To let your cat back out on the streets is to expose him once more to the risks of becoming a stray again. You are not breaking natural laws; you are establishing a new, happy life the stray deserves.

14

Conclusion: corrects misconception

Warning

DISCUSSION QUESTIONS

1. Explain why the steps in this process could or could not be arranged in a different order.
2. Characterize the tone (see pages 220–23) of Roth's essay.
3. After reading Roth's essay would you be more likely to adopt a stray cat? Does your answer stem from Roth's content, her manner of presentation, or both?

SUGGESTION FOR WRITING ■ Write an essay that provides directions for selecting a riding horse, hunting dog, or household pet other than a cat. Be sure to include the reason for any action whose purpose is not obvious, and provide cautionary warnings whenever necessary.

Walter Kiechel III

HOW TO GIVE A SPEECH

Walter Kiechel III (born 1946) is a native of Nebraska but grew up in Alexandria, Virginia. In 1968, he graduated from Harvard University. After five years of naval service, he returned to Harvard where, in 1977, he received advanced degrees in law and business administration. That same year, he joined the staff of Fortune *as a reporter-researcher. Subsequently, he became an associate editor and writer, then was made a member of the magazine's board of editors, and finally was promoted to assistant managing editor. Kiechel writes a column titled "Office Hours" that deals with issues of managerial psychology and sociology and also edits the magazine's "Money and Markets" section. A collection of his "Office Hours" columns has been published under the title* Office Hours: A Guide to the Managerial Life. *In our selection, Kiechel offers neophyte speechmakers tips for improving their effectiveness.*

Looking for an easy way to reduce even a strong, self-confident manager to a nail-biting mass of insecurities? Just ask him to give a speech to an unfamiliar audience. If he can't get out of accepting, he'll probably devote several sweaty

1

hours to writing out his remarks or, if he is senior enough, delegate the awful task of composition to some underling. When the hour of execution arrives, he will stride manfully to the podium, assume a quasi-fetal stance, and proceed to read his text word by droning word. Not for nothing does pop research indicate that the average American fears speaking before a group more than he fears death. As Paul Nelson, dean of Ohio University's college of communication, observes, "Death is faster."

2   Choose life, even if it means working to become a better speaker. Why don't more managers take up the challenge? "Most businessmen are worried that they're going to come across like someone else," argues Charles Windhorst, co-founder of Communispond. It's a firm that teaches executives that the trick in fact is to have all the mechanical stuff down so pat that the authentic, worth-listening-to you comes through undistorted. Learn the basics and get out of your own way.

3   The basics begin when you're invited to speak. While the folks asking may have a foggy idea of what they want you to talk on, their none-too-clear guidelines probably leave you ample room to set your own topic. Don't be in a hurry here. First, the experts universally agree, you should find out as much as you can about your audience.

4   Who are these people—what age, sex, and line of work—and why will they be assembled? If they're mostly women, you will want to use more examples that feature you know whom. Are they coming to hear you more or less voluntarily, or is their attendance required? Captive audiences are harder to grab. When are you supposed to talk to them? If it's right after a meal or at the end of the day, expect Coma City; leading off in the morning often means that you'll lose 15 minutes to your hosts' unavailing attempts to start on time. Maybe most important, why do they want to hear from *you,* of all people?

5   Much of this dope you can get by grilling the person who had the temerity to invite you. For the ultimate in analysis, though, nothing beats spending a little time with your prospective audience. Robert Waterman Jr., whose co-authorship of *In Search of Excellence* propelled him into big-time speakerdom, finds that if he's to exhort some company's troops, for example, it helps a lot to poke around the corporation for a day or so beforehand talking to everybody he can. He can then address their specific concerns.

6   Once you have a feel for your audience, consult your mental inventory of what interests you these days. Not just what you know or can amass facts on, but what you care about. Dale Carnegie said it 70 years ago, and the experts are still saying it: If you're not excited about your subject, you won't be able to excite your audience about it either. To find your topic, look for where your concerns intersect with their wants and needs. Decide on your purpose—whether to inform, persuade, or entertain. Then give your impending address what Max Wortman, a management professor at the University of Tennessee and a popular speaker, calls a "schmaltzy" title. Not "Current Realities and Future Trends in the Brake Shoe Industry"; rather "What the Future Holds, and Why We Probably Can't Get There From Here."

7   Now all you have to do is compose and deliver the sucker. In putting it together, bear in mind that this is an oral, not a written communication. This means you should use short, simple words, go long on personal pronouns—I, me, you, we—and repeat your main points, since the listener won't be able to go back and reread whatever puzzled him. To achieve the right effect, try composing initially with a Dictaphone or cassette recorder, says Fern Johnson, a professor of communication at the University of Massachusetts at Amherst. If others write the

TEACHING STRATEGY

Ask students to assess whether they could or could not prepare and present a speech in front of strangers by following the directions in this essay. Why or why not? Students might also identify those types of processes that are easier to teach people through written instructions and those that are more difficult.

CLASSROOM ACTIVITY

Ask students to bring in short articles or chapters on carrying out some activity. Divide the class into small groups and distribute the copies; then ask the groups to compare Kiechel's tone with that of the other pieces of writing and determine which is most effective and why.

talk for you, make sure that they too observe the basic principle. Dorothy Sarnoff, a Manhattanite who has taught public speaking to many a celebrity, tells of asking 20 or so U.S. State Department speechwriters whether they ever spoke aloud the remarks they prepared for senior diplomats. None ever did. And you wondered why we're in trouble around the globe.

In thinking about how to structure what you say, go back to the purpose you decided on. As Communispond's Windhorst observes, the standard tell-'em-what-you're-gonna-tell-'em, tell-'em, and tell-'em-what-you-told-'em works fine if your goal is to inform. If you're out to persuade, though, you're probably better off laying out the problem, marshaling the evidence for your view, then ending with a call to action.

8

At the beginning of your remarks, you want to get the audience on your side—and fast. Research suggests that they make up their minds on whether to like you, and to listen to you, within a minute or two after you start out. Audacious you can, of course, attempt to win them over with a joke. Be careful, though: Make sure that you can actually tell a funny story—not everyone can—and that the joke leads naturally into the body of your speech. The best openers, the experts advise, are probably tales from your own experience: sometimes self-deprecating, not necessarily thigh-slappers, but calculated to show the audience that you're pretty much like them. Or worse.

9

The standard wisdom says you probably can't hope to put across more than three main points. Listeners should get a sense of movement, of progression, from one part of the speech to the next. Consider using rhetorical questions to alert them to transitions. You needn't be highfalutin, though. Some of the hottest speakers on the corporate circuit—Tom Peters, Waterman's co-author, for example—seem to do nothing but string together story after story.

10

In framing your conclusion, figure out precisely what you want your listeners to take away. An impulse to act? Lay out with gory specificity what they should do, whether it's writing their Congressman, selling more brake shoes, or razing Carthage. A better understanding of your subject? Summarize your main points. A warm, happy feeling? Leave 'em laughing. Time your remarks to run a bit shorter than the period allotted; besides surprising your listeners no end, this may cause them to want more, and to invite you back another time.

11

Once you know what you're going to say, put it into a form you can talk from. To keep you from reading, the Communispond firm recommends using your own miserably hand-drawn pictures, or ideographs, one for each major idea. If you simply must have the words in front of you, at least break down your text into natural five- or six-word phrases, one to a line, triple-spaced, with brackets to indicate the phrases that make up a single thought.

12

You can now attend to the truly mechanical. If you're going to use so-called visual aids—and you probably should if your audience is large—keep them simple, one phrase or idea per slide or overhead transparency. Determine in as much detail as possible how the room will be set up. Will there be a podium, for instance? How tall? If the answer is two inches below your height in stiletto heels, ask that other arrangements be made. Ensure that someone checks out the microphone before you go on.

13

Rehearse, but try to avoid getting it down so well that you're bored with it. A final pre-speaking tip from Ohio University's Nelson: Write your own introduction. The audience is going to form an impression about you so quickly that if Mr. It-Gives-Me-Great-Pleasure stumbles through your entire potted bio—the four degrees, the military service, the time you spent heading the Thule office—you

14

DISCUSSION QUESTIONS (p. 390)

1. An activity that inspires such universal fear and trembling clearly requires directions for coping. Thus Kiechel establishes the rationale for his essay.

2. While the phrasing in paragraph 1 could have been handled differently and "businessmen" in paragraph 2 could have been "business people," little else in the essay suggests that women are slighted. Two women speaking authorities are cited in paragraph 7, the reference in paragraph 13 to the podium being "below your height in stiletto heels" obviously indicates a female manager, and in paragraph 15 Kiechel refers to "*Madame* President" and "*Mr.* First Vice President." Sandwiched in between these last two references is "*Mr.* It-Gives-Me-Great Pleasure" in paragraph 14.

3. The major steps, and the actions involved in each, are as follows: A. Assessing your audience: 1. Asking the person who invited you to talk; 2. Talking directly with the prospective audience. B. Choosing your subject: 1. Determining what interests you; 2. Relating your interests to your audience's wants and needs; 3. Choosing a title. C. Preparing to give the speech: 1. Choosing appropriate diction; 2. Structuring the speech; 3. Preparing the opening; 4. Choosing the main points; 5. Framing the conclusion; 6. Preparing speaking aids; 7. Checking features of the speaking place; 8. Rehearsing the speech. D. Giving the speech: 1. Creating a favorable first impression; 2. Speaking energetically; 3. Maintaining proper eye contact; 4. Maintaining audience interest; 5. Ending strongly.

4. Some noteworthy examples include the following: Paragraph 2: "Choose life, even if it means. . . ." and "the mechanical stuff." Paragraph 4: "harder to grab" and "Coma City." Paragraph 5: "this dope," "exhort some company's troops," and "poke around." Paragraph 6: "these days" and "schmaltzy." Paragraph 7: "the sucker." Paragraph 8: "the standard tell-'em-what-you're-gonna-tell-'em. . . ." Paragraph 10: "highfalutin." Paragraph 11: "gory." Paragraph 14: "Mr. It-Gives-Me-Great-Pleasure" and "potted." Paragraph 15: "stuffy nonsense." Paragraph 16: "trot out." Paragraph 17: "sure-fire gag line."

5. We feel it's better to point out fragments to students before they call the "error" to our attention. Paragraph 6: "Not just what you know. . . ." and "Not 'Current Realities and Future'. . . ." Paragraph 9: "Or worse." Kiechel uses the fragments intentionally as part of his humorous informality. Caution students against using fragments until they can handle correct sentences.

6. Expert opinions are cited in paragraphs 1–2, 3 (universally), 5–8, 9–10 (expert consensus), 12, 14, 16, and 17. Such opinions lend authority to the presentation and indicate that it has been well researched.

7. Although there are obvious differences, learning about your audience, being excited about your subject, determining your purpose, and creating a sense of progression from one part to the next are important in both speaking and writing.

15   may lose them before you stand up. Furnish him instead with a brief, down-to-earth account of yourself that stresses what you have in common with your listeners.

With appropriate fanfare, you take the podium. Stand up straight, look out at your audience, smile if it's appropriate, and then launch right in, with no boring "Thank you" or "Madam President, Mr. First Vice President. . ." Put more energy into talking than you usually do; this isn't the time or place for the stuffy nonsense that says that a good manager never raises his voice or gestures with his hands. Indeed, if you can just forget about those appendages, you may free them to do their own helpful thing, whether it's the grand sweep of a big idea, a short jab for emphasis, or the clenched fist of intensity.

16   Maintain eye contact with your audience. If you're a novice, and nervous, try to find two or three friendly faces, people who seem to be laughing at your stories and nodding along with your witty *aperçus*. When you look up from your text, look at them. As Dean Nelson notes, the nodders are more likely to be women, who aren't socialized like males to keep a poker face. As you grow more experienced, you'll be able to sweep the room with your gaze, exchanging glances with the neutrals and eventually even with the hostiles. What you're looking for is not just encouragement, but also any sense that you may be losing the crowd. When you see them beginning to stare at the floor, react: Rephrase your last point to make it clearer, tell them again how vital your subject is to them, trot out one of your punchier anecdotes. You may also want to hasten to the close, dropping the lesser points that stand in your way.

17   Finish strong, not trailing off or adding another feeble "thank you." Give 'em a great quote, a passionate, punctuated request, or a sure-fire gag line. Leave the vivid air signed with your honor, to borrow Stephen Spender's phrase. Then sit down and just wait for the applause.

DISCUSSION QUESTIONS

1. Why do you think Kiechel begins by noting that both managers and the average American dread giving a speech?
2. In paragraph 1 Kiechel refers to a manager and the average American as "him" or "he." Do you think the essay slights women? Be specific.
3. What are the major steps of this process? The actions which make up these steps? Be specific.
4. No law decrees that a set of directions must be presented in a serious and formal manner. Point out several examples of humorous informality in Kiechel's essay.
5. Identify the two sentence fragments in paragraph 6 and the one in paragraph 9. How can you justify their inclusion?
6. Show where and explain why Kiechel cites expert opinions to support his ideas.
7. How are preparing a speech and preparing an essay similar?

SUGGESTION FOR WRITING ■ Write an essay that provides directions for some nail-biting activity, perhaps asking the boss for a raise, informing your spouse or parents that you caused major damage to the family car, or explaining to your parents why you have decided to drop one of your courses. Use humor if it seems appropriate.

Alexander Petrunkevitch

FROM THE SPIDER AND THE WASP

Alexander Petrunkevitch (1875–1964) was a professor of zoology at Yale University for over a third of a century. He was born in Russia and emigrated to the United States in 1903, holding teaching positions at several universities before going to Yale. He gained international recognition for his investigations of spiders and his writings on them, in particular his Index Catalogue of Spiders of North, Central, and South America *(1911) and* An Inquiry into the Natural Classification of Spiders *(1933). A man of wide-reaching interests, Petrunkevitch also produced historical and philosophical works as well as translations of Russian poetry. The following selection, excerpted from a 1952* Scientific American *article, describes a natural process and analyzes the behavior of its two participants.*

In the adult stage the [pepsis] wasp lives only a few months. The female produces but a few eggs, one at a time at intervals of two or three days. For each egg the mother must provide one adult tarantula, alive but paralyzed. The mother wasp attaches the egg to the paralyzed spider's abdomen. Upon hatching from the egg, the larva is many hundreds of times smaller than its living but helpless victim. It eats no other food and drinks no water. By the time it has finished its single Gargantuan meal and become ready for wasphood, nothing remains of the tarantula but its indigestible chitinous skeleton.

The mother wasp goes tarantula-hunting when the egg in her ovary is almost ready to be laid. Flying low over the ground late on a sunny afternoon, the wasp looks for its victim or for the mouth of a tarantula burrow, a round hole edged by a bit of silk. The sex of the spider makes no difference, but the mother is highly discriminating as to species. Each species of Pepsis requires a certain species of tarantula, and the wasp will not attack the wrong species. In a cage with a tarantula which is not its normal prey, the wasp avoids the spider and is usually killed by it in the night.

Yet when a wasp finds the correct species, it is the other way about. To identify the species the wasp apparently must explore the spider with her antennae. The tarantula shows an amazing tolerance to this exploration. The wasp crawls under it and walks over it without evoking any hostile response. The molestation is so great and so persistent that the tarantula often rises on all eight legs, as if it were on stilts. It may stand this way for several minutes. Meanwhile the wasp, having satisfied itself that the victim is of the right species, moves off a few inches to dig the spider's grave. Working vigorously with legs and jaws, it excavates—like a machine—a hole 8 to 10 inches deep with a diameter slightly larger than the spider's girth. Now and again the wasp pops out of the hole to make sure that the spider is still there.

When the grave is finished, the wasp returns to the tarantula to complete her ghastly enterprise. First she feels it all over once more with her antennae. Then her behavior becomes more aggressive. She bends her abdomen, protruding her sting, and searches for the soft membrane at the point where the spider's

1 **PERSPECTIVE**

Petrunkevitch uses relatively formal diction and, except for a couple of fleeting lapses, betrays no personal feelings toward the process he is describing. This combination is ideal for conveying the objectivity associated with scientific inquiry.

2 **CLASSROOM ACTIVITY**

Bring in several short process analysis articles from *Scientific American, Omni,* or some similar scientific periodical aimed at intelligent lay readers and distribute each to a small group of students.

3 Have the groups compare Petrunkevitch's style with that of the other articles, and in the new processes, identify the steps and note any deviations from objectivity.

4

legs join its body—the only spot where she can penetrate the horny skeleton. From time to time, as the exasperated spider slowly shifts ground, the wasp turns on her back and slides along with the aid of her wings, trying to get under the tarantula for a shot at the vital spot. During all this maneuvering, which can last for several minutes, the tarantula makes no move to save itself. Finally the wasp corners it against some obstruction and grasps one of its legs in her powerful jaws. Now at last the harassed spider tries a desperate but vain defense. The two contestants roll over and over on the ground. It is a terrifying sight and the outcome is always the same. The wasp finally manages to thrust her sting into the soft spot and holds it there for a few seconds while she pumps in the poison. Almost immediately the tarantula falls paralyzed on its back. Its legs stop twitching; its heart stops beating. Yet it is not dead, as is shown by the fact that if taken from the wasp it can be restored to some sensitivity by being kept in a moist chamber for several months.

5   After paralyzing the tarantula, the wasp cleans herself by dragging her body around the ground and rubbing her feet, sucks the drop of blood oozing from the wound in the spider's abdomen, then grabs a leg of the flabby, helpless animal in her jaws and drags it down to the bottom of the grave. She stays there for many minutes, sometimes for several hours, and what she does all that time in the dark we do not know. Eventually she lays her egg and attaches it to the side of the spider's abdomen with a sticky secretion. Then she emerges, fills the grave with soil carried bit by bit in her jaws, and finally tramples the ground all around to hide any trace of the grave from prowlers. Then she flies away, leaving her descendant safely started in life.

6   In all this the behavior of the wasp evidently is qualitatively different from that of the spider. The wasp acts like an intelligent animal. This is not to say that instinct plays no part or that she reasons as man does. But her actions are to the point; they are not automatic and can be modified to fit the situation. We do not know for certain how she identifies the tarantula—probably it is by some olfactory or chemo-tactile sense—but she does it purposefully and does not blindly tackle a wrong species.

7   On the other hand, the tarantula's behavior shows only confusion. Evidently the wasp's pawing gives it no pleasure, for it tries to move away. That the wasp is not simulating sexual stimulation is certain because male and female tarantulas react in the same way to its advances. That the spider is not anesthetized by some odorless secretion is easily shown by blowing lightly at the tarantula and making it jump suddenly. What, then, makes the tarantula behave as stupidly as it does?

8   No clear, simple answer is available. Possibly the stimulation by the wasp's antennae is masked by a heavier pressure on the spider's body, so that it reacts as when prodded by a pencil. But the explanation may be much more complex. Initiative in attack is not in the nature of tarantulas; most species fight only when cornered so that escape is impossible. Their inherited patterns of behavior apparently prompt them to avoid problems rather than attack them. For example, spiders always weave their webs in three dimensions, and when a spider finds that there is insufficient space to attach certain threads in the third dimension, it leaves the place and seeks another, instead of finishing the web in a single plane. This urge to escape seems to arise under all circumstances, in all phases of life, and to take the place of reasoning. For a spider to change the pattern of its web is as impossible as for an inexperienced man to build a bridge across a chasm obstructing his way.

DISCUSSION QUESTIONS

1. This process is divided into six steps: Hunting for a victim (paragraph 2), determining that the victim is the right species (first part of paragraph 3), digging the victim's grave (last part of paragraph 3), paralyzing the victim (paragraph 4), laying an egg on the victim (middle part of paragraph 5), and burying the victim (last part of paragraph 5). Point out to students that step 4 involves a series of substeps: feeling the victim all over once more, searching for a spot to insert the poison, battling the victim, and inserting the poison. Similarly, step 5 involves the wasp's cleaning herself, dragging the victim into the grave, and laying the egg.

2. Petrunkevitch's attitude is basically, but not entirely, objective. In a few places the writing reflects his emotional reactions. In paragraph 4, the wasp's enterprise is called "ghastly," and the sight of the two contestants rolling on the ground is "terrifying." In paragraph 7, the spider is said to behave "stupidly." These examples suggest that Petrunkevitch is sympathetic toward the spider.

In a way the instinctive urge to escape is not only easier but often more efficient than reasoning. The tarantula does exactly what is most efficient in all cases except in an encounter with a ruthless and determined attacker dependent for the existence of her own species on killing as many tarantulas as she can lay eggs. Perhaps in this case the spider follows its usual pattern of trying to escape, instead of seizing and killing the wasp, because it is not aware of its danger. In any case, the survival of the tarantula species as a whole is protected by the fact that the spider is much more fertile than the wasp.

9

DISCUSSION QUESTIONS

1. Into how many steps is this natural process divided? In which paragraph or paragraphs is each discussed?
2. Characterize Petrunkevitch's attitude toward his topic. Is it completely objective, or does Petrunkevitch sometimes reveal his personal feelings? If he does, indicate where.
3. Petrunkevitch uses a number of transitional words and phrases to ensure a smooth flow of ideas. Indicate those transitional devices and the paragraphs in which they are found.
4. Where does the conclusion begin and what is its purpose?

SUGGESTION FOR WRITING ■ **Write an essay explaining some process you perform frequently. Possibilities include flossing your teeth, brewing a pot of coffee, or preparing for a date.**

Richard Selzer

THE KNIFE

Richard Selzer (born 1928) grew up in Troy, New York, where his father was a family doctor. He attended Union College and Albany Medical College. After service in the United States Army, he completed three years of postdoctoral training at Yale University and joined its medical faculty. Selzer's writings, which include both short stories and essays, focus on medical topics and have appeared in an array of popular magazines. In "The Knife," Selzer traces the course of an operation while meditating on the nature of his calling.

One holds the knife as one holds the bow of a cello or a tulip—by the stem. Not palmed nor gripped nor grasped, but lightly, with the tips of the fingers. The knife is not for pressing. It is for drawing across the field of skin. Like a slender fish, it waits, at the ready, then, go! It darts, followed by a fine wake of red. The flesh parts, falling away to yellow globules of fat. Even now, after so many times, I still marvel at its power—cold, gleaming, silent. More, I am still struck with a kind of dread that it is I in whose hand the blade travels, that my hand is its vehicle, that

1

3. Paragraph 3: "Meanwhile," "Now and again." Paragraph 4: "When the grave is finished," "First," "Then," "From time to time," "Finally," "Now at last," "Finally," "Almost immediately," "Yet." Paragraph 5: "After paralyzing," "then," "Eventually," "Then," "Finally," "Then." Most of these words and phrases simply signal the passage of time. However, "When the grave is finished" (paragraph 4) echoes "Meanwhile the wasp . . . moves off . . . to dig the spider's grave" (paragraph 3), and "Yet" (paragraph 4) signals a contrast between what precedes and what follows it.
4. Paragraphs 8 and 9 form the conclusion and try to account for the "stupid" behavior of the spider. The preceding two paragraphs contrast the behavior of the adversaries and set the stage for the conclusion.

PERSPECTIVE
Selzer uses formal-informal language that in spots takes on a formal cast, as evidenced by a rather poetic tone. The essay is notable for revealing the emotions that underlie a process in which personal feelings should presumably play little or no part.

yet again this terrible steel-bellied thing and I have conspired for a most unnatural purpose, the laying open of the body of a human being.

2   A stillness settles in my heart and is carried to my hand. It is the quietude of resolve layered over fear. And it is this resolve that lowers us, my knife and me, deeper and deeper into the person beneath. It is an entry into the body that is nothing like a caress; still, it is among the gentlest of acts. Then stroke and stroke again, and we are joined by other instruments, hemostats and forceps, until the wound blooms with strange flowers whose looped handles fall to the sides in steely array.

3   There is sound, the tight click of clamps fixing teeth into severed blood vessels, the snuffle and gargle of the suction machine clearing the field of blood for the next stroke, the litany of monosyllables with which one prays his way down and in: *clamp, sponge, suture, tie, cut.* And there is color. The green of the cloth, the white of the sponges, the red and yellow of the body. Beneath the fat lies the fascia, the tough fibrous sheet encasing the muscles. It must be sliced and the red beef of the muscles separated. Now there are retractors to hold apart the wound. Hands move together, part, weave. We are fully engaged, like children absorbed in a game or the craftsmen of some place like Damascus.

4   Deeper still. The peritoneum, pink and gleaming and membranous, bulges into the wound. It is grasped with forceps, and opened. For the first time we can see into the cavity of the abdomen. Such a primitive place. One expects to find drawings of buffalo on the walls. The sense of trespassing is keener now, height-ened by the world's light illuminating the organs, their secret colors revealed—maroon and salmon and yellow. The vista is sweetly vulnerable at this moment, a kind of welcoming. An arc of the liver shines high and on the right, like a dark sun. It laps over the pink sweep of the stomach, from whose lower border the gauzy omentum is draped, and through which veil one sees, sinuous, slow as just-fed snakes, the indolent coils of the intestine.

5   You turn aside to wash your gloves. It is a ritual cleansing. One enters this temple doubly washed. Here is man as microcosm, representing in all his parts the earth, perhaps the universe.

6   I must confess that the priestliness of my profession has ever been impres-sed on me. In the beginning there are vows, taken with all solemnity. Then there is the endless harsh novitiate of training, much fatigue, much sacrifice. At last one emerges as celebrant, standing close to the truth lying curtained in the Ark of the body. Not surplice and cassock but mask and gown are your regalia. You hold no chalice, but a knife. There is no wine, no water. There are only the facts of blood and flesh.

7   And if the surgeon is like a poet, then the scars you have made on countless bodies are like verses into the fashioning of which you have poured your soul. I think that if years later I were to see the trace from an old incision of mine, I should know it at once, as one recognizes his pet expressions.

8   But mostly you are a traveler in a dangerous country, advancing into the moist and jungly cleft your hands have made. Eyes and ears are shuttered from the land you left behind; mind empties itself of all other thought. You are the root of groping fingers. It is a fine hour for the fingers, their sense of touch so enhanced. The blind must know this feeling. Oh, there is risk everywhere. One goes lightly. The spleen. No! No! Do not touch the spleen that lurks below the left leaf of the diaphragm, a manta ray in a coral cave, its bloody tongue protruding. One poke and it might rupture, exploding with sudden hemorrhage. The filmy omentum

must not be torn, the intestine scraped or denuded. The hand finds the liver, palms it, fingers running along its sharp lower edge, admiring. Here are the twin mounds of the kidneys, the apron of the omentum hanging in front of the intestinal coils. One lifts it aside and the fingers dip among the loops, searching, mapping territory, establishing boundaries. Deeper still, and the womb is touched, then held like a small muscular bottle—the womb and its earlike appendages, the ovaries. How they do nestle in the cup of a man's hand, their power all dormant. They are frailty itself.

There is a hush in the room. Speech stops. The hands of the others, assistants and nurses, are still. Only the voice of the patient's respiration remains. It is the rhythm of a quiet sea, the sound of waiting. Then you speak, slowly, the terse entries of a Himalayan climber reporting back.   9

"The stomach is okay. Greater curvature clean. No sign of ulcer. Pylorus,   10
duodenum fine. Now comes the gallbladder. No stones. Right kidney, left, all
right. Liver . . . uh-oh."

Your speech lowers to a whisper, falters, stops for a long, long moment,   11
then picks up again at the end of a sigh that comes through your mask like a last
exhalation.

"Three big hard ones in the left lobe, one on the right. Metastatic deposits.   12
Bad, bad. Where's the primary? Got to be coming from somewhere."

The arms shifts direction and the fingers drop lower and lower into the   13
pelvis—the body impaled now upon the arm of the surgeon to the hilt of the
elbow.

"Here it is."   14

The voice goes flat, all business now.   15

"Tumor in the sigmoid colon, wrapped all around it, pretty tight. We'll take   16
out a sleeve of the bowel. No colostomy. Not that, anyway. But, God, there's a lot
of it down there. Here, you take a feel."

You step back from the table, and lean into a sterile basin of water, resting   17
on stiff arms, while the others locate the cancer. . . .

What is it, then, this thing, the knife, whose shape is virtually the same as it 18
was three thousand years ago, but now with its head grown detachable? Before
steel, it was bronze. Before bronze, stone—then back into unremembered time.
Did man invent it or did the knife precede him here, hidden under ages of
vegetation and hoofprints, lying in wait to be discovered, picked up, used?

The scalpel is in two parts, the handle and the blade. Joined, it is six inches 19
from tip to tip. At one end of the handle is a narrow notched prong upon which
the blade is slid, then snapped into place. Without the blade, the handle has a
blind, decapitated look. It is helpless as a trussed maniac. But slide on the blade,
click it home, and the knife springs instantly to life. It is headed now, edgy,
leaping to mount the fingers for the gallop to its feast.

Now is the moment from which you have turned aside, from which you   20
have averted your gaze, yet toward which you have been hastened. Now the
scalpel sings along the flesh again, its brute run unimpeded by germs or other
frictions. It is a slick slide home, a barracuda spurt, a rip of embedded talon. One
listens, and almost hears the whine—nasal, high, delivered through that gleaming
metallic snout. The flesh splits with its own kind of moan. It is like the penetration
of rape.

The breasts of women are cut off, arms and legs sliced to the bone to make   21

4. Paragraphs 6, 7, and 8 constitute extended comparisons that attempt to establish the essential character of surgery and its practitioners. Briefer comparisons in paragraphs 1, 2, 3, 4, 9, 19, 20, 21, and 22 play more modest and varied roles. Thus, the comparison in paragraph 1 emphasizes the delicacy with which a scalpel is held, the one in paragraph 20 points up the violence of the cutting, and the one in paragraph 21 reveals the tension that the surgery entails. Together, the comparisons help readers visualize just what this operation, and by extension all surgery, involves.

5. They are "Do not touch the spleen" and "The filmy omentum must not be torn, the intestine scraped or denuded." These warnings call attention to the dangerous nature of the proceeding and the strain the surgeon undergoes.

6. Everything done to this point is merely a prelude to the surgeon's main task, the actual exploration for cancer. Now that the search is about to start, the members of the operating team pause in dread anticipation of what might be found.

7. The fragment suggests that inasmuch as illness and injury are unavoidable, the knife's work never ceases for long. Because the fragment is more forceful and emphatic than a complete sentence, it provides an especially effective ending for the essay.

ready for the saw, eyes freed from sockets, intestines lopped. The hand of the surgeon rebels. Tension boils through his pores, like sweat. The flesh of the patient retaliates with hemorrhage, and the blood chases the knife wherever it is withdrawn.

22   Within the belly a tumor squats, toadish, fungoid. A gray mother and her brood. The only thing it does not do is croak. It too is hacked from its bed as the carnivore knife lips the blood, turning in it in a kind of ecstasy of plenty, a gluttony after the long fast. It is just for this that the knife was created, tempered, heated, its violence beaten into paper-thin force.

23   At last a little thread is passed into the wound and tied. The monstrous booming fury is stilled by a tiny thread. The tempest is silenced. The operation is over. On the table, the knife lies spent, on it side, the bloody meal smear-dried upon its flanks. The knife rests.

24   And waits.

DISCUSSION QUESTIONS

1. Cite several parts of the essay to show that despite Selzer's use of medical terms he is writing for a lay audience.
2. Point out examples of effective description in paragraph 3 and explain what they contribute to the process.
3. Identify the signals that Selzer uses to help the reader follow the course of the operation.
4. Selzer includes numerous comparisons in his essay. Identify them and discuss their purpose.
5. Even though Selzer is not providing directions for someone to follow, he includes three warnings to himself in paragraph 8. What are they? What purpose do they serve?
6. In paragraph 9, Selzer notes that a hush occurs, speech and movement cease, and quiet prevails. Explain why.
7. Discuss the meaning and effectiveness of the sentence fragment that ends the essay.

SUGGESTION FOR WRITING ■ Select some activity you're familiar with—perhaps planning a party, programming a computer, or dieting successfully—and describe the steps involved, using appropriate comparisons and figurative language.

Illustration

OVERVIEW OF ILLUSTRATION ESSAYS

Three of the four illustration essays offer multiple examples to make their point. One features a single, extended example. Three are serious and one is humorous. Three use informal language, and the remaining one uses colloquial language. One has an unstated point, and the others have stated points.

James Thurber

COURTSHIP THROUGH THE AGES

James Thurber (1894–1961) is widely regarded as one of this country's finest twentieth-century humorists. A native of Ohio, Thurber attended Ohio State University and then worked as a reporter and columnist for several papers in this country and abroad. In 1927, he became associated with The New Yorker *and in the succeeding years produced a steady flow of stories, reminiscences, and cartoons for that magazine. Collections of his works include* The Owl in the Attic *(1931),* My Life and Hard Times *(1933),* Let Your Mind Alone! *(1937),* Fables for Our Times *(1940),* My World—and Welcome to It *(1942),* The Thurber Carnival *(1945), and* Thurber Country *(1952). The following selection, which originally appeared in* The New Yorker, *offers a humorous look at the difficulties encountered by the male of the species when a-wooing he would go.*

1   Surely nothing in the astonishing scheme of life can have nonplussed Nature so much as the fact that none of the females of any of the species she created really cared very much for the male, as such. For the past ten million years Nature has been busily inventing ways to make the male attractive to the female, but the whole business of courtship, from the marine annelids up to man, still lumbers heavily along, like a complicated musical comedy. I have been reading the sad and absorbing story in Volume 6 (Cole to Dama) of the *Encyclopaedia Britannica*. In this volume you can learn all about cricket, cotton, costume designing, crocodiles, crown jewels, and Coleridge but none of these subjects is so interesting as the Courtship of Animals, which recounts the sorrowful lengths to which all males must go to arouse the interest of a lady.

Introduction: provides background

2   We all know, I think, that Nature gave man whiskers and a mustache with the quaint idea in mind that these would prove attractive to the female. We all know that, far from attracting her, whiskers and mustaches only made her nervous and gloomy, so that man had to go in for somersaults, tilting with lances, and performing feats of parlor magic to win her attention; he also had to bring her candy, flowers, and the furs of animals. It is common knowledge that in spite of all these "love displays" the male is constantly being turned down, insulted, or thrown out of the house. It is rather comforting, then, to discover that the peacock, for all his gorgeous plumage, does not have a particularly easy time in courtship; none of the males in the world do. The first peahen, it turned out, was only faintly stirred by her suitor's beautiful train. She would often go quietly to sleep while he was whisking it around. The *Britannica* tells us that the peacock actually had to learn a certain little trick to wake her up and revive her interest: he had to learn to vibrate his quills so as to make a rustling sound. In ancient times

Point to be illustrated

Body: paragraphs 2–7

First examples: support main point, as do all examples

397

man himself, observing the ways of the peacock, probably tried vibrating his whiskers to make a rustling sound; if so, it didn't get him anywhere. He had to go in for something else; so, among other things, he went in for gifts. It is not unlikely that he got this idea from certain flies and birds who were making no headway at all with rustling sounds.

3   One of the flies of the family Empidae, who had tried everything, finally hit on something pretty special. He contrived to make a glistening transparent balloon which was even larger than himself. Into this he would put sweetmeats and tidbits and he would carry the whole elaborate envelope through the air to the lady of his choice. This amused her for a time, but she finally got bored with it. She demanded silly little colorful presents, something that you couldn't eat but that would look nice around the house. So the male Empis had to go around gathering flower petals and pieces of bright paper to put into his balloon. On a courtship flight a male Empis cuts quite a figure now, but he can hardly be said to be happy. He never knows how soon the female will demand heavier presents, such as Roman coins and gold collar buttons. It seems probable that one day the courtship of the Empidae will fall down, as man's occasionally does, of its own weight.

4   The bowerbird is another creature that spends so much time courting the female that he never gets any work done. If all the male bowerbirds became nervous wrecks within the next ten or fifteen years, it would not surprise me. The female bowerbird insists that a playground be built for her with a specially constructed bower at the entrance. This bower is much more elaborate than an ordinary nest and is harder to build; it costs a lot more, too. The female will not come to the playground until the male has filled it up with a great many gifts: silvery leaves, red leaves, rose petals, shells, beads, berries, bones, dice, buttons, cigar bands, Christmas seals, and the Lord knows what else. When the female finally condescends to visit the playground, she is in a coy and silly mood and has to be chased in and out of the bower and up and down the playground before she will quit giggling and stand still long enough even to shake hands. The male bird is, of course, pretty well done in before the chase starts, because he has worn himself out hunting for eyeglass lenses and begonia blossoms. I imagine that many a bowerbird, after chasing a female for two or three hours, says the hell with it and goes home to bed. Next day, of course, he telephones someone else and the same trying ritual is gone through with again. A male bowerbird is as exhausted as a night-club habitué before he is out of his twenties.

5   The male fiddler crab has a somewhat easier time, but it can hardly be said that he is sitting pretty. He has one enormously large and powerful claw, usually brilliantly colored, and you might suppose that all he had to do was reach out and grab some passing cutie. The very earliest fiddler crabs may have tried this, but, if so, they got slapped for their pains. A female fiddler crab will not tolerate any caveman stuff; she never has and she doesn't intend to start now. To attract a female, a fiddler crab has to stand on tiptoe and brandish his claw in the air. If any female in the neighborhood is interested—and you'd be surprised how many are not—she comes over and engages him in light badinage, for which he is not in the mood. As many as a hundred females may pass the time of day with him and go on about their business. By nightfall of an average courting day, a fiddler crab who has been standing on tiptoe for eight or ten hours waving a heavy claw in the air is in pretty sad shape. As in the case of the male of all species, however, he gets out of bed next morning, dashes some water on his face, and tries again.

ILLUSTRATION 399

The next time you encounter a male web-spinning spider, stop and reflect that he is too busy worrying about his love life to have any desire to bite you. Male web-spinning spiders have a tougher life than any other males in the animal kingdom. This is because the female web-spinning spiders have very poor eyesight. If a male lands on a female's web, she kills him before he has time to lay down his cane and gloves, mistaking him for a fly or a bumblebee who has tumbled into her trap. Before the species figured out what to do about this, millions of males were murdered by ladies they called on. It is the nature of spiders to perform a little dance in front of the female, but before a male spinner could get near enough for the female to see who he was and what he was up to, she would lash out at him with a flat-iron or a pair of garden shears. One night, nobody knows when, a very bright male spinner lay awake worrying about calling on a lady who had been killing suitors right and left. It came to him that this business of dancing as a love display wasn't getting anybody anywhere except the grave. He decided to go in for web-twitching, or strand-vibrating. The next day he tried it on one of the nearsighted girls. Instead of dropping in on her suddenly, he stayed outside the web and began monkeying with one of its strands. He twitched it up and down and in and out with such a lilting rhythm that the female was charmed. The serenade worked beautifully; the female let him live. The *Britannica's* spider-watchers, however, report that this system is not always successful. Once in a while, even now, a female will fire three bullets into a suitor or run him through with a kitchen knife. She keeps threatening him from the moment he strikes the first low notes on the outside strings, but usually by the time he has got up to the high notes played around the center of the web, he is going to town and she spares his life.

6 | Fifth example

Even the butterfly, as handsome a fellow as he is, can't always win a mate merely by fluttering around and showing off. Many butterflies have to have scent scales on their wings. Hepialus carries a powder puff in a perfumed pouch. He throws perfume at the ladies when they pass. The male tree cricket, Oecanthus, goes Hepialus one better by carrying a tiny bottle of wine with him and giving drinks to such doxies as he has designs on. One of the male snails throws darts to entertain the girls. So it goes, through the long list of animals, from the bristle worm and his rudimentary dance steps to man and his gift of diamonds and sapphires. The golden-eye drake raises a jet of water with his feet as he flies over a lake; Hepialus has his powder puff, Oecanthus his wine bottle, man his etchings. It is a bright and melancholy story, the age-old desire of the male for the female, the age-old desire of the female to be amused and entertained. Of all the creatures on earth, the only males who could be figured as putting any irony into their courtship are the grebes and certain other diving birds. Every now and then a courting grebe slips quietly down to the bottom of a lake and then, with a mighty "Whoosh!" pops out suddenly a few feet from his girl friend, splashing water all over her. She seems to be persuaded that this is a purely loving display, but I like to think that the grebe always has a faint hope of drowning her or scaring her to death.

7 | Sixth example: discusses series of animals

I will close this investigation into the mournful burdens of the male with *Britannica's* story about a certain Argus pheasant. It appears that the Argus displays himself in front of a female who stands perfectly still without moving a feather. . . . The male Argus the *Britannica* tells about was confined in a cage with a female of another species, a female who kept moving around, emptying ashtrays and fussing with lampshades all the time the male was showing off his

8 | Conclusion: final example

400   READER

DISCUSSION QUESTIONS

1. Thurber suggests throughout the essay that his primary interest is man, not animals. Paragraph 1: "the marine annelids up to man. . . ." Paragraph 2: His first illustration deals with man and "In ancient times man himself. . . ." Paragraphs 3 and 4: Thurber attributes human qualities to the fly and the bowerbird. Depending on the level of your class, you might introduce and discuss personification. Paragraph 6: The female spider strikes "with a flat-iron or a pair of garden shears" and "will fire three bullets into a suitor or run him through with a kitchen knife." Paragraph 7: "from the bristle worm and his rudimentary dance steps to man. . . ." and ". . . man [has] his etchings." Paragraph 8: Thurber's final illustration deals with man.

2. At the end of paragraph 2, Thurber indicates that the peacock got the idea of vibrating its quills from certain flies and birds. Paragraphs 3 and 4 then provide examples of a fly and a bird. Paragraph 4 ends by mentioning the exhaustion of the bowerbird; then paragraph 5 takes up the idea of exhaustion by mentioning the exhausting courtship rite of the fiddler crab. Paragraph 6 moves on to discuss the creature with the toughest courting problem of all those mentioned, and paragraph 7 moves away from a very ugly creature to a beautiful one. Students write more effectively if we reinforce the idea of coherence.

3. Thurber cites the *Encyclopaedia Britannica* to lend authority to his illustrations, which might otherwise seem made up. Of course, the *Encyclopaedia* does not attribute human behavior to its examples, as Thurber humorously does.

talents. Finally, in disgust, he stalked away and began displaying in front of his water trough. He reminds me of a certain male (*Homo sapiens*) of my acquaintance who one night after dinner asked his wife to put down her detective magazine so that he could read a poem of which he was very fond. She sat quietly enough until he was well into the middle of the thing, intoning with great ardor and intensity. Then suddenly there came a sharp, disconcerting *slap!* It turned out that all during the male's display, the female had been intent on a circling mosquito and had finally trapped it between the palms of her hands. The male in this case did not stalk away and display in front of a water trough; he went over to Tim's and had a flock of drinks and recited the poem to the fellas. I am sure they all told bitter stories of their own about how their displays had been interrupted by females. I am also sure that they all ended up singing "Honey, Honey, Bless Your Heart."

DISCUSSION QUESTIONS

1. In paragraph 1 Thurber notes that he will be dealing with the courtship of animals, and the remainder of the selection appears to do just that. What evidence suggests that his main interest is not in the mating of animals at all?
2. Point out the linking techniques that Thurber uses in moving from paragraph 2 through paragraph 7.
3. Why do you think Thurber cites the *Encyclopaedia Britannica* in paragraphs 1, 2, 6, and 8?
4. Explain why the ending "Honey, Honey, Bless Your Heart" is or is not effective.
5. Is Thurber writing primarily to inform? To entertain? To do both? Discuss.

SUGGESTION FOR WRITING ■ Write an essay illustrating the ways that men court women or women court men. Provide at least three examples and aim for a light, humorous tone.

Martin Gottfried

RAMBOS OF THE ROAD

Martin Gottfried is a native of New York City and a writer on theatrical matters. Born in 1933, he earned an A.B. degree at Columbia University and then, after attending law school, served two years in the military intelligence branch of the U.S. Army. Following his discharge in 1959, he spent four years as a music and movie critic and since 1963 has worked as a drama critic. He has authored several books on the theater as well as magazine articles on a variety of topics. In our selection, Gottfried examines the driving behavior of all-too-many motorists.

1   The car pulled up and its driver glared at us with such sullen intensity, such hatred, that I was truly afraid for our lives. Except for the Mohawk haircut he didn't have, he looked like Robert DeNiro in "Taxi Driver," the sort of young man who, delirious for notoriety, might kill a president.

ILLUSTRATION **401**

He was glaring because we had passed him and for that affront he pursued us to the next stoplight so as to express his indignation and affirm his masculinity. I was with two women and, believe it, was afraid for all three of us. It was nearly midnight and we were in a small, sleeping town with no other cars on the road.

When the light turned green, I raced ahead, knowing it was foolish and that I was not in a movie. He didn't merely follow, he chased, and with his headlights turned off. No matter what sudden turn I took, he followed. My passengers were silent. I knew they were alarmed, and I prayed that I wouldn't be called upon to protect them. In that cheerful frame of mind, I turned off my own lights so I couldn't be followed. It was lunacy. I was responding to a crazy *as* a crazy.

"I'll just drive to the police station," I finally said, and as if those were the magic words, he disappeared.

Elbowing Fenders: It seems to me that there has recently been an epidemic of auto macho—a competition perceived and expressed in driving. People fight it out over parking spaces. They bully into line at the gas pump. A toll booth becomes a signal for elbowing fenders. And beetle-eyed drivers hunch over their steering wheels, squeezing the rims, glowering, preparing the excuse of not having seen you as they muscle you off the road. Approaching a highway on an entrance ramp recently, I was strong-armed by a trailer truck so immense that its driver all but blew me away by blasting his horn. The behemoth was just inches from my hopelessly mismatched coupe when I fled for the safety of the shoulder.

And this is happening on city streets, too. A New York taxi driver told me that "intimidation is the name of the game. Drive as if you're deaf and blind. You don't hear the other guy's horn and you sure as hell don't see him."

The odd thing is that long before I was even able to drive, it seemed to me that people were at their finest and most civilized when in their cars. They seemed so orderly and considerate, so reasonable, staying in the right-hand lane unless passing, signaling all intentions. In those days you really eased into highway traffic, and the long, neat rows of cars seemed mobile testimony to the sanity of most people. Perhaps memory fails, perhaps there were always testy drivers, perhaps—but everyone didn't give you the finger.

A most amazing example of driver rage occurred recently at the Manhattan end of the Lincoln Tunnel. We were four cars abreast, stopped at a traffic light. And there was no moving even when the light had changed. A bus had stopped in the cross traffic, blocking our paths: it was normal-for-New-York-City gridlock. Perhaps impatient, perhaps late for important appointments, three of us nonetheless accepted what, after all, we could not alter. One, however, would not. He would not be helpless. He would go where he was going even if he couldn't get there. A Wall Street type in suit and tie, he got out of his car and strode toward the bus, rapping smartly on its doors. When they opened, he exchanged words with the driver. The doors folded shut. He then stepped in front of the bus, took hold of one of its large windshield wipers and broke it.

The bus doors reopened and the driver appeared, apparently giving the fellow a good piece of his mind. If so, the lecture was wasted, for the man started his car and proceeded to drive directly *into the bus*. He rammed it. Even though the point at which he struck the bus, the folding doors, was its most vulnerable point, ramming the side of a bus with your car has to rank very high on a futility index. My first thought was that it had to be a rental car.

Lane merger: To tell the truth, I could not believe my eyes. The bus driver opened his doors as much as they could be opened and he stepped directly onto the hood of the attacking car, jumping up and down with both his feet. He then

2

3

4

5

6

7

8

9

10

4. This ending is effective because it makes the same point the other illustrations do: despite rejections, the males will try again. This is Nature's law. But note also how Thurber suggests the irony in Nature's law.

5. While Thurber makes a point about the difficulties and frustrations of males, he seems mainly intent on entertaining us with his humorous approach.

PERSPECTIVE

Gottfried's essay discusses a problem that has resulted in freeway shootings in some parts of the country. In keeping with the topic, the essay maintains a serious tone throughout while shading it to reflect different emotional responses at different points of the essay. The opening four paragraphs communicate the sense of fear that Gottfried felt when chased by the driver he had passed. In paragraph 10, the finale of the bus-ramming episode, a note of incredulity creeps in as Gottfried notes that "I could not believe my eyes" at the "exercise in absurdity" that had just been played out. And in the final paragraph, he becomes indignant as he attacks the bullies who "represent an America that derides the values of decency and good manners. . . ." Shading an overall tone in this manner enhances the effectiveness of any writing.

TEACHING STRATEGY

Various writers have commented on the pressures of living in a technological society. Ask students to identify as many pressures as they can and then to speculate on possible links between these pressures and the driving behavior that Gottfried illustrates.

CLASSROOM ACTIVITIES

1. Ask students, working in small groups, to list other kinds of auto macho behavior that Gottfried might have mentioned but didn't.
2. Have students, working in small groups, suggest steps that individual drivers and organizations concerned with driver safety might take to decrease auto macho behavior.

DISCUSSION QUESTIONS

1. The thesis statement is the first sentence of paragraph 5.
2. The introduction consists of the first four paragraphs. The anecdote of the driver who pursued Gottfried is designed to draw the reader into the essay. In addition, the introduction helps clarify the meaning of "auto macho" in the thesis statement.
3. One example may have been regarded as atypical. In addition, several examples demonstrate that auto macho takes many forms.
4. Gottfried uses order of climax, as indicated by his characterization of the final example as "A most amazing example of driver rage" (paragraph 8) and by the extraordinarily ridiculous behavior of the driver.
5. Paragraph 11 points out that auto macho extends far beyond "the nuts of the world," affecting, in a milder way, everyone who drives. Paragraph 12 offers a psychiatrist's explanation for its prevalence.
6. Gottfried points out that the implications of auto macho extend beyond our highway behavior. If, as he contends, it represents "an America that derides the values of decency and good manners," then we can expect this outlook to affect other aspects of American life.
7. This question should prompt a spirited discussion.

retreated into the bus, closing the doors behind him. Obviously a man of action, the car driver backed up and rammed the bus again. How this exercise in absurdity would have been resolved none of us will ever know for at that point the traffic unclogged and the bus moved on. And the rest of us, we passives of the world, proceeded, our cars crossing a field of battle as if nothing untoward had happened.

11   It is tempting to blame such belligerent, uncivil and even neurotic behavior on the nuts of the world, but in our cars we all become a little crazy. How many of us speed up when a driver signals his intention of pulling in front of us? Are we resentful and anxious to pass him? How many of us try to squeeze in, or race along the shoulder at a lane merger? We may not jump on hoods, but driving the gantlet, we seethe, cursing not so silently in the safety of our steel bodies on wheels—fortresses for cowards.

12   What is it within us that gives birth to such antisocial behavior and why, all of a sudden, have so many drivers gone around the bend? My friend Joel Katz, a Manhattan psychiatrist, calls it, "a Rambo pattern. People are running around thinking the American way is to take the law into your own hands when anyone does anything wrong. And what constitutes 'wrong'? Anything that cramps your style."

13   It seems to me that it is a new America we see on the road now. It has the mentality of a hoodlum and the backbone of a coward. The car is its weapon and hiding place, and it is still a symbol even in this. Road Rambos no longer bespeak a self-reliant, civil people tooling around in family cruisers. In fact, there aren't families in these machines that charge headlong with their brights on in broad daylight, demanding we get out of their way. Bullies are loners, and they have perverted our liberty of the open road into drivers' license. They represent an America that derides the values of decency and good manners, then roam the highways riding shotgun and shrieking freedom. By allowing this to happen, the rest of us approve.

DISCUSSION QUESTIONS

1. Identify the thesis statement of this essay.
2. What paragraphs make up the introduction? Besides starting the essay, what function do they perform?
3. Why are several examples a better choice for this essay than one extended example?
4. In what order does Gottfried arrange his examples?
5. What does Gottfried accomplish in paragraphs 11-12?
6. What function, other than ending the essay, is served by the final paragraph?
7. Judging from your experience, how prevalent are road Rambos of the type that Gottfried discusses?

SUGGESTION FOR WRITING ■ Write an illustration essay exploring the behavior, good or bad, that you have experienced on campus, in the workplace, or while engaged in some activity such as shopping. Use several examples, arrange them in an appropriate order, and try to account for the behavior.

ILLUSTRATION   **403**

Mark Twain

Corn-Pone Opinions

Samuel Langhorne Clemens (1835–1910), who later adopted the pen name Mark Twain, was born in Florida, Missouri, and grew up in the Mississippi River town of Hannibal, Missouri. After working as a printer, steamboat pilot, and western journalist, he turned to lecturing and fiction writing and soon achieved fame as a humorist. Today Twain is regarded as one of this country's foremost realistic writers and satirists. His reputation rests firmly on such works as The Adventures of Tom Sawyer *(1875),* The Prince and the Pauper *(1881),* The Adventures of Huckleberry Finn *(1884),* A Connecticut Yankee in King Arthur's Court *(1889), and* Life on the Mississippi *(1883). In our essay, Twain examines the way we form our opinions and finds it wanting.*

Fifty years ago, when I was a boy of fifteen and helping to inhabit a Missourian village on the banks of the Mississippi, I had a friend whose society was very dear to me because I was forbidden by my mother to partake of it. He was a gay and impudent and satirical and delightful young black man—a slave—who daily preached sermons from the top of his master's woodpile, with me for sole audience. He imitated the pulpit style of the several clergymen of the village, and did it well, and with fine passion and energy. To me he was a wonder. I believed he was the greatest orator in the United States and would some day be heard from. But it did not happen; in the distribution of rewards he was overlooked. It is the way, in this world. 1

He interrupted his preaching, now and then, to saw a stick of wood; but the sawing was a pretense—he did it with his mouth; exactly imitating the sound the bucksaw makes in shrieking its way through the wood. But it served its purpose; it kept his master from coming out to see how the work was getting along. I listened to the sermons from the open window of a lumber room at the back of the house. One of his texts was this: 2

"You tell me whar a man gits his corn pone, en I'll tell you what his 'pinions is." 3

I can never forget it. It was deeply impressed upon me. By my mother. Not upon my memory, but elsewhere. She had slipped in upon me while I was absorbed and not watching. The black philosopher's idea was that a man is not independent, and cannot afford views which might interfere with his bread and butter. If he would prosper, he must train with the majority; in matters of large moment, like politics and religion, he must think and feel with the bulk of his neighbors, or suffer damage in his social standing and in his business prosperities. He must restrict himself to corn-pone opinions—at least on the surface. He must get his opinions from other people; he must reason out none for himself; he must have no first-hand views. 4

I think Jerry was right, in the main, but I think he did not go far enough. 5

1. It was his idea that a man conforms to the majority view of his locality by calculation and intention. 6

This happens, but I think it is not the rule. 7

2. It was his idea that there is such a thing as a first-hand opinion; an original opinion; an opinion which is coldly reasoned out in a man's head, by a 8

PERSPECTIVE

Although most students know of Twain's reputation as a humorous writer, few realize that as he aged his writings became increasingly bitter and pessimistic. This essay, written in Twain's darker period, shows flashes of humor in the earlier part, but the overall tone is one of disgust at human stupidity.

TEACHING STRATEGIES

1. This essay was published in 1923. You might have students discuss to what extent Twain's opinions are valid in the 1990s. The discussion might lead to an illustration essay.
2. Ask students to identify several examples of parallelism and discuss their effectiveness. Furthermore, depending on the sophistication of your class, you could have them comment on the distinguishing features of Twain's style.
3. Ask why Twain concludes with statements dripping with irony. The answer, of course, requires an understanding of the whole essay.

CLASSROOM ACTIVITY

Have the class identify as many current fads as they can. List the fads on the board and then discuss them. This activity could lead to a writing assignment.

searching analysis of the facts involved, with the heart unconsulted, and the jury room closed against outside influences. It may be that such an opinion has been born somewhere, at some time or other, but I suppose it got away before they could catch it and stuff it and put it in the museum.

9   I am persuaded that a coldly-thought-out and independent verdict upon a fashion in clothes, or manners, or literature, or politics, or religion, or any other matter that is projected into the field of our notice and interest, is a most rare thing—if it has indeed ever existed.

10   A new thing in costume appears—the flaring hoopskirt, for example—and the passers-by are shocked, and the irreverent laugh. Six months later everybody is reconciled; the fashion has established itself; it is admired, now, and no one laughs. Public opinion resented it before, public opinion accepts it now, and is happy in it. Why? Was the resentment reasoned out? Was the acceptance reasoned out? No. The instinct that moves to conformity did the work. It is our nature to conform; it is a force which not many can successfully resist. What is its seat? The inborn requirement of self-approval. We all have to bow to that; there are no exceptions. Even the woman who refuses from first to last to wear the hoopskirt comes under that law and is its slave; she could not wear the skirt and have her own approval; and that she *must* have, she cannot help herself. But as a rule our self-approval has its source in but one place and not elsewhere—the approval of other people. A person of vast consequences can introduce any kind of novelty in dress and the general world will presently adopt it—moved to do it, in the first place, by the natural instinct to passively yield to that vague something recognized as authority, and in the second place by the human instinct to train with the multitude and have its approval. An empress introduced the hoopskirt, and we know the result. A nobody introduced the bloomer, and we know the result. If Eve should come again, in her ripe renown, and reintroduce her quaint styles— well, we know what would happen. And we should be cruelly embarrassed, along at first.

11   The hoopskirt runs its course and disappears. Nobody reasons about it. One woman abandons the fashion; her neighbor notices this and follows her lead; this influences the next woman; and so on and so on, and presently the skirt has vanished out of the world, no one knows how nor why, nor cares, for that matter. It will come again by and by and in due course will go again.

12   Twenty-five years ago, in England, six or eight wine glasses stood grouped by each person's plate at a dinner party, and they were used, not left idle and empty; today there are but three or four in the group, and the average guest sparingly uses about two of them. We have not adopted this new fashion yet, but we shall do it presently. We shall not think it out; we shall merely conform, and let it go at that. We get our notions and habits and opinions from outside influences; we do not have to study them out.

13   Our table manners, and company manners, and street manners change from time to time, but the changes are not reasoned out; we merely notice and conform. We are creatures of outside influences; as a rule we do not think, we only imitate. We cannot invent standards that will stick; what we mistake for standards are only fashions, and perishable. We may continue to admire them, but we drop the use of them. We notice this in literature. Shakespeare is a standard, and fifty years ago we used to write tragedies which we couldn't tell from—from somebody else's; but we don't do it any more, now. Our prose standard, three quarters of a century ago, was ornate and diffuse; some authority or other changed it in the direction of compactness and simplicity, and conformity fol-

ILLUSTRATION **405**

lowed, without argument. The historical novel starts up suddenly, and sweeps the land. Everybody writes one, and the nation is glad. We had historical novels before; but nobody read them, and the rest of us conformed—without reasoning it out. We are conforming in the other way, now, because it is another case of everybody.

The outside influences are always pouring in upon us, and we are always obeying their orders and accepting their verdicts. The Smiths like the new play; the Joneses go to see it, and they copy the Smith verdict. Morals, religions, politics, get their following from surrounding influences and atmospheres, almost entirely; not from study, not from thinking. A man must and will have his own approval first of all, in each and every moment and circumstance of his life—even if he must repent of a self-approved act the moment after its commission, in order to get his self-approval *again:* but, speaking in general terms, a man's self-approval in the large concerns of life has its source in the approval of the peoples about him, and not in a searching personal examination of the matter. Mohammedans are Mohammedans because they are born and reared among the sect, not because they have thought it out and can furnish sound reasons for being Mohammedans; we know why Catholics are Catholics; why Presbyterians are Presbyterians; why Baptists are Baptists; why Mormons are Mormons; why thieves are thieves; why monarchists are monarchists; why Republicans are Republicans and Democrats, Democrats. We know it is a matter of association and sympathy, not reasoning and examination; that hardly a man in the world has an opinion upon morals, politics, or religion which he got otherwise than through his associations and sympathies. Broadly speaking, there are none but corn-pone opinions. And broadly speaking, corn-pone stands for self-approval. Self-approval is acquired mainly from the approval of other people. The result is conformity. Sometimes conformity has a sordid business interest—the bread-and-butter interest—but not in most cases. I think. I think that in the majority of cases it is unconscious and not calculated; that it is born of the human being's natural yearning to stand well with his fellows and have their inspiring approval and praise—a yearning which is commonly so strong and so insistent that it cannot be effectually resisted, and must have its way.

A political emergency brings out the corn-pone opinion in fine force in its two chief varieties—the pocketbook variety, which has its origin in self-interest, and the bigger variety, the sentimental variety—the one which can't bear to be outside the pale; can't bear to be in disfavor; can't endure the averted face and the cold shoulder; wants to stand well with his friends, wants to be smiled upon, wants to be welcome, wants to hear the precious words, *"He's* on the right track!" Uttered, perhaps by an ass, but still an ass of high degree, an ass whose approval is gold and diamonds to a smaller ass, and confers glory and honor and happiness, and membership in the herd. For these gauds many a man will dump his life-long principles into the street, and his conscience along with them. We have seen it happen. In some millions of instances.

Men think they think upon great political questions, and they do; but they think with their party, not independently; they read its literature, but not that of the other side; they arrive at convictions, but they are drawn from a partial view of the matter in hand and are of no particular value. They swarm with their party, they feel with their party, they are happy in their party's approval; and where the party leads they will follow, whether for right and honor, or through blood and dirt and a mush of mutilated morals.

In our late canvass half of the nation passionately believed that in silver lay

14

15

16

17

DISCUSSION QUESTIONS (p. 406)

1. Twain notes, in paragraph 9, that "... a coldly-thought-out and independent verdict upon a fashion in clothes, or manners, or literature, or politics, or religion, or any other matter ... is a most rare thing. ...." Because no single example could illustrate the lack of independent thinking on all of these matters, a whole series of examples is required.

2. This essay has a nine-paragraph introduction that ends with Twain's thesis statement. This lengthy introduction allows Twain to present a detailed discussion of the character and views of his friend Jerry as well as to offer a criticism of the views that acts as a springboard for his own thoughts. At the time Twain wrote this essay, fashion favored a more leisurely style than is now in vogue. By conforming to the prevailing mode, Twain ironically and unintentionally lends support to his thesis.

3. Twain arranges his examples in a sequence that moves from trivial matters such as fashions in literature and clothing to more serious concerns—religion and political questions. This principle of presentation allows for some flexibility. Thus Twain might have reversed the order in which he discusses clothing and literature or religion and politics, but he could not logically have used an order intermingling trivial and serious concerns.

4. Twain is making the point that although he examined both questions carefully, he found no evidence that people arrived at their views concerning silver and tariffs through the exercise of logic.

5. The tone of the essay reflects Twain's disillusionment with human beings. This attitude is perhaps most readily apparent in the thesis statement but finds expression at many other places in the essay. In paragraph 10, for example, Twain notes that "It is our nature to conform; it is a force which not many can successfully resist. What is its seat? The inborn requirement of self-approval. We all have to bow to that. . . ." In paragraph 13, he declares that "We cannot invent standards that will stick; what we mistake for standards are only fashions, and perishable." In paragraph 15, he declares that in order to avoid the stigma of being held in political disfavor, "a man will dump his life-long principles into the street, and his conscience along with them." And note the highly sarcastic words that end the essay.

salvation, the other half as passionately believed that that way lay destruction. Do you believe that a tenth part of the people, on either side, had any rational excuse for having an opinion about the matter at all? I studied that mighty question to the bottom—came out empty. Half of our people passionately believe in high tariff, the other half believe otherwise. Does this mean study and examination, or only feeling? The latter, I think. I have deeply studied that question, too—and didn't arrive. We all do no end of feeling, and we mistake it for thinking. And out of it we get an aggregation which we consider a boon. Its name is Public Opinion. It is held in reverence. It settles everything. Some think it the Voice of God.

DISCUSSION QUESTIONS

1. Why do you think Twain uses several examples rather than a single extended one?
2. What part of the essay constitutes the introduction? What is Twain's thesis?
3. Discuss the order in which Twain arranges his examples.
4. In paragraph 17, Twain says that after studying two important questions he "came out empty" and "didn't arrive." Explain what he means by these expressions.
5. How would you characterize the tone (see pages 220–23) of this essay? Refer to the text when answering.

SUGGESTION FOR WRITING ■ Write a rebuttal to Twain by citing examples of friends and acquaintances who hold nonconformist views on such matters as religion, politics, family relationships, education, or recreation and who can rationally defend their positions.

Ellen Goodman

THE COMPANY MAN

Ellen Goodman (born 1941) is a native of Massachusetts and a 1963 graduate of Radcliffe College. A journalist since graduation, she has worked as a researcher and reporter for Newsweek, *a feature writer for the* Detroit Free Press *and the* Boston Globe, *and a columnist for the Washington Post Writers Group, as well as a commentator on CBS Radio's* Spectrum *show and NBC-TV's* Today Show. *She has also contributed articles to* Ms., McCall's, *and the* Village Voice. *Book-length publications include* Turning Points *(1979) and two collections of newspaper columns,* Close to Home *(1979) and* At Large *(1981). In 1980, she received a Pulitzer Prize for commentary. Our selection, taken from* At Large, *depicts a workaholic whose total dedication to his job killed him.*

PERSPECTIVE

Unlike the other writers in this section, Goodman uses a single extended example. Because her company man typifies the type A workaholic, no other examples are needed. The style is informal, the tone matter-of-fact, and because the topic does not lend itself to humor, there is none. The essay ends on an ironic note when Phil's boss, thinking about Phil's replacement, asks, "Who's been working the hardest?"

1   He worked himself to death, finally and precisely, at 3:00 A.M. Sunday morning.

ILLUSTRATION 407

The obituary didn't say that, of course. It said that he died of a coronary thrombosis—I think that was it—but everyone among his friends and acquaintances knew it instantly. He was a perfect Type A, a workaholic, a classic, they said to each other and shook their heads—and thought for five or ten minutes about the way they lived.

This man who worked himself to death finally and precisely at 3:00 A.M. Sunday morning—on his day off—was fifty-one years old and a vice-president. He was, however, one of six vice-presidents, and one of three who might conceivably—if the president died or retired soon enough—have moved to the top spot. Phil knew that.

He worked six days a week, five of them until eight or nine at night, during a time when his own company had begun the four-day week for everyone but the executives. He worked like the Important People. He had no outside "extracurricular interests," unless, of course, you think about a monthly golf game that way. To Phil, it was work. He always ate egg salad sandwiches at his desk. He was, of course, overweight, by 20 to 25 pounds. He thought it was okay, though, because he didn't smoke.

On Saturdays, Phil wore a sports jacket to the office instead of a suit, because it was the weekend.

He had a lot of people working for him, maybe sixty, and most of them liked him most of the time. Three of them will be seriously considered for his job. The obituary didn't mention that.

But it did list his "survivors" quite accurately. He is survived by his wife, Helen, forty-eight years old, a good woman of no particular marketable skills, who worked in an office before marrying and mothering. She had, according to her daughter, given up trying to compete with his work years ago, when the children were small. A company friend said, "I know how much you will miss him." And she answered, "I already have."

"Missing him all these years," she must have given up part of herself which had cared too much for the man. She would be "well taken care of."

His "dearly beloved" eldest of the "dearly beloved" children is a hard-working executive in a manufacturing firm down South. In the day and a half before the funeral, he went around the neighborhood researching his father, asking the neighbors what he was like. They were embarrassed.

His second child is a girl, who is twenty-four and newly married. She lives near her mother and they are close, but whenever she was alone with her father, in a car driving somewhere, they had nothing to say to each other.

The youngest is twenty, a boy, a high-school graduate who has spent the last couple of years, like a lot of his friends, doing enough odd jobs to stay in grass and food. He was the one who tried to grab at his father, and tried to mean enough to him to keep the man at home. He was his father's favorite. Over the last two years, Phil stayed up nights worrying about the boy.

The boy once said, "My father and I only board here."

At the funeral, the sixty-year-old company president told the forty-eight-year-old widow that the fifty-one-year-old deceased had meant much to the company and would be missed and would be hard to replace. The widow didn't look him in the eye. She was afraid he would read her bitterness and, after all, she would need him to straighten out the finances—the stock options and all that.

Phil was overweight and nervous and worked too hard. If he wasn't at the office, he was worried about it. Phil was a Type A, a heart-attack natural. You could have picked him out in a minute from a lineup.

(paragraph numbers in margin: 2, 3, 4, 5, 6, 7, 8, 9, 10, 11, 12, 13, 14)

TEACHING STRATEGIES

1. Ask students to consider the whole essay and then comment on the curt statement at the end of paragraph 3.

2. Ask students to list the characteristics of a type B, or laid-back, personality. They might consider the person's approach to his or her job, family, recreation, and neighbors. This list could launch the writing suggestion that follows Goodman's essay.

DISCUSSION QUESTIONS (p. 408)

1. The type A (the medical profession's term for a prime heart attack candidate) is a hard-driving workaholic bent on getting to the "top spot" (paragraph 3). Such a person is unable to relax and enjoy any type of family relationship or any recreational activities that seem unproductive.

2. By these omissions Goodman suggests that Phil could be any number of people working for any number of companies. The type she is illustrating is found in many places.

3. By illustrating the life and death of a workaholic, Goodman is sounding an alert to others caught up in the same lethal rut. Her essay is an implicit argument against workaholism.

4. By focusing on one illustration rather than several, Goodman can present a fully rounded portrait of a workaholic and the shattering impact of workaholism on its victim's family. Had Goodman used several illustrations, no such portrait would have emerged, lessening the reader's realization of the seriousness of the condition.

5. Phil spent so much time at the office and so little with his children that his son had to ask neighbors about his father's personality. Ironically the neighbors, just like Phil's family, probably didn't know him either.

6. As the headnote indicates, this essay was originally published as a newspaper column where short paragraphs are standard fare.

15   So when he finally worked himself to death, at precisely 3:00 A.M. Sunday morning, no one was really surprised.

16   By 5:00 P.M. the afternoon of the funeral, the company president had begun, discreetly of course, with care and taste, to make inquiries about his replacement. One of three men. He asked around: "Who's been working the hardest?"

DISCUSSION QUESTIONS

1. Goodman says that Phil was "a perfect type A" (paragraph 2). After reflecting on her essay, explain the characteristics of this type.
2. Why do you think Goodman doesn't supply Phil's last name or the name of the company he works for?
3. What idea is Goodman trying to put across?
4. Unlike the essay by Thurber, Goodman's uses one longer illustration rather than several shorter ones. Why?
5. What is the significance of Phil's oldest son going "around the neighborhood researching his father, asking the neighbors what he was like" (paragraph 9)? Why were they embarrassed?
6. How do you account for Goodman's relatively short paragraphs?

SUGGESTION FOR WRITING ■ Using one extended example, write an essay that illustrates the lifestyle of a laid-back employee or friend. Your paper need not, of course, feature a death.

Classification

OVERVIEW OF
CLASSIFICATION ESSAYS

The classification essays display various levels of language and types of diction. Two use highly informal language, along with light-hearted humor. A third is also written informally, but the diction is somewhat more sophisticated. The remaining essay uses formal-informal language and moderately sophisticated diction.

Eric Berne

CAN PEOPLE BE JUDGED BY THEIR APPEARANCE?

Eric Berne (1910–1970) was born in Montreal, Quebec, and earned his medical degree at McGill University. Following graduation, he studied at the Yale Psychiatric Clinic and the New York Psychoanalytic Institute and became a U.S. citizen in 1943. During World War II, Berne served in the Army Medical Corps and later was a consultant to the Surgeon General. He also practiced psychiatry in New York and California. Berne was the author of several books on psychiatry, two of which, Games People Play *(1964) and* Layman's Guide to Psychiatry and Psychoanalysis *(1957, 1968), gained wide popular attention. In our selection, taken from the second edition of the latter book, Berne offers an explanation of why some people act the way they do.*

Everyone knows that a human being, like a chicken, comes from an egg. At a very early stage, the human embryo forms a three-layered tube, the inside layer of which grows into the stomach and lungs, the middle layer into bones, muscle, joints, and blood vessels, and the outside layer into the skin and nervous system.

Usually these three grow about equally, so that the average human being is a fair mixture of brains, muscles, and inward organs. In some eggs, however, one layer grows more than the others, and when the angels have finished putting the child together, he may have more gut than brain, or more brain than muscle. When this happens, the individual's activities will often be mostly with the overgrown layer.

We can thus say that while the average human being is a mixture, some people are mainly "digestion-minded," some "muscle-minded," and some "brain-minded," and correspondingly digestion-bodied, muscle-bodied, or brain-bodied. The digestion-bodied people look thick; the muscle-bodied people look wide; and the brain-bodied people look long. This does not mean the taller a man is the brainier he will be. It means that if a man, even a short man, looks long rather than wide or thick, he will often be more concerned about what goes on in his mind than about what he does or what he eats; but the key factor is slenderness and not height. On the other hand, a man who gives the impression of being thick rather than long or wide will usually be more interested in a good steak than in a good idea or a good long walk.

Medical men use Greek words to describe these types of body-build. For the man whose body shape mostly depends on the inside layer of the egg, they use the word *endomorph*. If it depends mostly upon the middle layer, they call him a *mesomorph*. If it depends upon the outside layer, they call him an *ectomorph*. We can see the same roots in our English words "enter," "medium," and

PERSPECTIVE

In making his classification, Berne almost totally ignores the largest category of humans, those who have "a fair mixture of brains, muscles, and inward organs." Why? Because his purpose is to acquaint readers with the personality quirks of three relatively uncommon types of individuals. Since the behavior patterns of the "mixture" category are more familiar, there is little need to discuss them.

1   Introduction: discusses development of three embryo layers

2   Body: paragraphs 2–14

3   Paragraphs 3–6: general characteristics, naming of three body types

4

409

"exit," which might just as easily have been spelled "ender," "mesium," and "ectit."

5   Since the inside skin of the human egg, or endoderm, forms the inner organs of the belly, the viscera, the endomorph is usually belly-minded; since the middle skin forms the body tissues, or soma, the mesomorph is usually muscle-minded; and since the outside skin forms the brain, or cerebrum, the ectomorph is usually brain-minded. Translating this into Greek, we have the viscerotonic endomorph, the somatotonic mesomorph, and the cerebrotonic ectomorph.

6   Words are beautiful things to a cerebrotonic, but a viscerotonic knows you cannot eat a menu no matter what language it is printed in, and a somatotonic knows you cannot increase your chest expansion by reading a dictionary. So it is advisable to leave these words and see what kinds of people they actually apply to, remembering again that most individuals are fairly equal mixtures and that what we have to say concerns only the extremes. Up to the present, these types have been thoroughly studied only in the male sex.

First category

7   If a man is definitely a thick type rather than a broad or long type, he is likely to be round and soft, with a big chest but a bigger belly. He would rather eat than breathe comfortably. He is likely to have a wide face, short, thick neck, big thighs and upper arms, and small hands and feet. He has overdeveloped breasts and looks as though he were blown up a little like a balloon. His skin is soft and smooth, and when he gets bald, as he does usually quite early, he loses the hair in the middle of his head first.

8   The short, jolly, thickset, red-faced politician with a cigar in his mouth, who always looks as though he were about to have a stroke, is the best example of this type. The reason he often makes a good politician is that he likes people, banquets, baths, and sleep; he is easygoing, soothing, and his feelings are easy to understand.

9   His abdomen is big because he has lots of intestines. He likes to take in things. He likes to take in food, and affection and approval as well. Going to a banquet with people who like him is his idea of a fine time. It is important for a psychiatrist to understand the nature of such men when they come to him for advice.

Second category

10   If a man is definitely a broad type rather than a thick or long type, he is likely to be rugged and have lots of muscle. He is apt to have big forearms and legs, and his chest and belly are well formed and firm, with the chest bigger than the belly. He would rather breathe than eat. He has a bony head, big shoulders, and a square jaw. His skin is thick, coarse, and elastic, and tans easily. If he gets bald, it usually starts on the front of the head.

11   Dick Tracy, Li'l Abner, and other men of action belong to this type. Such people make good lifeguards and construction workers. They like to put out energy. They have lots of muscles, and they like to use them. They go in for adventure, exercise, fighting, and getting the upper hand. They are bold and unrestrained, and love to master the people and things around them. If the psychiatrist knows the things which give such people satisfaction, he is able to understand why they may be unhappy in certain situations.

Third category

12   The man who is definitely a long type is likely to have thin bones and muscles. His shoulders are apt to sag, and he has a flat belly with a dropped stomach, and long, weak legs. His neck and fingers are long, and his face is shaped like a long egg. His skin is thin, dry, and pale, and he rarely gets bald. He looks like an absent-minded professor and often is one.

Though such people are jumpy, they like to keep their energy and don't   13
fancy moving around much. They would rather sit quietly by themselves and
keep out of difficulties. Trouble upsets them, and they run away from it. Their
friends don't understand them very well. They move jerkily and feel jerkily. The
psychiatrist who understands how easily they become anxious is often able to
help them get along better in the sociable and aggressive world of endomorphs
and mesomorphs.

In the special cases where people definitely belong to one type or another,   14
then, one can tell a good deal about their personalities from their appearance.
When the human mind is engaged in one of its struggles with itself or with the
world outside, the individual's way of handling the struggle will be partly determined by his type. If he is a viscerotonic he will often want to go to a party where
he can eat and drink and be in good company at a time when he might be better
off attending to business; the somatotonic will want to go out and do something
about it, master the situation, even if what he does is foolish and not properly
figured out, while the cerebrotonic will go off by himself and think it over, when
perhaps he would be better off doing something about it or seeking good company to try to forget it.

| Connection between body type, personality |

Since these personality characteristics depend on the growth of the layers of   15
the little egg from which the person developed, they are very difficult to change.
Nevertheless, it is important for the individual to know about these types, so that
he can have at least an inkling of what to expect from those around him, and can
make allowances for the different kinds of human nature, and so that he can
become aware of and learn to control his own tendencies, which may sometimes
guide him into making the same mistakes over and over again in handling his
difficulties.

| Conclusion: value of understanding three personalities |

DISCUSSION QUESTIONS

1. Even though Berne applies scientific labels to the three categories of people he discusses, the essay isn't written for scientists. What audience is Berne trying to reach? How do you know?
2. Point out the significance of the following sentence in paragraph 6: "So it is advisable to leave these words and see what kinds of people they actually apply to, remembering again that most individuals are fairly equal mixtures and that what we have to say concerns only the extremes."
3. In what order does Berne organize his categories? Would another order have worked as well? Why or why not?
4. How does Berne organize the discussion within each of his categories?

SUGGESTION FOR WRITING ■ Write an essay that classi-
fies your friends according to their political beliefs, taste in clothes, preferences in movies, or habits of study.

DISCUSSION QUESTIONS

1. This essay is addressed to intelligent, well-educated lay people. The writing is re-laxed, including figurative language ("when the angels have finished putting the child together"), homely phrasing ("He . . . looks as though he were blown up a little like a balloon," "His ab-domen is big because he has lots of intestines"), and refer-ences to politicians, comic-strip characters, and absent-minded professors. The use of scientific terms is confined to paragraphs 4–6, after which these terms are aban-doned in favor of terms like "thick type," "broad type," and "long type."
2. This sentence serves two purposes. First, it reminds us that most people don't fall

into one of the three categories discussed in the essay. (This point is first mentioned in paragraph 2.) More important, it signals a shift from a general discussion of the three types to specific explanations and examples of each category.

3. He begins by describing the type of person that results when the inner layer of the embryo develops too much and ends by describing the type that develops when the outer layer develops too much. The progression is from physically oriented to mentally oriented people. It would seem disorganized to sandwich the mentally oriented type between the others.

4. The discussion begins with basic physical information about the type, offers examples, provides behavorial information, and ends by pointing out the importance of the information to psychiatrists.

PERSPECTIVE

Like Thurber's "Courtship Through the Ages," this essay links humans and animals. Fury, however, compares humans to animals, while Thurber attributes human qualities to nonhuman creatures. Either approach helps achieve a comic effect. Some students may ask why many of Fury's paragraphs are so brief. Such paragraphs, of course, are common in newspapers and in articles appearing in magazines aimed at the mass market.

Kathleen Fury

IT'S ONLY A PAPER WORLD

Kathleen Fury (born 1941) is a native New Yorker and a graduate of Purdue University (1964). Since graduation Fury has worked as a writer and magazine editor. She has held editorships with Redbook, Ladies Home Journal, *and* Savvy, *and is currently a regular contributor to* Working Woman. *She is the author of a 1985 book,* Dear 60 Minutes. *In the essay we have chosen, Fury takes a lighthearted look at the different kinds of "paper pushers" in a modern office.*

1   Many experts claimed that the computer age heralded the advent of the paperless office. Clearly, this is not to be. If anything, offices are overwhelmed by even more paper, much of it now with sprocket holes.

2   Humankind is adapting, fortunately. According to the dictates of our varied individual natures, we have developed ways of coping with our changing ecosystem.

3   The beaver uses paper to build. It may not be exactly clear to observers just what she's building, but deep in her genetic code she knows.

4   On one side of the typical beaver's desk leans a foot-high stack of papers. Close by is a vertical file stuffed with bulging folders, some waving in the air, unable to touch bottom. In between, the beaver constructs a clever "dam" to prevent the entire structure from falling over: Her two-tier In/Out box supports the pile and allows movement of papers from one place to another.

5   Incredibly, to nonbeaver observers, the beaver has an uncanny ability to locate a two-month-old report buried within the pile. With deft precision, she can move her hand four millimeters down the pile and extract what she's looking for, confident that the dam will hold.

6   In this way, the beaver has evolved a protective mechanism that makes her invaluable within the organization, for nobody else, including her secretary, can find anything on her desk. When the beaver goes away on vacation, her department simply ceases work until she returns. She is thus assured that the cliché "nobody's indispensable" doesn't apply to her.

7   The squirrel's desk, by contrast, is barren. Throughout the year, in all kinds of weather, the squirrel energetically stores away what her brain tells her she may need someday. In her many file cabinets, drawers and bookcases she neatly stores memos, letters, printouts and receipts she believes will nourish her in the months and years to come.

8   Unlike her co-worker the beaver, the squirrel does not always know exactly where she has hidden a particular item. She knows she *has* it but is not skilled at remembering the exact location.

9   Like the maple tree, which produces enough seeds to reforest a continent, the squirrel illustrates nature's method of "overkill." By saving and storing everything, she increases her chance of retrieving something.

10   Of necessity, squirrels have developed the ability to move through a wide territorial range. When a squirrel moves on to another job, as she tends to do rather often due to lack of space, management must hire a special team of search-and-destroy experts to go through her files.

11   Nature's scavengers, her "clean-up crew," crows are regarded with wary

admiration by squirrels and beavers, who recognize their contribution to keeping the corporate ecosystem tidy.

Crows are responsible for such paper-management advice as "Act on it—or throw it away." They are deeply drawn to paper shredders, trash compactors and outsized waste receptacles and will buy them if they happen to work in purchasing. 12

Crows belie the common epithet "birdbrained," for it has taken centuries of evolution to create a mind disciplined enough to know with certainty that it is OK to throw the CEO's Statement of Corporate Policy in the wastebasket after a glance. 13

Other species, who must adapt to the corporate food chain, quickly learn not to address any crow with a sentence that begins, "Do you have a copy of. . .?" 14

The clever bees are among the wonders of the corporate world. A bee neither hoards nor destroys paper; she redistributes it, moving from office to office as if between flowers. 15

Her methods are various and unpredictable, but there is no madness in them. Sometimes she arrives in an office with paper in hand and, distracting a colleague with conversation, simply leaves the paper inconspicuously on his desk. Sometimes she moves paper through seemingly legitimate channels, sending it through interoffice mail with ingenious notes like "Please look into this when you get a chance." More often, she employs the clever notation invented by bees, "FYI." 16

Whatever her method, she ensures that paper floats outward and does not return to her. Students of human behavior have come to call this cross-pollination "delegation," though to the bee it is simply a genetic imperative. 17

While others of the species hoard, distribute and destroy paper, the possum follows the evolutionary dictates of all marsupials and carries it with her. 18

Instead of a pouch, the office possum has a briefcase—in some cases, several. It is large and soft sided to accommodate her needs. Some possums, as an auxiliary system, carry handbags large enough to hold legal-size files. When a possum needs to retrieve paper, she goes not to a file cabinet or an In box but to her bags. She protects her paper by carrying it with her at all times—to her home, to the health club, to lunch. 19

Though she has no natural predators, the possum's habits create special risks. She must spend considerable time at the lost-and-found department of theaters and restaurants and knows by heart the telephone number of the taxi commissioner. One of her arms is longer than the other. 20

But in nature, all things serve a purpose. And if the office burned down, the lowly possum would be the sole possessor of the paper that is the raison d'être of all the other animals. 21

DISCUSSION QUESTIONS

1. How would you explain the term "sprocket holes" in paragraph 1?
2. What does Fury mean in paragraph 17 when she refers to the bee's habit of distributing paper as a "genetic imperative"?
3. Speaking of the possum Fury says that "One of her arms is longer than the other" (paragraph 20). Why?
4. Point out the transitions that Fury uses to link her various categories.

7. Since offices today are "overwhelmed" with paper, Fury points out in humorous fashion the ways that different types handle this deluge.

PERSPECTIVE

Baker's essay, like the one by Kathleen Fury, is an example of broad humor and thus is ideally suited for the informal writing style. More subtle humor, such as that found in E. M. Forster's "My Wood" (pages 434–36), requires a correspondingly more sophisticated writing style.

TEACHING STRATEGIES

1. Since students often use humor freely in their conversations, they assume that writing in a humorous vein flows as easily. Not so. Writing with effective humor requires considerable skill. You might want to discuss with your class how Baker achieves his humor.
2. Baker uses dashes in paragraphs 1, 4, 11, and 12. You could ask students to examine these uses and then formulate guidelines for the proper uses of the dash.

DISCUSSION QUESTIONS

1. The references to science and scientists—of course Baker presents no scientific evidence and names no researchers—are clearly intended to add a spurious note of authority to his ridiculous assertion that inanimate objects have brains and plot against humans. Thus these references heighten the humor.
2. Baker discusses his first category in paragraphs 2–4, his second in paragraphs 6–10, and his third in paragraphs 11–14. Paragraph 5 provides a transition between the first and second categories. The categories are arranged in order of climax as

5. Explain why you think Fury does or does not consider this to be a complete classification in which all categories are discussed.
6. Indicate why the concluding paragraph of the essay is effective.
7. Reflect on the essay and then suggest Fury's purpose in writing this classification.

SUGGESTION FOR WRITING ■ **Write an essay classifying the members of some group that you encounter regularly. You might, for example, classify the shoppers in a mall, the members in a sports or entertainment group, the members of your church or synagogue, or the students in a particular class.**

Russell Baker

THE PLOT AGAINST PEOPLE

Russell Baker (born 1925) is a native of Virginia and a graduate of Johns Hopkins University, where he earned an A.B. degree in 1947. Following seven years at the Baltimore Sun, *Baker joined the Washington bureau of the* New York Times. *In 1962, he transferred to New York City and began writing the "Observer" column for the paper, swiftly gaining a reputation as an adroit humorist. His book-length publications include volumes of fiction, autobiography, and verse, as well as several collections of his newspaper columns, the most recent of which,* There's a Country in My Cellar, *appeared in 1991. He has also contributed articles to numerous popular magazines. His writings have won him several honors, including the Pulitzer Prize in 1979. In our selection, from an "Observer" column, Baker gives his humor full rein as he exposes the dastardly machinations of inanimate objects against humans.*

1   Inanimate objects are classified scientifically into three major categories—those that break down, those that get lost, and those that don't work.

2   The goal of all inanimate objects is to resist man and ultimately to defeat him, and the three major classifications are based on the method each object uses to achieve its purpose. As a general rule, any object capable of breaking down at the moment when it is most needed will do so. The automobile is typical of the category.

3   With the cunning peculiar to its breed, the automobile never breaks down while entering a filling station which has a large staff of idle mechanics. It waits until it reaches a downtown intersection in the middle of the rush hour, or until it is fully loaded with family and luggage on the Ohio Turnpike. Thus it creates maximum inconvenience, frustration, and irritability, thereby reducing its owner's lifespan.

4   Washing machines, garbage disposals, lawn mowers, furnaces, TV sets, tape recorders, slide projectors—all are in league with the automobile to take their turn at breaking down whenever life threatens to flow smoothly for their enemies.

5   Many inanimate objects, of course, find it extremely difficult to break down. Pliers, for example, and gloves and keys are almost totally incapable of breaking down. Therefore, they have had to evolve a different technique for resisting man.

They get lost. Science has still not solved the mystery of how they do it, and no man has ever caught one of them in the act. The most plausible theory is that they have developed a secret method of locomotion which they are able to conceal from human eyes. [6]

It is not uncommon for a pair of pliers to climb all the way from the cellar to the attic in its single-minded determination to raise its owner's blood pressure. Keys have been known to burrow three feet under mattresses. Women's purses, despite their great weight, frequently travel through six or seven rooms to find hiding space under a couch. [7]

Scientists have been struck by the fact that things that break down virtually never get lost, while things that get lost hardly ever break down. A furnace, for example, will invariably break down at the depth of the first winter cold wave, but it will never get lost. A woman's purse hardly ever breaks down; it almost invariably chooses to get lost. [8]

Some persons believe this constitutes evidence that inanimate objects are not entirely hostile to man. After all, they point out, a furnace could infuriate a man even more thoroughly by getting lost than by breaking down, just as a glove could upset him far more by breaking down than by getting lost. [9]

Not everyone agrees, however, that this indicates a conciliatory attitude. Many say it merely proves that furnaces, gloves, and pliers are incredibly stupid. [10]

The third class of objects—those that don't work—is the most curious of all. These include such objects as barometers, car clocks, cigarette lighters, flashlights and toy-train locomotives. It is inaccurate, of course, to say that they *never* work. They work once, usually for the first few hours after being brought home, and then quit. Thereafter, they never work again. [11]

In fact, it is widely assumed that they are built for the purpose of not working. Some people have reached advanced ages without ever seeing some of these objects—barometers, for example—in working order. [12]

Science is utterly baffled by the entire category. There are many theories about it. The most interesting holds that the things that don't work have attained the highest state possible for an inanimate object, the state to which things that break down and things that get lost can still only aspire. [13]

They have truly defeated man by conditioning him never to expect anything of them. When his cigarette lighter won't light or his flashlight fails to illuminate, it does not raise his blood pressure. Objects that don't work have given man the only peace he receives from inanimate society. [14]

DISCUSSION QUESTIONS

1. Baker refers to science in paragraphs 1, 6, 8, and 13. How do you account for these references in an essay that is so obviously tongue-in-cheek?
2. In which paragraphs does Baker discuss his first, second, and third categories? How are the categories arranged?
3. Point out features that contribute to Baker's very informal style.
4. Discuss Baker's use of specific details to develop his categories. What other objects might he have included in each category?
5. For what audience does Baker write? How do you know?
6. Many essays end with some sort of conclusion, but Baker's does not. How do you account for the omission?

---

evidenced by the statements "The third class . . . is the most curious of all" and "things that don't work have attained the highest state possible for an inanimate object. . . ."

3. Baker's style is marked by ordinary words and a considerable number of short sentences. Most of the sentences follow a loose arrangement. Although contractions, another mark of informality, are not prevalent in the essay, Baker does use the word "don't" four times (in paragraphs 1, 11, 13, and 14) and "won't" once, in paragraph 14.

4. When discussing his first category, Baker focuses on the automobile and its diabolical penchant for breaking down at the time that will cause the owner the greatest grief. Other objects in the category receive only brief attention. Moving to the second category, Baker focuses on pliers, keys, and purses, noting the incredible journeys they sometimes take to frustrate their owners. Objects in the third category receive relatively little attention; Baker merely names a few and states that after a short time they quit working. Other promising candidates: category one—snowblowers and electric shavers; category two—eyeglass cases and address books; category three—windup toys and electric timers.

5. Baker writes for a general audience, as shown by his informal language and the fact that the essay first appeared in the *New York Times*, a newspaper with several million readers.

6. Conclusions, of course, reinforce the main points of writing. Baker's main point, that inanimate objects are out to get humans, is so ridiculous that "reinforcing" it through a conclusion is unnecessary.

SUGGESTION FOR WRITING ■ Write an essay classifying the annoyances that you find particularly bothersome. Possibilities might include sets of directions that are flawed in different ways, the kinds of misbehavior exhibited by people in long lines, or the various inadequacies of service people such as salesclerks and receptionists. Use either a serious or a humorous tone.

Lewis Thomas

THE TECHNOLOGY OF MEDICINE

Lewis Thomas (born 1913) has won widespread recognition as one of our most perceptive writers on medical topics. A native of Flushing, New York, he earned his medical degree at Harvard (1937) and then held positions as a pathologist and medical administrator at several universities. In 1973, he became president of the Sloan-Kettering Cancer Center in New York. In 1971, he started writing a column called "Notes of a Biology Watcher" for the New England Journal of Medicine. *These contributions became very popular, and in 1974 were collected in a book,* The Lives of a Cell: Notes of a Biology Watcher, *which won the National Book Award. A second collection of columns from the same journal,* The Medusa and the Snail: Further Notes of a Biology Watcher, *appeared in 1979. Most recent books include the autobiographical* The Youngest Science: Notes of a Medical Watcher *(1983) and* Late Night Thoughts on Listening to Mahler's Ninth Symphony *(1983). In our selection, originally published in the* New England Journal of Medicine, *Thomas classifies and evaluates three categories of medical technology.*

1   Technology assessment has become a routine exercise for the scientific enterprises on which the country is obliged to spend vast sums for its needs. Brainy committees are continually evaluating the effectiveness and cost of doing various things in space, defense, energy, transportation, and the like, to give advice about prudent investments for the future.

2   Somehow medicine, for all the $80-odd billion that it is said to cost the nation, has not yet come in for much of this analytical treatment. It seems taken for granted that the technology of medicine simply exists, take it or leave it, and the only major technologic problem which policy-makers are interested in is how to deliver today's kind of health care, with equity, to all the people.

3   When, as is bound to happen sooner or later, the analysts get around to the technology of medicine itself, they will have to face the problem of measuring the relative cost and effectiveness of all the things that are done in the management of disease. They make their living at this kind of thing, and I wish them well, but I imagine they will have a bewildering time. For one thing, our methods of managing disease are constantly changing—partly under the influence of new bits of information brought in from all corners of biologic science. At the same time, a great many things are done that are not so closely related to science, some not related at all.

In fact, there are three quite different levels of technology in medicine, so unlike each other as to seem altogether different undertakings. Practitioners of medicine and the analysts will be in trouble if they are not kept separate. [4]

1. First of all, there is a large body of what might be termed "nontechnology," impossible to measure in terms of its capacity to alter either the natural course of disease or its eventual outcome. A great deal of money is spent on this. It is valued highly by the professionals as well as the patients. It consists of what is sometimes called "supportive therapy." It tides patients over through diseases that are not, by and large, understood. It is what is meant by the phrases "caring for" and "standing by." It is indispensable. It is not, however, a technology in any real sense, since it does not involve measures directed at the underlying mechanism of disease. [5]

It includes the large part of any good doctor's time that is taken up with simply providing reassurance, explaining to patients who fear that they have contracted one or another lethal disease that they are, in fact, quite healthy. [6]

It is what physicians used to be engaged in at the bedside of patients with diphtheria, meningitis, poliomyelitis, lobar pneumonia, and all the rest of the infectious diseases that have since come under control. [7]

It is what physicians must now do for patients with intractable cancer, severe rheumatoid arthritis, multiple sclerosis, stroke, and advanced cirrhosis. One can think of at least twenty major diseases that require this kind of supportive medical care because of the absence of an effective technology. I would include a large amount of what is called mental disease, and most varieties of cancer, in this category. [8]

The cost of this nontechnology is very high, and getting higher all the time. It requires not only a great deal of time but also very hard effort and skill on the part of physicians; only the very best of doctors are good at coping with this kind of defeat. It also involves long periods of hospitalization, lots of nursing, lots of involvement of nonmedical professionals in and out of the hospital. It represents, in short, a substantial segment of today's expenditures for health. [9]

2. At the next level up is a kind of technology best termed "halfway technology." This represents the kinds of things that must be done after the fact, in efforts to compensate for the incapacitating effects of certain diseases whose course one is unable to do very much about. It is a technology designed to make up for disease, or to postpone death. [10]

The outstanding examples in recent years are the transplantations of hearts, kidneys, livers, and other organs, and the equally spectacular inventions of artificial organs. In the public mind, this kind of technology has come to seem like the equivalent of the high technologies of the physical sciences. The media tend to present each new procedure as though it represented a breakthrough and therapeutic triumph, instead of the makeshift that it really is. [11]

In fact, this level of technology is, by its nature, at the same time highly sophisticated and profoundly primitive. It is the kind of thing that one must continue to do until there is a genuine understanding of the mechanisms involved in disease. In chronic glomerulonephritis, for example, a much clearer insight will be needed into the events leading to the destruction of glomeruli by the immunologic reactants that now appear to govern this disease, before one will know how to intervene intelligently to prevent the process, or turn it around. But when this level of understanding has been reached, the technology of kidney replacement will not be much needed and should no longer pose the huge problems of logistics, cost, and ethics that it poses today. [12]

DISCUSSION QUESTIONS

1. Paragraphs 1 and 2 contrast the amount of technology assessment carried out in nonmedical scientific disciplines and in medicine. Paragraph 3 points out the difficulties that analysts will face when they do cope with the technology of medicine. Thomas uses the "funnel technique" to ease his readers into the categories.
2. The categories are arranged according to the level of technology involved in each, from the lowest level to the highest, from the least effective to the most effective. This is the most logical arrangement for Thomas to use. If he had begun by discussing the most highly technical category, everything following that discussion would have seemed anticlimactic. Furthermore, since Thomas ends with a plea for giving priority to the third category, it is logical that his discussion should lead up to that category.
3. In each case, Thomas begins by explaining and illustrating what he means by that level of technology and then moves to consider its costs.
4. Halfway technology involves no understanding of underlying disease mechanisms and is very costly. High technology is based on an understanding of disease mechanisms and is relatively inexpensive as well as relatively easy to administer.

13   An extremely complex and costly technology for the management of coronary heart disease has evolved—involving specialized ambulances and hospital units, all kinds of electronic gadgetry, and whole platoons of new professional personnel—to deal with the end results of coronary thrombosis. Almost everything offered today for the treatment of heart disease is at this level of technology, with the transplanted and artificial hearts as ultimate examples. When enough has been learned to know what really goes wrong in heart disease, one ought to be in a position to figure out ways to prevent or reverse the process, and when this happens the current elaborate technology will probably be set to one side.

14   Much of what is done in the treatment of cancer, by surgery, irradiation, and chemotherapy, represents halfway technology, in the sense that these measures are directed at the existence of already established cancer cells, but not at the mechanisms by which cells become neoplastic.

15   It is a characteristic of this kind of technology that it costs an enormous amount of money and requires a continuing expansion of hospital facilities. There is no end to the need for new, highly trained people to run the enterprise. And there is really no way out of this, at the present state of knowledge. If the installation of specialized coronary-care units can result in the extension of life for only a few patients with coronary disease (and there is no question that this technology is effective in a few cases), it seems to me an inevitable fact of life that as many of these as can be will be put together, and as much money as can be found will be spent. I do not see that anyone has much choice in this. The only thing that can move medicine away from this level of technology is new information, and the only imaginable source of this information is research.

16   3. The third type of technology is the kind that is so effective that it seems to attract the least public notice; it has come to be taken for granted. This is the genuinely decisive technology of modern medicine, exemplified best by modern methods of immunization against diphtheria, pertussis, and the childhood virus diseases, and the contemporary use of antibiotics and chemotherapy for bacterial infections. The capacity to deal effectively with syphilis and tuberculosis represents a milestone in human endeavor, even though full use of this potential has not yet been made. And there are, of course, other examples: the treatment of endocrinologic disorders with appropriate hormones, the prevention of hemolytic disease of the newborn, the treatment and prevention of various nutritional disorders, and perhaps just around the corner the management of Parkinsonism and sickle-cell anemia. There are other examples, and everyone will have his favorite candidates for the list, but the truth is that there are nothing like as many as the public has been led to believe.

17   The point to be made about this kind of technology—the real high technology of medicine—is that it comes as the result of a genuine understanding of disease mechanisms, and when it becomes available, it is relatively inexpensive, and relatively easy to deliver.

18   Offhand, I cannot think of any important human disease for which medicine possesses the outright capacity to prevent or cure where the cost of the technology is itself a major problem. The price is never as high as the cost of managing the same diseases during the earlier stages of no-technology or halfway technology. If a case of typhoid fever had to be managed today by the best methods of 1935, it would run to a staggering expense. At, say, around fifty days of hospitalization, requiring the most demanding kind of nursing care, with the obsessive concern for details of diet that characterized the therapy of that time,

with daily laboratory monitoring, and, on occasion, surgical intervention for abdominal catastrophe, I should think $10,000 would be a conservative estimate for the illness, as contrasted with today's cost of a bottle of chloramphenicol and a day or two of fever. The halfway technology that was evolving for poliomyelitis in the early 1950s, just before the emergence of the basic research that made the vaccine possible, provides another illustration of the point. Do you remember Sister Kenny, and the cost of those institutes for rehabilitation, with all those ceremonially applied hot fomentations, and the debates about whether the affected limbs should be totally immobilized or kept in passive motion as frequently as possible, and the masses of statistically tormented data mobilized to support one view or the other? It is the cost of that kind of technology, and its relative effectiveness, that must be compared with the cost and effectiveness of the vaccine.

Pulmonary tuberculosis had similar episodes in its history. There was a sudden enthusiasm for the surgical removal of infected lung tissue in the early 1950s, and elaborate plans were being made for new and expensive installations for major pulmonary surgery in tuberculosis hospitals, and then INH and streptomycin came along and the hospitals themselves were closed up. 19

It is when physicians are bogged down by their incomplete technologies, by the innumerable things they are obliged to do in medicine when they lack a clear understanding of disease mechanisms, that the deficiencies of the health-care system are most conspicuous. If I were a policy-maker, interested in saving money for health care over the long haul, I would regard it as an act of high prudence to give high priority to a lot more basic research in biologic science. This is the only way to get the full mileage that biology owes to the science of medicine, even though it seems, as used to be said in the days when the phrase still had some meaning, like asking for the moon. 20

DISCUSSION QUESTIONS

1. Thomas classifies three different degrees of medical technology, yet he doesn't start to deal with these categories until paragraph 4. Why?
2. Discuss the arrangement of the categories in this essay. What is the basis for the arrangement? Why is this arrangement the most logical choice?
3. Study the discussions *within* each of the three categories, and then point out what type of information Thomas includes and the order in which he presents it.
4. What are the differences between "halfway technology" and "the real high technology"?
5. Why would Thomas "give high priority to a lot more basic research in biologic science" (paragraph 20)?
6. What audience do you think Thomas is trying to reach? Explain your answer.

SUGGESTION FOR WRITING ■ **Write an essay classifying the levels of expertise in some profession or trade you know about. For example, you might classify the workers in a dental office, the nursing personnel in a hospital, the employees in an accounting department, or the personnel in a law firm.**

5. Basic research in biological science will allow scientists to discover the basic mechanisms underlying various diseases and to develop medicines—antibiotics, hormones, and the like—that will interrupt the mechanisms and thus stop the disease. Doing this will eliminate the need for and the expenses of the first two categories.

6. As the headnote indicates, this essay originally appeared in the *New England Journal of Medicine,* so obviously physicians form the audience. Nevertheless, Thomas uses language that an educated lay audience could easily understand. Generally, he cites diseases and illnesses with which such readers are familiar—diphtheria, arthritis, multiple sclerosis, coronary thrombosis—and he avoids complex medical terminology.

OVERVIEW OF COMPARISON ESSAYS (pp. 420–33)

Four of the essays in this section are comparisons, and one is an analogy. Three comparisons use the alternating pattern. Two of them focus entirely on differences, and the other, while primarily concerned with differences, devotes some attention to similarities. The remaining comparison uses the block pattern and deals entirely with differences. Like all analogies, ours calls attention to the similarities that underlie two seemingly dissimilar things. In it, the writer likens the passage of grief to the return to a house that has withstood a cruel winter. One essay combines informal and colloquial diction, two fall into the formal–informal category, and two use devices like descriptive language, parallelism, and rhythmic sentences to give the writing a formal cast.

Comparison

Comparison

Bruce Catton

GRANT AND LEE: A STUDY IN CONTRASTS

Title sets up differences

Bruce Catton (1899–1978) was a nationally recognized expert on the Civil War. Born in Petoskey, Michigan, he attended Oberlin College, then worked as a reporter for several large newspapers. Between 1942 and 1948, he held several positions in the U.S. government, and then became an editor of American Heritage *magazine. His first book on the Civil War,* Mr. Lincoln's Army, *appeared in 1951 and was followed by* Glory Road *(1952) and* A Stillness at Appomattox *(1953). This last book won the Pulitzer Prize and the National Book Award and established Catton's reputation as a Civil War historian. In the years that followed, Catton continued to write other books on the Civil War, including a centennial trilogy:* The Coming Fury *(1961),* Terrible Swift Sword *(1962), and* Never Call Retreat *(1965). In 1972, he published the autobiographical* Waiting for the Morning Train: An American Boyhood *and followed it two years later with* Michigan: A Bicentennial History. *Our Catton selection comes from a collection of essays by eminent historians. In it, Catton points out differences as well as similarities in the two foremost military adversaries of the Civil War.*

Introduction: paragraphs 1–3; background; significance of following contrasts

1   When Ulysses S. Grant and Robert E. Lee met in the parlor of a modest house at Appomattox Court House, Virginia, on April 9, 1865, to work out the terms for the surrender of Lee's Army of Northern Virginia, a great chapter in American life came to a close, and a great new chapter began.

2   These men were bringing the Civil War to its virtual finish. To be sure, other armies had yet to surrender, and for a few days the fugitive Confederate government would struggle desperately and vainly, trying to find some way to go on living now that its chief support was gone. But in effect it was all over when Grant and Lee signed the papers. And the little room where they wrote out the terms was the scene of one of the poignant, dramatic contrasts in American history.

3   They were two strong men these oddly different generals, and they represented the strengths of two conflicting currents that, through them, had come into final collision.

Body: paragraph 4 to first part, paragraph 16; alternating pattern throughout

4   Back of Robert E. Lee was the notion that the old aristocratic concept might somehow survive and be dominant in American life.

First difference paragraphs 4–6: Lee's background, character

5   Lee was tidewater Virginia, and in his background were family, culture, and tradition . . . the age of chivalry transplanted to a New World which was making its own legends and its own myths. He embodied a way of life that had come down through the age of knighthood and the English country squire. America was a land that was beginning all over again, dedicated to nothing much more complicated than the rather hazy belief that all men had equal rights and should have an

420

equal chance in the world. In such a land Lee stood for the feeling that it was somehow of advantage to human society to have a pronounced inequality in the social structure. There should be a leisure class, backed by ownership of land; in turn, society itself should be keyed to the land as the chief source of wealth and influence. It would bring forth (according to this ideal) a class of men with a strong sense of obligation to the community; men who lived not to gain advantage for themselves, but to meet the solemn obligations which had been laid on them by the very fact that they were privileged. From them the country would get its leadership; to them it could look for the higher values—of thought, of conduct, or personal deportment—to give it strength and virtue.

Lee embodied the noblest elements of this aristocratic ideal. Through him, 6 the landed nobility justified itself. For four years, the Southern states had fought a desperate war to uphold the ideals for which Lee stood. In the end, it almost seemed as if the Confederacy fought for Lee; as if he himself was the Confederacy . . . the best thing that the way of life for which the Confederacy stood could ever have to offer. He had passed into legend before Appomattox. Thousands of tired, underfed, poorly clothed Confederate soldiers, long since past the simple enthusiasm of the early days of the struggle, somehow considered Lee the symbol of everything for which they had been willing to die. But they could not quite put this feeling into words. If the Lost Cause, sanctified by so much heroism and so many deaths, had a living justification, its justification was General Lee.

Grant, the son of a tanner on the Western frontier, was everything Lee was 7 not. He had come up the hard way and embodied nothing in particular except the eternal toughness and sinewy fiber of the men who grew up beyond the mountains. He was one of a body of men who owed reverence and obeisance to no one, who were self-reliant to a fault, who cared hardly anything for the past but who had a sharp eye for the future.

Paragraphs 7–9: Grant's background, character

These frontier men were the precise opposites of the tidewater aristocrats. 8 Back of them, in the great surge that had taken people over the Alleghenies and into the opening Western country, there was a deep, implicit dissatisfaction with a past that had settled into grooves. They stood for democracy not from any reasoned conclusion about the proper ordering of human society, but simply because they had grown up in the middle of democracy and knew how it worked. Their society might have privileges, but they would be privileges each man had won for himself. Forms and patterns meant nothing. No man was born to anything, except perhaps to a chance to show how far he could rise. Life was competition.

Yet along with this feeling had come a deep sense of belonging to a 9 national community. The Westerner who developed a farm, opened a shop, or set up in business as a trader could hope to prosper only as his own community prospered—and his community ran from the Atlantic to the Pacific and from Canada down to Mexico. If the land was settled, with towns and highways and accessible markets, he could better himself. He saw his fate in terms of the nation's own destiny. As its horizons expanded, so did his. He had, in other words, an acute dollars-and-cents stake in the continued growth and development of his country.

And that, perhaps, is where the contrast between Grant and Lee becomes 10 most striking. The Virginia aristocrat, inevitably, saw himself in relation to his own region. He lived in a static society which could endure almost anything except change. Instinctively, first loyalty would go to the locality in which that society

Second difference Lee's loyalty

existed. He would fight to the limit of endurance to defend it, because in defending it he was defending everything that gave his own life its deepest meaning.

11   The Westerner, on the other hand, would fight with an equal tenacity for the broader concept of society. He fought so because everything he lived by was tied to growth, expansion, and a constantly widening horizon. What he lived by would survive or fall with the nation itself. He could not possibly stand by unmoved in the face of an attempt to destroy the Union. He would combat it with everything he had, because he could only see it as an effort to cut the ground out from under his feet.

12   So Grant and Lee were in complete contrast, representing two diametrically opposed elements in American life. Grant was the modern man emerging; beyond him, ready to come on the stage, was the great age of steel and machinery, of crowded cities and a restless burgeoning vitality. Lee might have ridden down from the old age of chivalry, lance in hand, silken banner fluttering over his head. Each man was the perfect champion of his cause, drawing both his strengths and his weaknesses from the people he led.

13   Yet it was not all contrast, after all. Different as they were—in background, in personality, in underlying aspiration—these two great soldiers had much in common. Under everything else, they were marvelous fighters. Furthermore, their fighting qualities were really very much alike.

14   Each man had, to begin with, the great virtue of utter tenacity and fidelity. Grant fought his way down the Mississippi Valley in spite of acute personal discouragement and profound military handicaps. Lee hung on in the trenches at Petersburg after hope itself had died. In each man there was an indomitable quality . . . the born fighter's refusal to give up as long as he can still remain on his feet and lift his two fists.

15   Daring and resourcefulness they had, too; the ability to think faster and move faster than the enemy. These were the qualities which gave Lee the dazzling campaigns of Second Manassas and Chancellorsville and won Vicksburg for Grant.

16   Lastly, and perhaps greatest of all, there was the ability, at the end, to turn quickly from war to peace once the fighting was over. Out of the way these two men behaved at Appomattox came the possibility of a peace of reconciliation. It was a possibility not wholly realized, in the years to come, but which did, in the end, help the two sections to become one nation again . . . after a war whose bitterness might have seemed to make such a reunion wholly impossible. No part of either man's life became him more than the part he played in this brief meeting in the McLean house at Appomattox. Their behavior there put all succeeding generations of Americans in their debt. Two great Americans, Grant and Lee— very different, yet under everything very much alike. Their encounter at Appomattox was one of the great moments of American history.

**Side notes (left margin):**

Grant's loyalty

Summary of significant differences

Transition paragraph signals switch to similarities

First similarity

Second similarity

Third similarity: notes order of climax

Conclusion: significance of the meeting

DISCUSSION QUESTIONS

1. Paragraph 3 contains the thesis statement.
2. Lee stood for the aristocratic, chivalric tradition, loyalty to his locality, and a belief in a privileged leisure class destined to be leaders. Grant stood for just the opposite—democracy, self-

---

DISCUSSION QUESTIONS

1. Where is Catton's thesis statement?
2. Summarize the way of life that Lee stood for, and then do the same for Grant.
3. Why do the differences between Grant and Lee receive more extended treatment than the similarities? Why are the similarities discussed last?
4. How would you characterize Catton's attitude toward the two men? Refer to specific parts of the essay when answering.

SUGGESTION FOR WRITING ■ **Write an essay comparing two past or present political or military figures—perhaps Abraham Lincoln and Jefferson Davis or Dwight Eisenhower and Erwin Rommel. Try for a balanced treatment and select an appropriate organization.**

Suzanne Britt

THAT LEAN AND HUNGRY LOOK

Suzanne Britt is a native of Winston-Salem, North Carolina, and an alumna of Salem College and Washington University. Since college, she has made a career of journalism. Her writings have appeared in several major newspapers, including the Baltimore Sun, *the* Des Moines Register and Tribune, *the* Raleigh News and Observer, *and the* New York Times, *as well as in* Newsweek *magazine. In 1982, a collection of her essays appeared under the title* Show and Tell. *The following essay first appeared in* Newsweek *and was then made the basis of a book* Skinny People Are Dull and Crunchy Like Carrots. *In the essay, Britt draws a distinction between thin and fat people—and between two different philosophies of life.*

Caesar was right. Thin people need watching. I've been watching them for most of my adult life, and I don't like what I see. When these narrow fellows spring at me, I quiver to my toes. Thin people come in all personalities, most of them menacing. You've got your "together" thin person, your mechanical thin person, your condescending thin person, your tsk-tsk thin person, your efficiency-expert thin person. All of them are dangerous. 1

In the first place, thin people aren't fun. They don't know how to goof off, at least in the best, fat sense of the word. They've always got to be adoing. Give them a coffee break, and they'll jog around the block. Supply them with a quiet evening at home, and they'll fix the screen door and lick S&H green stamps. They say things like "there aren't enough hours in the day." Fat people never say that. Fat people think the day is too damn long already. 2

Thin people make me tired. They've got speedy little metabolisms that cause them to bustle briskly. They're forever rubbing their bony hands together and eying new problems to "tackle." I like to surround myself with sluggish, inert, easygoing fat people, the kind who believe that if you clean it up today, it'll just get dirty again tomorrow. 3

Some people say the business about the jolly fat person is a myth, that all of us chubbies are neurotic, sick, sad people. I disagree. Fat people may not be chortling all day long, but they're a hell of a lot *nicer* than the wizened and shriveled. Thin people turn surly, mean and hard at a young age because they never learn the value of a hot-fudge sundae for easing tension. Thin people don't like gooey soft things because they themselves are neither gooey nor soft. They are crunchy and dull, like carrots. They go straight to the heart of the matter while 4

---

reliance, loyalty to the nation, the chance to advance as far as ability would allow. (Catton's purpose is to contrast these two opposing outlooks.)

3. The differences between Grant and Lee (paragraphs 4–12) receive more extended treatment than the similarities because they represent the two conflicting currents that came into final collision with the outbreak of the Civil War. Similarities are discussed last because one of these similarities is the ability of both men to begin reconciliation and help the two sides "become one nation again."

4. Catton obviously admires, perhaps even eulogizes, the two men. Paragraphs 12 ("Each man was the perfect champion of his cause. . . .") through 16 ("Their behavior there put all succeeding generations of Americans in their debt.") suggest this attitude.

PERSPECTIVE

Students often assume that writing a humorous essay is easy. In fact, it is a demanding task that requires the careful choice of words, phrasing, and language devices needed to achieve just the right effect. Because Britt has clearly mastered the craft of humorous writing, you might explore with students how she makes us laugh.

TEACHING STRATEGIES

1. Follow up Discussion Question 4 by exploring the irony in paragraph 9. Britt's "one," "two," "three" methodical rationale for rejection is ironic in view of her statement in paragraph 4 that fat people let things "stay all blurry and hazy and vague." Furthermore, in paragraph 9 she says "The important thing is. . . ," yet note the last three sentences of paragraph 4.

2. Ask the class to identify some of the concrete details Britt uses to clarify her assertions about thin and fat people. Then ask what these details accomplish.

3. Point out the clichés and the sentence fragment in paragraph 7. Then ask why Britt uses them and whether they are effective.

4. Call attention to the alliteration in paragraph 12. Then ask students to discuss whether it is effective or overdone and to supply reasons for their answers.

CLASSROOM ACTIVITY

Have small groups of students generate contrasts between strict and non-strict parents or teachers, amusing and boring dates, health-conscious and non-health-conscious people, or other dissimilar groups. These contrasts might be presented as reports to the class and serve as the prelude to a writing assignment. Remind students to write with some clear purpose in mind and not merely to list contrasts.

DISCUSSION QUESTIONS (p. 425)

1. Britt's prime purpose is to entertain, as shown by her humorous language: ". . . your mechanical thin person, your condescending thin person, your tsk-tsk thin person. . . ." (paragraph 1); "They've got speedy little metabolisms that cause them to bustle briskly." (paragraph 3); "Thin people . . . are neither gooey nor soft. They are crunchy and dull, like carrots." (paragraph 4); and "They think these 2,000-point plans lead to happiness."(paragraph 8). A secondary purpose is to contrast two different philosophical outlooks—that of the relaxed, easy-going person and that of the intense, driven person.

2. Britt charges that thin people don't know when to goof off (paragraphs 2 and 3), have unpleasant personalities (paragraph 4), believe in logic (paragraphs 5–9), and oppress others (paragraphs 10–12). These short

fat people let things stay all blurry and hazy and vague, the way things actually are. Thin people want to face the truth. Fat people know there is no truth. One of my thin friends is always staring at complex, unsolvable problems and saying, "The key thing is . . ." Fat people never say that. They know there isn't any such thing as the key thing about anything.

5   Thin people believe in logic. Fat people see all sides. The sides fat people see are rounded blobs, usually gray, always nebulous and truly not worth worrying about. But the thin person persists. "If you consume more calories than you burn," says one of my thin friends, "you will gain weight. It's that simple." Fat people always grin when they hear statements like that. They know better.

6   Fat people realize that life is illogical and unfair. They know very well that God is not in his heaven and all is not right with the world. If God was up there, fat people could have two doughnuts and a big orange drink anytime they wanted it.

7   Thin people have a long list of logical things they are always spouting off to me. They hold up one finger at a time as they reel off these things, so I won't lose track. They speak slowly as if to a young child. The list is long and full of holes. It contains tidbits like "get a grip on yourself," "cigarettes kill," "cholesterol clogs," "fit as a fiddle," "ducks in a row," "organize" and "sound fiscal management." Phrases like that.

8   They think these 2,000-point plans lead to happiness. Fat people know happiness is elusive at best and even if they could get the kind thin people talk about, they wouldn't want it. Wisely, fat people see that such programs are too dull, too hard, too off the mark. They are never better than a whole cheesecake.

9   Fat people know all about the mystery of life. They are the ones acquainted with the night, with luck, with fate, with playing it by ear. One thin person I know once suggested that we arrange all the parts of a jigsaw puzzle into groups according to size, shape and color. He figured this would cut the time needed to complete the puzzle by at least 50 percent. I said I wouldn't do it. One, I like to muddle through. Two, what good would it do to finish early? Three, the jigsaw puzzle isn't the important thing. The important thing is the fun of four people (one thin person included) sitting around a card table, working a jigsaw puzzle. My thin friend had no use for my list. Instead of joining us, he went outside and mulched the boxwoods. The three remaining fat people finished the puzzle and made chocolate, double-fudged brownies to celebrate.

10   The main problem with thin people is they oppress. Their good intentions, bony torsos, tight ships, neat corners, cerebral machinations and pat solutions loom like dark clouds over the loose, comfortable, spread-out, soft world of the fat. Long after fat people have removed their coats and shoes and put their feet up on the coffee table, thin people are still sitting on the edge of the sofa, looking neat as a pin, discussing rutabagas. Fat people are heavily into fits of laughter, slapping their thighs and whooping it up, while thin people are still politely waiting for the punch line.

11   Thin people are downers. They like math and morality and reasoned evaluation of the limitations of human beings. They have their skinny little acts together. They expound, prognose, probe and prick.

12   Fat people are convivial. They will like you even if you're irregular and have acne. They will come up with a good reason why you never wrote the great American novel. They will cry in your beer with you. They will put your name in the pot. They will let you off the hook. Fat people will gab, giggle, guffaw, gallumph, gyrate and gossip. They are generous, giving and gallant. They are

gluttonous and goodly and great. What you want when you're down is soft and jiggly, not muscled and stable. Fat people know this. Fat people have plenty of room. Fat people will take you in.

DISCUSSION QUESTIONS

1. Cite passages from Britt's essay to show that she is trying to entertain us.
2. Britt asserts that thin people have four shortcomings. What are they, and where is each discussed? In what order are these shortcomings arranged?
3. Why do you think Britt uses the alternating pattern rather than the block pattern to organize her essay?
4. In paragraph 11 Britt charges that thin people like to make "reasoned evaluation of the limitations of human beings." In what way is this statement ironic?

SUGGESTION FOR WRITING ■ Write an essay comparing the attitudes of two people, one efficient and organized, the other inefficient and disorganized. Focus your paper on three or four points of comparison and organize them in the alternating pattern.

Mark Twain

INNOCENCE AND EXPERIENCE: DIFFERENT VIEWS OF THE RIVER[1]

A biographical sketch of Mark Twain appears on page 403. In this excerpt from Life on the Mississippi *(1881), Twain compares how the Mississippi River appeared to him before and after he became a pilot.*

Now when I had mastered the language of this water, and had come to know every trifling feature that bordered the great river as familiarly as I knew the letters of the alphabet, I had made a valuable acquisition. But I had lost something, too. I had lost something which could never be restored to me while I lived. All the grace, the beauty, the poetry, had gone out of the majestic river! I still kept in mind a certain wonderful sunset which I witnessed when steamboating was new to me. A broad expanse of the river was turned to blood; in the middle distance the red hue brightened into gold, through which a solitary log came floating, black and conspicuous; in one place a long, slanting mark lay sparkling upon the water; in another the surface was broken by boiling, tumbling rings, that were as many-tinted as an opal; where the ruddy flush was faintest, was a smooth spot that was covered with graceful circles and radiating lines, ever so delicately traced; the shore on our left was densely wooded, and the somber shadow that fell from this forest was broken in one place by a long, ruffled trail that shone like silver; and high above the forest wall a clean-stemmed dead tree waved a single

1

[1]Editors' title.

---

comings are arranged in order of climax, as shown by the first sentence in paragraph 10: "The main problem with thin people. . . ."
3. The alternating pattern is more appropriate because of the large number of details that Britt presents. The discussion of each difference is completed in one spot. The block pattern would have forced the reader to keep going back to grasp each specific difference clearly.
4. The statement is ironic because earlier in the essay Britt notes that fat people are more aware of human limitations than are thin people. In paragraph 4 she says that fat people realize "there is no truth" and "there isn't any such thing as the key thing about anything." In paragraph 6 she notes that "Fat people realize that life is illogical and unfair. They know very well that God is not in his heaven and that all is not right with the world." In short, fat people are better grounded on the matter of human limitations than thin people, who are always bringing limitations up.

PERSPECTIVE

This selection presents Twain in sober guise rather than as the more familiar humorist/satirist. To acquaint students with Twain's other side, have them read "Corn-Pone Opinions" (pages 403–6), and then ask them to compare the tone of the two essays.

TEACHING STRATEGIES

1. Ask students to analyze the figurative language in this essay and comment on its function and effectiveness.
2. Ask students to discuss the function and effectiveness of the rhetorical questions in paragraph 3.

CLASSROOM ACTIVITY

Divide the class into small groups and have them contrast how they viewed college before enrolling and how they view it now. The discussions could lead to reports presented to the whole class and ultimately to a paper.

DISCUSSION QUESTIONS

1. Twain uses the block pattern. Since paragraph 1 presents one scene viewed at one particular time, it can't be fragmented. Paragraph 2 follows the sequence in paragraph 1, and thus it also can't be fragmented.
2. The key thrust of the comparison is the sense of losing "the grace, the beauty, the poetry" that Twain felt when he came to know the river well as a pilot. Twain draws attention to this loss by the repetition.
3. "Bewitched" suggests that Twain was under some type of spell, and indeed he was—the spell of "grace," "beauty," and "poetry" cast by the "majestic river."
4. In paragraph 1 the sun, the log, and the mark didn't "mean" or "refer" to anything. Twain simply enjoyed these items for their sensuous beauty. In paragraph 2 the items have become much more practical, helping Twain navigate the river as a pilot.
5. The tone of paragraph 1 is rapturous and stems from sensuous descriptive details. The tone of paragraph 2 is factual and created by flat, everyday language. Each of the specific details mentioned in paragraph 1 is mentioned again in paragraph 2 but without any descriptive coloration.
6. The analogy between a riverboat pilot and a doctor is especially apt. With the experienced doctor, as with the experienced pilot, surface beauty—of the woman, of the river—loses its interest except as the mark of a subsurface condition.

leafy bough that glowed like a flame in the unobstructed splendor that was flowing from the sun. There were graceful curves, reflected images, woody heights, soft distances; and over the whole scene, far and near, the dissolving lights drifted steadily, enriching it every passing moment with new marvels of coloring.

2   I stood like one bewitched. I drank it in, in a speechless rapture. The world was new to me, and I had never seen anything like this at home. But as I have said, a day came when I began to cease from noting the glories and the charms which the moon and the sun and the twilight wrought upon the river's face; another day came when I ceased altogether to note them. Then, if that sunset scene had been repeated, I should have looked upon it without rapture, and should have commented upon it, inwardly, after this fashion: "This sun means that we are going to have wind to-morrow; that floating log means that the river is rising, small thanks to it; that slanting mark on the water refers to a bluff reef which is going to kill somebody's steamboat one of these nights, if it keeps on stretching out like that; those tumbling 'boils' show a dissolving bar and a changing channel there; the lines and circles in the slick water over yonder are a warning that that troublesome place is shoaling up dangerously; that silver streak in the shadow of the forest is the 'break' from a new snag, and he has located himself in the very best place he could have found to fish for steamboats; that tall dead tree, with a single living branch, is not going to last long, and then how is a body ever going to get through this blind place at night without the friendly old landmark?"

3   No, the romance and beauty were all gone from the river. All the value any feature of it had for me now was the amount of usefulness it could furnish toward compassing the safe piloting of a steamboat. Since those days, I have pitied doctors from my heart. What does the lovely flush in a beauty's cheek mean to a doctor but a "break" that ripples above some deadly disease? Are not all her visible charms sown thick with what are to him the signs and symbols of hidden decay? Does he ever see her beauty at all, or doesn't he simply view her professionally and comment upon her unwholesome condition all to himself? And doesn't he sometimes wonder whether he has gained most or lost most by learning his trade?

DISCUSSION QUESTIONS

1. Does Twain use the block or alternating pattern to organize his comparison? Why is his choice appropriate?
2. Why does Twain begin and end with references to something lost?
3. Why is "bewitched" at the start of paragraph 2 an appropriate word to describe Twain's reaction to the sunset in paragraph 1?
4. In paragraph 2 Twain says that "This sun means . . . ," "that floating log means . . . ," and "that slanting mark on the water refers. . . ." Point out the significance of the verbs Twain uses.
5. How do the tones (see pages 220–24) of paragraphs 1 and 2 differ?
6. Why do you suppose that Twain concludes by comparing doctors and steamboat pilots?

SUGGESTION FOR WRITING ■ **Write an essay comparing your original perceptions of and current reactions to a place you've re-visited after a period of time—for example, Las Vegas, Disneyland, or a national park.**

Richard Rodriguez

PRIVATE LANGUAGE, PUBLIC LANGUAGE

Richard Rodriguez (born 1944) is a native of San Francisco who is of Mexican ancestry. After learning English in the elementary grades, he went on to earn a baccalaureate degree in English at Stanford University (1967) and graduate degrees at Columbia University (1969) and the University of California at Berkeley (1975). Rejecting job offers from several major universities, he spent the next six years writing Memory: The Education of Richard Rodriguez *(1982), a book that traces his educational odyssey while attacking bilingual education and affirmative action. Rodriguez is now a full-time writer whose articles have appeared in a variety of scholarly magazines. In the following essay Rodriguez explores his contrasting childhood perceptions regarding English and his native Spanish.*

I remember to start with that day in Sacramento—a California now nearly thirty years past—when I first entered a classroom, able to understand some fifty stray English words. 1

The third of four children, I had been preceded to a neighborhood Roman Catholic school by an older brother and sister. But neither of them had revealed very much about their classroom experiences. Each afternoon they returned, as they left in the morning, always together, speaking in Spanish as they climbed the five steps of the porch. And their mysterious books, wrapped in shopping-bag paper, remained on the table next to the door, closed firmly behind them. 2

An accident of geography sent me to a school where all my classmates were white, many the children of doctors and lawyers and business executives. All my classmates certainly must have been uneasy on that first day of school—as most children are uneasy—to find themselves apart from their families in the first institution of their lives. But I was astonished. 3

The nun said, in a friendly but oddly impersonal voice, 'Boys and girls, this is Richard Rodriguez.' (I heard her sound out: *Rich-heard Road-ree-guess.*) It was the first time I had heard anyone name me in English. 'Richard,' the nun repeated more slowly, writing my name down in her black leather book. Quickly I turned to see my mother's face dissolve in a watery blur behind the pebbled glass door. 4

Many years later there is something called bilingual education—a scheme proposed in the late 1960s by Hispanic-American social activists, later endorsed by a congressional vote. It is a program that seeks to permit non-English-speaking children, many from lower-class homes, to use their family language as the language of school. (Such is the goal its supporters announce.) I hear them and 5 am forced to say no: It is not possible for a child—any child—ever to use his family's language in school. Not to understand this is to misunderstand the public uses of schooling and to trivialize the nature of intimate life—a family's 'language.'

6   Memory teaches me what I know of these matters; the boy reminds the adult. I was a bilingual child, a certain kind—socially disadvantaged—the son of working-class parents, both Mexican immigrants.

7   In the early years of my boyhood, my parents coped very well in America. My father had steady work. My mother managed at home. They were nobody's victims. Optimism and ambition led them to a house (our home) many blocks from the Mexican south side of town. We lived among *gringos* and only a block from the biggest, whitest houses. It never occurred to my parents that they couldn't live wherever they chose. Nor was the Sacramento of the fifties bent on teaching them a contrary lesson. My mother and father were more annoyed than intimidated by those two or three neighbors who tried initially to make us unwelcome. ('Keep your brats away from my sidewalk!') But despite all they achieved, perhaps because they had so much to achieve, any deep feeling of ease, the confidence of 'belonging' in public was withheld from them both. They regarded the people at work, the faces in crowds, as very distant from us. They were the others, *los gringos*. That term was interchangeable in their speech with another, even more telling, *los americanos*.

8   I grew up in a house where the only regular guests were my relations. For one day, enormous families of relatives would visit and there would be so many people that the noise and the bodies would spill out to the backyard and front porch. Then, for weeks, no one came by. (It was usually a salesman who rang the doorbell.) Our house stood apart. A gaudy yellow in a row of white bungalows. We were the people with the noisy dog. The people who raised pigeons and chickens. We were the foreigners on the block. A few neighbors smiled and waved. We waved back. But no one in the family knew the names of the old couple who lived next door; until I was seven years old, I did not know the names of the kids who lived across the street.

9   In public, my father and mother spoke a hesitant, accented, not always grammatical English. And they would have to strain—their bodies tense—to catch the sense of what was rapidly said by *los gringos*. At home they spoke Spanish. The language of their Mexican past sounded in counterpoint to the English of public society. The words would come quickly, with ease. Conveyed through those sounds was the pleasing, soothing, consoling reminder of being at home.

10   During those years when I was first conscious of hearing, my mother and father addressed me only in Spanish; in Spanish I learned to reply. By contrast, English (*inglés*), rarely heard in the house, was the language I came to associate with *gringos*. I learned my first words of English overhearing my parents speak to strangers. At five years of age, I knew just enough English for my mother to trust me on errands to stores one block away. No more.

11   I was a listening child, careful to hear the very different sounds of Spanish and English. Wide-eyed with hearing, I'd listen to sounds more than words. First, there were English (*gringo*) sounds. So many words were still unknown that when the butcher or the lady at the drugstore said something to me, exotic polysyllabic sounds would bloom in the midst of their sentences. Often the speech of people in public seemed to me very loud, booming with confidence. The man behind the counter would literally ask, 'What can I do for you?' But by being so firm and so clear, the sound of his voice said that he was a *gringo*; he belonged in public society.

I would also hear then the high nasal notes of middle-class American speech. The air stirred with sound. Sometimes, even now, when I have been traveling abroad for several weeks, I will hear what I heard as a boy. In hotel lobbies or airports, in Turkey or Brazil, some Americans will pass, and suddenly I will hear it again—the high sound of American voices. For a few seconds I will hear it with pleasure, for it is now the sound of *my* society—a reminder of home. But inevitably—already on the flight headed for home—the sound fades with repetition. I will be unable to hear it anymore. 12

When I was a boy, things were different. The accent of *los gringos* was never pleasing nor was it hard to hear. Crowds at Safeway or at bus stops would be noisy with sound. And I would be forced to edge away from the chirping chatter above me. 13

I was unable to hear my own sounds, but I knew very well that I spoke English poorly. My words would not stretch far enough to form complete thoughts. And the words I did speak I didn't know well enough to make into distinct sounds. (Listeners would usually lower their heads, better to hear what I was trying to say.) But it was one thing for *me* to speak English with difficulty. It was more troubling for me to hear my parents speak in public: their high-whining vowels and guttural consonants; their sentences that got stuck with 'eh' and 'ah' sounds; the confused syntax; the hesitant rhythm of sounds so different from the way *gringos* spoke. I'd notice, moreover, that my parents' voices were softer that those of *gringos* we'd meet. 14

I am tempted now to say that none of this mattered. In adulthood I am embarrassed by childhood fears. And, in a way, it didn't matter very much that my parents could not speak English with ease. Their linguistic difficulties had no serious consequences. My mother and father made themselves understood at the county hospital clinic and at government offices. And yet, in another way, it mattered very much—it was unsettling to hear my parents struggle with English. Hearing them, I'd grow nervous, my clutching trust in their protection and power weakened. 15

There were many times like the night at a brightly lit gasoline station (a blaring white memory) when I stood uneasily, hearing my father. He was talking to a teenaged attendant. I do not recall what they were saying, but I cannot forget the sounds my father made as he spoke. At one point his words slid together to form one word—sounds as confused as the threads of blue and green oil in the puddle next to my shoes. His voice rushed through what he had left to say. And, toward the end, reached falsetto notes, appealing to his listener's understanding. I looked away to the lights of passing automobiles. I tried not to hear anymore. But I heard only too well the calm, easy tones in the attendant's reply. Shortly afterward, walking toward home with my father, I shivered when he put his hand on my shoulder. The very first chance that I got, I evaded his grasp and ran on ahead into the dark, skipping with feigned boyish exuberance. 16

But then there was Spanish. *Español*: my family's language. *Español*: the language that seemed to me a private language. I'd hear strangers on the radio and in the Mexican Catholic church across town speaking in Spanish, but I couldn't really believe that Spanish was a public language, like English. Spanish speakers, rather, seemed related to me, for I sensed that we shared—through our langauge—the experience of feeling apart from *los gringos*. It was thus a ghetto Spanish that I heard and I spoke. Like those whose lives are bound by a barrio, I was reminded by Spanish of my separateness from *los otros, los gringos* in power. But more intensely than for most barrio children—because I did not live in a 17 barrio—Spanish seemed to me the language of home. (Most days it was only at home that I'd hear it.) It became the language of joyful return.

18

A family member would say something to me and I would feel myself specially recognized. My parents would say something to me and I would feel embraced by the sounds of their words. Those sounds said: *I am speaking with ease in Spanish. I am addressing you in words I never use with* los gringos. *I recognize you as someone special, close, like no one outside. You belong with us. In the family.*

19

(Ricardo.)

20

At the age of five, six, well past the time when most other children no longer easily notice the difference between sounds uttered at home and words spoken in public, I had a different experience. I lived in a world magically compounded of sounds. I remained a child longer than most; I lingered too long, poised at the edge of language—often frightened by the sounds of *los gringos*, delighted by the sounds of Spanish at home. I shared with my family a language that was startlingly different from that used in the great city around us.

21

For me there were none of the gradations between public and private society so normal to a maturating child. Outside the house was public society; inside the house was private. Just opening or closing the screen door behind me was an important experience. I'd rarely leave home all alone or without reluctance. Walking down the sidewalk, under the canopy of tall trees, I'd warily notice the—suddenly—silent neighborhood kids who stood warily watching me. Nervously, I'd arrive at the grocery store to hear there the sounds of the *gringo*—foreign to me—reminding me that in this world so big, I was a foreigner. But then I'd return. Walking back toward our house, climbing the steps from the sidewalk, when the front door was open in summer, I'd hear voices beyond the screen door talking in Spanish. For a second or two, I'd stay, linger there, listening. Smiling, I'd hear my mother call out, saying in Spanish (words): 'Is that you, Richard?' All the while her sounds would assure me: *You are home now; come closer; inside. With us.*

22

'*Sí*,' I'd reply.

23

Once more inside the house I would resume (assume) my place in the family. The sounds would dim, grow harder to hear. Once more at home, I would grow less aware of that fact. It required, however, no more than the blurt of the doorbell to alert me to listen to sounds all over again. The house would turn instantly still while my mother went to the door. I'd hear her hard English sounds. I'd wait to hear her voice return to soft-sounding Spanish, which assured me, as surely as did the clicking tongue of the lock on the door, that the stranger was gone.

24

Plainly, it is not healthy to hear such sounds so often. It is not healthy to distinguish public words from private words so easily. I remained cloistered by sounds, timid and shy in public, too dependent on voices at home. And yet it needs to be emphasized: I was an extremely happy child at home. I remember many nights when my father would come back from work, and I'd hear him call out to my mother in Spanish, sounding relieved. In Spanish, he'd sound light and free notes he never could manage in English. Some nights I'd jump up just at hearing his voice. With *mis hermanos* I would come running into the room where he was with my mother. Our laughing (so deep was the pleasure!) became screaming. Like others who know the pain of public alienation, we transformed the knowledge of our public separateness and made it consoling—the reminder

DISCUSSION QUESTIONS

1. Rodriguez establishes that when he entered school English was unfamiliar to him. He knew only about fifty English words, his brother and sister spoke only Spanish outside of class, and he had never heard the English form of his name until his teacher spoke it. Later parts of the essay explore his childhood attitudes toward English and Spanish.

2. The main point is that family language—by which Rodriguez means the language of a particular household—cannot be used in the classroom because it carries with it emotions and associations that only the members of that household can know. This point is stated in paragraph 5.

3. These paragraphs reveal that the Rodriguez family members, though accepted by their neighbors, were nevertheless outsiders—separated of intimacy. Excited, we joined our voices in a celebration of sounds. *We are speaking now the way we never speak out in public. We are alone—together,* voices sounded, surrounded to tell me. Some nights, no one seemed willing to loosen the hold sounds had on us. At dinner, we invented new words. (Ours sounded Spanish, but made sense only to us.) We pieced together new words by taking, say, an English verb and giving it Spanish endings. My mother's instructions at bedtime would be lacquered with mock-urgent tones. Or a word like *si* would become, in several notes, able to convey added measures of feeling. Tongues explored the edges of words, especially the fat vowels. And we happily sounded that military drum roll, the twirling roar of the Spanish *r*. Family language: my family's sounds. The voices of my parents and sisters and brother. Their voices insisting: *You belong here. We are family members. Related. Special to one another. Listen!* Voices singing and sighing, rising, straining, then surging, teeming with pleasure that burst syllables into fragments of laughter. At times it seemed there was steady quiet only when, from another room, the rustling whispers of my parents faded and I moved closer to sleep.

DISCUSSION QUESTIONS

1. What does Rodriguez accomplish in his first four paragraphs? What connection do you see between these paragraphs and later parts of the essay?
2. What is Rodriguez's main point? Where is it stated?
3. Discuss the significance of paragraphs 7–9.
4. Why did his parents' difficulties with English cause Rodriguez such concern?
5. In paragraph 16 Rodriguez tells us that he "looked away to the lights of passing automobiles" and that he "ran on ahead into the dark. . . ." Explain these actions.
6. Rodriguez does not begin to develop his discussion of Spanish—the private language—until paragraph 17. Why do you think this discussion didn't occur earlier in the essay?
7. Explain why the concluding paragraph is effective.

SUGGESTION FOR WRITING ■ Write a comparison essay
discussing some noteworthy difference between you, or some group you belong to, and the larger public. The difference may be one of race, ethnic background, religion, or lifestyle. Demonstrate clearly how the difference affects your relationship with that public.

Marjorie Waters

COMING HOME

Marjorie Waters was born and educated in upstate New York. A free-lance writer who works in Boston, she has authored numerous articles in popular and literary magazines, as well as one longer work, The Victory

from those around them by unease, a different lifestyle, and, perhaps most important of all, a different language. Thus the paragraphs lead smoothly to Rodriguez's examination of his early outlook toward English and Spanish.
4. To the young Rodriguez, his parents represent security in a non-Hispanic world. When he hears them struggle to express themselves in English, he has less confidence in their "protection" and "power" (paragraph 15).
5. Rodriguez was embarrassed by his father's rather unsuccessful attempts to communicate with the English-speaking gas-station attendant. Because he has lost confidence in his father's protective powers, he temporarily rejects his parent.
6. To build a case for the special nature of a family's language, Rodriguez must first demonstrate the family's separation from white society. Reversing the order would make the paragraphs on separation seem anticlimactic.
7. Paragraph 24 reiterates the connection between a family's language and its intimate life. Note how the tone, tender and nostalgic, reinforces the connection.

PERSPECTIVE

An analogy can be likened to an epiphany that illuminates and allows us to grasp the essential meaning or nature of some concept or state of mind through comparison. Thus Waters helps us grasp the nature of her recovery from grief by comparing it to the return to her old house that has survived a severe winter. If you have an especially capable class, you might make this point when you present analogy.

TEACHING STRATEGIES

1. Point out that this analogy is effective because the familiar item is well known (the return to a house), the items have significant similarities and offer revealing insights, and the analogy is not overextended or contrived.
2. The greeting "old friend" at the end of paragraph 1 establishes the house as something Waters once knew well and enjoyed. Likewise, we find out that she once knew and enjoyed a pre-grief lifestyle. Thus "old friend" helps set up the analogy to come and prepares for her reclaiming both the house and her life. In this light, you might ask students to comment on the significance of "old friend."

CLASSROOM ACTIVITY

Divide the class into small groups and have them discuss possibilities for developing analogies based on some of the writing suggestions listed at the end of Chapter 9. These discussions might lead to a writing assignment.

DISCUSSION QUESTIONS

1. The house had been assaulted by the elements of nature and, despite showing some effects of this assault, was still basically sound. Similarly, as paragraphs 5 and 6 make clear, Waters herself had been assaulted by grief after an unexpected death. And despite experiencing some traumatic effects, she also had emerged from the grief intact and feeling like herself again. Thus in this sentence Waters starts to lay the foundation (although unannounced: see answer 2) for her analogy.
2. Waters wants readers of her first four paragraphs to concentrate on and understand only the house and how she acclimated to it. That done, she then introduces the analogy at the start

Garden Kids' Book (1988). In the essay that follows, Ms. Waters draws an analogy between a house that has weathered a severe winter and an individual who has weathered a period of severe grief.

1   After the cruelest of winters, the house still stood. It was pale, washed clean by elements gone wild, and here and there a shutter dangled from a broken hinge. But the structure was sound; the corners had held. I walked around it slowly, studying every detail: the fine edge where window frame met clapboard, the slice of shadow across the roofline, the old wooden railing around the porch. When I climbed the stairs toward the door, I heard the floorboards groan beneath my weight as they had always done. Hello yourself, old friend, I said.

2   Inside, I made those rooms my own again, drew the curtains back, threw open the window, pulled the covers from the furniture, slapped all the upholstery with my hands. I could feel fresh air move in through open windows, replacing a season's worth of staleness with a smell of moist earth, a hint of flowers. After all the months of darkness light poured again into the house, fell in familiar angled patterns across furniture, walls, and floors. Where light beams passed through moving air, even the dust seemed alive; I watched it swirl, dance, resettle.

3   I made myself at home, kicked off my shoes so I could feel the floors beneath my feet again. I tilted my head, read the titles on the spines of all my books. I played old songs I hadn't heard in months, felt the summer music move through me as if my muscles were the strings. It carried me from room to room while I swept away the mustiness of winter, shook the rugs, cleaned cobwebs out of corners, hung laundered linens on the line to whip dry in the outdoor air. I pulled closed boxes out of closets and unwrapped all my things, slowly, one by one. I held and turned them in my hands before I put them out again on shelves, in cupboards and drawers. And when I had each room all full of me again, I showered and washed away the last of winter's claims in hot lather and steam.

4   Night fell and brought a chill to the air outside. I built a fire in the stove, drank tea that smelled of oranges and spice. I warmed my fingers round the cup and thought of how my house would look to passers-by, drowsy and content, with soft rectangles of light on the ground below the windows, a breath of smoke from the chimney. She's come back, they would say as they walked through the dark night. She's home again.

5   For me, the end of grief was a homecoming like this one, a returning to myself made sweeter by the long separation. I remember well the months that had followed that most unexpected death, when I felt cut loose, caught in my own cold storm, far away from all that made me feel at home. I wondered if I would ever again belong to any time or place. People spoke to me of sadness and loss, as if they were burdens to carry in my hands. I nodded in agreement, afraid to tell them that I felt no burdens, only weightlessness. I thought the world had pulled itself away from me, that I would drift, beyond reach, forever.

6   But winter ends, and grief does pass. As I had reclaimed my house and made it my own again, so I slowly reclaimed my life. I resumed my small daily rituals: a cup of coffee with a friend, long walks at sunset. I felt like myself again, and when I laughed, it was my own laugh I heard, rich and full. I had feared that, in my absence, the space that I had left behind would close over from disuse, but I returned to find that my house still stood, even after the cruelest of winters.

DISCUSSION QUESTIONS

1. Consider the essay as a whole and then point out the significance of this sentence in paragraph 1: "But the structure was sound; the corners had held."
2. Waters does not introduce her analogy at the start of the essay. Suggest why. Where are we first aware of her analogy?
3. Why do you think Waters, in paragraph 5, doesn't identify the person who died?
4. Reread the "As . . . so . . . " sentence in paragraph 6. What can you learn from its structure that can help you write your own analogy?
5. Does this analogy further explain the familiar by presenting information on the unfamiliar, or does it explain the unfamiliar by likening it to the familiar?
6. What does Waters accomplish by beginning and ending her essay with ". . . the cruelest of winters"?

SUGGESTION FOR WRITING ■ **Write an analogy that helps explain a time of great joy in your life. Feel free either to reveal or conceal the actual joy. Announce your analogy at the point which seems most effective.**

of paragraph 5, confident that the reader will now comprehend it.
3. Who died is unimportant to understanding the writer's purpose: to point out similarities between the reopening of a closed house and the recovery from grief, whatever its source.
4. The "as . . . so . . ." (or "just as . . . so also . . .") pattern is a common one in analogies because it clearly links the similarities. Students might well use this pattern when writing their own analogies.
5. Waters explains the somewhat unfamiliar (the recovery from grief) by likening it to the more familiar (the return to a house).
6. In paragraph 1 the phrase refers to the house; in paragraph 6 it refers to Waters' recovery from grief. Thus the two similarities under discussion are tied together.

OVERVIEW OF CAUSE-AND-EFFECT ESSAYS (pp. 434–47)

One of the four cause-and-effect essays explores causes, two explore effects, and one, while emphasizing causes, pays some attention to effects. Three of the four writers draw upon personal experience. Of these three essays, one uses gentle irony to make a philosophical point, and two of them have a serious tone, although one ends on a humorous note. All three use informal language. The remaining writer relies on formal-informal language and achieves an objective tone by citing case histories and statistics.

Cause and Effect

E. M. Forster

MY WOOD

E. M. Forster (1879–1970) was born in London and educated at King's College, Cambridge, where he received baccalaureate degrees in classics (1900) and history (1901). For the next eighteen years, he spent much of his time outside England, living in Greece and Italy, visiting India, and during World War I serving with the Red Cross in Egypt. After the war, Forster returned to England and, except for a brief stint in India as a Maharajah's private secretary, remained there the rest of his life. Forster's novels include Where Angels Fear to Tread *(1905),* The Longest Journey *(1907),* A Room with a View *(1908),* Howard's End *(1910), and* A Passage to India *(1924). His short stories have been collected in two volumes,* The Celestial Omnibus *(1911) and* The Eternal Moment *(1928). After 1928, Forster focused on nonfiction, producing, among other books,* Abinger Harvest *(1936), a collection of essays and literary criticism from which our selection comes. In it, Forster notes the effects that owning property had on him.*

Introduction: provides background

Signals essay of effects

Body: paragraph 2 to first part, paragraph 7 First effect

1   A few years ago I wrote a book which dealt in part with the difficulties of the English in India. Feeling that they would have had no difficulties in India themselves, the Americans read the book freely. The more they read it the better it made them feel, and a cheque to the author was the result. I bought a wood with the cheque. It is not a large wood—it contains scarcely any trees, and it is intersected, blast it, by a public foot path. Still, it is the first property that I have owned, so it is right that other people should participate in my shame, and should ask themselves, in accents that will vary in horror, this very important question: What is the effect of property upon the character? Don't let's touch economics; the effect of private ownership upon the community as a whole is another question—a more important question, perhaps, but another one. Let's keep to psychology. If you own things, what's their effect on you? What's the effect on me of my wood?

2   In the first place, it makes me feel heavy. Property does have this effect. Property produces men of weight, and it was a man of weight who failed to get into the Kingdom of Heaven. He was not wicked, that unfortunate millionaire in the parable, he was only stout; he stuck out in front, not to mention behind, and as he wedged himself this way and that in the crystalline entrance and bruised his well-fed flanks, he saw beneath him a comparatively slim camel passing through the eye of a needle and being woven into the robe of God. The Gospels all through couple stoutness and slowness. They point out what is perfectly obvious, yet seldom realized: that if you have a lot of things you cannot move about a lot,

434

that furniture requires dusting, dusters require servants, servants require insurance stamps, and the whole tangle of them makes you think twice before you accept an invitation to dinner or go for a bathe in the Jordan. Sometimes the Gospels proceed further and say with Tolstoy that property is sinful; they approach the difficult ground of asceticism here, where I cannot follow them. But as to the immediate effects of property on people, they just show straightforward logic. It produces men of weight. Men of weight cannot, by definition, move like the lightning from the East unto the West, and the ascent of a fourteen-stone[1] bishop into a pulpit is thus the exact antithesis of the coming of the Son of Man. My wood makes me feel heavy.

In the second place, it makes me feel it ought to be larger.

The other day I heard a twig snap in it. I was annoyed at first, for I thought that someone was blackberrying, and depreciating the value of the undergrowth. On coming nearer, I saw it was not a man who had trodden on the twig and snapped it, but a bird, and I felt pleased. My bird. The bird was not equally pleased. Ignoring the relation between us, it took fright as soon as it saw the shape of my face, and flew straight over the boundary hedge into a field, the property of Mrs. Henessy, where it sat down with a loud squawk. It had become Mrs. Henessy's bird. Something seemed grossly amiss here, something that would not have occurred had the wood been larger. I could not afford to buy Mrs. Henessy out, I dared not murder her, and limitations of this sort beset me on every side. . . . A boundary protects. But—poor little thing—the boundary ought in its turn to be protected. Noises on the edge of it. Children throw stones. A little more, and then a little more, until we reach the sea. . . . And after all, why should even the world be the limit of possession? A rocket containing a Union Jack, will, it is hoped, be shortly fired at the moon. Mars. Sirius. Beyond which. . . . But these immensities ended by saddening me. I could not suppose that my wood was the destined nucleus of universal dominion—it is so very small and contains no mineral wealth beyond the blackberries. Nor was I comforted when Mrs. Henessy's bird took alarm for the second time and flew clean away from us all, under the belief that it belonged to itself.

In the third place, property makes its owner feel that he ought to do something to it. Yet he isn't sure what. A restlessness comes over him, a vague sense that he has a personality to express—the same sense which, without any vagueness, leads the artist to an act of creation. Sometimes I think I will cut down such trees as remain in the wood, at other times I want to fill up the gaps between them with new trees. Both impulses are pretentious and empty. They are not honest movements toward money-making or beauty. They spring from a foolish desire to express myself and from an inability to enjoy what I have got. Creation, property, enjoyment form a sinister trinity in the human mind. Creation and enjoyment are both very good, yet they are often unattainable without a material basis, and at such moments property pushes itself in as a substitute, saying, "Accept me instead—I'm good enough for all three." It is not enough. It is, as Shakespeare said of lust, "The expense of spirit in a waste of shame": it is "Before, a joy proposed; behind, a dream." Yet we don't know how to shun it. It is forced on us by our economic system as the alternative to starvation. It is also forced on us by an internal defect in the soul. By the feeling that in property may lie the

Second effect

Third effect

[1] A stone is a British unit of weight equal to fourteen pounds.

germs of self-development and of exquisite or heroic deeds. Our life on earth is, and ought to be, material and carnal. But we have not yet learned to manage our materialism and carnality properly; they are still entangled with the desire for ownership. . . .

6   And this brings us to our fourth and final point: the blackberries.

7   Blackberries are not plentiful in this meagre grove, but they are easily seen from the public footpath which traverses it, and all too easily gathered. Foxgloves, too—people will pull up the foxgloves, and ladies of an educational tendency even grub for toad stools to show them on the Monday in class. Other ladies, less educated, roll down the bracken in the arms of their gentlemen friends. There is a paper, there are tins. Pray, does my wood belong to me or doesn't it? And, if it does, should I not own it best by allowing no one else to walk there? There is a wood near Lyme Regis, also cursed by a public footpath, where the owner has not hesitated on this point. He has built high stone walls on each side of the path, and has spanned it by bridges, so that the public circulate like termites while he gorges on the blackberries unseen. He really does own his wood, this able chap. . . . And perhaps I shall come to this in time. I shall wall in and fence out until I really taste the sweets of property. Enormously stout, endlessly avaricious, pseudo-creative, intensely selfish, I shall weave upon my forehead the quadruple crown of possession until those nasty Bolshies come and take it off again and thrust me aside into the outer darkness.

DISCUSSION QUESTIONS

1. Forster focuses first on the physical effect of owning property (the wood makes him feel heavy), then turns to three effects of ownership on attitude (the wood makes him become greedy, feel he should do something to the property, and become selfish). This arrangement seems natural and logical.
2. Forster mentions these references to lend authority to his insights.
3. These expressions include "blast it" and "Don't let's" (paragraph 1); "stuck out in front, not to mention behind," "wedged himself this way and that," "bruised his well-fed flanks," and "a lot" (paragraph 2); "blackberrying," "a loud squawk," and "poor little thing" (paragraph 4); and "grub," "gorges," "chap," and "nasty Bolshies" (paragraph 7).
4. Most Americans today probably would not share Forster's views, but this question might elicit some interesting responses from your class.

DISCUSSION QUESTIONS

1. How does Forster arrange his discussion of effects? Why do you think he chose that arrangement?
2. Why do you think Forster's essay mentions the Bible, Tolstoy, and Shakespeare?
3. Forster writes in a casual, informal style. Point out several examples of expressions that contribute to this informality.
4. To what extent do you think that most Americans today would agree with what Forster, an Englishman, said over fifty years ago about the effects that owning property had on him?

SUGGESTION FOR WRITING ■ Write an essay explaining how some new possession, such as an automobile, a home computer, a videocassette player-recorder, or a new wardrobe affected your outlook and behavior. Try to maintain a light, playful tone.

Carll Tucker

FEAR OF DEARTH

Carll Tucker, a native of New York City, has reviewed books and movies for the Village Voice *and served as editor and columnist for the* Saturday Review. *Since 1983, he has edited the* Patent Trader *magazine. In this selection, he considers a contemporary paradox: the popularity of the unenjoyable activity of jogging.*

I hate jogging. Every dawn, as I thud around New York City's Central Park reservoir, I am reminded of how much I hate it. It's so tedious. Some claim jogging is thought conducive; others insist the scenery relieves the monotony. For me, the pace is wrong for contemplation of either ideas or vistas. While jogging, all I can think about is jogging—or nothing. One advantage of jogging around a reservoir is that there's no dry shortcut home. 1

From the listless looks of some fellow trotters, I gather I am not alone in my unenthusiasm: Bill-paying, it seems, would be about as diverting. Nonetheless, we continue to jog; more, we continue to *choose* to jog. From a practically infinite array of opportunities, we select one that we don't enjoy and can't wait to have done with. Why? 2

For any trend, there are as many reasons as there are participants. This person runs to lower his blood pressure. That person runs to escape the telephone or a cranky spouse or a filthy household. Another person runs to avoid doing anything else, to dodge a decision about how to lead his life or a realization that his life is leading nowhere. Each of us has his carrot and stick. In my case, the stick is my slackening physical condition, which keeps me from beating opponents at tennis whom I overwhelmed two years ago. My carrot is to win. 3

Beyond these disparate reasons, however, lies a deeper cause. It is no accident that now, in the last third of the twentieth century, personal fitness and health have suddenly become a popular obsession. True, modern man likes to feel good, but that hardly distinguishes him from his predecessors. 4

With zany myopia, economists like to claim that the deeper cause of everything is economic. Delightfully, there seems no marketplace explanation for jogging. True, jogging is cheap, but then not jogging is cheaper. And the scant and skimpy equipment which jogging demands must make it a marketer's least favored form of recreation. 5

Some scout-masterish philosophers argue that the appeal of jogging and other body-maintenance programs is the discipline they afford. We live in a world in which individuals have fewer and fewer obligations. The work week has shrunk. Weekend worship is less compulsory. Technology gives us more free time. Satisfactorily filling free time requires imagination and effort. Freedom is a wide and risky river; it can drown the person who does not know how to swim across it. The more obligations one takes on, the more time one occupies, the less threat freedom poses. Jogging can become an instant obligation. For a portion of his day, the jogger is not his own man; he is obedient to a regimen he has accepted. 6

life. Students could brainstorm possibilities in small groups and then use the discussions as the springboard for a paper. Remind students to check the third model outline in Chapter 10 for the organizational pattern of causal chains.

DISCUSSION QUESTIONS

1. Tucker uses the fragment intentionally to prepare for his focus on causes. Regarding fragments, we feel it's better to point them out to students than to have them call the "error" to our attention.

2. The reasons in paragraph 3 are relatively unimportant, and each is confined to relatively few people. Tucker gets these reasons out of the way before moving on to more important reasons.

3. Paragraph 5 discusses economic reasons, paragraph 6 discipline–obligation reasons, paragraph 7 theological reasons, and paragraph 9 "fear of dearth." These reasons are arranged from least to most important. The economic reason is essentially dismissed, the discipline one is plausible, and the theological one goes "one step further." But in paragraph 9 he explains what drives us "even more."

4. Tucker means that people with too much free time have problems occupying that time. Regular jogging can become part of the answer.

5. The four sentences immediately following offer supporting evidence for the statement. You may want to point out the parallel structure of these sentences.

6. The "we" tend to jog for reasons related to survival; the "I" (Tucker) jogs for practical reasons.

7. This question should prompt an interesting and revealing discussion. It could be used as a springboard for a writing assignment.

7   Theologians may take the argument one step further. It is our modern irreligion, our lack of confidence in any hereafter, that makes us anxious to stretch our mortal stay as long as possible. We run, as the saying goes, for our lives, hounded by the suspicion that these are the only lives we are likely to enjoy.

8   All of these theorists seem to me more or less right. As the growth of cults and charismatic religions and the resurgence of enthusiasm for the military draft suggest, we do crave commitment. And who can doubt, watching so many middle-aged and older persons torturing themselves in the name of fitness, that we are unreconciled to death, more so perhaps than any generation in modern memory?

9   But I have a hunch there's a further explanation of our obsession with exercise. I suspect that what motivates us even more than a fear of death is a fear of dearth. Our era is the first to anticipate the eventual depletion of all natural resources. We see wilderness shrinking; rivers losing their capacity to sustain life; the air, even the stratosphere, being loaded with potentially deadly junk. We see the irreplaceable being squandered, and in the depths of our consciousness we are fearful that we are creating an uninhabitable world. We feel more or less helpless and yet, at the same time, desirous to protect what resources we can. We recycle soda bottles and restore old buildings and protect our nearest natural resource—our physical health—in the almost superstitious hope that such small gestures will help save an earth that we are blighting. Jogging becomes a sort of penance for our sins of gluttony, greed, and waste. Like a hairshirt or a bed of nails, the more one hates it, the more virtuous it makes one feel.

10   That is why *we* jog. Why *I* jog is to win at tennis.

DISCUSSION QUESTIONS

1. Does Tucker focus on causes or effects? How does the sentence fragment that ends paragraph 2 relate to this focus?

2. What function does paragraph 3 serve?

3. Identify the causes or effects that Tucker discusses. In what order are they presented?

4. Explain the meaning of this sentence in paragraph 6: "Freedom is a wide and risky river; it can drown the person who does not know how to swim across it." Relate this sentence to the focus on causes or effects.

5. Explain how Tucker defends his contention in paragraph 9 that we are anticipating "the eventual depletion of all natural resources."

6. Why are "we" and "I" italicized in paragraph 10?

7. If you are a jogger or an exercise enthusiast, do you know why? If you are a couch potato, do you know why? Discuss.

SUGGESTION FOR WRITING ■ **Write an essay explaining the causes or effects of the popular preoccupation with dieting, sleek cars, fashionable clothes, or something similar.**

Brent Staples

BLACK MEN AND PUBLIC SPACE

Brent Staples is a journalist whose academic background in psychology and upbringing in the poor and largely black industrial town of Chester, Pennsylvania, have uniquely equipped him to address black problems and concerns. After earning A.B. and M.A. degrees, Staples worked as a college instructor and employee of a management firm while completing his Ph.D. at the University of Chicago in 1982. In 1983, he became a reporter for the Chicago Sun-Times *and three years later accepted a position with* The New York Times, *where he now serves on that paper's editorial board. In our selection, Staples examines the fear and hostility that blacks in public places sometimes arouse.*

My first victim was a woman—white, well dressed, probably in her early twenties. I came upon her late one evening on a deserted street in Hyde Park, a relatively affluent neighborhood in an otherwise mean, impoverished section of Chicago. As I swung onto the avenue behind her, there seemed to be a discreet, uninflammatory distance between us. Not so. She cast back a worried glance. To her, the youngish black man—a broad six feet two inches with a beard and billowing hair, both hands shoved into the pockets of a bulky military jacket—seemed menacingly close. After a few more quick glimpses, she picked up her pace and was soon running in earnest. Within seconds she disappeared into a cross street.

That was more than a decade ago. I was twenty-two years old, a graduate student newly arrived at the University of Chicago. It was in the echo of that terrified woman's footfalls that I first began to know the unwieldy inheritance I'd come into—the ability to alter public space in ugly ways. It was clear that she thought herself the quarry of a mugger, a rapist, or worse. Suffering a bout of insomnia, however, I was stalking sleep, not defenseless wayfarers. As a softy who is scarcely able to take a knife to a raw chicken—let alone hold one to a person's throat—I was surprised, embarrassed, and dismayed all at once. Her flight made me feel like an accomplice in tyranny. It also made it clear that I was indistinguishable from the muggers who occasionally seeped into the area from the surrounding ghetto. That first encounter, and those that followed, signified that a vast, unnerving gulf lay between nighttime pedestrians—particularly women—and me. And I soon gathered that being perceived as dangerous is a hazard in itself. I only needed to turn a corner into a dicey situation, or crowd some frightened, armed person in a foyer somewhere, or make an errant move after being pulled over by a policeman. Where fear and weapons meet—and they often do in urban America—there is always the possibility of death.

In that first year, my first away from my hometown, I was to become thoroughly familiar with the language of fear. At dark, shadowy intersections, I could cross in front of a car stopped at a traffic light and elicit the *thunk, thunk, thunk, thunk* of the driver—black, white, male, or female—hammering down the door locks. On less traveled streets after dark, I grew accustomed to but never comfortable with people crossing to the other side of the street rather than pass me. Then there were the standard unpleasantries with policemen, doormen,

1

2

3

bouncers, cabdrivers, and others whose business it is to screen out troublesome individuals *before* there is any nastiness.

4   I moved to New York nearly two years ago and I have remained an avid night walker. In central Manhattan, the near-constant crowd cover minimizes tense one-on-one street encounters. Elsewhere—in SoHo, for example, where sidewalks are narrow and tightly spaced buildings shut out the sky—things can get very taut indeed.

5   After dark, on the warrenlike streets of Brooklyn where I live, I often see women who fear the worst from me. They seem to have set their faces on neutral, and with their purse straps strung across their chests bandolier-style, they forge ahead as though bracing themselves against being tackled. I understand, of course, that the danger they perceive is not a hallucination. Women are particularly vulnerable to street violence, and young black males are drastically overrepresented among the perpetrators of that violence. Yet these truths are no solace against the kind of alienation that comes of being ever the suspect, a fearsome entity with whom pedestrians avoid making eye contact.

6   It is not altogether clear to me how I reached the ripe old age of twenty-two without being conscious of the lethality nighttime pedestrians attributed to me. Perhaps it was because in Chester, Pennsylvania, the small, angry industrial town where I came of age in the 1960s, I was scarcely noticeable against a backdrop of gang warfare, street knifings, and murders. I grew up one of the good boys, had perhaps a half-dozen fistfights. In retrospect, my shyness of combat has clear sources.

7   As a boy, I saw countless tough guys locked away; I have since buried several, too. They were babies, really—a teenage cousin, a brother of twenty-two, a childhood friend in his mid-twenties—all gone down in episodes of bravado played out in the streets. I came to doubt the virtues of intimidation early on. I chose, perhaps unconsciously, to remain a shadow—timid, but a survivor.

8   The fearsomeness mistakenly attributed to me in public places often has a perilous flavor. The most frightening of these confusions occurred in the late 1970's and early 1980's, when I worked as a journalist in Chicago. One day, rushing into the office of a magazine I was writing for with a deadline story in hand, I was mistaken for a burglar. The office manager called security and, with an ad hoc posse, pursued me through the labyrinthine halls, nearly to my editor's door. I had no way of proving who I was. I could only move briskly toward the company of someone who knew me.

9   Another time I was on assignment for a local paper and killing time before an interview. I entered a jewelry store on the city's affluent Near North Side. The proprietor excused herself and returned with an enormous red Doberman pinscher straining at the end of a leash. She stood, the dog extended toward me, silent to my questions, her eyes bulging nearly out of her head. I took a cursory look around, nodded, and bade her good night.

10   Relatively speaking, however, I never fared as badly as another black male journalist. He went to nearby Waukegan, Illinois, a couple of summers ago to work on a story about a murderer who was born there. Mistaking the reporter for the killer, police officers hauled him from his car at gunpoint and but for his press credentials would probably have tried to book him. Such episodes are not uncommon. Black men trade tales like this all the time.

11   Over the years, I learned to smother the rage I felt at so often being taken for a criminal. Not to do so would surely have led to madness. I now take

DISCUSSION QUESTIONS

1. This paragraph, the essay's introduction, presents a well-told anecdote that draws the reader into the body of the essay while illustrating its main point: that blacks have the capacity to alter public space in ugly ways.

2. The thesis statement is the third sentence of paragraph 2.

3. This sentence is a time signal that establishes when Staples first became aware of the problems that his blackness could create for whites. Together with the incidents that occur at later times, it shows the problem to be long-standing and important, presumably to other blacks as well as Staples.

4. By presenting himself as a peaceful person—"a softy who is scarcely able to take a knife to a raw chicken" (paragraph 2)—Staples establishes a contrast between what he is perceived to be and what he is. Thus he reminds his readers that it is a mistake to judge others by their appearance.

5. Paragraphs 1 and 2 follow a single cause–multiple

precautions to make myself less threatening. I move about with care, particularly late in the evening. I give a wide berth to nervous people on subway platforms during the wee hours, particularly when I have exchanged business clothes for jeans. If I happen to be entering a building behind some people who appear skittish, I may walk by, letting them clear the lobby before I return, so as not to seem to be following them. I have been calm and extremely congenial on those rare occasions when I've been pulled over by the police.

And on late-evening constitutionals I employ what has proved to be an 12 excellent tension-reducing measure: I whistle melodies from Beethoven and Vivaldi and the more popular classical composers. Even steely New Yorkers hunching toward nighttime destinations seem to relax, and occasionally they even join in the tune. Virtually everybody seems to sense that a mugger wouldn't be warbling bright, sunny selections from Vivaldi's *Four Seasons*. It is my equivalent of the cowbell that hikers wear when they know they are in bear country.

DISCUSSION QUESTIONS

1. Discuss the effectiveness of Staples's opening paragraph.
2. Identify the thesis statement of the essay.
3. Consider the essay as a whole and then point out the significance of the first sentence in paragraph 2.
4. What does Staples accomplish by mentioning at several points in the essay his distaste for violence?
5. Which patterns of causal analysis, discussed on pages 118–20, do you find in this essay?
6. Trace Staples's changing responses to the fear and hostility that he encounters.

SUGGESTION FOR WRITING ■ Write a cause-and-effect essay exploring your reactions to some actual or perceived threat to you. Possibilities might include engine trouble on a plane flight, a snowstorm that traps you in your car, or recurring head, chest, or stomach pains that send you to your doctor. Include your reactions both at the time and afterward.

Alex Taylor III

WHY WOMEN MANAGERS ARE BAILING OUT

Alex Taylor III (born 1945) is a writer on business and finance at Time Warner, Inc., where he is an associate editor of Fortune. *Previous experience includes working as a business news writer at the* Detroit Free Press *and a news reporter, producer, and anchor at three Midwestern television stations. Born in Greenwich, Connecticut, Taylor graduated*

effect pattern: Staples's appearance triggers flight by the women he encounters and surprise, embarrassment, and dismay, as well as some frightening realizations, in himself. The same pattern holds for paragraphs 3, 4, and 5, which briefly mention other unpleasant incidents stemming from Staples's blackness. In paragraphs 6 and 7, Staples shifts to a single effect–multiple cause pattern that links his peaceful nature to the fights, killings, and jailings that were part of his childhood. With paragraphs 8, 9, and 10, Staples turns to a single cause–single effect pattern to relate three potentially dangerous incidents that he experienced or knew about. For the essay's conclusion, which shows his assessment of his experiences, he again uses a single cause–multiple effect pattern.

6. Following the first incident, Staples experiences surprise, embarrassment, and dismay (paragraph 2). As incidents multiply and sometimes seem to pose danger for him, he develops feelings of fear (paragraphs 8 and 9) and later, in retrospect, rage (paragraph 11) at being continually regarded as a criminal. Finally, to reassure people who might feel endangered, he resorts to a pattern of behavior that makes him seem less threatening.

PERSPECTIVE

The cause-and-effect essays demonstrate how purpose affects a piece of writing. Forster, Tucker, and Staples all present personal insights—with which others might disagree—on their topics. They write informally in the first person. In contrast, Taylor, who writes in the third person and uses formal-informal language, has produced an objective report which is unlikely to trigger serious disagreement.

TEACHING STRATEGIES

1. Ask students to compare Taylor's essay with the one written by either Forster or Tucker and try to account for the differences in language, content, point of view, and tone. Suggest that students consider these matters in light of the writers' purposes. The ensuing discussion can provide an excellent opportunity to discuss the role of purpose in shaping these elements.

2. Ask students to evaluate the audience Taylor has in mind and to defend their conclusions with references to the essay.

3. Taylor relies on a number of direct quotations. Ask students to locate some examples, point out how and why he establishes the qualifications of those quoted, and discuss the reasons for using quotations.

4. Ask students to comment on the effectiveness of Taylor's opening sentence and to indicate what they can learn from it.

5. To reinforce the notion of coherence, have students examine paragraphs 10–22 and point out how they are connected.

CLASSROOM ACTIVITY

Organize students into small groups and have them brainstorm some of the reasons people quit jobs—domineering bosses, unsafe conditions, poor pay, health considerations, burnout, and the like. Each group could present its conclusions in a report delivered to the entire class. A writing assignment might follow.

with a B.A. in history from Middlebury College and an M.A. in journalism from the University of Missouri. He is a member of the adjunct faculty of the Columbia Graduate School of Journalism. In this essay, Taylor examines a recent business phenomenon, the exodus of large numbers of women from the ranks of management.

1   When the history of the last quarter of the 20th century in the U.S. is written, scholars may well conclude that the nation's most important social development has been the rise to positions of power and influence of its most vigorous majority: American women. So many women have come flocking into the labor force—fully 70% of all American women aged 25 to 54 are today at work for pay or actively seeking jobs—that more Americans are now employed than ever before. . . .

2   But there is a cloud, no bigger than a woman's hand, on the horizon. Many women, including some of the best educated and most highly motivated, are dropping out of the managerial work force. A disquieting number of the dropouts are the pioneering women who have struggled so hard, often in the face of prejudice and economic adversity, to earn the valued passport to high executive rank in corporate America, the Master of Business Administration degree.

3   A decade ago scarcely one newly minted MBA in eight was a woman. Today the proportion has risen dramatically and hearteningly to one in three. Yet the fact that many of those who led the way ten years ago have begun to bail out presents worrisome auguries not only for the female MBAs, but also for women of all kinds in the work force. If the MBAs cannot find gratification there, can *any* women?

4   To take just two examples:

5   Earning a master's degree in management from Northwestern University's Kellogg School in 1976 represented a personal triumph for Kathleen Mattox. She attended classes at night while working full time as a sales representative, first for American Hospital Supply and then for Abbott Laboratories. This enabled her to pay about half the $24,000 cost of her degree. Upon graduation she went to work for Bristol-Myers as an associate product manager in its medical devices subsidiary, based in Warsaw, Indiana.

6   Mattox thrived on the heavy travel to such cities as Hong Kong, Singapore, and Sydney, but both she and her husband chafed at Warsaw's provincialism. When she was recruited by 3M to work in St. Paul, she leaped at the chance. But the job, supervising a 15-person marketing department for orthopedic products, proved too demanding. "I was the youngest person in that job and one of only two women holding jobs like it," she recalls. "I was working my buns off, and there was a lot of emotional pressure." Already rocky, the marriage, her second, failed.

7   In 1983 Mattox decided she had had enough of big companies. She quit 3M to start her own marketing consulting firm, catering to clients in the health-care business. Working out of a converted bedroom in her home, she still puts in long hours on occasion, but now she has what she wants. Says she: "There are no hassles and it's great. I just want to live in the style to which I've become accustomed as a self-employed person. I have no visions of grandeur."

8   Another member of the class of '76, Mary Beth Deyerle took her MBA from the University of Chicago and then got her first job at Texas Commerce Bank in Houston. She soon discovered that she was earning $500 a year less than a man

with similar experience in the same job. "At first I was kind of angry, especially with this talk about equality," she says. "Finally I accepted it." Three years later she left the bank to have her first child, even though she was due a promotion to assistant vice president. "A lot of women MBAs feel guilty if they stay home. An MBA is an aggressive person. You want something for yourself—money, power, whatever. To give it all up is a cop-out in a way." For the first 18 months Deyerle missed her job, but now, after the birth of her second child, she has no plans to return. Says she: "I don't think you can both be a mother and work every day without it taking a big toll on you."

Not so long ago such defections would have gone unnoticed. Women were expected to work only a few years before marrying or having children. But times have radically changed, particularly with the awarding of substantial numbers of MBAs to women beginning in the mid-1970s. These women were supposed to lead the charge into the corridors of corporate power. Now many of these would-be leaders are retreating.   9

Fortune analyzed the career paths of men and women who received MBAs in 1976 from 17 of the most selective business schools. The analysis shows that of those whose first jobs were identifiable from school records, the same percentage of women MBAs as men—69%—went to work for large corporations or professional firms. Ten years later, of those who reported their current job situations on alumni questionnaires, about the same percentage—44% of the men and 43% of the women—still worked for such employers.   10

But there is one major difference between male and female MBAs. After ten years significantly more women than men have dropped off the management track. That is, they have left positions where they either managed other people or were clearly on their way to doing so. Fully 30% of the 1,039 women from the class of '76 reported they are either self-employed or unemployed or they listed no occupation. Men bail out too, but the percentage is much smaller. Some 21% of the 4,255 men listed either self-employment or no occupation on the alumni questionnaires.   11

Even those numbers probably understate the difference. Telephone interviews with a random sample of over 50 of the women in the 30% indicate that many work only part time out of their homes, or do not work at paying jobs at all. Phone interviews with 50 men chosen at random from the 21% found that 29 are in fact working for companies, 19 are self-employed, and only two are unemployed. . . .   12

This attrition in the managerial work force comes at a critical time for working women. Companies have had visible numbers of female managers for two decades or so. But the unspoken expectation back in the 1960s and early 1970s was that any women who had persevered and become managers had put child-rearing behind them or forgone families entirely. Women MBAs from 1976 and the classes that followed are among the first trying to juggle the demands of full-time jobs with family life. If these women decide their careers are not worth the struggle, their example may deter younger women coming along behind them. Corporations will lose a supply of talented executives.   13

Why are women dropping out? First, they find it hard to get ahead—harder, they think, than it is for men. Says Donald Johnson of the New York executive search firm of Johnson Smith & Knisely: "When they reach their mid-30s and early 40s, women feel the men surging ahead of them. They aren't winding up in the important jobs." Mary Anne Devanna, a research coordinator at Columbia's Grad-   14 uate School of Business who has studied the careers of MBAs, observes: "Women are making rational decisions. The probability that they will make chairman of the board is less than that of men, so if higher responsibility isn't going to be forthcoming, now is the time to quit."

15   At the majority of companies, the most successful women still find themselves stuck just below the level of vice president. A new study by Korn/Ferry International, the executive recruiting firm, shows that at Fortune 500 industrial and service companies women account for only 2% of senior executives—defined as vice presidents and above, but excluding the president and chairman.

16   Women also suspect they are not paid as well as their male classmates. They are often right. Research at the University of Pittsburgh indicates that MBA women who joined accounting firms in 1973 were earning an average of $6,400 less than their male counterparts ten years later. Women who received MBAs from Pitt between 1973 and 1982 earned an average of $9,000 less in 1983 than men from the same graduating classes. When differences in work experience and job type were eliminated, women still made $2,200 less.

17   There are several theories to explain why women seem to feel more unhappiness with corporate life than men do. One is that women more often find themselves stifled by organizational rigidity. Ardis Burst left Harvard Business School in 1976 "fueled with rockets," she says. But after the birth of her first child, she quit her job at General Foods as an associate product manager in the Maxwell House division. Says she of life in a big company: "There's a lack of autonomy. The homogeneity is difficult to live with. The only real reward was money and, further down the line, power, but the trade-off didn't seem worth it." Burst is now writing a book on management, and says she will never go back to a large corporation.

18   A second theory holds that women are still shunted away from exciting operating assignments into staff jobs in the "three p's": purchasing, personnel, and public relations. Yet another theory maintains that the number of women managers has not yet reached the critical mass needed for them to function comfortably in the corporate world.

19   In their forthcoming book, *Success and Betrayal: The Crisis of Women in Corporate America*, authors Sarah Hardesty and Nehama Jacobs, who interviewed 100 women, contend that the level of discontent is far higher than generally acknowledged. They blame part of it on women's own unrealistic expectations, expectations buoyed by stories of individual successes and by the pronouncements of the women's movement about how fulfilling work outside the home supposedly is.

20   The demands of raising a family are probably the biggest factor driving women out of the corporation. Says Allan Cox, a Chicago executive recruiter: "We have more women than before who are having second thoughts about everything-for-the-career. When the baby comes along, the six-week maternity leave becomes a two-year maternity leave." The notion of the so-called superwoman who successfully manages job and family is far less popular than it was a few years ago. "My perception is that women have given up the goal of being superwomen because it is impossible," observes Eleanor G. May, a University of Virginia Business School professor. "Only a few people can cope, and if you talk to them you discover that they aren't coping satisfactorily, and the stress is greater than they should be handling."

21   Some research even suggests that having a family can hurt women's ca-

reers. In her study of Columbia MBAs from the classes of '69 through '72, Mary Ann Devanna found that only 58% of the women were married, compared with 73% of the men. She concluded: "Women are still asked to pay a significant price for their economic success by limiting the probability that they will also marry." Josephine Olson, a researcher at the University of Pittsburgh, also observes that women who have a managerial career are less likely to have a husband and children. "Why is not clear," Olson says. "Do the MBAs consciously choose to make sacrifices in their personal lives for their careers? Or are the women who are less interested in being wives and mothers the ones who are most interested in being managers?"

No one knows the answer. But women's priorities change as they grow older. The career-minded 25-year-old dynamo is often more concerned about marriage and a family a few years later. Brooke Banbury-Masland, a management specialist at Data General Corp., and Daniel Brass, a Penn State professor, studied 94 MBA women whose average age was 30. They found marriage had overtaken career as what the women valued most. The authors concluded: "As more of the women married, careers did not decrease in importance, but the importance of marriage increased significantly. In response to the statement, 'I feel that a career can take the place of marriage,' most of the sample strongly disagreed."   22

More and more women are deciding to leave companies to go to work for themselves. The number of self-employed women surged from 2.1 million in 1980 to 2.6 million in 1985. The most popular areas to start businesses in are consulting, retail sales, and educational services, followed closely by public relations, real estate, and advertising. . . .   23

The two-career couple, a phenomenon that has become widespread, creates strains that can lead to work force defections. Consider the day-to-day life of Ilene Gordon, a graduate of M.I.T.'s Sloan School of Management and now a vice president of Packaging Corp. of America. Gordon operates on a schedule that would derail Amtrak. Both she and her husband, vice president with the Booz Allen consulting firm, travel frequently for work; sometimes they rendezvous at the airport and take a limo home together. Sunday is the only day of the week they eat dinner with their two small children. Gordon functions on six hours of sleep a night and seems to thrive. She concedes that "I'm probably missing out on some important moments in my daughter's life, but I think I'm getting plenty. Besides, my children have each other."   24

Even the best organized household can be thrown off-balance, though. When the baby sitter does not arrive or a nursery closes down unexpectedly, parents are faced with a decision about who will stay home with the child. Opportunities for one spouse to change jobs or relocate can become traumatic decisions. Couples complain that they have everything except time together.   25

Most companies have been slow to change the aspects of corporate life that drive women out. One problem is that corporations lack data on the phenomenon. Phyllis Silverman, who directed a study of corporate policies on parental leave for Catalyst, a research group that studies issues relating to women in the workplace, says: "Companies are not keeping statistics on how many women leave, how many come back, and how many remain a year after they return from maternity leave. Corporate information is all based on anecdotal evidence about 'that woman' who took maternity leave and never came back." Some executives fear that figures showing an exodus of women due to frustration and lack of promotion could open the way to lawsuits for sex discrimination.   26

27   A number of organizations, though are beginning to awaken to the problem. . . . It has already become acute at certain Big Eight accounting firms, where more than half of new hires are women. At Touche Ross, for example, women have been leaving to work for client companies, where the hours and travel are more predictable. In response the firm is experimenting with a four-day workweek for mothers of young children who want to stay on the partnership track. The short-week path takes ten to 12 years rather than the traditional eight to ten years, but keeps women in the running. Touche Ross refuses to disclose how many women are partners now, and will say only that several junior women are using the short-week path.

28   At other companies women seeking to vary their work schedules are encouraged to cut their own deals with bosses. Corporations generally avoid formal policies on such arrangements as flexible working hours, work at home, shortened workweeks, or job sharing. Despite the publicity generated about telecommuting, for instance, only two companies—Pacific Bell and Mountain Bell—are known to have programs that allow managers to work at home on computer terminals. Lack of flexibility can hurt. Janie Witham, a 1976 Indiana University MBA, was on a managerial career track at IBM—legendary for its consideration of employees—for eight years. She ended up quitting, though, because the company would not allow her to work part time after the birth of her child. . . .

29   Corporations will be under increasing pressure to develop better policies for child care. Many already provide referral services and some have supported independent day-care centers, but only a handful have opened their own on-premise facilities or provided financial assistance for at-home baby sitters.

30   One of the few major U.S. corporations with its own day-care center is Campbell Soup. Some 125 children—80 are on the waiting list—aged 2 months to 5 years spend their day in a center across the street from Campbell's Camden, New Jersey, headquarters. The company picks up half the weekly tab, which can total $95. Campbell President R. Gordon McGovern says the center cuts absenteeism, reduces distractions at work, and enables the company to hire people it could not hire before.

31   Consultants urge companies to survey employees to find out exactly what kind of child care they need. The simplest solution is to give workers more time off, such as when a child is sick. But that's tough to do with managers. Other possibilities include direct payments for child care through a flexible benefits system that also allows workers without children to direct the payments to other purposes. Such benefits are tax deductible to the employer and tax free to the employee, and would remain so under the tax reform bill. Some companies provide counseling on child care and steer parents toward community care programs, which they may also help subsidize. Most employers find they do not want their own day-care centers on the premises. For one thing, parents do not like to commute with their children. For another, the threat of lawsuits against child-care providers has sent insurance premiums spiraling.

32   So what is a company to do? Corporate management is by its nature a consultative process, difficult to pull off unless all the managers are present. But efficient companies should be able to afford women managers more flexibility in their hours, particularly at the beginning and end of the workday. Establishing a separate career track for women to permit extended leaves of absence may seem like perpetuation of their treatment as persons apart. But it may be the only way to keep them in the corporate fold. Companies will have to recognize, too, that

nowadays their best future executives are often married to other promising managers. These busy people may not be willing to relocate or work a 70-hour week.

The tougher challenge for corporations will be to overcome the remaining, sometimes extraordinarily subtle barriers to women's advancement. If employers are serious about treating women equitably, they obviously will have to put them in the same jobs, provide them with the same support, and give them the same power as men. 33

As Rosabeth Kanter [a professor at Harvard Business School] notes, companies have found a place in the managerial work force for the superwoman who came to the job unencumbered by outside obligations. Now, if they want the benefit of her brains, they will have to find a place for the woman with a family. The woman, in short, who is merely human. 34

DISCUSSION QUESTIONS

1. Besides starting the essay, what does Taylor accomplish in his opening paragraph?
2. What purpose do the two examples detailed in paragraphs 5–8 serve? Explain why the essay would have been less effective without these examples.
3. In what part of the essay does Taylor deal with causes? What are these causes? In what order are they arranged?
4. Where does Taylor deal with effects? What are these effects?
5. Note that Taylor concludes his essay with a sentence fragment. How would you justify this fragment?
6. Do you think it would be discriminating against men to grant women managers the special concessions the essay names? Why or why not?

SUGGESTION FOR WRITING ■ Write an essay explaining why you changed your mind about some important matter. For example, you might tell why you altered a decision to attend a certain college or follow a certain career or why you switched your views on marriage, religion, or politics. End the essay by briefly noting one or more effects of the change.

---

going to work for themselves (paragraph 23). Then, turning his attention to employers, he points out that Touche Ross is experimenting with a four-day work week for mothers of young children (paragraph 27), some companies encourage women to negotiate flexible work schedules (paragraph 28), and other companies have established day-care centers for the children of female employees (paragraphs 29 and 30) or are being urged to survey women about their child-care preferences (paragraph 31).

5. Taylor attempts to conclude with punch by using a fragment that calls attention to itself and highlights the situation of the woman who can't be manager, wife, and mother all at once. We always tell our students that even though professional writers sometimes use fragments, complete sentences are expected in freshman English.

6. These questions should prompt a spirited discussion.

OVERVIEW OF DEFINITION ESSAYS (pp. 448–56)

Three of the essays in this section define abstract terms, and one defines a concrete term. In developing their essays, two writers use brief definitions in the form of metaphors (for example, "Waiting is a kind of suspended animation" and "Speaking correct English is 'white'"), a third uses an essential definition, and the fourth uses a variant form of an essential definition that is presented as a question. All four essays employ formal-informal language, one with a noticeable formal slant, and all incorporate some of the other writing strategies.

Lance Morrow

WAITING AS A WAY OF LIFE

Lance Morrow (born 1939) was born in Lewisburg, Pennsylvania, and attended Harvard University, graduating in 1963. After a short stint at the Washington Star*, he moved to* Time *magazine, where he is now a senior writer. His writings for* Time *include numerous cover stories and essays; and he has also authored one book,* The Chief: A Memoir of Fathers and Sons*, in which he explores his relationship with his father. In 1981, he received a National Magazine Award for his essays in* Time*. In our selection, Morrow explores the various facets of one of life's unpleasant necessities: waiting.*

PERSPECTIVE

Most students should be receptive to Morrow's essay since waiting—in cafeteria, registration, book-buying, and library checkout lines—is an all-too-familiar part of their college experience. Students, however, may not have viewed life's waits as burdensome, rendering us helpless and powerless.

Introduction: notes negative aspects of waiting and some ways of coping

1   Waiting is a kind of suspended animation. Time solidifies: a dead weight. The mind reddens a little with anger and then blanks off into a sort of abstraction and fitfully wanders, but presently it comes up red and writhing again, straining to get loose. Waiting casts one's life into a little dungeon of time. It is a way of being controlled, of being rendered immobile and helpless. One can read a book or sing (odd looks from the others) or chat with strangers if the wait is long enough to begin forming a bond of shared experience, as at a snowed-in airport. But people tend to do their waiting stolidly. When the sound system went dead during the campaign debate in 1976, Jerry Ford and Jimmy Carter stood in mute suspension for 27 minutes, looking lost.

Body: paragraphs 2–10

Development by single example

2   To enforce a wait, of course, is to exert power. To wait is to be powerless. Consider one minor, almost subliminal form. The telephone rings. One picks up the receiver and hears a secretary say, "Please hold for Mr. Godot." One sits for perhaps five seconds, the blood pressure just beginning to cook up toward the red line, when Godot comes on the line with a hearty "How are ya?" and business proceeds and the moment passes, Mr. Godot having established that he is (subtly) in control, that his time is more precious than his callee's. (Incidentally, the only effective response to hearing the secretary's "Please hold for . . ." is to hang up without explanation. After two or three times, Mr. Godot himself will place the call, as he should have done at the start.)

Development by single example

3   But the "please hold" ploy is a mere flicker in the annals of great and horrible waiting. Citizens of the Soviet Union would think it bourgeois decadence to complain about such a trifle. The Soviets have turned waiting into a way of life. The numb wait is their negotiating style: a heavy, frozen, wordless impassivity designed to madden and exhaust the people across the table. To exist in the Soviet Union is to wait. Almost perversely, when Soviet shoppers see a line forming, they simply join it, assuming that some scarce item is about to be offered

for sale. A study published by *Pravda* calculates that Soviet citizens waste 37 billion hours a year standing in line to buy food and other basic necessities. To bind an entire people to that kind of life is to do a little of the work of the Gulag in a different style.

Waiting is a form of imprisonment. One is doing time—but why? One is being punished not for an offense of one's own but often for the inefficiencies of those who impose the wait. Hence the peculiar rage that waits engender, the sense of injustice. Aside from boredom and physical discomfort, the subtler misery of waiting is the knowledge that one's most precious resource, time, a fraction of one's life, is being stolen away, irrecoverably lost.

4 | Development by cause and effect

Americans have ample miseries of waiting, of course—waits sometimes connected with affluence and leisure. The lines to get a passport in Manhattan last week stretched around the block in Rockefeller Center. Travelers waited four and five hours just to get into bureaucracy's front door. A Washington *Post* editorial writer reported a few days ago that the passengers on her 747, diverted to Hartford, Conn., on the return flight from Rome as a result of bad weather in New York City, were forced to sit on a runway for seven hours because no customs inspectors were on hand to process them.

5 | Development by two brief examples

The great American waits are often democratic enough, like traffic jams. Some of the great waits have been collective, tribal—waiting for the release of the American hostages in Iran, for example. But waiting often makes class distinctions. One of the more depressing things about being poor in America is the endless waiting in welfare or unemployment lines. The waiting rooms of the poor are forlorn, but in fact almost all waiting rooms are spiritless and blank-eyed places where it always feels like 3 in the morning.

6 | Paragraphs 6 and 7: development by comparison

One of the inestimable advantages of wealth is the immunity that it can purchase from serious waiting. The rich do not wait in long lines to buy groceries or airplane tickets. The help sees to it. The limousine takes the privileged right out onto the tarmac, their shoes barely grazing the ground.

7

People wait when they have no choice or when they believe that the wait is justified by the reward—a concert ticket, say. Waiting has its social orderings, its rules and assumptions. Otherwise peaceful citizens explode when someone cuts into a line that has been waiting a long time. It is unjust; suffering is not being fairly distributed. Oddly, behavioral scientists have found that the strongest protests tend to come from the immediate victims, the people directly behind the line jumpers. People farther down the line complain less or not at all, even though they have been equally penalized by losing a place.

8 | Development by cause and effect, comparison

Waiting is difficult for children. They have not yet developed an experienced relationship with time and its durations: "Are we there yet, Daddy?" There can be pleasant, tingling waits, of course, full of fantasies, and they are often connected with children: the wait for the child to arrive in the first place, the wait for Christmas, for summer vacation. Children wait more intensely than adults do. Sheer anticipation makes their blood jump in a lovely way.

9 | Development by comparison

Waiting can have a delicious quality ("I can't wait to see her." "I can't wait for the party"), and sometimes the waiting is better than the event awaited. At the other extreme, it can shade into terror: when one waits for a child who is late coming home or—most horribly—has vanished. When anyone has disappeared, in fact, or is missing in action, the ordinary stress of waiting is overlaid with an unbearable anguish of speculation: Alive or dead?

10 | Development by comparison

Conclusion: contains an ironic twist

Waiting can seem an interval of nonbeing, the blank space between events

11

1. Morrow's purpose might be stated in this way: to wait is to be controlled, powerless, even imprisoned. Several parts of the essay convey this notion. Paragraph 1: "straining to get loose," "little dungeon of time," "way of . . . being rendered immobile and helpless." Paragraph 2: "exert power" and "to be powerless," "he is (subtly) in control." Paragraph 3: the Soviet "negotiating style" and the reference to "the Gulag." Paragraph 4: "form of imprisonment" and "stolen away, irrecoverably lost." Paragraphs 5–10 show various manifestations of waiting and the resultant helplessness.

2. Morrow writes for a general, intelligent audience, one that does not consist of a certain age group and that is not marked by specialized knowledge or particular interests. His examples are drawn from all levels—children, rich, poor—and they will be familiar to most of us: traffic jams, American hostages in Iran, waiting for concert tickets. In addition, his sentences and words, as well as the notation that the essay originally appeared in *Time*, suggest this general, intelligent audience.

PERSPECTIVE

Students, both before and after graduation, are likely to formulate personal notions about what success means to them. In the 1990s, greed seems to be less of a driving force than it was for some in the 1980s. As a result, Shames's essay should provide relevant reading.

and the outcomes of desires. It makes time maddeningly elastic: it has a way of seeming to compact eternity into a few hours. Yet its brackets ultimately expand to the largest dimensions. One waits for California to drop into the sea or for "next year in Jerusalem" or for the Messiah or for the Apocalypse. All life is a waiting, and perhaps in that sense one should not be too eager for the wait to end. The region that lies on the other side of waiting is eternity.

DISCUSSION QUESTIONS

1. What is Morrow's purpose in writing this definition? Cite specific parts of the essay to defend your answer.

2. For what audience does he write? How do you know?

SUGGESTION FOR WRITING ■ **Write an essay that defines speed or efficiency as a way of life. Use the methods of development that seem most appropriate.**

Laurence Shames

THE SWEET SMELL OF SUCCESS ISN'T ALL THAT SWEET

Laurence Shames (born 1951) is a native of Newark, New Jersey, and a graduate of New York University. After completing his education, he began a career as a nonfiction writer, contributing to such publications as Playboy, McCall's, Esquire, Vanity Fair, *and the* New York Times. *A 1986 book,* The Big Time: The Harvard Business School's Most Successful Class and How It Shaped America, *explores the contributions of the 1949 graduating class to the worlds of business and public service. Shames's writings reflect a strong concern for values, a concern apparent in the following selection, which attacks contemporary attitudes about success.*

1   John Milton was a failure. In writing "Paradise Lost," his stated aim was to "justify the ways of God to men." Inevitably, he fell short of accomplishing that and only wrote a monumental poem. Beethoven, whose music was conceived to transcend Fate, was a failure, as was Socrates, whose ambition was to make people happy by making them reasonable and just. The inescapable conclusion seems to be that the surest, noblest way to fail is to set one's own standards titanically high.

2   The flip-side of that proposition also seems true, and it provides the safe but dreary logic by which most of us live: The surest way to succeed is to keep one's strivings low—or at least to direct them along already charted paths. Don't set yourself the probably thankless task of making the legal system better; just shoot at becoming a partner in the firm. Don't agonize over questions about where your

talents and proclivities might most fulfillingly lead you; just do a heads-up job of determining where the educational or business opportunities seem most secure.

After all, if "success" itself—rather than the substance of the achievements that make for success—is the criterion by which we measure ourselves and from which we derive our self-esteem, why make things more difficult by reaching for the stars?

What is this contemporary version of success really all about?

According to certain beer commercials, it consists in moving up to a premium brand that costs a dime or so more per bottle. Credit-card companies would have you believe success inheres in owning their particular piece of plastic.

If these examples sound petty, they are. But take those petty privileges, weave them into a fabric that passes for a value system and what you've got is a national mood that has vast motivating power that can shape at least the near future of the entire company.

Under the flag of success, modern-style, liberal arts colleges are withering while business schools are burgeoning—and yet even business schools are having an increasingly hard time finding faculty members, because teaching isn't considered "successful" enough. Amid a broad consensus that there is a glut of lawyers and an epidemic of strangling litigation, record numbers of young people continue to flock to law school because, for the individual practitioner, a law degree is still considered a safe ticket.

The most sobering thought of all is that today's M.B.A.'s and lawyers are tomorrow's M.B.A.'s and lawyers: Having invested so much time and money in their training, only a tiny percentage of them will ever opt out of their early chosen fields. Decisions made in accordance with today's hothouse notions of ambition are locking people into careers that will define and also limit their activities and yearnings for virtually the rest of their lives.

Many, by external standards, will be "successes." They will own homes, eat in better restaurants, dress well and, in some instances, perform socially useful work. Yet there is a deadening and dangerous flaw in their philosophy: It has little room, little sympathy and less respect for the noble failure, for the person who ventures past the limits, who aims gloriously high and falls unashamedly short.

That sort of ambition doesn't have much place in a world where success is proved by worldly reward rather than by accomplishment itself. That sort of ambition is increasingly thought of as the domain of irredeemable eccentrics, of people who haven't quite caught on—and there is great social pressure not to be one of them.

The result is that fewer people are drawn to the cutting edge of noncommercial scientific research. Fewer are taking on the sublime, unwinnable challenges of the arts. Fewer are asking questions that matter—the ones that can't be answered. Fewer are putting themselves on the line, making as much of their minds and talents as they might.

The irony is that today's success-chasers seem obsessed with the idea of *not settling*. They take advanced degrees in business because they won't settle for just a so-so job. They compete for slots at law firms and investment houses because they won't settle for any but the fastest track. They seem to regard it as axiomatic that "success" and "settling" are opposites.

Yet in doggedly pursuing the rather brittle species of success now in fashion, they are restricting themselves to a chokingly narrow swath of turf along the entire range of human possibilities. Does it ever occur to them that, frequently,

3

4

5

6

7

8

9

10

11

12

13

success is what people settle for when they can't think of something noble enough to be worth failing at?

DISCUSSION QUESTIONS

1. Shames clearly signals his ironic intent by emphasizing the noble aims of Milton, Beethoven, and Socrates and by noting that although Milton failed to "justify the ways of God to men," he did produce a "monumental poem." Indeed, the fact that Shames cites men whose achievements have survived for centuries shows that he doesn't seriously consider them failures.

2. Shames is making the point that we define success by the trappings associated with financial advancement rather than by the actual accomplishment. The trappings include such things as the premium beer and credit cards mentioned in paragraph 5 and the homes, elegant meals, and fine clothing alluded to in paragraph 9. Because this distinction highlights the contemporary definition of success, Shames positions it ahead of the paragraphs that elaborate upon it.

3. The essay uses the following writing strategies: Paragraph 1: examples; paragraph 3: comparison; paragraph 5: examples and brief definitions; paragraph 7: comparison and examples; paragraph 9: comparison; paragraphs 10 and 11: cause (10) and effect (11); paragraphs 12 and 13: cause (12) and effect (13).

4. A rhetorical question produces a stronger emphasis than an assertion; thus it draws reader attention.

5. This question should prompt a stimulating discussion.

PERSPECTIVE

Although this essay is about blacks, other groups—racial, religious, ethnic, and national—bear burdens of harmful definition, while yet others enjoy the advantages of favorable definition. The

DISCUSSION QUESTIONS

1. In paragraph 1 Shames asserts that Milton, Beethoven, and Socrates were failures. How do you know that he doesn't intend these statements to be taken seriously?

2. Shames notes in paragraph 3 that " 'success' itself—rather than the substance of the achievements that make for success—" seems to be the touchstone by which we measure our worth. What do you think he means? Why is the distinction positioned at this point?

3. What writing strategies does Shames use to develop his essay? Where does he use them?

4. Why do you think Shames ends his essay with a rhetorical question, that is, one for which no answer is expected?

5. To what extent do you agree with Shames's idea of success? Discuss.

SUGGESTION FOR WRITING ■ Write a definition essay explaining how the popular view of responsibility, greed, marriage, single life, friendship, or some other concept needs redefining. Use whatever writing strategies advance your purpose.

William Raspberry

THE HANDICAP OF DEFINITION

William Raspberry (born 1935) grew up in Okolona, Mississippi, and received his education at Indiana Central College, where he earned a Bachelor of Science degree in 1958. In college, he worked as a reporter for the Indianapolis Recorder *and following graduation continued with that publication until he entered the army. In 1962, after his military service, he began working for the* Washington Post, *an association that continues to the present. Raspberry now authors a nationally syndicated column dealing with current issues, such as criminal justice and minority concerns. In this essay, he discusses the ramifications of current views on what it means to be black.*

1   I know all about bad schools, mean politicians, economic deprivation and racism. Still, it occurs to me that one of the heaviest burdens black Americans—and black children in particular—have to bear is the handicap of definition: the question of what it means to be black.

2   Let me explain quickly what I mean. If a basketball fan says that the Boston Celtics' Larry Bird plays "black," the fan intends it—and Bird probably accepts it—as a compliment. Tell pop singer Tom Jones he moves "black" and he might grin in appreciation. Say to Teena Marie or The Average White Band that they sound "black" and they'll thank you.

But name one pursuit, aside from athletics, entertainment or sexual performance in which a white practitioner will feel complimented to be told he does it "black." Tell a white broadcaster he talks "black," and he'll sign up for diction lessons. Tell a white reporter he writes "black," and he'll take a writing course. Tell a white lawyer he reasons "black" and he might sue you for slander. 3

What we have here is a tragically limited definition of blackness, and it isn't only white people who buy it. 4

Think of all the ways black children can put one another down with charges of "whiteness." For many of these children, hard study and hard work are "white." Trying to please a teacher might be criticized as acting "white." Speaking correct English is "white." Scrimping today in the interest of tomorrow's goals is "white." Educational toys and games are "white." 5

An incredible array of habits and attitudes that are conducive to success in business, in academia, in the non-entertainment professions are likely to be thought of as somehow "white." Even economic success, unless it involves such "black" undertakings as numbers banking, is defined as "white." 6

And the results are devastating. I wouldn't deny that blacks often are better entertainers and athletes. My point is the harm that comes from too narrow a definition of what is black. 7

One reason black youngsters tend to do better at basketball, for instance, is that they assume they can learn to do it well, and so they practice constantly to prove themselves right. 8

Wouldn't it be wonderful if we would infect black children with the notion that excellence in math is "black" rather than white, or possibly Chinese? Wouldn't it be of enormous value if we could create the myth that morality, strong families, determination, courage and love of learning are traits brought by slaves from Mother Africa and therefore quintessentially black? 9

There is no doubt in my mind that most black youngsters could develop their mathematical reasoning, their elocution and their attitudes the way they develop their jump shots and their dance steps: by the combination of sustained, enthusiastic practice and the unquestioned belief that they can do it. 10

In one sense, what I am talking about is the importance of developing positive ethnic traditions. Maybe Jews have an innate talent for communication; maybe the Chinese are born with a gift for mathematical reasoning; maybe blacks are naturally blessed with athletic grace. I doubt it. What is at work, I suspect, is assumption, inculcated early in their lives, that this is a thing our people do well. 11

Unfortunately, many of the things about which blacks make this assumption are things that do not contribute to their career success—except for that handful of the truly gifted who can make it as entertainers and athletes. And many of the things we concede to whites are the things that are essential to economic security. 12

So it is with a number of assumptions black youngsters make about what it is to be a "man": physical aggressiveness, sexual prowess, the refusal to submit to authority. The prisons are full of people who, by this perverted definition, are unmistakably men. 13

But the real problem is not so much that the things defined as "black" are negative. The problem is that the definition is much too narrow. 14

Somehow, we have to make our children understand that they are intelligent, competent people, capable of doing whatever they put their minds to and making it in the American mainstream, not just in a black subculture. 15

definition may be imposed from inside or outside the group, or it may be the result of interior and exterior forces acting together. Whatever its origin, definition, favorable or unfavorable, plays an important role in shaping the status and prospects of individuals. For this reason, it is important that students understand its operation, especially in regard to themselves.

TEACHING STRATEGY

Ask students to speculate on the causes of the present definition of "black" and what steps might be taken to develop a more positive and helpful definition.

CLASSROOM ACTIVITY

You might have students consider their race, religion, ethnic background, or social class and then develop definitions of them. To avoid one-sidedness, students should consider both favorable and unfavorable elements. This activity could lead to a definition paper.

DISCUSSION QUESTIONS

1. Raspberry demonstrates that he is aware of other major factors that affect blacks negatively. Despite these factors, however, he regards the question of what it means to be black as one of the "heaviest burdens" borne by his race.

2. Illustration is used in paragraphs 2, 3, 5, 6, and 11; comparison in paragraphs 2, 3, 15, and 16; and cause and effect in paragraphs 2, 3, 5–8, 10, and 11. A brief definition occurs in paragraph 13.

3. The purpose of a rhetorical question is not to elicit a response but to provide greater emphasis than an assertion. By using these questions, Raspberry calls the reader's attention forcefully to points he considers especially important.

4. The short sentence helps to undercut the preceding "maybe" sentences. In addition, a short sentence, sandwiched between two longer ones, hits with greater emphasis.

5. As the headnote to this essay indicates, Raspberry is a syndicated columnist. He therefore follows the journalistic practice of using short paragraphs, which are easier to read than longer ones.

6. The final two paragraphs make the point that blacks must be convinced they are intelligent, capable people who can succeed in the mainstream world.

16   What we seem to be doing, instead, is raising up yet another generation of young blacks who will be failures—by definition.

DISCUSSION QUESTIONS

1. Why does Raspberry start his essay by listing the four factors mentioned in his opening sentence?

2. What writing strategies does Raspberry use to develop his definition? Refer to specific parts of the essay when answering.

3. Raspberry uses two rhetorical questions in paragraph 9. Read them again and then develop a definition that indicates what a rhetorical question is and what it achieves.

4. Discuss the effect that Raspberry achieves by using the short sentence "I doubt it" in paragraph 11.

5. How do you account for the short paragraphs that Raspberry uses?

6. What is the function of the final two paragraphs of the essay?

SUGGESTION FOR WRITING ■ Write an essay defining what it means to be male, female, black, Hispanic, or a member of some other group. Use three or more writing strategies to develop your essay.

PERSPECTIVE

Rigid bureaucratic policies enforced by inflexible people have frustrated all of us at one time or another. It is of course much easier to mouth the words, "I'm sorry, but that's the policy here" than it is to make individual adjustments for specific circumstances. "The Bureaucrat" should make for interesting reading.

TEACHING STRATEGIES

1. Ask the class to explain the statement in paragraph 1 that "it is the bureaucrat who makes the milieu, not the other way around" and why this statement is positioned at the outset.

2. You might discuss the parallelism, and even the alliteration, in paragraph 10.

3. Have students explain the meaning and significance of the following statements: Paragraph 13: ". . . one who,

Citicorp N. A.

THE BUREAUCRAT

At one time or another, almost everyone has run afoul of bureaucratic bungling and red tape. Why do such difficulties occur so often? In the selection below, the anonymous author defines "bureaucrat" and clears up the mystery for us.

1   Bureaucracy is a state of mind. True, every bureaucrat needs an organization, a milieu—to choose another useful word from the French—but it is the bureaucrat who makes the milieu, not the other way around.

2   Most of us associate bureaucracy and all its attendant evils with large organizations, especially governments, and we are not surprised to see it getting worse. As the earth's population grows and computers multiply along with the people, burgeoning bureaucracy appears a natural consequence. What Thomas Carlyle, a hundred years ago, could dismiss contemptuously as "the Continental nuisance called 'Bureaucracy'" is now to become the fate of all humanity because there are so many of us.

3   Before resigning ourselves to the inevitable, however, we might pause to consider that one of the most pervasive bureaucracies the world has ever known was oppressing the population of the Nile Valley 5,000 years ago, when there were fewer people in the entire world than now live in North America. Add to this the thought that the same number of people can be organized into (*a*) an army,

(*b*) a crowd or (*c*) a mob, and it is clear that something more must be involved than time and numbers.

What distinguishes each of the aforementioned groups is not how many people it contains, nor where they happen to congregate, but their purpose for being there. And so it is with the bureaucrat.

The true bureaucrat is any individual who has lost sight of the underlying purpose of the job at hand, whether in government, industry—or a bank. The purpose of a library, for example, is to facilitate the reading of books. Yet to a certain type of librarian, perfection consists of a well-stocked library with a place for every book—and every book in its place. The reader who insists on taking books home, leaving empty spaces on shelves, is this librarian's natural enemy.

It is a cast of mind invulnerable even to the vicissitudes of war. We see it in James Jones's novel *From Here to Eternity* where American soldiers under surprise attack by Japanese planes at the outbreak of World War II rush to the arsenal for weapons, only to find the door barred by a comrade-in-arms loudly proclaiming that he cannot pass out live ammunition without a written request signed by a commissioned officer.

One of these custodians forgot the purpose of a library, the other, the purpose of an army. Both illustrate how, in institutionalized endeavors, means have a way of displacing the ends they are originally designed to serve. In fact, it is one of the bureaucrat's distinguishing features that, for him or for her, the means *become* the ends.

The struggle to prevent this subtle subversion is—or should be—a continual challenge to every policymaker in any organization, public or private. Bureaucrats love any policy and can be counted on to enforce it faithfully, as in, "I'm sorry, but that's the policy here." Unfortunately, they don't understand what a policy is.

A policy is a standard solution to a constantly recurring problem, not an inviolable law. As a weapon in the hands of literal-minded people, however, a "firm policy" can be as deadly as a repeating rifle. When matters finally become intolerable, the harassed administrator will usually "change the policy." Of course, this never helps because the problem was not the policy in the first place, but the manner of its application.

Every college student seeking entry into a course for which he lacks the exact prerequisite, every shopper trying to return a gift without receipt of purchase, every bank customer seeking to correct an error in an account is in danger of discovering that the rules imagined by Joseph Heller are in service wherever rote is more revered than reason.

The application of binary logic to human affairs through electronic computers has done nothing to retard the spread of *Catch 22* into the wider world. And thus the thought occurs that modern bureaucracy does, after all, present some problems new to history. Nothing lends itself so readily to "a standard solution to a constantly recurring problem" as a computer.

In the best of all possible worlds we might look forward to the day when computers handle all standard solutions, freeing human brains to concentrate on the singular and the exceptional. In the real world, it does not always work out that way—as anyone knows who has ever become trapped in a two-way correspondence with a computer and appealed in vain for human intervention.

A favorite student protest sign of the sixties read, "I am a Human Being. Do not fold, spindle or mutilate." What they objected to is real, only the fault is not in

(marginal paragraph numbers: 4, 5, 6, 7, 8, 9, 10, 11, 12, 13)

having forgotten his purpose, redoubles his efforts." Paragraph 14: "We has met the enemy, and they is us."
4. Ask what is accomplished by beginning and ending the essay with the assertion that "Bureaucracy is a state of mind." The answer of course requires an understanding of the entire essay.

CLASSROOM ACTIVITY

Divide the class into small groups and ask students to identify and describe examples of bureaucrats. They might start with college bureaucrats they have encountered. The group discussions could culminate in reports that are presented to the entire class and serve as the springboard for a writing assignment.

DISCUSSION QUESTIONS (p. 456)

1. The first sentence of paragraph 5 is the essential definition of "bureaucrat," and the first sentence of paragraph 9 is the essential definition of "policy." Note that if the core of an extended definition is an essential definition, that essential definition need not be placed in the opening paragraph.
2. Paragraph 3 is developed indirectly by negation—pointing out what a bureaucracy *isn't*. ". . . it is clear

that something more must be involved than time and numbers." This statement corrects the misconception, raised in paragraph 2, that bureaucracy is a natural consequence of population growth. Paragraphs 5 and 6 are developed by illustrations, the librarian and the comrade-in-arms.

3. The purpose is to caution readers about the dangers of a bureaucrat who adheres rigidly to policy. The illustrations in paragraphs 5 and 6, the discussion of policy in paragraph 9, the cautions against letting means become ends in paragraphs 7 and 13, and the caution not to be a bureaucrat in paragraph 15 all relate to this purpose.

4. The essay says that the struggle against bureaucracy challenges "every policy-maker in any organization, public or private" (paragraph 8) and urges the reader "not to be a bureaucrat" (paragraph 15). Thus it is aimed at people who could become bureaucrats.

14   our computers, but in ourselves. It lies in our human propensity to let means become ends, and all too often to resemble Santayana's description of a fanatic; one who, having forgotten his purpose, redoubles his efforts.

14   We can denounce the bureaucrats and condemn their works, but they will not go away. They have been with us since the dawn of history, and if they seem to be getting worse, it is because *we* are getting worse. For, in the words of the comic strip *Pogo*: "We has met the enemy, and they is us."

15   Bureaucracy is a state of mind, and the best way to fight it—whether you work for government, industry, a private foundation or a bank—is not to be a bureaucrat. Or at least try not to.

DISCUSSION QUESTIONS

1. Where does the essential definition of *bureaucrat* appear? The essential definition of *policy*?

2. What methods of writing are used to develop paragraphs 3, 5, and 6?

3. What seems to be the purpose of this essay? Refer to specific parts of the text to explain your answer.

4. To what audience is it addressed? Again, when answering cite appropriate examples.

SUGGESTION FOR WRITING ■ Write a definition of a corporate raider or a politician. Aim your essay at a specific audience and develop it with several strategies of writing.

Argument

Edward I. Koch

DEATH AND JUSTICE

Edward Koch (born 1924) is a native of New York, a veteran of World War II, and a graduate of New York University, where he earned a law degree in 1948. For some two decades after graduation, he practiced law in New York City, during which time he began playing an active role in Democratic party politics. In 1966, he became a district leader and three years later was elected to the City Council. Between 1969 and 1977, he served in the U.S. House of Representatives, where he became known for his strong liberal stance on social issues. In 1977, he waged a successful campaign for mayor of New York, pledging to cut crime and reduce wasteful spending. He held the mayor's office until 1990. While mayor, Koch authored two books: Mayor *(1984), an examination of his city's politics, and* Politics *(1985), which records his years as a political fledgling. The following essay, which critiques the views of those opposed to capital punishment, reflects Koch's long-term commitment to crime fighting.*

Last December a man named Robert Lee Willie, who had been convicted of raping and murdering an 18-year-old woman, was executed in the Louisiana state prison. In a statement issued several minutes before his death, Mr. Willie said: "Killing people is wrong. . . . It makes no difference whether it's citizens, countries, or governments. Killing is wrong." Two weeks later in South Carolina, an admitted killer named Joseph Carl Shaw was put to death for murdering two teenagers. In an appeal to the governor for clemency, Mr. Shaw wrote: "Killing is wrong when I did it. Killing is wrong when you do it. I hope you have the courage and moral strength to stop the killing."

It is a curiosity of modern life that we find ourselves being lectured on morality by cold-blooded killers. Mr. Willie previously had been convicted of aggravated rape, aggravated kidnapping, and the murders of a Louisiana deputy and a man from Missouri. Mr. Shaw committed another murder a week before the two for which he was executed, and admitted mutilating the body of the 14-year-old girl he killed. I can't help wondering what prompted these murderers to speak out against killing as they entered the death-house door. Did their new-found reverence for life stem from the realization that they were about to lose their own?

Life is indeed precious, and I believe the death penalty helps to affirm this fact. Had the death penalty been a real possibility in the minds of these murderers, they might well have stayed their hand. They might have shown moral awareness before their victims died, and not after. Consider the tragic death of Rosa Velez, who happened to be home when a man named Luis Vera burglarized her apart-

Four of the five argument essays rely primarily upon rational appeal, and the remaining one combines emotional and ethical appeal. Three of the essayists offer authoritative opinion and statistical findings, one cites historical facts, and one relies upon personal experience and enlightened common sense. Four of the essays use formal-informal language, and one is highly formal. All draw upon writing strategies discussed in the rhetoric section.

PERSPECTIVE

Koch makes his case for the death penalty by refuting, one after the other, opposition arguments against capital punishment. Perhaps because the issue is so controversial, Koch takes special care to project a favorable image of himself both near the beginning and at the end of his essay. The primary appeal, however, is rational.

1 | Introduction: paragraphs 1 and 2
Examples

2 | Provides background

3 | Body: paragraphs 3–14
Proposition of fact

Development by example

457

ment in Brooklyn. "Yeah, I shot her," Vera admitted. "She knew me, and I knew I wouldn't go to the chair."

Author's qualifications

4   During my 22 years in public service, I have heard the pros and cons of capital punishment expressed with special intensity. As a district leader, councilman, congressman, and mayor, I have represented constituencies generally thought of as liberal. Because I support the death penalty for heinous crimes of murder, I have sometimes been the subject of emotional and outraged attacks by voters who find my position reprehensible or worse. I have listened to their ideas. I have weighed their objections carefully. I still support the death penalty. The reasons I maintained my position can be best understood by examining the arguments most frequently heard in opposition.

Author's qualifications

Ethical appeal

First refutation: rejects emotional appeal

5   1. *The death penalty is "barbaric."* Sometimes opponents of capital punishment horrify with tales of lingering death on the gallows, of faulty electric chairs, or of agony in the gas chamber. Partly in response to such protests, several states such as North Carolina and Texas switched to execution by lethal injection. The condemned person is put to death painlessly, without ropes, voltage, bullets, or gas. Did this answer the objections of death penalty opponents? Of course not. On June 22, 1984, The *New York Times* published an editorial that sarcastically attacked the new "hygienic" method of death by injection, and stated that "execution can never be made humane through science." So it's not the method that really troubles opponents. It's the death itself they consider barbaric.

Concedes point
Rational appeal: analogy

6   Admittedly, capital punishment is not a pleasant topic. However, one does not have to like the death penalty in order to support it any more than one must like radical surgery, radiation, or chemotherapy in order to find necessary these attempts at curing cancer. Ultimately we may learn how to cure cancer with a simple pill. Unfortunately, that day has not yet arrived. Today we are faced with the choice of letting the cancer spread or trying to cure it with the methods available, methods that one day will almost certainly be considered barbaric. But to give up and do nothing would be far more barbaric and would certainly delay the discovery of an eventual cure. The analogy between cancer and murder is imperfect, because murder is not the "disease" we are trying to cure. The disease is injustice. We may not like the death penalty, but it must be available to punish crimes of cold-blooded murder, cases in which any other form of punishment would be inadequate and, therefore, unjust. If we create a society in which injustice is not tolerated, incidents of murder—the most flagrant form of injustice—will diminish.

Ethical appeal: concedes point

Second refutation

7   2. *No other major democracy uses the death penalty.* No other major democracy—in fact, few other countries of any description—are plagued by a murder rate such as that in the United States. Fewer and fewer Americans can remember the days when unlocked doors were the norm and murder was a rare and terrible offense. In America the murder rate climbed 122 percent between 1963 and 1980. During that same period, the murder rate in New York City increased by almost 400 percent, and the statistics are even worse in many other cities. A study at M.I.T. showed that based on 1970 homicide rates a person who lived in a large American city ran a greater risk of being murdered than an American soldier in World War II ran of being killed in combat. It is not surprising that the laws of each country differ according to differing conditions and traditions. If other countries had our murder problem, the cry for capital punishment would be just as loud as it is here. And I daresay that any other major democracy

Evidence: statistics

where 75 percent of the people supported the death penalty would soon enact it into law.

3. *An innocent person might be executed by mistake.* Consider the work of Adam Bedau, one of the most implacable foes of capital punishment in this country. According to Mr. Bedau, it is "false sentimentality to argue that the death penalty should be abolished because of the abstract possibility that an innocent person might be executed." He cites a study of the 7,000 executions in this country from 1893 to 1971, and concludes that the record fails to show that such cases occur. The main point, however, is this. If government functioned only when the possibility of error didn't exist, government wouldn't function at all. Human life deserves special protection, and one of the best ways to guarantee that protection is to assure that convicted murderers do not kill again. Only the death penalty can accomplish this end. In a recent case in New Jersey, a man named Richard Biegenwald was freed from prison after serving 18 years for murder; since his release he has been convicted of committing four murders. A prisoner named Lemuel Smith, who, while serving four life sentences for murder (plus two life sentences for kidnapping and robbery) in New York's Green Haven Prison, lured a woman corrections officer into the chaplain's office and strangled her. He then mutilated and dismembered her body. An additional life sentence for Smith is meaningless. Because New York has no death penalty statute, Smith has effectively been given a license to kill.

But the problem of multiple murder is not confined to the nation's penitentiaries. In 1981, 91 police officers were killed in the line of duty in this country. Seven percent of those arrested in the cases that have been solved had a previous arrest for murder. In New York City in 1976 and 1977, 85 persons arrested for homicide had a previous arrest for murder. Six of these individuals had two previous arrests for murder, and one had four previous murder arrests. During those two years the New York police were arresting for murder persons with a previous arrest for murder on the average of one every 8.5 days. This is not surprising when we learn that in 1975, for example, the median time served in Massachusetts for homicide was less than two-and-a half years. In 1976 a study sponsored by the Twentieth Century Fund found that the average time served in the United States for first-degree murder is ten years. The median time served may be considerably lower.

4. *Capital punishment cheapens the value of human life.* On the contrary, it can be easily demonstrated that the death penalty strengthens the value of human life. If the penalty for rape were lowered, clearly it would signal a lessened regard for the victims' suffering, humiliation, and personal integrity. It would cheapen their horrible experience, and expose them to an increased danger of recurrence. When we lower the penalty for murder, it signals a lessened regard for the value of the victim's life. Some critics of capital punishment, such as columnist Jimmy Breslin, have suggested that a life sentence is actually a harsher penalty for murder than death. This is sophistic nonsense. A few killers may decide not to appeal a death sentence, but the overwhelming majority make every effort to stay alive. It is by exacting the highest penalty for the taking of human life that we affirm the highest value of human life.

5. *The death penalty is applied in a discriminatory manner.* This factor no longer seems to be the problem it once was. The appeals process for a condemned prisoner is lengthy and painstaking. Every effort is made to see that the

8 | Third refutation |

| Evidence: statistics |

| Established truths |

| Development by examples |

| Emotional appeal |

9 | Evidence: statistics |

10 | Fourth refutation |

| Rational appeal: analogy |

11 | Fifth refutation |

verdict and sentence were fairly arrived at. However, assertions of discrimination are not an argument for ending the death penalty but for extending it. It is not justice to exclude everyone from the penalty of the law if a few are found to be so favored. Justice requires that the law be applied equally to all.

12   6. *Thou shalt not kill*. The Bible is our greatest source of moral inspiration. Opponents of the death penalty frequently cite the sixth of the Ten Commandments in an attempt to prove that capital punishment is divinely proscribed. In the original Hebrew, however, the Sixth Commandment reads, "Thou Shalt Not Commit Murder," and the Torah specifies capital punishment for a variety of offenses. The biblical viewpoint has been upheld by philosophers throughout history. The greatest thinkers of the 19th century—Kant, Locke, Hobbes, Rousseau, Montesquieu, and Mill—agreed that natural law properly authorizes the sovereign to take life in order to vindicate justice. Only Jeremy Bentham was ambivalent. Washington, Jefferson, and Franklin endorsed it. Abraham Lincoln authorized executions for deserters in wartime. Alexis de Tocqueville, who expressed profound respect for American institutions, believed that the death penalty was indispensable to the support of social order. The United States Constitution, widely admired as one of the seminal achievements in the history of humanity, condemns cruel and inhuman punishment, but does not condemn capital punishment.

13   7. *The death penalty is state-sanctioned murder*. This is the defense with which Messrs. Willie and Shaw hoped to soften the resolve of those who sentenced them to death. By saying in effect, "You're no better than I am," the murderer seeks to bring his accusers down to his own level. It is also a popular argument among opponents of capital punishment, but a transparently false one. Simply put, the state has rights that the private individual does not. In a democracy, those rights are given to the state by the electorate. The execution of a lawfully

condemned killer is no more an act of murder than is legal imprisonment an act of kidnapping. If an individual forces a neighbor to pay him money under threat of punishment, it's called extortion. If the state does it, it's called taxation. Rights and responsibilities surrendered by the individual are what give the state its power to govern. This contract is the foundation of civilization itself.

14   Everyone wants his or her rights, and will defend them jealously. Not everyone, however, wants responsibilities, especially the painful responsibilities that come with law enforcement. Twenty-one years ago a woman named Kitty Genovese was assaulted and murdered on a street in New York. Dozens of

neighbors heard her cries for help but did nothing to assist her. They didn't even call the police. In such a climate the criminal understandably grows bolder. In the presence of moral cowardice, he lectures us on our supposed failings and tries to equate his crimes with our quest for justice.

15   The death of anyone—even a convicted killer—diminishes us all. But we are diminished even more by a justice system that fails to function. It is an illusion to let ourselves believe that doing away with capital punishment removes the murderer's deed from our conscience. The rights of society are paramount. When we protect guilty lives, we give up innocent lives in exchange. When opponents of capital punishment say to the state: "I will not let you kill in my name," they are also saying to murderers: "You can kill in your *own* name as long as I have an excuse for not getting involved."

16   It is hard to imagine anything worse than being murdered while neighbors do nothing. But something worse exists. When those same neighbors shrink back from justly punishing the murderer, the victim dies twice.

DISCUSSION QUESTIONS

1. Why do you think Koch ends paragraph 2 with a question rather than a direct statement of his opinion?
2. Why does Koch tell us in paragraph 8 that Bedau is "one of the most implacable foes of capital punishment in this country"?
3. Why do you think Koch devotes most of his essay to refuting opposition arguments?

SUGGESTION FOR WRITING ■ Write an essay that argues against capital punishment and that refutes Koch's evidence. If you agree with Koch, select another controversial issue (perhaps a particular solution to the waste disposal or street crime problem), take a position, and argue for it.

Barbara Ehrenreich

TEACH DIVERSITY—WITH A SMILE

Barbara Ehrenreich, a native of Butte, Montana, was born in 1941. After completing an undergraduate degree at Reed College, she earned a doctorate at Rockefeller University. Ehrenreich's writings, shaped by a liberal perspective, offer sharp commentary on an array of political and social issues. Her book-length works include a study of the failings of America's public-health empire and several books on gender issues. Her articles have appeared in a variety of magazines, including Esquire, Vogue, Nation, New Republic, *and* Time, *among others. In our selection, Ehrenreich offers her thoughts on the significance of multicultural education and the tactics of its supporters and opponents.*

Something had to replace the threat of communism, and at last a workable substitute is at hand. "Multiculturalism," as the new menace is known, has been denounced in the media recently as the new McCarthyism[1], the new fundamentalism, even the new totalitarianism—take your choice. According to its critics, who include a flock of tenured conservative scholars, multiculturalism aims to toss out what it sees as the Eurocentric bias in education and replace Plato with Ntozake Shange and traditional math with the Yoruba number system. And that's just the beginning. The Jacobins[2] of the multiculturalist movement, who are described

[1]McCarthyism features the use of indiscriminate and often baseless accusations, together with intimidating investigative methods, to achieve one's purpose. The term refers to Senator Joseph McCarthy, who in the early 1950s resorted to these practices to unearth supposed Communists in the government and elsewhere.

[2]The Jacobins were political extremists who conducted a reign of terror against their opponents during the French Revolution.

462

1. Supporters of multi-cultural education contend that monoculturalism focuses too narrowly on Western individuals and ideas. Their opponents respond by arguing that Western European thought has been the chief force shaping American culture and therefore deserves the emphasis it receives. Ask students to consider both viewpoints, taking into account America's history and present world position, and then assess their relative merits.

2. Have students identify where Ehrenreich uses exaggeration and then speculate on her reasons for doing this.

3. Ask students to pinpoint and name other rhetorical strategies that Ehrenreich uses in her argument.

4. You might ask students to defend or criticize the use of speech codes to protect females, blacks, Hispanics, and non-mainstream campus groups against abusive language.

DISCUSSION QUESTIONS

1. Although Ehrenreich favors the teaching of multiculturalism, she tempers her position with a caveat that multiculturalists need to regain the humor of "self-mockery" (paragraph 8) that doesn't take political correctness over-seriously.

2. The proposition—one of value—consists of the final two sentences of the essay. It asserts the superiority of multiculturalsim because it is "richer, livelier and ultimately more fun."

derisively as P.C., or politically correct, are said to have launched a campus reign of terror against those who slip and innocently say "freshman" instead of "freshperson," "Indian" instead of "Native American" or, may the Goddess forgive them, "disabled" instead of "differently abled."

2 So you can see what is at stake here: freedom of speech, freedom of thought, Western civilization and a great many professional egos. But before we get carried away by the mounting backlash against multiculturalism, we ought to reflect for a moment on the system that the P.C. people aim to replace. I know all about it; in fact it's just about all I *do* know, since I—along with so many educated white people of my generation—was a victim of monoculturalism.

3 American history, as it was taught to us, began with Columbus' "discovery" of an apparently unnamed, unpeopled America, and moved on to the Pilgrims serving pumpkin pie to a handful of grateful red-skinned folks. College expanded our horizons with courses called Humanities or sometimes Civ, which introduced us to a line of thought that started with Homer, worked its way through Rabelais and reached a poignant climax in the pensées of Matthew Arnold. Graduate students wrote dissertations on what long-dead men had thought of Chaucer's verse or Shakespeare's dramas; foreign languages meant French or German. If there had been high technology in ancient China, kingdoms in black Africa or women anywhere, at any time, doing anything worth noticing, we did not know it, nor did anyone think to tell us.

4 Our families and neighborhoods reinforced the dogma of monoculturalism. In our heads, most of us '50s teenagers carried around a social map that was about as useful as the chart that guided Columbus to the "Indies." There were "Negroes," "whites" and "Orientals," the latter meaning Chinese and "Japs." Of religions, only three were known—Protestant, Catholic and Jewish—and not much was known about the last two types. The only remaining human categories were husbands and wives, and that was all the diversity the monocultural world could handle. Gays, lesbians, Buddhists, Muslims, Malaysians, Mormons, etc., were simply off the map.

5 So I applaud—with one hand, anyway—the multiculturalist goal of preparing us all for a wider world. The other hand is tapping its fingers impatiently, because the critics are right about one thing: when advocates of multiculturalism adopt the haughty stance of political correctness, they quickly descend to silliness or worse. It's obnoxious, for example, to rely on university administrations to enforce P.C. standards of verbal inoffensiveness. Racist, sexist and homophobic thoughts cannot, alas, be abolished by fiat but only by the time-honored methods of persuasion, education and exposure to the other guy's—or, excuse me, woman's—point of view.

6 And it's silly to mistake verbal purification for genuine social reform. Even after all women are "Ms." and all people are "he or she," women will still earn only 65¢ for every dollar earned by men. Minorites by any other name, such as "people of color," will still bear a hugely disproportionate burden of poverty and discrimination. Disabilities are not just "different abilities" when there are not enough ramps for wheelchairs, signers for the deaf or special classes for the "specially" endowed. With all due respect for the new politesse, actions still speak louder than fashionable phrases.

7 But the worst thing about the P.C. people is that they are such poor

advocates for the multicultural cause. No one was ever won over to a broader, more inclusive view of life by being bullied or relentlessly "corrected." Tell a 19-year-old white male that he can't say "girl" when he means "teen-age woman," and he will most likely snicker. This may be the reason why, despite the conservative alarms, P.C.-ness remains a relatively tiny trend. Most campuses have more serious and ancient problems: faculties still top-heavy with white males of the monocultural persuasion; fraternities that harass minorities and women; date rape; alcohol abuse; and tuition that excludes all but the upper fringe of the middle class.

So both sides would be well advised to lighten up. The conservatives ought   8
to realize that criticisms of the great books approach to learning do not amount to totalitarianism. And the advocates of multiculturalism need to regain the sense of humor that enabled their predecessors in the struggle to coin the term P.C. years ago—not in arrogance but in self-mockery.

Beyond that, both sides should realize that the beneficiaries of multi-   9
culturalism are not only the "oppressed peoples" on the standard P.C. list (minorities, gays, etc.). The "unenlightened"—the victims of monoculturalism—are oppressed too, or at least deprived. Our educations, whether at Yale or at State U. were narrow and parochial and left us ill-equipped to navigate a society that truly is multicultural and is becoming more so every day. The culture that we studied was, in fact, *one* culture and, from a world perspective, all too limited and ingrown. Diversity is challenging, but those of us who have seen the alternative know it is also richer, livelier and ultimately more fun.

DISCUSSION QUESTIONS

1. Explain the meaning of "with a Smile" in the essay's title.
2. Identify the writer's proposition. Is it one of fact, policy, action, or value?
3. While supporting multiculturalism, Ehrenreich offers several criticisms of the behavior that its supporters sometimes display. What are her specific objections? How are they arranged?
4. What kinds of support does Ehrenreich use? Refer to specific parts of the essay when answering.
5. What problems does Ehrenreich consider more serious than those stressed by multiculturalists?
6. Read the discussion of conclusions on pages 189–92 and then identify the kind Ehrenreich uses and discuss its effectiveness.

SUGGESTION FOR WRITING ■ Drawing upon printed
sources and using at least two kinds of support, write an argument defending monocultural education. If you favor multicultural education, follow the guidelines above and write an argument that shows how it is "preparing us all for a wider world," as Ehrenreich asserts in paragraph 5.

---

3. Ehrenreich objects to multiculturalist efforts to have universities enforce politically correct language (paragraph 5), to their mistaking "verbal purification for genuine social reform" (paragraph 6), and to their efforts to win converts by bullying (paragraph 7). These objections are arranged by order of climax, as shown by the first sentence of paragraph 7.

4. Paragraph 1 and the first part of paragraph 2 use material that has appeared in the media. (Because the criticisms have been so widespread, Ehrenreich cites no specific sources.) The remainder of paragraph 2 and paragraphs 3 and 4 are based on Ehrenreich's personal experience. Paragraphs 5, 6, and 7 are grounded in what is essentially enlightened common sense, making assertions that few fair-minded people would seriously question.

5. In paragraph 6, Ehrenreich notes that women suffer from disproportionately low wages, that minorities are burdened by poverty and discrimination, and that the disabled receive little help in coping with their handicaps. In paragraph 7, she criticizes the makeup of college faculties, the harassing practices of fraternities, date rape, alcohol abuse, and high tuition fees. All of these matters clearly overshadow the drive for "verbal purification."

6. Besides presenting the proposition, Ehrenreich's two-paragraph conclusion offers a recommendation to each side in the multiculturalism controversy. This is a logical follow-up to her criticisms of their tactics and thus an effective ending.

Andrew Kupfer

WHAT TO DO ABOUT DRUGS

Andrew Kupfer holds a Bachelor of Arts degree in anthropology from Brandeis University and advanced degrees in regional and urban planning from the London School of Economics and Cambridge University. He worked as a planner for the New York City Department of Housing Preservation and Development and as a copyeditor for the American Institute of Physics. In 1982, he began working for Fortune *as a reporter. Since 1988, he has been an associate editor for that magazine. In our selection, Kupfer offers his suggestions for coping with one of our most pressing social problems.*

1   Drugs are dangerous. Even users agree on that. Yet the U.S. seems to be getting nowhere in its war against them. In frustration, large numbers of Americans, including academics, members of Congress, and some big city mayors, are talking about waving a white flag. Legalize the stuff, some of them say, and be done with it. Let multinational companies take the business—and the profits—away from criminals. Stop the gunfights, the car bombs, the street crime, the bribes. Drug barons can sell their fleets of airplanes and go back to stealing cars, or whatever they were doing when all this started.

2   The idea is tantalizing, but simplistic. It addresses only one aspect of drug use—the prevailing criminality—without raising the question of how people can be persuaded not to use drugs in the first place. Moreover, legalization would have different effects on the markets for different drugs. At best it is not a solution but a trade-off: lower crime, perhaps, in return for the risk of greater drug use, addiction, and health costs.

3   Still, as Ronald Reagan used to say about the economy when he was running for President in 1980, what we're doing now isn't working. America needs a radical rethinking of its stance toward drugs. There might even be a place for legalization as part—but only part—of a carefully crafted policy that seeks to create a legal market for marijuana separate from that for heroin, cocaine, and its cheaper derivative crack. The money and police time freed up by legalizing pot could help pay for a more effective crackdown on hard drugs plus more programs for rehabilitation of addicts.

4   Legalization of all drugs is a last-stand position based not on the notion that hard drugs are good for people, but on the widespread perception that the government has thrown all its resources into the struggle and failed. That perception is flawed. Despite the tough rhetoric, the war on drugs has been less than total. The Administration's most recent policy is Zero Tolerance, which is supposed to mean just that. The smallest pinch of drugs found in a million-dollar yacht would be enough to justify seizure. No holds barred, nobody gets off. The reality is different. Yachts were seized, then given back. Punishment of offenders is wildly inconsistent. A Florida court in May convicted Carlos Lehder, a handsome pilot who looks as if he stepped out of a television thriller. He faces a prison sentence of life plus 150 years for smuggling cocaine into the U.S. About the same time, a judge in Manhattan put on probation a woman convicted of attempting to sell 174 vials of crack. As long as street sellers go free, Carlos Lehder's colleagues in the Colombian cartel can keep on producing and shipping cocaine to the U.S.

Nor can it be said that society is uniformly tough on drug users. When   5
traces of drugs were found in the body of a railroad engineer, killed when he
rammed into the rear of a standing train last spring in New York, his union
resisted the understandable call for mandatory drug testing. Job seekers in other
kinds of work aren't so keen on testing either.

Probably Americans have no stomach for pushing drug law enforcement   6
anywhere near the max. In Malaysia, after all, drug trafficking is punished by
hanging. The task is to develop a policy in line with American concepts of civil
liberties and within the limits of U.S. resources.

A first step is to decide that a drug-free society should not be the goal of   7
policy. The thinking behind Zero Tolerance, says Dr. David F. Musto, professor of
psychiatry at Yale, "is part of a typically American ideal about the perfectibility
of man." Total success is unattainable and policymakers who try to achieve it will
overlook intermediate measures that may do a better job of helping people kick
the habit or keep from developing one in the first place.

One of those steps could be the unthinkable: legalization of marijuana.   8
Since the early 1970s aging flower children have pushed for legal pot on grounds
of—as they would put it—common sense. They argue that the drug is nonaddic-
tive, widely used, and probably no worse a health hazard than alcohol. This "Why
not?" approach never got anywhere, because it was easily countered with "Why?"
Who needed another social problem no worse than alcohol? Now some surprising
data from the Netherlands suggest that there might be a more compelling reason
to legalize marijuana.

Pot has already been decriminalized in some U.S. states, though not com-   9
pletely legalized. Possessing small amounts of marijuana is punishable only by a
small fine in New York, Ohio, California, Oregon, and seven other states; it could
result in prison elsewhere. In places where the harsher laws remain on the books,
police often put a low priority on making arrests for small transactions involving
marijuana and hashish, because of limits on the number of cops, courtrooms, and
jail cells. The result is de facto decriminalization in much of the country at the
local level. Still, the Drug Enforcement Administration (DEA) continues to watch
out for marijuana use and U.S. Customs officers might confiscate your car if they
catch you bringing in some joints from Mexico. Drug enforcement agents still
spend a lot of time and money chasing down foreign suppliers.

The importance of a legal market for marijuana is that it could help steer   10
young people away from hard drugs by breaking the connection between marijuana smokers and drug pushers. The chief agent in the descent of people into
hard drugs is the pusher. In the inner cities especially, pushers are walking
drugstores, selling marijuana and hashish, barbiturates, stimulants, cocaine, and
heroin. The first sample is usually free. Data from the National Institute of Drug
Abuse show that, aside from alcohol, marijuana is the first drug most young
people try. It they are buying pot on the street, as most of them must, then they
will be exposed to the rest of the pharmacopeia.

The Netherlands provides a fascinating example of how creating a separate   11
market for marijuana and hashish can help cut heroin use. As hard drugs washed
across the world in the late 1960s and early 1970s, many young people in the
Netherlands became addicted. A dozen years ago, in an attempt to reverse the
trend, the government tripled the jail term for trafficking in hard drugs. At
the same time officials declared that they would not prosecute anyone found with
less than 30 grams of marijuana and hashish, though laws against the drugs
remained on the books.

12   Since then small amounts have been sold openly by operators of coffee-houses in Amsterdam, usually under the watchful eye of the police. "Because we want separation of markets," says ministry of justice drug policy adviser M. A. A. van Capelle, "we're interested in keeping a small market in soft drugs so people will know where to get it." Police don't look too closely into where the coffee-houses get their supplies, but if proprietors start mixing in hard drugs or sell amounts of pot deemed excessive, the place is shut down. The result is that a youngster curious about pot can buy it and use it in a safe place. He won't be arrested and he won't be exposed to pushers of hard drugs.

13   The Dutch worried at first that their new policy would cause a surge in marijuana use. In fact, according to the government, consumption has fallen. This decline may reflect the growing disaffection with drugs characteristic of the post-Flower Power era, but it is no less noteworthy that it occurred in a period of more open availability. The real payoff, though, is that use of heroin, the hard drug of choice in the Netherlands, has fallen too, particularly among young people. In 1981, 14% of heroin addicts were under 22; today the figure is 4.8%.

14   Critics of legalization will argue that the United States is not the Nether-lands. Indeed not. The U.S. is a more heterogeneous society, with no institution quite comparable to the friendly Dutch coffeehouse. Americans might not be as comfortable relying on the discretion of local cops in the enforcement of—or in winking at—marijuana laws. Another approach here could be to legalize mari-juana outright and make liquor stores the point of sale. The age restriction could be the same as for alcohol. The government could tax pot, with the revenue used to finance hard-drug treatment programs. If pot were taxed like cigarettes, it would generate an estimated $11 billion a year. Some $1.2 billion in state and federal money is now spent annually on drug treatment.

15   Legal pot would likely be a home-grown U.S. industry, removing it still further from the criminal elements in the international drug trade. American-grown marijuana now satisfies 25% of domestic demand, up from 9% when Reagan took office. The U.S. Drug Enforcement Administration believes that the U.S. will be the world's largest producer by the early 1990s, and soon after that a net exporter. Marijuana is already the largest cash crop in California.

16   Doctors still differ about the damage marijuana smoking inflicts, though they are beginning to agree that prolonged regular use may be risky, particularly to short-term memory and the lungs (marijuana contains tar, like cigarettes). As does alcohol, marijuana impairs perception, coordination, and memory. Long-term effects on the brain and the lungs are not yet known. The heart works harder, increasing blood pressure, a risk to people with hypertension. THC, the active ingredient, lowers the concentration of reproductive hormones in the bloodstream. But occasional use is unlikely to cause lasting health problems, and most people tend to use marijuana for only a short period of their lives.

17   A larger concern is whether more people would use marijuana if sanctions were removed. No one knows for sure. The ranks of drinkers grew by only about 10% after Prohibition ended. A recent survey of high school seniors across the nation by the University of Michigan shows that while fewer are smoking mari-juana, the vast majority (85%) find it readily available. Those who don't probably haven't been looking.

18   The case against legalizing hard drugs is twofold. First and foremost, the possibility of an explosion of addiction is too grave a risk regardless of any supposed benefits. Second, many of those benefits are illusory. One of the argu-ments for legalization is that the price would drop dramatically with the elimina-

tion of the huge criminal-risk premium, and addicts would no longer have to steal to support their habits. Dr. Mitchell S. Rosenthal, president of Phoenix House, a New York-based drug rehabilitation center, disputes that. For many addicts, he points out, crime is the way they earn money for all their needs, not just for drugs; because they are addicts they are unsuited to ordinary occupations. "If you give somebody free drugs you don't turn him into a responsible employee, husband, or father," says Rosenthal. "A large number of drug addicts have serious underlying problems."

Some advocates of legalization point to the British system of the 1950s, 19 when heroin was available to addicts by prescription. The number of addicts remained stable for many years, and almost all were known to doctors. The aim was to wean addicts from the drug, but if doctors could not, they gave small doses that prevented withdrawal without producing a high. That ended with the worldwide drug boom of the 1970s. With drugs flooding into the country illegally, doctors could no longer control an addict's habit. Addicts will go for a kick if they can find one. Unable to get enough heroin from doctors, they turned to the illegal market. The prescription system died out.

Even if a separate, legal market for marijuana were successful in slowing 20 the growth of hard-drug users, the U.S. would still have to contend with those already hooked. That means continued, even increased, pressure on heroin and cocaine dealers, but with a more balanced effort than the U.S. has been pursuing. The emphasis has been on stopping drugs in the source countries. The huge profits of drug producers have worked against that approach. The drug barons are so rich they have managed to bribe high officials and sometimes whole governments. "In the long run the real answer to the drug problem is not interdiction," says Robert Stutman, special agent in charge of the Drug Enforcement Administration office in New York. "Even using the military won't make a major difference." Peter Reuter, a senior economist at the Rand Corp., points out that since prices are so high, a drug dealer can still make big money even if lawmen seize most of a shipment.

But there are some steps the U.S. can take. International cooperation may 21 be the most promising. Countries where drugs are produced once took the view that drug use was an American problem. Now that they are discovering that the number of addicts within their borders is growing, they have become more willing to explore joint action against drug producers and dealers.

At home, the U.S. needs a unified, coordinated policy that extends from 22 federal drug enforcement officers down to local judges and cops. Agents from the DEA and the FBI conducted separate undercover investigations into laundering of Colombian drug money. Both operations hit pay dirt, but did there have to be two?

More enforcement dollars should be pushed down to the street. New York 23 City officials claim to have had great luck with Operation Pressure Point, which focused police manpower on the streets of the Lower East Side. Says Sterling Johnson Jr., special narcotics prosecutor for the city: "Pressure Point was a tremendous success in taking the community back, literally, from the drug dealers." Mark Kleiman, a lecturer on criminal justice at Harvard University's Kennedy School of Government, says that if police are active in the streets, they can increase the time a drug user must spend to find dope. "If you are a heavy user and the probability of not connecting is great," says Kleiman, "that becomes a strong argument for getting into a treatment program."

If an addict looks for a program, however, he had better be able to get in. In 24

DISCUSSION QUESTIONS

1. Kupfer signals at the outset of his argument that he disagrees with the legalization of drugs. "In frustration" and "waving a white flag" both suggest surrender to a situation as a last-chance alternative. He explains in paragraph 4 that such an attitude is "flawed." His rejection of legalization leads him to what he proposes instead (see answer 2). This essay thus pairs nicely with the following one by Hamill, which argues for legalization.

2. Kupfer has a two-sentence proposition, one of action, located in paragraph 3: "America needs a radical rethinking. . . . There might even be a place for legalization. . . ."

3. Kupfer explains in paragraph 10 that if marijuana were legalized, people would not have to buy it from drug pushers on the street. It is these pushers who also sell the hard drugs which lead to serious problems. A Netherlands experiment with separation of markets led to lower consumption not only of heroin but also of marijuana. (paragraphs 11–13).

4. Kupfer cites authoritative opinion in paragraphs 7, 12, 18, 20, 23, 24, 26, and 27.

5. Kupfer refutes the argument for legalization of *all* drugs in paragraphs 2, 4–6, 18 and 19.

6. This sentence summarizes Kupfer's main argument: provide a separate market for marijuana by legalizing it and at the same time put increased pressure on heroin and cocaine dealers as part of a balanced campaign against hard drugs. Since no one can forecast precisely the effects of legalized marijuana, Kupfer says that this action "could" prove beneficial. Students should be cautioned against making unjustified claims.

7. Reading these paired essays exposes students to the

New York City, New Haven, and Portland, Oregon, the waiting list for treatment can be several months long. Not every addict would avail himself of help even with limitless facilities, but it is unconscionable that people must be turned away when billions are being spent on interdiction that at most raises the street price of drugs by a few dollars. When a drug user is ready to go for help, he should be able to do so without a long wait. "One of the differences between drug users and us is time scale," says David Turner, director of the Standing Conference on Drug Abuse, based in London. "We want things immediately, but we can cope with delay. An addict is used to taking heroin and getting immediate relief. It's not surprising that if he is told he can have an appointment in four weeks, he will probably forget about it."

25   The best solution to the drug problem is societal change. That takes a long time. A good start is instilling an understanding of the potential hazards of drug use at an early age. Signs are that the numerous school programs across the country are beginning to work. The University of Michigan survey shows drug use among high school seniors down 13.6% since 1982. (The survey excludes teenagers who have dropped out, however, the biggest group of crack users.)

26   The role that education can play is apparent in Massachusetts, which has developed a range of curricula for kindergarten to the 12th grade. "The program is really one part hard facts about drug education and three parts comprehensive health education," says Marianne Lee, deputy director of the Massachusetts Governor's Alliance Against Drugs. "A fourth of all children live in a home where there is a substance-abuse problem. We teach kids how to deal with that, and how to keep their self-esteem intact." Since 1984 the number of high school students who have tried illicit drugs has dropped 11%, vs. a national decline of 7%. The downside is that alcohol use remains high in Massachusetts; 61% of students said they had used it at least once in the 30 days before the survey.

27   Is the Just Say No campaign helping? "It's not enough to tell kids to say no," says Lee. "We have to give them a reason to say no." Perhaps the phrase has had to bear more weight than it was meant to. Originally coined as a slogan for very young children, it was latched onto as a motto by drug treatment programs of all types. More sophisticated kids are not impressed by it.

28   Some educators worry that legalizing marijuana while continuing a tough stance toward hard drugs might send a confusing message. But American society transmits many conflicting signals about addictive substances. For example, while the Surgeon General rails against smoking, Congress continues to subsidize tobacco growing. A policy of compromise could give an outlet to people who wish to experiment with soft drugs and their small intoxications, deglamorizing those drugs while vilifying those that are deadly. That just might help break the spiral of criminality and violence without throwing open the doors of chemical invention to those who may not be able to resist.

DISCUSSION QUESTIONS

1. With the essay as a whole in mind, point out the significance of the following sentence in paragraph 1: "In frustration, large numbers of Americans, including academics, members of Congress, and some big city mayors, are talking about waving a white flag."

2. What is Kupfer's proposition and where is it located? Is it one of fact, policy, action, or value?

3. According to Kupfer, how would a separate legal market for marijuana help in the fight against hard drugs—heroin, cocaine, and crack?

4. Point out several places where Kupfer uses authoritative opinion as evidence.

5. Where does he refute, that is, counter the arguments of, opposing positions?

6. Consider the essay as a whole and then comment on the significance of the following sentence in paragraph 28: "A policy of compromise could give an outlet to people who wish to experiment with soft drugs and their small intoxications, deglamorizing those drugs while vilifying those that are deadly."

7. Kupfer's views on legalizing all drugs differ markedly from those of Hamill in the following essay (pages 469–80). Read Hamill's essay and then evaluate their differing attitudes.

differing viewpoints in an argument, teaches them to weigh both sides before forming their own opinions, and allows you to generate a class debate which, considering the topic, should be a spirited one.

SUGGESTION FOR WRITING ■ **Write an essay favoring (or opposing) the death penalty for certain crimes but not others. Support your argument with well-chosen, authoritative opinions.**

Pete Hamill

FACING UP TO DRUGS: IS LEGALIZATION THE SOLUTION?

Pete Hamill (born 1935) is a native of Brooklyn, New York, and attended Pratt Institute and Mexico City College. Following jobs as a sheet-metal worker and advertising designer, he turned to journalism, becoming a reporter for the New York Post *in 1960. Since then, he has written and reported for a great many periodicals, including among others the* Saturday Evening Post, New York Daily News, Village Voice, Cosmopolitan, Playboy, *and* Reader's Digest. *He is the author of an array of novels and screenplays and has authored the scripts for several recordings with music. In the selection we present, Hamill recommends a controversial way of dealing with the problem of drugs.*

Hard drugs are now the scariest fact of New York life. They have spread genuine fear among ordinary citizens. They have stained every neighborhood in every borough, respecting no boundaries of class or color or geography. They have destroyed marriages, corrupted cops and banks, diminished productivity, fed the wild spiral of rents and condominium prices, overwhelmed the public hospitals, and filled the prisons to bursting.

The price of the drug scourge increases by the day. Hard drugs have injured thousands of families, some named Zaccaro and Kennedy, many others less well known. They have ruined uncountable numbers of careers and distorted others. Last year, when Dwight Gooden was sent off to the Smithers clinic, hard drugs almost certainly cost the Mets a championship. Gooden's friend, the brilliant pitcher Floyd Youmans of the Montreal Expos, learned no lesson from this; he was recently suspended indefinitely after once more failing a drug test. But Gooden and Youmans are not isolated cases, young men ensnared by the life-

1

2

PERSPECTIVE

A few years ago, public opinion was overwhelmingly against the legalization of drugs as a way of dealing with the problems they cause. As the drug situation has worsened, however, legalization has gained more advocates, Hamill among them. Students should note that Hamill recommends legalization only on a 10-year trial basis. If the results don't prove satisfactory, the present system could be reinstated. Hamill's plan, then, represents a variation upon the usual pro-legalization stance and, like Kupfer's, illustrates that multiple options are often possible.

TEACHING STRATEGIES

1. Teaching strategies 1–3 and 5 that accompany the preceding essay by Kupfer could also apply to this essay.
2. Ask students to explain why the opening paragraph is effective. Possible answers include the arresting statement in the first sentence and the parallelism that helps set up the argument for legalization.
3. Ask students to examine Hamill's use of colons in paragraphs 7, 12, 14, 15, 34, 40, and 52 and then formulate some guidelines for the proper use of colons.
4. Although his essay is grounded on rational appeal, Hamill also uses emotional and ethical appeals to strengthen his argument. Ask students to identify these appeals and comment on their effectiveness.

CLASSROOM ACTIVITIES

1. Divide the class into small groups and have students brainstorm to determine what educational steps would be most effective in combatting drug use. Their conclusions could be presented as reports to the entire class.
2. These same groups might explore and present reports on such options as mandatory, random (and this of course is the key word) drug tests and other possibilities not dealt with at length by Kupfer or Hamill. Any or all of these reports could serve as the basis for a writing assignment.

style of the poor neighborhoods of Tampa. Hard drugs have damaged the lives of pitcher Steve Howe, prizefighter Aaron Pryor, and football players Mercury Morris, Hollywood Henderson, and Don Reese, to mention only a few. Many other talented Americans, with no excuses to make about poverty or environment, have been hurt by hard drugs. And they cost Len Bias, Janis Joplin, Jimi Hendrix, Jim Morrison, and John Belushi their lives.

3   These terrible examples seem to make no difference; for the druggies, there are no cautionary tales. All over New York today, thousands of people are playing with drugs as if nothing will happen to *them*. And in this dense and dangerous city, such a taste for folly usually results in corpses.

4   New York, of course, is not unique. With the drug plague spreading all over the United States, the Feds now estimate that the country's cocaine-user population is now at 5.8-million. These new druggies include prep-school students, bankers, policemen, railroad workers, pilots, factory hands, stockbrokers, journalists, and—with the arrival of crack—vast numbers of the urban poor. According to the National Institute on Drug Abuse, the average age of first-time drug-users in the United States is now thirteen.

5   The drug trade is one of the most successful of all multinational capitalist enterprises, brilliantly functioning on the ancient rules of supply and demand. The demand is insatiable, the supply apparently limitless. In a business estimated by the president's South Florida Task Force to gross more than $100 billion a year, there are fortunes, large and small, to be made. And the art of the drug deal always contains the gun. As the authority of the old mob faded in the seventies (with the breakup of the Istanbul–Marseilles–New York pipeline), new bad guys moved in: Cubans and Colombians first; then, as the cocaine business flourished, Bolivians and Dominicans. Israeli hoodlums out of Brighton Beach took a big hunk of the heroin trade. And 30 to 40 Jamaican "posses" began operating in the United States, starting with marijuana and hashish, then moving hard into the cocaine trade. The Shower Posse works out of the Bronx, the Spangler Posse in Brooklyn, the Dunkirk Boys in Harlem. Experts say the posses killed about 350 people last year, and the number could be much higher (more than 200 homicides here last year involved Jamaicans). Now the word on the street is that the Pakistanis are moving into town, with an endless supply of heroin from home.

6   But the advent of crack has led to the true decentralization of the drug trade. The old days of iron control by the Gambino or Bonanno families are clearly over. Small groups of violent entrepreneurs now run the trade in individual housing projects, on specific streets, in the vicinity of valued high schools. Men have been killed in disputes over control of a single street corner. Such drug gangs as the Vigilantes in Harlem, the Wild Bunch in Bed-Stuy, and the Valley Boys in the northeast Bronx are young and deadly. And unless something is done, they are here to stay.

7   They all have guns, including automatic weapons, and they have a gift for slaughter that makes some people nostalgic for the old Mafia. Nearly every morning, the newspapers carry fresh bulletins from the drug wars, full of multiple homicides and the killing of women and children. The old hoodlums were sinister bums who often killed one another, but they had some respect for the innocence of children. Not this set. The first indication that the rules of the game had changed dawned on us in 1982. In February of that year, on the Grand Central Parkway, the eighteen-month-old daughter and the four-month-old son of a Colombian drug-dealer were destroyed by shotgun blasts and automatic weapons,

after their parents had been blown away. One Dominican dealer was forced to watch the disembowelment of his wife before being shotgunned to death. In Jackson Heights, according to New York *Newsday*, the favored method of execution is now the "Colombian necktie": The throat is cut and the tongue pulled through the slit to hang down upon the chest. The drug gangs are not misunderstood little boys. Their violence is at once specific and general: When they get rid of a suspected informer, they send chilling lessons to many others. Yet most of us read about their mayhem as if it were taking place in some barbarous and distant country and not the city that also contains the Metropolitan Museum.

It isn't as if these people are simply breaking the law; in some places, the law doesn't even exist. Whole neighborhoods in Brooklyn and Queens have been abandoned to the rule of the men with the Uzis, the MAC-10s, and the 9-mm. pistols. When police officer Edward Byrne was stationed outside the South Jamaica home of a witness in a drug case, the bad guys just walked up and killed him. When police officer George Scheu started crusading last year against drug-dealers in his Flushing neighborhood, he was shot down and killed outside his home. These actions remind us of the criminal anarchy in Colombia, where scores of police officers, judges, and public officials (including the minister of justice) have been assassinated by the drug caudillos. The new drug gangs enforce their power with violence, demonstrating that they can successfully murder witnesses and cops who might get in the way. When the first prosecutor is killed, there may be outrage in New York, but there will be no surprise. 8

Officers of the law are not the only casualties. Every weekend, discos erupt in gunfire as drug gangs fight over money or women or the ambiguous intentions of a smile. Every other week, innocent bystanders are shot down, provided a day of tabloid mourning, swiftly forgotten. 9

These killers are servicing a huge number of New Yorkers. The population of the stupefied can no longer be accurately counted. It is estimated that New York heroin addicts number about 200,000, or ten full-strength army divisions. But nobody knows how many people are using cocaine or crack. Some cops say it is more than a million. This might be hyperbole, the result of what some perceive to be anti-drug hysteria. But nobody who lives in New York can deny the daily evidence of the drug plague. 10

You see blurred-out young men panhandling for crack money from Columbus Avenue to Wall Street. Every night, wide-eyed, gold-bedecked teenage crackheads do 75 miles an hour on the Henry Hudson Parkway, racing one another in BMWs. In the age of AIDS, schoolgirls are hooking on street corners. Thousands of other young New Yorkers, whacked on drugs, are now incapable of holding jobs or acquiring the basic skills that might make a decent life possible. They amble around the ghettos. They fill the welfare hotels. They mill about the Port Authority bus terminal. They careen through subway cars, sometimes whipping out knives or pistols. The eyes of the heroin-users are glazed, their bodies filthy. The shooters among them often share "works," knowing that dirty needles can give them AIDS; they choose to risk an agonizing death in order to get high. The crackheads are wilder—eyes pinwheeling, speed-rapping away, or practicing various menacing styles. Smack or crack: They'd rather do either than go to a ball game, love someone, raise a child, listen to music, read a book, or master a difficult craft. 11

All of us are paying for this sick and disastrous binge. Crime in New York, after tailing off for a few years, has risen drastically. The reason is simple: Most 12 junkies don't work. To feed their habits, addicts must either deal or steal. A Justice Department study released last winter showed that 79 percent of men arrested in New York for serious crimes tested positive for recent use of illegal drugs, 63 percent for cocaine. In 1977, there were 505 cops in this city's Narcotics Division; today, there are nearly 1,200. They made 35,774 drug-related arrests last year and estimate that 40 percent of the city's murders (there were 1,672 in 1987) were drug-related. In the first three months of this year, murder was up 10 percent in the city; car theft, 18.2 percent; assault, 9.4 percent; larceny, 5 percent; robbery, 4 percent. New Yorkers must come up with billions of tax dollars to pay for the police work involved, along with the cost of the druggies' hospital treatment, the operation of various clinics, and welfare payments to those who are so blitzed they can't support themselves.

13   With the pervasive use of hard drugs, and the enormous profits involved, it is no surprise that policemen all over the country have been dirtied, most sickeningly in Miami. But there is evidence that the corruption goes beyond cases of underpaid street cops looking the other way for their kids' tuition. A few years ago, a veteran agent became the first FBI man to plead guilty to cocaine-trafficking. Assistant U.S. Attorney Daniel N. Perlmutter, a rising star in Rudolph Giuliani's office, went to jail for stealing cocaine and heroin from a safe where evidence was stored.

14   No wonder Jesse Jackson was able to make drugs a major part of this year's presidential campaign. No wonder a *New York Times*/CBS News poll in March showed that Americans were far more concerned with drug-trafficking than with Central America, arms control, terrorism, or the West Bank. Americans have learned one big thing in the past few years: There has been a war on drugs, all right, and we have lost. Nobody knows this better than New Yorkers.

15   The ancient question is posed: What is to be done? The drug culture is now so pervasive, the drug trade so huge, powerful, and complex, that there are no simple answers. But the attack on the problem must deal with the leading actors in this squalid drama: dealers and users. That is, any true war on drugs must grapple with the problems of supply and demand.

SUPPLY

16   It is one of the more delicious ironies of the Cold War era that the bulk of the cocaine and heroin supply comes from countries that used to be called part of the free world. While trillions have been spent on national security, the security of ordinary citizens has been destroyed by countries that are on our side. The cocaine cartel is headquartered in Medellín, Colombia. Most coca leaves are produced in Bolivia and Peru, where they are turned into coca paste for processing in Colombia. Most heroin is coming from Pakistan, Thailand, Turkey, and Mexico. The Colombians and Mexicans also produce much of the marijuana crop that is grown outside the United States.

17   The big supply-side coke-dealers control processing and distribution, leaving the grungy details of retailing to thousands of Americans. Many Caribbean islands are crucial to distribution, as was Panama until the indictment of Noriega. Mexico also is used as a transshipment point for huge supplies of cocaine and heroin that it does not produce. In all these countries, the governments themselves have been corrupted by the trade. The government of Colombia has virtually surrendered to the violence of the drug barons, while the governments of

Panama and Bolivia are flat-out drug rings. Some Caribbean nations—the Bahamas in particular—have been accused of the same partnership with traffickers. The civilian government of Haiti was recently overthrown by the military in a dispute over the drug trade. In Mexico, the corruption is low-level in many places but is said to involve higher-ups in various state governments. In Thailand and Pakistan, drug-traffickers ply their trade with little interference from their governments; Thailand is more worried about Vietnam than about 110th Street, and Pakistan is making too much money off the war in Afghanistan to care about junkies in the United States.

Frustrated Americans have demanded that something drastic be done about the drug traffic. And over the past few years, the following measures have been advocated: 18

1. *War.* This is one of the most frequently voiced demands, what Maxwell Smart would have called the old let's-go-in-and-bomb-the-bejesus-out-of-them plan. Massachusetts senator John Kerry and Los Angeles police chief Daryl Gates are among those who have suggested military action. After all, if the United States is truly the most powerful nation on earth, why can't it *go to the source?*

From 1839 to 1842, the British actually did fight a war in China over drugs.   19
But in the case of the Opium War, the British were the drug-pushers. They went ashore in China and killed a lot of Chinese in the name of their holy cause (opium was produced in British India, sold in China), the equivalent of Colombia's attacking the United States for the right to sell cocaine.

But a United States war against the drug-producing countries would be a   20
forbiddingly expensive enterprise. You can't do it with one or two Grenada-style public-relations spectacles. And a war against one country—say, Colombia— would have no effect; the bad guys would just move next door. To use military force effectively to stop the production of poppies and coca leaves, the United States would have to attack all of the offending countries *at the same time.*

But it is hard to imagine a simultaneous declaration of war against Panama,   21
Colombia, Peru, Bolivia, Mexico, Turkey, Thailand, and Pakistan, with a smaller expedition against the Bahamas. We have had some comical adventurers in the National Security Council lately, but none *that* comical. There are 80 million people in Mexico alone, with rugged, mountainous terrain through the center of the country and dense jungles in the southern regions. Bolivia is twice the size of France and also mountainous. In Pakistan, American troops would face all the guns the CIA has been supplying to the anti-Communist Afghans, many of whom have been ripped off by Pakistani gangsters. Another war in Southeast Asia (to cut off the Thai supply) would be no fun, but it would carry its own ironies, since much of the current mass stupefaction in America can be traced to the Vietnam era.

The logistics of Drug War One would be staggering; planes, ships, and   22
rockets would be sent on their way to three continents. In every country from Turkey to Thailand, an American invasion would unite most of the local population on nationalist grounds. (We had a mild sample of that recently in the wholly owned CIA subsidiary of Honduras when the arrest of a drug-dealer by U.S. agents led to the burning down of one of the embassy buildings, along with several nights of anti-U.S. rioting.) Various international agreements would get in the way (the Organization of American States is unlikely to authorize a mass invasion of its own most important member states). U.S. casualties in such a worldwide operation would be very heavy as local armies and nationalist guerrilla

bands descended upon the invaders, prepared to die, as they say, for their country. In the event that the Americans won all of these simultaneous wars, they would then have to occupy those countries for a generation if they truly hoped to wipe out the sources of drugs. The cost of a dozen huge garrisons would finish off the already precarious U.S. economy.

23   2. *Economic pressure.* On paper, this sounds like a more rational means of eradicating drugs. The United States (and the other leading industrial countries) would cut off credits, foreign aid, and all legitimate trade with the drug-producing countries. Presumably, the governments of those countries would then realize swiftly that they must get rid of the drug barons and would dispatch their own soldiers to wipe them out. While wielding the economic Big Stick, the United States would hold out the carrots of crop replacement, expanded foreign aid, guaranteed purchase of legitimate crops. (Bolivia, for example, went heavily into coca-leaf production in the seventies after its cotton industry collapsed with the fall of worldwide cotton prices. This followed the sharp decline of its tin industry.) The idea would be to create as much domestic pain as possible, so the local governments would get out of the drug racket—or crush it.

24   Unfortunately, the recent fiasco in Panama showed us on a small scale that this probably wouldn't work. Again, nationalism would be a major factor (in Panama, most people blamed the U.S. for their plight, not Noriega). And in using economic sanctions, the U.S. could not make distinctions among drug-dealers; Washington would have to be as tough on NATO ally Turkey as it is on Bolivia, as ferocious against Thailand and Pakistan as against Colombia and Mexico.

25   But U.S. companies also need most of these countries as markets. Economic sanctions work both ways; all American goods would be stopped at other nations' borders, thus closing plants all over our own country. Mexico would stop paying its multi-billion-dollar debt to U.S. banks, which would then collapse—perhaps pulling the entire country into a major depression.

26   3. *Moral persuasion.* Don't even bother.

27   4. *The sealing of the borders.* Again, this would cost uncountable billions. We have a 5,426-mile undefended border with Canada. It was crossed without problem by Prohibition rumrunners, vaulted for decades by Mafia drug-peddlers, and is easily traversed these days by the cocaine-runners. The 1,942-mile border with Mexico is a sieve. In spite of tough immigration laws, several million illegal aliens are expected to cross it this year; well-financed drug-runners with their fleets of small aircraft and trucks are unlikely to be stopped.

28   Enlisting the Armed Forces as border guards almost certainly would only complicate matters—as the Israelis have learned on the West Bank, soldiers are not policemen. Chasing druggies back home to Mexico or Canada (in "hot pursuit") could lead to an international incident every other day. The first time a private plane flown by some orthodontist with a defective radio was shot down over Toronto, the plan would be abandoned.

29   America's miles of coastline are guarded by an underfinanced, undermanned Coast Guard. Florida alone has 580 miles of coast, and there are more than 120,000 pleasure boats registered in southern Florida. Smugglers have become very sophisticated about penetrating our feeble defenses. The South Florida Task Force—headed by Vice-President George Bush and supported by the Drug Enforcement Administration, the FBI, the Customs Service, the U.S. Army (which supplied Cobra helicopters), the Bureau of Alcohol, Tobacco & Firearms, the

Internal Revenue Service, the Coast Guard, the U.S. Navy (whose warships gave the Coast Guard support), the U.S. Border Patrol, the U.S. Marshals, and the Treasury Department—has been a colossal flop. After more than six years of this effort, there are more drugs on the streets than ever before, and their lower prices (down from $47,000 a kilo for cocaine six years ago to about $12,000 now) indicate that all those well-photographed record-setting busts haven't stopped the flow.

The reason is simple. The demand and the profits are enormous. So it's no surprise that when the government concentrates its efforts in one spot (as it did in southern Florida), the druggies simply go elsewhere: to the Florida panhandle, the bayous of Louisiana, the shores of Mississippi. Many even follow the old rumrunner trails, dropping anchor off Montauk and using small boats to make runs against the unguarded shores of Long Island. One unexpected consequence of the patchwork War on Drugs has been the spread of the trade to places that once were free of it. Brilliant.

5. *Draconian measures, including the death penalty.* Mayor Koch and others have called for the death penalty for big-time drug-dealers. The problem is that most of them don't live here. For every Carlos Lehder, convicted recently after a long trial in Florida, there are thousands of others whose immunity is guaranteed by use of violence.

But if the death penalty is to be employed to solve the drug problem, why should it be limited to the few foreign wholesalers who are extradited and tried here? To be fair, you would have to attack every participant in the production and distribution systems. That is, you would have to do more than fry a few thousand pushers; you would have to execute every crooked cop, every corrupt banker who launders drug money, every politician who is on the take. You would also have to lock up all members of the CIA involved in the *contra* drug-running scheme (persuasively described in Leslie Cockburn's *Out of Control*) and strap them into the electric chair, along with their bosses and whoever in the White House collaborated in these operations. The death penalty for drug-dealing is a slogan, not a solution. Even if exceptions were made for ideological zealots, the state would have to kill several hundred thousand people. And the drugs would continue to flow.

DEMAND

One night a year ago, I had dinner with a Mexican diplomat and asked him about the drug problem in Mexico. He said, "You have to understand something: If thousands of North American yuppies suddenly decided tomorrow to get high by shoving bananas up their noses—and they were willing to pay $10 a banana—Mexico would bloom in bananas."

His point was a simple one: The drug problem in the United States is one of demand, not of production. Poor countries are like poor people—in order to survive, they will sell whatever the market demands. In our time, in this country and this city, the market demands hard drugs.

There have been a variety of suggestions about dealing with the insatiable appetite that Americans have developed for cocaine and heroin.

1. *Willpower.* This is the Nancy Reagan plan, beautifully described by a

recent beauty contestant as "Just Say Don't." It is primarily directed at teenagers, imploring them to resist the peer pressure that could lead to using drugs. A few weeks ago, I asked some New York street kids about this program. They just laughed and laughed.

37   2. *Education*. This is getting better. In the past, the country paid a heavy price for lies told in the name of education (marijuana will lead to heroin, etc.). Television has been playing a more responsible role lately, with a variety of series and programs about the cost and consequences of drugs (*48 Hours on Crack Street*; the two Peter Jennings specials on ABC). If this effort is sustained, we may begin to see a slow, steady decline in drug use (the way cigarette-smoking began to wane after the truth was told about its connection to lung cancer and heart disease). The great risk is that education about drugs will merely provoke curiosity and lead to wider use. Kids always think they are immortal.

38   3. *Treatment*. I visited a drug-treatment center in Suffern a few weeks ago. The facilities were secure, the 28-day program tough, the staff dedicated. There were exactly 28 beds for junkies. There are 250,000 smack addicts in New York State alone. Around the state, there are about 5,000 beds available to treat heroin addicts. Obviously, not everyone who wants treatment can get it. Those who have summoned all the desiccated vestiges of their pride and hope in order to enter a treatment program should be able to do so. But this, too, will cost many billions if all the country's addicts are to be handled by such programs.

39   4. *More Draconian measures*. This would follow examples set in China, Singapore, and a few other places. It would attack both dealer and user, supply and demand. All would be subject to heavy prison sentences (or the electric chair, if the death-penalty advocates had their way). The user would be considered as guilty as the seller.

40   Again, those good old Draconian measures make better rhetoric than reality. In New York, the Rockefeller drug law was one such measure. Put into effect in 1973, this was the "nation's toughest" drug legislation: For possession of two ounces of heroin, the minimum sentence was 15 to 25 years in prison; the maximum was life. A repeat conviction for possessing any stimulant or hallucinogen "with intent to sell" sent a felon to jail for one to eight and a half, again with a maximum of life. Probation, alternate sentences, and plea bargaining were forbidden. Yes, a lot of bad guys did go to jail, and by 1975, 91 percent of convicted drug felons were serving maximum prison sentences.

41   But these measures also helped cause the current crisis. The courts were soon jammed with accused drug felons demanding jury trials. The spending of many additional millions on judges and new courtrooms didn't ease the problem. And it was also now worth killing cops to avoid doing life in Attica. The old mob *did* respond to the new laws. Many of them got out of the smack racket (with the usual exceptions), but that only opened the way for the Cubans and Colombians. Judges began releasing first offenders and low-level dealers for the simple reason that there was no room in our prisons: They were already packed with druggies. And as cops became more cynical about the justice system, corruption became more possible.

42   New Yorkers are already the most heavily taxed Americans. It's unlikely that they would agree to billions of dollars in additional taxes to pay for another 30 prisons or an additional 500 judges to deal with all the users and pushers in the state. Nor would anybody be happy paying even more for welfare to handle the women and children left behind by the imprisoned druggies.

WHAT IS TO BE DONE?

After watching the results of the plague since heroin first came to Brooklyn   43
in the early fifties, after visiting the courtrooms and the morgues, after wandering
New York's neighborhoods to see for myself, and after consuming much of the
literature on drugs, I've reluctantly come to a terrible conclusion: The only solution is the complete legalization of these drugs.

I did not originate this idea, of course. In the past year, the mayors of   44
Baltimore, Washington, and Minneapolis have urged that legalization be looked
into. Various shapers of public opinion, including such conservatives as William
F. Buckley Jr. and Milton Friedman, have done the same. Many have cited articles
in such publications as *The Economist, Foreign Policy*, and the British medical
journal *The Lancet*, all suggesting that the only solution is legalization.

Legalization doesn't mean endorsement. Cigarettes, liquor, and prescription   45
drugs such as Valium are now legal, though neither government nor society
endorses their use. Any citizen can now endanger his health with cigarettes (and
300,000 people die each year from smoking-related illnesses). Or make a mess of
his life with whiskey (alcohol abuse costs us more than $100 billion a year). Or
take too many Valiums and die. These drugs, however, have become respectable
over the years. State banquets are often marked by the drinking of toasts, in which
the drug called liquor is offered in honor of the distinguished visitor. Business,
politics, and love affairs are often conducted with the lubricant of alcohol. I have
no patience anymore for drunks, and I can't abide the company of cokeheads and
junkies. But every sensible citizen must recognize that the current system under
which some drugs are legal and others are not is hypocritical.

I think a ten-year experiment with legalization is worth the risk. If it doesn't   46
accomplish its goals, legislators could always go back to the present disastrous
system. And we might learn that we can live without hypocrisy.

The strongest argument for legalization is economic. We simply don't have   47
the money to deal with eliminating supply or demand. Too many Americans want
this stuff, and we are again falling into the trap created by Prohibition: We try to
keep people from buying things they want, we cite moral reasons as our motives,
and we create a criminal organization that will poison all of our lives for decades.
The old mob was the child of Prohibition. A new mob, infinitely more ruthless, is
certain to come out of the present crisis. That can be prevented by eliminating the
illegal profits that fund and expand the power of the drug gangs.

How would legalization work? A few possibilities: 48

1. Marijuana—not a hard drug, of course, but described as one in the
debate—could be the first to be legalized. About 20 million Americans smoke
grass on a regular basis and about 400,000 are arrested every year for possession.
Mark Kleiman, former director of policy analysis for the Criminal Division of the
Justice Department, estimates that legalizing the sale of marijuana would save
about $500 million in law-enforcement costs and produce about $7 billion in
revenues. Those numbers alone should settle this part of the argument.

Pot could be sold openly in licensed liquor stores all over the country   49
(legalization must be national; if it were limited to New York, every pothead,
cokehead, and junkie in the country would soon arrive here). All laws now
applicable to selling liquor (used legally by 100 million Americans) would apply
to marijuana. Citizens would be arrested for driving under the influence. The
weed could not be sold to minors. Advertising would be restricted. All taxes—

including those on domestic farmers and importers—would be applied to drug treatment, education, and research for the duration of the ten-year experiment.

50   2. Heroin could be legalized a year later, dispensed through a network of neighborhood health stations and drugstores. While the old British system of registering addicts was in effect, the number of those receiving daily maintenance doses was low (about 500 in London). In the late sixties, the system was changed. The number of dispensing doctors was reduced nationwide to a few hundred (from thousands), and new registered addicts were required to enter methadone programs. The number of addicts soared. Obviously, the old system was better.

51   After legalization, this vile drug would be banned from commercial sale. The price would be very low (25 cents a dose), perhaps even free. All current addicts would have to register within six months of the passage of the enabling legislation. They would be supplied with identity cards resembling driver's licenses, showing their faces. They would also be given the opportunity to go drug-free through a greatly expanded system of treatment centers (funded by the marijuana tax and import fees). Their records would be kept confidential, but they would have to register.

52   Presumably, this would accomplish two things: (1) take the profits out of heroin sales and (2) contain the present addict population. Most junkies support their habits by dealing; they create new addicts to have more customers. There would be no economic point to creating new junkies. The street junkie also would gain relief from the degrading process of making his day's connection. He would stop stealing from old ladies, his family, and strangers. He would no longer have to risk AIDS infection by sharing works.

53   The mechanics would be difficult; some junkies need five or six doses a day, and if you hand them the supply all at once, they are likely to sell some of it to others. The cost of six separate needles a day for 200,000 junkies would be very high. New junkies would be a different problem. Certainly, there would be a continuing, if diminished, supply of young addicts, for a variety of reasons. Some would get heroin from family members who are junkies, the way young alcoholics have been known to raid the family liquor cabinet. There will always be sick old junkies ready to corrupt the young and others who may want to spread their personal misery to as many as possible. But new junkies would be able to enter the system only by telling the authorities how they got turned on. And this would be a point where one of those good old Draconian measures would be useful. Part of the law could mandate life sentences for anyone who created a new junkie.

54   3. Cocaine could be legalized soon after heroin and sold in its conventional forms through liquor stores. The same regulations that govern the sale and use of liquor and marijuana would apply. The drug barons of the world could then go legitimate. The drug-user would have a regulated supply of cocaine that was not cut with Ajax or speed. He would pay a variety of prices depending on quality, as the drinker does for various wines, liquors, and champagnes. Even the crack-users, at the bottom of the social scale of coke-users, would be able to buy cocaine legally, thus putting the hoodlums out of business. If the customers wanted to go home, then, and cook up some crack in the microwave (all they would need is cocaine hydrochloride, baking soda, and water or ammonia), they could do so. If they then sold it to kids, they would end up doing life.

55   I say all of this with enormous reluctance. I hate the idea of living in a country that is drowning in drugs. I know that if drugs were freely available, some

of the most damaged people in society could fall into degradation, as many of the poor have across the years in countries where alcohol is legal. There would be casualties everywhere, and the big-city ghettos might suffer terribly (although the assumption that blacks and Hispanics automatically would fall into addiction faster than others is a kind of racism). I know that it would be strange to travel around the world and be an automatic drug suspect, my luggage searched, my body frisked, a citizen of the drug country. Alas, while researching this article, I realized that I live in that country now.

There are good and decent arguments against legalization that go beyond the minor problems of embarrassment and humiliation. The most obvious is that the number of addicts might increase dramatically as legalization and easy access tempted millions of citizens to experiment. History suggests that this is likely to happen, at least for a while. One study shows that the number of drinkers in this country increased by more than 60 percent after the end of Prohibition, returning to the level reached before the noble experiment. Forty years after the British drug-dealers won the Opium War, the number of opium addicts in China had risen to 90 million. In laboratory experiments with cocaine, animals keep taking larger and larger amounts of the drug, until they die. Dr. Frank H. Gawin, director of stimulant abuse, treatment, and research at Yale University, said recently, "I would be terrified to live in a cocaine-legalized society."

Another objection is that nobody knows whether legalization would work—and if it drastically increased the number of addicts over a ten-year period, reversing the process might be impossible. So I'm not suggesting that legalization would transform this violent city into Pericles' Athens. But all of us know that the present system doesn't work. And if the tax revenues from sales of legal drugs could fund real treatment programs, if we treated drug addiction the way we treat alcoholism (as a health problem instead of a crime problem), if education more powerfully stressed that all drug abuse is the pastime of idiots, an experiment with legalization might be worth the attendant risks.

Some of those risks could be covered by specific proposals in the new laws. Congress could insist, for example, that all law-enforcement money freed by legalization be used to attack the deeper problems of poverty, housing, family disintegration, and illiteracy, which make life in the ghettos so hopeless and drugs so tempting. With any luck, we then might see the number of drug-users decline as more citizens realized drugs' heavy costs and as the young realized that it isn't very hip to make yourself stupid. Certainly, as the huge illicit profits vanished, the level of urban violence would be swiftly reduced.

The police who have been diverted to the drug wars could be employed against more terrible crimes. The strain on the courts and prisons would ease, leading to a criminal-justice system that guarantees more thoughtful prosecutions, fairer trials, and certain punishment for malefactors.

Legalization wouldn't be a license to go wild. Drug use would continue to be regulated, perhaps in a tougher way, with heavy penalties for doctors, nurses, pilots, train engineers, and others who have heavy social responsibilities. The Armed Forces could continue to forbid the use of drugs. Employers could insist that they don't want drug-users working for them any more than they want drunks. There would be sad and tragic examples of people fallen into the gutter, as there have always been with alcohol. A few hustlers would work the margins of the legal-drug business, trying to avoid taxes and duties. But we would rid ourselves of a lot of hypocrisy. We would be forced to face some truths about

56

57

58

59

60

paragraph 45 opens with a refutation of sorts. By saying "Legalization doesn't mean endorsement," Hamill anticipates and answers a likely objection to his proposal.

5. It is probably necessary for Hamill to concede these points. Most informed people are aware of them. But students should note that he counters these concessions in paragraph 57: "The present system doesn't work" and "an experiment with legalization might be worth the attendant risks." Generally speaking, it doesn't weaken an argument to acknowledge that the opposition has some merit. Whether Hamill's concessions are major must be decided by each individual.

6. The fragments are as follows: Paragraph 7: "Not this set." Paragraph 30: "Brilliant." Paragraph 61: "Perhaps." These fragments help Hamill make his points with added punch, and they also help vary the pace of the writing. Have students substitute complete sentences for the fragments and then notice the different effects.

7. This question, which of course has no precise answer, should spark a stimulating class discussion. You might use the discussion as the basis for a writing assignment.

King's speech is a masterful example of emotional and ethical argument. Drawing upon the full resources of formal diction, he exhorts his followers to persist in the peaceful pursuit of equality, holding forth the vision of a transfigured nation, purged of racism and basking in brotherhood. In our discussion of the emotional appeal (pages 149–50), we stress its power to "win the hearts and the help" of its audience. In this connection, you might point out that King's speech was instrumental in the pas-

ourselves, deprived at last of the comforting figures of those foreign ogres who are supposed to be corrupting all these poor innocent Americans.

61   Perhaps, along the way, we might even discover why so many millions of Americans insist on spending their days and nights in a state of self-induced mental impairment. Perhaps. For now, we just have to discover a way to get home alive.

DISCUSSION QUESTIONS

1. Hamill does not state his proposition at the beginning of his argument. What is his proposition and where is it located? Is it one of fact, policy, action, or value? Why do you think he delayed offering it?

2. Think of the essay as a whole and then indicate what function paragraph 15 serves.

3. Hamill uses statistics, authoritative opinion, and personal experience as evidence. Point out examples of each.

4. Where does Hamill refute, that is, point out shortcomings in, opposing positions? What do these refutations accomplish?

5. Hamill concedes, in paragraphs 55–57, that there are some "good and decent arguments against legalization." Do you think that this acknowledgment weakens his argument? Explain.

6. Paragraphs 7, 30, and 61 contain intentional sentence fragments. Identify them and explain why they are effective.

7. Do you agree with the complete legalization favored by Hamill, the limited legalization favored by Kupfer (pages 464–69), or a position not advocated by either? Defend your answer.

SUGGESTION FOR WRITING ■ Write an argument favoring (or opposing) the legalization of casino gambling or doctor-assisted suicides for terminally ill patients. Develop your essay with appropriate statistics, authoritative opinions, and personal experience.

Martin Luther King, Jr.

I HAVE A DREAM

Martin Luther King, Jr. (1929–1968) has earned lasting fame for his part in the civil rights struggles of the 1950s and 1960s. Born in Atlanta, Georgia, he was ordained a Baptist minister in his father's church in 1947. A year later, he graduated from Morehouse College, then went on to take a Bachelor of Divinity degree at Crozier Theological Seminary (1951) and a Ph.D. in philosophy at Boston University (1954), after which he accepted a pastorate in Montgomery, Alabama. King's involvement with civil rights grew when he organized and led a boycott that succeeded in desegregating Montgomery's bus system. In 1957, he founded and became the first president of the Southern Christian Leadership Conference and assumed a leading role in the civil rights movement. King advocated a policy of nonviolent protest based on the beliefs of Thoreau and Gandhi and never veered from it despite many acts of violence directed at him. The success of King's crusade helped bring about the passage of the Civil Rights Act of 1964 and the Voting Rights Act of 1965 and won him the Nobel Peace Prize in 1964. King was assassinated on April 4, 1968, in Memphis. Since then, his birthday, January 15, has been made a national holiday. The speech "I Have a Dream" was delivered August 28, 1963, at the Lincoln Memorial in Washington, D.C., before a crowd of 200,000 people who had gathered to commemorate the centennial of the Emancipation Proclamation and to demonstrate for pending civil rights legislation. It stands as one of the most eloquent pleas ever made for racial justice.

I am happy to join with you today in what will go down in history as the greatest demonstration for freedom in the history of our nation. 1

Five score years ago, a great American, in whose symbolic shadow we stand today, signed the Emancipation Proclamation. This momentous decree came as a great beacon light of hope to millions of Negro slaves who had been seared in the flames of withering injustice. It came as a joyous daybreak to end the long night of their captivity. 2

But one hundred years later, the Negro still is not free; one hundred years later, the life of the Negro is still sadly crippled by the manacles of segregation and the chains of discrimination; one hundred years later, the Negro lives on a lonely island of poverty in the midst of a vast ocean of material prosperity; one hundred years later, the Negro is still languishing in the corners of American society and finds himself in exile in his own land. 3

So we've come here today to dramatize a shameful condition. In a sense we've come to our nation's capital to cash a check. When the architects of our republic wrote the magnificent words of the Constitution and the Declaration of Independence, they were signing a promissory note to which every American was to fall heir. This note was the promise that all men, yes, black men as well as white men, would be guaranteed the unalienable rights of life, liberty, and the pursuit of happiness. 4

It is obvious today that America has defaulted on this promissory note in so far as her citizens of color are concerned. Instead of honoring this sacred obligation, America has given the Negro people a bad check; a check which has come back marked "insufficient funds." But we refuse to believe that the bank of justice is bankrupt. We refuse to believe that there are insufficient funds in the great vaults of opportunity of this nation. And so we've come to cash this check, a check that will give us upon demand the riches of freedom and the security of justice. 5

We have also come to this hallowed spot to remind America of the fierce urgency of now. This is no time to engage in the luxury of cooling off or to take the tranquilizing drug of gradualism. Now is the time to make real the promises of democracy; now is the time to rise from the dark and desolate valley of segregation to the sunlit path of racial justice; now is the time to lift our nation from the quicksands of racial injustice to the solid rock of brotherhood; now is the time to make justice a reality for all of God's children. It would be fatal for the nation to 6

sage of the Civil Rights Act of 1964 and the Voting Rights Act of 1965, which together have helped transform the status of America's blacks.

TEACHING STRATEGIES

1. You might reinforce the circumstances, explained in the biographical note on King, that prompted this speech. Many students will probably not be old enough to recall it.
2. Ask the class to identify and discuss the effectiveness of some of King's allusions. Responses could be tied to a discussion of audience and what assumptions King makes about his listeners.
3. Ask students why King links his dream to the broader concept of the American dream.
4. In paragraph 9 King mentions a number of injustices suffered by blacks. Discuss how the situation has changed today. Also discuss whether whites, native Americans, Mexican-Americans, senior citizens, teenagers, or the handicapped are victims of injustice. Views on contemporary discrimination might lead to an argument essay on how to cope with it.
5. Throughout his campaign for civil rights, King consistently rejected the use of violence. Are there any situations where violence is justified? A discussion of this question might also lead to an argument essay.

DISCUSSION QUESTIONS (p. 483)

1. The speech was delivered as the capstone of a march to commemorate Lincoln's signing of the Emancipation Proclamation 100 years before, so it is only fitting that King begin as he does. Moreover, by mentioning Lincoln and the Emancipation Proclamation, King draws attention to the hopes that blacks experienced a century before and that are paralleled by those stirring in the blacks of his day, while reminding his listeners that the original hopes still haven't been realized.

2. King's proposition is implied. It might be stated as follows: Today, black Americans do not enjoy the rights guaranteed by the Declaration of Independence and Constitution, but if they persevere in the nonviolent struggle for civil rights they can win these rights for themselves and their children.

3. King's immediate purpose is twofold: to inspire his followers to continue their struggle for racial justice and to prick the consciences of white Americans. To inspire his followers, he points out the rewards that they will reap if they avoid despair and continue to persevere. To appeal to white consciences, he notes that America has not lived up to the ideal expressed in the Declaration of Independence and the Constitution (paragraph 4) and points out some of the abuses and burdens that blacks must put up with (paragraphs 9 and 10). By doing all these things King hopes to accomplish a third, less immediate purpose: to win congressional and presidential support for the civil rights legislation then being considered.

4. King's primary audience is his followers in the civil rights movement. In addition, he hopes to reach white Americans, many of whom were indifferent or hostile toward his aims.

5. King's speech has four main parts. In paragraphs 3–7 he reminds his listeners of the bleak situation in which blacks find themselves and of the need for change. In paragraphs 8–10 he exhorts them to take heart and continue their struggle for justice without succumbing to bitterness and hatred. In paragraphs 11 through the first part of para-

overlook the urgency of the moment. This sweltering summer of the Negro's legitimate discontent will not pass until there is an invigorating autumn of freedom and equality.

7   Nineteen sixty-three is not an end, but a beginning. And those who hope that the Negro needed to blow off steam and will now be content will have a rude awakening if the nation returns to business as usual. There will be neither rest nor tranquility in America until the Negro is granted his citizenship rights. The whirlwinds of revolt will continue to shake the foundations of our nation until the bright day of justice emerges.

8   But there is something that I must say to my people, who stand on the worn threshold which leads into the palace of justice. In the process of gaining our rightful place, we must not be guilty of wrongful deeds. Let us not seek to satisfy our thirst for freedom by drinking from the cup of bitterness and hatred. We must forever conduct our struggle on the high plain of dignity and discipline. We must not allow our creative protests to degenerate into physical violence. Again and again we must rise to the majestic heights of meeting physical force with soul force. The marvelous new militancy, which has engulfed the Negro community, must not lead us to a distrust of all white people. For many of our white brothers, as evidenced by their presence here today, have come to realize that their destiny is tied up with our destiny. And they have come to realize that their freedom is inextricably bound to our freedom. We cannot walk alone. And as we walk, we must make the pledge that we shall always march ahead. We cannot turn back.

9   There are those who are asking the devotees of Civil Rights, "When will you be satisfied?" We can never be satisfied as long as the Negro is the victim of the unspeakable horrors of police brutality; we can never be satisfied as long as our bodies, heavy with the fatigue of travel, cannot gain lodging in the motels of the highways and the hotels of the cities; we cannot be satisfied as long as the Negro's basic mobility is from a smaller ghetto to a larger one; we can never be satisfied as long as our children are stripped of their selfhood and robbed of their dignity by signs stating "For White Only"; we cannot be satisfied as long as the Negro in Mississippi cannot vote and a Negro in New York believes he has nothing for which to vote. No! No, we are not satisfied, and we will not be satisfied until "justice rolls down like waters and righteousness like a mighty stream."

10   I am not unmindful that some of you have come here out of great trials and tribulations. Some of you have come fresh from narrow jail cells. Some of you have come from areas where your quest for freedom left you battered by the storms of persecution and staggered by the winds of police brutality. You have been the veterans of creative suffering. Continue to work with the faith that unearned suffering is redemptive. Go back to Mississippi. Go back to Alabama. Go back to South Carolina. Go back to Georgia. Go back to Louisiana. Go back to the slums and ghettos of our Northern cities, knowing that somehow this situation can and will be changed. Let us not wallow in the valley of despair.

11   I say to you today, my friends, that even though we face the difficulties of today and tomorrow, I still have a dream. It is a dream deeply rooted in the American dream. I have a dream that one day this nation will rise up and live out the true meaning of its creed, "We hold these truths to be self-evident, that all men are created equal." I have a dream that one day on the red hills of Georgia, sons of former slaves and the sons of former slave owners will be able to sit down together at the table of brotherhood. I have a dream that one day even the state of Mississippi, a state sweltering with the heat of injustice, sweltering with the heat of oppression, will be transformed into an oasis of freedom and justice. I have a

dream that my four little children will one day live in a nation where they will not be judged by the color of their skin, but by the content of their character.

I HAVE A DREAM TODAY! 12

I have a dream that one day down in Alabama—with its vicious racists, with 13 its Governor having his lips dripping with the words of interposition and nullification—one day right there in Alabama, little black boys and black girls will be able to join hands with little white boys and white girls as sisters and brothers.

I HAVE A DREAM TODAY! 14

I have a dream that one day every valley shall be exalted, every hill and 15 mountain shall be made low. The rough places will be plain and the crooked places will be made straight, "and the glory of the Lord shall be revealed, and all flesh shall see it together."

This is our hope. This is the faith that I go back to the South with. With this 16 faith we will be able to hew out of the mountain of despair, a stone of hope. With this faith we will be able to transform the jangling discords of our nation into a beautiful symphony of brotherhood. With this faith we will be able to work together, to pray together, to struggle together, to go to jail together, to stand up for freedom together, knowing that we will be free one day. And this will be the day. This will be the day when all of God's children will be able to sing with new meaning, "My country 'tis of thee, sweet land of liberty, of thee I sing. Land where my fathers died, land of the pilgrim's pride, from every mountain side, let freedom ring." And if America is to be a great nation, this must become true.

So let freedom ring from the prodigious hilltops of New Hampshire; let 17 freedom ring from the mighty mountains of New York; let freedom ring from the heightening Alleghenies of Pennsylvania; let freedom ring from the snowcapped Rockies of Colorado; let freedom ring from the curvaceous slopes of California. But not only that. Let freedom ring from Stone Mountain of Georgia; let freedom ring from Lookout Mountain of Tennessee; let freedom ring from every hill and mole hill of Mississippi. "From every mountainside, let freedom ring."

And when this happens, and when we allow freedom to ring, when we let 18 it ring from every village and every hamlet, from every state and every city, we will be able to speed up that day when all of God's children, black men and white men, Jews and Gentiles, Protestants and Catholics, will be able to join hands and sing in the words of the old Negro spiritual: "Free at last. Free at last. Thank God Almighty, we are free at last."

DISCUSSION QUESTIONS

1. Why do you think King begins with a reference to Lincoln?
2. Does this speech have a stated or an implied proposition? What is the proposition?
3. What does King hope to accomplish by the speech? How does he go about achieving his aim(s)?
4. What is the audience for the speech?
5. How does King organize his speech? How does this organization advance his purpose?
6. Which type(s) of argumentative appeal does King use? Cite appropriate parts of the speech.
7. What kinds of stylistic devices does King use? Where do they occur? How do they increase the effectiveness of the speech?

graph 16, he lays out his hopes for the future, and in the remainder of the speech he foresees victory.

6. King's speech is a masterful example of emotional and ethical appeal. Emotion is evident in every part of the speech, but perhaps most strongly in paragraph 9, which points out the injustices still suffered by blacks, and in paragraphs 16–19, which set out King's dreams for the future. In calling for racial justice, King emerges as a deeply ethical individual, an impression that is enhanced by his rejection of physical violence (paragraph 8) and his religious allusions (paragraphs 6, 15, 16, and 18).

7. King relies heavily on metaphors and repetition to accomplish his purpose. Metaphors abound throughout the speech. Brief examples include "beacon light of hope" and "flames of withering injustice" (paragraph 2); "Manacles of segregation," "chains of discrimination," and "vast oceans of material prosperity" (paragraph 3); "sweltering summer . . . discontent," and "invigorating autumn of freedom" (paragraph 6); "bright day of justice" (paragraph 7); "palace of justice" and "cup of bitterness and hatred" (paragraph 8); "Storms of persecution," "winds of police brutality," and "valley of despair" (paragraph 10); "table of brotherhood," "heat of injustice, sweltering with the heat of oppression," and "oasis of freedom and justice" (paragraph 11); and "mountain of despair," "stone of hope," and "beautiful symphony of brotherhood" (paragraph 16). Paragraphs 4 and 5 constitute an extended metaphor or analogy that likens the rights guaranteed by the Constitution and Bill of Rights to a promissory note drawn on a bank. This extended metaphor includes two short metaphors: "bank of justice" and "vaults of opportunity."

Repetition is likewise prominently featured in much of
the speech. In paragraph 3
we have "one hundred years
later," in paragraph 6 *"Now* is
the time," in paragraph 9
"We can never be satisfied"
and variations thereon, and in
paragraph 10 "Go back." This
technique reaches its climax
with the powerful and moving repetition of "I have a
dream" (paragraphs 11–15)
and "Let freedom ring" (paragraphs 17 and 18). Other stylistic devices include balanced
sentences "from the dark and
desolate valley of segregation
to the sunlit path of racial
justice" and "from the quicksands of racial injustice to the
solid rock of brotherhood"
(paragraph 6) and similes
"until justice rolls down like
waters and righteousness like
a mighty stream" (paragraph
9). Metaphors and similes add
vividness to the speech, thus
strengthening the listeners'
grasp of the ideas presented.
Repetition helps drum the
points home and at the same
time adds rhythm, and therefore emotional force, to the
message.

SUGGESTION FOR WRITING ■ **Write an essay calling for some major social or political change. For example, you might recommend that the country enact national health insurance, institute a peacetime draft, ban smoking in all public places, amend the Constitution to ban or legalize abortions, establish federally funded day-care centers for working mothers, or offer all workers a 30-day leave of absence without pay.**

Mixing the Writing Strategies

OVERVIEW OF MIXING
THE WRITING STRATEGIES
Although all three essays in
this section combine several
writing strategies, one is fundamentally argument, one
fundamentally illustration, and
one fundamentally comparison. The argument essay uses
statistics to help make its
point, the comparison essay
uses the block pattern of organization, and the illustration
essay relies on several brief
examples rather than a single
extended one. One essay uses
technical diction, one informal
diction, and one formal-
informal diction.

As we noted on page 163, most essays mix various writing strategies for assorted purposes. This section features three examples. Margin notations on the Commoner essay point out the interplay of several strategies, and the discussion questions following the Klass and Greenfield essays direct your attention to the strategies these writers use.

Barry Commoner

WHY WE HAVE FAILED

Title indicates causes

Barry Commoner (born 1917) is one of our best-known writers on environmental matters. Born in New York, he earned his undergraduate degree at Columbia University (1937) and graduate degrees at Harvard University (1938 and 1941). Following graduation, Commoner embarked on an academic career that has led him to the directorship of the Center for the Biology of Natural Systems at New York's Queens College. He is a member of numerous professional organizations and has held executive positions with a number of them. In addition, he has served on the editorial boards of numerous publications. His books include Science and Survival *(1966),* The Closing Circle: Nature, Man, and Technology *(1971),* The Poverty of Power *(1976), and* The Politics of Energy *(1979). He has edited several volumes on energy as well as written hundreds of journal articles. In our example, from the journal published by the environmental group Greenpeace, he criticizes our way of handling environmental problems and proposes a radically different approach.*

In 1970, in response to growing concern, the U.S. Congress began a massive effort to undo the pollution damage of the preceding decades. In short order, legislators in Washington passed the National Environmental Protection Act (NEPA) and created the Environmental Protection Agency (EPA) to administer it. These two events are the cornerstone of what is indisputably the world's most vigorous pollution control effort, a model for other nations and a template for dozens of laws and amendments passed since. Now, nearly 20 years later, it is time to ask an important and perhaps embarrassing question: how far have we progressed toward the goal of restoring the quality of the environment?

Introduction: narrative

The answer is indeed humbling. Apart from a few notable exceptions, environmental quality has improved only slightly, and in some cases worsened. Since 1975, emissions of sulfur dioxide and carbon monoxide are down by about

Body: paragraphs 2–21

485

Effects: paragraphs
2 and 3

19 percent, but nitrogen oxides are up about 4 percent. Overall improvement in major pollutants amounts to only about 15 to 20 percent, and the rate of improvement has actually slowed considerably.

3   There are several notable and heartening exceptions. Pollution levels of a few chemicals—DDT and PCBs in wildlife and people, mercury in the fish of the Great Lakes, strontium 90 in the food chain and phosphate pollution in some local rivers—have been reduced by 70 percent or more. Levels of airborne lead have declined more than 90 percent since 1975.

Argument by illustrations

4   The successes explain what works and what does not. Every success on the very short list of significant environmental quality improvements reflects the same remedial action: production of the pollutant has been stopped. DDT and PCB levels have dropped because their production and use have been banned. Mercury is much less prevalent because it is no longer used to manufacture chlorine. Lead has been taken out of gasoline. And strontium has decayed to low levels because the United States and the Soviet Union had the good sense to stop the atmospheric nuclear bomb tests that produced it.

Argument by comparison

5   The lesson is plain: pollution prevention works; pollution control does not. Only where production technology has been changed to eliminate the pollutant has the environment been substantially improved. Where it remains unchanged, where an attempt is made to trap the pollutant in an appended control device—the automobile's catalytic converter or the power plant's scrubber—environmental improvement is modest or nil. When a pollutant is attacked at the point of origin, it can be eliminated. But once it is produced, it is too late.

Illustrations

Cause: paragraphs 6 and 7

6   Most of our environmental problems are the inevitable result of the sweeping technological changes that transformed the U.S. economic system after World War II: the large, high-powered cars; the shift from fuel-efficient railroads to gas-guzzling trucks and cars; the substitution of fertilizers for manure and crop rotation and of toxic synthetic pesticides for ladybugs and birds.

Illustrations

7   By 1970, it was clear that these technological changes were the root cause of environmental pollution. But the environmental laws now in place do not address the technological origin of pollutants. I remember the incredulity in Senator Edmund Muskie's voice during NEPA hearings when he asked me whether I was really testifying that the technology that generated postwar economic progress was also the cause of pollution. I was.

Cause and effect

8   Because environmental legislation ignored the origin of the assault on environmental quality, it has dealt only with its subsequent problems—in effect defining the disease as a collection of symptoms. As a result, all environmental legislation mandates only palliative measures. The notion of preventing pollution—the only measure that really works—has yet to be given any administrative force.

Argument by illustrations:
paragraphs 9 and 10

9   The goal established by the Clean Air Act in 1970 could have been met if the EPA had confronted the auto industry with a demand for fundamental changes in engine design, changes that were practical and possible. And had American farmers been required to reduce the high rate of nitrogen fertilization, nitrate water pollution would now be falling instead of increasing.

10   If the railroads and mass transit were expanded, if the electric power system were decentralized and increasingly based on cogenerators and solar sources, if American homes were weatherized, fuel consumption and air pollution would be sharply reduced. If brewers were forbidden to put plastic nooses on six-packs of beer, if supermarkets were not allowed to wrap polyvinyl chloride film around

everything in sight, if McDonald's restaurants could rediscover the paper plate, if the use of plastics was cut back to those things considered worth the social costs (say artificial hearts or video tape), then we could push back the petrochemical industry's toxic invasion of the biosphere.

Of course, all this is easier said than done. I am fully aware that what I am proposing is no small thing. It means that sweeping changes in the major systems of production—agriculture, industry, power production and transportation— would be undertaken for a social purpose: environmental improvement. This represents social (as contrasted with private) governance of the means of production—an idea that is so foreign to what passes for our national ideology that even to mention it violates a deep-seated taboo.

11

Effect

Comparison

The major consequence of this powerful taboo is the failure to reach the goals in environmental quality that motivated the legislation of the 1970s.

12

Effect

In the absence of a prevention policy, the EPA adopted a convoluted pollution control process. First, the EPA must estimate the degree of harm represented by different levels of the numerous environmental pollutants. Next, some "acceptable" level of harm is chosen (for example, a cancer risk of one in a million) and emission and/or ambient concentration standards that can presumably achieve that risk level are established.

13

Process: paragraphs 13 and 14

Illustration

Polluters are then expected to respond by introducing control measures (such as automobile exhaust catalysts or power plant stack scrubbers) that will bring emissions to the required levels. If the regulation survives the inevitable challenges from industry (and in recent years from the administration itself), the polluters will invest in the appropriate control systems. Catalysts are attached to cars, and scrubbers to the power plants and trash-burning incinerators. If all goes well—and it frequently does not—at least some areas of the country and some production facilities are then in compliance with the regulation.

14

Illustrations

The net result is that an "acceptable" pollution level is frozen in place. Industry, having invested heavily in equipment designed to reach just the required level, is unlikely to invest in further improvements.

15

Effect

Clearly, this process is the opposite of the preventive approach to public health. It strives not for the continuous improvement of environmental health, but for the social acceptance of some, hopefully low, risk to health. By contrast, the preventive approach aims at progressively reducing the risk to health. It does not mandate some socially convenient stopping point. The medical professions, after all, did not decide that the smallpox prevention program could stop when the risk reached one in a million. They kept on, and the disease has now been wiped out worldwide.

16

Comparison

Analogy

How do you decide when to stop, where to set the standard for acceptable pollution? The current fashion is to submit the question to a risk/benefit analysis. Since the pollutants' ultimate effect can often be assessed by the number of lives lost, the risk/benefit analysis requires that a value be placed on human life. Such reckoning often bases that value on lifelong earning power, so that a poor person's life is worth less than a rich person's. So, on the risk/benefit scale, the poor can be exposed to more pollution than the rich. In fact, this is what is happening in the United States: the burden of an environmental risk—say the siting of a municipal incinerator or a hazardous waste landfill—falls disproportionally on poor people, who lack the political and financial clout to deter the risk.

17

Comparison

Effect
Illustrations

In this way, risk/benefit analysis—a seemingly straightforward numerical computation—conceals a profound, unresolved moral question: should poor peo-

18

Effects

ple be subjected to a more severe environmental burden than rich people, simply because they lack the resources to evade it? Since in practice the risk/benefit equation masquerades as science, it relieves society of the duty to confront this question. One result of failing to adopt the preventive approach is that the regulatory agencies have been driven into positions that seriously diminish the force of social morality.

19   The fate of Alar, the pesticide used to enhance the marketability of apples, provides a recent instructive example of what prevention means. Like many other petrochemical products, Alar poses a health risk. It has been proven to induce cancer in test animals. As in many other such cases, a debate has flourished over the extent of the hazard to people, especially children, and over what standards should be applied to limit exposure to "acceptable" levels.

20   In June, Alar broke out of the pattern when the manufacturer, Uniroyal, decided that regardless of the toxicological uncertainties, Alar would be taken off the market. They acted simply because parents were unhappy about raising their children on apple juice that represented *any* threat to their health. Food after all, is supposed to be good for you.

21   This is a clear-cut example of the benefits of prevention, as opposed to control. Pollution prevention means identifying the source of the pollutant in the production process, eliminating it from that process and substituting a more environmentally benign method of production. This differentiates it from source reduction (reducing the amount of the pollutant produced, either through altering processes or simple housekeeping) and pollution control. Once a pollutant is eliminated, the elaborate system of risk assessment, standard setting and the inevitable debates and litigation become irrelevant.

22   Instituting the practice of prevention rather than control will require the courage to challenge the taboo against questioning the dominance of private interests over the public interest. But I suggest that we begin with an open public discussion of what has gone wrong, and why. That is the necessary first step on the road toward realizing the nation's unswerving goal—restoring the quality of the environment.

Margin notes:

Illustration: paragraph 19 and 20

Argument Definition

Comparison Definition

Effects

Conclusion: Effect

DISCUSSION QUESTIONS

1. This sentence draws attention to itself because its length contrasts markedly with that of the preceding sentences in the paragraph. As a result, the short sentence hits with impact and helps emphasize Commoner's point about technology causing pollution.
2. The parallelism gives the writing continuity, rhythm, and balance. In addition, the detailing of possibilities and their beneficial effects leads Commoner to his proposal (in paragraph 11) for social rather than private governance of the means of production.
3. This question should spark a lively class discussion.

DISCUSSION QUESTIONS

1. Discuss the effectiveness of the short sentence ("I was.") that ends paragraph 7.
2. Why do you think Commoner uses the "If . . . , then . . . " pattern of expression in paragraph 10?
3. Do you agree with the approach that Commoner proposes in paragraph 11? Why or why not?

SUGGESTION FOR WRITING ■ Write an essay showing why someone or some organization has succeeded at some endeavor. Select a situation you know well and then develop it with an appropriate mixture of writing strategies.

Perri Klass

SHE'S YOUR BASIC L.O.L. IN N.A.D.

Perri Klass (born 1958) has pursued dual careers as physician and writer. A native of Trinidad, she was brought to the United States by her parents, attended schools in New York and New Jersey, and in 1986 graduated from Harvard Medical School. Her fiction writings include one novel, Recombinations *(1985), a short-story collection,* I Am Having an Adventure *(1986), and numerous short stories in popular magazines. Her essays have appeared in a variety of newspapers and magazines, as well as in a collection entitled* A Not Entirely Benign Procedure *(1987). In our essay, Klass examines the gains and losses that result from understanding and using medical jargon.*

"Mrs. Tolstoy is your basic L.O.L. in N.A.D., admitted for a soft rule-out M.I.," the intern announces. I scribble that on my patient list. In other words Mrs. Tolstoy is a Little Old Lady in No Apparent Distress who is in the hospital to make sure she hasn't had a heart attack (rule out a myocardial infarction). And we think it's unlikely that she has had a heart attack (a *soft* rule-out). 1

If I learned nothing else during my first three months of working in the hospital as a medical student, I learned endless jargon and abbreviations. I started out in a state of primeval innocence, in which I didn't even know that "s̄ C.P., S.O.B., N/V" meant "without chest pain, shortness of breath, or nausea and vomiting." By the end I took the abbreviations so for granted that I would complain to my mother the English Professor, "And can you believe I had to put down *three* NG tubes last night?" 2

"You'll have to tell me what an NG tube is if you want me to sympathize properly," my mother said. NG, nasogastric—isn't it obvious? 3

I picked up not only the specific expressions but the patterns of speech and the grammatical conventions; for example, you never say that a patient's blood pressure fell or that his cardiac enzymes rose. Instead, the patient is always the subject of the verb: "He dropped his pressure." "He bumped his enzymes." This sort of construction probably reflects the profound irritation of the intern when the nurses come in the middle of the night to say that Mr. Dickinson has disturbingly low blood pressure. "Oh, he's gonna hurt me bad tonight," the intern may say, inevitably angry at Mr. Dickinson for dropping his pressure and creating a problem. 4

When chemotherapy fails to cure Mrs. Bacon's cancer, what we say is, "Mrs. Bacon failed chemotherapy." 5

"Well, we've already had one hit today, and we're up next, but at least we've got mostly stable players on our team." This means that our team (group of doctors and medical students) has already gotten one new admission today, and it is our turn again, so we'll get whoever is next admitted in emergency, but at least most of the patients we already have are fairly stable, that is, unlikely to drop their pressures or in any other way get suddenly sicker and hurt us bad. Baseball metaphor is pervasive: A no-hitter is a night without any new admissions. A player is always a patient—a nitrate player is a patient on nitrates, a unit player is a patient in the intensive-care unit and so on, until you reach the terminal player. 6

7   It is interesting to consider what it means to be winning, or doing well, in this perennial baseball game. When the intern hangs up the phone and announces, "I got a hit," that is not cause for congratulations. The team is not scoring points; rather, it is getting hit, being bombarded with new patients. The object of the game from the point of view of the doctors, considering the players for whom they are already responsible, is to get as few new hits as possible.

8   These special languages contribute to a sense of closeness and professional spirit among people who are under a great deal of stress. As a medical student, it was exciting for me to discover that I'd finally cracked the code, that I could understand what doctors said and wrote and could use the same formulations myself. Some people seem to become enamored of the jargon for its own sake, perhaps because they are so deeply thrilled with the idea of medicine, with the idea of themselves as doctors.

9   I knew a medical student who was referred to by the interns on the team as Mr. Eponym because he was so infatuated with eponymous terminology, the more obscure the better. He never said "capillary pulsations" if he could say "Quincke's pulses." He would lovingly tell over the multinamed syndromes—Wolff-Parkinson-White, Lown-Ganong-Levine, Henoch-Schonlein—until the temptation to suggest Schleswig-Holstein or Stevenson-Kefauver or Baskin-Robbins became irresistible to his less reverent colleagues.

10   And there is the jargon that you don't ever want to hear yourself using. You know that your training is changing you, but there are certain changes you think would be going a little too far.

11   The resident was describing a man with devastating terminal pancreatic cancer. "Basically he's C.T.D.," the resident concluded. I reminded myself that I had resolved not to be shy about asking when I didn't understand things. "C.T.D.?" I asked timidly.

12   The resident smirked at me. "Circling The Drain."

13   The images are vivid and terrible. "What happened to Mrs. Melville?"

14   "Oh, she boxed last night." To box is to die, of course.

15   Then there are the more pompous locutions that can make the beginning medical student nervous about the effects of medical training. A friend of mine was told by his resident, "A pregnant woman with sickle-cell represents a failure of genetic counseling."

16   Mr. Eponym, who tried hard to talk like the doctors, once explained to me, "An infant is basically a brainstem preparation." A brainstem preparation, as used in neurological research, is an animal whose higher brain functions have been destroyed so that only the most primitive reflexes remain, like the sucking reflex, the startle reflex and the rooting reflex.

17   The more extreme forms aside, one most important function of medical jargon is to help doctors maintain some distance from their patients. By reformulating a patient's pain and problems into a language that the patient doesn't even speak, I suppose we are in some sense taking those pains and problems under our jurisdiction and also reducing their emotional impact. This linguistic separation between doctors and patients allows conversations to go on at the bedside that are unintelligible to the patient. "Naturally, we're worried about adeno-C.A.," the intern can say to the medical student, and lung cancer need never be mentioned.

18   I learned a new language this past summer. At times it thrills me to hear myself using it. It enables me to understand my colleagues, to communicate

DISCUSSION QUESTIONS

1. Klass develops her essay primarily by a substantial number of illustrations of medical jargon and abbreviations. These examples are found in the title as well as in paragraphs 1–7, 9, 11–12, and 14–17.

2. Definition: paragraphs 1–4, 6, 7, 12, 14, 16, 17; cause and/or effect: paragraphs 2–4, 8–15, 17, and 18; narration: paragraph 9; analogy: in paragraphs 6 and 7, Klass develops a type of analogy between a baseball team and a hospital team.

effectively in the hospital. Yet I am uncomfortably aware that I will never again notice the peculiarities and even atrocities of medical language as keenly as I did this summer. There may be specific expressions I manage to avoid, but even as I remark them, promising myself I will never use them, I find that this language is becoming my professional speech. It no longer sounds strange in my ears—or coming from my mouth. And I am afraid that as with any new language, to use it properly you must absorb not only the vocabulary but also the structure, the logic, the attitudes. At first you may notice these new alien assumptions every time you put together a sentence, but with time and increased fluency you stop being aware of them at all. And as you lose that awareness, for better or for worse, you move closer and closer to being a doctor instead of just talking like one.

DISCUSSION QUESTIONS

1. Klass develops her essay by using one primary writing strategy and several secondary ones. Identify her primary strategy and point out where she uses it.
2. Where does she use definition? Cause and/or effect? Narration? Analogy?
3. How does Klass use contrast when she evaluates medical jargon?
4. Klass tells us in paragraph 17 that the use of jargon to describe medical conditions helps in "reducing their emotional impact." Explain what she means.
5. Point out why the last sentence in paragraph 18 is an appropriate ending for the essay.

SUGGESTION FOR WRITING ■ Write an essay that clarifies the jargon used in some profession or that used by fitness fanatics, social climbers, dieters, students, or some other people with shared values. Use several writing strategies to make your point.

3. Klass draws a contrast between the desirable and undesirable uses of medical jargon. Such jargon establishes an effective means of communication between medical professionals, contributes to "closeness and professional spirit" (paragraph 8), helps doctors "maintain some distance from their patients" (paragraph 17), and enables Klass to feel that she's "cracked the code" (paragraph 8). On the other hand, "C.T.D." (paragraphs 11 and 12), "boxed" (paragraph 14), the sickle-cell reference (paragraph 15), and Mr. Eponym's uses (paragraph 9) leave something to be desired.
4. Jargon helps establish some distance and thus diminishes the doctor's emotional involvement with the patient.
5. Klass reflects on the new language she learned during her first three months working as a medical student in the hospital. In addition, "for better or for worse" sums up the contrasting feelings discussed in answer 3.

Jeff Greenfield

THE BLACK AND WHITE TRUTH ABOUT BASKETBALL

Jeff Greenfield (born 1943) is a native of New York City, where he now pursues a dual career in writing and TV broadcasting. A graduate of the University of Wisconsin and the Yale Law school, he served on the staffs of New York mayor John Lindsay and Senator Robert Kennedy before turning full time to his present occupations. His short pieces have appeared in many well-known magazines, and he has authored books on television, sports, and politics. In our selection, Greenfield offers his explanation for the dominating role played by blacks in professional basketball.

The dominance of black athletes over professional basketball is beyond dispute. Two-thirds of the players are black, and the number would be greater

PERSPECTIVE

It is possible that some will see racist overtones in this differentiation between "black" and "white" styles of basketball. In paragraph 4, however, Greenfield cautions that he is "talking about culture, not chromosomes." And in the final paragraph he observes how the two styles "fit together" on the court and result in "a fusion of cultures."

were it not for the continuing practice of picking white bench warmers for the sake of balance. Over the last two decades, no more than three white players have been among the ten starting players on the National Basketball Association's All-Star team, and in the last quarter century, only two white players—Dave Cowens and Larry Bird of the Boston Celtics—have ever been chosen as the NBA's Most Valuable Player.

2   And at a time when a baseball executive can lose his job for asserting that blacks lack "the necessities" to become pro sports executives and when the National Football League only in 1989 had its first black head coach, the NBA stands as a pro sports league that hired its first black head coach in 1968 (Bill Russell) and its first black general manager in the early 1970s (Wayne Embry of the Milwaukee Bucks). What discrimination remains—lack of equal opportunity for speaking engagements and product endorsements—has more to do with society than with basketball.

3   This dominance reflects a natural inheritance: Basketball is a pastime of the urban poor. The current generation of black athletes are heirs to a tradition more than half a century old. In a neighborhood without the money for bats, gloves, hockey sticks and ice skates, or shoulder pads, basketball is an eminently accessible sport. "Once it was the game of the Irish and Italian Catholics in Rockaway and the Jews on Fordham Road in the Bronx," writes David Wolf in his brilliant book, *Foul!* "It was recreation, status, and a way out." But now the ethnic names have been changed: Instead of the Red Holzmans, Red Auerbachs, and the McGuire brothers, there are Julius Ervings and Michael Jordans, Ralph Sampsons and Kareem Abdul-Jabbars. And professional basketball is a sport with national television exposure and million-dollar salaries.

4   But the mark on basketball of today's players can be measured by more than money or visibility. It is a question of style. For there is a clear difference between "black" and "white" styles of play that is as clear as the difference between 155th Street at Eighth Avenue and Crystal City, Missouri. Most simply (remembering we are talking about culture, not chromosomes), "black" basketball is the use of superb athletic skill to adapt to the limits of space imposed by the game. "White" ball is the pulverization of that space by sheer intensity.[1]

5   It takes a conscious effort to realize how constricted the space is on a basketball court. Place a regulation court (ninety-four by fifty feet) on a football field, and it will reach from the back of the end zone to the twenty-one yard line; its width will cover less than a third of the field. On a baseball diamond, a basketball court will reach from home plate to first base. Compared to its principal indoor rival, ice hockey, basketball covers about one-fourth the playing area. Moreover, during the normal flow of the game, most of the action takes place on the third of the court nearest the basket. It is in this dollhouse space that ten men, each of them half a foot taller than the average man, come together to battle each other.

6   There is, thus, no room; basketball is a struggle for the edge: the half step with which to cut around the defender for a lay-up, the half second of freedom

---

[1]This distinction has nothing to do with the question of whether whites can play as "well" as blacks. In 1987, the Detroit Pistons' Isaiah Thomas quipped that the Celtics' Larry Bird was "a pretty good player," but would be much less celebrated and wealthy if he were black. As Thomas later said, Bird is one of the greatest pro players in history. Nor is this distinction about "smart," although the Los Angeles Lakers' Magic Johnson is right in saying that too many journalists ascribe brilliant strategy by black players to be solely due to "innate" ability.

with which to release a jump shot, the instant a head turns allowing a pass to a teammate breaking for the basket. It is an arena for the subtlest of skills: the head fake, the shoulder fake, the shift of body weight to the right and the sudden cut to the left. Deception is crucial to success; and to young men who have learned early and painfully that life is a battle for survival, basketball is one of the few pursuits in which the weapon of deception is a legitimate tactic rather than the source of trouble.

If there is, then, the need to compete in a crowd, to battle for the edge, then the surest strategy is to develop the *unexpected*: to develop a shot that is simply and fundamentally different from the usual methods of putting the ball in the basket. Drive to the hoop, but go under it and come up the other side; hold the ball at waist level and shoot from there instead of bringing the ball up to eye level; leap into the air, but fall away from the basket instead of toward it. All these tactics, which a fan can see embodied in the astonishing play of the Chicago Bulls' Michael Jordan, take maximum advantage of the crowding on the court. They also stamp uniqueness on young men who may feel it nowhere else. 7

"For many young men in the slums," David Wolf writes, "the school yard is the only place they can feel true pride in what they do, where they can move free of inhibitions and where they can, by being spectacular, rise for the moment against the drabness and anonymity of their lives. Thus, when a player develops extraordinary 'school yard' moves and shots . . . [they] become his measure as a man." 8

So the moves that begin as tactics for scoring soon become calling cards. You don't just lay the ball in for an uncontested basket; you take the ball in both hands, leap as high as you can, and slam the ball through the hoop. When you jump in the air, fake a shot, bring the ball back to your body, and throw up a shot, all without coming back down, you have proved your worth in uncontestable fashion. 9

This liquid grace is an integral part of "black" ball, almost exclusively the province of the playground player. Some white stars like Bob Cousy, Billy Cunningham, and Doug Collins had it, and the Celtics' Kevin McHale has it now: the body control, the moves to the basket, the free-ranging mobility. Most of them also possessed the surface ease that is integral to the "black" style; an incorporation of the ethic of mean streets—to "make it" is not just to have wealth but to have it without strain. Whatever the muscles and organs are doing, the face of the "black" star almost never shows it. Magic Johnson of the Lakers can bring the ball downcourt with two men on him, whip a pass through an invisible opening, cut to the basket, take a return pass, and hit the shot all with no more emotion than a quick smile. So stoic was San Antonio Spurs' great George Gervin that he earned the nickname "Ice Man." (Interestingly, a black coach like former Celtics' coach K. C. Jones exhibited far less emotion on the bench than a white counterpart like Dick Motta or Jack Ramsey.) 10

If there is a single trait that characterizes "black" ball it is leaping ability. Bob Cousy, ex-Celtic great and former pro coach, says that "when coaches get together, one is sure to say, 'I've got the one black kid in the country who can't jump.' When coaches see a white boy who can jump or who moves with extraordinary quickness, they say, 'He should have been born black, he's that good.' " 11

Don Nelson, now a top executive with the Golden State Warriors, recalls that back in 1970, Dave Cowens, then a relatively unknown graduate of Florida State, prepared for his rookie pro season by playing in the Rucker League, an outdoor competition in Harlem playgrounds that pits pros against college kids 12 and playground stars. So ferocious was Cowens's leaping ability, Nelson says, that "when the summer was over, everyone wanted to know who the white son of a bitch was who could jump so high." That's another way to overcome a crowd around the basket—just go over it.

13   Speed, mobility, quickness, acceleration, "the moves"—all of these are catch-phrases that surround the "black" playground athlete, the style of play. So does the most racially tinged of attributes, "rhythm." Yet rhythm is what the black stars themselves talk about: feeling the flow of the game, finding the tempo of the dribble, the step, the shot. It is an instinctive quality (although it stems from hundreds of hours of practice), and it is one that has led to difficulty between system-oriented coaches and free-form players. "Cats from the street have their own rhythm when they play," said college drop-out Bill Spivey, onetime New York high school star. "It's not a matter of somebody setting you up and you shooting. You *feel* the shot. When a coach holds you back, you lose the feel and it isn't fun anymore."

14   When legendary Brooklyn playground star Connie Hawkins was winding up his NBA career under Laker coach Bill Sharman, he chafed under the methodical style of play. "He's systematic to the point where it begins to be a little too much. It's such an action-reaction type of game that when you have to do everything the same way, I think you lose something.

15   There is another kind of basketball that has grown up in America. It is not played on asphalt playgrounds with a crowd of kids competing for the court; it is played on macadam driveways by one boy with a ball and a backboard nailed over the garage; it is played in gyms in the frigid winter of the rural Midwest and on Southern dirt courts. It is a mechanical, precise development of skills (when Don Nelson was an Iowa farm boy, his incentive to make his shots was that an errant rebound would land in the middle of chicken droppings). It is a game without frills, without flow, but with effectiveness. It is "white" basketball: jagged, sweaty, stumbling, intense. Where a "black" player overcomes an obstacle with finesse and body control, a "white" player reacts by outrunning or overpowering the obstacle.

16   By this definition, the Boston Celtics are a classically "white" team. They rarely suit up a player with dazzling moves; indeed, such a player would probably make Red Auerbach swallow his cigar. Instead, the Celtics wear you down with execution, with constant running, with the same play run again and again and again. The rebound by Robert Parrish triggers the fast break, as everyone races downcourt; the ball goes to Larry Bird, who pulls up and takes the shot or who drives and then finds Reggie Lewis or Kevin McHale free for an easy basket.

17   Perhaps the most definitively "white" position is that of the quick forward, one without great moves to the basket, without highly developed shots, without the height and mobility for rebounding effectiveness. So what does he do?

18   He runs. He runs from the opening jump to the final buzzer. He runs up and down the court, from base line to base line, back and forth under the basket, looking for the opening, the pass, the chance to take a quick step, the high percentage shot. To watch San Antonio's Mark Olberding or Detroit's Bill Laimbeer, players without speed or obvious moves, is to wonder what they are doing in the NBA—until you see them swing free and throw up a shot that, without demanding any apparent skill, somehow goes in the basket more frequently than the shots of many of their more skilled teammates. And to have watched the New York Knicks' (now U.S. Senator) Bill Bradley, or the Celtics' John Havlicek, is to have watched "white" ball at its best.

DISCUSSION QUESTIONS

1. This is primarily a comparison essay. The title suggests that Greenfield will compare black and white players, and the strategy becomes apparent in the first paragraph.
2. Paragraphs 1–4 serve as the introduction. The first two paragraphs demonstrate that blacks dominate the game of basketball. Paragraph 3 con-

Havlicek or Lambeer, or the former Laker Kurt Rambis, stand in dramatic contrast to Michael Jordan or to the Philadelphia 76ers' legend, Julius Erving. Erving had the capacity to make legends come true, leaping from the foul line and slam-dunking the ball on his way down; going up for a lay-up, pulling the ball to his body, and driving under and up the other side of the rim, defying gravity and probability with impossible moves and jumps. Michael Jordan of the Chicago Bulls has been seen by thousands spinning a full 360 degrees in midair before slamming the ball through the hoop. 19

When John Havlicek played, by contrast, he was the living embodiment of his small-town Ohio background. He would bring the ball downcourt, weaving left, then right, looking for a path. He would swing the ball to a teammate, cut behind the pick, take the pass, and release the shot in a flicker of time. It looked plain, unvarnished. But it was a blend of skills that not more than half a dozen other players in the league possessed. 20

To former pro Jim McMillian, a black who played quick forward with "white" attributes, "it's a matter of environment. Julius Erving grew up in a different environment from John Havlicek. John came from a very small town in Ohio. There everything was done the easy way, the shortest distance between two points. It's nothing fancy; very few times will he go one-on-one. He hits the lay-up, hits the jump shot, makes the free throw, and after the game you look up and say, 'How did he hurt us that much?' " 21

"White" ball, then, is the basketball of patience, method, and sometimes brute strength. "Black" ball is the basketball of electric self-expression. One player has all the time in the world to perfect his skills, the other a need to prove himself. These are slippery categories, because a poor boy who is black can play "white" and a white boy of middle-class parents can play "black." Bill Cartwright of the Chicago Bulls and Steve Alford of the Golden State Warriors are athletes who seem to defy these categories. 22

And what makes basketball the most intriguing of sports is how these styles do not necessarily clash; how the punishing intensity of "white" players and the dazzling moves of the "blacks" can fit together, a fusion of cultures that seems more and more difficult in the world beyond the out-of-bounds line. 23

DISCUSSION QUESTIONS

1. What primary writing strategy does Greenfield use to develop his essay? At what point does this strategy become evident?
2. Which paragraphs serve as the introduction? What does each accomplish?
3. Identify the thesis sentence of the essay.
4. Where does Greenfield use narration? Process? Illustration? Classification? Cause and Effect? Definition?
5. Explain the organization of the essay.
6. What does Greenfield accomplish in his final paragraph?

SUGGESTION FOR WRITING ■ **Write an essay that accounts for the dominance of blacks in some other sport, in a type of music such as jazz or the blues, or in some other appropriate field. Use several writing strategies to develop the paper.**

tends that this domination stems from the socioeconomic situation of youthful black players. Paragraph 4 defines the "black" and "white" styles of play, which Greenfield explores in the body of the paper.
3. The thesis statement consists of the final two sentences of paragraph 4, which point out the difference between the black and white styles of playing basketball.
4. Narration: paragraph 12; process: paragraphs 2, 9, 10, 16, 19, and 20; illustration: paragraphs 3, 7, 10, 12, 14, 15, 16, 18, 19, 20, and 21; classification: paragraph 22; cause and effect: paragraphs 3, 5, 6, 7, 8, and 9; definition: paragraphs 4, 13, 15, and 22. You might explain to students that the essay can be viewed as an implicit argument and that its contentions are therefore open to question. To illustrate, if the black domination of basketball has its roots in the cramped playing field and the lack of "money for bats, gloves, hockey sticks and ice skates, or shoulder pads" (paragraph 3), then how can we account for the many black professional football and baseball players, who presumably faced the same constraints? Isn't it possible that one or more other factors may also play a part in black success?
5. Paragraphs 1–4 make up the introduction; paragraphs 5–14 focus primarily on the black style of play; paragraphs 15–21 look primarily on the white style; and paragraphs 22–23 form the conclusion. The essay uses the block pattern of organization for its comparisons.
6. This paragraph points out that the two styles of play are complementary, not antagonistic. It also offers a poignant contrast between the "fusion of cultures" on the basketball court and their growing separation elsewhere in society.

HANDBOOK

Sentence Elements

Learning the parts of English sentences won't in itself improve your writing, but it will equip you to handle errors at the sentence level. Before you can identify and correct unwarranted shifts from past to present time, for example, you need to know about verbs and their tenses. Similarly, recognizing and correcting pronoun case errors require a knowledge of what pronouns are and how they are used. In this section we first cover subjects and predicates, then complements, appositives, and the parts of speech, and finally phrases and clauses.

SUBJECTS AND PREDICATES

The subject of a sentence tells who or what it is about. A *simple subject* consists of a noun (that is, a naming word) or a noun substitute. A *complete subject* consists of a simple subject plus any words that limit or describe it.

The predicate tells something about the subject and completes the thought of the sentence. A *simple predicate* consists of one or more verbs (words that show action or existence); a *complete predicate* includes any associated words also. In the following examples the simple subjects are underlined once and the simple predicates twice. The subjects and predicates are separated with slash marks.

William / laughed.

Mary / has moved.

Sarah / painted the kitchen.

The student over there in the corner / is majoring in art.

A sentence can have a compound subject (two or more separate subjects), a compound predicate (two or more separate predicates), or both.

The elephants and their trainer / bowed to the audience and left the ring.

Sentences that ask questions don't follow the usual simple subject–simple predicate order. Instead, the order may be reversed; or if the simple predicate consists of two verbs, the simple subject may come between them.

When is / your / theme due? (Simple subject follows simple predicate.)

Has / Joan / walked her pygmy goat yet? (Simple subject comes between verbs.)

499

have writing centers that administer such tests.
2. Conduct special work-
shops, either on a particular
day or for part of a class period, for students with low
pre-test scores.

EXERCISE ANSWERS

1. The full <u>moon</u> / <u>rose</u>
majestically over the mountain
peak.
2. <u>John</u> / <u>was</u> ill on the
day of the big test.
3. The <u>boys</u> and <u>girls</u> /
<u>laughed</u> and <u>splashed</u>
happily in the pool.
4. That <u>man</u> by the door /
<u>is</u> my uncle.
5. The <u>judge</u> / <u>revoked</u>
Rudy's parole and <u>ordered</u>
him to jail.
6. The tall <u>oak</u> / <u>shaded</u>
almost the entire back yard.
7. My favorite <u>subject</u> / <u>is</u>
history.
8. <u>Mr. Eames</u> / <u>has bought</u>
a wicker chair for his living
room.
9. <u>Has</u> / <u>Denise</u> / <u>mentioned</u>
her promotion to the chief
accountant?
10. <u>Mary</u> / <u>had</u> a little lamb
stew for lunch.

PERSPECTIVE

Students often confuse the
different types of complements. When you teach complements, it is important to
stress that the four types
function differently. Otherwise
students may see them simply
as words that follow the verb.

CLASSROOM ACTIVITIES

1. Have students complete
the following sentences with
a direct object. The instructor
corrected _____ . The old man
carried _____ . For lunch, the

Usage Considerations. Because subjects are such important sentence elements, think carefully about each one you write so that your sentences won't be vague or misleading. Read the example below.

Our *government* has failed to enact any health insurance plan.

This statement can be expressed more precisely:

Congress has failed to enact any health insurance plan.

The *President* has vetoed the proposed health insurance plan.

Paying close attention to subjects lets you present your ideas more accurately and clearly.

EXERCISE ■ **Place a slash mark between the complete subject and the complete predicate; then underline the simple subject once and the verb(s) twice. If a subject comes between two verbs, set it off with two slash marks.**

1. The full moon rose majestically over the mountain peak.
2. John was ill on the day of the big test.
3. The boys and girls laughed and splashed happily in the pool.
4. That man by the door is my uncle.
5. The judge revoked Rudy's parole and ordered him to jail.
6. The tall oak shaded almost the entire back yard.
7. My favorite subject is history.
8. Mr. Eames has bought a wicker chair for his living room.
9. Has Denise mentioned her promotion to the chief accountant?
10. Mary had a little lamb stew for lunch.

COMPLEMENTS

A complement is a word or word group that forms part of the predicate and helps complete the meaning of the sentence. Complements fall into four categories: direct objects, indirect objects, subject complements, and object complements.

A *direct object* names whatever receives, or results from, the action of a verb.

The millwright repaired the *lathe*. (Direct object receives action of verb *repaired*.)

Hilary painted a *picture*. (Direct object results from action of verb *painted*.)

They took *coffee* and *sandwiches* to the picnic. (Direct objects receive action of verb *took*.)

As the last sentence shows, a sentence may have a compound direct object—two or more separate direct objects.

An *indirect object* identifies someone or something that receives whatever is named by the direct object.

Doris lent *me* her calculator. (Indirect object *me* receives *calculator,* the direct object.)

Will and Al bought their *boat* new sails. (Indirect object *boat* receives *sails,* the direct object.)

An indirect object can be converted to a prepositional phrase that begins with *to* or *for* and follows the direct object.

Doris lent her calculator *to me.*

Will and Al bought new sails *for their boat.*

A *subject complement* follows a linking verb—one that indicates existence rather than action. It renames or describes the subject.

Desmond is a *carpenter.* (Complement *carpenter* renames subject *Desmond.*)

The lights are too *bright* for Percy. (Complement *bright* describes subject *lights.*)

An *object complement* follows a direct object and renames or describes it.

The council named Donna *treasurer.* (Object complement *treasurer* renames direct object *Donna.*)

The audience thought the play *silly.* (Object complement *silly* describes direct object *play.*)

Usage Considerations. Like subjects, direct objects can be revised for greater precision, as these examples show.

John sent *a gift.*

John sent *a giant coloring book as a birthday gift.*

Often, you can carry the revision one step further by adding an indirect object, subject complement, or object complement to the sentence.

John sent *his niece* a giant coloring book as a birthday gift. (indirect object added)

*A*PPOSITIVES

An appositive is a noun or word group serving as a noun that follows another noun or noun substitute and expands its meaning. Appositives may be restrictive or nonrestrictive. Restrictive appositives distinguish whatever they modify from other items in the same class. They are written without commas.

My sister *Heidi* is a professional golfer. (Appositive *Heidi* distinguishes her from other sisters.)

I have just read a book by the novelist *Henry James.* (Appositive *Henry James* distinguishes him from other novelists.)

Nonrestrictive appositives provide more information about whatever they

football star ate _____ and _____ . The monkey broke _____ .

2. Have students complete the following sentences with an indirect object. John sent _____ roses. The lunchroom served _____ cold mashed potatoes. The lawyer mailed _____ the contract. My brother bought _____ the latest U2 CD.

PERSPECTIVE

The use of restrictive and nonrestrictive appositives is often a sign of a student's increasing syntactical maturity and therefore should be encouraged.

CLASSROOM ACTIVITY

When introducing appositives, you might explain how to use them effectively. Use sentence-combining exercises, such as the following, that require students to join two separate sentences, employing either a restrictive or nonrestrictive appositive.

1. My brother is an avid fly fisherman. His name is David.
2. Jimmy Carter plays an important role in supervising elections in foreign countries. Jimmy Carter is a former U.S. President.
3. Charles Ives is known for writing very discordant music. Charles Ives is a famous American composer.
4. Wallace Stevens worked for an insurance company. Wallace Stevens was a poet.
5. He suffered from angina. Angina is a kind of heart condition.

modify. This sort of appositive is set off by a pair of commas except at the end of a sentence; then it is preceded by a single comma.

> Nicolai Karpov, *the Rusitarian Consul,* was interviewed on TV last week. (Appositive names *Karpov's* occupation.)

> Todd plans to major in paleontology, *the study of fossils.* (Appositive defines *paleontology.*)

Usage Considerations. When a brief definition is necessary, appositives can help you improve your sentences.

> John Cage wrote hundreds of pieces for prepared piano.

> John Cage, *a twentieth century avant-garde composer,* wrote hundreds of pieces for prepared pianos, *instruments with odds and ends stuck between their strings to provide unusual effects.*

Don't, however, clutter your writing with appositives that provide unneeded information; the overload will impede and irritate your reader.

EXERCISE ■ **Identify each italicized item as a direct object (DO), an indirect object (IO), a subject complement (SC), an object complement (OC), or an appositive (AP).**

1. Harry is a *student* in business administration.
2. Mr. Ames gave his *son* money for the movies.
3. The study group found Kant's philosophy *difficult.*
4. Dan lost his *umbrella* in the subway.
5. Speed Spedowski, *our best pitcher,* won twenty-three games last season.
6. Bill borrowed several *tapes* for the party.
7. The newspaper named Melissa *editor.*
8. Nelson was *overjoyed* at winning the essay contest.
9. Yesterday, Count Dracula found a *bat* in his belfry.
10. My cousin *Sally* has a vacation house in Maine.

PARTS OF SPEECH

Traditional English grammar classifies words into eight parts of speech: *nouns, pronouns, verbs, adjectives, adverbs, prepositions, conjunctions,* and *interjections.* This section discusses these categories as well as verbals, phrases, and clauses, which also serve as parts of speech.

Nouns

Nouns name persons, places, things, conditions, ideas, or qualities. Some nouns, called *proper nouns,* identify one-of-a-kind items like the following:

Combinations

1. My brother David is an avid fly fisherman.
2. Jimmy Carter, former U.S. President, plays an important role in supervising elections in foreign countries.
3. Charles Ives, a famous American composer, is known for writing very discordant music.
4. The poet Wallace Stevens worked for an insurance company.
5. He suffered from angina, a kind of heart condition.

EXERCISE ANSWERS

1. SC   6. DO
2. IO   7. OC
3. OC   8. SC
4. DO   9. DO
5. AP   10. AP

PERSPECTIVE

Far too often the parts of speech are glossed over as rather obvious and unremarkable elements of our language. Clearly, however, our grammatical world should not be taken for granted. Consider, for example, a language that is less noun-centered than ours or one that is richer in adjectives. Obviously, these features would have an enormous impact on how people would conceive of the world.

CLASSROOM ACTIVITY

Have students describe simple, everyday events, such as sunrise, teeth-brushing, walking to class, without using nouns. The subsequent frustration should reveal the importance of nouns and be an excellent topic of discussion. In addition, the very effort to avoid nouns will, like the pink elephant an individual noun

France   Christmas
Pacific Ocean   North Dakota
George Washington   Mona Lisa
Pulitzer Prize   World Series
Spirit of St. Louis   Wyandotte Corporation
Declaration of Independence   Miami–Dade Junior College

Mount Everest, on the border of *Tibet* and *Nepal,* was named for *Sir George Everest,* an Englishman.

Common nouns name general classes or categories of items and include abstract, concrete, and collective nouns.

Abstract Nouns.   An abstract noun names a condition, idea, or quality—something we can't see, feel, or otherwise experience with our five senses.

arrogance   harmony   sickness
envy   liberalism   understanding
fear   love

His *desire* to win caused him to cheat.

Mary felt great *loyalty* to her family.

Concrete Nouns.   A concrete noun identifies something that we can experience with one or more of our senses.

man   desk   pillow   needle
bicycle   lemon   airplane   pan
building   piston   carton   smoke

The *air* was thin at the *peak* of the *mountain.*

The *hammer* had a broken *handle.*

Collective Nouns.   A collective noun is singular in form but stands for a group or collection of items.

assembly   committee   crowd   flotilla   herd
bunch   congregation   delegation   gang   tribe
class   convoy   family   group   troop

The *jury* filed into the courtroom to announce its verdict.

The *flock* of geese settled onto the lake.

Usage Considerations.   Good writing demands precise, potent nouns. If you carefully select your nouns, you can help sharpen your message. Ill-chosen nouns, on the other hand, suggest poor thinking. Note how the vague word "freedom" robs the following sentence of any specific meaning.

Our *freedom* needs to be protected.

What did the writer have in mind? Here are a few possibilities.

Our *right to own guns* needs to be protected.

tries not to think about, bring them to mind.

CLASSROOM ACTIVITIES

1. Have students write sentences in which every noun is a proper noun, and allow them to make up a proper name for each object. This exercise will help them see the difference between proper and common nouns and how common nouns contribute to our ability to think and communicate.
2. You might have students try to create their own common noun (class term) and then find a definition for it. For example, a "flusterjet" might be any student who is excessively nervous just before an exam.

CLASSROOM ACTIVITY

Have students list as many nouns as possible, perhaps allowing them to refer to textbooks, then determine which are abstract and which are concrete. For example, use the nouns "arrogance" and "smoke," pointing out that while we can see only the symptoms of arrogance, we can clearly see smoke itself.

CLASSROOM ACTIVITY

Have students identify activities that a class can do as a group. For example, a class might make an average test score, produce a book with chapters written by individual students, and so on.

Our *private behavior* needs to be protected.

Our *national sovereignty* needs to be protected.

Even when meaning does not present problems, sentences can be sharpened by careful attention to nouns. Note the greater precision of the second sentence below.

Our *dog* has a savage bite.

Our *pit bull* has a savage bite.

EXERCISE ■ **Identify the nouns in the following sentences.**

1. Jeremy has undertaken the task of learning conversational German this summer.
2. Scrabble is a pleasant game to play on a cold, wet evening.
3. The chairperson will tell you about the decision of the committee.
4. The tree was covered with blossoms around which many bees buzzed.
5. My new apartment is in Miami, Florida.
6. His intelligence and humor make him a very popular lecturer.
7. A Rolls-Royce will provide decades of transportation for its owner.
8. Marcy Johnson jumped in her car, revved its engine, and roared off down the road.
9. The woods are beautiful this time of year.
10. In three months I will finish my enlistment in the army.

Pronouns

Pronouns, which take the place of nouns in sentences, help you avoid the awkward repetition of nouns.

If Brad doesn't like the *book,* take *it* back to the library.

There are eight categories of pronouns: *personal, relative, interrogative, demonstrative, reflexive, intensive, indefinite,* and *reciprocal.*

Personal Pronouns.　Personal pronouns refer to one or more clearly identified persons, places, or things.

Subjective	*Objective*	*Possessive*
I	me	my, mine
you	you	your, yours
he	him	his
she	her	her, hers
it	it	its
we	us	our, ours
you	you	your, yours
they	them	their, theirs

Subjective pronouns serve as the subjects of sentences or clauses; objective pronouns serve as direct and indirect objects; and possessive pronouns show possession or ownership. *My, your, our,* and *their* always precede nouns and thus function as possessive adjectives. *His* and *its* may or may not precede nouns.

He bought a sport shirt. (pronoun as subject)

Donald saw *them.* (pronoun as direct object)

Simon lent *her* ten dollars. (pronoun as indirect object)

That car is *theirs.* (pronoun showing ownership)

Relative Pronouns.   A relative pronoun relates a subordinate clause—a word group that has a subject and a predicate but does not express a complete idea—to an antecedent in the main part of its sentence. The relative pronouns include the following:

who	whose	what	whoever	whichever
whom	which	that	whomever	whatever

Who in its various forms refers to people, *which* to things, and *that* to either people or things.

Mary Beth Cartwright, *who* was arrested last week for fraud, was Evansville's "Model Citizen" two years ago. (The antecedent of *who* is *Mary Beth Cartwright.*)

He took the typewriter, *which* needed cleaning, to the repair shop. (The antecedent of *which* is *typewriter.*)

David Bullock is someone *whom* we should definitely hire. (The antecedent of *whom* is *someone.*)

Montreal is a city *that* I've always wanted to visit. (The antecedent of *that* is *city.*)

Which typically introduces nonrestrictive clauses, that is, clauses that provide more information about whatever they modify (see page 561).

The palace, *which* was in bad condition a century ago, is finally going to be restored. (Clause adds information about palace.)

That is typically used in other situations, especially to introduce restrictive clauses: those that distinguish the things they modify from others in the same class (see page 561).

The used car *that* I bought last week at Honest Bill's has already broken down twice. (Clause distinguishes writer's used car from others.)

Interrogative Pronouns.   Interrogative pronouns introduce questions. All of the relative pronouns except *that* also function as interrogative pronouns.

who	which	whoever	whichever
whom	what	whomever	whatever
whose			

What is the matter?

Who asked you?

Whatever do you mean?

him. I tried to cheer him up by reassuring him that his girlfriend loves him, and that is what matters. I suspect that he doesn't believe me. He finally went and had a terrible time. In the end, though, he and I had to laugh about the whole event.

PERSPECTIVE

Relative pronouns help writers formulate more complex sentences. You might introduce relative clauses through sentence-combining exercises.

CLASSROOM ACTIVITY

Have students combine the following sentences using relative pronouns:

1. He owns the Toyota Camry. The Toyota Camry has a broken headlight.
2. George Bush was once the director of the CIA. George Bush is now President.
3. The streets are peppered with potholes. The streets will be paved this spring.
4. The word-processing program works very well. I purchased the word-processing program last year.
5. *Buddenbrooks* is a novel. I have always wanted to read *Buddenbrooks.*

Combinations

1. He owns the Toyota Camry that has a broken headlight.
2. George Bush, who was once the director of the CIA, is now President.
3. The streets that are peppered with potholes will be paved this spring. OR The streets, which are peppered with potholes, will be paved this spring.

pro

When *what* and *which* are followed by nouns, they act as adjectives, not pronouns.

Which movie should we see?

Demonstrative Pronouns.   As their name suggests, demonstrative pronouns point things out. There are four such pronouns.

4. The word-processing program that I purchased last year works very well.
5. *Buddenbrooks* is a novel that I have always wanted to read.

this	these
that	those

This and its plural *these* identify recent or nearby things:

This is the play to see.

These are the times that try men's souls.

That and its plural *those* identify less recent or more distant things:

That is Mary's house across the road.

Those were very good peaches you had for sale last week.

Reflexive and Intensive Pronouns.   A reflexive pronoun reverses the action of a verb, making the doer and the receiver of the action the same. An intensive pronoun lends emphasis to a noun or pronoun. The two sets of pronouns are identical.

myself	herself	ourselves
yourself	itself	yourselves
himself	oneself	themselves

My father cut *himself* while shaving. (reflexive pronoun)

The President *himself* has asked me to undertake this mission. (intensive pronoun)

Don't substitute a reflexive pronoun for a personal pronoun.

   Faulty   Jill and *myself* are going to a movie.

Revision   Jill and *I* are going to a movie.

   Faulty   Give the tickets to John and *myself.*

Revision   Give the tickets to John and *me.*

Sometimes you'll hear people say things like "He made it *hisself,*" "They're only fooling *theirself,*" or "They bought *theirselves* sodas." Such forms are nonstandard. Say "himself" and "themselves" instead.

Indefinite Pronouns.   The pronouns in this group refer to unidentified persons, places, or things. The group includes the following:

anybody	everything	one
anyone	nobody	somebody
anything	no one	someone
everybody	nothing	something
everyone		

These words consistently act as pronouns. Other words may function either as indefinite pronouns or as adjectives:

all	any	most	few	much
another	each	either	many	neither

Here are some examples:

Everyone is welcome. (indefinite pronoun)

Many are called, but *few* are chosen. (indefinite pronouns)

Many men but only a *few* women attend the Air Force Academy. (adjectives)

Reciprocal Pronouns. The two reciprocal pronouns show an interchange of action between two or more parties. *Each other* is used when two parties interact, *one another* when three or more do.

Pam and Patty accidentally gave *each other* the same thing for Christmas. (two persons)

The members of the football team joyfully embraced *one another* after their victory. (more than two persons)

Usage Considerations. Many students handle pronouns carelessly, damaging the clarity of their writing. Problems include letting the same pronoun stand for different nouns or using a pronoun where detailed, vivid language would be more effective. The following sentence illustrates poor pronoun usage.

My brother loves fly fishing. He thinks *it* is the only way to spend a summer weekend. In fact, whenever he's off work, he'll do *it.*

Rewritten as follows, the passage has been notably improved.

My brother loves fly fishing. He thinks that *wading a stream and casting leisurely for trout* is the only way to spend a summer weekend. In fact, whenever he's off work, he *can be found up to his hips in water, offering his hand-tied flies to the waiting rainbows.*

EXERCISE ■ **Identify each pronoun in the following sentences and indicate its type.**

1. This is the kind of movie that I like.
2. Everyone in the class came to the party she gave at term's end.
3. If you feel thirsty, pour yourself a glass of lemonade.
4. That is a terrible-looking chair. Who would buy it anyhow?
5. What do you think Sally and Bill bought each other for Christmas?
6. I myself will take the blame for anything that goes wrong with the experiment.
7. Don't ask me to change; I like myself just as I am.
8. The children splashed one another with water from the pool.
9. Nobody whom I know has ever won anything playing Lotto.
10. This is the best city in the Midwest for anyone who likes fine dining.

pro

TEACHING STRATEGY

While many students are likely to be familiar with most kinds of pronouns, few use sentences that employ reciprocal pronouns. To give students practice, have them list things people might do to each other or one another and then write sentences built around these activities, using the appropriate pronouns. For example, Steve and his brother shot each other while hunting. The members of the class shook hands with one another.

EXERCISE ANSWERS

1. This (demonstrative), that (relative), I (personal)
2. Everyone (indefinite), she (personal)
3. you (personal), yourself (reflexive)
4. That (demonstrative), Who (interrogative), it (personal)
5. What (interrogative), you (personal), each other (reciprocal)
6. I (personal), myself (intensive), anything (indefinite), that (relative)
7. me (personal), I (personal), myself (reflexive), I (personal)
8. one another (reciprocal)
9. Nobody (indefinite), whom (relative), I (personal), anything (indefinite)
10. This (demonstrative), anyone (indefinite), who (relative)

Verbs

A verb indicates action or existence: what something is, was, or will be. Verbs fall into three classes: *action verbs, linking verbs,* and *helping verbs.*

Action Verbs.   As its name suggests, an action verb expresses action. Some action verbs are transitive, others intransitive. A *transitive* verb has a direct object which receives or results from the action and rounds out the meaning of the sentence.

The photographer *took* the picture.

Without the direct object, this sentence would not express a complete thought. In contrast, an *intransitive* verb requires no direct object to complete the meaning of the sentence.

Lee Ann *gasped* loudly.

Little Tommy Tucker *sings* for his supper.

Many action verbs can play both transitive or intransitive roles, depending on the sentences they are used in.

Kari *rode* her bicycle into town. (transitive verb)

Karl *rode* in the front seat of the car. (intransitive verb)

Linking Verbs.   A linking verb shows existence—what something is, was, or will be—rather than action. Linking verbs are intransitive and tie their subjects to subject complements. Some subject complements are nouns or noun substitutes that rename their subjects. Others are adjectives that describe their subjects.

Ms. Davis *is* our new director. (Complement *director* renames subject *Ms. Davis.*)

The soup *was* lukewarm. (Complement *lukewarm* describes subject *soup.*)

The most common linking verbs are forms of the verb *to be* (*is, are, am, was, were, be, being, been*). Some other verbs that may function as linking verbs are *seem, become, appear, remain, feel, look, smell, sound,* and *taste.*

Helping Verbs.   Helping verbs accompany action or linking verbs, allowing them to express with great precision matters such as possibility, obligation, and time. Common helping verbs include the following:

has	been	had (to)
have	do	shall
had	does	will
am	did	going (to)
is	used (to)	about (to)
are	may	would
was	might	should
were	must	ought (to)
be	have (to)	can
being	has (to)	could

I *shall ask* him. (helping verb *shall* with action verb *ask*)

The driver *was being lifted* onto a stretcher. (helping verbs *was* and *being* with action verb *lifted*)

You *have been* good. (helping verb *have* with linking verb *been*)

The patient *will feel* better soon. (helping verb *will* with linking verb *feel*)

We *might go* to Corvallis next weekend. (helping verb *might* with action verb *go*)

Helping verbs usually appear next to the main verbs, but they don't have to:

Ellen *will* undoubtedly *resign.*

Combinations of two or more verbs are called verb phrases.

Usage Considerations. Energetic writing requires energetic verbs. Don't take verbs for granted; revise them as necessary in order to strengthen a sentence. Note the improved precision of the second example sentence.

I *gave* the maitre d' a ten-dollar bill.

I *slipped* the maitre d' a ten-dollar bill.

EXERCISE ■ **Identify each verb in the following sentences and indicate its type.**

1. If Butch and Jim need transportation, my car will be available.
2. Please write your name on your quiz before you give it to me.
3. Marvin has been sitting in front of the TV all morning.
4. I will be watching the Detroit Pistons play tonight.
5. The movie offered lots of action, but the plot was poor.
6. Christine's assistance on this project has been invaluable.
7. William must have finished the yard work by now.
8. Teresa will probably be elected president of the club.
9. Robert has donated his pet buffalo to the zoo.
10. Will you be a little less noisy, please?

EXERCISE ANSWERS
1. need (action), will (helping), be (linking)
2. write (action), give (action)
3. has been (helping), sitting (action)
4. will be (helping), watching (action), play (action)
5. offered (action), was (linking)
6. has (helping), been (linking)
7. must have (helping), finished (action)
8. will be (helping), elected (action)
9. has (helping), donated (action)
10. Will (helping), be (linking)

Principal Parts. Verbs change in form to show time (tense) distinctions. For every action verb, tenses are built from three principal parts: *present, past,* and *past participle.* The present is the principal part you would look up in the dictionary (*win, skip, go,* and so on). If the subject of a verb is a singular pronoun (*he, she, it*) or a singular noun, add an *s* or *es* to the dictionary form (*wins, skips, goes*). Most verbs have identical past and past participles.

	Present	*Past*	*Past Participle*
I, you, we, they	talk	talked	talked
He, she, it, Henry	talks	talked	talked
I, you, we, they	stand	stood	stood
He, she, it, the decision	stands	stood	stood

Of the remaining verbs, most have different past and past participles.

	Present	Past	Past Participle
I, you, we, they	swim	swam	swum
He, she, it, the boy	swims	swam	swum
I, you, we, they	bite	bit	bitten
He, she, it, the dog	bites	bit	bitten

With a few verbs, the past and past participles are identical to the dictionary form.

	Present	Past	Past Participle
I, you, we, they	set	set	set
He, she, it	sets	set	set

If you're uncertain about the principal parts of a verb, check your dictionary.

Tense.   English has six basic tenses: present, past, future, present perfect, past perfect, future perfect. They are formed from the principal parts of action and linking verbs, either alone or combined with helping verbs.

The *present tense* is formed from the present principal part of the main verb. It shows present condition and general or habitual action, indicates permanent truths, tells about past events in the historical present, and sometimes denotes action at some definite future time.

Helen *looks* beautiful in her new gown. (present condition)

John *works* on the eighteenth floor. (general action)

I *brush* my teeth each morning. (habitual action)

The sun *rises* in the East. (permanent truth)

On November 11, 1918, the guns *fall* silent, and World War I *comes* to an end. (historical present)

Monday, I *begin* my new job. (future action)

The *past tense* is based on the past principal part of the verb. The past tense shows that a condition existed or an action was completed in the past. The verb tense leaves the time indefinite, but surrounding words may specify it.

Paul *was* angry with his noisy neighbors. (past condition, time indefinite)

Sandy *received* a long letter yesterday. (past action, time specified by *yesterday*)

The *future tense* combines *shall* or *will* and the present principal part of the main verb. It indicates that a condition will exist or an action will take place in the future.

You *will feel* better after a good night's sleep. (future condition)

I *shall attend* the concert next week. (future action)

The *present perfect* tense is formed with *has* or *have* and the past participle of the main verb. It shows that a past condition or action, or its effect, continues until the present time.

The players *have been* irritable since they lost the homecoming game. (Condition continues until present.)

Juanita *has driven* a United Parcel Service truck for five years. (Action continues until present.)

William *has repaired* the snow blower. (Effect of action continues until present although the action itself was completed in the past.)

The *past perfect* tense combines *had* and the past participle of the main verb. It refers to a past condition or action that was completed before another past condition or action.

He *had been* in the army two years when the war ended. (Past perfect condition occurred first.)

Vivian moved into the house that she *had built* the summer before. (Past perfect action occurred first.)

The *future perfect* tense is formed from the verbs *shall have* or *will have* plus the past participle of the main verb. It shows that a condition or an action will have been completed at some time in the future. Surrounding words specify time.

Our sales manager *will have been* with the company ten years next July. (Condition will end.)

By the end of this year, I *shall have written* the great American novel. (Action will be completed.)

Each of these basic tenses has a *progressive tense* that indicates action in progress. The progressive tense always includes some form of the verb *to be* followed by a present participle, a verb that ends in *-ing.*

Present progressive	I *am running.*
Past progressive	I *was running.*
Future progressive	I *shall be running.*
Present perfect progressive	I *have been running.*
Past perfect progressive	I *had been running.*
Future perfect progressive	I *shall have been running.*

Voice.   Transitive verbs have two voices: active and passive. A verb is in the *active voice* when the subject carries out the action named by the verb.

Barry *planned* a picnic. (Subject *Barry* performs action.)

A verb is in the *passive voice* when the subject receives the action. The performer may be identified in an accompanying phrase or go unmentioned.

A picnic *was planned* by Barry. (The phrase *by Barry* identifies the performer.)

The picnic *was canceled.* (The performer goes unmentioned.)

A passive construction always uses a form of *to be* and the past participle of an action verb. Like other constructions, the passive may show past, present, or future time.

Amy *is paid* handsomely for her investment advice. (present tense)

I *was warned* by a sound truck that a tornado was nearby. (past tense)

I *will be sent* to Ghana soon by the Peace Corps. (future tense)

I *have been awarded* a sizable research grant. (present perfect tense)

The city *had been shelled* heavily before the infantry moved in. (past perfect tense)

By the end of this month, the site for our second factory *will have been chosen.* (future perfect tense)

To convert a sentence from the passive to the active voice, make the performer the subject, the original subject the direct object, and drop the form of *to be.*

The treaty *was signed* by the general. (passive)

The general *signed* the treaty. (active)

Technical and scientific writing commonly use the passive voice to explain processes since their flat, impersonal tone adds an air of scientific objectivity and authority. Other kinds of writing, however, avoid the passive voice except when it is desirable to conceal the doer of the action or when the action is more significant than the actor. See pages 203–4 for more information on usage.

EXERCISE ■ Identify each verb in the following sentences, indicate its tense, and note any use of the passive voice.

1. They will have arrived in Tokyo by this evening.
2. This TV program is relayed to Europe by satellite.
3. The Krause Corporation's new headquarters building will be dedicated June 30.
4. The school psychologist was asked whether she had any explanation for Tim's odd behavior.
5. We have been told we face yet another 15 percent staff cutback.
6. Nancy bought a new Michael Jackson CD.
7. The Northrups will start their vacation tomorrow.
8. Leslie works in the Sales Department of IBM.
9. Norman darted into the basement when he saw the funnel-shaped cloud.
10. Nick has earned three *A*'s and one *B* this semester.
11. In 1992, my family left the town where we had lived for fifteen years.
12. With any luck, by decade's end a worldwide nuclear disarmament pact will have been signed.

Mood.   The mood of a verb shows whether the writer regards a statement as a

1. fact
2. command or request
3. wish, possibility, condition contrary to fact, or the like.

English has three moods: the indicative, imperative, and subjunctive.

A sentence in the *indicative mood* states a real or supposed fact or asks a question.

Nancy *graduates* from high school tomorrow.

We *lived* in Oakmont when Rachel was born.

He *had been* a sailor during the war.

Has Joe *asked* anyone to the prom yet?

Most verbs are used in the indicative mood.

A sentence in the *imperative mood* delivers a command or makes a request.

Leave the room immediately! (command)

Please *turn* the CD player down. (request)

The subject of a sentence in the imperative mood is always *you*. Although ordinarily unstated, the subject sometimes appears in the sentence.

You leave the room immediately!

The *subjunctive mood* is used

1. in *if, as if,* and *as though* clauses to express a wish, a possibility, or an action or a condition contrary to fact
2. in *that* clauses expressing orders, demands, requests, resolutions, proposals, or motions
3. with modal auxiliaries to express wishes, probability, possibility, permission, requirements, recommendations, suggestions, and conditions contrary to fact.

To express a present or future wish, possibility, condition or action in an *if, as if,* or *as though* clause, use *were* with any personal pronoun or noun serving as the subject of the clause.

If only Stan *were* less gullible! (present wish contrary to fact)

Even if Kay *were* to explain, Mary wouldn't believe her. (future possibility)

Arthur is behaving as if he *were* a millionaire. (present condition contrary to fact)

To express a wish, possibility, or condition contrary to past facts, use *had been* or *had* plus the past participle of an action verb.

If the engine *had been lubricated*, the bearing wouldn't have burned out. (past condition contrary to fact)

Alice looked as if she *had lost* her best friend. (condition expressed in clause occurs before action of verb *looked*)

When writing *that* clauses expressing orders, demands, requests, resolutions, proposals, or motions, use *be* or the present plural form of an action verb.

I move that they *be* rewarded for their bravery.

The group proposed that Margaret *go* to the scene of the accident and *inspect* it personally.

10. "has earned," present perfect
11. "left," past; "had lived," past perfect
12. "will have been signed," future perfect, passive

TEACHING STRATEGY

Assign a short paper that provides an opportunity to write in the subjunctive. For example, students could specify what changes they would make in the university if they were its president or speculate what might occur in the next ten years.

CLASSROOM ACTIVITY

Because students are relatively unfamiliar with the subjunctive mood, you might have them complete the following sentences: I wish _____. If only _____. Even if _____. Most students act as if _____. If the class had been easier, _____. The dorm room looked as if _____. I would like to suggest that students _____. Because I've had this course _____. A longer school year _____.

In other *that* clauses, use the appropriate indicative form of the verb.

> I know that they *were* rewarded for their bravery.

> The group believed that Margaret *had gone* to the scene of the accident and *inspected* it personally.

The modal auxiliaries include the helping verbs *can, could, may, might, must, shall, will, would, should,* and *ought to.* The examples below illustrate the meanings they can express.

1. Wishes (*could, would*)

> I wish I *could* shimmy like my sister Kate.

> The Republicans wish the Democrats *would* go away and vice versa.

2. Probability (*should*)

> Because I've studied diligently, I *should* do better on my next chemistry test.

3. Possibility (*may, might, can, could*)

> High interest rates *could* cause our housing industry to collapse.

> I *might* stay up to watch the eclipse of the moon tonight.

4. Permission (*can, may*)

> The public *can* use these tennis courts every afternoon.

> You *may* leave as soon as you've finished filing these folders.

5. Requirements (*must*)

> The landlord has raised our rent again; we *must* find another apartment.

6. Recommendations, suggestions (*should, ought to*)

> Randy *should* see a doctor about his chest pains.

> The nuclear powers *ought to* reduce their stockpiles of atomic weapons.

7. Conditions contrary to fact (*could*)

> If only I *could* live my life over!

EXERCISE ANSWERS

1. SUB	**6.** SUB
2. IND	**7.** SUB
3. SUB	**8.** IMP
4. IMP	**9.** SUB
5. IND	**10.** IND

EXERCISE ■ **For each of the following sentences, identify the mood as indicative (IND), imperative (IMP), or subjunctive (SUB).**

1. Terry requested that the next regular meeting be postponed for a week.
2. Hot chocolate is an excellent bedtime drink.
3. Sally should learn to curb her sharp tongue.
4. Tell me all about the movie you saw last night.
5. Someone in the crowd shrieked loudly at the sudden thunderclap.
6. If I were boss here, I'd raise everybody's wages.
7. The latest drop in interest rates should spur consumer spending.
8. Don't ever use that tone of voice to me again.

9. Werner Heisenberg may have slept here.
10. Where did you buy that attractive blouse?

Adjectives

An adjective *modifies* a noun or pronoun by describing it, limiting it, or otherwise making its meaning more exact.

The *brass* candlestick stood next to the *fragile* vase. (*Brass* modifies *candlestick,* and *fragile* modifies *vase.*)

The cat is *long-haired* and *sleek.* (*Long-haired* and *sleek* modify *cat.*)

There are three general categories of adjectives: limiting, descriptive, and proper.

Limiting Adjectives.   A limiting adjective identifies or points out the noun or pronoun it modifies. It may indicate number or quantity. Several categories of pronouns can serve as limiting adjectives, as can numbers and nouns.

Whose briefcase is on the table? (interrogative adjective)

The couple *whose* car was stolen called the police. (relative adjective)

This restaurant has the best reputation for gourmet food. (demonstrative adjective)

Some people have no social tact at all. (indefinite adjective)

Sally swerved *her* car suddenly to avoid an oncoming truck. (possessive adjective)

Three people entered the lecture hall late. (number as adjective)

The *schoolgirl* look is fashionable this year. (noun as adjective)

Descriptive Adjectives.   A descriptive adjective names a quality, characteristic, or condition of a noun or pronoun. Two or more of these adjectives, members of the largest category of adjectives, may modify the same noun or pronoun.

The *yellow* submarine belongs to the Beatles.

He applied *clear* lacquer to the table top.

The *slim, sophisticated* model glided onto the runway.

The child wore a *thick, green, quilted* jacket.

Proper Adjectives.   A proper adjective is derived from a proper noun and is always capitalized.

Harwell is a *Shakespearean* actor.

Articles as Adjectives.   Articles appear immediately before nouns and can therefore be considered adjectives. There are three articles in English: *a, an,* and *the. The* points to a specific item, *a* and *an* do not. *A* precedes words beginning with consonant sounds; *an* precedes words with vowel sounds, making pronunciation easier.

PERSPECTIVE

Some students avoid adjectives as though such descriptive additions might infect their writing. Others write essays that are soggy with adjectives. In discussing adjectives, you might have students assess their own use of them.

TEACHING STRATEGIES

1.   Have students review several essays in the Reader to determine where adjectives have been used and to what effect. Be sure the review is not confined to narration and description essays; students need to realize that adjectives play an important role in all writing, not just "literary" essays.
2.   Have students review one of their own drafts to determine where they need adjectives to help limit their nouns and where they have used adjectives to excess.

CLASSROOM ACTIVITY

Have students identify adjectives that might help limit and qualify a long list of nouns. Discuss the different effects the use of these adjectives would have. You might note that adjectives help answer the question, "What kind of ____?" Sample nouns: dog, man, house, woman, student, child, boy, car, tire, tree, star, restaurant, potatoes, and so on.

adj

The right word at *the* right moment can save a friendship. (Definite articles suggest there is one right word and one right moment.)

A right word can save *a* friendship. (Indefinite articles suggest there may be several right words and friendships.)

I think I'd like *an* apple with my lunch. (No particular apple is specified.)

Sometimes the definite article refers to a class of items.

The tiger is fast becoming an endangered species.

Context shows whether such a sentence refers to particular items or entire classes.

Comparison with Adjectives.   Adjectives may be used to show comparison. When two things are compared, shorter adjectives usually add *-er* and longer adjectives add *more*. When three or more things are compared, shorter adjectives usually add *-est* and longer ones add *most*.

John is *taller* than Pete. (short adjective comparing two things)

Sandra seems *more* cheerful than Jill today. (long adjective comparing two things)

John is the *tallest* of the three brothers. (short adjective comparing three things)

Sandra is the *most* cheerful girl in the class. (longer adjective comparing more than three things)

Some adjectives, like the examples below, have irregular forms for comparisons.

good—better—best

bad—worse—worst

Don't use the *-est* form of the shorter adjective for comparing just two things.

Faulty   This is the *smallest* of the two castles.

Instead, use the *-er* form.

Revision   This is the *smaller* of the two castles.

Position of Adjectives.   Most adjectives come immediately before the words they modify. In a few set expressions (for example, heir *apparent*), the adjective immediately follows the word it modifies. Similarly, adjective pairs sometimes appear in a follow-up position for added emphasis (The rapids, *swift* and *dangerous,* soon capsized the raft). Sometimes adjectives also serve as subject complements and follow their subjects (The puppy was *friendly*).

Usage Considerations.   Some students overuse adjectives, but most underuse them. Review your sentences carefully to see where adding or cutting adjectives can increase the impact of your writing.

My Buick is the talk of my friends.

My *dilapidated, old, rusty, fenderless, 1970* Buick is the talk of my friends.

My *rusty, fenderless, 1970* Buick is the talk of my friends.

TEACHING STRATEGY

To reinforce the material on comparisons, try combining it with the section on comparison errors on pages 548–49.

The first sentence lacks adjectives that show why the car is discussed. Sentence two overcorrects this fault by including two adjectives that repeat the information provided by the others. The final sentence strikes the proper balance.

adv

EXERCISE ■ **Identify the adjectives in the following sentences.**

1. Tom is a very unhappy person.
2. Paul has an aunt who writes long, chatty letters to him regularly.
3. Sean ate an English muffin and drank a cup of black coffee.
4. Barton has an unusual sideboard in his dining room.
5. The tired carpenter tossed his tools into the red truck and drove home.
6. After buying a few gifts, Linda and Audrey took a slow stroll around the resort town.
7. Harvey ate three hamburgers and four helpings of salad at the picnic.
8. From the hilltop, the view was beautiful.
9. The weather is so hot and humid that we can't do a bit of work.
10. The glass blower deftly made an attractive vase.

Adverbs

An adverb modifies a verb, an adjective, another adverb, or a whole sentence. Adverbs generally answer questions such as "how?" "when?" "where?" "how often?" and "to what extent?"

The floodwaters receded *very* slowly. (Adverb modifies adverb and answers the question "how?")

My sister will visit me *tomorrow*. (Adverb modifies verb and answers the question "when?")

The coach walked *away* from the bench. (Adverb modifies verb and answers the question "where?")

The tire is *too* worn to be safe. (Adverb modifies adjective and answers the question "how much?")

The teller is *frequently* late for work. (Adverb modifies adjective and answers the question "how often?")

Unfortunately, the game was canceled because of rain. (The adverb modifies the whole sentence but does not answer any question.)

Formation of Adverbs. Most adverbs are formed by adding *-ly* to adjectives.

The wind is *restless*. (*Restless* is an adjective modifying *wind*.)

He walked *restlessly* around the room. (*Restlessly* is an adverb modifying *walked*.)

Many common adverbs, however, (*almost, never, quite, soon, then, there,* and *too*) lack *-ly* endings.

I *soon* realized that pleasing my boss was impossible.

This movie is *too* gruesome for my taste.

Furthermore, some words such as *better, early, late, hard, little, near, only, straight,* and *wrong* do double duty either as adjectives or adverbs.

We must have taken a *wrong* turn. (*Wrong* is an adjective modifying the noun *turn.*)

Where did I go *wrong?* (*Wrong* is an adverb modifying the verb *go.*)

Comparison with Adverbs.   Like adjectives, adverbs can show comparison. When two things are compared, shorter adverbs add *more.* When three or more things are compared, *most* is used.

Harold works *more* efficiently than Don. (adverb comparing two people)

Of all the people in the shop, Harold works the *most* efficiently. (adverb comparing more than three people)

Some adverbs, like some adjectives, use irregular forms for comparisons:

well—better—best

much—more—most

Position of Adverbs.   Adverbs are more movable than any other part of speech. Usually, adverbs that modify adjectives and other adverbs appear next to them to avoid confusion.

Her *especially* fine tact makes her a welcome guest at any party. (Adverb *especially* modifies adjective *fine.*)

The novel was *very* badly written. (Adverb *very* modifies adverb *badly.*)

Adverbs that modify verbs, however, can often be shifted around in their sentences without causing changes in meaning.

Quickly, he slipped through the doorway.

He slipped *quickly* through the doorway.

He slipped through the doorway *quickly.*

Usage Considerations.   You can often sharpen the meaning of a sentence by adding a well-chosen adverb.

The student squirmed in his chair.

The student squirmed *anxiously* in his chair.

Including the adverb *anxiously* in the second sentence shows the mental state of the student.

Be careful, however, not to overuse adverbs as they can bog down your writing.

EXERCISE ■ **Identify the adverbs in the following sentences.**

1. Harold is late more frequently than any other member of the crew.
2. After dinner, the children went outdoors and played noisily.
3. The doctor told Albert his illness, though quite serious, would respond well to treatment.
4. Lucy stepped quickly to the door and listened intently to the howling wind.
5. I often wish I could study less hard without my grades suffering.
6. The pirate ship glided swiftly and silently toward the sleeping town.
7. The tired, perspiring runner staggered wearily across the finish line.
8. You'll have to work very fast to keep up with Jody.
9. Regrettably, I will be unable to attend the meeting tomorrow.
10. The forced march was too difficult for the new marine recruits.

Prepositions

A preposition links its object—a noun or noun substitute—to some other word in the sentence and shows a relationship between them. The relationship is often one of location, time, means, or reason or purpose. The word group containing the preposition and its object makes up a prepositional phrase.

The new insulation *in* the attic keeps my house much warmer now. (Preposition *in* links object *attic* to *insulation* and shows location.)

We have postponed the meeting *until* tomorrow. (Preposition *until* links object *tomorrow* to *postponed* and shows time.)

The tourists traveled *by* automobile. (Preposition *by* links object *automobile* to *traveled* and shows means.)

Warren swims *for* exercise. (Preposition *for* links object *exercise* to *swims* and shows reason or purpose.)

The following list includes the most common prepositions, some of which consist of two or more words.

above	beside	in	out of
after	between	instead of	over
against	by	into	since
along with	by reason of	like	through
among	contrary to	near	to
at	during	next to	toward
because of	except	of	under
before	for	on	with
below	from	onto	without

Many of these combine to form additional prepositions: *except for, in front of, by way of, on top of,* and the like.

Certain prepositions sometimes occur in close association with certain verbs, *con*

forming verb units with altered meanings. When this happens, we call the prepositions verb particles. Here is an example.

> The instructor let Jeff make *up* the test.

Note the great difference between the meaning of the foregoing sentence and "The instructor let Jeff make the test."

Usage Considerations.   It is easy to use a small group of prepositions over and over in your writing. This habit often results in imprecise or misleading sentences. To avoid this problem, think carefully about your choice of prepositions as you revise. Read the following example:

> He walked *by* the railroad tracks on his way home.

Note that two interpretations are possible.

> He walked *along* the railroad tracks on his way home.

> He walked *past* the railroad tracks on his way home.

Clearly you would use the preposition that conveys your intended meaning.

EXERCISE ■ **Identify the prepositions and their objects in the following sentences.**

 1. I finally finished waxing the car just before the rainstorm.
 2. Aloe lotion will give you instant relief from sunburn.
 3. For reasons of security, this gate must be kept locked at all times.
 4. Shortly after dark, the group arrived at the camp.
 5. Across the street, George was working on his roof.
 6. At the end of the concert, everyone in the hall stood and applauded.
 7. Helen sprinkled the roast with a blend of herbs.
 8. Because of an error, all of the information in the computer was lost.
 9. During intermission, Joyce stepped outside for a breath of fresh air.
 10. The huge jet taxied slowly onto the runway.

Conjunctions

Conjunctions serve as connectors, linking parts of sentences or whole sentences. These connectors fall into three groups: coordinating conjunctions, subordinating conjunctions, and conjunctive adverbs.

Coordinating Conjunctions.   Coordinating conjunctions connect terms of equal grammatical importance: words, word groups, and simple sentences. These conjunctions can occur singly (*and, but, or, nor, for, yet, so*) or in pairs called correlative conjunctions (*either–or, neither–nor, both–and,* and *not only–but also*). The elements that follow correlative conjunctions must be parallel; that is, have the same grammatical form.

Tom *and* his cousin are opening a video arcade. (Coordinating conjunction connects nouns.)

Shall I serve the tea in the living room *or* on the veranda? (Coordinating conjunction connects phrases.)

I am going to Europe this summer, *but* Marjorie is staying home. (Coordinating conjunction connects simple sentences.)

Amy *not only* teaches English *but also* writes novels. (Correlative conjunctions connect parallel predicates.)

You can study nursing *either* at Ferris State University *or* at DeWitt College. (Correlative conjunctions connect parallel phrases.)

Friendship is *both* pleasure *and* pain. (Correlative conjunctions connect parallel nouns.)

Subordinating Conjunctions.

Like relative pronouns, subordinating conjunctions introduce subordinate clauses, relating them to independent clauses, which can stand alone as complete sentences. Examples of subordinating conjunctions include *because, as if, even though, since, so that, whereas,* and *whenever* (see page 527 for a more complete list).

I enjoyed the TV program *because* it was so well acted. (Conjunction connects *because it was so well acted* to rest of sentence.)

Whenever you're ready, we can begin dinner. (Conjunction connects *whenever you're ready* to rest of sentence.)

Conjunctive Adverbs.

These connectors resemble both conjunctions and adverbs. Like conjunctions, they serve as linking devices between elements of equal rank. Like adverbs, they function as modifiers, showing such things as similarity, contrast, result or effect, addition, emphasis, time, and example. The following list groups the most common conjunctive adverbs according to function.

Similarity: likewise, similarly
Contrast: however, nevertheless, on the contrary, on the other hand, otherwise
Result or effect: accordingly, as a result, consequently, hence, therefore, thus
Addition: also, furthermore, in addition, in the first place, moreover
Emphasis or clarity: in fact, in other words, indeed, that is
Time: afterwards, later, meanwhile, subsequently
Example: for example, for instance, to illustrate

The job will require you to travel a great deal; *however,* the salary is excellent.

Sean cares nothing for clothes; *in fact,* all of his socks have holes in their toes.

An interjection is an exclamatory word used to gain attention or to express strong feeling. It has no grammatical connection to the rest of the sentence. An interjection is followed by an exclamation point or a comma.

Hey! Watch how you're driving! (strong interjection)

Oh, is the party over already? (mild interjection)

con

pbr

Usage Considerations. You can add variety to your writing by varying the conjunctions you use. If you consistently rely on the conjunction *because*, try substituting *as* or *since*. Likewise, you might periodically replace *if* with *provided that*.

When you have choppy sentences, try combining them by using a conjunction.

> You can buy smoked salmon at Sally's Seafoods. You can buy it at Daane's Thriftland as well.

> You can buy smoked salmon *either* at Sally's Seafoods *or* at Daane's Thriftland.

The revision is much smoother than the original sentence pair.

EXERCISE ■ **Identify the coordinating conjunctions (CC), subordinating conjunctions (SC), conjunctive adverbs (CA), and interjections (I) in the following sentences.**

1. The car was not only dented but also dirty.
2. While Roger was at the movies, his brother bought a model airplane.
3. Heavens, what's all the fuss about anyhow?
4. Either the Coles or the Thurlows will drive us to the airport.
5. Although they felt under the weather, Marie and Sally attended the dance.
6. The candidate's views matched those of his audience; consequently, he received warm applause.
7. Neither William nor his brother has ever traveled out of the state.
8. Sandra is no academic slouch; indeed, she was valedictorian of her high school class.
9. I plan to go sailing tomorrow, but Nicole will stay home.
10. Curses! Sherlock has foiled yet another of my dastardly schemes.
11. Mark refused to wear his seat belt; therefore, he was ticketed by the police.
12. I'd like to buy this suit, but I just can't afford it.

*P*HRASES AND CLAUSES

Phrases

A phrase is a group of words that lacks a subject and a predicate and serves as a single part of speech. This section discusses four basic kinds of phrases: *prepositional phrases, participial phrases, gerund phrases,* and *infinitive phrases*. The last three are based on participles, gerunds, and infinitives, verb forms known as verbals. A fifth type of phrase, the verb phrase, consists of sets of two or more verbs (*has fixed, had been sick, will have been selected,* and the like).

Prepositional Phrases. A prepositional phrase consists of a preposition, one or more objects, and any associated words. These phrases serve as adjectives or adverbs.

The picture *over the mantel* was my mother's. (prepositional phrase as adjective)

He bought ice skates *for himself*. (prepositional phrase as adverb modifying verb)

The toddler was afraid *of the dog*. (prepositional phrase as adverb modifying adjective)

Our visitors arrived late *in the day*. (prepositional phrase as adverb modifying another adverb)

Frequently, prepositional phrases occur in series. Sometimes they form chains in which each phrase modifies the object of the preceding phrase. At other times some or all of the phrases may modify the verb or verb phrase.

John works *in a clothing store / on Main Street / during the summer*.

Here the first and third phrases serve as adverbs modifying the verb *works* and answering the questions "where?" and "when?" while the second phrase serves as an adjective modifying *store*.

On occasion, especially in questions, a preposition may be separated from its object, making the phrase difficult to find.

This is the book *that* I've been looking *for*.

What are you shouting *about?*

Participial Phrases. A participial phrase consists of a participle plus associated words. Participles are verb forms that, when used in participial phrases, function as adjectives or adverbs. A present participle ends in *-ing* and indicates an action currently being carried out. A past participle ends in *-ed, -en, -e, -n, -d,* or *-t* and indicates some past action.

The chef *preparing dinner* trained in France. (present participial phrase as adjective)

The background, *sketched in lightly*, accented the features of the woman in the painting. (past participial phrase as adjective)

She left *whistling a jolly melody*. (present participial phrase as adverb)

A perfect participial phrase consists of *having* or *having been* plus a past participle and any associated words. Like a past participial phrase, it indicates a past action.

Having alerted the townspeople about the tornado, the sound truck returned to the city garage. (perfect participial phrase)

Having been alerted to the tornado, the townspeople sought shelter in their basements. (perfect participial phrase)

Some participial phrases that modify persons or things distinguish them from others in the same class. These phrases are written without commas. Other phrases provide more information about the persons or things they modify and are set off with commas.

The man *fixing my car* is a master mechanic. (Phrase distinguishes man fixing car from others.)

Mr. Welsh, *fatigued by the tennis game,* rested in the shade. (Phrase provides more information about Mr. Welsh.)

Gerund Phrases. A gerund phrase consists of a gerund and the words associated with it. Like present participles, gerunds are verb forms that end in *-ing*. Unlike participles, though, they function as nouns rather than as adjectives or adverbs.

Kathryn's hobby is *collecting stamps.* (gerund phrase as subject complement)

Kathryn's hobby, *collecting stamps,* has made her many friends. (gerund phrase as appositive)

He devoted every spare moment to *overhauling the car.* (gerund phrase as object of preposition)

Infinitive Phrases. An infinitive phrase consists of the present principal part of a verb preceded by *to (to fix, to eat),* together with any accompanying words. These phrases serve as adjectives, adverbs, and nouns.

This looks like a good place *to plant the shrub.* (infinitive phrase as adjective)

Lenore worked *to earn money for college.* (infinitive phrase as adverb)

My goal is *to have my own business some day.* (infinitive phrase as noun)

Gerunds can often be substituted for infinitives and vice versa.

To repair this fender will cost two hundred dollars. (infinitive phrase as subject)

Repairing this fender will cost two hundred dollars. (gerund phrase as subject)

At times the *to* in an infinitive may be omitted following verbs such as *make, dare, let,* and *help.*

Kristin didn't dare *(to) move* a muscle.

The psychiatrist helped me *(to) overcome* my fear of flying.

Verbals Not in Phrases. Participles, gerunds, and infinitives can function as nouns, adjectives, or adverbs, even when they are not parts of phrases.

That *sunbathing* woman is a well-known model. (participle as adjective)

Dancing is fine exercise. (gerund)

The children want *to play.* (infinitive as noun)

If you're looking for a job, Sally is the person *to see.* (infinitive as adjective)

I'm prepared *to resign.* (infinitive as adverb)

Usage Considerations. Phrases can often help clarify or develop the information in a sentence.

Original My brother is fishing.

CLASSROOM ACTIVITY

Students need to recognize that phrases are used to develop sentences. To make this point, have students complete the following sentences by supplying appropriate phrases. Prepositional phrases: The book _____ belongs to Jack Welbell. The car went skidding _____ . The old boxer was afraid _____ . My house is located _____ _____ . Participial phrases: That man _____ was once a spy. The sidewalks _____ were still icy. Our car _____ was left by the side of the road. Having _____ , Steve sat back quietly in his seat. Having been _____ , the class raced for the door. Gerund phrases: I devote every spare moment to _____ . _____ _____ occupied most of my weekend _____ . Politicians seem to enjoy _____ . _____ has helped me invest my money wisely. Infinitive phrases: My goal is _____ . He worked very hard _____ . The library is not a good place _____ . Sally decided _____ .

Revision   My brother is fishing *for trout just below Barnes Dam on Sidewinder Creek.* (prepositional phrases added)

Original   The boat barely made shore.

Revision   The boat, *listing heavily and leaking badly,* barely made shore. (participial phrases added)

To avoid ponderous sentences, don't, however, weigh them down with phrases, as in the following example.

My brother is fishing for trout just below Barnes Dam on Sidewinder Creek *near Perry Pass in the mountains of Central Colorado.*

EXERCISE ■ **Identify the italicized phrases as prepositional, participial, gerund, or infinitive and tell whether each is used as a noun, an adjective, or an adverb.**

1. *Walking the dog in the rain* made me grouchy for the rest of the day.
2. *To ride the Orient Express* was Marian's fondest ambition.
3. *Opening the door a tiny crack,* Michelle stared with horror at the scene before her.
4. Sue Ellen works *in a grocery store* during the summer.
5. Tom couldn't decide which refrigerator *to buy his mother.*
6. Old-fashioned in every way, Chester shaves himself *with a straight razor.*
7. Dave loves *flying a crop-duster plane.*
8. *Glaring angrily at the class,* the teacher shouted for silence.
9. This calculator can't be used *to determine cube roots.*
10. The car *for me* must be small, inexpensive, and cheap to run.
11. The most interesting part of the trip, *visiting Cawdor Castle,* came on our third day in Scotland.
12. Some of the houses have lost their roofs *because of the storm.*
13. *Having sounded the alarm,* the trumpeter took shelter in the castle.
14. *Picking blueberries* is a pleasant way to spend a summer morning.
15. The soprano moved downstage *to sing an aria.*

EXERCISE ANSWERS

1. gerund, noun
2. infinitive, noun
3. participial, adjective
4. prepositional, adverb
5. infinitive, adjective
6. prepositional, adverb
7. gerund, noun
8. participial, adjective
9. infinitive, adverb
10. prepositional, adjective
11. gerund, noun
12. prepositional, adverb
13. participial, adjective
14. gerund, noun
15. infinitive, adverb

Clauses

A clause is a word group that includes a subject and a predicate. An *independent clause,* sometimes called a main clause, expresses a complete thought and can function as a simple sentence. A *subordinate clause,* or dependent clause, cannot stand by itself. Subordinate clauses may serve as nouns, adjectives, or adverbs.

Noun Clauses.   A noun clause can serve in any of the ways that ordinary nouns can.

What the neighbor told John proved to be incorrect. (noun clause as subject)

The woman asked *when the bus left for Spokane.* (noun clause as direct object)

I'll give a reward to *whoever returns my billfold.* (noun clause as object of preposition *to*)

Noun clauses normally begin with one of the following words:

Relative Pronouns		*Subordinating Conjunctions*
who	whoever	when
whom	whomever	why
whose	that	where
what	whatever	how
which	whichever	whether

The relative pronoun *that* is sometimes omitted from the beginning of a clause that acts as a direct object.

Dr. Kant thinks *(that) he knows everything.*

If a clause is serving as a noun, you can replace it with the word *something* or *someone,* and the sentence will still make sense.

Dr. Kant thinks *something.*

If the clause is serving as an adjective or an adverb, making the substitution turns the sentence into nonsense.

The person *who wins the lottery* will receive two million dollars.

The person *someone* will receive two million dollars.

Adjective Clauses. Like ordinary adjectives, adjective clauses modify nouns and noun substitutes.

Give me one reason *why you feel the way you do.* (Adjective clause modifies noun.)

I'll hire anyone *that Dr. Stone recommends.* (Adjective clause modifies pronoun.)

Generally, adjective clauses begin with one of the following words:

Relative Pronouns	*Subordinating Conjunctions*
who	when
whom	where
whose	why
what	after
which	before
that	

Sometimes the word that introduces the clause can be omitted.

The chair *(that) we ordered last month* has just arrived. (pronoun *that* omitted but understood)

The man *(whom) we were talking to* is a movie producer. (pronoun *whom* omitted but understood)

Sometimes, too, a preposition comes ahead of the introductory pronoun.

The grace *with which Nelson danced* made the onlookers envious.

An adjective clause may be restrictive and distinguish whatever it modifies from others in the same class, or it may be nonrestrictive and provide more information about whatever it modifies.

Flora wiped up the cereal *that the baby had spilled.* (restrictive clause)

Harriet Thomas, *who was born in Alaska,* now lives in Hawaii. (nonrestrictive clause)

As these examples show, restrictive clauses are not set off with commas, but nonrestrictive clauses are.

Adverb Clauses. These clauses modify verbs, adjectives, adverbs, and sentences, answering the same questions that ordinary adverbs do.

You may go *whenever you wish.* (Adverb clause modifies verb.)

Sandra looked paler *than I had ever seen her look before.* (Adverb clause modifies adjective.)

Darryl shouted loudly *so that the rescue party could hear him.* (Adverb clause modifies adverb.)

Unless everyone cooperates, this plan will never succeed. (Adverb clause modifies whole sentence.)

The word or word group that introduces an adverb clause is always a subordinating conjunction. Here are the most common of these conjunctions, grouped according to the questions they answer.

When? after, as, as soon as, before, since, until, when, whenever, while
Where? where, wherever
How? as if, as though
Why? as, because, now that, since, so that
Under what conditions? although, if, once, provided that, though, unless
To what extent? than

Occasionally in an adverb clause, the omission of one or more words won't hurt its meaning. Such a construction is called an *elliptical clause.*

While (he was) making a sandwich, Garth hummed softly. (*he was* omitted but understood)

Unlike noun and adjective clauses, adverb clauses can often be moved about in their sentences.

Garth hummed softly *while (he was) making a sandwich.*

Usage Considerations. Like phrases, clauses can help develop sentences as well as smooth out choppiness.

Original   The old grandfather clock ticked loudly through the night.

Revision   The old grandfather clock *that my great-aunt gave me before she died* ticked loudly through the night. (clause adds information)

Original   The chemistry professor insisted on lab safety. He had been hurt in a lab explosion the previous year.

cl

> **Revision**   The chemistry professor, *who had been hurt in a lab explosion the previous year*, insisted on lab safety. (clause adds smoothness)

To avoid clumsiness, avoid overloaded sentences like the one below.

> The old grandfather clock that my great-aunt gave me before she died *and that I took with me to England when my company transferred me there for two years* ticked loudly through the night.

EXERCISE ■ Identify the italicized clauses as noun, adjective, or adverb.

1. Why do Bill's parents always give him *whatever he wants?*
2. Steve pitched *as if a big-league scout were watching him.*
3. Gary is the only golfer *who putted well today.*
4. The dog barked loudly *because he was hungry.*
5. *Why anyone would want to skydive* is beyond me.
6. The secretary *Julie hired last month* has already received a raise.
7. I can't believe *that Beth has to work all weekend.*
8. Square dancing is an activity *that millions enjoy.*
9. The woman glanced impatiently at her watch *while awaiting the bus.*
10. Charlotte Bronte wrote her best works *before she was thirty-five.*
11. The family *for whom this house was built* can no longer afford the mortgage payments.
12. The committee will award a plaque to *whichever student wins the spelling bee.*

Editing to Correct Sentence Errors

Accepted usage improves the smoothness of your prose, makes your writing easier to understand, and demonstrates that you are a careful communicator. These assets, in turn, increase the likelihood that the reader will accept your ideas.

When you've finished revising the first draft of a piece of writing, edit it with a critic's eye to ensure that you eliminate all errors. Circle sentences or parts of them that are faulty or suspect. Then check your circled items against this section of the Handbook, which deals with the most common errors in college writing.

SENTENCE FRAGMENTS

A sentence fragment is a group of words that fails to qualify as a sentence but is capitalized and punctuated as if it were a sentence. To be a sentence, a word group must (1) have a subject and a verb and (2) make sense by itself. The first of the following examples has a subject and a verb; the second does not. Neither makes sense by itself.

> If you want to remain.
> His answer to the question.

Methods of Revision. Eliminating a sentence fragment is not hard. Careful reading often shows that the fragment goes with the sentence that comes just before or just after it. And sometimes two successive fragments can be joined. Note how we've corrected the fragments (italicized) in the following pairs.

Faulty	*Having been warned about the storm*. We decided to stay home.
Revision	Having been warned about the storm, we decided to stay home.
Faulty	*After eating*. The dog took a nap.
Revision	After eating, the dog took a nap.
Faulty	Sally went to work. *Although she felt sick.*
Revision	Sally went to work although she felt sick.
Faulty	Dave bought a new suit. *Over at Bentley's.*
Revision	Dave bought a new suit over at Bentley's.

529

frag

Faulty	*That bronze clock on the mantel. Once belonged to my grandmother.*
Revision	That bronze clock on the mantel once belonged to my grandmother.

Joining a fragment to a sentence or to another fragment works only if the problem is simply one of mispunctuation. If the fragment stems from an improperly developed thought, revise the thought into correct sentence form.

Punctuating Your Corrections. When you join a fragment to the following sentence, you need not place a comma between the two unless the fragment has six or more words or if omitting a comma might cause a misreading. When joining a fragment to the preceding sentence, omit a comma unless there is a distinct pause between the two items. The preceding examples illustrate these points.

Intentional Fragments. Fragments are commonly used in conversation and the writing that reproduces it. Professional writers also use fragments to gain special emphasis or create special effects. Pages 204–5 discuss these applications.

CONNECTED DISCOURSE EXERCISE ■ Identify and correct the sentence fragments in the following letter.

Dear Phone Company:

Recently I received a phone bill for over $500. While I do use the phone fairly extensively. Most of the calls I make are local ones. In this case, many of the calls on my bill were to other countries. Including a phone call to New Delhi, India. I can hardly be held responsible for these calls. Especially since I don't know anyone who lives overseas. Since the only long-distance call I made was to Kalamazoo, Michigan. I have deducted the charges for all the other long-distance calls from my bill and am sending you the balance. In order to prevent this type of error from happening again. Would you please have a representative determine why these charges appeared on my bill?

Sincerely,

Desperate

EXERCISE ■ Twelve main clauses paired with fragments are shown below. In each case identify the sentence (S) and the fragment (F) and then eliminate the fragment.

1. The clerk handed the package to the customer. And walked swiftly away from the counter.

2. Exhausted by his efforts to push the car out of the snowbank. Paul slumped wearily into the easy chair.
3. The dinner honored three retirees. One of them my father.
4. After tidying up the kitchen. My parents left for the movies.
5. If Dr. Frankenstein's experiment is a success. He'll throw a monster party to celebrate.
6. Even though Ned studied very hard. He had trouble with the test.
7. The dog barked at the stranger. And chased him from the property.
8. By leaving the ballpark before the last out was made. We avoided the after-game crowd.
9. The Corellis bought a shag rug. To put in front of the fireplace.
10. I'd like you to meet Bruce Dalton. My closest friend in high school.
11. By taking Amtrak. We escaped the strain of driving to Chicago.
12. Fred told Martha. That he was playing tennis Monday afternoon.

RUN-ON SENTENCES AND COMMA SPLICES

ro cs

A run-on, or fused, sentence occurs when one sentence runs into another without anything to mark their junction. A comma splice occurs when only a comma marks the junction. These errors lead your readers to think that you are hasty or careless. Here are several examples.

Run-on sentence Laura failed to set her alarm she was late for work.

Comma splice Violets are blooming now, my lawn is covered with them.

Run-on sentence Rick refused to attend the movie he said he hated horror shows.

Comma splice Perry watched the road carefully, he still missed his turn.

Run-on sentence Janet worked on her term paper her friend studied for a calculus test.

Comma splice Janet worked on her term paper, her friend studied for a calculus test.

Testing for Errors. To check out a possible comma splice or fused sentence, read what precedes and follows the comma or suspected junction and see whether the two parts can stand alone as sentences. If *both parts* can stand alone, there is an error. Otherwise, there is not.

Darryl is a real troublemaker, someday he'll find himself in serious difficulty.

Examination of the parts preceding and following the comma shows that each is a complete sentence:

Darryl is a real troublemaker.
Someday he'll find himself in serious difficulty.

PERSPECTIVE

Comma splices and run-ons occur most frequently when the subject of the second sentence is a pronoun that refers to an antecedent in the previous sentence. In such cases, the writer erroneously believes that pronoun and antecedent must be in the same sentence. Errors also occur because the sentences are so closely linked in meaning that the student feels the need to bind them somehow. Finally, students sometimes omit implicit subordinating or coordinating conjunctions.

TEACHING STRATEGY

Have students review their own writing to identify where and why they produce comma splices and run-ons. Because many students think that a pronoun and its antecedent cannot appear in separate sentences, stress that they can.

The writer has therefore committed a comma splice that needs correction.

Methods of Revision. You can correct run-on sentences and comma splices in several ways.

1. Create two separate sentences.

Revision   Violets are blooming now. My lawn is covered with them.

Revision   Rick refused to attend the movie. He said he hated horror shows.

2. Join the sentences with a semicolon.

Revision   Violets are blooming now; my yard is covered with them.

Revision   Rick refused to attend the movie; he said he hated horror shows.

3. Join the sentences with a comma and a coordinating conjunction (*and, but, or, nor, for, yet, so*).

Revision   Laura failed to set her alarm, *so* she was late for work.

Revision   Perry watched the road carefully, *but* he still missed his turn.

4. Join the sentences with a semicolon and a conjunctive adverb (see page 521).

Revision   Laura failed to set her alarm; *consequently*, she was late for work.

Revision   Violets are blooming now; *in fact*, my yard is covered with them.

5. Introduce one of the sentences with a subordinating conjunction (see pages 521, 527).

Revision   *Because* Laura failed to set her alarm, she was late for work.

Revision   Janet worked on her term paper *while* her friend studied for a calculus test.

As our examples show, you can often correct an error in several ways.

CONNECTED DISCOURSE EXERCISE ■ Identify and correct the comma splices and run-on sentences in the following letter.

Dear Desperate:

We are sorry to hear that you are having difficulty paying your bill, it is, however, your responsibility. Unfortunately we have no way to prevent you from making overseas calls, you have to curb your own tendency to reach out and touch your friends. Following your instructions, we are sending a technician to remove your phone. Please be home this Friday morning he will arrive then. Even though we will

ro cs

EXERCISE ANSWER

Dear Desperate:

We are sorry to hear that you are having difficulty paying your bill; it is, however, your responsibility. Unfortunately we have no way to prevent you from making overseas calls; you have to curb your own tendency to reach out and touch your friends. Following your instructions, we are sending a technician to remove your phone. Please be home this Friday morning, for he will arrive then. Even though we will remove your phone, you are still responsible for the unpaid portion of remove your phone, you are still responsible for the unpaid portion of your bill, it is your financial obligation. We would dislike referring this matter to a collection agency, it could ruin your credit rating.

Sincerely,

Your friendly phone representative

EXERCISE ■ **Indicate whether each item is correct (C), is a run-on sentence (RO), or contains a comma splice (CS) and then correct the faulty items.**

1. Lee is a difficult person he becomes angry whenever he doesn't get his own way.
2. The student appeared puzzled by the instructor's answer to his question, but he said nothing more.
3. The doctor warned Allan about his high cholesterol level, he went on a high-fiber diet.
4. Sally researched her topic thoroughly and wrote her report carefully as a result she received an *A*.
5. It's nice to see you again; we should get together more often.
6. The horse stumbled and nearly fell in the backstretch, nevertheless it managed to finish second.
7. Janice thought the exercises would be easy, after finishing them she found that her whole body ached.
8. I've just started to take up chess, you can hardly expect me to play well.
9. I'd like to help you out which way did you come in?
10. The company's profits increased steadily all year; threfore, it gave its employees a Christmas bonus.

SUBJECT–VERB AGREEMENT

A verb should agree in number with its subject. Singular verbs should have singular subjects, and plural verbs should have plural subjects.

Correct My *boss is* a grouch. (singular subject and verb)

Correct The *apartments have* two bedrooms. (plural subject and verb)

Ordinarily, matching subjects and verbs causes no problems. The following special situations, however, can create difficulties.

Subject and Verb Separated by a Word Group. Sometimes a word group that includes one or more nouns comes between the subject and the verb. When this happens, match the verb with its subject, not a noun in the word group.

Correct Our *basket* of sandwiches *is* missing.

your bill. It is your financial obligation. We would dislike referring this matter to a collection agency since it could ruin your credit rating.

Sincerely,

Your friendly phone representative

EXERCISE ANSWERS

1. RO (person. He / person; he / person because he)
2. C
3. CS (level; therefore, / level, so)

sv agr

4. RO (carefully. As a result, / carefully; as a result,)
5. C
6. CS (backstretch. Nevertheless, / backstretch; nevertheless,)
7. CS (easy, but / easy. But)
8. CS (chess. You / chess; you / chess; therefore, you / chess, so you)
9. RO (out. Which / out; which)
10. C

PERSPECTIVE

Errors in subject–verb agreement rarely occur because students misunderstand the rules. In most cases, errors happen because students lose track of the subject.

Correct   Several *books* required for my paper *are* not in the library.

Correct   Mr. *Schmidt,* along with his daughters, *runs* a furniture store.

Correct   The old *bus,* crammed with passengers, *was* unable to reach the top of the hill.

Two Singular Subjects.   Most singular subjects joined by *and* take a plural verb.

Correct   The *couch* and *chair were* upholstered in blue velvet.

Sentences like the one above almost never cause problems. With subjects like *restoring cars* and *racing motorcycles,* however, singular verbs are often mistakenly used.

Faulty   *Restoring cars* and *racing motorcycles consumes* most of Frank's time.

Revision   *Restoring cars* and *racing motorcycles consume* most of Frank's time.

When *each* or *every* precedes the subjects, use a *singular* verb in place of a plural.

Correct   Every *book* and *magazine was* badly water-stained.

Singular subjects joined by *or, either–or,* or *neither–nor* also take singular verbs.

Correct   A *pear* or an *apple is* a nice afternoon snack.

Correct   Neither *rain* nor *snow slows* our letter carrier.

Finally, use a singular verb when two singular subjects joined by *and* name the same person, place, or thing.

Correct   My *cousin* and business *partner is* retiring next month.

Cousin and *partner* refer to the same person.

One Singular and One Plural Subject.   When one singular subject and one plural subject are joined by *or, either–or,* or *neither–nor,* match the verb with the closer of the two.

Correct   Neither *John* nor his *parents were* at home.

Correct   Neither his *parents* nor *John was* at home.

As these examples show, the sentences are usually smoother when the plural subject follows the singular.

Collective Nouns as Subjects.   Collective nouns (*assembly, class, committee, family, herd, majority, tribe,* and the like) are singular in form but stand for groups or collections of people or things. Ordinarily, collective nouns are considered to be singular and therefore take singular verbs.

Correct   The *class is* writing a test.

Correct   The *herd was* clustered around the water hole.

Sometimes, though, a collective noun refers to the separate individuals making up the grouping, and then it requires a plural verb.

Correct   The *jury are* in dispute about the verdict.

Sentences in Which the Verb Comes Ahead of the Subject.

Sentences that begin with words such as *here, there, how, what,* and *where* fall into this category. With such sentences, the verb must agree with the subject that follows it.

Correct   Here *is* my *house.*

Correct   Where *are* my *shoes?*

Correct   There *is* just one *way* to solve this problem.

Correct   There *go* my *chances* for a promotion.

sv agr

CONNECTED DISCOURSE EXERCISE ■ Identify and correct the subject–verb agreement errors in the following letter.

Regional Accounts Manager:

One of your area phone representatives have seriously misread a letter I submitted with my bill. I refused to pay for long-distance overseas calls since neither I nor my roommate know anyone who live overseas. Instead of deducting the calls from my bill, she sent someone to remove my phone. Now my phone, along with many of my valuable possessions, have been removed. Unfortunately the technician, whom I allowed into my apartment only after carefully checking his credentials, were a thief. He locked me in a closet and cleared out the apartment. I have called the police, but I also expect the phone company to reimburse me for my losses. There is only two choices. Either the stolen items or a check covering the loss need to be sent to me immediately. Otherwise I am afraid I will be forced to sue. A jury are sure to rule in my favor. In addition, I expect to find that those overseas calls has been deducted from my bill.

                   Sincerely,

                   Desperately Desperate

EXERCISE ANSWER

Regional Accounts Manager:

One of your area phone representatives has seriously misread a letter I submitted with my bill. I refused to pay for long-distance overseas calls since neither I nor my roommate knows anyone who lives overseas. Instead of deducting the calls from my bill, she sent someone to remove my phone. Now my phone, along with many of my valuable possessions, has been removed. Unfortunately the technician, whom I allowed into my apartment only after carefully checking his credentials, was a thief. He locked me in a closet and cleared out the apartment. I have called the police, but I also expect the phone company to reimburse me for my losses. There are only two choices. Either the stolen items or a check covering the loss needs to be sent to me immediately. Otherwise I am afraid I will be forced to sue. A jury is sure to rule in my favor. In addition, I expect to find that those overseas calls have been deducted from my bill.

Sincerely,

Desperately Desperate

EXERCISE ■ **Choose the correct verb form from the pair in parentheses.**

1. The pictures in the drawing room of the mansion (has, have) been insured for twelve million dollars.
2. Every dish and piece of stainless that I own (is, are) dirty.
3. Look! There (is, are) Kathy and her friend Marge.
4. Reading novels and watching TV (takes, take) up most of Stanley's time.
5. Each of these proposals (represents, represent) a great amount of work.
6. Two hamburgers or a hot beef sandwich (makes, make) an ample lunch.
7. (Has, Have) either of the orchids blossomed yet?
8. The automobile with the broken headlights and dented sides (was, were) stopped by the police.
9. The tribe (believes, believe) that this river is sacred.
10. My grandmother's brooch, along with her earrings, (has, have) been missing for a week.
11. Neither the supervisor nor the union stewards (seems, seem) concerned about the department's poor safety record.
12. Those men loitering on the corner by the drugstore (looks, look) like troublemakers.

PRONOUN-ANTECEDENT AGREEMENT

The antecedent of a pronoun is the noun or pronoun to which it refers. Just as subjects should agree with their verbs, pronouns should agree with their antecedents: singular antecedents require singular pronouns, and plural antecedents require plural pronouns. Ordinarily, you will have no trouble matching antecedents and pronouns. The situations below, however, can cause problems.

Indefinite Pronouns as Antecedents.   Indefinite pronouns include words like *each, either, neither, any, everybody, somebody,* and *nobody.* Whenever an indefinite pronoun is used as an antecedent, the pronoun that refers to it should be singular.

> *Faulty*   *Neither* of the actors had learned *their* lines.

> *Revision*   *Neither* of the actors had learned *his* lines.

When the gender of the antecedent is unknown, you may follow it with *his or her,* or if this results in awkwardness, rewrite the sentence in the plural.

> *Correct*   *Anyone* who has studied *his or her* assignments properly should do well on the test.

> *Correct*   *Those* who have studied *their* assignments should do well on the test.

Occasionally, a ridiculous result occurs when a singular pronoun refers to an indefinite pronoun that is obviously plural in meaning. When this happens, rewrite the sentence to eliminate the problem.

Faulty   *Everybody* complained that the graduation ceremony had lasted too long, but I didn't believe *him.*

Revision   Everybody complained that the graduation ceremony had lasted too long, but I didn't agree.

Two Singular Antecedents.   Two or more antecedents joined by *and* ordinarily call for a plural pronoun.

Correct   Her briefcase and umbrella were missing from *their* usual place on the hall table.

When *each* or *every* precedes the antecedent, use a singular pronoun.

Correct   Every college and university must do *its* best to provide adequate student counseling.

Singular antecedents joined by *or, either–or,* or *neither–nor* call for singular pronouns.

Correct   Neither Carol nor Irene had paid *her* rent for the month.

Applying this rule can sometimes yield an awkward or foolish sentence. When this happens, rewrite the sentence to avoid the problem.

Faulty   Neither James nor Sally has finished *his or her* term project.

Revision   James and Sally have not finished *their* term projects.

Singular antecedents joined by *and* that refer to the same person, place, or thing use a singular pronoun.

Correct   My *cousin* and business *partner* is retiring to *his* condo in Florida next month.

Singular and Plural Antecedents.   If one singular and one plural antecedent are joined by *or, either–or,* or *neither–nor,* the pronoun agrees with the closer one.

Correct   Either Terrence James or the Parkinsons will let us use *their* lawn mower.

Correct   Either the Parkinsons or Terrence James will let us use *his* lawn mower.

Sentences of this sort are generally smoother when the plural subject follows the singular.

Collective Nouns as Antecedents.   When a collective noun is considered a single unit, the pronoun that refers to it should be singular.

Correct   The *troop* of scouts made *its* way slowly through the woods.

When the collective noun refers to the separate individuals in the group, use a plural pronoun.

Correct   The staff lost *their* jobs when the factory closed.

EXERCISE ANSWER

Dear Desperately Desperate:

We were sorry to hear about the theft from your apartment. Apparently a gang of con artists recently had its base of operations in your community. They posed as repair technicians and presented false credentials to customers expecting their phones to be repaired. Someone also must have intercepted your mail and written his or her own response since we have no record of any previous letter from you. Clearly neither the

representative you mentioned nor the phony phone technician could have held a position with our company. Our technicians must provide us with their fingerprints and take periodic lie detector tests. Further, our representatives will not answer correspondence since it is not a part of their job description. For these reasons, we do not believe we are responsible for your losses. However, a review of our records does show that you owe $500; we have included a copy of the bill in case you have misplaced the original.

Sincerely,

Accounts Manager

EXERCISE ANSWERS

1. his or her
2. their
3. their
4. his or her
5. its
6. her
7. their
8. its
9. her
10. its

CONNECTED DISCOURSE EXERCISE ■ Identify and correct the pronoun–antecedent agreement errors in the following letter.

Dear Desperately Desperate:

We were sorry to hear about the theft from your apartment. Apparently a gang of con artists recently had their base of operations in your community. It posed as repair technicians and presented false credentials to anyone expecting their phone to be repaired. Someone also must have intercepted your mail and written their own response since we have no record of any previous letter from you. Clearly neither the representative you mentioned nor the phony phone technician could have held their position with our company. Every one of our technicians must provide us with their fingerprints and take periodic lie detector tests. Further, none of our representatives will answer correspondence since it is not a part of their job description. For these reasons, we do not believe we are responsible for your losses. However, a review of our records does show that you owe $500; we have included a copy of the bill in case you have misplaced the original.

Sincerely,

Accounts Manager

EXERCISE ■ Choose the right pronoun from the pair in parentheses.

1. If everybody does (his or her, their) part, the pageant should go smoothly.
2. Neither Greg nor the Snows had remembered to make (his, their) reservations at the ski lodge.
3. The graduating class filed by the principal and received (its, their) diplomas.
4. Each of the performers nervously waited (his or her, their) turn to audition.
5. Every boot and shoe I own needs to have (its, their) laces replaced.
6. Either Laurie or Alicia will show (her, their) slides at the party.
7. Dave and Bill loudly voiced (his, their) complaints about the restaurant's service.
8. Pleased with the performance, the audience showed (its, their) pleasure by applauding loudly.
9. Either the Talbots or Nancy Dunn will lend us (her, their) lawnmower.
10. Samantha's mother told her to put every toy and game back in (its, their) proper storage place.

Avoiding Faulty Pronoun Reference

TEACHING STRATEGY

This section can easily be combined with the section on pronoun-antecedent agreement. As students check their drafts for pronoun agreement, they might also determine whether the pronouns have appropriate and clear antecedents.

Any pronoun except an indefinite pronoun should refer to just one noun or noun substitute—its antecedent. Reference problems result when the pronoun has two or more antecedents, a hidden antecedent, or no antecedent. These errors can cause mixups in meaning as well as ridiculous sentences.

More Than One Antecedent. The following sentences lack clarity because their pronouns have two possible antecedents rather than just one.

Faulty   Take the screens off the windows and wash *them*.

Faulty   Harry told Will that *he* was putting on weight.

The reader can't tell whether the screens or the windows should be washed or who is putting on weight.

Sometimes we see a sentence like this one:

Faulty   If the boys don't eat all the Popsicles, put *them* in the freezer.

In this case, we know it's the Popsicles that should be stored, but the use of *them* creates an amusing sentence.

Correct these faults by replacing the pronoun with a noun or by rephrasing the sentence.

Revision   Wash the windows after you have taken off the screens.

Revision   Take off the screens so that you can wash the windows.

Revision   Harry told Will, "I am (you are) putting on weight."

Revision   Put any uneaten Popsicles in the freezer.

Hidden Antecedent. An antecedent is hidden if it takes the form of an adjective rather than a noun.

Faulty   The movie theater is closed today, so we can't see *one*.

Faulty   As I passed the tiger's cage, *it* lunged at me.

To correct this fault, replace the pronoun with the noun used as an adjective or switch the positions of the pronoun and the noun and make any needed changes in their forms.

Revision   The theater is closed today, so we can't see a movie.

Revision   As I passed its cage, the tiger lunged at me.

No Antecedent. A no-antecedent sentence lacks any noun to which the pronoun can refer. Sentences of this sort occur frequently in everyday conversation but should be avoided in formal writing. The examples below illustrate this error.

Faulty   The lecture was boring, but *they* took notes anyway.

Faulty   On the news program, *it* told about a new crisis in the Persian Gulf.

pr ref

To set matters right, substitute a suitable noun for the pronoun or reword the sentence.

> *Revision*   The lecture was boring, but the students took notes anyway.

> *Revision*   The news program told about a new crisis in the Persian Gulf.

Sometimes a *this, that, it,* or *which* will refer to a whole idea rather than a single noun. This usage is acceptable provided the writer's meaning is obvious, as in this example.

> *Correct*   The instructor spoke very softly, *which* meant we had difficulty hearing him.

Problems occur, however, when the reader can't figure out which of two or more ideas the pronoun refers to.

> *Faulty*   Ginny called Sally two hours after the agreed-upon time and postponed their shopping trip one day. *This* irritated Sally very much.

What caused Sally to be irritated—the late call, the postponement of the trip, or both? Again, rewording or adding a clarifying word will correct the problem.

> *Revision*   Ginny called Sally two hours after the agreed-upon time and postponed their shopping trip one day. This *tardiness* irritated Sally very much.

> *Revision*   Ginny called Sally two hours after the agreed-upon time and postponed their shopping trip one day. Ginny's *change of plans* irritated Sally very much.

The first of these examples illustrates the addition of a clarifying word; the second illustrates rewriting.

CONNECTED DISCOURSE EXERCISE ■ Identify and correct any faulty pronoun references in the following memorandum.

TO: Director of Food Services, Groan University

FROM: Vice-President of College Services

DATE: February 19, 19--

SUBJECT: Student Complaints about Cafeteria

Complaints about food quality and cafeteria hours are common but easily resolved. They can be extended by simply installing vending machines. It might not make for a nutritious meal, but it certainly will undercut some of the dissatisfaction. Of course, no matter how good the food, they will complain. Still, you can partially defuse those complaints by having students list their major concerns and then meeting them. Of

pr ref

EXERCISE ANSWER

TO: Director of Food Services, Groan University

FROM: Vice-President of College Services

DATE: February 19, 19--

SUBJECT: Student Complaints about Cafeteria

Complaints about food quality and cafeteria hours are common but easily resolved. The cafeteria hours can be extended by simply installing vending machines. Snack food might not make for a nutritious meal, but it certainly will undercut some of the dissatisfaction. Of course, no matter how good the food, students will complain. Still, you can partially defuse those complaints by having students list their major concerns and then meeting the common objections. Of course, you can always increase student satisfaction by purchasing a soft ice cream machine and offering ice cream cones for dessert.

course, you can always increase student satisfaction by purchasing a soft ice cream machine and offering it for dessert.

EXERCISE ■ Indicate whether each sentence is correct (C) or contains a faulty pronoun reference (F) and then correct any faulty sentences.

1. Ann told Jennifer that the boss wanted to see her.
2. Because the ring hurt her finger, Ruth took it off.
3. At the farmer's market they sell many kinds of produce.
4. I like the food in Mexican restaurants because it is very spicy.
5. They tell me that the company's profits have risen five percent this quarter.
6. Knowing that my friends like hot dogs, I grilled them at the picnic.
7. When Jeffrey rose to make his speech, they all started laughing.
8. In the paper, it told about the state's budget crisis.
9. While we stood by the horse barn, they started neighing.
10. As soon as Teresa removed the leash from the dog, it ran into the street.
11. Warren gloated about his business coup to all his friends, which surprised them greatly.
12. Everyone dreams, and we have several of them every night.

AVOIDING UNWARRANTED SHIFTS IN PERSON

Pronouns can be in the first person, second person, or third person. *First-person* pronouns identify people who are talking or writing about themselves, *second-person* pronouns identify people being addressed directly, and *third-person* pronouns identify persons or things that are being written or spoken about. The following table sorts pronouns according to person.

First Person	*Second Person*	*Third Person*
I	you	he
me	your	she
my	yours	it
mine	yourself	his
we	yourselves	her
us		hers
our		its
ours		one
ourselves		they
		their
		theirs
		indefinite pronouns

All nouns are in the third person. As you revise, be alert for unwarranted shifts from one person to another.

shft

are especially likely to occur if students are not sure whether to use "one" or "you."

Faulty	I liked *my* British vacation better than *my* vacation in France and Italy because *you* didn't have language problems.
Revision	I liked *my* British vacation better than *my* vacation in France and Italy because *I* didn't have language problems.
Faulty	Holidays are important to *everyone*. They boost *your* spirits and provide a break from *our* daily routine.
Revision	Holidays are important to *everyone*. They boost *one's* spirits and provide a break from *one's* daily routine.
Faulty	The taller the *golfer,* the more club speed *you* will have with a normally paced swing.
Revision	The taller the *golfer,* the more club speed *he* or *she* will have with a normally paced swing.

As these examples show, the shift can occur within a single sentence or when the writer moves from one sentence to another.

Some shifts in person, however, are warranted. Read the following correct sentence:

Correct	*I* want *you* to deliver these flowers to Ms. Willoughby by 3 o'clock. *She* needs them for a party.

Here the speaker identifies himself or herself (I) while speaking directly to a listener (you) about someone else (she). In this case, shifts are needed to get the message across.

EXERCISE ANSWER

Good health is clearly important to you. But it is your responsibility to ensure your own good health. You can start with simple exercises. We would like to provide you with a low-impact aerobics video tape for only $9. We guarantee that the more out of shape you are, the quicker you will notice the benefits. The way your body feels affects the quality of your life. Let our tape help you to a better life.

EXERCISE ANSWERS

1. S. Because many of our tour guides . . . , we soon . . . .

2. S. We like the location . . . ; we are close . . . .

3. C.

4. C.

5. S. If you complete . . . , you can expect . . . . / Anyone who completes a degree in vocational education can expect . . . .

CONNECTED DISCOURSE EXERCISE ■ Identify and correct the unwarranted shifts in person in the following paragraph.

Good health is clearly important to everyone. But it is one's responsibility to ensure one's own good health. You can start with simple exercises. We would like to provide you with a low-impact aerobics video tape for only $9. We guarantee that the more out of shape the customer, the quicker you will notice the benefits. The way our bodies feel affects the quality of our lives. Let our tape help you to a better life.

EXERCISE ■ Indicate whether the sentence is correct (C) or contains an unwarranted shift in person (S). Correct faulty sentences.

1. Because many of our tour guides spoke very poor English, the tourists soon became quite frustrated.

2. We like the location of our new house very much; you are close to a couple of large shopping centers.

3. If you want me to invite Gary to the party, I'll call him right now.

4. Be sure you tell the bakery clerk that we will need the cake by tomorrow noon.

5. If you complete a degree in vocational education, anyone can expect a rewarding career.

6. Once we learn to ride a bicycle, a person never forgets how.

7. Anyone wishing to make the trip to Chicago should make your own hotel reservations.

8. After we had finished the test, the instructor told the students she would return it on Thursday.

9. Each year planeloads of Americans fly to Europe and visit the countries from which our ancestors came.

10. Our company has a very liberal vacation policy; you get four weeks off each year.

6. S. Once we learn . . . , we never forget how. / Once anyone learns . . . , he or she never forgets how.

7. S. Anyone wishing . . . should make his or her own hotel reservations.

8. S. After we . . . , the instructor told us . . . .

9. S. . . . visit the countries from which their ancestors came.

10. S. Our company . . . ; we get . . . . / This company . . . ; employees get . . . .

USING THE RIGHT PRONOUN CASE

Case means the changes in form that a personal pronoun (see pages 504–5) undergoes to show its function in a sentence. English has three cases: the *subjective,* the *nonsubjective* (objective), and the *possessive*. The following chart shows the different forms.

Subjective Form	Nonsubjective Form	Possessive Form
I	me	my, mine
he	him	his
she	her	her, hers
we	us	our, ours
you	you	your, yours
they	them	their, theirs
who	whom	whose

The subjective case is used for subjects and subject complements, the nonsubjective for direct objects, indirect objects, and objects of prepositions. The possessive case shows ownership and is also used with gerunds.

The following pointers will help you select the proper pronoun as you revise.

We and Us Preceding Nouns.
Nouns that serve as subjects take the pronoun *we*. Other nouns take the pronoun *us*.

Correct   *We* tourists will fly home tomorrow. (*We* accompanies the subject.)

Correct   The guide showed *us* tourists through the cathedral. (*Us* accompanies a nonsubject.)

If you can't decide which pronoun is right, mentally omit the noun and read the sentence to yourself, first with one pronoun and then with the other. Your ear will indicate the correct form.

My mother made (we, us) children vanilla pudding for dessert.

Omitting *children* shows immediately that *us* is the right choice.

case

PERSPECTIVE

Students often make mistakes in selecting a pronoun case because they have internalized a faulty set of rules. It is not unusual for students to object to the correct form because it sounds odd to them. In some cases of course the rules are changing. For instance, some linguists suggest that the *who/whom* distinction will soon disappear. Still, until this change is definitively established, it is not difficult for students to learn this distinction. After all, whom could it hurt?

TEACHING STRATEGY

To counteract the effects of faulty rules, have students repeat the correct form until it seems less odd.

> *Correct*   My mother made *us* children vanilla pudding for dessert.

Pronouns Paired with Nouns.   When such a combination serves as the subject of a sentence or accompanies the subject, use the subject form of the pronoun. When the combination plays a nonsubject role, use the nonsubject form of the pronoun.

> *Correct*   Arlene and *I* plan to join the Peace Corps. (*I* is part of the compound subject.)

> *Correct*   Two people, Mary and *I*, will represent our school at the meeting. (*I* is part of a compound element accompanying the subject.)

> *Correct*   The superintendent told Kevin and *him* that they would be promoted soon. (*Him* is part of a compound nonsubject.)

> *Correct*   The project was difficult for Jeffrey and *him* to complete. (*Him* is part of a compound nonsubject.)

Again, mentally omitting the noun from the combination will tell you which pronoun is correct.

Who and Whom in Dependent Clauses.   Use *who* for the subjects of dependent clauses; otherwise use *whom*.

> *Correct*   The Mallarys prefer friends *who are interested in the theater.* (*Who* is the subject of the clause.)

> *Correct*   Barton is a man *whom very few people like.* (*Whom* is not the subject of the clause.)

A simple test will help you decide between *who* and *whom*. First, mentally isolate the dependent clause. Next, block out the pronoun in question and then insert *he* (or *she*) and *him* (or *her*) at the appropriate spot in the remaining part of the clause. If *he* (or *she*) sounds better, *who* is right. If *him* (or *her*) sounds better, *whom* is right. Let's use this test on the sentence below.

> The woman *who(m) Scott is dating* works as a mechanical engineer.
> Scott is dating (she, her.)

Clearly *her* is correct; therefore, *whom* is the proper form.

> *Correct*   The woman *whom Scott is dating* works as a mechanical engineer.

Pronouns as Subject Complements.   In formal writing, pronouns that serve as subject complements (see page 501) always take the subject form.

> *Correct*   It is *I*.

> *Correct*   It was *she* who bought the old Parker mansion.

This rule, however, is often ignored in informal writing.

> It's *her*.

> That's *him* standing over by the door.

Comparisons Using *than* or *as . . . as*.   Comparisons of this kind often make no direct statement about the second item of comparison. When the second naming word is a pronoun, you may have trouble choosing the right one.

> Harriet is less outgoing than (*they, them*).

> My parents' divorce saddened my sister as much as (*I, me*).

Not to worry. Expand the sentence by mentally supplying the missing material. Then try the sentence with each pronoun and see which sounds right.

> Harriet is less outgoing than (*they, them*) are.

> My parents' divorce saddened my sister as much as it did (*I, me*).

Obviously *they* is the right choice for the first sentence, and *me* is the right choice for the second one.

> ***Correct***   Harriet is less outgoing than *they* are.

> ***Correct***   My parents' divorce saddened my sister as much as it did *me*.

Pronouns Preceding Gerunds.   Use the possessive form of a pronoun that precedes a gerund (see page 524).

> I dislike *their* leaving without saying goodbye.

> Ted can't understand *her* quitting such a good job.

This usage emphasizes the action named by the gerund instead of the person or persons performing it. Thus, in the above sentences, the possessive form of the pronoun signals that it's the *leaving* the writer dislikes and the *quitting* that Ted can't understand. The persons involved are secondary.

When the pronoun precedes a participle (see page 523), it should be in the nonsubject case. The emphasis is then on the actor rather than the action.

> Jennifer caught *them* listening to records instead of studying.

In this example, Jennifer caught the listeners, not the listening.

If you have trouble deciding between the nonsubject and possessive forms of a pronoun, ask yourself whether you want to emphasize the action or the actor; then proceed accordingly.

case

CONNECTED DISCOURSE EXERCISE ■ **Identify and correct the pronoun case errors in the following paragraph.**

Between my brother and I, we are always able to pull at least five good-sized trout a day from the creek behind our house. Us rural trout fishermen just seem to have the knack. Of course, those city fishermen whom insist on employing artificial flies won't appreciate our methods even if they can't do as well as us. We just let our bait,

EXERCISE ANSWER

Between my brother and me, we are always able to pull at least five good-sized trout a day from the creek behind our house. We rural trout fishermen just seem to have the knack. Of course, those city fishermen who insist on employing artificial flies won't appreciate our methods even if they can't do as well as we do. We just let our bait, usually a juicy worm, float downstream to the waiting trout. Of course, my brother won't let the fishing interfere with his sleeping. In fact, it was he that developed the idea of looping the line around his toe so that he would wake up when a trout took the bait. Others have told my brother and me that this method is dangerous, but neither of us has lost a toe yet. Of course, the people whom we invite to dinner don't complain about our

methods, and they seem to enjoy the fish.

EXERCISE ANSWERS

1. who	**7.** I
2. I	**8.** me
3. We	**9.** me
4. whom	**10.** his
5. I	**11.** they
6. us	**12.** her

PERSPECTIVE

Writers of course legitimately shift tenses to reflect changes in time. Student problems arise chiefly because events can be presented from more than one temporal perspective. A narrative of a past event could be presented in either the past or the present tense. For instance, the sample paragraph in the text uses the present to describe an event that is clearly past. Students can easily shift focus without knowing it. When proofreading at the sentence level, they overlook the changes in tense. Furthermore, some students forget to put tense endings on some or all of their verbs.

usually a juicy worm, float downstream to the waiting trout. Of course, my brother won't let the fishing interfere with him sleeping. In fact, it was him that developed the idea of looping the line around his toe so that he would wake up when a trout took the bait. Others have told my brother and I that this method is dangerous, but neither of us has lost a toe yet. Of course, the people who we invite to dinner don't complain about our methods, and they seem to enjoy the fish.

EXERCISE ■ Choose the right form of the pronoun for each of the following sentences.

1. Cherie is the one student (who, whom) I believe has the potential to become a professional acrobat.
2. Two of us, Carrie and (I, me), will have a soft drink stand at the county fair.
3. (We, Us) Greens pride ourselves on our beautiful lawns.
4. Ken Conwell is the only candidate (who, whom) I like in this election.
5. Brookfield has richer friends and a more luxurious lifestyle than (I, me).
6. The friendly student told (we, us) freshmen that we were in the wrong building.
7. As youngsters, Bill and (I, me) used to play cowpersons and Native Americans.
8. My uncle has given Sandra and (I, me) tickets for tonight's Bach concert.
9. The instructor was cross with Darryl and (I, me) for talking in class.
10. There is no reason for (him, his) dismissing my request so bluntly.
11. I am as confused as (they, them) by the newspaper account of the accident.
12. The church awarded Connie and (she, her) certificates for their long Sunday school service.

CONSISTENCY IN SHOWING TIME

Inconsistencies occur when a writer shifts from the past tense to the present or vice versa without a corresponding shift in the time of the events being described. The following paragraph contains an uncalled-for shift from the present tense to the past.

As *The Most Dangerous Game* opens, Sanger Rainsford, a famous hunter and author, and his old friend Whitney are standing on the deck of a yacht and discussing a mysterious island as the ship passes near it. Then, after everyone else has gone to bed, Rainsford manages to fall overboard. He swims to the island and ends up at a chateau owned by General Zaroff, a refugee from the Communist takeover in Russia. Zaroff, bored with hunting animals, has turned to hunting humans on his desert island. Inevitably, Rainsford is turned out into the jungle to be hunted down. There were [shift to past tense] actually four hunts over a three-day period, and at the end of the last one, Rainsford jumped into the sea, swam across a cove to the chateau, and killed Zaroff in the general's own bedroom. Afterward he sleeps [shift back to present tense] and decides "he had never slept in a better bed."

The sentence with the unwarranted shift in tense should read as follows:

> There are actually four hunts over a three-day period, and at the end of the last one, Rainsford jumps into the sea, swims across a cove to the chateau, and kills Zaroff in the general's own bedroom.

The time shift in the quotation part of the final sentence is justified because the sleeping has occurred before Rainsford's thoughts about it.

CONNECTED DISCOURSE EXERCISE ■ Identify and correct any inconsistencies in showing time in the following passage.

There is no better time to go swimming than at night. The summer after I had graduated from high school, I worked for a landscaping company. After a sweaty day mowing lawns and digging up gardens, all of us who worked there would jump into the back of Dick's old pick-up and rattle out to Woods Lake. It is just dark as we arrive. The moon is beautiful, reflected in that black mirror set in a frame of hills. We stumble down a small, sandy hill to the beach, where we strip off our dusty jeans and sweaty shirts before plunging into the cool reflection of stars.

EXERCISE ■ Indicate whether each sentence is correct (C) or contains an unwarranted shift (S) in tense. Then correct the faulty sentences.

1. Although the alarm rang, Bob continues to lie in bed.
2. When autumn arrives, we often go for long walks in the woods.
3. John is writing his dissertation but found the job tough going.
4. When the trapeze artist fell into the net, the audience gasps loudly.
5. The flames died slowly down as the firefighters directed their hoses toward the building.
6. Edward walks for half an hour before he ate dinner.
7. Sarah had many friends but sees them infrequently.
8. As Elaine walked toward the garden, a rabbit scampers quickly away.
9. Before their guests arrived, the Kleinhans dusted and vacuumed the entire house.
10. Dark, sinister-looking clouds roll in, and rain started to fall.

AVOIDING MISUSE OF ADJECTIVES AND ADVERBS

Beginning writers often use adjectives when they should use adverbs and also confuse the comparative and superlative forms of these parts of speech when making comparisons.

Misusing Adjectives for Adverbs.
Although most adjectives can be misused as adverbs, the following seven, listed with the corresponding adverbs, cause the most difficulty.

Adjectives	*Adverbs*
awful	awfully
bad	badly
considerable	considerably
good	well
most	almost
real	really
sure	surely

The following sentences show typical errors.

> **Faulty**   Bryan did *good* in his first golf lesson. (*good* mistakenly used to modify verb *did*)

> **Faulty**   *Most* every graduate from our auto service program receives several job offers. (*Most* mistakenly used to modify adjective *every*)

> **Faulty**   The speech was delivered *real* well. (*real* mistakenly used to modify adverb *well*)

Because adverbs modify verbs, adjectives, and other adverbs (see page 517), and adjectives modify nouns and noun substitutes (see page 515), the above sentences clearly require adverbs.

> **Revision**   Bryan did *well* in his first golf lesson.

> **Revision**   *Almost* every graduate from our auto service program receives several job offers.

> **Revision**   The speech was delivered *really* well.

If you can't decide whether a sentence requires an adjective or an adverb, determine the part of speech of the word being modified and proceed accordingly.

Confusing the Comparative and Superlative Forms in Comparisons.
The comparative form of adjectives and adverbs is used to compare two things, the superlative form to compare three or more things. Adjectives with fewer than three syllables generally add *-er* to make the comparative form and *-est* to make the superlative form (tall, tall*er*, tall*est*). Adjectives with three or more syllables generally add *more* to make the comparative and *most* to make the superlative

(enchanting, *more* enchanting, *most* enchanting), as do most adverbs of two or more syllables (loudly, *more* loudly, *most* loudly).

When making comparisons, beginning writers sometimes mistakenly use double comparatives or double superlatives.

Faulty   Harry is *more taller* than James. (double comparative)

Faulty   The Chrysler Building has the *most splendidest* lobby I've ever seen. (double superlative)

The correct versions read as follows:

Revision   Harry is *taller* than James.

Revision   The Chrysler Building has the *most splendid* lobby I've ever seen.

In addition, writers may erroneously use the superlative form, rather than the comparative form, to compare two things.

Faulty   Barry is the *richest* of the two brothers.

Faulty   Jeremy is the *most talented* of those two singers.

Here are the sentences correctly written.

Revision   Barry is the *richer* of the two brothers.

Revision   Jeremy is the *more talented* of those two singers.

Reserve the superlative form for comparing three or more items.

Correct   Barry is the *richest* of the three brothers.

Correct   Jeremy is the *most talented* of those four singers.

CONNECTED DISCOURSE EXERCISE ■ **Identify and correct the adjective–adverb errors in the following paragraph.**

This year our football team is outstanding. Spike Jones, our quarterback, has been playing real good this past season. Stan Blunder, the most talented of our two ends, hasn't dropped a pass all season. The team can most always count on Stan to catch the crucial first-down pass. Of course, the team wouldn't be where it is today without John Schoolyard's good coaching. He has made this team much more better than it was even a year ago. Only the kicking team has done bad this season. Of course, with this most wonderfulest offense, the players haven't gotten much practice. The good news is, then, that we can sure expect to watch some terrific college football for years to come.

and adverbs, have them construct, and say aloud, sentences that use the appropriate forms. Some students have an aversion to expressions like "He plays football really well," which they regard as "uppity." When such feelings surface, you might discuss dialects. Whatever their feelings, students need to recognize that edited American English is the common currency of the professions.

mis adj/adv

EXERCISE ANSWER

This year our football team is outstanding. Spike Jones, our quarterback, has been playing really well this past season. Stan Blunder, the more talented of our two ends, hasn't dropped a pass all season. The team can almost always count on Stan to catch the crucial first-down pass. Of course, the team wouldn't be where it is today without John Schoolyard's good coaching. He has made this team much better than it was even a year ago. Only the kicking team has done badly this season. Of course, with this wonderful offense, the players haven't gotten much practice. The good news is, then, that we can surely expect to watch some terrific college football for years to come.

mm

EXERCISE ■ **For each of the following sentences, choose the proper word from the pair in parentheses.**

1. A person can become (stronger, more stronger) by lifting weights.
2. Canvasback Dunn is clearly the (less, least) formidable of the two main challengers for Killer McGurk's boxing crown.
3. Diane did (good, well) on her chemistry test.
4. (Most, Almost) all our salaried employees have degrees in business administration or engineering.
5. Carol wore the (silliest, most silliest) hat I've ever seen to the masquerade party.
6. Don was hurt (bad, badly) in the auto accident.
7. Brad was the (funniest, most funniest) of all the performers at the comedy club.
8. Clear Lake is the (deeper, deepest) of the three lakes in our county.
9. Linda has made a (real, really) outstanding contribution to the project.
10. If you follow this diet you'll be (thinner, more thinner) in ten days.

*A*VOIDING MISPLACED MODIFIERS

A misplaced modifier is a word or word group that is improperly separated from the word it modifies. When separation of this type occurs, the sentence often sounds awkward, ridiculous, or confusing.

Usually, you can correct this error by moving the modifier next to the word it is intended to modify. Occasionally, you'll also need to alter some of the phrasing.

Faulty   There is a bicycle in the basement *with chrome fenders*. (The basement appears to have chrome fenders.)

Faulty   David received a phone call from his uncle *that infuriated him*. (The uncle appears to have infuriated David.)

Revision   There is a bicycle *with chrome fenders* in the basement.

Revision   David received an *infuriating* phone call from his uncle. (Note the change in wording.)

In shifting the modifier, don't inadvertently create another faulty sentence.

Faulty   Fritz bought a magazine with an article about Michael Jackson *at the corner newsstand*. (The article appears to tell about Jackson's visit to the corner newsstand.)

Faulty   Fritz bought a magazine *at the corner newsstand* with an article about Michael Jackson. (The corner newsstand appears to have an article about Jackson.)

Revision   *At the corner newsstand,* Fritz bought a magazine with an article about Michael Jackson.

As you revise, watch also for *squinting modifiers*—that is, modifiers positioned so that the reader doesn't know whether they are supposed to modify what comes ahead of them or what follows them.

> **Faulty**   The man who was rowing the boat *frantically* waved toward the onlookers on the beach.

Is the man rowing frantically or waving frantically?

Correct this kind of error by repositioning the modifier so that the ambiguity disappears.

> **Revision**   The man who was *frantically* rowing the boat waved toward the onlookers on the beach.

> **Revision**   The man who was rowing the boat waved *frantically* toward the onlookers on the beach.

EXERCISE ■ Indicate whether each sentence is correct (C) or contains a misplaced modifier (MM). Correct faulty sentences.

1. The boss asked me after lunch to type a special report.
2. Brenda returned the cottage cheese to the store that had spoiled.
3. The hikers tramped through the woods wearing heavy boots.
4. The movie was heavily advertised by the studio before sneak previews were shown.
5. Mark mailed a package to his friend sealed with masking tape.
6. The woman packing her suitcase hastily glanced out the window at the commotion in the yard.
7. We bought a dictionary that was bound in leather at the local bookstore.
8. Jerry bought a Navajo rug for his bedroom in New Mexico.
9. Workers have uncovered an archaeological discovery in the local gravel pit of great importance.
10. The guide pointed out the Rembrandt painting to the tourists over the fireplace.

AVOIDING DANGLING MODIFIERS

A dangling modifier is a phrase or clause that lacks clear connection to the word or words it is intended to modify. As a result, sentences are inaccurate, often comical. Typically, the modifier leads off the sentence, although it can also come at the end.

Sometimes the error occurs because the sentence fails to specify who or what is modified. At other times, the separation is too great between the modifier and what it modifies.

> **Faulty**   *Walking in the meadow,* wildflowers surrounded us. (The wildflowers appear to be walking in the meadow.)

> **Faulty**   Dinner was served *after saying grace.* (The dinner appears to have said grace.)

EXERCISE ANSWERS

1. MM. After lunch, the boss / a special report after lunch.
2. MM. the cottage cheese that had spoiled to the store.
3. MM. Wearing heavy boots, the hikers / The hikers, wearing heavy boots,
4. C.
5. MM. a package sealed with masking tape.
6. MM. hastily packing her suitcase / glanced hastily / out the window hastily
7. MM. At the local bookstore, we / We bought a leather-bound dictionary at
8. MM. In New Mexico, Jerry bought
9. MM. a very important archaeological discovery / In the local gravel pit, workers
10. MM. the Rembrandt painting over the fireplace.

> **Faulty**   *Fatigued by the violent exercise,* the cool shower was very relaxing. (The cool shower appears to have been fatigued.)

The first of these sentences is faulty because the modifier is positioned too far away from *us.* The other two are faulty because they do not identify who said grace or found the shower relaxing.

You can correct dangling modifiers in two basic ways. First, leave the modifier unchanged and rewrite the main part of the sentence so that it begins with the term actually modified. Second, rewrite the modifier so that it has its own subject and verb, thereby eliminating the inaccuracy.

> **Revision**   *Walking in the meadow,* we were surrounded by wildflowers. (The main part of the sentence has been rewritten.)

> **Revision**   *As we walked in the meadow,* wildflowers surrounded us. (The modifier has been rewritten.)

> **Revision**   Dinner was served *after we had said grace.* (The modifier has been rewritten.)

> **Revision**   *Fatigued by the violent exercise,* Ted found the cool shower very relaxing. (The main part of the sentence has been rewritten.)

> **Revision**   *Because Ted was fatigued by the violent exercise,* the cool shower was very relaxing. (The modifier has been rewritten.)

Ordinarily, either part of the sentence can be rewritten, but sometimes only one part can.

EXERCISE ■ Indicate whether each sentence is correct (C) or contains a dangling modifier (DM). Correct faulty sentences.

1. Dancing at the wedding reception, my feet hurt.
2. Working in the yard, Pete was drenched by the sudden cloudburst.
3. Looking out the window, a velvety lawn ran down to the river's edge.
4. Having mangy fur, our parents wouldn't let us keep the stray cat.
5. Because of memorizing all the definitions, Pam scored 100 on the spelling test.
6. Reminiscing about my army days, a run-in with my drill sargeant came to mind.
7. Unaware of what had happened, the confusion puzzled Nan.
8. At the age of eight, my father wrote a best-selling novel.
9. While eating dinner, an explosion rocked the house.
10. Laden with packages, the mail carrier tried to lift the mail bag.

*A*VOIDING NONPARALLELISM

Nonparallelism results when equivalent ideas follow different grammatical forms. One common kind of nonparallelism occurs with words or word groups in pairs or in a series.

Faulty   Althea enjoys *jogging, to bike,* and *to swim.*

Faulty   The superintendent praised the workers *for their productivity* and *because they had an excellent safety record.*

Faulty   The banner was *old, faded,* and *it had a rip.*

Note how rewriting the sentences in parallel form improves their smoothness.

Revision   Althea enjoys *jogging, biking,* and *swimming.*

Revision   The superintendent praised the workers for *their productivity* and *their excellent safety record.*

Revision   The banner was *old, faded,* and *ripped.*

Nonparallelism also occurs when correlative conjunctions (*either . . . or, neither . . . nor, both . . . and,* and *not only . . . but also*) are followed by unlike elements.

Faulty   That sound *either <u>was a thunderclap</u> or <u>an explosion</u>.*

Faulty   The basement was *not only <u>poorly lighted</u> but also <u>it had a foul smell</u>.*

Ordinarily, repositioning one of the correlative conjunctions will solve the problem. Sometimes, however, one of the grammatical elements must be rewritten.

Revision   That sound was *either <u>a thunderclap</u> or <u>an explosion</u>.* (*Either* has been repositioned.)

Revision   The basement was *not only <u>poorly lighted</u> but also <u>foul smelling</u>.* (The element following *but also* has been rewritten.)

EXERCISE ■ Indicate whether each sentence is correct (C) or nonparallel (NP). Correct faulty sentences.

1. The lemonade was cold, tangy, and refreshing.
2. Although he had practiced for several days, the scout could neither tie a square knot nor a bowline.
3. This job will involve waiting on customers, and you will need to maintain our inventory.
4. My summer job at a state park gave me experience in repairing buildings, the operation of heavy equipment, and assisting park visitors.
5. To maintain his rose bushes properly, Sam fertilizes, sprays, prunes, and waters them according to a strict schedule.
6. Once out of high school, Barry plans either to join the navy or the air force.
7. My favorite sports are swimming, golfing, and to bowl.
8. Janice's leisure activities include collecting coins, reading, and she also watches TV.
9. In two weeks, Marilyn will be moving to Manhattan and work for a stockbroker.
10. This house not only is poorly planned but also too expensive.

also _____ . The instructor warned the class about _____ , _____ , and _____ . A good education requires _____ and _____ . That sound was either a(n) _____ or a(n) _____ .

//

EXERCISE ANSWERS
1. C.
2. NP. could tie neither
3. NP. waiting on customers and maintaining our inventory.
4. NP. operating heavy equipment
5. C.
6. NP. to join either
7. NP. and bowling.
8. NP. and watching TV.
9. NP. and working
10. NP. is not only

AVOIDING FAULTY COMPARISONS

A faulty comparison results if you (1) mention one of the items being compared but not the other, (2) omit words needed to clarify the relationship, or (3) compare different sorts of items. Advertisers often offend in the first way.

> ***Faulty***   Irish tape has better adhesion.

With what other tape is Irish tape being compared? Scotch tape? All other transparent tape? Mentioning the second term of a comparison eliminates reader guesswork.

> ***Revision***   Irish tape has better adhesion than any other transparent tape.

Two clarifying words, *other* and *else*, are frequently omitted from comparisons, creating illogical sentences.

> ***Faulty***   Sergeant McNabb has made more arrests than any officer in his precinct.
>
> ***Faulty***   Stretch French is taller than anyone on his basketball team.

The first sentence is illogical because McNabb is one of the officers in his precinct and therefore cannot be more conscientious than any officer in the precinct. Similarly, because French is a member of his basketball team, he can't be taller than anyone on his team. Adding *other* to the first sentence and *else* to the second corrects matters.

> ***Revision***   Sergeant McNabb has made more arrests than any *other* officer in his precinct.
>
> ***Revision***   Stretch French is taller than anyone *else* on his basketball team.

Comparing unlike items is perhaps the most common kind of comparison error. Here are two examples.

> ***Faulty***   The cities in California are larger than North Dakota.
>
> ***Faulty***   The cover of this book is much more durable than the other book.

The first sentence compares the cities of California with a state, while the second compares the cover of a book with a whole book. Correction consists of rewriting each sentence so that it compares like items.

> ***Revision***   The cities in California are larger than *those in* North Dakota.
>
> ***Revision***   The cover of this book is much more durable than *that of* the other book.

comp

EXERCISE ANSWER

TO: All Residency Hall Advisors in Knuckles Hall

FROM: John Knells, Residency Hall Director

DATE: March 13, 19--

SUBJECT: Noise in Residence Hall

CONNECTED DISCOURSE EXERCISE ■ Identify and correct the misplaced modifiers, dangling modifiers, nonparallelism, and faulty comparisons in the following memorandum.

TO: All Residency Hall Advisors in Knuckles Hall

FROM: John Knells, Residency Hall Director

DATE: March 13, 19--

SUBJECT: Noise in Residence Hall

Recently I received a report from a student that deeply disturbed me. Apparently, after quiet hours students still have visitors in their rooms, are playing their stereos loudly, and are even staging boxing matches in the halls. The student who wrote me desperately tries to study. However, he is often forced to leave his room disturbed by the noise. He was not the only one to complain. You should know that we have had more complaints about Knuckles Hall than any dorm on campus. Since discussing this problem with you at the last staff meeting, things haven't seemed to get any better. The rules are not only poorly enforced but also they are completely ignored. Your job performance is worse than the students. If you don't improve immediately, I will be forced to dismiss you.

EXERCISE ■ Indicate whether each sentence is correct (C) or contains a faulty comparison (FC). Correct any faulty comparison.

1. The houses on Parkdale Street are more modest than Windsor Terrace.
2. Maxine has more seniority than any other member of her department.
3. The finish on the dresser is not as smooth as the end table.
4. In contrast to your yard, I have an underground sprinkling system.
5. My mother's homemade jam has more flavor than any jam I've eaten.
6. Of the two singers, Dorothy has a much stronger voice than Elaine.
7. The dresses sold at J.C. Penney's are much less expensive than the Tres Chic Shoppe.
8. Frontline reports show that during June our side lost fewer tanks.
9. The extravagance of the Cashes is greater than any other couple I know.
10. Alan received a higher midterm test score than anyone in his class.

Recently I received a deeply disturbing report from a student. Apparently, after quiet hours students still have visitors in their rooms, play their stereos loudly, and even stage boxing matches in the halls. The student who wrote me tries desperately to study. However, disturbed by the noise, he is often forced to leave his room. He was not the only one to complain. You should know that we have had more complaints about Knuckles Hall than about any other dorm on campus. Since I discussed this

comp

problem with you at the last staff meeting, things haven't seemed to get any better. The rules are not only poorly enforced but also completely ignored. Your job performance is worse than the students' behavior. If you don't improve immediately, I will be forced to dismiss you.

EXERCISE ANSWERS

1. FC. than those on / than the houses on
2. C.
3. FC. that on / the finish on
4. FC. mine has / my yard has
5. FC. than that of any other
6. C.
7. FC. than those sold at /than the ones sold at / than the dresses sold at
8. FC. fewer tanks than the enemy. / than during the previous month. / than during any other month.
9. FC. than that of / than the extravagance of
10. FC. than anyone else

Punctuation marks indicate relationships among different sentence elements. As a result, these marks help clarify the meaning of written material. Similarly, a knowledge of mechanics—capitalization, abbreviations, numbers, and italics—helps you avoid distracting inconsistencies.

This part of the Handbook covers the fundamentals of punctuation and mechanics. Review it carefully when you edit your final draft.

APOSTROPHES

Apostrophes (') show possession, mark contractions, and indicate plurals that are singled out for special attention.

Possession.   Possessive apostrophes usually show ownership. (*Mary's cat*). Sometimes, though, they identify the works of creative people (*Hemingway's novels*) or indicate an extent of time or distance (*one hour's time, one mile's distance*).

Possessive apostrophes are used with nouns and with pronouns like *someone, no one, everybody, each other,* and *one another.* The possessive form is easily recognized because it can be converted to a prepositional phrase beginning with *of.*

The collar of the dog

The whistle of the wind

The intention of the corporation

The birthday of Scott

To show possession with pronouns, singular nouns, and plural nouns that do not end in an *s,* add an apostrophe followed by an *s.*

Someone's car is blocking our drive. (possessive of pronoun *someone*)

The *manager's* reorganization plan will take effect next week. (possessive of singular noun *manager*)

The *women's* lounge is being redecorated. (possessive of plural noun *women*)

The *boss's* orders must be obeyed. (possessive of singular noun *boss*)

With singular nouns that end in *s,* the possessive is sometimes formed by merely adding an apostrophe at the end (James' helmet). The preferred usage, however, is *'s* (James's helmet) unless the addition of the *s* would make it awkward to pronounce the word.

> *Moses's* followers entered the Promised Land. (awkward pronunciation of *Moses's*)
> *Moses'* followers entered the Promised Land. (nonawkward pronunciation of *Moses'*)

Plural nouns ending in *s* form the possessive by adding only an apostrophe at the end.

> All the *ladies'* coats are on sale today. (possessive of plural noun *ladies*)

> The *workers'* lockers were moved. (possessive of plural noun *workers*)

To show joint ownership by two or more persons, use the possessive form for the last-named person only. To show individual ownership, use the possessive form for each person's name.

> Ronald and *Joan's* boat badly needed overhauling. (joint ownership)

> *Laura's* and *Alice's* term projects are almost completed. (individual ownership)

Hyphenated nouns form the possessive by adding *'s* to the last word.

> My *mother-in-law's* house is next to mine.

> Never use an apostrophe with the possessive pronouns *his, hers, whose, its, ours, yours, theirs.*

> This desk is *his;* the other one is *hers.* (no apostrophes needed)

Contractions.   Contractions of words or numbers omit one or more letters or numerals. An apostrophe shows exactly where the omission occurs.

> *Wasn't* that a disappointing concert? (contraction of *was not*)

> Around here, people still talk about the blizzard of *'79.* (contraction of 1979)

Don't confuse the contraction *it's,* meaning *it is* or *it has,* with the possessive pronoun *its,* which should never have an apostrophe. If you're puzzled by an *its* that you've written, try this test. Expand the *its* to *it is* or *it has* and see whether the sentence still makes sense. If it does, the *its* is a contraction and needs the apostrophe. If the result is nonsense, the *its* is a possessive pronoun and does not get an apostrophe. Here are some examples.

> *Its* awfully muggy today.

> *Its* been an exciting trip.

> Every dog has *its* day.

The first example makes sense when the *its* is expanded to *it is.*

> *It is* awfully muggy today.

The second makes sense when the *its* is expanded to *it has*.

> *It has* been an exciting trip.

Both of these sentences therefore require apostrophes.

> *It's* awfully muggy today.

> *It's* been an exciting trip.

The last sentence, however, turns into nonsense when the *its* is expanded.

> Every dog has *it is* day.

> Every dog has *it has* day.

In this case, the *its* is a possessive pronoun and requires no apostrophe.

> Every dog has *its* day.

Plurals.   To improve clarity, the plurals of letters, numbers, symbols, and words being singled out for special attention are written with apostrophes.

> Mind your *p's* and *q's*. (plurals of letters)

> Your *5's* and *6's* are hard to tell apart. (plurals of numbers)

> The formula was sprinkled with *Π's* and *Σ's*. (plurals of symbols)

> Don't use so many *however's* and *therefore's* in your writing. (plurals of words)

Apostrophes are often used to form the plurals of abbreviations.

> How many *rpm's* does this shaft turn at? (plural of abbreviation for revolutions per minute)

When no danger of confusion exists, an *s* alone will suffice.

> During the late *1960s*, many university students demanded changes in academic life.

EXERCISE ANSWER

TO: The Records Office Staff

FROM: The Assistant Registrar

DATE: January 27, 19--

SUBJECT: Faulty Student Transcripts

Recently, we have had too many student complaints about handwritten transcripts. Apparently it's hard to tell the B's and D's apart. One staff member's handwriting is totally illegible. This staff's carelessness is unacceptable. Someone's even gone so far as to write grade changes in pencil, which allows students to make changes. This can't

CONNECTED DISCOURSE EXERCISE ■ Supply, delete, or relocate apostrophes as necessary in the following memorandum.

TO: The Records Office Staff

FROM: The Assistant Registrar

DATE: January 27, 19--

SUBJECT: Faulty Student Transcripts

Recently, we have had too many student complaints' about handwritten transcripts. Apparently its hard to tell the Bs and Ds apart. One staff members' handwriting is totally illegible. This staffs carelessness is unacceptable. Someones even gone so far as to write grade change's in pencil, which allows students to make changes. This cant continue. In a short time, John and Marys student assistants will be typing the past transcripts into our new computer system. Once grades are entered, the computers ability to generate grade reports will solve this problem. Until that time, lets make an effort to produce clear and professional-looking transcripts.

continue. In a short time, John and Mary's student assistants will be typing the past transcripts into our new computer system. Once grades are entered, the computer's ability to generate grade reports will solve this problem. Until that time, let's make an effort to produce clear and professional-looking transcripts.

EXERCISE ■ Supply apostrophes where necessary to correct the following sentences.

1. The bosss speech reviewed the companys safety record.
2. Lets find out whats wrong with Melanys bicycle.
3. Dave and Marvins fiancées are identical twins.
4. Its highly unlikely that this movie will ever earn back its production costs when its released.
5. Sues test score was higher than all her friends test scores.
6. There are two *ls* and two *es* in the name Colleen.
7. When everyones ready, well start the slide show.
8. Alice overloads her sentences with *consequentlys* and *accordinglys*.
9. Somebodys car is blocking the Petersons driveway.
10. Ill ask whether we can swim in Julies pool this morning.
11. Everyones views will be aired at todays meetings.
12. The class of 69 was the largest in our high schools 70-year history.

EXERCISE ANSWERS
1. boss's, company's
2. Let's, what's, Melany's
3. Marvin's
4. It's highly, it's released.
5. Sue's, friends'
6. *l's, e's*
7. everyone's, we'll
8. *consequently's, accordingly's*
9. Somebody's, Petersons'
10. I'll, Julie's
11. Everyone's, today's
12. '69, school's

*C*OMMAS

Since commas (,) occur more frequently than any other mark of punctuation, it's vital that you learn to use them correctly. When you do, your sentence structure is clearer, and your reader grasps your meaning without having to reread.

Commas separate or set off independent clauses, items in a series, coordinate adjectives, introductory elements, places and dates, nonrestrictive expressions, and parenthetical expressions.

Independent Clauses. When you link two independent clauses with a coordinating conjunction (*and, but, or, nor, for, yet,* or *so*), put a comma in front of the conjunction.

> Arthur is majoring in engineering, *but* he has decided to work for a clothing store following graduation.

> The water looked inviting, *so* Darlene decided to go for a swim.

Don't confuse a sentence that has a compound predicate (see page 499) with a sentence that consists of two independent clauses.

TEACHING STRATEGIES

1. Students should learn not only where commas are positioned but also where they aren't. The most common inappropriate locations for commas are (a) between the subject and the verb, the verb and its object, and the preposition and its object; (b) before a subordinating conjunction joining a dependent clause to a sentence; and (c) before a prepositional phrase. It helps to stress these errors at the appropriate time.

2. Students often overload on comma rules. Sometimes it is easier to introduce a new comma rule each week, mak-

560

HANDBOOK

TEACHING STRATEGY

Have students who are still confused try this approach. Whenever they find two apparent sentences joined by a coordinating conjunction, have them place a finger over the conjunction and see whether the word group on either side can stand as an independent sentence. If both can, the student should use a comma. Some students, however, will probably still not see the point. Often, they are confused because they have trouble understanding that a pronoun can be the subject of an independent clause, something you probably will have to reexplain to them.

PERSPECTIVE

Some students have learned that a comma should not be used before the last item in a series. Although the popular press often omits the final comma, many businesses still prefer its inclusion. You might explain this variation to your students.

TEACHING STRATEGY

Have students test for coordinate adjectives by mentally inserting an "and" between the pair in question. If the meaning does not change, the adjectives are coordinate, and a comma is required.

TEACHING STRATEGIES

1. Sometimes students suspect that a sentence has an introductory element, but they don't know for sure. When this happens, have them reposition the suspected element at the end of the sentence. If it is indeed an introductory element, the meaning of the sentence will not

Tom watered the garden and mowed the lawn. (single sentence with compound predicate)

Tom watered the garden, *and* Betty mowed the lawn. (sentence with two independent clauses)

Here's a simple test. Read what follows the comma. Unless that part can stand alone as a sentence, don't use a comma.

Items in a Series. A series consists of three or more words, phrases, or clauses following on one another's heels. Whenever you write a series, separate its items with commas.

Sarah, Paul, and *Mary* are earning *A*'s in advanced algebra. (words in a series)

Nancy strode *across the parking lot, through the revolving door,* and *into the elevator.* (phrases in a series)

The stockholders' report said *that the company had enjoyed record profits during the last year, that it had expanded its work force by 20 percent,* and *that it would soon start marketing several new products.* (clauses in a series)

Coordinate Adjectives. Use commas to separate coordinate adjectives—those that modify the same noun or noun substitute and can be reversed without altering the meaning of the sentence.

Andrea proved to be an efficient, cooperative employee.

Andrea proved to be a cooperative, efficient employee.

When reversing the word order wrecks the meaning of the sentence, the adjectives are not coordinate and should be written without a comma.

Many new brands of video cassette recorders have come on the market lately.

Reversing the adjectives *many* and *new* would turn this sentence into nonsense. Therefore, no comma should be used.

Introductory Elements. Use commas to separate introductory elements—words, phrases, and clauses—from the rest of the sentence. When an introductory element is short and the sentence will not be misread, you can omit the comma.

Correct   After bathing, Jack felt refreshed.

Correct   Soon I will be changing jobs.

Correct   Soon, I will be changing jobs.

Correct   When Sarah smiles her ears wiggle.

Correct   When Sarah smiles, her ears wiggle.

The first example needs a comma; otherwise, the reader might become temporarily confused.

After bathing Jack . . .

Always use commas after introductory elements of six or more words.

> *Correct*   Whenever I hear the opening measure of Beethoven's *Fifth Symphony,* I get goose bumps.

Places and Dates.
Places include mailing addresses and geographical locations. The following sentences show where commas are used.

> Sherry Delaney lives at 651 Daniel Street, Memphis, Tennessee 38118.

> I shall go to Calais, France, next week.

> Morristown, Oklahoma, is my birthplace.

Note that commas appear after the street designation and the names of cities, countries, and states, except when the name of the state is followed by a zip code. Dates are punctuated as shown in the following example.

> On Sunday, June 9, 1991, Elaine received a degree in environmental science.

Here, commas follow the day of the week, the day of the month, and the year. With dates that include only the month and the year, commas are optional.

> *Correct*   In July 1989 James visited Scotland for the first time.

> *Correct*   In July, 1989, James visited Scotland for the first time.

Nonrestrictive Expressions.
A nonrestrictive expression supplies added information about whatever it modifies. This information, however, is *nonessential* and does not affect the basic meaning of the sentence. The two sentences below include nonrestrictive expressions.

> Senator Conwell, *the senior senator from this state,* faces a tough campaign for reelection.

> My dog, *frightened by the thunder,* hid under my bed while the storm raged.

If we delete the phrase *the senior senator from this state* from the first sentence, we still know that Senator Conwell faces a tough reelection battle. Likewise, if we delete *frightened by the thunder* from the second sentence, we still know that the dog hid during the storm.

Restrictive expressions, which are written *without commas,* distinguish whatever they modify from other persons, places, or things in the same category. Unlike nonrestrictive expressions, they are almost always *essential* sentence elements. Omitting a restrictive expression alters the meaning of the sentence, and the result is often nonsense.

> Any person *caught stealing from this store* will be prosecuted.

Dropping the italicized part of this sentence leaves us with the absurd statement that any person, not just those caught stealing, faces prosecution.

Parenthetical Expressions.
A parenthetical expression is a word or a word group that links one sentence to another or adds information or emphasis to the sentence in which it appears. Parenthetical expressions include the following:

be materially altered. Note that the preceding sentence passes this test.
2. Students sometimes mistake complete subjects for introductory phrases: Studying late at night, isn't always the best strategy. (incorrect) Studying late at night isn't always the best strategy. (correct) In most cases, the "move" test will usually reveal the error. "Isn't always the best strategy, studying late at night" just doesn't make sense, even to an undiscriminating eye.

TEACHING STRATEGY

Because students often fail to put needed commas after names of places and dates, ask them to proofread with this oversight in mind.

TEACHING STRATEGY

You might combine this unit with the earlier one on relative pronouns (page 505), where supplementary sentence-combining exercises are provided. Students can best learn how such expressions work, and especially the difference between restrictive and nonrestrictive expressions, by constructing some themselves. A few more sentence-combining pairs follow:

James Johnson has been arrested for embezzlement. James Johnson was our head accountant.

Anybody has a toothache. Anybody should go to the dentist.

A man has a broken leg. A man should not go skiing.

The President of the United States has a good grasp of foreign affairs. The President of the United States was once the head of the CIA.

Combined Sentences

James Johnson, our head accountant, has been arrested for embezzlement.

Anybody who has a toothache should go to the dentist.

A man who has a broken leg should not go skiing.

The President of the United States, once the head of the CIA, has a good grasp of foreign affairs.

Clarifying phrases
Names and titles of people being addressed directly
Abbreviations of degree titles and of *junior* and *senior* following people's names
Echo questions
"Not" phrases
Adjectives that come after, rather than before, the words they modify

The examples that follow show the uses of commas.

All of Joe's spare time seems to center around reading. Kevin, *on the other hand,* enjoys a variety of activities. (phrase linking two sentences together)

Myra Hobbes, *our representative in Seattle,* is being transferred to Spokane next month. (clarifying phrase)

I think, *Jill,* that you'd make a wonderful teacher. (name of person addressed directly)

Tell me, *Captain,* when the cruise ship is scheduled to sail. (title of person addressed directly)

Harley Kendall, *Ph.D.,* will be this year's commencement speaker. (degree title following name)

Peter Bradley, *Jr.,* has just taken over his father's plumbing business. (personal abbreviation following name)

Alvin realizes, *doesn't he,* that he stands almost no chance of being accepted at West Point? (echo question)

Mathematics, *not home economics,* was Tammy's favorite high school subject. ("not" phrase)

The road, *muddy and rutted,* proved impassable. (adjectives following word they modify)

EXERCISE ANSWER

Dear Loy Norrix Knight:

While we know you will be busy this summer, we hope you will take the time to join us for the 20-year reunion of the graduating class of 1972. The reunion will include a cocktail hour, a buffet dinner, and a dance. For your entertainment we are going to bring in a professional band and a band starring some of your good old high school chums. John McLeary, who is now a well-known professional nightclub performer, will serve as the emcee. Do you remember him hosting our senior-year assemblies?

CONNECTED DISCOURSE EXERCISE ■ Add or delete commas as necessary in the following letter.

Dear Loy Norrix Knight:

While we know you will be busy this summer we hope you will take time to join us for the 20-year reunion of the graduating class of 1972. The reunion will include a cocktail hour a buffet dinner and a dance. For your entertainment we are going to bring in a professional band and a band starring some of your good, old high school chums. John Mcleary who is now a well-known professional nightclub performer will serve as the emcee. Do you remember him hosting our senior-year assemblies?

Yes many of your former, hardworking teachers will be at the reunion. You can thank them for the difference they made in your life or you can tell them what you've thought of them all these years. This reunion will also be your opportunity to catch up on the lives of your former friends find out what that old flame now looks like and brag a little about your own successes. And if you are really lucky you might even be able to sneak a dance with your high school prom partner.

We hope you will make plans, to join us here at the Kalamazoo Hilton, on July 28 1992 at 7 p.m. Wear your best 1970's style clothes. Remember revisiting the past, can be fun.

                                    Sincerely,

                                    The Reunion Committee

Yes, many of your former, hardworking teachers will be at the reunion. You can thank them for the difference they made in your life, or you can tell them what you've thought of them all these years. This reunion will also be your opportunity to catch up on the lives of your former friends, find out what that old flame now looks like, and brag a little about your own successes. And if you are really lucky, you might even be able to sneak a dance with your high school prom partner.

We hope you will make plans to join us here at the Kalamazoo Hilton on July 28, 1992, at 7 p.m. Wear your best 1970s style clothes. Remember, revisiting the past can be fun.

Sincerely,

The Reunion Committee

EXERCISE ■ Supply commas as necessary to correct the following sentences.

1. Before leaving Jim stopped to say goodbye to Lisa.
2. Although our prices continue to go up people will probably keep buying our video games.
3. This store's burglar alarm system which is very outdated should be replaced immediately.
4. Stepping into the cool pleasant bake shop Annette bought a large cinammon doughnut for a snack.
5. Mr. Kowalski was born in Warsaw Poland and became a United States citizen on February 15 1975.
6. The brakes on our car aren't working so we'll have to take the bus.
7. The moviegoing couple bought popcorn candy bars and large Cokes at the lobby concession stand.
8. For more information about the Scotland tour write Doreen Campbell 218 Riverdale Street St. Clair Shores Michigan 48082.
9. Joyce Cone our advertising manager has been elected president of the National Advertising Association.
10. Tell me Mr. Franklin why you'd like to work for our company.

EXERCISE ANSWERS

1. leaving,	7. popcorn,
2. up,	bars,
3. system,	8. tour,
outdated,	Campbell,
4. cool,	Street,
shop,	Shores,
5. Warsaw,	9. Cone,
Poland,	manager,
15,	10. me,
6. working.	Franklin,

PERSPECTIVE

As they do with other punctuation marks, students tend to overuse the semicolon once they have learned its applications. For many inexperienced writers, semicolons seem like a bargain, providing the force of the period

SEMICOLONS

The main use of the semicolon (;) is to separate independent clauses, which may or may not be connected with a conjunctive adverb (see page 521). Other uses include separating and the continuity of the comma, making it possible to avoid comma splices forever. Warn students about excessive semicolons in their writing. Students need to realize that semicolons are a specialized punctuation mark, not simply a way of avoiding subordinating conjunctions, coordinating conjunctions, and periods and, when used excessively, they can result in an artificially formal style.

CLASSROOM ACTIVITY

The following passage contains too many semicolons and is, as a result, excessively stilted. Have students revise the passage so that it is more effective.

Yesterday was impossibly hot; even the squirrels tried to sneak into the air-conditioned malls. Everyone had his or her air conditioner set on high; I really worried about a power failure. Just imagine a power failure in such heat; it would be terrible. The results would include fans, essential in this weather, coming to a standstill; re-

;

frigerators, now without power, turning into stinking coffins for rotten food; air conditioning, because of the blackout, would be unavailable anywhere; and hospitals, jammed with victims of heat prostration, would overflow.

Possible Revision

Yesterday was so impossibly hot that even the squirrels tried to sneak into the air-conditioned malls. Because everyone's air conditioner was set on high, I really worried about a power failure. Just imagine a power failure in such heat. Fans would come to a standstill. Refrigerators

two or more series of items
items containing commas in a single series
independent clauses that contain commas and are connected with a coordinating conjunction.

Independent Clauses.

The examples that follow show the use of semicolons to separate independent clauses.

The fabric in this dress is terrible; its designer must have been asleep at the swatch. (no conjunctive adverb)

Steve refused to write a term paper; *therefore*, he failed the course. (conjunctive adverb *therefore* joining independent clauses)

Conjunctive adverbs can occur within, rather than between, independent clauses. When they do, set them off with commas.

Marsha felt very confident. Jane, *on the other hand*, was nervous and uncertain. (conjunctive adverb within independent clause)

To determine whether a pair of commas or a semicolon and comma are required, read what comes before and after the conjunctive adverb. Unless both sets of words can stand alone as sentences, use commas.

Two or More Series of Items.

With sentences that have two or more series of items, writers often separate the series with semicolons in order to lessen the chances of misreading.

My duties as secretary include typing letters, memos, and purchase orders; sorting, opening, and delivering mail; and making plane and hotel reservations for traveling executives.

The semicolons provide greater clarity than commas would.

Comma-Containing Items Within a Series.

When commas accompany one or more of the items in a series, it's often better to separate the items with semicolons instead of commas.

The meal included veal, which was cooked to perfection; asparagus, my favorite vegetable; and brown rice, prepared with a touch of curry.

Once again, semicolons provide greater clarity than additional commas.

Independent Clauses with Commas and a Coordinating Conjunction.

Ordinarily, a comma is used to separate independent clauses joined by a coordinating conjunction. When one or more of the clauses have commas, however, a semicolon provides clearer separation.

The long, black limousine pulled up to the curb; and Jerry, shaking with excitement, watched the President alight from it.

The semicolon makes it easier to see the two main clauses.

CONNECTED DISCOURSE EXERCISE ■ **Add and delete semicolons as appropriate in the following letter. You may have to substitute semicolons for commas.**

Dear Student:

Our college, as you are well aware, has been going through a number of changes, and these developments, both in the registration system and the curriculum, will continue next year. In the end these improvements will only benefit you; but we know that many of you have been anxious about the exact nature of the changes. To answer your questions, we have arranged an open forum with Linda Peters, president of the college, Drake Stevens, the registrar, and Jerry Mash, vice-president of academic affairs. The meeting will be held in Johnston Hall; 2 p.m.; March 23. Please come with your questions, this is your opportunity to put your fears to rest.

Sincerely,

John X. Pelle
Dean of Students

EXERCISE ■ **Supply semicolons wherever they are necessary or desirable in the following sentences. You may have to substitute semicolons for commas. If a sentence is correct, write C.**

1. The garage sale included women's coats, hats, and purses, men's shoes, shirts, and ties, and children's scarves, mittens, and rubbers.
2. James couldn't stand his sarcastic boss, therefore, he quit his job.
3. Our house is far too small, we should start looking for a larger one.
4. Morris wanted to work for a company that was small, environmentally responsible, and located in a midsize city, and finally, after a dozen job interviews, he went to work for Greenland, Inc.
5. This has been a good year for raspberries, I've gotten over thirty quarts from my small patch of bushes.
6. The road ahead has been washed out by a flood; you'll have to make a detour.
7. After touring the company's facilities, we had lunch with Giles Seymour, its president, Cheryl James, its sales manager, and Daryl Brewer, its research director.
8. Penny is a real cat lover; in fact, she has six.
9. The instructor, angry with the noisy class, shouted for silence, and the students, startled by his outburst, quieted down.
10. During Jim's trip to Russia, he visited Moscow, its capital, St. Petersburg, founded by Peter the Great, and Volgograd, formerly known as Stalingrad.

would turn into stinking coffins for rotten food. Worst of all, no air conditioning would be available anywhere. The hospitals would be jammed to overflowing with victims of heat prostration.

EXERCISE ANSWER

Dear Student:

Our college, as you are well aware, has been going through a number of changes; and these developments, both in the registration system and the curriculum, will continue next year. In the end these improvements will only benefit you, but we know that many of you have been anxious about the exact nature of the changes. To answer your questions, we have arranged an open forum with Linda Peters, president of the college; Drake Stevens, the registrar; and Jerry Mash, vice-president of academic affairs. The meeting will be held in

;

Johnston Hall, 2 p.m., March 23. Please come with your questions; this is your opportunity to put your fears to rest.

Sincerely,

John X. Pelle

Dean of Students

EXERCISE ANSWERS

1. purses; ties;
2. boss;
3. small;
4. city;
5. raspberries;
6. C.
7. president; manager;
8. C.
9. silence;
10. capital; Great;

PERSPECTIVE

In some ways, you have been teaching end marks throughout this Handbook. Whether you are helping students to identify sentences or to avoid comma splices, you need to refer to end marks. Although most college instructors would like to take these marks for granted, many students have problems with them. Inexperienced writers sometimes fail to use them. Why? Mina Shaughnessy has suggested that these writers see the period as ending a thought, something they don't like to do since it seems so hard for them to get started again. Furthermore, students usually don't construct sentences one at a time. Halfway through one sentence, they are already thinking of the next. As a result, they may link everything together with commas.

. ? !

TEACHING STRATEGIES

1. Usually students who avoid end marks do include some punctuation marks at the sentence breaks. Have students review their writing to identify places where they need end marks. Often, checking for comma splices and run-ons will solve the end mark problem. However, to avoid the danger that inexperienced writers will become obsessive about using periods and produce a series of short, choppy sentences, this check should be made during proofreading.
2. Teaching end marks allows you to explore matters of style. Have students read over their drafts, note where

PERIODS, QUESTION MARKS, AND EXCLAMATION POINTS

Since periods, question marks, and exclamation points signal the ends of sentences, they are sometimes called *end marks*. In addition, periods and question marks function in several other ways.

Periods.   Periods (.) end sentences that state facts or opinions, give instructions, make requests that are not in the form of questions, and ask indirect questions—those that have been rephrased in the form of a statement.

Linda works as a hotel manager. (Sentence states fact.)

Dean Harris is a competent administrator. (Sentence states opinion.)

Clean off your lab bench before you leave. (Sentence gives instruction.)

Please move away from the door. (Sentence makes request.)

I wonder whether Ruthie will be at the theater tonight. (Sentence asks indirect question.)

Periods also follow common abbreviations as well as a person's initials.

Mr.	Sr.	P.M.
Mrs.	B.C.	a.s.a.p.
Ms.	A.D.	St.
Dr.	A.M.	Corp.

Mark Valentini, Jr., has consented to head the new commission on traffic safety.

Writers today often omit periods after abbreviations for the names of organizations or government agencies, as the following examples show.

ABC	FBI	IRS
ACLU	FHA	NAM
AFL-CIO	GM	USAF

An up-to-date college dictionary will indicate whether a certain abbreviation should be written without periods.

Periods also precede decimal fractions and separate numerals standing for dollars and cents.

0.81 percent	$5.29
3.79 percent	$0.88

Question Marks.   A question mark (?) ends a whole or a partial sentence that asks a direct question (one that repeats the exact words of the person who asked it).

Do you know how to operate this movie projector? (whole sentence asking a direct question)

Has Cinderella scrubbed the floor? Swept the hearth? Washed the dishes? (sentence and sentence parts asking direct questions)

Dr. Baker—wasn't she your boss once?—has just received a promotion to sales manager. (interrupting element asking a direct question)

The minister inquired, "Don't you take this woman to be your lawful wedded wife?" (quotation asking a direct question)

A question mark in parentheses may be used to indicate uncertainty about some piece of information.

Winfield reached America in 1721 (?) and spent the rest of his life in Philadelphia.

Exclamation Points.   Exclamation points (!) are used to express strong emotion or especially forceful commands.

Darcy! I never expected to see you again!

Sam! Turn that radio down immediately!

Help! Save me!

Use exclamation points sparingly; otherwise, they will quickly lose their force.

CONNECTED DISCOURSE EXERCISE ■ Add, change, or remove end marks as necessary in the following passage.

It was horrifying, the mob of screaming fans grabbed Jack Slitherhips as he left the concert hall. Soon all I could see were his arms reaching for help. But it never came. Why do fans act this way. I am left wondering whether they love or hate their idols? They tore the clothes off Slitherhips, they tore out patches of his hair, someone even snatched his false teeth. Is this any way to treat a fading rock star. Jack is now in the hospital in a complete body cast; when I finally got to see him, he mumbled that he was giving up show business, he plans to settle down on a small farm. Who can blame him?

EXERCISE ■ Supply periods, question marks, or exclamation points wherever they are necessary. You may have to change existing punctuation marks. If a sentence is correct, write C.

1. The instructor asked Margie why she hadn't finished her process paper.
2. The videotape of the movie *Casablanca* retails for $2995.
3. Good lord, quit popping that gum before you drive me nuts.
4. Lock the front door before you go to bed.
5. Where do you plan to spend your vacation this year.
6. While you were in Los Angeles, did you tour a movie studio shop on Rodeo Drive see a TV broadcast.
7. Would you be interested in having dinner with me tonight.
8. When it's 5 PM in California, it's 8 PM in New York.

end marks are used, and then consider their findings in light of questions like these: Are my sentences too short and choppy? Have I supplied needed question marks? Used any unnecessarily? Should I combine certain sentences by substituting a semicolon, conjunctive adverb, or some other form of conjunction for the period? Have I overused exclamation points?

EXERCISE ANSWER
(There is more than one way to punctuate this passage.)

It was horrifying. The mob of screaming fans grabbed Jack Slitherhips as he left the concert hall. Soon all I could see were his arms reaching for help. But it never came. Why do fans act this way? I am left wondering whether they love or hate their idols. They tore the clothes off Slitherhips. They tore out patches of his hair. Someone even snatched his false teeth. Is this any way to treat a fading rock star? Jack is now in the hospital in a complete body cast. When I fi-

.?!

nally got to see him, he mumbled that he was giving up show business to settle down on a small farm. Who can blame him!

You might have students try several different methods of punctuating this passage, including some changes in sentence structure, to see the stylistic effect.

EXERCISE ANSWERS

1. C.	**7.** tonight?
2. $29.95	**8.** P.M./P.M.
3. lord! nuts!	**9.** 8.5
/ nuts!	
4. C.	**10.** Crickets?
5. year?	**11.** located.
6. studio?	**12.** C.
Drive?	
broadcast?	

9. The interest rate on my house mortgage is a modest 85 percent.
10. Buddy Holly—wasn't his band called the Crickets—is sometimes called the father of rock and roll.
11. The safety inspector asked the building supervisor where the fire extinguishers were located?
12. Be sure to return these books to the library today.

COLONS, DASHES, PARENTHESES, AND BRACKETS

Colons, dashes, parentheses, and brackets separate and enclose, thereby clarifying relationships among the various parts of a sentence.

Colons.   Colons (:) introduce appositives, formal lists, and explanations following words that could stand alone as a complete sentence.

His aim in life is grandiose: to corner the market in wheat. (appositive)

Three students have been selected to attend the conference: Lucille Perkins, Dan Blakely, and Frank Napolis. (list)

Three factors account for the financial problems of most farmers: (1) high interest rates, (2) falling land values, and (3) the strong dollar, which makes it difficult to sell crops abroad. (explanation)

The first of the following sentences is incorrect because the words preceding the colon can't stand alone as a sentence.

Faulty   The tools needed for this job include: a hacksaw, a file, and a drill.

Revision   The tools needed for this job include a hacksaw, a file, and a drill.

Colons are frequently used to introduce formal quotations that extend beyond a single sentence.

The speaker stepped to the lectern and said: "I am here to ask for your assistance. Today several African nations face a food crisis because drought has ruined their harvests. Unless we provide help quickly, thousands of people will die of starvation."

In such situations, the material preceding the quotation need not be a complete sentence.

Colons also separate hours from minutes (8:20 A.M.), salutations of business letters from the body of the letters (Dear Ms. Stanley:), titles of publications from subtitles (*The Careful Writer: A Guide to English Usage*), numbers indicating ratios (a 3:2:2 ratio), and chapter from verse in biblical references (Luke 6:20–49).

Dashes.   Like colons, dashes (—) set off appositives, lists, and explanations but are used in less formal writing. A dash emphasizes the material it sets off.

Only one candidate showed up at the political rally—Jerry Manders. (appositive)

The closet held only three garments—an out-at-the-elbows sportscoat, a pair of blue jeans, and a tattered shirt. (list)

I know what little Billy's problem is—a soiled diaper. (explanation)

Dashes set off material that interrupts the flow of thought within a sentence.

Her new car—didn't she get it just three months ago?—has broken down twice.

Similarly, dashes are used to mark an interrupted segment of dialogue.

"I'd like to live in England when I retire."

"In England? But what will your wife—?"

"My wife likes the idea and can hardly wait for us to make the move."

Dashes set off parenthetical elements containing commas, and a dash can set off comments that follow a list.

The comedian—short, fat, and squeaky-voiced—soon had everyone roaring with laughter. (parenthetical element with commas)

A brag, a blow, a tank of air—that's what Senator Conwell is. (comment following a list)

Type a dash as two unspaced hyphens and leave no space between it and the words on either side of it.

Parentheses. Parentheses ( ) are used to enclose numbers or letters that designate the items in a formal list and to set off incidental material within sentences. Except in the kind of list shown in the first example below, a comma does not usually precede a parenthesis.

Each paper should contain (1) an introduction, (2) several paragraphs developing the thesis statement, and (3) a conclusion.

Some occupations (computer programming, for example) may be overcrowded in ten years.

If the material in parentheses appears within a sentence, don't use a capital letter or period, even if the material is itself a complete sentence.

The use of industrial robots (one cannot foresee their consequences) worries some people today.

If the material in parentheses is written as a separate sentence, however, then punctuate it as you would a separate sentence.

Paula's angry outburst surprised everyone. (She had seemed such a placid person.)

If the material in parentheses comes at the end of a sentence, put the final punctuation after the closing parenthesis.

This company was founded by Willard Manley (1876–1951).

In contrast to dashes, parentheses de-emphasize the material they enclose.

It frequently takes students five years to earn a college diploma. Wasn't it supposed to take four years?

The movie star had the politicians completely captivated. The movie star was beautiful, charming, and witty.

He certainly made a spectacle of himself. He was blowing her kisses, waving his handkerchief, and yelling out her name.

Combinations

They offer only one thing for breakfast—cold oatmeal.

It frequently takes students five years—wasn't it supposed to take four?—to earn a college diploma.

The movie star—beautiful, charming, and witty—had the politicians completely captivated.

He certainly made a spectacle of himself—blowing her kisses, waving his handkerchief, and yelling out her name.

PERSPECTIVE

Students are often confused about when to use parentheses, when commas, and when dashes. In some cases, the difference is really a matter of style; however, these punctuation marks do produce different effects. While commas tend to incorporate the set-off material into the sentence, parentheses tend to exclude it. Dashes, if anything, tend to draw attention to the material.

Brackets.   In quoted material, brackets [ ] enclose words or phrases that have been added to make the message clearer. They are also used with the word *sic* (Latin for "thus") to point out errors in quoted material.

> "This particular company [Zorn Enterprises, Inc.] pioneered in the safe disposal of toxic wastes," the report noted. (The bracketed name is added to the original.)

> "[Carl Sagan's] expertise in science has made him a popular figure on the lecture circuit," his friend stated. (The bracketed name replaces *his* in the original.)

> "The principle [sic] cause of lung cancer is cigarette smoking," the article declared. (The word *principal* is misspelled "principle" in the original.)

To call attention to an error, follow it immediately with the bracketed *sic*. The reader will then know that the blame rests with the original writer, not with you.

CONNECTED DISCOURSE EXERCISE ■ Supply any necessary or appropriate colons, dashes, parentheses, and brackets in the following letter.

Wayout Auto Company

We at Oldfield Sales a subsidiary of Jip, Inc., have had a serious problem with the cars we ordered from your company for leasing to our customers who will probably never return to us again. Two major parts fell off while the cars were sitting in the customers' driveways the exhaust system and the transmission. If this had happened while they were driving thank goodness it didn't, our customers could have been killed. Just imagine what that especially once it got into the newspapers would have done to our business. We must hold you to your claim that "while our cars are the cheapest sic on the market, we garnishee sic every car we sell." We expect immediate reimbursement for all the cars we purchased from you plus one million dollars to cover the damage to our reputation. A menace, a rip-off, a bad business deal, that's what your cars are. If you don't issue a formal recall for all your vehicles by 530 p.m., Friday, July 23, we will be forced to forward this matter to the federal government.

Sincerely,

Ken Swindelle
Service Manager

[ ]

EXERCISE ■ **Supply colons, dashes, parentheses, and brackets wherever they are necessary.**

1. Worthington's new house mansion would be a better term has twenty-eight rooms.
2. This resort offers unsurpassed facilities for three winter sports ice skating, skiing, and tobogganing.
3. Two long meetings, a shopping trip, a dinner engagement I've had a busy day!
4. The main parts of the pressure tester include 1 an indicator dial, 2 a hose connection, 3 a damper valve, and 4 a sensing unit.
5. At the tone, the time will be 330 P.M. exactly.
6. The headline stated, "Students Voice They're *sic* Disapproval of Tuition Hike."
7. "His Charles Darwin's book *On the Origin of Species* touched off a controversy that still continues," the lecturer declared.
8. One major social problem will remain with us for several decades the population explosion.
9. On Wall Street today, advancing stocks outpaced decliners by a 43 ratio.
10. I'll bet I can guess what you'd like for your birthday a new bike.
11. A few movie sequels *Godfather II*, for example have received as much critical praise as their parent films.
12. I listen to music for several reasons sometimes for excitement, sometimes for relaxation, sometimes for nostalgia, and sometimes for fun.

a rip-off, a bad business deal--that's what your cars are. If you don't issue a formal recall for all your vehicles by 5:30 p.m., Friday, July 23, we will be forced to forward this matter to the federal government.

Sincerely,

Ken Swindelle
Service Manager

EXERCISE ANSWERS

1. house— / term—
2. sports:
3. engagement—
4. (1) (2) (3) (4)
5. 3:30
6. [*sic*]
7. [Charles Darwin's]
8. decades:
9. 4:3
10. birthday—
11. (*Godfather II*, for example)
12. reasons:

*Q*UOTATION MARKS

Quotation marks (" ") set off direct quotations, titles of short pieces of writing, subdivisions of books, and expressions singled out for special attention.

Direct Quotations. A direct quotation repeats a speaker's or writer's exact words.

"Tell me about the movie," said Debbie. "If you liked it, I may go myself."

The placement director said, "The recruiter for Procter and Gamble will be on campus next Thursday to interview students for marketing jobs." (spoken comment)

"The U.S. trade deficit is expected to reach record levels this year," *The Wall Street Journal* noted. (written comment)

Jackie said the party was "a total flop."

As these sentences show, a comma or period that follows a direct quotation goes inside the quotation marks. When a quotation is a sentence fragment, the comma preceding it is omitted.

When an expression like "he said" interrupts a quoted sentence, use commas to set off the expression. When the expression comes between two complete

PERSPECTIVE

The use of quotation marks with direct quotations is a matter of responsible reporting as well as of proper punctuation. Students need to appreciate that these marks allow us to distinguish between a paraphrase and the exact words of a source. This difference can be important, and failure to make the proper distinction can have legal ramifications.

ETHICAL ISSUE

A journalist recently interviewed the superintendent of schools in a large city. During the interview, the superintendent suggested that students didn't seem to have the intellectual capacity to handle the traditional curriculum. To enliven the interview, the journalist later wrote in her article the following sentence: "Superintendent Jameson insisted that 'the students in this city are too stupid to cope with a traditional curriculum.' " When called to task, the journalist argued that though the superintendent never said those exact words, the quote did capture the essence of his comment and so was appropriate. Discuss with students whether the journalist was justified, and if not, why not.

TEACHING STRATEGY

Have students interview classmates, or even faculty members, on a topic of interest. Then they could prepare papers that make appropriate use of quotation marks, exchange papers, and check each other's work for the use of quotes. Or you could make a presentation to the class and have them report on it, using quotation marks. Be prepared to chuckle when

" "

you see how students represent what you say.

quoted sentences, use a period after the expression and capitalize the first word of the second sentence.

> "Hop in," said Jim. "Let me give you a ride to school."

> "Thank you," replied Kelly, opening the car door and sliding into the front seat.

> "I can't remember," said Jim, "when we've had a worse winter."

Titles of Short Works and Subdivisions of Books.   These short works include magazine articles, essays, short stories, chapters of books, one-act plays, short poems, songs, and television and radio programs.

> The article was titled "The Real Conservatism." (article)

> Last night I read John Cheever's "The Enormous Radio," "Torch Song," and "The Swimmer." (short stories)

> Many John Denver fans consider "Take Me Home, Country Roads" to be his greatest piece of music. (song)

Here, as with direct quotations, a comma or period that follows a title goes inside the quotation marks.

Expressions Singled Out for Special Attention.   Writers who wish to call the reader's attention to a word or symbol sometimes put it within quotation marks.

> The algebraic formula included a "π," a "Θ," and a "Δ."

> "Bonnets" and "lifts" are British terms for car hoods and elevators.

More frequently, however, these expressions are printed in italics (page 582).
   Again, any commas and periods that follow expressions set off by quotation marks go inside the marks.

Quotation Marks Within Quotation Marks.   When a direct quotation or the title of a shorter work appears within a direct quotation, use single quotation marks (' ').

> "I heard the boss telling the foreman, 'Everyone will receive a Christmas bonus,' " John said.

> The instructor told the class, "For tomorrow, read Ernest Hemingway's 'The Killers.' "

Note that the period goes inside of both the single and the double quotation marks.

Positioning of Semicolons, Colons, and Question Marks. Position semicolons and colons that come at the end of quoted material after, not before, the quotation marks.

> Marcia calls Francine "that greasy grind"; however, I think Marcia is simply jealous of Francine's abilities.

> There are two reasons why I liked "Dallas": the plot was interesting, and the acting was good.

When a question mark accompanies a quotation, put it outside the quotation marks if the whole sentence rather than the quotation asks the question.

> Why did Cedric suddenly shout, "This party is a big bore"?

Put the question mark inside the quotation marks if the quotation, but not the whole sentence, asks a question or if the quotation asks one question and the whole sentence asks another.

> Marie asked, "What college is your brother planning to attend?" (The quoted material, not the whole sentence, asks the question.)

> Whatever possessed him to ask, "What is the most shameful thing you ever did?" (The whole sentence and the quoted material ask separate questions.)

CONNECTED DISCOURSE EXERCISE ■ Use quotation marks correctly in the following paragraph.

Mr. Silver recently lectured our class on Stephen Crane's The Bride Comes to Yellow Sky. One thing we shouldn't forget, Mr. Silver insisted, is that the town is deliberately named Yellow Sky. What is the significance of Crane's choice of the words Yellow Sky? Mr. Silver pointed out a number of possible associations, including cowardice, the setting sun, the open expanse of the West, freedom, the sand in the concluding passage. The story, Mr. Silver stated, is drenched in color words. For example, he pointed out, in the first three paragraphs alone Crane mentions vast flats of green grass, brick-colored hands, new black clothes, and a dress of blue cashmere.

EXERCISE ■ Supply properly positioned quotation marks wherever they are necessary.

1. Jeffrey called the novel's plot a hopeless mishmash.
2. I think, said Tom, that I'll go to Chicago for the weekend.
3. What poem has the lines Home is the sailor, home from the sea,/ And the hunter home from the hills?
4. Denise tells everyone, I prefer classical music; however, her CD collection includes only hard rock and country music.
5. Nearly every educated American now knows what the Russian words glasnost and perestroika mean.
6. At last my paper is finished, John said happily. Now I can start typing it.
7. Does anyone here know what the word dilatory means?
8. Why did Neil's wife ask him, How would you like me to dispose of your remains?
9. William asked his son, What movie do you plan to see?
10. Larry called the following movies my all-time favorites: *Casablanca, Gone with the Wind*, and *Patton*.

10. "my all-time favorites":
11. "The expression 'go for broke' first entered main-stream American English dur-ing World War II," the instructor told her class.
12. "extirpate" "root out, abolish, exterminate."

11. The expression go for broke first entered mainstream American English during World War II, the instructor told her class.
12. Sarah didn't realize that extirpate means root out, abolish, exterminate.

*H*YPHENS

Hyphens(-) are used to join compound adjectives and nouns, compound numbers and word–number combinations, and certain prefixes and suffixes to the words with which they appear. In addition, hyphens help prevent misreadings and awk-ward combinations of letters or syllables.

Compound Adjectives and Nouns. Hyphens are often used to join separate words that function as single adjectives and come before nouns. Typical examples follow.

Howard is a very *self-contained* person.

The *greenish-yellow* cloud of chlorine gas drifted toward the village.

Betty's *devil-may-care* attitude will land her in trouble someday.

When the first word of the compound is an adverb ending in *-ly* or when the compound adjective follows the noun it modifies, no hyphen is used.

The *badly* burned crash victim was rushed to the hospital.

The color of the chlorine gas was *greenish yellow.*

When two or more compound adjectives modify the same last term, the sentence will flow more smoothly if that term appears just once, after the last item in the series. The hyphens accompanying the earlier items in the series are kept, however.

Many seventeenth-, eighteenth-, and nineteenth-century costumes are on display in this museum.

Hyphenated nouns include such expressions as the following:

secretary-treasurer   good-for-nothing
sister-in-law   man-about-town

Here is a sentence with hyphenated nouns.

Denton is *editor-in-chief* of the largest newspaper in this state.

Compound Numbers and Word–Number Combinations. Hyphens are used to separate two-word numbers from twenty-one to ninety-nine and fractions that have been written out.

Marcy has worked *twenty-one* years for this company.

One-fourth of my income goes for rent.

Similarly, hyphens are used to separate numerals from units of measurement that follow them.

This chemical is shipped in *50-gallon* drums.

Prefixes and Suffixes.   A prefix is a word or set of letters that precedes a word and alters its meaning. A suffix is similar but comes at the end of the word. Although most prefixes are not hyphenated, the prefixes *self-* and *all-* do get hyphens, as does the suffix *-elect* and the prefix *ex-* when it accompanies a noun.

This stove has a *self-cleaning* oven.

Let Claire Voyant, the *all-knowing* soothsayer, read your future in her crystal ball.

Ethel is the *chairperson-elect* of the club.

Several *ex-teachers* work in this department.

A prefix used before a capitalized term is always hyphenated.

The *ex-FBI* agent gave an interesting talk on the operations of that agency.

Preventing Misreadings and Awkward Combinations of Letters and Syllables.   Hyphens help prevent misreadings of certain words and also break up awkward combinations of letters and syllables between certain prefixes and suffixes and their core words.

The doctor *re-treated* the wound with a new antibiotic. (The hyphen prevents the misreading *retreated*.)

The company plans to *de-emphasize* sales of agricultural chemicals. (The hyphen prevents the awkward repetition of the letter *e* in *deemphasize*.)

Between Syllables.   Whenever you have to split a word between two lines, place a hyphen at the end of the first line to show the division. The word is always broken, and the hyphen inserted, between syllables. (Any good dictionary shows the syllable divisions of each word it includes.) Never divide a one-syllable word or leave two letters to be placed on the second line, even if those two letters constitute a syllable.

EXERCISE ■ **Supply hyphens wherever they are necessary. If the sentence is correct, write C.**

1. The task of residing the house will take three days.
2. Margaret is the most selfsufficient person that I've ever met.
3. Judge Grimm gave the convicted arsonist a ten to twenty year prison sentence.
4. Nearly three fourths of our chemistry majors go on to graduate school.
5. When I was thirty five years old, I quit my job and opened my own small business.
6. Most of my exsoldier friends belong to veterans' organizations.
7. Jeremiah's antigovernment tirades have caused most of his friends to avoid him.
8. The orange red flowers growing next to the house contrasted strongly with the dark gray of its walls.

EXERCISE ANSWERS
1. re-siding
2. self-sufficient
3. ten- to twenty-year
4. three-fourths
5. thirty-five
6. ex-soldier
7. anti-government
8. orange-red
9. 90-day
10. senator-elect
11. shell-like / blue-gray
12. dyed-in-the-wool

9. My new electric coffee grinder comes with a 90 day guarantee on parts and labor.
10. What national problems concern our new senatorelect the most?
11. The picture consisted of a series of vaguely shelllike shapes against a blue gray background.
12. He's a dyed in the wool villain if there ever was one.

CAPITALIZATION

cap

Capitalize the first word in any sentence, the pronoun *I*, proper nouns and adjectives, titles used with—or in place of—names, and the significant words in literary and artistic titles.

Proper Nouns. A proper noun names one particular person, group of persons, place, or thing. Such nouns include names of the following:

Persons
Organizations
Racial, political, and religious groups
Countries, states, cities, and streets
Companies and buildings
Geographical locations and features
Days, months, and holidays
Trademarks
Languages
Ships and aircraft
Names of academic degrees and the abbreviations for them
Sacred writings and pronouns standing for God and Jesus
Titles used in place of names

The sentences below show the capitalization of proper nouns.

Sigmund works for the *National Psychoanalytical Institute*, an organization that has done much to advance the science of psychiatry.

How much does this roll of *Saran Wrap* cost?

Gwen Greene moved to *Paris, France,* when her father became the consul there.

On *Friday, October* 13, 1989, *George Bush* visited our city.

Larry has a *Master of Arts* degree, and his sister has a *Ph.D.*

My father works for the *Ford Motor Company,* but I work for *Chrysler.*

Do not capitalize words like *institute, college, company, or avenue* unless they form part of a proper name. Likewise, do not capitalize the names of courses unless they start a sentence, are accompanied by a course number, or designate a language.

I have a 95 average in *Economics* 112 but only a 73 average in sociology.

Harry plans to take intermediate *German* in his junior year.

Do you plan to attend *Drew College* or some other college?

Proper Adjectives. Adjectives created from proper nouns are called proper adjectives. Like the nouns themselves, they should be capitalized.

> Lolita Martinez, our class valedictorian, is of *Mexican* ancestry. (*Mexican* is derived from the proper noun *Mexico*.)

Abbreviations. As a general rule, capitalize abbreviations only if the words they stand for are capitalized.

> Milton DeWitt works for the *IRS*. (*IRS* is capitalized because "Internal Revenue Service" would be.)

> The flask holds 1,500 *cc* of liquid. (The abbreviation *cc* is not capitalized because "cubic centimeters" would not be.)

A few abbreviations are capitalized even though all or some of the words they stand for aren't. Examples include TV (television) and VCR (videocassette recorder). Others are shown on pages 578–79.

Personal Titles. Capitalize a personal title if it precedes a name or is used in place of a name. Otherwise, do not capitalize.

> The division is under the command of *General* Arnold Schafer.

> Tell me, *Doctor,* do I need an operation?

> The *dean* of our Engineering Division is Dr. Alma Haskins.

Many writers capitalize titles of high rank when they are used in place of names.

> The *President* will sign this bill tomorrow.

> The *president* will sign this bill tomorrow.

Either usage is acceptable.

Titles of Literary and Artistic Works. When citing the title of publications, pieces of writing, movies, television programs, paintings, sculptures, and the like, capitalize the first and last words and all other words except *a, an, the,* coordinating conjunctions, and one-syllable prepositions.

> Last week I played *Gone with the Wind* on my VCR and read Christopher Isherwood's *Goodbye to Berlin*. (The preposition *with*, the article *the*, and the preposition *to* are not capitalized.)

> John is reading a book called *The Movies of Abbott and Costello*. (The preposition *of* and the coordinating conjunction *and* are not capitalized.)

> My favorite TV show is "Murder, She Wrote." (All the words in the title are capitalized.)

Note that the titles of literary and artistic works are italicized and that the titles of TV programs are set off by quotation marks.

cap

EXERCISE ANSWERS

1. *The American Family Cookbook.*
2. Federal National Mortgage Association / Washington, D.C. / July.
3. Sergeant Brockway
4. ACLU Midville / Christmas
5. Boyle City / Judge Martha Berkowicz.
6. Delta Corporation
7. Wheaties / Mother.
8. Elizabethan / English / Queen Elizabeth
9. Friday
10. Professor.

EXERCISE ■ **Identify any word or abbreviation that should be capitalized in the following sentences.**

1. The recipe for this stew comes from *the american family cookbook.*
2. My cousin has accepted a job with the federal national mortgage association and will move to washington, d.c. in july.
3. The announcement said that sergeant brockway had received a second lieutenant's commission.
4. The aclu has asked midville to scrap its ordinance prohibiting christmas religious displays on private property.
5. The newest municipal judge in boyle city is judge martha berkowicz.
6. Unless sales increase markedly in the next quarter, the delta corporation will be forced into bankruptcy.
7. We need to buy some wheaties, mother.
8. During the elizabethan period of english history, which takes its name from queen elizabeth I, many poems and other writings were dedicated to the queen.
9. In the summer, I close my shop each friday at noon.
10. What are your postretirement plans, professor?

*A*BBREVIATIONS

Items that are abbreviated include certain personal titles, names of organizations and agencies, Latin terms, and scientific and technical terms.

Personal Titles.   Abbreviate *Mister, Doctor,* and similar titles when they come just ahead of a name, and *Junior, Senior,* and degree titles when they follow names.

Will *Mr.* Harry Babbitt please come to the front desk?

Arthur Compton, *Sr.,* is a well-known historian; his son, Arthur Compton, *Jr.,* is a television producer.

This article on marital discord was written by Irma Quarles, *Ph.D.*

Names of Organizations and Agencies.   Many organizations and agencies are known primarily by their initials rather than their full names. Several examples follow.

AAA	FBI	NBC
CARE	FHA	NATO
CIA	IBM	UNESCO

Latin Terms.   Certain Latin terms are always abbreviated; others are abbreviated when used with dates or times.

e.g. (*exempli gratia:* for example)
i.e. (*id est:* that is)

ab

etc. (*et cetera:* and [the] others)
vs. (*versus:* against)
A.D. (*anno Domini:* in the year of our Lord)
A.M. or a.m. (*ante meridiem:* before noon)
P.M. or p.m. (*post meridiem:* after noon)

The play starts at 8 *P.M.*

Many writers (*e.g.,* Dylan Thomas and Truman Capote) have had serious problems with alcohol.

For consistency with A.D., the term "before Christ" is abbreviated as B.C.

Scientific and Technical Terms.   For brevity's sake, scientists and technicians abbreviate terms of measurement that repeatedly occur. Terms that the reader would not know are written out the first time they are used, and they are accompanied by their abbreviation in parentheses. Unfamiliar organizations and agencies that are mentioned repeatedly are handled in like manner.

The viscosity of the fluid measured 15 centistokes (cks) at room temperature.

Common practice calls for writing such abbreviations without periods unless they duplicate the spelling of some word.

Standard dictionaries list common abbreviations. When you don't recognize one, look it up. Use abbreviations sparingly in essays. If you're unsure about what is appropriate, don't abbreviate.

EXERCISE ■ **Supply abbreviations wherever they are necessary or are customarily used.**

ab

1. The conference on poverty in the 1980s will be chaired by Roland Reagan, Doctor of Philosophy.
2. When writing, don't use Latin terms like *id est* and *exempli gratia* except as comments in parentheses and footnotes.
3. The United Nations Educational, Scientific, and Cultural Organization sponsors programs in primary education throughout the Third World.
4. My physics instructor, Doctor Seth Greenfield, Junior, has just completed a textbook on optics.
5. The thermometer on my front porch says that the temperature is 77° Fahrenheit (25° Celsius).
6. At 10:20 *ante meridiem*, the local TV station announced that a tornado had been sighted near Leesville.
7. This fall, the Columbia Broadcasting System will air nine new sitcoms.
8. Which would you prefer, Mister Bartleby, tea or coffee?
9. To begin the test, place a 50-gram sample of ore in a 1,000-milliliter beaker.
10. International Business Machines will begin marketing a new line of personal computers next week.

EXERCISE ANSWERS
1. Ph.D.
2. *i.e./e.g.*
3. UNESCO (no "the" before abbreviation)
4. Dr./Jr.
5. 77°F/25°C
6. 10:20 A.M.
7. CBS (no "the" before abbreviation)
8. Mr.
9. 50-gm/1,000-ml
10. IBM

Numbers

Some instructors ask their students to use figures for numbers larger than ninety-nine and to spell out smaller numbers.

> Boise is *100* miles from here.

> Boise is *ninety-nine* miles from here.

Other instructors prefer that students switch to figures beginning with the number ten.

> My son will be *nine* years old on his next birthday.

> My son will be *10* years old on his next birthday.

With either practice, the following exceptions apply.

Numbers in a Series.   Write all numbers in a series the same way regardless of their size.

> Gatsby has *64* suits, *110* shirts, and *214* ties.

> In just one hour the emergency room personnel handled *two* stabbings, *five* shootings, and *sixteen* fractures.

> We have *150* salespeople, *51* engineers, and *7* laboratory technicians.

Dates.   Use figures for dates that include the year.

> February *14, 1985* (not February 14th, 1985)

When the date includes the day but not the year, you may use figures or spell out the number.

> June 9
> June ninth
> the ninth of June

Page Numbers and Addresses.   Use figures for page numbers and street numbers in addresses.

> Check the graph on page *415*.

> I live at *111* Cornelia Street, and my office is at *620* Fifth Avenue.

Numbers Beginning Sentences.   Spell out any number that begins a sentence. If this requires three or more words, rephrase the sentence so that the number comes after the opening and numerals can be used.

> The year *1980* was a good one for this wine.

> *Sixty thousand* fans jammed the stadium.

> An army of *265,000* troops assaulted the city. (If this number began the sentence, five words—an excessive number—would be needed to write it out.)

num

Decimals, Percentages, Times. Use figures for decimals and percentages as well as for expressions of time that are accompanied by A.M. or P.M.

The shaft is *0.37*-inch in diameter.

Last year the value of my house jumped *25* percent.

The plane leaves here at *9:50* A.M. and reaches New Orleans at *2:30* P.M.

One Number Following Another. When one number comes immediately after another, spell out the first number, if smaller than 100, and use numerals for the second one. If the first number is larger than 100, use numerals for it and spell out the second one.

We ordered *six 30*-gallon drums of solvent for the project.

The supplier shipped us *600 thirty*-gallon drums by mistake.

As noted earlier, this rule does not apply to dates that include the year.

EXERCISE ■ **Identify any miswriting of numbers in the following sentences and rewrite these numbers correctly.**

1. 50,000 people ride this city's buses each day.
2. The article on page fifty-nine of this week's issue of *Time* discusses Madonna's latest video.
3. Next Saturday at one-thirty P.M., the city will test its emergency warning sirens.
4. My grandparents' golden wedding anniversary was July seventeen, nineteen ninety-one.
5. Mildred has 500 books, two hundred CDs, and fifty-five videocassettes.
6. It is not uncommon for credit-card holders to pay interest rates of eighteen percent or more.
7. Laura's plane will leave for New York at two-thirty P.M. on May the sixteenth.
8. The thickness of this piece needs to be increased by fifteen hundredths of an inch.
9. The address of the National Trust for Historic Preservation is seventeen eighty-five Massachusetts Avenue, N.W., Washington, D.C. 20036.
10. The store ordered one thousand twenty-pound bags of de-icing salt for November delivery.

EXERCISE ANSWERS
1. Fifty thousand
2. page 59
3. 1:30 P.M.
4. July 17, 1991.
5. 500 books, 200 CDs, and 55 videocassettes.
6. 18 percent
7. 2:30 P.M. / May 16
8. 0.15 inch.
9. 1785 Massachusetts Avenue N.W.
10. 1,000 twenty-pound

ital

---

*I*TALICS

Italics are used for the titles of longer publications, the names of vehicles and vessels, foreign words and phrases, and expressions singled out for special attention. When writing or typing papers, use underlining to represent italics.

Titles of Longer Publications and Artistic Works. These items may include the following:

books	record albums	long musical works and poems
magazines	paintings	plays
newspapers	movies	sculptures

As noted on page 572, quotation marks are used for the titles of articles, short stories, short poems, one-act plays, and other brief pieces of writing.

Last night I finished F. Scott Fitzgerald's *The Great Gatsby* and read two articles in *The New Yorker*. (book, magazine)

Michelangelo's *David* is surely one of the world's greatest sculptures. (sculpture)

The *Detroit Free Press* had praise for the revival of Tennessee Williams's play *The Glass Menagerie*. (newspaper, play)

Stephen Vincent Benét's poem *John Brown's Body* won a Pulitzer Prize in 1929. (book-length poem)

Do not use italics when naming the Bible or its parts.

Joanna's favorite book of the Bible is the Book of Ecclesiastes, part of the Old Testament.

Names of Vehicles and Vessels.   Names of particular airplanes, ships, trains, and spacecraft are italicized.

The plane in which Charles Lindbergh flew over the Atlantic Ocean was named *The Spirit of St. Louis.*

Foreign Expressions.   Use italics to identify foreign words and phrases that have not yet made their way into the English language.

The writer has a terribly pessimistic *weltanschauung*. (philosophy of life)

This season, long skirts are the *dernier cri*. (the latest thing)

When such expressions become completely assimilated, the italics are dropped. Most dictionaries use an asterisk (*), a dagger (†), or other symbol to identify expressions that need italicizing.

Expressions Singled Out for Special Attention.   These include words, letters, numerals, and symbols.

The Greek letter *pi* is written Π.

I can't tell whether this letter is meant to be an *a* or an *o* or this number a *7* or a *9.*

In England, the word *lorry* means truck.

As noted on page 572, quotation marks sometimes replace italics for this purpose.

EXERCISE ANSWER

Because I can speak Russian fluently, I was recruited by the CIA while still at Boston College. I suspected that it was Professor Hogsbottom, a political science teacher, who had suggested that they consider me. After all, he had been a general during World

CONNECTED DISCOURSE EXERCISE ■ Use hyphens, capitalization, abbreviations, numbers, and italics properly in the following passage.

Because I can speak russian fluently, I was recruited by the

central intelligence agency while still at Boston college. I suspected that

it was professor Hogsbottom, a Political Science teacher, who had suggested that they consider me. After all, he had been a General during World War Two and still had connections with the intelligence community. It turned out that my brother in law was responsible; he was an ex FBI agent. Soon I was an american spy located, of all places, in England. Who would suspect that we had to spy on the english? For 3 years I posed as a british aristocrat who was a general bon vivant and man about town. I went by the alias of Mister Henry Higgins, Junior. Everyone, of course, wanted to know if I had seen My Fair Lady. Personally I thought the whole thing was a monty python style joke until I found a position in the british secret service. Who could have believed the british kept so many secrets from their american allies? For twenty one years I spied on the british without anyone suspecting that I was an all american boy. I did find out recently, however, that because of my fluent russian they had suspected me of being a russian spy and had been feeding me false information all along.

War II and still had connections with the intelligence community. It turned out that my brother-in-law was responsible; he was an ex-FBI agent. Soon I was an American spy located, of all places, in England. Who would suspect that we had to spy on the English? For three years I posed as a British aristocrat who was a general *bon vivant* and man-about-town. I went by the alias of Mr. Henry Higgins, Jr. Everyone, of course, wanted to know if I had seen *My Fair Lady*. Personally I thought the whole thing was a Monty-Python-style joke until I found a position in the British secret service. Who could have believed the British kept so many secrets from their American allies? For twenty-one years I spied on the British without anyone suspecting that I was an all-American boy. I did find out recently, however, that because of my fluent Russian they had suspected me of being a Russian spy and had been feeding me false information all along.

EXERCISE ■ Supply italics wherever they are necessary.

1. To keep abreast of the business news, I read both Investor's Daily and Forbes.
2. Next week, Boris is taking the Siberian Express to Irkutsk, Siberia.
3. Of all my art prints, I like Erte's Fishbowl best.
4. According to fashion forecasts, miniskirts will be de rigueur next summer.
5. My uncle served on the cruiser Indianapolis during World War II.
6. Because Pam lost her brother's copy of Moby Dick, she bought him a new one.
7. Sometimes when I try to print a b I make a d instead.
8. Let's rent videotapes of Alfred Hitchcock's Rear Window and Rebecca for the weekend.
9. The latest revival of Arthur Miller's play The Crucible has received much critical praise.
10. In Scotland, the term lum refers to a chimney.

ital

EXERCISE ANSWERS

1. *Investor's Daily* / *Forbes*
2. *Siberian Express*
3. *Fishbowl*
4. *de rigueur*
5. *Indianapolis*
6. *Moby Dick*
7. *b* / *d*
8. *Rear Window* / *Rebecca*
9. *The Crucible*
10. *lum*

sp

"Why the big deal about accurate spelling?"

"Does it really make that much difference if I have an *i* and an *e* turned around or if I omit a letter when spelling a word?"

Students frequently question the importance of proper spelling. Perhaps the answer is suggested by the following sentence, taken from a student essay:

I spent over seven hours *studing* one day last week.

The omission of a *y* in *studing* changes the person from one who is studious to one who is a dreamer. Not only does inaccurate spelling smack of carelessness, but also it sometimes drastically alters meaning.

Although there is no sure-fire way of becoming a good speller, you can minimize the difficulties by learning basic spelling rules, applying helpful spelling tips, and memorizing the proper spelling of troublesome words.

SPELLING RULES

The following four rules should ease spelling pains.

Rule 1. If a word has the double vowels[1] *ie* or *ei* and the combination has a long *e* sound (as in *me*), use *ie* except after *c*. If the combination has an *a* sound, use *ei*.

ie (*as long* e)	ei *after* c	ei (*as* a)
achieve	deceive	freight
belief	receive	neighbor
grieve	receipt	reign
piece	perceive	weigh

The main exceptions to this rule include *either, financier, leisure, neither, seize, species,* and *weird.*

Rule 2. If a one-syllable word (example: *sin*) ends in a single consonant preceded by a single vowel, double the consonant before adding a suffix (see page 575) that starts with a vowel. Apply the same rule with a word of two or more syllables (example: *admit*) if the final syllable is accented and ends with a single consonant preceded by a vowel.

[1]The vowels are *a, e, i, o,* and *u.* The consonants are the remaining letters of the alphabet.

"Dear Mom, Wud you belive I lost my job at the offise today? I gess sumwun thair doesnt like me."

From *Recess Time*, The Best Cartoons from *The Kappan*, edited by Kristin Herzog, 1983.

"th" in "bathroom." If you see errors of this sort, help students by teaching them the right pronunciation. (d) Confusion of homophones. Some students consistently confuse words like "know" and "no." When this is the source of the misspelling, bring the homophones to the student's attention. (e) Difficulty in seeing the structure of words. Some students blur syllables or even omit some. As a result, "parallel" becomes "parall." Such students must first learn how to sound out the word, then how to break it into its syllables. (f) Poor visual memory. Some students are poor readers and have little visual memory. Have such students copy the correctly spelled word in different colored ink, break it into its key parts, and compare the copy to the original. Some students even benefit from writing a word in the air with their hands while they say it.

3. Mina Shaughnessy's book *Errors and Expectations* has such important suggestions about approaching extremely weak spellers that they are worth repeating here. (a) "Assume at the outset that the misspellings of young adults can be brought under control" (175). (b) "Begin by teaching the student to observe himself as a speller" (175). (c) "Before attempting to work on individual errors, make certain the student understands certain terms and operations" (177). (d) "If possible start to work on misspellings that can be controlled by the application of rules" (177). (e) "Develop an awareness of the main dis-

Words with Single Syllables	*Words with Two or More Syllables*
rig — rigged	admit — admittance
sin — sinned	control — controller
stop — stopping	equip — equipped

If the accent does not fall on the last syllable, do not double the final consonant.

audit — audited	chatter — chattered
counsel — counselor	simmer — simmering

Rule 3. If a word ends in *y* preceded by a single consonant, change the *y* to an *i* unless you are adding the suffix *-ing*.

y changed to **i**	*y retained*
beauty — beautiful	fury — furious
fury — furious	defy — defying
easy — easily	dry — drying
vary — various	vary — varying

sp

crepancies between the student's pronunciation of words and the models of pronunciation upon which the spelling system is based" (179). (f) "Develop an awareness of the ways in which pronunciation helps the speller" (179). (g) "Develop the student's ability to discriminate among graphemic options" (181). (h) "Teach the use of the dictionary" (185).

4. The term "dyslexia" should be reserved for a very specific neurological condition that causes students to have problems processing what they hear and see. Usually a student with dyslexia will show pronounced reversals of letters or even confuse letters like *d*'s and *b*'s. Some students will wrongly identify themselves as dyslexic to explain their spelling problems. When a student seems to have excessive problems mastering spelling and you suspect a learning difficulty, refer him or her to your school's testing service or office of student developmental services. Even students with mild dyslexia can be helped. A student's learning disability should not be a call to surrender but rather a challenge to be overcome.

Rule 4. If a word ends in a silent *e*, the *e* is usually dropped when a suffix starting with a vowel is added.

blue — bluish	fame — famous
dense — density	grieve — grievous

In a few cases, the *e* is retained to avoid pronunciation difficulties or confusion with other words.

dye — dyeing (not dying)	singe — singeing (not singing)
shoe — shoeing (not shoing)	

The *e* is also retained when it is preceded by a soft *c* sound (pronounced like the letter *s*) or a soft *g* sound (pronounced like the letter *j*) and the suffix being added starts with an *a* or an *o*.

peace — peaceable	courage — courageous
change — changeable	manage — manageable

HELPFUL SPELLING TIPS

Here are some tips that can further improve your spelling.

1. Examine each problem word carefully, especially prefixes (*aud*ience, *aud*ible), suffixes (superintend*ent*, descend*ant*), and double consonants (sate*ll*ite, roo*mm*ate, and co*ll*apsible).
2. Sound out each syllable carefully, noting its pronunciation. Words like *height*, *governor*, and *candidate* are often misspelled because of improper pronunciation.
3. Make a list of your problem words and review them periodically. Concentrate on each syllable and any unusual features (arc*t*ic, ambig*uous*).
4. Use any crutches that will help: there is *gain* in *bargain*; to *breakfast* is to *break a fast*; a disease causes *dis-ease*.
5. When you copy anything from the blackboard or a textbook, copy it carefully. Writing a word correctly helps you to spell it correctly the next time.
6. Buy a good collegiate dictionary and look up the words you don't know how to spell. (See pages 211–13 for more information on dictionaries.)

LIST OF TROUBLESOME WORDS

Students frequently misspell the words in the following list. Study these words carefully until the correct spelling becomes automatic. Then have a friend read them to you while you write them down. Tag the ones you misspell and whenever you revise a paper check especially for these words.

abandoned	absorption	accept	accidentally
abbreviate	absurd	access	accommodate
absence	academy	accessible	accomplish
absorb	accelerate	accident	accumulate

sp

accustom
achieve
achievement
acknowledge
acknowledgment
acquaintance
acquire
acquit
acquitted
address
advice
advise
aerial
aggravate
aggravated
aggression
aggressive
aging
alcohol
allege
alleviate
alley(s)
allot
allotted
allowed
all right
already
although
altogether
always
amateur
ambiguous
among
analysis (analyses)
analyze
anonymous
anxiety
apartment
apparent
appearance
appreciate
appropriate
architecture
arctic
argue
arguing
argument
arithmetic
ascent
assassin

assent
assistance
assistant
athlete
athletics
attempt
attendance
average
bachelor
balance
balloon
barbarous
barbiturate
beautiful
beggar
believe
beneficial
benefit
benefited
biscuit
boundary
bourgeois
breathe
Britain
bulletin
bureau
bureaucracy
business
cafeteria
calendar
camouflage
campaign
candidate
carburetor
carriage
carrying
casual
category
causal
ceiling
cellar
cemetery
changeable
changing
characteristic
chauffeur
chief
colloquial
colonel
column

commission
commit
commitment
committed
committee
committing
comparatively
competent
competition
concede
conceive
condemn
condescend
confident
congratulations
connoisseur
conqueror
conscience
conscientious
conscious
consistency
consistent
conspicuous
contemptible
continuous
controversy
convenience
convenient
coolly
cooperate
corollary
corps
corpse
correlate
counterfeit
courteous
criticism
criticize
cruelty
curiosity
curriculum
dealt
deceit
deceive
decent
decision
defendant
defense
definite
definitely

dependent
descendant
descent
describe
description
desert
desirable
despair
desperate
dessert
develop
development
difference
dilemma
disappear
disastrous
discernible
disciple
discipline
discussion
disease
dissatisfied
dissipate
dominant
drunkenness
echoes
ecstasy
efficiency
efficient
eighth
eligible
eliminate
embarrass
emphasis
employee
engineer
enthusiastic
environment
equal
equip
equipment
equipped
equivalent
especially
exaggerate
exceed
excellent
except
excerpt
excess

excitement	inevitable	mysterious	potatoes
exercise	infinitely	necessary	practice
existence	ingenious	neither	precede
experience	ingenuous	nevertheless	precedent
extraordinary	innocent	niece	precious
extremely	intelligent	noticeable	predominant
fallacy	interest	obedience	preference
familiar	interfere	occasion	preferred
fascinate	irresistible	occasionally	prejudice
fascist	irresponsible	occur	preparation
February	jeopardy	occurred	privilege
fiery	judgment	occurrence	probably
finally	judicial	occurring	procedure
financier	knowledge	official	proceed
foreign	knowledgeable	omission	professor
foreword	laboratory	omit	prominent
forfeit	legitimate	omitted	pronounce
forward	leisure	omitting	pronunciation
friend	library	opinion	propaganda
fulfill	license	opponent	propagate
gaiety	lightning	opportunity	propeller
gases	loneliness	optimistic	prophecy
gauge or gage	loose	original	prophesy
genius	lose	outrageous	prostate
genuine	magnificent	pamphlet	prostrate
government	maintain	parallel	protein
grammar	maintenance	paralysis	psychiatry
guarantee	maneuver	parliament	psychology
guard	manual	particularly	pursue
handkerchief	marriage	pastime	pursuit
harass	mathematics	patent	quantity
height	mattress	peaceable	questionnaire
heroes	meant	perceive	quiet
hindrance	medicine	perfectible	quite
hygiene	medieval	perform	quiz
hypocrisy	mediocre	permanent	quizzes
hysterical	melancholy	permissible	realize
illiterate	miniature	perseverance	receipt
illogical	minute	persuade	receive
illusion	miscellaneous	physical	recipe
immediate	mischievous	physician	recognizable
implement	misspell	picnic	recommend
impromptu	modifies	picnicked	refer
inadequate	modify	playwright	reference
incident	modifying	pleasant	referring
incidentally	moral	pleasurable	reign
independent	morale	politician	relevant
indict	mortgage	possess	relieve
indispensable	mosquitoes	possession	religious
individual	muscle	possible	remembrance

reminisce
reminiscence
reminiscent
rendezvous
repellent
repentance
repetition
representative
resemblance
resistance
restaurant
rhetoric
rhyme
rhythm
roommate
sacrifice
sacrilege
sacrilegious
safety
salary
sandwich
scarcely
scene
scenic
schedule
science
secretary
seize
sensible
separate
sergeant
severely
siege
similar
simultaneous
sincerely
skeptical
skiing
skillful
skis
society
sophomore
source
specifically
specimen
sponsor
spontaneous
statistics
steely
strategy

studying
subtle
subtlety
subtly
succeed
success
successful
succinct
suffrage
superintendent
supersede
suppose
suppress
surprise
syllable
symmetry
sympathize
synonym
synonymous
tangible
tariff
technical
technique
temperament
temperature
temporary
tenant
tendency
thorough
thought
through
traffic
trafficking
tragedy
tranquillity
or tranquility
transcendent
transcendental
transfer
transferred
transferring
translate
tries
truly
twelfth
typical
tyrannical
tyranny
unanimous
unconscious

undoubtedly
unmistakable
unnecessary
until
unwieldy
urban
urbane
usage
useful
using
usual
usually
vacancy
vacillate
vacuum
valuable
vegetable
vengeance
victorious
village
villain
waive
warrant
warring
weather
Wednesday
weird
whether
whole
wholly
wield
wintry
wiry
worshiped
or worshipped
wreak
wreck
writing
written
yield

sp

Glossary of Word Usage

TEACHING STRATEGY

There are several ways of handling these word usage problems. Make students responsible for mastering a specific number of commonly confused words each week (15 is about right). Or refer students to the glossary whenever they make a mistake. Probably a combination of the approaches is best. Students should be aware that there are troublesome words and be responsible for identifying and correcting the errors in their writing.

SUGGESTED INSTRUCTOR READINGS

Chomsky, C. "Reading, Writing, and Phonology." *Harvard Education Review* 40 (1970): 287–309. Demonstrates how spelling is not a function of pronunciation but rather is based on lexical considerations. Also shows how this attitude should influence our teaching.

D'Eloia, S. "The Uses—and Limits—of Grammar." *Journal of Basic Writing* 1 (1977): 1–20. Argues that instruction in formal grammar does little to improve student writing and that it is more effective to place our instruction within the context of student writing.

Dobie, A.B. "Orthographical Theory and Practice, or How to Teach Spelling." *Journal of Basic Writing* 5 (1986): 41–48. Shows how the differences between orthography and pronunciation can result in very specific practices for the teaching of spelling.

The English language has many words and expressions that confuse writers and thereby lessen the precision and effectiveness of their writing. These troublesome items include the following:

> Word pairs that sound alike or almost alike but are spelled differently and have different meanings
> Word pairs that do not sound alike but still are often confused
> Words or phrases that are unacceptable in formal writing

The following glossary identifies the most common of these troublemakers. Familiarize yourself with its contents. Then consult it as you revise your writing if you have even the slightest doubt about the proper use of a word, phrase, or expression.

a, an   Use *a* with words beginning with a consonant sound (even if the first written letter is a vowel); use *an* with words beginning with a vowel or a vowel sound.

> *a* brush, *a* student, *a* wheel, *a* risky situation, *a* once-in-a-lifetime opportunity

> *an* architect, *an* apple, *an* unworthy participant, *an* interesting proposal, *an* honest politician

accept, except   *Accept* is a verb meaning "to receive" or "to approve." *Except* is used as a verb or a preposition. As a verb, *except* means "to take out, exclude, or omit." As a preposition, it means "excluding," "other than," or "but not."

> She *accepted* the bouquet of flowers.

> Linda *excepted* Sally from the list of guests. (verb)

> All of Linda's friends *except* Sally came to the party. (preposition)

access, excess   *Access* is a noun meaning "means or right to enter, approach, or use." In the computer field it is a verb meaning "gain entrance to." *Excess* is an adjective meaning "too much; more than needed; lack of moderation."

> I have *access* to a summer cottage this weekend.

> The code permits users to *access* the computer.

> The airline booked an *excess* number of passengers on that flight.

adapt, adopt   To *adapt* is "to adjust," often by modification. To *adopt* is to "take as one's own."

He *adapted* to the higher elevations of the Rocky Mountains.

She *adopted* the new doctrine expounded by the prophet.

adverse, averse   *Adverse* is an adjective meaning "unfavorable." *Averse* is an adjective meaning "disinclined" or "feeling distaste for."

Adverse circumstances caused the ceremony to be postponed.

Martha was *averse* to naming all the guilty children.

advice, advise   *Advice* is a noun meaning "a recommendation about how to deal with a situation or problem." *Advise* is a verb meaning "to recommend or warn."

The young man followed his sister's *advice*.

Mr. Smith *advised* John to buy 10,000 shares of the stock.

affect, effect   Although both words may function as nouns and verbs, usually *affect* is a verb and *effect* is a noun. The verb *affect* means "to influence, cause a change in, or arouse the emotions of." The noun *affect* is a technical term in psychology and refers to feeling. The noun *effect* means "result or outcome." The verb *effect* means "to bring about or achieve."

His speech *affected* me greatly. (verb)

The *effect* of the announcement was felt immediately. (noun)

The doctor was soon able to *effect* a cure. (verb)

aggravate   *Aggravate* is a verb meaning "to intensify or make worse" an existing situation. The use of *aggravate* to mean "annoy" or "anger" is colloquial.

> *Colloquial*   Susan's behavior at the dance really *aggravated* me.

> *Standard*   Marcy's interference only *aggravated* the conflict between Bill and Nadine.

ain't   This nonstandard term for *isn't* or *aren't* is unacceptable in college writing.

all ready, already   *All ready* means "completely prepared" or "everyone is ready." *Already* means "previously, even now, even then."

The scouts are *all ready* for the camp out.

When we arrived we found he had *already* gone.

The report is *already* a week overdue.

all right, alright   *Alright* is a nonstandard spelling of *all right* and is not acceptable in college writing.

all together, altogether   *All together* means "all in one place" or "in unison." *Altogether* is an adverb meaning "completely, entirely."

The family was *all together* at the wedding.

All together, men, push!

Mr. Doe is *altogether* at fault for writing the letter.

Kolln, M. "Closing the Books on Alchemy." *College Composition and Communication* 32 (1981): 139–51. Argues that we should still teach grammar to ensure a shared vocabulary and conceptual framework.

Kroll, B. and J. Schafer. "Error Analysis and the Teaching of Composition." *College Composition and Communication* 29 (1978): 242–48. Explains how we can effectively observe the pattern in student errors, determine the source of those errors, and then provide the most effective instruction.

Pooley, R. C. *The Teaching of English Usage.* 2nd ed. Urbana, IL: NCTE, 1974. It is important to recognize that there is a history to the public attitude about usage errors. Pooley reviews public attitudes about usage from the 1700s to the present and analyzes typical usage problems.

Shaughnessy, M. P. *Errors and Expectations: A Guide for the Teacher of Basic Writing.* New York: Oxford UP, 1977. If there is any one work that today's writing teacher must read, this is it. Shaughnessy provides a careful analysis of the reasons weaker students have problems with grammar, punctuation, spelling, and vocabulary and offers very specific, carefully considered, and tested teaching methods.

Summey, G., Jr. *American Punctuation.* New York: Ronald, 1949. Provides both a brief history of punctuation and a trenchant *usage*

discussion of all the
conventions of punctuation.
Williams, J. M. *Style: Ten
Lessons in Clarity and
Grace.* 2nd ed. Glenview,
IL: Scott, 1985. Helps to
connect issues of grammar
and error to issues of style.

allusion, delusion, illusion   An *allusion* is an indirect reference. A *delusion* is a mistaken belief, often part of a psychological condition. An *illusion* is a deceptive appearance presented to the sight or created by the imagination.

> In his sermon, the minister made many *allusions* to the New Testament.

> He suffers from the *delusion* that he is a millionaire.

> They wore makeup to give the *illusion* of beauty.

a lot, alot   *Alot* is an erroneous spelling of the two words *a lot.* The phrase *a lot* is usually colloquial; in formal writing replace it with "many."

already   See *all ready, already.*

alright   See *all right, alright.*

alternately, alternatively   *Alternately* means "occurring by turns, one after the other." *Alternatively* means "providing a choice between two items."

> The U.S. flag has seven red and six white stripes, arranged *alternately.*

> Highway 44 offers the most direct route to Junction City. *Alternatively,* Highway 88 is much more scenic.

altogether   See *all together, altogether.*

among, between   Use *between* when referring to two things and *among* when referring to more than two.

> He divided the candy *between* Allan and Stephanie.

> He divided the candy *among* the five children.

amoral, immoral   *Amoral* means "outside or beyond the moral order or code." *Immoral* simply means "not moral."

> The movie, which takes no clear position on the behavior it depicts, seems curiously *amoral.*

> Murder is an *immoral* act.

amount, number   *Amount* refers to total quantities, things in bulk, or weight. *Number* refers to countable things. Never use *amount* when referring to people.

> Cassandra inherited a large *amount* of money.

> Cassandra now has a large *number* of friends.

an, a   See *a, an.*

and/or   Although often used in commercial and legal documents, this combination should be avoided in other writing.

angry, mad   *Mad* means "insane," although it is often used colloquially to mean "annoyed" or "angry." To be precise, use *mad* only to mean insane.

> *Colloquial*   I was *mad* at Debbie.

> *Standard*   I was *angry* with Debbie.

any, any other   Do not use *any* when you mean *any other*. Using *any* in the following example would mean that Theresa is more qualified than herself.

Theresa is more qualified than *any other* candidate.

anyone, any one   *Anyone* means "any person." *Any one* means "any single person or thing."

I can whip *anyone* in this room.

I saw three movies last week but didn't like *any one* of them.

appraise, apprise   *Appraise* means "to determine the value of something." *Apprise* means "to notify" or "to tell."

The jeweler *appraised* the gold brooch at $1,500.

Having been *apprised* of the situation, the family priest was able to reconcile the parents and the children.

apt, liable, likely   Both *apt* and *liable* express a tendency or inclination. *Liable* suggests something unpleasant or likely to result in legal action. It should be used only when the event may have unpleasant consequences.

We are *liable* to miss the train.

My lawyer said that I was *liable* for the damage my car had caused.

If the probable consequences are not unpleasant, *apt* is the better word.

I am *apt* to buy books if we go to the shopping center.

Likely merely implies strong probability.

Sandra is *likely* to pass this course without any difficulty.

around   *Around* is colloquial use for "approximately" or "about."

Colloquial   She arrived *around* 10:00 P.M.
The blouse cost *around* $15.

Standard   She arrived at *approximately* 10:00 P.M.
The blouse cost *about* $15.

as   *As* is frequently used as a weak substitute for *because, since, when,* and *while.*

Weak   She ran out of the house *as* it was on fire.

Better   She ran out of the house *because* it was on fire.

As should not be used in place of *whether* or *that.*

Nonstandard   I don't know *as* I like her.

Standard   I don't know *that* I like her.
I don't know *whether* I like her.

as, like   *As* may be used as a conjunction that introduces an adverb clause, but *like* should not be used this way.

Unacceptable   *Like* my father always said, "You can fool some of the people all of the time."

> *Standard*   *As* my father always said, "You can fool some of the people all of the time."

Like may, however, be used as a preposition.

> In times *like* this, it's hard not to despair.

> Any woman *like* Sally can expect a successful career in business.

assure, ensure, insure   To *assure* is "to make safe from risk, to guarantee" or "to convince." *Ensure* and *insure* can be variant spellings meaning "to make certain." *Insure*, however, is now generally associated with the business of insurance.

> The counselor tried to *assure* the students that they had made a wise choice.

> The captain *assured* them that they would be rescued.

> The father, wanting to *ensure* his son's college education, applied for a federally *insured* loan.

averse   See *adverse, averse.*

awful, awfully   In everyday speech, *awful* is used to describe things disagreeable or objectionable: "an *awful* movie," "an *awful* character." *Awfully* is used colloquially as an intensifier: "*awfully* nice," "*awfully* bad." Unless they are used to mean "solemnly impressive," however, both words should be avoided in formal writing.

> The *awful* majesty of the cathedral silenced the chattering tourists.

awhile, a while   *A while*, consisting of the noun *while* and the article *a*, means "a period of time." *Awhile* is an adverb meaning "for a short time."

> Dinner will be served in *a while*.

> Sit *awhile* and tell me the latest gossip.

bad, badly   *Bad* is an adjective. *Badly* is an adverb. *Badly* is colloquial when used to mean "very much."

> *Unacceptable*   She feels *badly* about her mistake.
> Tom behaved *bad* at the circus.

> *Colloquial*   I want a new car *badly*.

> *Standard*   She feels *bad* about her mistake. (adjective as subject complement)
> Tom behaved *badly* at the circus. (adverb)
> I want a new car *very much*.

being as, being that   When used as substitutes for *because* or *since*, these expressions are nonstandard.

> *Nonstandard*   *Being that* I was the first in line, I was able to purchase choice tickets.

> *Standard*   *Because* I was first in line, I was able to purchase choice tickets.

beside, besides   Both words are prepositions, but they have different meanings. *Beside* means "at the side of," and *besides* means "in addition to."

Sheila and Bill sat *beside* the trailer to eat their lunch.

Besides Harvey, Seymour is coming to dinner.

between   See *among, between.*

breath, breathe   *Breath* is a noun and *breathe* is its verb counterpart.

Nicole stepped outside the stuffy cabin for a *breath* of fresh air.

The cabin was so stuffy that Nicole could hardly *breathe.*

broke   *Broke,* when used to mean "without money," is colloquial.

Colloquial   Because Shelley was *broke,* she had to miss the movie.

Standard   Because Shelley *had no money,* she had to miss the movie.

can, may   *Can* refers both to permission and to the ability to do something, while *may* refers to permission only.

I think I *can* pass the exam on Friday. (ability)

My mother says I *can* go to the movies. (permission)

May I take the test next Monday? (permission)

When used to denote permission, *can* lends a less formal air to writing than does *may.*

cannot, can not   The use of *cannot* is preferred unless the writer wishes to italicize the *not* for emphasis.

You *cannot* expect a raise this year.

No, you can *not* expect a raise this year.

can't hardly   This nonstandard form for *cannot, can't,* or *can hardly* is unacceptable in college writing.

can't help but   In college writing, this colloquial phrase should be revised to the simpler *I can't help* or *I cannot help.*

Colloquial   I *can't help but* wish that I were going to the concert.

Standard   I *can't help* wishing that I were going to the concert.

capital, capitol   *Capital* means "a city that serves as a seat of government." *Capitol* means "a building in which a state legislature meets" or "the building in which Congress meets."

Dover is the *capital* of Delaware.

The *capitol* in Dover is popular with visitors.

censor, censure   To *censor* is "to judge"—literature, movies, letters, and the like—and to decide what material is unfit to be read or seen. To *censure* is "to judge harshly" or "find fault with."

> The warden *censored* all the prisoners' mail.

> The judge *censured* Clyde's criminal behavior.

childish, childlike   Both of these terms mean "like a child." *Childish*, however, has a negative connotation.

> He is fifty-two years old, but he behaves in a *childish* manner.

> Jon's face has a *childlike* quality that everyone likes immediately.

cite, sight, site   *Cite* means "to mention or quote as an example," *sight* means "to see" or "a view," and *site* means "a location."

> Cheryl *cited* Abraham Lincoln's Emancipation Proclamation in her talk.

> He was able to *sight* the enemy destroyers through the periscope.

> The building *site* is a woody area south of town.

climactic, climatic   *Climactic* is an adjective that means "of, being, or relating to a climax." *Climatic* is an adjective meaning "of or relating to a climate."

> Riding the roller coaster was the *climactic* event of Alice's day.

> The *climatic* features of Arizona are desirable to many people.

complement, compliment   Both words can act as nouns or verbs. As a noun, *complement* means "something that completes or makes up the whole." As a verb, it means "to complete or perfect." As a noun, *compliment* means "a flattering or praising remark." As a verb, it means "to flatter or praise."

> A *complement* of navy personnel boarded the foreign freighter. (noun)

> This fruit will *complement* the meal nicely. (verb)

> Scott paid Sara Jane a lovely *compliment* at the time of her graduation. (noun)

> Mother *complimented* me for cleaning my room. (verb)

conscience, conscious   *Conscience* refers to the sense of moral right or wrong. *Conscious* refers to the awareness of one's feelings or thoughts.

> Edgar's *conscience* forced him to return the money.

> Basil was not *conscious* of his angry feelings.

Do not confuse *conscious* with *aware*; although these words are similar in meaning, one is *conscious* of feelings or actions but *aware* of events.

contemptible, contemptuous   *Contemptible* means "deserving of contempt." *Contemptuous* means "displaying contempt."

> Peter's drunkenness is *contemptible*.

> Mary is *contemptuous* of Peter's drunkenness.

continual, continuous   *Continual* means "frequently or regularly repeated." *Continuous* means "uninterrupted."

> The telephone's *continual* ringing made the morning a nightmare.

> His wound caused him *continuous* pain for a week.

could have, could of   *Could of* is an unacceptable substitute for *could have* because a preposition cannot substitute for a verb.

> **Nonstandard**   I *could of* gone with my parents to Portugal.

> **Standard**   I *could have* gone with my parents to Portugal.

council, counsel   A *council* is a group of people that governs or advises. *Counsel* can be used as both a noun and a verb. The noun means "advice," and the verb means "to advise."

> The city *council* meets on the second Tuesday of every month.

> The lawyer's *counsel* was sound. (noun)

> The psychologist *counsels* many abused children. (verb)

couple   *Couple* denotes two things and should not be used to refer to more than that number.

criteria, criterion   *Criterion* is always singular, *criteria* always plural.

> The primary *criterion* for performing this job is manual dexterity.

> Manual dexterity is but one of many *criteria* on which you will be judged.

cute   *Cute*, an overused colloquialism, should be avoided; it has too many connotations to be used precisely in writing.

data   *Data* is the plural of *datum*. Today, however, it is usually used with a singular verb.

> **Acceptable**   These *data* are incorrect.

> **Acceptable**   This *data* is incorrect.

definite, very definite   Since *definite* means "precise" or "unmistakable," *very definite* is repetitive. One really cannot be more definite than *definite*.

delusion   See *allusion, delusion, illusion*.

desert, deserts, dessert   *Desert* is land that is arid. With the accent on the last syllable, it is a verb meaning "to abandon." *Deserts* means "that which is deserved." *Dessert* is food served after dinner.

> The Sonoran *desert* is full of plant life.

> You'll get your just *deserts* if you *desert* me now.

> They had cheesecake for *dessert* every Thursday night.

device, devise   *Device* is a noun meaning "a mechanical contrivance, gadget, or tool." *Devise* is a verb meaning "to plan or invent."

This new *device* gives us better gas mileage.

We must *devise* a new approach to our problem.

different from, different than   *Different from* is preferred over *different than*.

His ideas on marriage were *different from* those of his wife.

Different than is accepted, however, when a clause follows and the *from* construction would be wordy.

>   *Acceptable*   Susan looks *different than* she did last summer.

>   *Wordy*   Susan looks *different from* the way she looked last summer.

discreet, discrete   To be *discreet* means to be "prudent, tactful, or careful of one's actions." *Discrete* means "distinct or separate."

Jack was always *discreet* when he talked to his grandparents.

When two atoms of hydrogen combine with one atom of oxygen, they are no longer *discrete* entities.

disinterested, uninterested   A person who is *disinterested* is impartial or unbiased. A person who is *uninterested* is indifferent or not interested.

We need a *disinterested* judge to settle the dispute.

Joe is completely *uninterested* in sports.

don't   This contraction for *do not* should never be used with singular subjects such as *he*, *she*, or *it*. Instead, use *doesn't*, the contraction for *does not*, with singular subjects.

>   *Nonstandard*   *Don't* he know how to spell?
>   She *don't* think of anyone except herself.
>   That mistake *don't* help your image.

>   *Standard*   *Doesn't* he know how to spell?
>   She *doesn't* think of anyone except herself.
>   That mistake *doesn't* help your image.

due to   *Due to* has always been acceptable following a linking verb.

Her success was *due to* hard work.

Purists, however, object to *due to* when it is used in other situations, especially in introductory phrases.

Due to the many requests we have had, not everyone who wishes tickets will receive them.

In such cases, it's best to recast the sentence.

Because we have had so many requests, not everyone who wishes tickets will receive them.

effect   See *affect, effect*.

e.g.   This abbreviation, from the Latin *exempli gratia,* means "for example." Avoid using it except in comments in parentheses and in footnotes.

elicit, illicit   *Elicit* is a verb that means "to draw forth." *Illicit* is an adjective meaning "not permitted."

> A good professor can always *elicit* responses from students.

> He was engaged in many types of *illicit* activities.

emigrate, immigrate   When people *emigrate,* they move out of a country. When people *immigrate,* they move into a country.

> The family *emigrated* from Poland.

> Many Russians *immigrated* to America.

eminent, imminent   *Eminent* means "prominent," whereas *imminent* means "about to happen."

> Niels Bohr was an *eminent* physicist.

> Our instruments show that an earthquake is *imminent.*

ensure   See *assure, ensure, insure.*

enthused, enthusiastic   *Enthused* is a colloquial word and should not be used in place of *enthusiastic.*

> **Colloquial**   John was *enthused* about the prospects for jobs in his hometown.

> **Standard**   John was *enthusiastic* about the prospects for jobs in his hometown.

especially, specially   The term *especially* means "particularly, notably." *Specially* means "for a specific purpose."

> He is an *especially* talented pianist.

> He was *specially* chosen to represent his group.

et al.   This expression, from the Latin *et alii,* means "and others," referring to people. Ordinarily, the abbreviation should be used only in footnotes and bibliographic entries.

etc.   This abbreviation, from the Latin *et cetera,* means "and other things" and is used in reference to objects rather than people. It should be avoided except in comments in parentheses or in footnotes. It should never be preceded by *and.*

everyone, every one   *Everyone* means "every person." *Every one* means "every particular person or thing."

> *Everyone* who wants to go to the ball game should let me know today.

> If you carefully check *every one* of your paragraphs, you can improve your writing.

except   See *accept, except.*

excess   See *access, excess.*

explicit, implicit *Explicit* means "clearly expressed" or "straightforward." *Implicit* means "implied" or "understood without direct statement."

You must state your needs *explicitly* if you want them fulfilled.

When I took on the project, I made an *implicit* commitment to see it through.

extant, extent *Extant* is an adjective meaning "still existing." *Extent* is a noun meaning "scope, size, range, limit."

The dodo bird is no longer *extant.*

From Nevada to Colorado is the *extent* of my travels.

farther, further The traditional distinction is that *farther* refers to physical distance and *further* to distance in time. *Further* is now generally accepted in either context. Only *further* should be used to mean "additional."

In the race for the Muscular Dystrophy Association, Janet ran *farther* than Cindy.

If you think *further* on the matter, I am certain we can reach an agreement.

Let me make one *further* point.

fewer, less *Fewer* refers to countable items. *Less* refers to quantity or degree.

Mrs. Smith has *fewer* dogs than cats.

There is *less* money in Joan's checking account than in Stanley's.

Jack was *less* ambitious in his later years.

Never use *less* to refer to people.

> **Nonstandard** *Less* people were there than I expected.

> **Standard** *Fewer* people were there than I expected.

flaunt, flout To *flaunt* is "to display in a showy way." To *flout* is "to express contempt" or "to show scorn."

Jay *flaunted* his handsome physique before all his friends.

Jerrold *flouted* the convention of dressing for dinner by arriving in tennis shoes.

formally, formerly *Formally* means "according to established forms, conventions, and rules; ceremoniously." *Formerly* means "in the past."

The ambassador *formally* greeted his dinner guests.

Formerly, smallpox was one of our most serious diseases.

funny *Funny* refers to something that is amusing. It should not be used to mean "odd" or "unusual" in college writing.

> **Colloquial** I felt *funny* visiting my old fourth-grade classroom.

> **Standard** I felt *odd* visiting my old fourth-grade classroom.

further See *farther, further.*

get   *Get*, in any of its many colloquial senses, should not be used in writing.

   Colloquial   Her way of looking at a man really *gets* me.
                 I'll *get* him if it's the last thing I do.

    Standard   Beth will *get* at least a *B* in this course.

good and   Replace this colloquial phrase with *very*.

   Colloquial   She is *good and* tired of the cafeteria food.

    Standard   She is *very* tired of the cafeteria food.

good, well   Do not mistakenly use *good* as an adverb when an adjective is required.

   Unacceptable   John did *good* on his first test.

    Standard   John is making *good* progress on his report.
                John is a *good* student.

Well can be used as an adjective meaning "in good health." Otherwise it should always be used as an adverb.

   Last week I had a bad cold, but now I am *well*. (adjective)

   John did *well* on his first test. (adverb)

got, gotten   Both are acceptable past-participle forms of the verb *to get*.

had ought, hadn't ought   Both are incorrect in formal writing. The correct forms are *ought* and *ought not*.

   I *ought* to start studying.

   You *ought* *not* to cut class again.

hanged, hung   People may be *hanged*. Objects may be *hung*.

   The prisoner was *hanged* at noon.

   Mavis *hung* the picture in the dining room.

hisself, theirself, theirselves   These are nonstandard forms of *himself* and *themselves*.

hopefully   *Hopefully* means "in a hopeful manner." In informal speaking, it is used to mean "it is hoped" or "I hope," but this usage is not correct in formal writing. (Compare this with *carefully*, which means "in a careful manner"; no one uses *carefully* to mean "it is cared.")

   Colloquial   *Hopefully*, it will not rain during the class picnic.

    Standard   *Hopefully* I bought a lottery ticket.

hung   See *hanged, hung*.

i.e.   This abbreviation, meaning "that is," comes from the Latin *id est*. Avoid using it except in comments in parentheses or footnotes.

if, whether   *If* is used to introduce adverb clauses, where it means "assuming that."

> *If* I finish my report on time, I'll attend the concert with you.

If and *whether* are often used interchangeably to introduce noun clauses that follow verbs such as *ask, say, doubt, know,* and *wonder.*

In formal writing, however, *whether* is preferred.

> *Less Desirable*   I don't know *if* we'll be able to see the North Star tonight.
>
> *More Desirable*   I don't know *whether* we'll be able to see the North Star tonight.

illicit   See *elicit, illicit.*

illusion   See *allusion, delusion, illusion.*

immigrate   See *emigrate, immigrate.*

imminent   See *eminent, imminent.*

immoral   See *amoral, immoral.*

implicit   See *explicit, implicit.*

imply, infer   To *imply* is "to indicate indirectly or give implication." To *infer* is "to conclude from facts, evidence, or indirect suggestions."

> Jack *implied* that he wanted a divorce.
>
> Doris *inferred* that Jack wanted a divorce.

incidence, incidents   *Incidents* are separate, countable experiences. *Incidence* refers to the rate at which something occurs.

> Two *incidents* during childhood led to her reclusiveness.
>
> The *incidence* of cancer in Japan is less than that in the United States.

incredible, incredulous   *Incredible* means "fantastic, unbelievable." *Incredulous* means "skeptical, disbelieving."

> That she could run so fast seemed *incredible.*
>
> Why is Bill wearing that *incredulous* look?

infer   See *imply, infer.*

ingenious, ingenuous   *Ingenious* means "clever and inventive." *Ingenuous* means "unsophisticated and innocent."

> Sue presented an *ingenious* solution to our problem.
>
> Mary's *ingenuous* comments amused everyone in the room.

in regards to   This is an incorrect use of *in regard to.*

insure   See *assure, ensure, insure.*

inter-, intra-   *Inter-* means "between or among." *Intra-* means "within."

> From Chicago to Milwaukee is an *interstate* drive of approximately ninety miles.

> From San Francisco to Los Angeles is an *intrastate* drive of about 400 miles.

in terms of   Avoid this vague, overused expression.

> ***Vague***   *In terms of* the price he is asking, I would not recommend purchasing Tom's car.

> ***Preferred***   *Because* of the price he is asking, I would not recommend purchasing Tom's car.

irregardless   This nonstandard form of *regardless* includes the repetitive elements of *ir* and *less*, both of which mean "without."

is when, is where   *Is when* properly refers only to time.

> April *is when* our lilac bush blooms.

Is where properly refers only to place.

> Athens *is where* I met him.

The following sentences are *faulty* because muckraking is not a place, and an abscess is not a time.

> Muckraking *is where* someone investigates corporate or governmental abuses of power.

> An abscess *is when* some spot in body tissue fills with pus.

These sentences should be rephrased to eliminate the faulty assertion.

> Muckraking is the investigation of corporate or governmental abuses of power.

> An abscess occurs when some spot in body tissue fills with pus.

its, it's, its'   *Its* is a possessive pronoun. *It's* is a contraction of *it is* or *it has.*

> The gold chair was ruined, for someone had torn *its* seat.

> *It's* all I have to offer. (It is all I have to offer.)

> *It's* been a difficult day. (It has been a difficult day.)

There is no correct use for *its'*.

kind of, sort of   In college writing, these are unacceptable substitutes for *somewhat, rather,* or *slightly.*

> ***Colloquial***   She is *sort of* angry.
> I am *kind of* glad she went away.

> ***Standard***   She is *somewhat* angry.
> I am *rather* glad she went away.

When *kind* and *sort* refer to a type, use them with singular nouns and verbs. With their plural forms, *kinds* and *sorts,* use plural nouns and verbs.

> **Unacceptable**   These *kind* of exams are difficult.
>
> **Standard**   This *kind* of exam is difficult.
> These *kinds* of exams are difficult.

In such constructions, be certain that *kind of* or *sort of* is essential to your meaning. Otherwise, these phrases are unnecessary.

later, latter   *Later* refers to time; *latter* points out the second of two items. If more than two items are listed, use *last* to refer to the final one.

> He arrived at the party *later* than he was expected.

> Although Professors Stein and Patterson both lectured during the course, only the *latter* graded the final exam.

> Of my three cats, Sheba, Tiger, and Spot, only the *last* still needs the vaccination.

lay, lie   *Lie* means "to recline" or "to remain in a particular position." It never takes a direct object. *Lay* means "to place" and always takes a direct object. These verbs are often confused, in part because the past tense of *lie* is *lay*. (The past tense of *lay* is *laid*.)

> If I *lie* here a minute, I shall feel better.

> *Lay* the book on the table, please.

> As I *lay* asleep, a robber entered my apartment and stole my stereo.

> He *laid* a hand on her shoulder.

leave, let   *Leave* means "to depart," and *let* means "to allow." Never use *leave* when *let* is meant.

> **Nonstandard**   *Leave* him figure it out alone.

> **Standard**   *Let* him figure it out alone.

lend, loan   Traditionally, *loan* has been classed as a noun and *lend* as a verb. Today, the use of *loan* as a verb is so commonplace that it is accepted as colloquial English.

> **Standard**   I have applied for a *loan* so that I can buy a car. (noun)
> Please *lend* me your class notes. (verb)

> **Colloquial**   Please *loan* me your class notes. (verb)

less   See *fewer, less.*

let   See *leave, let.*

liable   See *apt, liable, likely.*

lie   See *lay, lie.*

like   See *as, like.*

likely See *apt, liable, likely.*

literally The word *literally* means "restricted to the exact, stated meaning." In formal writing, use *literally* only to designate factual statements.

> **Colloquial**   It was 65°, but I was *literally* freezing.
>
> **Standard**   Our dog was *literally* foaming at the mouth.
>   It was 65°, but I was *very* cold.

loan See *lend, loan.*

loose, loosen, lose *Loose* can be used as both a verb and an adjective. As a verb, it means "untie or unfasten"; as an adjective, it means "unattached, unrestrained, not confined." *Loosen* is a verb meaning "undo or ease." *Lose* can be used only as a verb meaning "mislay, fail to win, unable to maintain."

> He *loosed* the restraints on the tiger. (verb)
>
> One should wear *loose* clothing when bowling. (adjective)
>
> When will Mrs. Brady *loosen* her control over young Tom?
>
> You would *lose* your nose if it were not attached to your face.

lots, lots of *Lots* and *lots of* colloquially mean "many, much, a large amount, or a great amount." Avoid these expressions in college writing.

> **Colloquial**   I've spent *lots of* money in my life.
>
> **Standard**   I have spent *much* money in my life.

mad See *angry, mad.*

many, much *Many* is used when referring to a certain quantity; *much* is used when referring to an indefinite amount or to abstract concepts.

> There are *many* students in the biology class.
>
> How did Betty learn so *much* in so little time?

may See *can, may.*

may be, maybe *May be* is always used as a verb phrase. *Maybe* is an adverb meaning "perhaps."

> I *may be* chairman of the board by next June.
>
> *Maybe* we will see Jim at home.

medium, media *Medium* is the singular form of this word; *media* is the plural.

> Television is the *medium* I use most to get the news.
>
> The *media* have given extensive coverage to the brain transplant story.

much See *many, much.*

myself   *Myself* is an intensive and a reflexive pronoun; it cannot substitute for a personal pronoun such as *I* or *me*.

> *Unacceptable*   Four other students and *myself* founded the club.

> *Standard*   Four other students and *I* founded the club.

nice   Do not use this word to mean "pleasing, enjoyable, attractive."

not hardly   This is a nonstandard variation of *hardly* and is inappropriate in college writing.

number   See *amount, number.*

of between, of from, off of   Eliminate the unnecessary *of* from these colloquial phrases.

> *Colloquial*   There was a crowd *of between* three and four thousand people at the contest.
> Get *off of* my property!

> *Standard*   The crowd at the contest numbered *between* three and four thousand people.
> Get *off* my property!

on account of   This is a nonstandard substitute for *because.*

> *Nonstandard*   The team was unable to practice *on account of* everyone was still upset over Tuesday's loss.

> *Standard*   The team was unable to practice *because* everyone was still upset over Tuesday's loss.

passed, past   *Passed* is a verb designating movement that has taken place. *Past* is a noun or an adjective designating a former time.

> The parade *passed* the reviewing stand at 10:30 A.M.

> In the *past*, few people were concerned about the environmental effects of pesticides.

> This *past* summer, I visited France.

patience, patients   *Patience* means "the ability to wait or endure without complaining." *Patients* are "people being treated by physicians or dentists."

> Thad's *patience* was exhausted by the slow service in the restaurant.

> Following the tornado, doctors in the emergency room treated over sixty *patients.*

persecute, prosecute   *Persecute* means "to harass persistently because of race, religion, or belief." *Prosecute* means "to bring legal suit against."

> Ethnic groups are often *persecuted.*

> The company will *prosecute* anyone caught stealing.

personal, personnel   *Personal* is an adjective meaning "private, individual." *Personnel* are the people working in an organization.

Religious preference is a *personal* matter that you do not have to reveal during a job interview.

The *personnel* of the sanitation department will not be involved in the city workers' strike.

plenty When used as an adverb, *plenty* should be replaced by *very*.

    Colloquial   That geology exam was *plenty* hard.

    Standard   That geology exam was *very* hard.

precede, proceed *Precede* means "to go before or ahead of." *Proceed* means "to go on" or "to go forward."

The ritual of sharpening his pencils always *preceded* doing his homework.

The guide then said, "If you will *proceed*, I will show you the paintings by da Vinci."

predominant, predominate *Predominant* is an adjective meaning "chief, main, most frequent." *Predominate* is a verb meaning "to have authority over others."

The *predominant* European influence on South American culture was Spanish.

In America, the will of the people should *predominate*.

presently *Presently* means "soon" rather than "at the present time." *Currently* is preferred for the second meaning.

I will be there *presently*.

Currently, I am otherwise engaged.

principal, principle *Principal*, which means "chief," "most important," or "the amount of money on which interest is computed," is used as both a noun and an adjective. *Principle* is used only as a noun and means "truths, beliefs, or rules generally dealing with moral conduct."

The *principal* suspect in the case was arrested last Friday by the police.

The *principal* of Lewiston High School is Alison Cooperstein.

At this interest rate, your *principal* will double in ten years.

His *principles* are unconventional.

proceed See *precede, proceed*.

prosecute See *persecute, prosecute*.

quiet, quite *Quiet* is an adjective meaning "silent, motionless, calm." *Quite* is an adverb meaning "entirely" or "to a considerable extent or degree."

The class grew *quiet* when the teacher walked in.

He is *quite* wrong.

The movie was *quite* good.

raise, rise   *Raise* is a transitive verb and therefore requires a direct object. *Rise*, its intransitive counterpart, takes no direct object.

> We plan to *raise* horses on our new farm.

> The temperature is expected to *rise* to 75°F tomorrow.

Raise can also be a noun meaning "an increase in pay."

> Tammy received a 25 percent *raise* last week.

real, really   *Real* is an adjective; *really* is an adverb.

> She had *real* plants decorating the bedroom.

When used as an adverb, *real* is a colloquialism and should be replaced with *really*.

> *Colloquial*   We had a *real* good time at the party.

> *Standard*   We had a *really* good time at the party.

reason is because, reason is that   The *reason is because* is colloquial and unacceptable in formal writing; the *reason is that* is the preferred usage.

> *Colloquial*   The *reason is because* I love her.

> *Standard*   The *reason is that* I love her.

respectfully, respectively   *Respectfully* means "with respect." *Respectively* indicates that the items in one series are related to those in a second series in the order given.

> Joseph should treat his parents *respectfully*.

> Tom, Anna, and Susan were assigned *Bleak House*, *Great Expectations*, and *Dombey and Son*, *respectively*, for their reports.

rise   See *raise, rise*.

sensual, sensuous   *Sensual* refers to bodily or sexual sensations. *Sensuous* refers to impressions experienced through the five senses.

> Singles bars offered *sensual* pleasures without emotional commitments.

> The Tivoli Garden provides many *sensuous* delights for visitors.

set, sit   Generally, *set* means "to place" and takes a direct object. *Sit* means "to be seated" and does not take a direct object.

> Alice *set* her glass on the mantel.

> May I *sit* in this chair?

When it refers to the sun, however, *set* is used without a direct object.

> As the sun *set*, we turned homeward.

shall, will   *Shall* is used in first-person (see page 541) questions and in specialized forms of writing such as military orders and laws. Otherwise, *will* is used.

Shall we go to the movies tonight?

The company *shall* fall into formation at precisely twelve noon.

No family home *shall* be assessed at more than 50 percent of its actual value.

should have, should of   *Should of* is an unacceptable substitute for *should have* because a preposition cannot substitute for a verb.

> ***Nonstandard***   I *should of* gone to the lake.

> ***Standard***   I *should have* gone to the lake.

[sic]   This Latin word, always enclosed in brackets, follows quoted errors in grammar, spelling, or information. Inclusion of [sic] indicates that the error appeared in the original, which is being quoted exactly.

sight   See *cite, sight, site.*

sit   See *set, sit.*

site   See *cite, sight, site.*

so   *So* is an acceptable coordinating conjunction but tends to add an informal effect to writing and should therefore be used sparingly. For example, "Tom said he was divorcing me, *so* I began to cry" would be more effective if restated as follows: "When Tom said he was divorcing me, I began to cry." Do not use *so* as a substitute for *extremely* or *very* except with adverb clauses beginning with *that.*

> ***Colloquial***   You are *so* careless in what you say.
> The discussion was *so* informative that I took many notes.

> ***Standard***   You are *very* careless in what you say.
> The discussion was *extremely* informative.

some   *Some* is colloquial and unacceptable in writing when used as an intensifier (We had *some* time of it!) or an adverb (He'll probably pout *some* after you leave).

sometime, some time, sometimes   *Sometime* means "at a future unspecified time," *some time* means "a span of time," and *sometimes* means "occasionally."

> We should get together *sometime* and play bridge.

> The weather has been hot for *some time.*

> *Sometimes* I go to dinner with Ethel.

sort of   See *kind of, sort of.*

specially   See *especially, specially.*

stationary, stationery   *Stationary* means "not moving" or "fixed." *Stationery* means "paper for writing letters."

> The circular part in the center must remain *stationary,* or the machine will not function.

> Sue always writes on scented *stationery.*

such, such . . . that The use of *such* when it means "very" or "extremely" is unacceptable unless it is followed by a *that* clause completing the thought.

> ***Colloquial*** They were *such* good cookies.

> ***Standard*** They were *such* good cookies *that* I asked Steve for his recipe.

suppose to, supposed to *Suppose to* is the nonstandard form of *supposed to*. In speech, it is difficult to hear the final *d* on *supposed,* and one may say *suppose to* without being detected; however, the correct written form is always *supposed to*.

sure, surely *Sure* is colloquial for the adverb *surely*.

> ***Colloquial*** You *sure* know how to make good coffee, Mrs. Olsen.

> ***Standard*** You *surely* know how to make good coffee, Mrs. Olsen.

Although *surely* is correct, it may sound too formal and insincere. Therefore, *certainly* is often a better word to use.

take and, try and Avoid these expressions. Simply eliminate them from the sentence or substitute *try to* for *try and*.

> ***Unacceptable*** If you *take and* cover the tomato plants, they probably won't freeze.
> I think you should *try and* settle your differences.

> ***Standard*** If you cover the tomato plants, they probably won't freeze.
> I think you should *try to* settle your differences.

than, then *Than* is used to make comparisons; *then* means "at that time, in that case."

> Jill is taller *than* her brother.

> First we will eat, and *then* we will discuss business.

that, which These two words have the same meaning. *That* may refer both to things and groups of people; *which*, only to things. When referring to things, *that* is generally used with clauses that distinguish the things they modify from others in the same class (restrictive clauses). *Which* is generally used with clauses that add information about the things they modify (nonrestrictive clauses).

> Any book *that* she likes is certain to be trashy. (restrictive clause)

> The Winthrop Building, *which* cost two million dollars to construct, could not now be duplicated for ten times that much. (nonrestrictive clause)

See page 561 of the Handbook for a more complete explanation of restrictive and nonrestrictive expressions.

their, there, they're These three separate words are often confused because they sound alike. *Their* is the possessive form of *they*. *There* is an expletive that appears at the beginning of a sentence and introduces the real subject, or it is an adverb meaning "in or at that place, at that point." *They're* is a contraction of *they are*.

It is *their* basketball.

There are many reasons why I cannot come.

Put the sofa down *there*.

They're going to be here soon.

theirself, theirselves   See *hisself, theirself, theirselves*.

then   See *than, then*.

there   See *their, there, they're*.

thorough, through   *Thorough* means "careful, complete, exact, painstaking." *Through* means "in one side and out the other, from end to end, from start to finish, over the whole extent of, finished."

Brenda has done a *thorough* job.

Let's run *through* the plan again.

thusly   *Thusly* is a nonstandard form of *thus*.

to, too, two   *To* is a preposition meaning "as far as, toward, until, onto." *Too* is an adverb meaning "excessively" or "also." *Two* is a number.

I'm going *to* the store.

Are you going *too?*

This car is *too* expensive for me.

There are *two* characters in the play.

toward, towards   Both forms are correct. *Toward* generally is used in the United States and *towards* in England.

try and   See *take and, try and*.

two   See *to, too, two*.

uninterested   See *disinterested, uninterested*.

unique   *Unique* means "without an equal" or "extremely unusual" and thus should not be modified by an adverb such as *very*.

use to, used to   *Use to* is the nonstandard form of *used to*. In speech it is difficult to hear the *d* on *used*, and one may say *use to* without being detected; however, the correct written form is always *used to*.

used to could   This phrase is nonstandard for *used to be able to*.

Nonstandard   I *used to could* run ten miles.

Standard   I *used to be able to* run ten miles.

very definite   See *definite, very definite*.

wander, wonder   *Wander* is a verb meaning "to move about without a plan or set destination." *Wonder* is a noun meaning "something causing surprise, admiration, or awe" or a verb meaning "to be curious about."

> Some people like to *wander* through shopping malls for recreation.
>
> That child is a *wonder* at mathematics.
>
> I *wonder* whether I have received an *A* on that test.

way, ways   *Ways* may be used to refer to two or more means or methods but not to time or distance.

> | *Unacceptable* | Timbuktu is a long *ways* from the United States. |
> | *Standard* | There are two *ways* of thinking about that issue. |
> | | Timbuktu is a long *way* from the United States. |

well   See *good, well*.

were, where   *Were* is the past form of the verb *to be* and is used with *we, you,* and *they*. *Where* is an adverb or a pronoun meaning "in, at, to, from a particular place or situation" or "which or what place."

> I'm sorry that you *were* ill yesterday.
>
> Mr. Morris will show you *where* to register.

where . . . at, to   *At* and *to* are unnecessary after *where*.

> | *Wordy* | *Where* are you taking the car *to*? |
> | | *Where* does she live *at*? |
> | *Standard* | *Where* are you taking the car? |
> | | *Where* does she live? |

whether   See *if, whether*.

which   See *that, which*.

who, whom   In formal writing, *who* should be used only as a subject in clauses and sentences and *whom* only as an object.

> | *Unacceptable* | *Who* are you taking to dinner on Friday? |
> | | I know *who* the boss will promote. |
> | | John is the candidate *whom* I think will be elected. |
> | *Standard* | *Whom* are you taking to dinner on Friday? |
> | | I know *whom* the boss will promote. |
> | | John is the candidate *who* I think will be elected. |

See page 544 of the Handbook for a fuller discussion of *who* and *whom*.

who's, whose   *Who's* is a contraction of *who is* or *who has,* and *whose* is the possessive form of *who*.

> *Who's* coming to see us tonight?

I would like to know *who's* been dumping trash in my yard.

Whose book is that?

will   See *shall, will.*

wise   Do not randomly add *wise* to the ends of nouns. Such word coinings are ineffective.

> *Ineffective*   Personality*wise*, Sheila is ideal for the job.

> *Standard*   Sheila has an *ideal personality* for the job.

wonder   See *wander, wonder.*

would have, would of   *Would of* is an unacceptable substitute for *would have*. A preposition cannot substitute for a verb.

> *Nonstandard*   I *would of* enjoyed seeing the Picasso exhibit.

> *Standard*   I *would have* enjoyed seeing the Picasso exhibit.

would have been, had been   When *would* occurs in the main part of a sentence, use *had been* (not *would have been*) in an "if" clause.

> *Nonstandard*   If the engine *would have been* lubricated, the bearing *would not* have burned out.

> *Standard*   If the engine *had been* lubricated, the bearing *would not* have burned out.

your, you're   *Your* is a possessive form of *you; you're* is a contraction of *you are.*

Where is *your* history book?

Tell me when *you're* ready to leave.

Author–Title Index

Subject Index

Gobbledygook, 228, 340–41
Guilt by association, 153

Hasty generalization, 151
Helping verbs, 508–9
Hyperbole. *See* Overstatement
Hyphens, 574–75

Idioms, 212
Illustration:
    example essays, 95–96, 397–408
    number of examples, 92–93
    organizing examples, 93–94
    planning and drafting, 94–95
    purpose, 91–92
    questions for drafting and
        revision, 94, 95
    revising, 95
    selecting examples, 92
    writing suggestions, 97
Imperative mood of verbs, 513
Implied topic sentence, 174
Indefinite pronouns, 506–7
Independent clauses, 525
Indicative mood of verbs, 513
Indirect objects, 500–501
Induction in argument, 144–45
Infinitive phrases, 524
Inquiry letters, 344–45
Intensive pronouns, 506
Interjections, 521
Interrogative pronouns, 505–6
Interrupted-order sentences, 200
Interview reports, 323–27
Intransitive verbs, 508
Introductions of essays, 186–88
Irony:
    kinds of, 255–56
    as literary element, 255–56
    as suggestive element, 227
Italics, 581–82

Jargon, 218
Job application letters, 348–51

Journal, keeping a, 13–14

Key words for paragraph
    coherence, 184

Library research paper:
    acknowledging and handling
        sources, 292–308
    adjusting topic, 279
    assembling a working
        bibliography, 270–80
    card catalog, 271–74
    choosing a topic, 267–68
    computerized card catalog, 274
    computerized databases, 275–78
    encyclopedias, 270–71
    example outline and paper,
        309–18
    learning about library, 266
    note taking, 280–86
    organizing and outlining, 287–88
    paraphrasing, 284
    periodical indexes, 275–78
    plagiarism, avoiding, 307–8
    quoting, 284–86, 304–7
    schedule for, 267
    summarizing, 282–83
    writing, 289–92
Limiting adjectives, 515
Linking verbs, 508
Literature, elements of:
    character, 250–52
    irony, 255–56
    narrator and point of view, 248–50
    plot, 246–48
    setting, 252–54
    symbols, 254–55
    theme, 257–58
Literature, writing papers about,
    259–63
Loose sentences, 198–99

Main clauses, 525

ACKNOWLEDGMENTS *(continued from p. iv)*

Russell Baker, "The Plot Against People." Copyright © 1968 by The New York Times Company. Reprinted by permission.

Carl Becker, *Freedom and Responsibility in the American Way of Life* (N.Y.: Vintage-Knopf, 1945).

Eric Berne, "Can People Be Judged by Their Appearance?" From *A Layman's Guide to Psychiatry and Psychoanalysis*. Copyright © 1947, 1957, 1968 by Eric Berne, renewed 1985 by Ellen Berne, Eric Berne, and Terence Berne. Reprinted by permission of Simon & Schuster, Inc.

Bruno Bettelheim, "Joey: A 'Mechanical Boy,' " *Scientific American* March 1959, p. 122.

Ray Allen Billington, "The Frontier Disappears," *The American Story*, ed. Earl Schenck Miers (Great Neck, N.Y.: Channel, 1956).

"The Brink of a Disaster," *America*, March 31, 1979, p. 247.

Suzanne Britt, "That Lean and Hungry Look," *Newsweek*, Oct. 9, 1977. Reprinted by permission of the author.

Claude Brown, *Manchild in the Promised Land* (N.Y.: Macmillan, 1965), p. 304.

James L. Buckley, "Three Cheers for the Snail Darter," *National Review*, September 14, 1979, pp. 1144–45.

"The Bureaucrat," Citicorp. Reprinted by permission. All rights reserved.

Gladys Hasty Carroll, *Sing Out the Glory* (Boston: Little Brown, and Co., 1958).

Rachel Carson, *Silent Spring*, (Boston: Houghton Mifflin, 1962).

Bruce Catton, "Grant and Lee: A Study in Contrasts," From *The American Story*, ed. Earl Schenck Miers. Reprinted by permission of U.S. Capital Historical Society.

John Ciardi, "Dawn Watch." From *Manner of Speaking*, by John Ciardi. Copyright © 1982 by Rutgers University Press. Reprinted by permission.

John Ciardi, "What Is Happiness?" in *Manner of Speaking* (New Brunswick, N.J.: Rutgers University Press, 1972).

Robert Claiborne, "Future Schlock," *The Nation*, January 25, 1971, p. 117.

Cecil Clutton and John Stanford, *The Vintage Motor-car* (N.Y.: Charles Scribner's Sons, 1955), p. 135.

Judith Coburn, "Dolores Huerta: La Pasionaria of the Farm Workers," *Ms.*, Nov. 1976, pp. 12–13.

Barry Commoner, "Why We Have Failed," from *Greenpeace*, Sept.–Oct., 1989 (all rights reserved).

Joseph Conrad, *Lord Jim* (N.Y.: Holt, Rinehart and Winston, 1957), p. 13.

"Controlling Phobias Through Behavior Modification," *USA Today*, August 1978.

Kelly Davis, "Health and High Voltage: 765 KV Lines," *Sierra*, July–August 1978.

Vine Deloria, Jr., "Custer Died for Your Sins," *Playboy*, Aug. 1969.

Lester del Ray, *The Mysterious Sky* (N.Y.: Chilton Book Company, 1964).

Magda Denes, In *Necessity and Sorrow: Life and Death in an Abortion Hospital* (N.Y.: Basic Books, 1976), p. xiv.

Robert Dick-Read, *Sanamu: Adventures in Search of African Art* (N.Y.: E.P. Dutton, 1964), pp. 228–29.

Joan Didion, "On Self-Respect," in *Slouching Toward Bethlehem* (N.Y.: Farrar, Straus and Giroux, 1968), pp. 143–44.

Annie Dillard, "A Total Eclipse" from *Teaching a Stone to Talk* by Annie Dillard. Copyright © 1982 by Annie Dillard. Reprinted by permission of Harper & Row, Publishers, Inc.

Leo Durocher, *Nice Guys Finish Last* (N.Y.: Simon & Schuster, 1975), p. 54.

Wayne Dyer, *What Do You Really Want for Your Children?* (New York: William Morrow, Inc., 1985).

Barbara Ehrenreich, "Teach Diversity—with a Smile." *Time*, April 8, 1991. Copyright © 1991 The Time Inc. Magazine Company. Reprinted by permission.

Loren Eiseley, "The Judgment of the Birds," in *The Immense Journey* (N.Y.: Random House, 1956), pp. 174–75.

Loren Eiseley, *The Unexpected Universe* (N.Y.: Harcourt Brace Jovanovich, 1969), p. 88.

Marian Engle, review of *The Goddess and Other Women*, by Joyce Carol Oates, *New York Times Book Review*, Nov. 24, 1974, p. 7.

Howard Ensign Evans, *Life on a Little-Known Planet* (N.Y.: E.P. Dutton, 1968), pp. 107–8.

Henry Fairlie, "A Victim Fights Back," *The Washington Post*, April 30, 1978.

David Finkelstein, "When the Snow Thaws," *The New Yorker*, Sept. 10, 1979, p. 127.

James F. Fixx, "What Running Can't Do For You," *Newsweek*, Dec. 18, 1978, p. 21. Copyright © 1978, Newsweek, Inc.

"Formlessness," From *Roget's International Thesaurus* by Robert L. Chapman. Copyright © 1977 by Harper & Row, Publishers, Inc. Reprinted by permission of the publisher.

E. M. Forster, "My Wood." From *Abinger Harvest*. Copyright 1936 and renewed 1964 by E. M. Forster. Reprinted by permission of Harcourt Brace Jovanovich, Inc.

Bruce Friedman, "Eating Alone in Restaurants." From *The Lonely Guy's Book of Life*. Copyright © 1979 by McGraw-Hill, Inc.

Otto Friedrich, "There are 00 Trees in Russia," *Harper's Magazine*, Oct. 1964.

Kathleen Fury, "It's Only a Paper World," *Working Woman*, August 1986. Reprinted by permission.

Gustavo A. Garotti, "How to Fight the Drug War," *Atlantic Monthly*, July, 1989.

Ellen Goodman, "The Company Man." From *At Large*. Copyright © 1981 by The Washington Post Company. Reprinted by permission of Summit Books, a division of Simon & Schuster, Inc.

Martin Gottfried, "Rambos of the Road," *Newsweek*, Sept. 8, 1986. Reprinted by permission of the author.

Jeff Greenfield, "The Black and White Truth About Basketball." *Esquire*, 1984. Reprinted by permission of Sterling Lord Literistic, Inc. Copyright © 1984, 1990 by Jeff Greenfield.

Amy Gross, "The Appeal of the Androgynous Man." *Mademoiselle*. Copyright © 1976 by The Condé Nast Publications, Inc. Reprinted by permission of Amy Gross.

Pete Hamill, "Facing Up to Drugs: Is Legalization the Answer?" Copyright © 1988, News America Publishing, Inc. All rights reserved. Reprinted by permission of *New York* magazine.

L. D. Hamilton, "Antibodies and Antigens," *The New Book of Knowledge* 1967, I, 317.

S. I. Hayakawa, *Language in Thought and Action*, 3rd ed. (N.Y.: Harcourt Brace Jovanovich, 1972), p. 50.

John Hersey, *Hiroshima* (N.Y.: Modern Library, 1946), p. 4.

Nancy K. Hill, "Scaling the Heights: The Teacher as Mountaineer," *The Chronicle of Higher Education*, June 16, 1980, p. 48.

Thomas Henry Huxley, "A Liberal Education and Where to Find It," *Macmillan's Magazine*, March 17, 1868.

Dina Ingber, "Computer Addicts," *Science Digest*, July 1981.

Washington Irving, "The Spectre Bridegroom," in *Selected Writings of Washington Irving*, ed. Saxe Commins (N.Y.: Modern Library, 1945), p. 53.

Bruce Jackson, "Who Goes to Prison: Caste and Careerism in Crime," *Atlantic Monthly*, Jan. 1966, p. 52.

Robert Jastrow, *Until the Sun Dies* (N.Y.: Norton, 1977).

Vernon E. Jordan Jr., "The New Negativism," *Newsweek*, Aug. 14, 1978, p. 13. Copyright © 1978, Newsweek, Inc.

Doris Kearns, "Who Was Lyndon Baines Johnson?", from *Lyndon Johnson and the American Dream* (N.Y.: Harper & Row, 1976).

Helen Keller, "Three Days to See," *Atlantic Monthly*, Jan. 1933, p. 35.

John F. Kennedy, "Inaugural Address," Washington, D.C. Jan. 20, 1961.

Walter Kiechel III, "How to Give a Speech, From *Fortune*, June 8, 1987. Reprinted by permission.

Martin Luther King, Jr., "I Have a Dream." Reprinted by permission of Joan Daves Agency. Copyright © 1963 by Martin Luther King, Jr., renewed 1991 by Coretta Scott King.

Martin Luther King, Jr., extracts from "Letter from Birmingham Jail," in *Why We Can't Wait* by Martin Luther King, Jr. Copyright © 1963, 1964 by Martin Luther King, Jr. Reprinted by permission of Harper & Row, Publishers, Inc.

Martin Luther King, Jr., "Pilgrimage to Nonviolence," in *Stride Toward Freedom* (N.Y.: Harper & Row, 1958), p. 84.

Perri Klass, "She's Your Basic L.O.L. in N.A.D." Reprinted by permission of the Putnam Publishing Group from *A Not Entirely Benign Procedure* by Perri Klass. Copyright © 1987 by Perri Klass. This essay originally appeared in the October 4, 1984, *New York Times*.

Marilyn Kluger, "A Time of Plenty," *Gourmet*, Nov. 1976, p. 22.

Edward I. Koch, "Death and Justice." Published by permission of *The New Republic*.

Andrew Kupfer, "What to Do about Drugs," from *Fortune*, June 20, 1988. Reprinted by permission.

Kenneth Labich, "The Scandal of Killer Trucks," *Fortune*, March 30, 1987.

Pär Lagerkvist, "Father and I," from *The Marriage Feast* (N.Y.: Hill & Wang, 1954). © 1954 by Albert Bonniers Vörlag.

Robert Lipsyte, *Sports World* (N.Y.: Quadrangle Books, 1975), p. ix.

John Lovesey, "A Myth is as Good as a Mile," *Sports Illustrated*, Nov. 9, 1964.

Marilyn Machlowitz, "Workaholism: What's Wrong with Being Married to Your Work?", *Working Woman*, May 1978, p. 51.

Malcolm X, *The Autobiography of Malcolm X* (N.Y.: Ballantine Books, 1964), p. 171.

Marshall Mandell, "Are You Allergic to Your House?", *Prevention*, Sept. 1979, p. 101.

Marya Mannes, "Wasteland," in *More in Anger* (Philadelphia: J.B. Lippincott, 1958), p. 40.

Margaret Mead, "New Superstitions for Old," from *A Way of Seeing* by Margaret Mead and Rhoda Metraux. Copyright © 1966 by Margaret Mead and Rhoda Metraux.

L. David Mech, "Where Can the Wolves Survive?", *National Geographic*, Oct. 1977, p. 536.

H. L. Mencken, "The Libido for the Ugly," Copyright 1927 by Alfred A. Knopf, Inc., and renewed 1955 by H. L. Mencken. Reprinted from *A Mencken Chrestomathy*, edited and annotated by H. L. Mencken, by permission of the publisher.

Thomas H. Middleton, "The Magic Power of Words," *Saturday Review*, Dec. 11, 1976, p. 90.

Don Ethan Miller, "A State of Grace: Understanding the Martial Arts," *Atlantic Monthly*, Sept. 1980. Copyright © 1980 by Don Ethan Miller.

Lance Morrow, "Waiting As a Way of Life," *Time*, July 23, 1984. Copyright © 1984 Time, Inc. Reprinted by permission.

George Orwell, excerpt from "Shooting an Elephant," in *Shooting an Elephant and Other Essays*, copyright 1950 by Sonia Brownell Orwell; renewed 1978 by Sonia Pitt-Rivers. Reprinted by permission of Harcourt Brace Jovanovich, Inc., and Martin Secker & Warburg Ltd.

Jo Goodwin Parker, "What is Poverty?" in George Henderson, *America's Other Children: Public Schools Outside Suburbia* (University of Oklahoma Press, 1971).

Nancy Perry, "Saving the Schools: How Business Can Help," from *Fortune*. Nov. 7, 1988.

Alexander Petrunkevitch, from "The Spider and the Wasp," *Scientific American*, August, 1952. Copyright © 1952 by Scientific American, Inc. All rights reserved.

J. Winston Porter, "We'll Trash *U.S.A. Today* too." from *U.S.A. Today*, July 11, 1988. All rights reserved.

William Raspberry, "The Handicap of Definition." From *Instilling Positive Images* by William Raspberry. Copyright © 1982, Washington Post Writers Group. Reprinted by permission.

Lord Richie-Calder, "The Doctor's Dilemma," *The Center Magazine*, Sept/Oct. 1971.

Edwin Arlington Robinson, "The Miller's Wife," *The Three Taverns*, Charles Scribner's Sons, 1920.

Edwin Arlington Robinson, "Richard Cory," *The Children of the Night*, Charles Scribner's Sons, 1897.

Richard Rodriguez, "Private Language, Public Language." From "Aria: A Memoir of a Bilingual Childhood" by Richard Rodriguez. Reprinted by permission of Georges Borchardt, Inc., for the author. Copyright © 1980 by Richard Rodriguez. First appeared in *The American Scholar*.

Philip Ross, "The Boy and the Bank Officer." From *New York*, March 13, 1979. Reprinted by permission of Roberta Pryor, Inc. Copyright © 1979 by Philip Ross.

Kathy Roth, "How to Adopt a Stray." Reprinted from *The Cat Catalog: The Ultimate Cat Book*, ed. by Judy Fireman. © 1976 Workman Publishing Company, New York. Reprinted by permission of the publisher.

Bertrand Russell, *The ABC of Relativity* (London: Allen and Unwin, 1965), pp. 46–47.

Bertrand Russell, "Respect for Law," *San Francisco Review*, Winter, 1958, pp. 63–65. Reprinted by permission of June Oppen Degnan.

Lewis Sawaquat, "For My Indian Daughter," *Newsweek*, Sept. 5, 1983. Reprinted by permission of the author.

Richard Selzer, "The Knife." From *Mortal Lessons*, Copyright © 1974, 1975, 1976 by Richard Selzer. Reprinted by permission of Simon & Schuster, Inc.

Laurence Shames, "The Sweet Smell of Success Isn't All That Sweet." Copyright © 1986 by The New York Times Company. Reprinted by permission.

QuickBooks® 2022

ALL-IN-ONE

by Stephen L. Nelson, MBA, CPA,
MS in Taxation

A Wiley Brand

QuickBooks® 2022 All-in-One For Dummies®

Published by: **John Wiley & Sons, Inc.,** 111 River Street, Hoboken, NJ 07030-5774, www.wiley.com

Copyright © 2022 by John Wiley & Sons, Inc., Hoboken, New Jersey

Published simultaneously in Canada

For general information on our other products and services, please contact our Customer Care Department within the U.S. at 877-762-2974, outside the U.S. at 317-572-3993, or fax 317-572-4002. For technical support, please visit https://hub.wiley.com/community/support/dummies.

Wiley publishes in a variety of print and electronic formats and by print-on-demand. Some material included with standard print versions of this book may not be included in e-books or in print-on-demand. If this book refers to media such as a CD or DVD that is not included in the version you purchased, you may download this material at http://booksupport.wiley.com. For more information about Wiley products, visit www.wiley.com.

Library of Congress Control Number: 2021948187

ISBN: 978-1-119-81721-5 (pbk); 978-1-119-81722-2 (ebk); 978-1-119-81723-4 (ebk)

SKY10031114_110321